AN INTRODUCTION TO GROUP WORK PRACTICE

SECOND EDITION

RONALD W. TOSELAND
UNIVERSITY AT ALBANY, STATE UNIVERSITY OF NEW YORK

ROBERT F. RIVAS
SIENA COLLEGE

ALLYN AND BACON
Boston   London   Toronto   Sydney   Tokyo   Singapore

Editor: Linda Scharp
Production Editor: Mary Ann Hopper
Text Designer: Robert Vega
Cover Designer: Robert Vega
Production Manager: Deidra M. Schwartz
Electronic Text Management: Marilyn Wilson Phelps, Matthew Williams, Jane Lopez,
    Karen L. Bretz

Copyright © 1995 by Allyn and Bacon
A Division of Paramount Publishing
160 Gould Street
Needham Heights, Massachusetts 02194

An earlier edition, entitled *An Introduction to Group Work Practice*, copyright © 1984
by Macmillan Publishing Company.

Library of Congress Cataloging-in-Publication Data
Ronald W. Toseland
    An introduction to group work practice / Ronald W. Toseland,
Robert F. Rivas.—2nd ed.
      p.   cm.
    Includes bibliographical references and index.
    ISBN 0-02-421132-X
    1. Social group work. 2. Leadership. I. Rivas, Robert F. II. Title
HV45.T68   1995
361.4—dc20   93-43431
                                                         CIP

Printed in the United States of America

10 9 8 7 6 5   99 98 97

CONTENTS

Chapter 3

Understanding Group Dynamics   69

Chapter 4

Leadership   93

PART II

The Planning Stage   141

Chapter 5

The Planning Stage   143

Chapter 9

Treatment Groups: Specialized Methods   *261*

Chapter 10

Task Groups: Foundation Methods   *295*

Chapter 11

Task Groups: Specialized Methods   *329*

PART V

The Ending Stage   *363*

Chapter 12

Evaluation   *365*

Chapter 13

Ending the Group's Work   *391*

Chapter 14

Case Examples   *411*

PREFACE

It has been ten years since the first edition of this text was published. Because it took almost five years to prepare the first edition, we were very gratified to learn that the text was being widely used by professionals and in undergraduate and graduate courses in Schools of Social Work throughout the United States and throughout the world. Although we believe that much of the original text remains timely, in recent years we received many inquiries about our plans to prepare a second edition. Based on the suggestions we received from fellow practitioners, scholars, and students we have revised each chapter of the original text.

Because we remain committed to presenting a coherent and organized overview of the field, the second edition includes a typology of treatment groups that has been expanded to include support groups, a growing area of group work practice. The typology of task groups has also been expanded to include groups to meet client, organizational, and community needs.

In the revised edition, we have continued to emphasize three focal areas for practice: (a) the individual group member, (b) the group as a whole, and (c) the environment in which the group functions. However, we have placed greater emphasis on the importance of the latter two focal areas because our experiences in supervising students and conducting workshops for professionals over the last ten years have revealed that group as a whole dynamics and the environment in which groups function are often neglected aspects of group work practice.

Because we remain keenly aware that students and practitioners want practical suggestions on how to proceed when facilitating treatment and task groups during each stage of their development, we have expanded the emphasis on practical leadership skills in each chapter dealing with the stages of group work practice. For example, the two middle stage chapters have been expanded to four. Chapters 8 and 10 describe the foundation methods for leading treatment and task groups during the middle stage, and Chapters 9 and 11 describe specialized procedures for leading treatment and task groups. In the new edition, there is also a revised and expanded chapter on leadership (Chapter 4) which includes new sections on working with culturally diverse groups, how to assess one's leadership style, and what to discuss with a potential co-leader prior to leading a group. We have also added full-length case examples of a treatment group and a task group in a new chapter (Chapter 14), and we have increased the number of examples in the other chapters to help illustrate the skills that can be used during each stage of the helping process.

We have made a host of other changes which we hope will make the text more useful for practitioners, students, and educators. For example, we have expanded the Appendix, including codes of ethics from two professional group work associations, a list of films that illustrate group work practice, additional references for specialized group work practice, and a bibliography on teleconference groups, a new and rapidly expanding area of group work practice. We have also included learning assignments at the end of each chapter.

The ideas expressed in this book have evolved over many years of study and practice. Some of the earliest and most powerful influences that have shaped this effort have resulted from our contact wiht Bernard Hill, Alan Klein, Sheldon Rose, and Max Siporin. Their contribution to the development of our thinking is evident throughout this book. Perhaps even more important, however, were their support and encouragement in the early years of our professional development and their belief in our ability to make a contribution to knowledge about group work practice.

Ths ideas in this book were also greatly influenced by Albert Alissi, Leonard Brown, Burton Gummer, Margaret Hartford, Grafton Hull, Jr., Norma Lang, Catherine Papell, William Reid, Beulah Rothman, Jerrold Shapiro, and Peter Vaughan. Their comments, suggestions, and reactions were invaluable in improving the quality of the book. We are also indebted to the many practitioners and students with whom we have worked over the years. Sharing practice experiences, discussing successes and failures, and giving and receiving constructive feedback helped us clarify and improve the ideas presented in this text.

We would also like to acknowledge the material support and encouragement given to us by our respective educational institutions. The administrative staff of the School of Social Welfare and the Rockefeller College of the University at Albany, State University of New York, and the administrative staff of Siena College have played important roles in helping us accomplish this project. In particular, we would like to acknowledge the editorial assistance of Ken Winston, Pat Oles, and Philip McCallion, and the secretarial assistance of B. J. Kelly. All have made important contributions to the preparation of this second edition.

But most important of all, we are especially grateful to our spouses, Sheryl Holland and Donna Allingham Rivas. Their personal and professional insights have done much to enrich this book. Without their continuous support and encouragement, we would not have been able to complete this work. A special note of thanks also goes to Becky, Stacey, and Heather for sacrificing some of their dads' time.

R.W.T.
R.F.R.

FOREWORD
by Max Siporin

It is a pleasure to welcome this second edition of *An Introduction to Group Work Practice* by Toseland and Rivas. Its popularity among helping professionals, and in education for the helping professions, particularly in social work, has been well deserved. The additions and modifications made here augment the book's strengths and contributions and enhance its usefulness for students and practitioners.

During this past decade, there has been a continuing expansion of interest in social group work and an increase in the number of its applications in a variety of helping methods and settings. Group work is no longer a neglected child; it now has a central place in the repertoire of helping methods used both to help people and to accomplish basic tasks in our society. The theoretical and technical knowledge and skills of group work are accepted as of basic importance in leading therapeutic and task groups. This book both espouses and contributes to this paradigmatic shift in our conceptual and action orientations within helping practice.

It is now well recognized that we live, develop our selves, take responsibility for our actions, and accomplish our life purposes as group members, in group roles and identities. We function in group contexts; in accord with group culture, norms, and beliefs; and with group nurture, resources, and support. Group work is a method of harnessing and directing these powerful group influences and resources for constructive ends. It expresses and implements needed social values: respect for and acceptance of human worth and diversity, interdependence, reciprocal mutual aid, altruism, and solidarity. These are basic values essential for individual, group, and community welfare. Group work thus represents social idealism in our striving for a democratic and just society. Such social values and behaviors are especially important in our time, which is characterized by much social conflict and violence, family and community fragmentation, and economic decline. Toseland and Rivas have placed group work in a historical tradition within social work of serving both a social cause and a technical function. They present a humanistic model of group work practice as a way of implementing these essential values and objectives.

Toseland and Rivas offer a systemic approach to practice, integrating concerns with individual, group, and organizational/community collectivities and situations. They thus articulate the person-situation perspective that has long been characteristic of social work and is now termed an ecological-systems approach. The increased attention to situational aspects of individual and group functioning is a recognition of how influential the larger organizational and community contexts are, and how their rewarding, limiting, and reinforcing aspects need to be assessed and dealt with in order to facilitate effective helping. Group work is also placed in an institutional context, as part of the system of social services that is a basic feature of our society.

The emphasis on task groups as well as treatment groups is particularly helpful because of the current shifts in our industrial and governmental organizations to a concern with using and empowering task groups and with ensuring effective group functioning. This recognizes the importance of individual and group performance in the achievement of both individual and group objectives. Concrete attainment of specific purposes, in terms of skilled task completion, is understood as a productive pathway to gain needed self-esteem and identity, as well as high group morale and productivity. Helpful ways of assessing and working with both types of groups, in terms of their stages of development, are explained in clear and practical terms, with illuminating examples and exercises. This material is presented with a concern for evaluating process and results of interventive activities and with accountability for the costs and effort involved.

The material on formulating and accomplishing concrete tasks, in the sections on task groups, is also applicable to therapeutic work with individuals and to work in treatment groups and support groups. The formerly fashionable "touchy-feely" approaches have been superseded by attention to specific objectives and tasks, not just in behavioral terms, but also in regard to modifying dysfunctional attitudes, feelings, beliefs, and cognitive schemas. Attention is paid as well to monitoring process, evaluating outcomes, and seeing to the maintenance of change for the long term. This trend is evident in work with therapy groups and in work with many types of support groups and community organization groups. The material presented here is responsive to this trend.

The new section on working with support groups meets an important need in our society for ways of facilitating and strengthening this life-giving resource in our communities. The values and benefits of active membership in support groups, including self-help groups, are now well documented. These types of groups are now considered instrumental in helping individuals deal with difficulties in social functioning, with mental disorder, and with many types of physical illnesses and conditions. The individualization of member needs requires attention to the diverse cultural, ethnic, racial, and religious backgrounds of individuals and groups, so that their mutual aid activities can be evoked and strengthened, in support groups as well as in therapy and task groups. The focus on individual and group tasks in such groups, and the provision of substantive programmatic and educational content, as illustrated here, are in line with pressing needs for such knowledge and skills.

Another contribution is the new material on task practice with community groups—with social action groups, coalitions, and delegate councils. Community development and organization practice meets a particular need in our diverse and fragmented communities to help with efforts toward community integration, inter-group harmony, and effective communal functioning and welfare. Positive community functioning is essential for individuals and families to function well in the systemic dynamics of their interdependence for an adaptive fit in mutual develop-ment and goal attainment. Well-functioning communities depend on work with constituent groups that represent communal as well as individual and family inter-ests and requirements. The material on community group work practice supports these efforts.

The expanded section on leadership theory and skills used with varied types of groups also meets an urgent need for knowledge and competence. The social authority of leading role models has been much eroded in recent years by preva-lent attacks on and rejections of what is considered oppressive, controlling, exploitive, and limiting of an individual's own interests and autonomy. In group work as conceived here, the model of the therapeutic guru as group leader that was fashionable in the not so distant past is replaced by a model of facilitative socio-emotional and practical task leadership that is better geared to democratic styles and to concrete accomplishment of group purposes. The leadership roles, styles, and skills discussed and illustrated throughout the book are of practical importance in asserting credible, meaningful, and competent authority. This is a social authority of leadership by the social group worker, as a legitimate represen-tative of group members, of the community, and of society, that can motivate, inspire, guide, and empower people and thus influence constructive attitudes and behavior change.

Toseland and Rivas offer a scholarly as well as a practical integration of the-ory and skill in their use of psychodynamic, behavioral, and task-centered orienta-tions. The discussions are grounded in solid empirical research and in extensive practice experience, with helpful references to the research literature and mean-ingful case illustrations.

This book remains an outstanding contribution to the theory and practice of social group work. It stands within the rich tradition of social work with groups and continues to lead us to new perspectives and helping behaviors in our work toward social betterment and social justice.

PART I

The Knowledge Base of Group Work Practice

CHAPTER 1

Introduction

This text is concerned with the practice of group work by professional social workers. Group work entails the deliberate use of intervention strategies and group processes to accomplish individual, group, and community goals using the value base and ethical practice principles of the social work profession. As one prepares to become an effective social work practitioner, it is important to realize the effect that groups have on people's lives. It is not possible to be a member of society without becoming a member of numerous groups and being influenced by others (Falck, 1988). Although it is possible to live in an isolated manner on the fringes of groups, our social nature makes this neither desirable nor healthy.

Groups provide the structure on which communities and the larger society are built. They provide formal and informal structure in the work place. But more important, they provide a means through which relationships with significant others are carried out. Participation in family groups, peer groups, and classroom groups helps members learn acceptable norms of social behavior, engage in satisfying social relationships, identify personal goals, and derive a variety of other benefits that result from participating in closely knit social systems. Experiences in social, church, recreation, interest, and work groups are essential in the development and maintenance of people and society.

THE FOCUS OF GROUP WORK PRACTICE

Social work practitioners use group work skills to help meet the needs of individual group members, the group as a whole, and the community. In this text, group work is conceptualized from a broad perspective. Group work involves the following:

1. Practice with a variety of treatment and task groups.
2. Work in three focal areas, that is, with individual group members, the group as a whole, and the group's environment.
3. Application of foundation skills and knowledge from a generalist approach to practice for leading many types of treatment and task groups.
4. Integration and use of specialized skills from differing approaches to practice for leading specific groups in particular situations.

This text is firmly grounded in a generalist approach to practice. To accomplish the broad mission and goals of the social work profession, generalist practitioners are expected to possess basic competencies that enable them to intervene effectively with individuals, families, groups, organizations, and communities. This text is designed to help generalist practitioners understand how group work can be used to help individuals, families, groups, organizations, and communities function as effectively as possible.

In many group work texts, little effort is made to examine the broad range of groups that may be used for helping purposes. Most texts focus almost exclusively on the use of groups for clinical practice. Scant mention is made of committees, teams, and other groups that are common in practice settings. Despite the distinctive emphasis of the social work profession on the interface between individuals and their social environment, in most group work texts, even less attention is paid to the use of groups in community practice. This text will examine the use of a broad range of treatment and task groups for practice with individuals, organizations, and communities.

Some prominent group workers (Hartford, 1971; Klein, 1972; Shulman, 1992) focus on the group as a whole as the unit of intervention and place less emphasis on work with individuals in the group. Others place their emphasis on changing individual group members within the group context (Garvin, 1987; Rose, 1989; Shaffer & Galinsky, 1989; Sundel, Glasser, Sarri, & Vinter, 1985). We believe both of these perspectives are useful. When leading any group, workers should direct their attention to individuals, the group as a whole, and the community in which the group functions. The worker focuses on individual members to help them accomplish their goals. The worker intervenes with the group as a whole to achieve an optimum level of group functioning and to ensure that the group accomplishes its purposes. The worker also assesses the group's environment and decides whether to help the group adapt to it or change it.

We believe the purpose of the group helps determine the emphasis that each of these focal areas should receive. For example, in a support group for recently separated people, the worker might focus on the development of mutual aid among members of the group as a whole. In an assertion training group, the worker might focus on assessing members' specific skills and deficits and developing individualized treatment plans.

In both cases, however, other focal areas should not be neglected. For example, in the support group it is necessary to help individual members develop plans for dealing with specific problems they are facing. In the assertion training group, it is important to enhance group cohesion, mutual sharing, and mutual aid in the group as a whole.

In both groups, attention must also be given to the community in which the group functions. For example, a close examination of the community in which members of the assertion training group function might suggest a need to make community services more responsive to members of the group. This may, in turn, lead to the development of a social action group to address this problem. Later in this text, we will examine in detail these three focal areas.

Another aspect of our conceptualization of group work practice is that workers draw on a broad base of knowledge and skills from generalist practice, which they apply to their work with a variety of specific treatment and task groups. The generalist approach emphasizes that social workers are called on to perform many roles in their professional lives. It suggests they have knowledge and skills that transcend specific roles—essential for effective practice. For example, knowledge about human development and generic skills such as empathic responding apply equally well to work with individuals, families, groups, and communities.

Although core generalist knowledge and skills are identified for both treatment and task groups throughout the text, more specialized skills are appropriate for particular types of groups. These specialized skills, which are frequently associated with specialized approaches to group work, are also explicated throughout this text.

Most experienced practitioners continue to learn by exposure to a variety of approaches to group work. Although some approaches are not easily integrated with one another—for example, behavioral and humanistic approaches—even widely divergent approaches have many commonalities. An eclectic use of specialized approaches can be helpful in deciding on the most effective methods for intervention in a particular group. Exclusive adherence to one approach may work well for a particular group in a particular situation, but it may not always work well when leading other groups in different situations. Rigid adherence to one approach tends to make a worker oblivious to other potentially useful methods. It can also distort a worker's assessment of a situation. A worker might mistakenly attempt to fit data from a situation to a particular practice approach, rather than choosing the practice approach to fit the situation. For these reasons, we believe that group workers can be most effective when they are familiar with several approaches to group work, and when they apply specialized knowledge and skills differentially depending on the particular group work endeavor.

Our approach also recognizes the interactional nature of the helping process (Maluccio, 1979). The interactional model of group leadership presented in Chapter 4 suggests some of the factors that workers should consider when deciding how to proceed with a group.

Organization of the Text

Group work can be understood as a series of activities carried out by the worker during the life of a group. While certain foundation activities, such as empathic responding, are essential throughout the life of the group, other activities—such as confrontation—are more appropriate during particular stages of a group's development (Rivas & Toseland, 1981; Shulman, 1981). Group workers' skillful use of specific foundation and stage-specific activities is guided by the developmental needs of the group as a whole and its individual members.

We have found that it is helpful to understand the practice of group work as consisting of six developmental stages:

1. Planning
2. Beginning

3. Assessment
4. Middle
5. Evaluation
6. Ending

These stages of group work correspond to predictable stages of group development. A group exhibits certain properties and processes during each stage of its development. The group worker's task is to engage in activities that facilitate the growth and development of the group during each stage.

This text is organized around the six stages of group work mentioned previously. Before discussing each stage, Part I of this text covers the knowledge base of group work practice. Chapter 1 introduces basic group work concepts and outlines the many types of groups that practitioners may work with in practice settings. Chapter 2 provides a basis for group work practice by examining the history and traditions of group work and by reviewing social science findings related to group processes. Chapter 3 provides a framework for examining group processes and group dynamics. Chapter 4 focuses on the processes and skills of group leadership and membership.

Part II describes in detail the methods and skills used by the worker in each stage of group work practice. Chapter 5 explains the worker's planning for the group. During the planning stage, the worker assesses the need for a group, considers potential group membership and sponsorship, and identifies the group's purpose. The worker also composes the group, recruits and orients members, and prepares for the first meeting by locating a suitable room and making other necessary arrangements.

Chapter 6 explains the skills necessary for beginning a group. This stage of group work occurs during the first few meetings of the group. As members begin face-to-face interaction, the worker helps build relationships by clarifying the group's purpose. During the beginning stage, the worker helps members get to know each other. Together, the worker and the members identify individual and group goals, and contracts are developed for work that will be accomplished during the middle stage of group work.

Chapter 7 focuses on the process of assessment. Assessment is conceptualized as a process that occurs at three levels: the individual group member, the group as a whole, and the group's environment. Chapter 7 discusses each of the levels of assessment and describes appropriate assessment methods.

Chapters 8 and 9 deal with the skills and activities the worker employs during the middle stage of work with treatment groups, and Chapters 10 and 11 focus on middle-stage skills with task groups. During the middle stage the worker helps members achieve their individual goals and helps the group accomplish its tasks.

The worker helps structure the group's work and helps build group dynamics that are conducive to achieving the expressive and instrumental goals of the group. Whereas Chapters 8 and 10 describe a variety of foundation activities that are useful in facilitating treatment and task groups with many objectives, Chapters 9 and 11 present specialized intervention activities for helping treatment and task groups accomplish specific objectives.

Chapter 12 describes how to evaluate group work practice. Chapter 13 explains the skills that can be used to end the group. The worker helps the group make the most of the time remaining to accomplish the group's tasks. The worker helps members generalize and maintain changes that have been made and helps them end their association.

VALUES AND ETHICS IN GROUP WORK PRACTICE

Practice Values

In social work, the focus of group work practice is influenced by a system of personal and professional values. These values affect workers' styles of intervention and the skills they use in working with clients. They also affect clients' reactions to the worker's efforts.

Values are beliefs that delineate preferences about how one ought or ought not to behave. They refer to some goal that is worth or not worth attaining (Rokeach, 1968). There is no such thing as value-free group work practice. All group workers operate on the basis of certain specific assumptions and values regarding the nature of human beings, the role of members, and the role of the group leader. Values influence the methods used to accomplish group and individual goals. Even a leader who is completely permissive and nondirective reveals the values embodied in such a stance.

A worker's actions in the group are affected by contextual values, client value systems, and the worker's personal value system (Morales & Sheafor, 1992). The context in which the group functions affects the values exhibited in the group. Contextual sources of values include the values of society, values of the agency sponsoring the group, and values of the social work profession. Brill (1990) has identified four values that are dominant in American society:

1. Judeo-Christian doctrine with its emphasis on the dignity and worth of people and people's responsibility for their neighbor.
2. Democratic values that emphasize equality and participation, including men's and women's rights to life, liberty, and the pursuit of happiness.
3. The Puritan ethic, which emphasizes men's and women's responsibility for themselves, and the central role of work in a moral life.
4. Social Darwinism, which emphasizes the survival of the strongest and the fittest in a long-term evolutionary process.

The organization and the community that are sponsoring the group are also part of the contextual value system that can influence a worker's stance toward the group. The health and social service organizations sponsoring the group have a history and a tradition with regard to the services they provide.

Before proposing to begin a group, the worker should become familiar with the agency's formal and informal values, which are embodied in the agency's policies, procedures, and practices. Are treatment groups a preferred method of delivering therapeutic services? Are decisions often made in task groups consisting of staff members, or are decisions imposed on staff by the agency's administrators? Becoming aware of the policies, procedures, and practices regarding the use of groups in a particular agency can help the worker prepare for possible resistance and evaluate and use sources of support within the agency.

Cultural and historical influences within communities can also influence how the group conducts its business. Community standards and values differ widely. Therefore, when planning a group, the worker needs to consider how cultural and historical influences within a community are likely to influence the group and its members.

The worker and the group are also affected by professional values. Important social work values summarized by Siporin (1975) include respecting the worth and dignity of the individual, respecting a person's autonomy and self-direction, facilitating a person's participation in the helping process, maintaining a nonjudgmental attitude, ensuring equal access to services and social provisions, and affirming the interdependence of the individual and society.

Beyond the values held by all professional social work practitioners, group workers share a special concern and interest in values that are basic to group work practice. Some of the key values of group work have been stated by Gisela Konopka (1983). She suggests that all group workers should agree on the importance of:

1. Participation and positive relations among people of different color, creed, age, national origin, and social class in the group.
2. The value of cooperation and mutual decision making embodied in the principles of a participatory democracy.
3. The importance of individual initiative within the group.
4. The importance of freedom to participate, including expressing thoughts and feelings about matters of concern to individual members or the group as a whole, and having the right to be involved in the decision-making process of the group.
5. The value of high individualization in the group so that each member's unique concerns are addressed.

These values are not absent in other aspects of social work practice, but in group work they are of central importance. The group is uniquely suited for the exercise of these values, and all group workers should give them their careful attention. As we have attended to these values when leading treatment and task groups over the years, we have found that three values have become particularly important to us.

First, we value members' ability to help one another. We value the power and the promise of relationships to help members grow and develop, to help them heal, to satisfy their needs for human contact and connectedness, and to promote a sense of unity and community. Thus, we strive to promote member-to-member helping relationships, and to de-emphasize the role of the leader as expert.

Second, we value groups' ability to empower people. Groups help members feel good about themselves and their abilities to make a difference in their own lives and in their community.

Third, we value the power of groups to promote understanding among people from diverse backgrounds. Members' respect and appreciation for one another grow as their relationships deepen. Thus, we believe strongly in the power of social group work to help bridge the gap that exists in modern society among people from diverse backgrounds.

In addition to values derived from the context of practice, the worker and the members bring their own values to the group. Each individual has a unique value system, and it is not possible to identify a general or common value system for all group members. Often, members are not clear about their own values or have not given them careful consideration. Part of the worker's task is to clarify his or her own values, to help the group members clarify their values, and to identify and resolve value conflicts between members and the larger society.

Although it is not possible to identify a common set of values for all group members, the worker should be especially sensitive to the effects that cultural diversity can have on values. For example, Lewis and Ho (1977) point out that in the Native American culture, although cooperation is an important value, it is considered impolite to offer advice, help, or opinion to someone unless it is solicited. Giordano (1973) suggests that group members with Irish ethnic backgrounds often prefer not to express their feelings openly, whereas Italian Americans are more likely to express their feelings freely.

Workers' personal value systems also affect how they practice. If workers are uncomfortable discussing certain value-laden topics, or if they impose their own values on the group, their work will be seriously impaired. Similarly, if they are not aware of the implications of their values, they are likely to conflict with members who have different values.

Workers who are not aware of their own values will also have difficulty when faced with ambiguous and value-laden situations. Sometimes the goals of the worker, the agency, the community, and the group members differ. This is often so with involuntary clients who are receiving the service of a worker at the request of law-enforcement officials or others in the community who find the client's behavior unacceptable. The more clear workers are about their own values and their own purposes and stances in relation to working with the group, the easier it will be for them to sort through conflicting goals and make their own purposes known to group members.

One of the best ways for workers to become aware of their own values and their own stance in working with a group is to obtain supervision and consultation on their work. Although workers will never become value-free, supervision and consultation can help them become aware of the values they bring to the group. Supervision can help workers modify or change values that are not consistent with those of the social work profession or helpful to their practice. Value clarification exercises can also help workers identify personal and professional values that might influence their work with a group (see, for example, Smith, 1977).

Practice Ethics

The National Association of Social Workers (NASW) has developed a code of ethics to guide the practice of its members. The code of ethics is an operational statement of the central values of the social work profession. Social workers who lead groups should be thoroughly familiar with it. It is available directly from NASW and is reproduced in many social work practice textbooks.

Corey and Corey (1987) point out that a code of ethics specifically for group workers is a helpful adjunct to the more general codes of ethics developed by professional associations. Two organizations, the Association for Specialists in Group Work (ASGW) and the American Group Psychotherapy Association (AGPA), have taken the lead in developing specific codes of ethics for group workers. The recently revised codes of ethics of both associations appear in Appendix A. Both codes focus on three main areas: (a) informed consent, (b) leader competence and training, and (c) the appropriate conduct of group meetings.

The first area includes telling members about the purpose and goals of the group and giving them information such as the potential risks of participation; the cost, timing, and duration of sessions; whether participation is voluntary; what is expected of group members during meetings; procedures to ensure confidentiality; and screening and termination procedures. In a survey of 300 group psychotherapists, Roback, Ochoa, Bloch, and Purdon (1992) found that the limits of confidentiality are rarely discussed with potential group members despite the fact that breaches of confidentiality by members are fairly common. Group leaders may also be required to report certain information, such as child abuse, even without the permission of a group member.

The second area covered in codes of ethics for group practitioners includes ensuring that workers have the proper education, training, and experience to lead a particular group. Practitioners should not offer a group, or use a procedure or technique within a group, without sufficient education, experience, and supervision to ensure that it is implemented properly. Practitioners should also seek out additional supervision and consultation when they anticipate or encounter difficulties with a particular group.

As they continue to practice, group workers have the additional responsibility to engage in ongoing professional development activities including workshops, seminars, and other professional educational opportunities. They should also keep up with current clinical and empirical findings that relate to their ongoing work with group members.

The third broad area in both codes of ethics focuses on ethical principles for the conduct of group meetings. These include ensuring that:

- Screening procedures lead to the selection of members whose needs and goals can be met by the group.
- Workers help members develop and pursue therapeutic goals.
- Members are protected from physical threats, intimidation, the imposition of worker and member values, and other forms of coercion and peer pressure that are not therapeutic.
- Members are treated fairly and equitably.
- Workers avoid exploiting members for their own gain.
- Appropriate referrals are made when the needs of a particular member cannot be met in the group.
- The worker engages in ongoing assessment, evaluation, and follow-up of members to ensure that the group meets their needs.

Galinsky and Schopler (1977) point out that violation of these ethical principals can be damaging to group members. They suggest, for example, that the harm encounter groups do to some members can be traced to inappropriate screening procedures and the failure of group workers to describe the risks and requirements of group membership. Similarly, Harold Lewis (1982) points out that although the NASW code of ethics indicates the primacy of clients' interests, workers sometimes choose to give primacy to their own definitions of clients' needs, or to give some group members' needs primacy over the needs of other members.

More recently, Lakin (1991) has pointed out that even well-intentioned, enthusiastic group workers can subtly violate ethical principals, and that these violations can be harmful to members. He presents evidence, for example, that pressures to conform in some feminist-oriented therapy groups can lead members to suppress particular opinions, thoughts, or points of view simply because they clash with the dominant ideology expressed in the group. Further, he points out that group dynamics are abused when they are developed for the purpose of ideological recruitment or persuasion rather than to address therapeutic needs. To guard against these potential ethical violations, he suggests that all group workers should consider the extent to which (a) workers' values are consonant with the needs and problems of group members, (b) workers are pushing their own agenda without regard to the needs and wishes of group members, and (c) each member's needs are individualized rather than treated as identical to those of other members.

DEFINITION OF GROUP WORK

The practice principles presented in this text are based on social work practice theory. However, as a method of practice, group work is used by a variety of helping professionals. Nurses, psychologists, counselors, psychiatrists, teachers, clergy, and others regularly employ treatment group methods in working with their clients. Managers, supervisors, administrators, staff-development specialists, politicians, and community organizers employ task group methods to carry out their job functions or the mandates of their organizations.

Although group work is used extensively in service delivery and agency functioning, it is infrequently identified as an important part of professional education and training. Nurses and physicians study medicine, teachers learn educational methods, managers and administrators concentrate on organizational theory; yet when these professionals begin to carry out the functions of their jobs, they frequently rely on group work as a method of practice. Therefore, although this text focuses on group work in the context of social work practice, the study of groups and group work can be useful in many different professions.

Many professions have contributed to the knowledge base of group work, so it is difficult to sort out each profession's contributions and viewpoints. It has been suggested that although group work has emerged as a conscious professional activity, there is little reason to believe that "there is conceptual agreement or even clarity regarding its definition, purposes, practice methods and techniques" (Alissi, 1980a, p. 3). Although approaches to group work are quite different, there is general agreement that each approach has its merits and particular practice applications. Therefore, a functional definition of group work should focus on the generic aspects of practice as well as allow for specialized approaches. The broad definition offered in this chapter allows beginning practitioners to understand the boundaries of group work as well as its many practice applications. It includes both treatment and task group practice. *Group work* can be defined as:

> Goal-directed activity with small groups of people aimed at meeting socio-emotional needs and accomplishing tasks. This activity is directed to individual members of a group and to the group as a whole within a system of service delivery.

This definition describes group work as goal-directed activity, which refers to planned, orderly worker activities carried out in the context of professional practice with people. Goal-directed activity has many purposes. For example, group workers may aim to support or educate members, help them socialize and achieve personal growth, or provide treatment for their problems and concerns.

Workers may also help members of a group develop leadership skills so they can take increasing responsibility for the group's development. At the same time, workers should enable their groups to change the social environment. This includes helping members gain greater control over the organizations and communities that affect their lives. Some writers advocate a person-in-situation view of practice (Klein, 1972; Pincus & Minahan, 1973; Schwartz & Zalba, 1971; Siporin, 1975). Others focus on techniques of individual change within small groups (Rose, 1989; Rose, 1991; Rose & LeCroy, 1991; Sarri, 1974; Vinter, 1967, 1985a). Both approaches are valuable, and attention should be given to both when groups set their goals.

The next component of the definition of group work refers to working with small groups of people. A large group may not allow for sufficient interaction. It is difficult to compose a large group around common purposes and common goals. The members of a large group sometimes think of themselves as an audience rather than as group members. Thus, the term *small group* implies the ability of members to identify themselves as members, to engage in interaction, and to exchange thoughts and feelings among themselves through verbal and nonverbal communication processes.

The definition of group work also indicates that workers practice with both treatment and task groups. Most workers are called upon both to help clients meet their personal needs and to help their agency or organization accomplish its tasks. For example, most direct service workers have many opportunities to work with both treatment and task groups.

Our definition of group work also emphasizes that the worker should have a dual focus within any group: goal-directed activities with individual members and with the group as a whole. The literature on group work is not particularly clear on this point. Some writers favor working with the goals of individual members (see, for example, Garvin & Glasser, 1971; Rose, 1989, 1991; Rose & LeCroy,

1991; Vinter, 1985a), while others emphasize working with the group as a whole as the primary focus of attention (see, for example, Klein, 1972; Schwartz & Zalba, 1971).

Few hold views that are mutually exclusive. Writers who emphasize the individual members as the primary client system usually note the importance of the group as a whole. Those who focus on the group as the primary client system frequently note the importance of individualizing the members' needs, concerns, and goals. Both the individuals and the group as a whole have life histories, developmental patterns, needs, goals, and characteristic patterns of behaving that should be of concern to the worker. Therefore, both the group as a whole and individual members should receive the attention of the worker.

The final portion of the definition of group work emphasizes that a group does not exist in a vacuum. It exists in relation to a community that sponsors, legitimizes, and influences its purposes, and to an existing service delivery system. Even self-help groups and groups conducted in private practice are influenced by organizational and community support, sponsorship, and sanction.

Usually, there is an exchange of influence between a group and its sponsoring agency. A group is often influenced by its sponsoring organization's resources, policies, goals, and mandates. At the same time, a group may be the catalyst for a needed change in agency policies or procedures. For example, an agency policy limits membership in a support group for young parents to a specific geographic area served by the agency. Because of the large number of single parents interested in attending the meetings, and the need for child care during meetings, the group highlights the need for child care services. In this example, the group is influenced by—and influences—the agency that sponsors it.

CLASSIFYING GROUPS

To understand the breadth of group work practice, it is helpful to become familiar with the variety of groups that can be led in practice settings. Because there are so many kinds of groups that workers may be called upon to lead, it is helpful to distinguish among them. In the following two sections, distinctions are made among groups on the basis of whether they are formed or occur naturally and whether they are treatment- or task-oriented.

Formed and Natural Groups

Formed groups are those that come together through some outside influence or intervention. They usually have some sponsorship or affiliation and are convened for a particular purpose. Some examples of formed groups are therapy groups, classroom groups, committees, social action groups, and teams. Natural groups come together spontaneously on the basis of naturally occurring events, interpersonal attraction, or the mutually perceived needs of members. They often lack formal sponsorship. Natural groups include family groups, peer groups, friendship networks, street gangs, and cliques.

This text is primarily concerned with formed groups. Natural groups are not given extensive coverage because of major differences between formed and natural groups. For example, natural groups such as families are neither planned nor constructed by a group worker. Generally, they have a longer developmental history, which has unique implications for the relationships established among members and hence for the interventions used by workers. For these reasons, a separate body of knowledge has been developed for work with natural groups. Work with families, for example, is a separate and distinct field of practice, using a separate body of knowledge and research, as well as distinct intervention techniques.

Despite the differences between formed and natural groups, many of the skills and techniques presented in this text are readily applicable to work with natural groups. We encourage group work practitioners to use the knowledge and skills presented in this text in their work with natural groups. Some efforts have already been made in this regard, such as attempts to use group work skills in working with the family unit (see, for example, Bell, 1975, 1981); working with gangs (see, for example, Spergel, 1966, 1969); and enhancing the social networks of those who are socially isolated (see, for example, Collins & Pancoast, 1970; Toseland, 1990a; Toseland, Decker, & Bliesner, 1979; Toseland, Sherman, & Bliven, 1981).

Purpose and Group Work

Formed groups can be classified according to the purposes for which they are organized. The term *purpose* can be defined as the general aims of a group. The importance of purpose in group work cannot be overemphasized. According to Wilson (1976), "the nature of the framework for the practice of group work depends on the purpose of the group [which is] served" (p. 41). A group's purpose identifies the reasons for bringing members together. As Klein (1972) notes, "purpose guides group composition" (pp. 31–32). It also helps guide the group's selection of goal-directed activities and define the broad parameters of the services to be delivered.

In this text, the term *treatment group* is used to signify a group whose major purpose is to meet members' socio-emotional needs. The purposes for forming treatment groups include meeting members' needs for support, education, therapy, growth, or socialization. In contrast, the term *task group* is used to signify any group in which the major purpose is neither intrinsically nor immediately linked to the needs of the members of the group. In task groups, the overriding purpose is to accomplish a mandate and complete the work for which the group was convened.

The concept of purpose in groups is sometimes difficult to understand because few groups exist for only one purpose. Most groups involve both meeting members' personal needs and accomplishing one or more group tasks. For example, in some approaches used in treatment groups, personal needs are met through a problem-solving approach or a task-centered approach (Garvin, Reid, & Epstein, 1976; Somers, 1976; Toseland; 1980). Treatment is conceptualized as a series of tasks to be accomplished. Completing these tasks is associated with a favorable outcome. A socialization group might, for example, plan and carry out a series of structured role plays to increase members' social skills. A growth group might engage in a series of exercises to increase members' self-awareness. In both cases, members have met their personal needs by participating in a group task. Thus, it is common for a treatment group to accomplish tasks as well as serve the socio-emotional needs of its members.

Treatment and Task Groups

In classifying groups as either treatment- or task-oriented, it is important to consider how the two types differ. Table 1–1 points out some of the major differences between treatment and task groups in terms of selected characteristics. The table is, in part, based on comparisons made by Klein (1972) and earlier by Jennings (1950). The bond present in a group is usually based on the purpose for which it is convened. Members of treatment groups are bonded by their common needs and common situations. Task group members create a common bond by working together to accomplish a task, carry out a mandate, or produce a product.

In treatment groups, roles are not set before the group forms, but develop through interaction among members. In task groups, members take on roles through a process of interaction and also are frequently assigned roles by the group. Roles that may be assigned include team leader, secretary, and fact finder.

TABLE 1–1
A comparison of task and treatment groups

	Type of Group	
Selected Characteristics	**Treatment**	**Task**
Bond	Members' personal needs	Task to be completed
Roles	Develop through interaction	Develop through interaction or are assigned
Communication Patterns	Open	Focused on the discussion of a particular task
Procedures	Flexible or formal, depending on the group	Formal agenda and rules
Composition	Based on common concerns, problems, or characteristics	Based on needed talents, expertise, or division of labor
Self-disclosure	Expected to be high	Expected to be low
Confidentiality	Proceedings usually private and kept within the group	Proceedings may be private but are sometimes open to the public
Evaluation	Success based on members meeting treatment goals	Success based on members accomplishing task or mandate, or producing a product

Communication patterns in treatment groups are open. Members are usually encouraged to interact with one another. Task group members are more likely to address their communications to the worker and to keep their communication focused on a particular group task. In some task groups, the amount that members communicate on a particular agenda item may be limited by the worker. In other task groups, members may limit their own communication because they believe they will not be well-received by the group.

Treatment groups often have flexible procedures for meetings, including a warm-up period, a period for working on members' concerns, and a period for summarizing the group's work. Task groups are more likely to have formalized rules that govern how members conduct group business and reach decisions.

Although a similar set of procedures can be used for composing both treatment and task groups, the actual composition of these types of groups may differ. For example, treatment groups are often composed of members with common concerns, problems, or abilities. Task groups are often composed of members with the necessary resources and expertise to accomplish the group's mission.

In treatment groups, members are expected to disclose their own concerns and problems. Therefore, self-disclosures may contain emotionally charged, personal concerns. In task groups, member self-disclosure is relatively infrequent. It is generally expected that members will confine themselves to discussions about accomplishing the group's task and will not share intimate, personal concerns.

The members of treatment groups often decide that the proceedings of the group should be confidential. The meetings of some task groups, such as treatment conferences and cabinets, may be private, but the meetings of other task groups, such as committees and delegate councils, are often described in minutes that may be circulated to interested persons and organizations.

The criteria for evaluating success also differ between treatment and task groups. Treatment groups are successful to the extent that they help members meet their individual treatment goals. Task groups are successful when they accomplish group goals, such as generating solutions to problems, planning strategies, or making correct decisions; or when they develop group products, such as a report, a set of regulations, or a series of recommendations concerning a particular community issue.

An example in which a worker is responsible for leading both types of groups may help illustrate the differences between treatment and task groups:

In the first group, the worker meets with adults who have recently become parents for the first time. The purpose of the group is to provide a forum for discussion about their adjustment to parenthood.

In the second group, the worker brings together several community representatives to study day-care resources and make recommendations to a government agency regarding changes in government support for day-care.

The parents group is classified as a treatment group because it is convened to meet the personal needs of its members. The group is bonded by its common purpose and the common needs and concerns of its members. It is expected that friendships might develop among group members and that members will help each other in their adjustment to parenthood. It is also expected that the feeling level and the level of self-disclosure will be high because of the similar characteristics of the members and the problems they face. Because members may self-disclose about personal issues, the proceedings of the group are confidential. Roles develop based on how members assist in accomplishing the purpose of the group and how members meet each other's needs.

Because parenting is a developmental phenomenon involving constant discovery and change, the procedures of the group are flexible, allowing members to share their immediate weekly concerns. The parents group is composed with the similarity of members' concerns in mind. Patterns of communication focus on the needs of members, such as adjusting to parenthood and becoming effective parents. To evaluate the success of the group, the worker focuses on members' satisfaction with the group experience and whether the group has met their needs.

In the group discussing day-care services, the focus is task-oriented, and the purpose is external to the personal needs of the members. Members are bonded by the common cause of improving day-care services. They are expected to reveal their personal viewpoints only to the extent that they contribute to the group's task. Personal feelings are occasionally shared, but factual data are given greater weight. The group is publicized and seeks outside, expert testimony to contribute to its deliberations. Confidentiality is impractical because it would hinder the accomplishment of the group's task. Roles are assigned by the worker. For example, members are appointed to subcommittees to collect needed data. Roles also develop depending on how each member contributes to the task of the group.

To facilitate an organized approach to the task, the group works from an agenda, which is published in advance to give participants time to prepare for the proceedings. To facilitate a division of labor and encourage different perspectives, the group is composed by selecting members who have some knowledge of day-care programs and needed areas of expertise. Patterns of communication focus on the task rather than on members' personal concerns. In evaluating the effectiveness of the group, the worker examines the group's decisions, actions, written reports and recommendations for clarity, thoroughness, and feasibility.

GROUP VS. INDIVIDUAL EFFORTS

There are several advantages and disadvantages to using a group rather than an individual effort to meet individual, organizational, and community needs. In describing these advantages and disadvantages, it is important to distinguish between the effectiveness and efficiency of treatment and task groups.

Advantages and Disadvantages of Treatment Groups

In relation to meeting client needs, Levine (1979) suggests that "group therapy can help with most anything that individual therapy can, providing an appropriate group is available and the individual will accept the group as the mode of treatment" (p. 11). Several writers have suggested that group treatment has advantages over individual treatment (Lieberman & Borman, 1979; Northen, 1982; Shulman, 1992; Toseland & Siporin, 1986; Yalom, 1985). Groups help members realize that they are not alone with their problems. They allow members to hear that others have similar concerns (Shulman, 1992; Yalom, 1985). They also give members the opportunity to help each other by being supportive, giving feedback, making suggestions, and providing useful information. Lieberman and Borman (1979) have noted the therapeutic benefit of the "helper-therapy principle" for members of groups that develop on a mutual aid basis. As members give and get help, they observe others achieving their goals. This process provides what Yalom (1985) refers to as an "installation of hope" that is absent in individual treatment.

Treatment groups provide other benefits that cannot be replicated in individual treatment. According to Northen (1982), group treatment is the preferred modality when a client's main problem concerns relationships with others. The presence of others gives members a chance to receive feedback that can help them in their efforts to change. Peer feedback can be particularly beneficial for adolescents and involuntary adult clients who may resist the suggestions of the worker, because he or she is viewed as an authority figure (Northen, 1982). It can also be beneficial for those who are socially isolated, such as older people who have lost peers and social roles, people who have been removed from their families, and people in hospitals and other institutions. Opportunities for vicarious learning are limited in individual treatment.

Groups can be valuable because they let members engage in reality testing (Gilbert, Miller, & Specht, 1980; Klein, 1972; Rose, 1989). Groups can develop into "social microcosms" (Yalom, 1985) in which members recreate problems they have experienced in the outside world. This can enable members to work through previously unsatisfying relationships with family members, peers, or friends (Konopka, 1963; Levine, 1979).

Groups can provide members with multiple opportunities to engage in role playing, test new skills, and rehearse new behaviors in the "safe" environment of the group (Rose, 1989). Opportunities to practice new behaviors with peers do not exist in individual treatment.

Although these advantages provide justification for using group work in treatment, several potential disadvantages of group treatment should be considered. Groups can encourage member conformity (Corey & Corey, 1987) and member dependency (Klein, 1972). When members open themselves up to other members through self-disclosure, they are vulnerable to harmful or unsupportive responses from them (Corey & Corey, 1987). Groups can scapegoat individual members (Konopka, 1963). Groups sometimes focus on a few particularly assertive or talkative members, creating a danger that these members' problems receive attention while other, less assertive or less talkative members receive little help (Shulman, 1992; Yalom, 1985).

In general, members can benefit from treatment groups when they have some ability to communicate with others, and when their concerns or problems lend themselves to group discussion. To the extent that certain group members, such as autistic children or schizophrenic adults, cannot communicate effectively, group work must be modified to include nonverbal program activities and, where appropriate, simple, brief verbal activities that are consistent with those members' skill levels. People who have an extreme need for privacy or confidentiality may also be unable to take part in group treatment without considerable support or reassurance. Groups are contraindicated for people whose behavior is so alien to others that it results in negative rather than positive interactions, or when it leads to the failure of others to continue with the group.

Empirical studies tend to support clinical reports of the effectiveness of treatment groups. In a comprehensive review of well-designed studies comparing group and individual treatment, Toseland and Siporin (1986) found that group treatment was more effective than individual treatment in 25 percent of the studies that were reviewed, whereas individual treatment was not found to be more effective than group treatment in any of the studies. Group work was also found to be more efficient than individual treatment, and to produce fewer dropouts from treatment.

Unfortunately, the empirical literature that was reviewed did not yield a clear pattern of the types of problems most effectively treated in groups. Subsequent work (Toseland, Rossiter, Peak, & Smith, 1990), however, has revealed that group treatment may be more effective than individual treatment for enhancing social supports, and less effective for dealing with intense, highly personal psychological problems.

Combined findings from the clinical and empirical literature suggest that social workers should consider recommending group treatment for individuals who suffer from isolation or who have other difficulties with interpersonal relationships, and individual treatment for those with highly personal psychological problems. Combinations of individual and group treatment appear to be effective for clients with both needs. It is always important to remember, however, that when recommending group or individual treatment, the practitioner should carefully consider individuals' needs and preferences before making any treatment decisions.

Advantages and Disadvantages of Task Groups

A group approach, as compared with an individual effort, also has advantages in helping individuals, organizations, and communities accomplish tasks. In working with groups of people in organizations and communities, democratic participation is often ideally desirable. Participation through group interaction helps members feel they have a stake in their organization or community. Resistance to change can be minimized when those who are to be affected are given the opportunity to participate in the change through group discussion (Bennis, Benne, & Chin, 1969; Resnick & Patti, 1980).

Group discussion, deliberation, and decision making can have other benefits. The increased quantity of information available in groups can be beneficial for generating alternative action plans, for problem solving, and for making decisions. Certain tasks are complex, requiring a pool of talents, expertise, or opinions for them to be completed in a satisfactory manner (Kiesler, 1978). The division of labor that occurs in well-run groups can also help members complete tasks quickly and efficiently.

Some disadvantages should be kept in mind when considering selecting a group approach for accomplishing tasks. For example, it has been suggested that group problem solving takes more time than individual problem solving (Hartford, 1971). Napier and Gershenfeld (1981) note that poorly run groups can make members feel frustrated, bored, or unappreciated. In addition, such groups often get little accomplished (Edson, 1977). Groups are also sometimes used to make simple decisions or solve simple problems that could be dealt with more easily by individuals. Under these conditions, group meetings can be costly to an organization and frustrating and unnecessary for group members.

Overall, findings about the effectiveness of group vs. individual problem solving and decision making have been equivocal (see, for example, Davis & Toseland, 1987; Hare, 1976; McGrath, 1984). In general, the advantages and disadvantages of using a group should be evaluated in relation to a particular situation and purpose. The needs of the group members and the requirements of the task should be given paramount consideration when deciding whether to use group work.

Although this text suggests that group work methods have a fairly wide applicability for many different types of individual, organizational, and community problems, these problems are sometimes best approached by using several practice methods. Thus, although group work is a valuable method by itself, within a generalist practice framework it is also valuable as part of larger planned change efforts that may use additional methods such as social casework or community organization to achieve particular goals (Anderson, 1981; Germain & Gitterman, 1980; Hartford, 1978; Pincus & Minahan, 1973; Siporin, 1975).

A TYPOLOGY OF TREATMENT AND TASK GROUPS

The broad distinctions between formed and natural groups and treatment and task groups can be further refined and developed into a classification system of the many types of groups workers may encounter in practice settings. One way to develop a classification system is to categorize treatment and task groups according to their primary purpose. Many writers have attempted to identify the primary purposes of the groups that workers may lead in practice settings. Hartford (1964) suggests groups may focus on "the social functioning, growth or change or rehabilitation of the group members" (p. 14). Schwartz (1974) suggests that groups are "an enterprise in mutual aid" (p. 218), and Murphy (1959) suggests that groups enhance members' "social functioning through a purposeful group experience" (pp. 34–35).

Other writers have attempted more ambitious classifications. For example, Douglas (1979) suggests that group purposes may include (a) individual growth and adjustment, (b) group development toward specific needs, and (c) social action, social change, and changing society through the group experience. Klein's (1972) "objectives for group workers" define a wide range of purposes for treatment and task groups. According to Klein, group purposes can include the following:

• Rehabilitation—restoring members to their former level of functioning.
• Habilitation—helping members grow and develop.
• Correction—helping members who are having problems with social laws or mores.
• Socialization—helping members learn how to get along with others and do what is socially acceptable.

- Prevention—helping members develop and function at an optimum level and helping them prepare for events that are likely to occur.
- Social action—helping members change their environment.
- Problem solving—helping members resolve complex issues and concerns.
- Developing social values—helping members develop a humanistic approach to living.

The rest of this chapter presents a typology of treatment groups and a typology of task groups that social workers will encounter in practice. The typologies are based on the primary purposes of each type of treatment and task group. Although groups with only one purpose rarely exist in practice, developing "pure" categories—that is, groups with a single purpose—is useful in illustrating differences between groups and in demonstrating the many ways that groups can be used in practice settings. For additional information about each type of group described, see Appendix B.

TREATMENT GROUPS

Five primary purposes for treatment groups are (a) support, (b) education, (c) growth, (d) therapy, and (e) socialization. In practice settings, there are innumerable variations of treatment groups that combine these five primary purposes. For example, a group for parents of children with Down syndrome might be oriented toward both education and growth. A group for alcoholics might have all five primary purposes. However, to show clearly the similarities and differences among types of groups, we have drawn up the treatment group typology shown in Table 1–2, which sets forth selected characteristics of typical treatment groups with one each of the five primary purposes. Table 1–2 can be used as a guide by workers who are planning to lead groups with only one purpose or groups that combine several purposes.

Support Groups

The description of the treatment typology begins with support groups because support is a common ingredient of many successful treatment groups. Support groups can be distinguished from other groups using supportive intervention strategies by their primary goal: to help members cope with stressful life events and revitalize and enhance their coping abilities to more effectively adapt to and cope with future stressful life events.

Some examples of support groups include the following:

- A group of children meeting at school to discuss the effects of divorce on their lives.
- A group of people diagnosed with cancer, and their families, discussing the effects of the disease and how to cope with it.
- A group of recently discharged psychiatric patients discussing their adjustment to community living.
- A group of single parents sharing the difficulties of raising children alone.

TABLE 1-2
A typology of treatment groups

	Purpose of the Group				
Selected Characteristics	**Support**	**Education**	**Growth**	**Therapy**	**Socialization**
Purpose	To help members cope with stressful life events and revitalize existing coping abilities	To educate through presentations, discussion, and experience	To develop members' potential, awareness, insight	To change behavior Correction, rehabilitation, coping and problem solving through behavior change interventions	To increase communication and social skills Improved interpersonal relationships through program activities, structured exercises, role plays, etc.
Leadership	A facilitator of empathic understanding and mutual aid	Leader as teacher and provider of structure for group discussion	Leader as facilitator and role model	Leader as expert, authority figure, or facilitator, depending on approach	Leader as director of the group's actions or programs
Focus	The ability of the individual to cope with a stressful life experience Communication and mutual aid	Individual learning focus Structuring of group for learning	Either member or group focus, depending on the approach Individual growth through the group experience	Focus on individual members' problems, concerns, or goals	Focus on the group as a medium for activity, participation, and involvement

22

Bond	Shared stressful experience, often stigmatizing	Common interest in learning, skills development	Common goals among members Contract to use group to grow	Common purpose with separate member goals Relationship of member with worker, group, or other members	A common activity, enterprise, or situation
Composition	Based on a shared life experience Often diverse	Similarity of education or skill level	Can be diverse Based on members' ability to work toward growth and development	Can be diverse or can be composed of people with similar problems or concerns	Depending on location of group and purpose, can be diverse or homogeneous
Communication	Much sharing of information, experiences, and coping strategies Frequent self-disclosure of emotionally charged material	Frequently leader-to-member, didactic Sometimes member-to-member during discussions Self-disclosure low	Highly interactive Members often take responsibility for communication in the group Self-disclosure moderate to high	Leader-to-member or member-to-member, depending on approach Self-disclosure moderate to high	Often represented in activity or nonverbal behavior Self-disclosure low to moderate and often nonverbal

Leadership of support groups is characterized by a facilitative approach that emphasizes helping members share their collective experiences in coping with a stressful event, such as the loss of a loved one or the onset of a serious illness. The group worker helps members share their experiences and empathically respond to each other. Simply recounting events, ventilating feelings, and reflecting upon coping efforts can promote self-understanding and help overcome loneliness, isolation, and despair. The group worker also helps members overcome feelings of alienation, stigmatization, and isolation by validating, affirming, and normalizing their experiences.

A major role of the worker is to facilitate hope in the future and motivate members to improve coping skills through self-help and mutual aid efforts. The worker fosters group norms that encourage members to share information and suggestions for more effective coping, and to try out new coping strategies. Because support is basic to many types of groups, these strategies for assisting members are also used, to varying degrees, in other treatment and task groups.

Strong emotional bonds often develop quickly in support groups because of members' shared experiences. Emotional bonding may also occur because members are stigmatized by the larger community, and find comfort and power in their association with each other. Frequently there is a high level of self-disclosure of emotionally charged material in support groups.

In addition to directly facilitating support groups, workers are often called upon to provide indirect assistance to support groups led by lay leaders. A worker might be asked to consult with the lay leader, serve as a referral source, or provide material assistance. Consultation may take the form of speaking at a meeting, helping the group resolve a problem in its functioning, or assisting members with specific problems or issues. The worker may be asked to refer appropriate individuals to a support group; provide a meeting place; or offer other support, such as help with printing a newsletter or distributing publicity.

Some writers have pointed out that professionals might interfere with the effective functioning of lay-led self-help support groups (Gartner & Riessman, 1984; Katz & Bender, 1987). The potential does exist for professionals to dominate, interfere with, or take over the functioning of such groups.

Members of self-help groups are sometimes wary of professional involvement because they fear it will compromise the autonomy and confidentiality of the group. This is particularly true of self-help groups such as Parents Anonymous, where members share concerns about child abuse or neglect—which are often considered socially stigmatizing.

Most evidence, however, suggests that there are strong connections between self-help support groups and professionals, and that both professionals and lay leaders benefit by cooperating with each other (Lieberman & Borman, 1979; Powell, 1987; Toseland & Hacker, 1982, 1985). Professionals gain an additional treatment resource that is often more flexible and responsive than the formal service system. Lay leaders have someone to turn to when they need particular types of expertise, resources, or assistance. Both can join forces when lobbying for additional community resources and services.

Educational Groups

The primary purpose of educational groups is to help members learn about themselves, their community, and their society. Educational groups are used in a variety of settings, including treatment agencies, schools, nursing homes, correctional institutions, and hospitals. Some examples of educational groups include the following:

- An adolescent sexuality group sponsored by a family planning agency.
- A "wellness-in-the-work-place" group designed by a social worker directing an employee assistance program.
- A group for prospective foster parents sponsored by a child welfare agency.
- A group sponsored by a community planning agency to help board members become more effective.

All educational groups are aimed at increasing members' information or skills. Most routinely involve presentations of information and knowledge by experts. They also often include opportunities for group discussion to foster learning. When leading educational groups, workers concentrate on both the individual learner and the group as a whole, as a vehicle for learning, reinforcement, and discussion.

Members of educational groups are bonded by a common interest in the material to be learned as well as by common characteristics, such as being an adolescent, a prospective foster parent, a union worker, or a board member. In composing educational groups, workers consider each member's knowledge of the subject matter and level of skills and experience, so that all members can get the most out of the learning process.

Some educational groups seek members with different levels of exposure to the subject matter so that beginners can learn from advanced members. When the group is small, there are usually opportunities for member-to-member communication and group discussion. Depending on the norms of the group and the subject under consideration, member self-disclosure varies from low to moderate. In general, a relatively low level of self-disclosure is expected in an educational group because the group is often structured around a presentation of material by the worker, a guest speaker, or a member. Usually, the material to be learned is seen as more important than the needs of members to self-disclose. However, workers often use a personalized approach to learning that emphasizes the developmental learning needs of individual members. This is especially true in residential and institutional settings where members' emotional or social functioning is impaired.

Other approaches to leading educational groups emphasize learning as a social experience. Workers who use this approach focus on group discussion and group activities rather than on didactic methods. Community center workers often use this approach to attract and hold the interest of members who participate in educational groups for personal enjoyment and enrichment.

Growth Groups

Growth-oriented groups are also found in a variety of settings. Such groups offer opportunities for members to become aware of, expand, and change their thoughts, feelings, and behaviors regarding self and others. The group is used as a vehicle to develop members' capabilities to the fullest. Growth groups focus on promoting socio-emotional health rather than remediating socio-emotional illness. Some examples of growth groups include the following:

• An encounter group for married couples.
• A values-clarification group for adolescents.
• A consciousness-raising group sponsored by a women's community center.
• A gay-pride group sponsored by a community health clinic serving the gay community in a large urban area.

Growth groups generally stress self-improvement and the potential of human beings to live a full and rewarding life, especially through improved relationships with others. They provide a supportive atmosphere in which individuals can gain insights, experiment with new behaviors, get feedback, and grow as human beings. The bond in growth groups stems from members' commitment to help one another develop their potential.

When composing growth groups, workers often select a diverse membership so that exposure to members with different characteristics will enhance growth. However, some growth groups are composed of members with similar characteristics to enhance intermember empathy and increase the supportive element of the group. In most growth-oriented groups, self-disclosure is moderate to high.

In this text, the term *growth* is used in its broadest sense. In the late 1960s and early 1970s, several new group work techniques for personal growth emerged during what has been referred to as the Human Potential Movement (Schutz, 1967). Several writers discuss these groups and the techniques that were employed to increase self-awareness and improve personal functioning (Howard, 1970; Schutz, 1967). Our broad interpretation of the term *growth* in group work stresses members coming together to develop their potential and increase their socio-emotional health, regardless of the techniques used to lead the group.

Therapy Groups

The therapy group is the type of group most easily identified and the type of group most frequently cited in the literature. Therapy groups help members change their behavior, cope with and ameliorate personal problems, or rehabilitate themselves after a social or health trauma. Although much of the emphasis is on support in therapy groups, they are distinguished from support groups by their focus on remediation and rehabilitation.

In group work practice, particular importance is often attached to leading therapy groups, even to the exclusion of other types of group work. This may be because of the importance attributed to the "medical model," which stresses therapy and treatment to bring "sick" or dysfunctional people back to health. As Konopka (1963) has noted, "the high status of psychiatry on the North American continent" helped to make the term *therapy* more precious and more important than the terms *casework* and *group work*, which are used by the social work profession (p. 33). Thus, remedial groups are often associated with the professionalism of group work as a method of practice. They are also frequently associated with a process of study, diagnosis, and treatment that is used to help group members achieve their individual goals (Vinter, 1967, 1985a).

Some examples of remedial groups include the following:

- A psychotherapy group for outpatients at a community mental health center.
- A group, sponsored by a voluntary health association, for people who want to stop smoking.
- A first-offenders group in a juvenile diversion program sponsored by a probation department.
- A hospital-sponsored group for people addicted to drugs.

In therapy groups, members come together to solve their problems. The group leader is often viewed as an expert, an authority figure, and a change agent. Members' problems are assessed and treatment goals are developed with the help of the worker. Although the group has a common purpose, each member may have a different problem with different symptoms. In addition, the etiology and development of each member's problem is unique. Therefore, to achieve individual goals, the worker often focuses on one member at a time. This approximates a one-to-one treatment relationship in a group. Depending on the approach or stance of the worker, the members of a therapy group may be expected to help each other work on their problems. The level of member self-disclosure is usually quite high but can depend somewhat on the types of problems experienced by group members.

Members of therapy groups have much to gain: relief from symptoms, loss of emotional pain, or resolution of a problem. Still, to ensure that members' needs are met, a good deal of planning usually takes place before the beginning of a therapy group. Therapeutic interventions are selected after a careful assessment of individual members, and the group is composed in relation to the members' problems. Often, members participate in an intake procedure so the worker can assess their interest in participating in the group, determine suitability for group treatment, and explain the purpose of the group. Although these procedures are also used with other types of groups, they are often emphasized when working with therapy groups.

Socialization Groups

Socialization groups are conducted in many settings (see, for instance, Boyd, 1938; Garvin, 1987; Klein, 1972). Such groups help members learn social skills and socially accepted behavior patterns so they can function effectively in the community. Socialization groups frequently use program activities such as games, role plays, or outings to help members accomplish individual goals (Middleman, 1968; Whittaker, 1985).

The personal needs of members and the goals of the group are often met through program activities rather than exclusively through group discussion.

Thus, socialization groups feature a "learning-through-doing" approach in which members improve their interpersonal skills by participating in program activities. Some examples of socialization groups include the following:

- A Catholic Youth Organization (CYO) activity group.
- A social club for outpatients of a psychiatric center.
- A monthly Vietnam Veterans evening social at a rural Veterans of Foreign Wars (VFW) post.
- A Parents Without Partners group, which includes picnics, dances, and other social activities.

Leadership in socialization groups can be directive or nondirective, depending on the complexity of program activities and the competencies of group members. Member participation is the key to successful individual and group outcomes. The group is a medium for activity, participation, and involvement—and members are bonded to each other through these activities. The composition of socialization groups can be based on the similar interests and needs of members or on the common experiences offered by a particular program activity.

There are at least three common forms of socialization groups: (a) social skills groups, (b) governance groups, and (c) recreation groups. Some social skills groups, such as assertiveness training groups, are formed for "normal" adults who wish to improve their existing skills. Unlike the other types of groups in our typology, social skills groups can be particularly useful for individuals who are unable or unwilling to communicate effectively and for those who have difficulty engaging in satisfying social relationships. Young children, shy adolescents, and mildly retarded adults are examples of client populations that can benefit from social skills groups. Program activities can help draw out these types of group members by helping them form meaningful relationships and learn social skills. Activities provide the basis for interaction and communication without the need for direct, verbal communication. Thus, by using program activities, group work can take place through nonverbal means.

In other cases, role plays, psychodrama, and other activities requiring verbal as well as nonverbal communication can be used to increase members' skills and promote socialization. The behavior displayed during these activities can also help a worker assess members' problems and plan effective interventions.

Governance groups are often found in residential settings, such as nursing homes, psychiatric hospitals, correctional facilities, and residential treatment centers. The purpose of these groups is to involve residents (of the unit, ward, floor, or cottage) in the daily governance of the institution. Although governance groups are closely related to task groups because they solve problems and make decisions, they have been classified as treatment groups because of their primary focus on the needs of members.

Through their participation in the governance process, members learn communication and conflict-resolution skills. They also learn to share with others, take responsibility for their actions, and participate in decision-making processes. The concept of a governance group is borrowed, in part, from the idea of the therapeutic community, where members have input into the rules that govern their behavior. Examples of governance groups include cottage meetings, ward meetings, resident councils, "family" meetings, and patient-rights meetings.

Participation in governance groups provides a method for members to identify with and become committed to the goals of the therapeutic community. It helps clarify members' roles, responsibilities, and rights within the community. All members of therapeutic communities are encouraged to attend meetings so that they have a voice in the way the community functions. In some settings, such as residential treatment centers, attendance may be required.

A third type of socialization group focuses on recreational activities. Much of the recent group work literature has understated the importance of recreational groups in meeting members' personal needs. The roots of group work can be traced to recreational groups like scouting, camping, sports, and club groups (Boyd, 1935; Slavson, 1945, 1946; Smith, 1935; Wilson, 1976). Recreation can be both an end and a means to an end. As an end, recreation can be a desirable leisure time activity. As a means, recreation can help a particular population become involved in an activity that has therapeutic benefits, such as increasing social skills.

Recreational groups are particularly important for working with children, adolescents, and adults in neighborhood centers. Because the groups are enjoyable, they are often helpful in engaging resistant clients such as gang members and pre-delinquent, latency-age children. They can help members learn community values and accepted norms of behavior, develop interpersonal skills, and feel a sense of belonging. In addition, recreational groups help members develop confidence in their ability to function as a part of a group and to function in other social situations. To carry out these important purposes, recreation groups require leaders who are skilled in both group work and the featured recreational mode or program activity.

TASK GROUPS

Task groups are common in most agencies and organizations. They are used to find solutions to organizational problems, to generate new ideas, and to make decisions. Task groups can have three primary purposes: (a) meeting client needs, (b) meeting organizational needs, and (c) meeting community needs.

Task groups whose primary purpose is to serve client needs include teams, treatment conferences, and staff development groups. Task groups whose primary purpose is to serve organizational needs include committees, cabinets, and boards of directors. Task groups whose primary purpose is to serve community needs include social action groups, coalitions, and delegate councils.

Selected characteristics of each type of group are presented in Table 1–3, and additional readings about each type of task group are listed in Appendix B. As with the treatment group typology, there is often some overlap between different types of task groups in actual practice situations. Thus, the typology should act as a heuristic guide for workers who may be called upon to lead different types of task groups, rather than a rigid classification system to which practitioners must adhere.

TABLE 1–3
A typology of task groups

Selected Characteristics	Client Needs		
	Teams	Treatment Conferences	Staff Development
Purpose	To engage in collaborative work on behalf of a client system	To develop, coordinate and monitor treatment plans	To educate members for better practice with clients
Leadership	Appointed by sponsoring agency	Neutral chair or chaired by member with most responsibility	Leader, supervisor, consultant, or educator
Focus	Build team to function smoothly High member focus	Decision-oriented Low member focus High client focus	Focus on staff members' needs and their performance with clients
Bond	Team spirit Needs of organization and client	Client system Treatment plan Inter- or intra-agency agreement	Continuing education needs Interest in client welfare Professional development
Composition	Often heterogeneous	Diversity by function, specialty, and expertise	Individuals with similar educational needs
Communication	Theoretically close, sometimes artificial or inspirational Low to moderate self-disclosure	Consideration of all points of view about the client system High disclosure	Leader-to-member Didactic and experiential instruction Member-to-member

Selected Characteristics	Organizational Needs		
	Committees	Cabinets	Board of Directors
Purpose	To discuss issues and accomplish tasks	To advise an executive officer about future directions or current policies and procedures	To govern an organization
Leadership	Appointed or elected	Appointed by chief executive officer of an organization	Officers designated by bylaws are nominated by subcommittee and approved by vote of the membership
Focus	A specific task or charge	The development of procedures and policies for organizational management	Policy making Governance Monitoring Fiscal control Fund-raising
Bond	Interest in a task	Loyalty to the organization and the chief executive officer	Commitment to the mission of the organization Service orientation
Composition	Diversity to aid decision making and division of labor	Appointment based on administrative responsibilities and expertise	Diverse members often selected for their status, power, influence in the community, expertise, representation of particular interest groups and constituencies
Communication	Relative to task Low member self-disclosure	Members present points of view based on their position in an organization To build a power base	Formal communication Parliamentary procedures Less formal in subcommittees Low member self-disclosure

TABLE 1–3, *continued*

Selected Characteristics	Community Needs		
	Social Action Groups	Coalitions	Delegate Councils
Purpose	To devise and implement social change tactics and strategies	To exert greater influence by sharing resources, expertise, and power bases of social action groups with common goals	To represent different organizations, chapters, or other units
Leadership	Indigenous leadership emerging from the groups Practitioner often is staffer or adviser	Often a charismatic or dedicated individual leading by consensus or elected by vote of the membership	Representatives appointed by the sponsoring organization
Focus	Consumer, community, social justice	Building consensus and a partnership for maximum influence	Collective input and action Equality of representation Focus on larger issues, concerns, and positions
Bond	Perception of injustice, inequity, or need for change	Interest in an issue Commitment to an ideological position	Larger purpose or community concern, rather than individual or agency concern
Composition	Based on common interest, shared purpose, and investment in community	Loose, temporary confederation of groups or organizations working in partnership to achieve a common goal	Diverse by definition Represents interest of sponsoring organization
Communication	Informal member-to-member discussion Formulation and implementation of tactics and strategies for change High member self-disclosure in relation to social problems	Formal or informal, depending on type of coalition Less formal in caucuses and subgroups Moderate member self-disclosure representing group interests	Provides a forum for communication among organizations Delegates are communication links between council and the sponsoring organization Low member self-disclosure

Groups to Meet Client Needs

Teams

Although empirical evidence for the effectiveness of interdisciplinary teams is limited (Halstead, 1976; Keith, 1991; Schmitt, Farrell, & Heinemann, 1988), team work is often considered the most effective method of delivering comprehensive social and health services to those in need (Brill, 1976; Kane, 1975). A *team* can be defined as:

> a number of individual staff members, each of whom possesses particular knowledge and skills, who come together to share their expertise with one another for a particular purpose. (Toseland, Palmer-Ganeles, & Chapman, 1986, p. 46)

Team members coordinate their efforts and work together on behalf of a particular client group. Some examples of teams include the following:

- An interdisciplinary group of professionals working on discharge planning with burn patients in a hospital.
- A group of professionals who deliver home-based hospice care.
- A number of researchers conducting a statewide welfare study.
- A group of professionals and aides who work with inpatients in a psychiatric hospital.

The functioning of the team is the responsibility of the team leader. Team leaders are often appointed by an administrator from the team's sponsoring agency, but in some settings they are elected or nominated by team members. The team leader is a facilitator and coordinator for the group and is accountable to the agency for the actions of the team. The team leader is responsible for conducting meetings, motivating team members, coordinating individual efforts, and ensuring effective team functioning.

In most, if not all cases, an agency sanctions the mutual involvement of team members on behalf of a particular client population. Often, the team is composed of members with different professional orientations, such as social work, nursing, physical and occupational therapy, and medicine. The team might also be composed of paraprofessionals, such as mental health therapy aides.

The agency and the team leader pay particular attention to how the team members work together as a group, which is frequently referred to as team building. Members are bonded by a team spirit that assists them in their work as a group rather than as a collection of individuals representing disparate concerns and professional agendas. At the same time, when building and maintaining an effective team, the worker should attend to members' unique personal and professional orientations. It is important to devote some time to team building and maintenance.

Ideally, team members should meet regularly to discuss their service delivery efforts and their functioning as a team (Abramson, 1989). Communication among team members varies according to the working situation of the team. Sometimes team members work independently of each other. For example, within a residential program for teen-agers, child-care workers might be considered important team members although they work different shifts.

To promote adequate communication and a coordinated team effort in such situations, it is a good practice to schedule meeting times when shifts overlap. Meetings should avoid focusing solely on service delivery—some time should be devoted to how members function as a group (Toseland, Palmer-Ganeles, & Chapman, 1986). Neglecting team functioning can lead to a variety of problems including interpersonal conflict and rivalry, duplication of effort, and uncoordinated or incomplete service.

Treatment Conferences

Treatment conferences meet for the purpose of developing, monitoring, and coordinating treatment plans for a particular client or client system. Members consider the client's situation and decide on a plan for working with the client. Some examples of treatment conferences include the following:

- An interdisciplinary group of professionals planning the discharge of a patient in a mental health facility.
- A group of child-care workers, social workers, nurses, and a psychiatrist determining a treatment plan for a child in residential treatment.
- A parole board considering testimony regarding the release of a prisoner in a correctional facility.
- A group of community mental health professionals considering treatment methods for a young man experiencing severe depression.

Although treatment conferences may, at first, appear similar to team meetings, they differ in five respects:

1. Members of a treatment conference might not all work together as do members of teams. They may be employees of different organizations who come to a treatment conference to discuss ways to coordinate their efforts on behalf of a particular client.
2. Participants may not have the same close working relationships and shared sense of purpose that are essential in teamwork. Members may not work together from day to day. In fact, they may never have met before the treatment conference.
3. Treatment conference groups might meet less frequently than teams, gathering as the need arises in particular situations.
4. The composition of the treatment conference group can vary considerably, depending on the client being discussed. In team meetings, the composition is relatively stable.
5. The plan of action might be carried out by only one member who is entirely responsible for the client's care. For example, during a treatment conference in a family service agency, a worker gets advice from colleagues about how to help a group member with a particularly difficult issue. The other members of the treatment conference have no direct contact with the client. In contrast, all members of a team usually have some contact with clients served by the team.

In treatment conferences, participants generally focus on one client at a time. Members who are familiar with the client contribute information that may be helpful in developing or improving a treatment plan. Other members, who might not be familiar with the client, can also contribute their expertise about how to most effectively treat the type of problem the client is experiencing. On the basis of this information, the group discusses the client's overall circumstances and considers alternative treatment plans. The group decides on one plan that they all agree will be the most helpful for the client.

Treatment conferences are oriented to decision making, problem solving, and coordinating the actions of members. The group focuses its attention on the needs of the client rather than on the needs of the group members. The bond that group members feel is based on their concern for a client and their commitment to an agreed-upon treatment plan.

Treatment conferences usually include all helping professionals who are working with a client. The group can also include consultants or experts who do not work directly with the client but who can contribute to the treatment plan by offering insight, resources, or advice. Treatment conference membership is diverse by design. Participants are invited because they have new insights and treatment opportunities based on their area of expertise and their unique experiences with a client.

It is the policy of some agencies to have clients and their spouses, parents, guardians, or significant others participate in treatment conferences. However, the staff of some agencies believe that inviting clients to treatment conferences may inhibit frank and open discussion. Also, some staff believe that the conflicting facts, multiple options in treatment planning, or emotionally charged issues that are sometimes discussed during treatment conferences can confuse or upset clients. These agencies sometimes invite the client and significant others to the portion of the treatment conference that occurs *after* treatment staff have had a private, freewheeling discussion about the client's situation. However, these agencies are in a minority. Most agencies simply opt not to have the client present at treatment conferences (Toseland, Ivanoff, & Rose, 1987).

No data are available to address when, or even if, it is best to invite clients and their significant others to treatment conferences. Still, because a client's right to self-determination is an important part of the value base of social work practice (Siporin, 1975), careful consideration should be given to soliciting clients' input into the treatment planning decisions that will affect their lives.

Treatment conference leadership can be determined in a variety of ways. In some agencies, the conferences are always led by the same person. This person might be the program director or a member of the staff, such as the social worker whose job includes responsibility for treatment coordination. Commonly, the designated leader is the worker with the most responsibility for, or involvement with, the client's care. In some agencies, leadership is rotated or a supervisor leads the meeting. In these situations, the leader can lend objectivity to the proceedings because he or she does not work directly with the client.

Staff Development Groups

The purpose of staff development groups is to improve services to clients by developing, updating, and refreshing workers' skills. Staff development groups provide workers with an opportunity to learn about new treatment approaches, resources, and community services; to practice new skills; and to review and learn from their previous work with clients. Examples of staff development groups include the following:

- A group of professionals who attend a series of seminars about pharmacology offered by a regional psychiatric center.
- An in-service development seminar on co-dependency for the staff of an alcoholism treatment agency.
- Group supervision offered by an experienced social worker for social workers who work in school districts where there are no supervisors.
- A program director who conducts a weekly supervisory group for paraprofessionals who work in a community outreach program for isolated elderly people.

Ideally, leaders of staff development groups are experts in a particular field. Often they also possess extensive experience and knowledge gathered through specialized training, study, and reflection on difficult practice issues.

The focus of staff development groups is on improving workers' skills so they can perform more effectively on behalf of their clients. The trainer or leader might use many methods to aid learning, including lectures, discussions, audio- and video-tape presentations, simulations, and live demonstrations. Members may be given the opportunity to practice new skills in the group, and to receive feedback from the trainer and the other members.

Members are bonded by their desire to improve their skills. Often they also share an interest in a similar client population or treatment method. They might also share in the camaraderie that comes from being at similar stages in their professional development.

In some staff development groups, the leader takes primary responsibility for the content of each session. The leader may make presentations, arrange for guest speakers, or prepare and conduct simulations and other staff development exercises. In other groups, members are responsible for structuring the group by taking turns presenting their work with particular clients.

Members are expected to risk opening their work to the scrutiny and critique of the rest of the group, and to participate in staff development exercises and discussions. They are also expected to learn from their own mistakes, and the mistakes of others in the group. Honest, frank, constructive communication and feedback among members is valued, as is a high level of self-disclosure.

Groups to Meet Organizational Needs

Committees

The most common type of task group is the committee. It is almost impossible to be associated with an agency or organization without having some contact with committees. Although they are most often used to meet organizational needs, in human service fields, organizational needs often overlap client needs. For example, a committee might meet to respond to a request by the United Way to improve service. The results of the committee's work are beneficial to both the agency and its clients.

A committee is made up of people who are appointed or elected to the group. Their task is to "accomplish a charge" (Pincus & Minahan, 1973, p. 61), which is delegated to the committee from a higher authority, such as organizational by-laws or an agency executive. Committees may be temporary creations (ad-hoc committees) or more permanent parts of the structure of an organization (standing committees).

Some examples of committees include the following:

- A group of young people responsible for recommending activities for the local community center.
- A group of employees assigned the task of studying and recommending changes in the agency's personnel policy.
- A group of social workers considering ways to improve service delivery to pregnant teen-agers.
- A group of staff members developing recommendations for an employee assistance program.

In these examples, members are concerned with producing reports, accomplishing tasks, issuing recommendations, or making decisions. In each example, the committee's work requires the collective wisdom of a number of people with varied viewpoints, expertise, and abilities.

Although members are expected to share their personal views during deliberations, the level of self-disclosure in committees is frequently low. In some cases, however, there are variations in the level of self-disclosure, depending on the norms that have developed in the committee and on the nature of the issues being discussed. For example, when the subject matter is of a sensitive nature, discussing personal viewpoints may require a high level of member self-disclosure.

Most committees tend to follow a standard set of procedures. Sometimes committees rely on those found in *Roberts Rules of Order* to conduct their meetings. In other cases, committees develop their own rules and regulations that control how members introduce and discuss issues, and how decisions are reached.

It is useful for each meeting to have an agenda, so committee members can follow the activity of the group and know what to expect during the rest of the meeting. The agenda provides structure, focus, and direction for the group. The chairperson is responsible for seeing that the agenda and the formalized procedures are carried out. The chairperson may be appointed by the authority that has given the committee its mandate or may be elected by committee or organization members.

Committees frequently deal with complex issues, requiring the group to divide large tasks into a series of smaller subtasks. Committees tend to assign roles to members to divide labor. When large committees deal with multiple issues or complex tasks, they frequently do much of their work through subcommittees, using the entire committee as a coordinating body or as a mechanism of approval for the recommendations of the subcommittees.

Subcommittees divide labor and expedite the completion of complex tasks. The larger committee authorizes the formation of one or more subcommittees from its membership to consider parts of a larger task or to research important questions relative to the overall task. Subcommittees report back to the larger committee.

The composition of subcommittees is the responsibility of the chairperson, who considers the qualifications and abilities of each committee member and selects subcommittee members on the basis of their ability to complete a particular task. In some cases, the chairperson may ask for volunteers rather than appoint members. This is particularly true when the subcommittee will deal with a particularly onerous task and highly motivated members are needed.

A committee is generally accountable to a higher authority. The power vested in a committee depends on the group's mandate and the extent to which its actions are binding. It is common for committees to be given the power to make recommendations rather than binding decisions.

The importance of the committee as a type of task group cannot be overemphasized. Most of the other types of task groups mentioned in our typology use elements of committee structure to complete their tasks. It can be argued that other forms of task groups such as cabinets and treatment conferences are special forms of committees.

Cabinets

Cabinets are designed to provide advice and expertise about policy issues to chief executive officers or other high-level administrators. Policies, procedures, and practices that affect the entire organization are discussed, developed, or modified in cabinets before being announced by a senior administrative officer. Cabinets also enable formal communications among senior administrators in an organization and help garner support for particular policies and procedures among senior and mid-level administrators.

Some examples of cabinet groups include the following:

- A meeting of section heads in a large state health department to discuss long-term care reimbursement policies.
- A weekly meeting of supervisory social work staff and the director of social services in a large municipal hospital.
- A series of meetings of senior United Way staff to discuss potential changes in methods of allocating money among member agencies.
- A meeting of department heads in a county social services department.

Cabinets focus their efforts on administrative and policy issues that may have important implications for the entire organization or subdivisions within it. Whereas committees often make recommendations to a higher authority outside the group, cabinet members often give advice about developing and changing policies and procedures directly to the chief executive officer or other administrator who leads the meeting. In some organizations, cabinets are delegated the authority to make decisions by the chief executive officer.

Unlike committee members, who may be elected or appointed, cabinet members are often appointed by the chief executive officer. Cabinet members are typically supervisors, department heads, or senior managers with powerful positions within the organization. Occasionally, the executive might ask an outside consultant to join the group because of his or her background and knowledge.

Authority and power are usually important in cabinets. Members often vie for the executive's attention and for the chance to influence policy decisions. Members sometimes take stances on policy issues that will benefit the program or section they lead within the larger organization.

The proceedings of cabinet meetings are often kept confidential. Self-disclosure is typically low, with members thinking strategically about how their statements on issues will effect their own standing within the group, and the likelihood that they will be able to influence current and future policy decisions.

Boards of Directors

There are two primary types of boards: the governing board and the advisory board (Conrad & Glenn, 1976). Under the articles of incorporation and the bylaws of not-for-profit organizations, governing boards—sometimes referred to as boards of trustees—are legally and financially responsible for the conduct of the organization.

The members of governing boards are stewards of the public trust, accountable to the state government, which granted the organization its charter; to the federal government, which granted tax-exempt status; and ultimately, to the public, whom the organization serves (Wolf, 1990). Members of advisory boards provide counsel and guidance to the management of an organization. However, they have no official power to make policy or fiscal decisions.

Some examples of board groups include the following:

- Trustees of a large public hospital.
- Members of the governing board of a family service agency.
- Individuals on the citizens advisory board to a county department of social services.
- Members of the board of a corporation that includes several affiliated social service and health agencies.

The primary functions of boards of directors are policy making, oversight of agency operations, ensuring the financial integrity and stability of the organization, and public relations. Boards of directors determine the mission and short- and long-range goals of the organization. They set personnel and operating policies. They offer counsel and advice to the chief executive officer, and monitor the organization's operations. They establish fiscal policy, set budgets, and install monitoring and auditing mechanisms. They also engage in fund-raising, hire the chief executive officer, and manage public relations.

Boards are not supposed to engage in the day-to-day operations of the organization, the hiring of staff (other than the executive director), or the details of programmatic decisions (Wolf, 1990).

The position and duties of the president, vice-president, secretary, treasurer, and any other officers of a board of directors are generally specified in the articles of incorporation and bylaws of the organization. The terms of these officers and how they are selected are specified in the board's operating procedures. Usually, officers are nominated by a subcommittee of the board, and elected to specified terms by the entire membership.

It has been estimated that 11.5 million people sit on the boards of not-for-profit agencies in the United States (Waldo, 1986). Board members are bonded by their commitment to the mission and goals of the organization and by their commitment to community service.

They are often a diverse group of individuals who are selected on the basis of their power, status, and influence in the community; their expertise; and their representation of particular interest groups and constituencies. For example, a board might contain lawyers who can provide advice on legal matters, accountants or bankers who can provide advice on fiscal matters, business people who can assist with fund-raising, advertising or other media experts who can help with public relations, and policy experts and consumers who can provide guidance on programmatic and service issues.

Written agendas are usually circulated before board meetings. Communication is often formal, following the rules of parliamentary procedure. Much of the actual work, however, is often conducted in less formal subcommittee meetings. Boards often have several standing and ad-hoc committees which report at board meetings and recommend actions in the form of motions. For example, the finance committee might recommend that the board approve the annual budget of the agency, the personnel committee might recommend a change in health benefits for employees, or the nominating committee might present a slate of new officers for board approval.

Groups to Meet Community Needs

Social Action Groups

Social action groups empower members to engage in collective action and planned change efforts to alter some aspect of their social or physical environment. They are often referred to as "grass roots" organizations because they arise from the concerns of individuals in the community who may have little individual power or status. Although the goals of social action groups are frequently linked to the needs of the individual members of the group, goal achievement generally also benefits people outside the group. Thus, social action groups serve the "common good" of both members and nonmembers.

Examples of social action groups include the following:

- A citizens group advocating increased police protection on behalf of the elderly population in a neighborhood.
- A group of social workers lobbying for increased funding for social services.
- A tenants group seeking support for a playground area in their housing complex.
- A group of staff members working to eliminate an unethical agency practice.

A worker involved in a social action group can assume one of many leadership roles, depending on the nature of the change effort and the needs of the group. A worker can assume an enabler role, helping the group acquire information or resources, determine priorities and procedures, and plan a strategy for action.

In working with tenants concerned about their rights, for example, the worker might help organize a tenant-rights group to help the individuals pursue their common goals. Alternatively, workers might take a directive role because of their expertise regarding the change effort. In a lobbying effort, for example, a worker might be particularly knowledgeable about techniques for influencing legislators. In this instance, the worker might be asked to speak for the social action group or might encourage the group to examine particular issues or use particular strategies, such as collaboration, bargaining, or conflict.

Although directive approaches to leading social action groups are sometimes useful and appropriate, the worker should be guided by the purpose of the group and the preferences of group members. The worker should make sure that a directive approach does not inhibit indigenous leadership from developing among members. Abels (1980) suggests that the worker should assume the role of an "instructed" advocate for the group. Using this approach, the worker's role is defined and limited by the social action group and includes four major goals: "(1) to help the group achieve its purpose, (2) to help the group remain together as a unit long enough to achieve these purposes, (3) to enable members to function in an autonomous manner, and (4) to help the group to come to terms with its community (environment)" (Abels, 1980, p. 327).

The composition of the social action group can vary depending on the nature and circumstances of the change effort. Sometimes workers take a leadership role in composing a social action group, while in other cases the group may form as a result of the interests of one or more concerned citizens. In the latter case, the worker is often asked to be a facilitator, enabler, or consultant, lending his or her expertise to the change effort without necessarily influencing the composition of the group.

When the worker does have a role in composing the group, consideration should be given to the level of support for the change effort among key community leaders. In some instances, the worker may seek members who can exert influence in the environment, or who have the diverse skills and resources needed to empower the group.

Communication patterns in social action groups also vary with the circumstances of the group. The worker helps the group develop open communication patterns so that all members have a chance to become involved. The worker also helps the group establish communication links with its environment. Good communication helps avoid misunderstandings and promotes a cooperative effort among all those who may have some stake in the change effort.

A more broadly conceived form of the social action group is what Pincus and Minahan (1973) call the "action system." An action system includes "those with whom the worker deals in his efforts to accomplish the tasks and achieve the goals of the change effort" (p. 61). The action system is similar to the social action group in that it is usually formed to engage in a planned change effort in the environment on behalf of a client system.

However, it may vary significantly from the social action group in terms of the worker's role, the bond that unites members, and the group's composition and communication. A worker usually forms an action system and directs it on behalf of a client system. In an action system, the worker frequently assumes the role of a change agent and a case manager as well as an enabler.

There may be other differences as well. Members of action systems may have little or no interaction with each other, and may rely on the worker to coordinate communication. This is rarely the case in social action groups. Members of action systems may be acting on behalf of a particular client rather than on behalf of other clients or for the common good. Despite these differences, action systems are related to social action groups and workers need to know group work skills to work with both action systems and social action groups.

Coalitions

Coalitions—or alliances, as they are sometimes called—are groups of organizations, social action groups, or individuals that come together to exert influence by sharing resources and expertise. Coalition members agree to pursue common goals, which they believe cannot be achieved by any of the members acting alone.

Some examples of coalitions include the following:

- A group of family planning and community health-care clinics who have formed a pro-choice coalition to influence state and federal legislation on abortion.
- Not-for-profit home-care agencies who gather to lobby for greater access to community care for the chronically ill elderly.
- Community agencies who want to bring public attention to the need for a community teen center.
- Business, community, and civic leaders who team up to explore ways to reduce racial tensions in a large urban area.

Despite scant attention to coalitions in the social work literature, the formation of coalitions as political and social forces to improve the responsiveness of the social environment to human beings has a long tradition in social group work. For example, Newstetter (1948) described principles for interagency collaboration that have formed the basis for more recent writings on the formation and development of coalitions (Gentry, 1987; Prigmore, 1974; Weisner, 1983).

Coalitions are often formed by a charismatic or dedicated individual who has high visibility and respect within the community. This individual helps organizations, groups, and individuals understand that they have common goals and purposes that could be better served by working together.

Because members of coalitions are often concerned about preserving their autonomy while joining with others in the group, coalitions sometimes experience conflict in establishing mutual goals, working agreements, plans of action, and equitable ways of sharing resources and accomplishments. Therefore, a primary task throughout coalition formation and development is building and maintaining consensus and a smooth partnership where efforts can be focused on the goals to be achieved, rather than intragroup rivalry. Charismatic leaders are helped in their efforts by the coalition members, who are bonded by their ideals, common ideology, and interest in a particular issue or set of issues.

Coalitions take many forms. Frequently, they are loose, temporary confederations of organizations or social action groups that coalesce to share resources and gain strength in numbers. In such informal coalitions, the autonomy of the individual members is strictly protected. Over time, however, some coalitions become more stable, long-term organizations, with centralized staff and resources.

Meetings may be characterized by ideologically fervent speechmaking and position taking. Much emphasis is placed on developing strategies to accomplish specific goals and coordinating activities involved in the action plan. Frequently, coalition meetings are characterized by formal interactions following the rules of parliamentary procedure. While parliamentary procedures are often not as strictly adhered to as in board meetings or delegate councils, they are used in coalitions to promote a sense of inclusion and belonging, so that members feel they have the opportunity to fully participate in the collective deliberations and decision making of the coalition. Much less formal give and take and freewheeling interaction are often found in caucuses during lengthy coalition meetings, and in subgroup and one-to-one discussions between coalition meetings. Also, less formal procedures are frequently found in ad-hoc, single-issue coalitions.

Delegate Councils

Delegate councils are task groups composed for the purposes of facilitating interagency communication and cooperation, studying communitywide social issues or social problems, engaging in collective social action, or governing large organizations. Members of delegate councils are appointed or elected by a sponsoring unit. The members' primary function is to represent the interests of their sponsoring unit during council meetings. A variation of the delegate council is the delegate assembly, which is usually larger.

Some examples of delegate councils include the following:

- A number of agency representatives who meet monthly to improve interagency communication.
- A group of elected representatives from local chapters of a professional organization who meet to approve the organization's budget.
- A state task force to study family violence composed of members appointed from each county.
- A yearly meeting of representatives from family service agencies throughout the county.

Representation is an important issue in delegate councils. A member represents a group of people, an agency, or another system. The member is often given authority to speak for the represented unit. Because the unit has agreed to participate by sending a representative, the represented unit generally agrees to abide by decisions made by the delegate council.

There are differing ways to achieve representation. The number of representatives for each sponsoring unit can vary with the size or importance of the unit. For example, legislative bodies frequently determine the number of representatives by considering the population of each voting district, county, or state, and apportioning an appropriate number of representatives for each district.

Other councils' representation may be dictated by a sanctioning authority to ensure control over policy decisions. For example, a consumer council for a large department of social service may have more employees than clients to ensure department control over the decisions made by the group.

Delegate councils provide an effective communications link among groups of people who otherwise might not be able to communicate in a formal way. For example, delegate councils frequently serve as a forum for communication among diverse human service agencies within a city, state, or nation. Such agencies might not otherwise communicate effectively with each other.

Delegate councils are usually concerned with broad issues that affect several agencies, a large segment of a population, or a group of people in a wide geographic area. They sometimes serve large numbers of people who have common interests and hold memberships in unions or professional organizations.

Delegate councils can be either discussion-oriented or action-oriented, or they may have components of both orientations. White House Conferences on Aging, for example, involve a series of delegate councils that discuss issues of concern to older Americans and make recommendations for government action.

Delegate councils are formed in a number of ways. Some councils are the product of ad-hoc task forces or coalitions that have been meeting informally for some time. Other councils begin with the support and sponsorship of a particular agency, and gradually establish their own identities, rules and procedures, and sources of funding. Representatives to delegate councils are either elected or appointed, and leadership is usually determined through an election.

Because council members are responsible for representing the views, interests, and positions of their sponsors to the delegate council, members often act formally on behalf of their constituencies. Delegates communicate with their sponsors regarding the proceedings of the council. The effectiveness of the delegate council depends on the ability of each delegate to achieve two-way communication between the council and the represented unit. The individual delegates are not expected to engage in a high level of personal self-disclosure because they are bound by a mandate to represent the collective views of a group of people.

SUMMARY

This introductory chapter provides a framework for studying and working with groups. Group work is a broad field of practice carried out by a variety of professionals. A definition of group work is offered that encompasses the breadth of group work practice and is sufficiently flexible to allow for specialized approaches and objectives.

To understand the types of groups that exist in practice, a distinction is made between treatment and task groups. Although some of the functions and objectives of task and treatment groups overlap, they are distinguished by a variety of characteristics. Despite these differences, group workers should understand that generic practice principles and generic stages of group development exist in all forms of group work practice.

This chapter also helps clarify the kinds of task and treatment groups often encountered in practice and illustrates the commonalities and differences among these groups. The typology of treatment groups distinguishes among those with five primary purposes: (a) support, (b) education, (c) growth, (d) therapy, and (e) socialization.

The typology of task groups distinguishes among nine types of task groups that are organized to serve three primary purposes: (a) meeting client needs, (b) meeting organizational needs, and (c) meeting community needs. Types of task groups that serve client needs include teams, treatment conferences, and staff development groups. Types of task groups that serve organizational needs include committees, cabinets, and boards of directors. Types of task groups that serve community needs include social action groups, coalitions, and delegate councils.

LEARNING ASSIGNMENTS

1. After reading Appendix A, interview an experienced group leader. Ask this person to identify three problems he or she has encountered while trying to implement social work values when practicing group work. For example, ask the person if he or she has encountered (a) violations of confidentiality, (b) conflicts between the rights of an individual member vs. the rights of the group, (c) problems in member-to-member and member-to-leader relationships within the group, and (d) problems in member-to-member and member-to-leader relationships outside the group. Ask how he or she has attempted to resolve these problems.

2. Observe a treatment group in a social service agency or in the community. Following the list of selected characteristics in Table 1–2, record your observations about the group. After you have observed the group answer the following questions:
    a. What was the primary purpose of the group? Was there more than one purpose?
    b. Comment on the role played by the leader in the group. Was the leader directive or nondirective?
    c. Was the focus of the group on the individual member or the group as a whole? To what extent was the focus on members' emotional needs vs. the tasks the group was convened to accomplish?
    d. What was the basis on which members bonded? Was the bond strong or weak?
    e. Describe the composition of the group. How were group members similar? How were they different?
    f. Describe the communication patterns you observed. Were all members involved in the interaction? What was the level of self-disclosure?

3. Interview two middle or upper managers in one or two social service agencies. Ask each person to list the task groups in which he or she is (a) a leader and (b) a member. Ask them to estimate the amount of time task group participation takes each week and the importance of this component of their jobs. Also, ask how well their education prepared them to be leaders and members of the task groups in which they are involved.

CHAPTER 2

Historical Developments

To develop a broad perspective concerning the potential uses of groups in practice settings, it is helpful to understand the developments that have occurred in the study of groups and in the practice of group work over the years. This historical perspective also gives the group worker a firm foundation upon which to build a knowledge base for effective group work practice.

Two general types of inquiries have enhanced our understanding of groups. One type has come from social scientists who have experimented with groups in laboratories. This inquiry has led to social science findings about basic properties and processes of groups. The other type has come from group work practitioners who have examined how groups function in practice settings. The results of both inquiries have led to improved methods for working with a variety of groups.

Practitioners often criticize the findings of social scientists as not being generalizable to "real world" practice settings. This is because social scientists frequently conduct their research in artificial laboratory settings, using short-term groups with participants who are not well-motivated. Despite criticisms, the results of laboratory studies have proved helpful to practitioners in their attempts to understand the forces that operate in small groups. In addition, some social scientists have used naturalistic observations to study the functioning of community groups, thereby overcoming the deficiencies of laboratory methods. For example, Bales (1955), Lewin (1947, 1948), Roethlisberger and Dickson (1939), Thrasher (1927), Whyte (1943) have developed their theories based on observations of groups functioning in community settings. Thus, studies undertaken by both practitioners and social scientists have been helpful in developing a knowledge base for group work practice.

In the following pages, historical developments within group work practice are examined and the influence of these developments on current practice trends is explored. Then there is a brief review of major social science findings that have implications for understanding group processes. The chapter concludes with a review of some major theories that currently influence group work practice.

KNOWLEDGE FROM GROUP WORK PRACTICE

Developments in the understanding of groups have come from a variety of fields. Social work, psychology, sociology, education, and recreation all have contributed to our knowledge base about working with groups. Today group work is a practice method used by members of many professional disciplines. Although there have been developments within education, recreation, counseling, and psychology, this historical review will concentrate on social work, the profession that has contributed most extensively to theory and practice about group work.

Casework began in England and the United States in charity organizations in the late 19th century, and group work grew up largely in English and American settlement houses. There were some exceptions to this trend. For example, as early as 1895, some people in the charity organization movement realized there was a need to organize the poor for social change as well as work with them one to one (Brackett, 1895). Group work was also used for therapeutic purposes in state mental institutions (Boyd, 1935) but much of the interest in group work stemmed from those who had led socialization groups, adult education groups, and recreation groups in settlement houses and youth service agencies (McCaskill, 1930).

It is often believed that group work is considerably younger than casework, but group work agencies actually started only a few years after casework agencies. There were courses for group workers in schools of social work in the early 1900s (Maloney, 1963), and both casework and group work were used by social workers in the early 20th century.

However, as Schwartz (1981) points out, the real historical difference between the two movements is that casework soon became identified with the social work profession, whereas group work did not become formally linked with social work until the National Conference of Social Work in 1935. The identification of group work with the social work profession increased during the 1940s (American Association of Group Workers, 1947), although group workers continued to maintain loose ties with recreation, adult education, and mental hygiene until 1955, when group workers joined with six other professional groups to form the National Association of Social Workers.

The use of group work in settlement houses and casework in charity organizations was not an accident. Group work—and the settlement houses where it was practiced—offered citizens the opportunity for education, recreation, socialization, and community involvement. Unlike the charity organizations, which focused on the diagnosis and treatment of the problems of the poor, settlement houses offered groups as an opportunity for citizens to gather to share their views, gain mutual support, and exercise the power derived from their association for social change.

The focus on innovative educational techniques and social change led to action. Compared with caseworkers, who relied on insight developed from psychodynamic approaches and on the provision of concrete resources, group workers relied on program activities to spur members to action. Program activities of all types were the media through which groups attained their goals (see, for example, Addams, 1909, 1926; Boyd, 1935, 1938; Smith, 1935). Activities such as camping, singing, group discussion, games, and arts and crafts were used for recreation, socialization, education, support, and rehabilitation. Unlike casework, which was largely focused on problem solving and rehabilitation, group work activities were used for enjoyment as well as to solve problems. Thus, the group work methods that developed from settlement house work had a different focus and a different goal than casework methods.

Differences between casework and group work can also be clearly seen in the helping relationship. Caseworkers sought out the most underprivileged victims of industrialization, treating "worthy" clients by providing them with resources and acting as examples of virtuous, hard-working citizens.

Although group workers also worked with the poor and impaired, they did not focus solely on the poorest cases nor on those with the most problems. They preferred the word *members* to *clients* (Bowman, 1935). They emphasized members' strengths rather than their weaknesses. Helping was seen as a shared relationship in which the group worker and the group members worked together for mutual understanding and action regarding their common concerns for their community. As concerns were identified, group members supported and helped one another, and the worker mediated between the demands of society and the needs of group members (Schwartz, 1981).

Shared interaction, shared power, and shared decision making placed demands on group workers that were not experienced by caseworkers. The number of group members, the fact that they could turn to one another for help, and the democratic decision-making processes that were encouraged meant that group workers had to develop skills different from those of caseworkers. Group workers used their skills to intervene in complex and often fast-paced group interactions while remaining aware of the welfare of all group members. Schwartz (1966) summed up the feelings engendered by the new group work method very well in the statement "there are so many of them and only one of me" (p. 572).

Between 1910 and 1920, those who were concerned with adult education, recreation, and community work began to realize the potential of group work. They began to understand that groups could be used to help people participate in their communities, to enrich people's lives, and to support people whose primary relationships were not satisfying. They saw that groups could help people learn social skills and problem-solving skills. They began to use groups to prevent delinquency and to rehabilitate those who were maladjusted (Addams, 1909, 1926).

It was during this time that some leaders of this movement began to write about the groups they saw operating in their own communities. Often they drew on their own practice experiences. Siporin (1980b), for example, describes the history of The Inquiry, an organization dedicated to the advancement of adult education that began in 1923. Among the members of The Inquiry were Eduard Lindeman, "the father" of adult education. In 1921, he published a book about community groups, titled *The Community*. Other members included Alfred Sheffield, who published several books about group discussion; Mary Follett, whose book *The New State*, published in 1918, described the organization of small community groups for political action, which she viewed as vital to the democratic process; Harrison Elliott, whose 1928 book *The Process of Group Thinking* examined interpersonal communication and interaction in small, problem-solving discussion groups; and Grace Coyle, who was developing her research on social processes in groups for her doctoral dissertation.

The work of those early writers suggests that group work was used for problem solving, discussion, and debate about social issues, as well as for social action, recreation, socialization, education, and for promoting harmony among different cultural and social groups.

Unlike the early writings of caseworkers, which emphasized improving practice outcomes by careful study, diagnosis, and treatment (Richmond, 1917), the early writings of group workers (Coyle, 1930, 1935) emphasized the processes that occurred during group meetings. For example, Grace Coyle, one of the first social workers to publish a text on groups, titled her 1930 work *Social Process in Organized Groups*, whereas the first text on casework, published in 1917 by Mary Richmond, was called *Social Diagnosis.*

The emphasis on group processes has remained throughout the history of group work. Group workers have always been concerned with how to best use the unique possibilities offered by the interaction of different people in a group. Thus, workers focus on the group as a whole as well as the individual members.

During the 1940s and 1950s, group workers began to use groups more frequently to provide therapy and remediation in mental health settings. In 1942, Fritz Redl started a group program for emotionally disturbed children in the Detroit area. These groups provided specialized diagnostic services unavailable at that time in child guidance centers (Reid, 1981). In the late 1940s, spurred by the work of Gisela Konopka, group services became an integral part of child guidance programs. In general, therapy groups were insight-oriented, relying less on program activities and more on diagnosis and treatment of members' problems (see, for example, Konopka, 1949, 1954; Redl, 1944; Trecker, 1956).

The emphasis on the use of groups for therapy and remediation was the result, in part, of the influence of Freudian psychoanalysis and ego psychology and, in part, of World War II, which created a severe shortage of trained workers to deal with mentally disabled war veterans. Interest in the use of groups in psychiatric settings continued into the 1950s, as can be seen in the proceedings of a national institute on this topic in 1955 (see Trecker, 1956).

The increased emphasis on diagnosis and treatment of the individual in the group could also be seen in the definition of group work accepted by the Commission of Social Work Practice of the newly formed National Association of Social Workers (Wilson, 1956). Other definitions of the social group work method were, however, somewhat broader. One widely accepted definition emphasized maintaining or improving the personal and social functioning of group members within a broad range of purposes, including (a) corrective, (b) preventive, (c) normal social growth, (d) personal enhancement, and (e) citizenship responsibility and participation (Hartford, 1964).

Although there was an increased emphasis in the 1940s and 1950s on using groups to improve the functioning of individual members, interest remained in using groups for recreational and educational purposes, especially in Jewish community centers and in youth organizations such as the Girl Scouts and the YWCA. During the 1950s and 1960s, groups were also used for community development and social action in neighborhood centers and community agencies. At the same time, there was an increase in the study of small groups as a social phenomenon. According to Hare (1976), the 1950s was the golden age of the study of groups.

During the 1960s the popularity of group services declined. This can be seen in accounts of well-known projects such as the Mobilization For Youth experiment (Weissman, 1969). Weissman stated, "the planners of Mobilization For Youth did not accord group work services a major role in the fight against delinquency" (p. 180). Work training programs and educational opportunities were viewed as more significant than group work services—except in the area of community organization, where the skill of group workers played an important role in organizing youths and adults around important social concerns.

Also, during the 1960s, the push toward a generic view of practice in schools of social work and the movement away from specializations in casework, group work, and community organization tended to weaken group work specializations in professional schools and reduce the number of professionals trained in group work as their primary mode of practice. Taken together, these factors contributed to the decline of group work in the 1960s.

During the 1970s interest in group work continued to wane. Fewer professional schools offered advanced courses in group work and fewer practitioners used it as a practice method. To increase awareness among practitioners about the potential benefits of groups, group workers throughout the United States and Canada came together in 1979 for the First Annual Symposium for the Advancement of Group Work. Each year since then, an annual group work symposium has been convened. These symposia bring together social group workers from the United States and other countries, who present clinical findings, research results, and workshops based on the work they have done with groups in their own communities.

During the 1980s and 1990s, attempts to revitalize group work within social work have continued and increased. The Association for the Advancement of Social Work with Groups (AASWG) has expanded into an international association with many affiliated local chapters. In addition to the annual symposia it sponsors, the AASWG has a person who is a liaison to the Council on Social Work Education to promote group work curriculum in schools of social work. The AASWG has also developed standards on group work education and submitted testimony to the Educational Standards Commission of the Council on Social Work Education.

Also, each year since 1985, a group of social work practitioners and educators, co-chaired by Sheldon Rose and Charles Garvin, has convened a seminar on group work research. The seminar is designed to promote research by encouraging participants to share findings and innovative methodological approaches, as well as to collaborate on social group work research endeavors.

Current Practice Trends

Treatment Groups

In an article that has had a profound effect on social work practice with groups, Papell and Rothman (1962) outlined three historically important models of group work practice, shown in Table 2–1, that are still widely used today. These three models are (a) the social goals model, (b) the remedial model, and (c) the reciprocal model.

The social goals model focuses on socializing members to democratic societal values. It values cultural diversity and the power of group action. It was used, and continues to be used, in settlement houses and in group work with youth organizations such as the Girl Scouts, the YWCA, and Jewish community centers. It also has been used by community development agencies to change societal norms and structures and improve the social welfare of all citizens.

The worker acts as an enabler who uses program activities, such as camping, discussions, and instructions about democratic processes, to socialize members. The worker also acts to empower members, by helping them make collective decisions and use their collective strength to make society more responsive to their needs.

In recent years, several writers have contributed significantly to the development of the social goals model, even though their work may not explicitly mention the model. Middleman (1980, 1982), for example, has made important contributions to the model by emphasizing the importance of program activities. Breton (1989), Cox (1988), Lee (1990), Parsons (1991), and Pernell (1986) have also made significant contributions by focusing on empowerment strategies in social group work. The writings of Klein (1953, 1970, 1972) and Tropp (1968, 1976) have also helped a great deal to refine the model. Tropp focused on how group development can be used to empower members to achieve the goals they have set for themselves. He was strongly opposed to the worker establishing goals for members, believing instead that groups could be growth-promoting only when the worker encouraged group self-direction toward common goals. Klein's writings emphasized the importance of matching members' needs to environmental opportunities for growth. Like Tropp, Klein emphasized the autonomy of group members and their freedom to pursue their own self-defined goals.

The remedial model focuses on restoring or rehabilitating individuals by helping them change their behavior. The worker acts as a change agent and intervenes in the group to achieve specific purposes determined by group members, the group worker, and society. The remedial model uses a leader-centered approach to group work, with the worker actively intervening in the group's process, often using step-by-step problem solving, task-centered, or behavioral methods. Garvin (1987), Rose (1989), and Vinter (1967), are often associated with this approach to group work.

With the increased attention to time-limited, goal-directed practice, and measurable treatment outcomes, this model has received increasing attention in the group work literature in recent years (see, for example, Cowger, 1980; Edleson &

Table 2-1
Three models of social group work

Selected Characteristics	Social Goals Model	Remedial Model	Reciprocal Model
Purpose and goals	Social consciousness, social responsibility, informed citizenship, and informed political and social action	To restore and rehabilitate group members who are behaving dysfunctionally	To form a mutual aid system among group members to achieve optimum adaptation and socialization
Agency	Settlement houses and neighborhood center settings	Formal agency setting, clinical outpatient or inpatient settings	Compatible with clinical inpatient and outpatient settings and neighborhood and community centers
Focus of work	Larger society, individuals within the context of the neighborhood and the social environment	Changing individual	Creating a self-help, mutual aid system among all group members
Role of the group worker	Role model and enabler for responsible citizenship	Change agent who engages in study, diagnosis, and treatment to help group members attain individual treatment goals	Mediator between needs of members and needs of the group and the larger society Enabler contributing data not available to the members
Type of group	Citizens, neighborhood, and community residents	Clients who are not functioning adequately and need help coping with life's tasks	Partners who work together sharing common concerns
Methods used in the group	Discussion, participation, consensus, developing and carrying out a group task, community organizing, and other program and action skills to help group members acquire instrumental skills about social action and communal living and change	Structured exercises, direct and indirect influence—within and outside of the group—to help members change behavior patterns	Shared authority where members discuss concerns, support one another, and form a cohesive social system to benefit one another

Adapted from Papell and Rothman, 1980a.

Syers, 1990; Rose, 1989; Schinke & Rose 1976; Schinke, Orlandi, Forgey, Rugg, & Douglas, 1992; Schinke, Gordon, & Weston, 1990; Sundel et al., 1985; Tolman & Edleson, 1989). It is used widely in inpatient and community-based settings with individuals who have severe behavioral problems and social skills deficits.

The third model presented by Papell and Rothman (1980a), the reciprocal model, is also sometimes referred to as the interactional model (see, for example, Reid, 1991). The model derives its name from the emphasis on the reciprocal relationship that exists between group members and society. Members both influence, and are influenced by, the environment. The worker acts as a mediator, helping group members find the common ground between their needs and societal demands. The worker also acts as a resource person who facilitates the functioning of the group, and helps members form a mutual aid system and explore new ways of coping with and adapting to environmental demands.

As contrasted with the remedial model, in which the work of the group is often focused on helping individual members with specific problems, the reciprocal model encourages workers to use group processes to foster a therapeutic environment in the group as a whole. The reciprocal model also encourages the worker to help the agency and the wider community better understand and meet individual members' needs. Gitterman and Shulman (1986), Schwartz (1976), and Shulman (1992) are best known for this group-centered, process-oriented approach to group work practice, but other authors such as Falck (1988), Glassman and Kates (1990), and Wasserman and Danforth (1988) have made important contributions to this approach. The approach has wide appeal because of its humanistic orientation, which emphasizes the potential for growth and development of group members, the activation of members' adaptive capacities through mutual aid efforts, and the attempt at making the social environment more responsive to members' needs.

The different foci of current practice models are equally valid, depending on the purposes, practice situations, and tasks facing the group. As mentioned in Chapter 1, groups can have many purposes. A remedial purpose, for example, may be appropriate for some populations and in some settings, such as outpatient community mental health clinics, alcohol and drug treatment centers, and residential centers for delinquent youth.

Mutual aid and shared, reciprocal responsibility are especially appropriate purposes for support groups designed to help members cope with distressing life events. They are also appropriate in self-help groups where reciprocal sharing of mutual concerns and the giving and receiving of support are central. For example, in Make Today Count, a medical self-help group for cancer patients, members are encouraged to share their concerns, experiences, and the reactions of their family members to help each other cope with their illness. In other groups, such as Parents Without Partners, program activities such as dances, dinners, and guest speakers are used to enhance the enjoyment of members and increase the beneficial effects of the group.

The usefulness and appropriateness of different practice models suggest that group workers should make differential use of group work methods, depending on the purposes, objectives, and goals of the groups they are leading. This view is shared by Reid (1981). In a comprehensive review of the history of group work, he concludes that there has always been more than one model of group work operating in the United States and that there will continue to be several models in use to meet the many purposes and goals of group work. Group work practice has an eclectic base, which developed as a response to diverse needs for educational, recreational, mental health, and social services. For additional information, the writings of Alissi (1980b), Lang (1972, 1979a, 1979b), Papell and Rothman (1980a, 1980b), and Roberts and Northen (1976) review in more detail the historical trends that have resulted in this eclectic base.

In recent years, there has also been a greater attempt to integrate different models of group work practice. Revisiting their earlier model-building efforts, Papell and Rothman (1980b) acknowledged that there had been a proliferation of practice models since they first defined their three practice models. Despite this, they asserted that there is a "mainstream model" of group work practice that incorporates elements of many different practice models. They suggested that this model was characterized by "common goals, mutual aid, and non-synthetic experiences" (p. 7). They pointed out that the fostering of a mutual aid system among members is a common ingredient of many seemingly polarized approaches to group work practice. They suggested that group development, and the creation of group structures for increasing the autonomy of members as the group develops, is also a common element of most current conceptualizations of group work practice.

Similarly, in considering the past, present, and future of group work in social work, Middleman and Wood (1990) also concluded that, in practice, there had been a blending of models of group work in recent years. They suggested that a mainstream model of social work with groups should include the worker (a) helping members develop a system of mutual aid, (b) understanding, valuing, and respecting group processes as powerful dynamics for change, (c) helping members become empowered for autonomous functioning within and outside the group, and (d) helping members "re-experience their groupness at the point of termination" (p. 11). Thus, they concluded that some clinical work with groups, especially that which focuses exclusively on one-to-one work with individual members within a group context, would be excluded from a mainstream model of social work with groups.

The first edition of this book, Toseland and Rivas (1984), also had as one of its primary goals bridging the schism between remedial and reciprocal approaches. The intent of the first edition, and this one, is to elucidate a core body of knowledge, values, skills, and procedures that are essential for professional, competent group work practice, regardless of ideological orientation.

Task Groups

With a few exceptions (Ephross & Vassil, 1988; Toseland & Ephross, 1987; Trecker 1946, 1980), little attention has been paid to task groups in the group work literature within the social work profession. Those who mention task groups spend only a brief portion of their texts on them (Brown, 1991; Garvin, 1987; Henry, 1992; Klein, 1972). Earlier in the history of group work, the journals *The*

Group, published between 1939 and 1955, and *Adult Leadership*, published from 1952 to 1977, devoted much of their space to articles about leading task groups. The distinction between task groups and treatment groups made today was not made in the earlier history of group work. Groups were used simultaneously for both task and treatment purposes (Siporin, 1980b). Recently, as can be seen in the bibliography in Appendix B, journals have devoted more attention to task groups.

Task groups have operated in social agencies since the settlement houses and charity organizations began more than 100 years ago. They are essential for effective client service and for the smooth operation of social agencies. The current need for expertise about task groups is becoming critical as more agencies than ever are using team approaches for service delivery. Siporin (1980b) states, "there is a need to give much more attention than we do at present in social work practice and in social work education to work with task groups" (p. 19). This text is designed to address this gap in the literature.

KNOWLEDGE FROM SOCIAL SCIENCE RESEARCH

According to Hare (1976), the scientific study of groups began at the turn of the century. A basic research question, which was asked at that time and continues to receive much attention today, concerns the extent to which being a part of a group influences the individual group member. Triplett (1898), for example, examined the effect that cyclists had on each other during races and found that a racer's competitiveness appeared to depend on the activities of others on the track. Taylor (1903) found that productivity increased among workers who were freed from the pressure to conform to the standards of other workers. Those early findings suggest that the presence of others has a significant influence on an individual group member. The presence of others tends to generate pressure to conform to the standards of behavior that are expected of those who belong to the group.

Other early social scientists also recognized the influence of groups on individual behavior. LeBon (1910) referred to the forces that were generated by group interaction as "group contagion" and "group mind," recognizing that people in groups react differently than individuals. McDougall (1920) extended the concept of the group mind. He noted the existence of groups as entities and pointed out a number of group-as-a-whole properties that could be studied as phenomena separate and distinct from properties affecting individuals working outside of a group.

The concept of a primary group was also an important contribution to the study of groups. Cooley (1909) defined a *primary group* as a small, informal group—such as a family or a friendship group—which has a tremendous influence on members' values, moral standards, and normative behaviors. The primary group was therefore viewed as essential in understanding socialization and development.

Few studies of small group processes were published between 1905 and 1920, but activity in these areas increased after World War I (Hare, 1976). Several experiments conducted during that time illustrated the powerful effects of group forces on the judgments and behavior of group members. Allport (1924), for example, found that the presence of others improved task performance. Sherif (1936) placed subjects in a darkened room with a pinpoint of light at one end. Known as the autokinetic effect, a stable light in a darkened room appears to move slightly. After Sherif determined an average range of perceived movement based on the responses of individual subjects, he placed them together in the darkened room. He found that the subjects modified their estimates of the amount the light moved based on the opinions of others in the group. The subjects continued to give these modified estimates after leaving the group.

Asch (1957), following up on Sherif's findings, placed confederates who had been instructed to give false estimates in a room with subjects who were asked to judge the length of a line in comparison to a standard line of a given length. Confederates were instructed to make incorrect responses in the presence of the subject. Would the subjects adhere to their correct judgments or alter their judgments based on the confederates' responses? The subjects altered their judgments to conform to those of the confederates 30 percent of the time even though the confederates' judgments were clearly incorrect.

After World War I, social scientists also began to study groups operating in the community. One of the earliest social scientists to study groups in their natural environments was Frederick Thrasher (1927). He studied gangs of delinquents in the Chicago area by becoming friendly with gang members and observing the internal operations of gangs. He noted that every member of a gang had a status within the group that was attached to his functional role in the gang. Thrasher also drew attention to the culture that developed within a gang, suggesting there was a common code that all members followed. The code was enforced by group opinion, coercion, and physical punishment. Thrasher's work and the works of Shaw (1930) and Whyte (1943) have influenced how group work is practiced with youths in settlement houses, neighborhood centers, and youth organizations.

Later, Sherif and his colleagues (Sherif & Sherif, 1953; Sherif, White, & Harvey, 1955; Sherif, 1956) relied on naturalistic observations of groups of boys in a summer camp to demonstrate how cohesion and intergroup hostility develop. Groups of boys who spent time together and had common goals, such as winning a tug-of-war, became more cooperative, developed a liking for one another, and felt solidarity with their teammates. At the same time, antagonism between groups increased. Bringing boys from different groups together only increased the tension until tasks were assigned that required the joint effort of boys from different groups.

Social scientists also learned more about people's behavior in groups from studies done in industry and in the U.S. Army. Perhaps the most famous of all industrial studies is the classic series of studies at Western Electric's Hawthorne Plant in Chicago (Roethlisberger, 1941; Roethlisberger & Dickson, 1939, 1975). These studies were designed to test whether piece-rate wage incentives increased the output of workers who assembled telephone equipment. The incentives were designed in such a way that wage increases gained by one team member would also benefit other team members. Management believed such a system would encourage individual productivity and increase group spirit and morale because all team members would benefit from the increase in productivity.

It was found that an informal group had developed among team members. Despite the opportunity to improve individual and group wages, workers did not produce more under the new incentive system. Results of the studies suggest that informal norms of what constituted a fair day's work governed the workers' behavior. Members of a work group that produced too much were ridiculed as being "rate busters" and those who produced too little were called "chiselers." Occasionally, more severe sanctions called "binging" were applied by team members when a worker did not conform to the team's notion of a fair day's work. "Binging" consisted of striking a fellow worker as hard as possible on the upper arm while verbally asking the worker to comply with the group's norms.

Studies conducted on combat units during World War II have also illustrated the powerful effects that small groups can have on the behavior of their members. For example, in describing the fighting ability of combat soldiers, Shils (1950) and Stouffer (1949) have suggested that the courage of the average soldier was only partially sustained by hatred of the enemy and the patriotic ideas of a democratic society. Their studies revealed that soldiers' loyalty to their particular unit strengthened their morale and supported them during periods of intense combat stress. Similarly, studies conducted in other settings by Cartwright and Lippitt (1961) and Lewin (1951) found that individuals needed social supports to uphold their values and beliefs and that when members diverge too greatly from a group's norms and values they will be punished or expelled from the group.

During the 1950s, an explosion of knowledge about small groups took place. Earlier experiments by Bales (1950), Jennings (1947, 1950), Lewin, Lippitt, and White (1939), and Moreno (1934) spurred interest in the study of both task and treatment groups. Some of the most important findings from this period are summarized in the work of Cartwright and Zander (1968), Hare (1976), Kiesler (1978), McGrath (1984), Nixon (1979), and Shaw (1976). Because they are reflected in a discussion of group dynamics and leadership in Chapters 3 and 4 of this text, they will not be repeated here. It is interesting to note, however, that the major themes of small group research that were initially developed in the first half of the 20th century—that is, conformity, communication and interaction patterns, leadership, interpersonal preference, and social perception—continue to dominate the research efforts of social scientists investigating the dynamics of small groups today.

INFLUENTIAL THEORIES

From knowledge about small groups accumulated over the years in laboratory and natural settings, investigators of group phenomena began to develop comprehensive theories to explain group functioning. An enormous variety of these theories exist (see Douglas, 1979). This chapter will consider five major theories: (a) psychoanalytic theory, (b) learning theory, (c) field theory, (d) social exchange theory, and (e) systems theory. Although we believe that a thorough knowledge of systems theory is basic to all group work practice, we have included other theories because they have been important influences on group work practice and we believe practitioners should be familiar with them. When continuing to improve and refine practice skills, group workers may want to examine these theories in greater depth.

Psychoanalytic Theory

Psychoanalytic theory has had an important influence on group work practice. In his work *Group Psychology and the Analysis of the Ego*, Freud (1922) set forth his theoretical formulations about groups and their influence on human behavior. Many of Freud's other works have also influenced group work practice. For example, commonly used terms such as *insight, ego strength,* and *defense mechanisms* originated in Freud's work. Although psychoanalytic theory focuses primarily on the individual, and Freud did not practice group psychotherapy, many of his followers, including Bion (1959), Redl (1942, 1944), Whitaker and Lieberman (1964), and Yalom (1985), have adapted psychoanalytic theory for working with groups. Psychoanalytic theory has also influenced the founders of other practice theories used in groups. These include Eric Berne's transactional analysis, Fritz Perl's gestalt therapy, and Frank Moreno's psychodrama.

According to psychoanalytic theory, group members act out in the group unresolved conflicts from early life experiences. In many ways, the group becomes a re-enactment of the family situation. Freud (1922), for example, describes the group leader as the all-powerful father figure who reigns supreme over group members. Group members identify with the group leader as the "ego ideal" (Wyss, 1973). Members form transference reactions to the group leader and to each other on the basis of their early life experiences. Thus, the interactions that occur in the group illustrate members' personality structures and defense mechanisms.

The group leader uses transference reactions to help members work through unresolved conflicts by exploring past behavior patterns and linking these patterns to current behaviors. The group leader might, for example, interpret the behavior of two group members who are struggling for the leader's attention as unresolved sibling rivalry. When interpretations made by the group worker are timed appropriately, members gain insight into their own behavior. According to psychoanalytic theory, insight is the essential ingredient in modifying and changing behavior patterns inside and outside of the group.

More recent conceptions of psychoanalytic group treatment (see, for example, Polansky, 1982; Yalom, 1985) have adapted and modified classical psychoanalytic theory to include a greater emphasis on the here-and-now experiences of group interaction. Emphasizing the here-and-now experiences of group members is useful in ensuring that members deal with issues of immediate concern to them. From an analysis of here-and-now behavior patterns in the group, the leader can help members reconstruct unresolved childhood conflicts. Through direct, mutual interpersonal communications, members build interpersonal skills, adaptive capacities, and ego strength, as well as gain insight into their behavior. The cohesiveness of the group allows members to reveal intimate details about their personal lives and to act out their conflicts in a safe, supportive environment.

Psychoanalytic theory has also been influential in furthering our understanding of how individuals behave in groups. Wilford Bion, who was psychoanalytically trained, developed the Tavastock approach to help people understand the primitive emotional processes that occur in groups. He suggested that group members often avoid the work of the group by reacting with flight-fight responses, and dependency, to the leader's authority (Bion, 1959).

A thorough discussion of psychoanalytic theory of group functioning is beyond the scope of this book. For further explanation of modern adaptations of psychoanalytic theory to group work practice, see Yalom (1985) and the *International Journal of Group Psychotherapy.*

Learning Theory

Perhaps no theory has stirred more controversy within social group work than learning theory. As with psychoanalytic theory, the primary focus of learning theory is on the behavior of individuals rather than on the behavior of groups. Thus, learning theory has largely ignored the importance of group dynamics. Also, like the early emphasis on primitive drives in psychoanalytic theory, the early emphasis on environmental contingencies and the de-emphasis of free-will lead some group workers to conclude that learning theory is deterministic. For these reasons, some view learning theory as antithetical to the values and traditions of growth, autonomy, and self-determination that are so much a part of the heritage of group work practice.

Despite the controversy, learning theory has had an important influence on current methods of group work practice. The emphasis on clear and specific goal setting, contracting, the influence of the environment on the group and its members, step-by-step treatment planning, measurable treatment outcomes, and evaluation can be traced, at least in part, to the influence of learning theory. The growing importance of short-term, structured psycho-educational groups attests to the important influence that learning theory principles have had on group work practice (Garvin, Reid, & Epstein, 1976; Middleman, 1980; Papell & Rothman, 1980b). For example, groups that focus on themes like social skills, assertiveness, relaxation, and parenting use learning theory principles and are found in many community and institutional settings. (For a detailed description of structured groups see Drum and Knott, 1977.)

According to social learning theory (Bandura, 1977b), the behavior of group members can be explained by one of three methods of learning. In the classical approach to learning theory, behavior becomes associated with a stimulus. For example, a worker responds by making a negative verbal comment each time a member turns and speaks to another member while the worker or other group members are speaking. After several times, the mere stimulus of the member turning, without speaking, will be enough to cue the worker to respond with a negative verbal comment.

A second and more common method of learning is called operant conditioning. In this paradigm, the behaviors of the group members and the worker are governed by the consequences of their actions. Thus, if member A acts in a certain way and member B reacts positively, member A will be likely to continue the behavior. Similarly, if a group worker receives negative feedback from group members about a particular behavior, the worker will be less likely to behave that way in the future.

Several writers (Feldman & Wodarski, 1975; Feldman, Caplinger, & Wodarski, 1983; Rose & Edleson, 1987) use operant learning theory principles in their approach to group work. For example, Rose (1989) suggests that tokens, praise, or other reinforcers can be used to increase desired behavior and decrease undesired behavior in the group or in the external environment.

In the group, the worker might use praise to increase member-to-member communications and negative verbal comments to decrease member-to-leader communications. To help a member with a problem he or she has experienced in the outside environment, such as being overweight, the group leader might ask the member to develop a plan that specifies self-imposed rewards for behavior that decreases caloric intake and self-imposed sanctions for behavior that increases caloric intake.

Bandura (1977b) has developed a third learning paradigm called social learning theory. If group members or the group worker were to wait for classical or operant conditioning to occur, behavior in groups would be learned very slowly. Bandura proposes that most learning takes place through observation and vicarious reinforcement or punishment. For example, when a group member is praised for a certain behavior, that group member and other group members reproduce the behavior later, hoping to receive similar praise. When a group member who performs a certain behavior is ignored or punished by social sanctions, other group members learn not to behave in that manner because such behavior results in a negative outcome.

In response to concerns that learning theory has not taken into consideration motivations, expectations, and other cognitive aspects of behavior, Mahoney (1974) and others have developed cognitive-behavioral approaches. Although learning theorists have not attempted to explain the functioning of groups as a whole, learning theory principles have been shown to be useful in helping members make desired changes. All group workers should be familiar with the basic principles of learning theory and cognitive behavior modification. Because of their particular relevance to treatment groups, we will draw on some of the principles of classical, operant, and social learning theories in our discussion of specialized methods for leading treatment groups in Chapter 9.

Field Theory

Kurt Lewin, more than any other social scientist, has come to be associated with the study of group dynamics. He conducted numerous experiments on the forces that account for behavior in small groups. For example, in an early study investigating leadership, Lewin, Lippett, and White (1939) created three types of groups with authoritarian, democratic, and laissez-faire leadership. The results of this study are reported in Chapter 4. Lewin and his colleagues were the first to apply the scientific method in developing a theory of groups. In 1944, he and his colleagues set up laboratories and formed the Research Center for Group Dynamics at the Massachusetts Institute of Technology.

According to Lewin's field theory, "a group has a life space, it occupies a position relative to other objects in this space, it is oriented toward goals, it locomotes in pursuit of these goals, and it may encounter barriers in the process of locomotion" (Shepard, 1964, p. 25). The unique contribution of field theory is that it views the group as a gestalt, that is, an entity of opposing forces that act to hold members in the group and to move the group along in its quest for goal achievement. According to Lewin (1947), groups are constantly changing to cope with their social situation, although there are times when a "quasi-stationary equilibrium" exists for all groups. In all cases, however, the behavior of individual group members and the group itself must be seen as a function of the total situation (Lewin, 1946).

In developing field theory, Lewin introduced several concepts to aid in understanding the forces at work in a group. Among these are (a) roles, which refer to the status, rights, and duties of group members; (b) norms, which are rules governing the behavior of group members; (c) power, which is the ability of members to influence one another; (d) cohesion, which is the amount of attraction the members of the group feel for one another and for the group; (e) consensus, which is the degree of agreement regarding goals and other group phenomena; and (f) valence, which is the potency of goals and objects in the life space of the group.

Lewin sought to understand the forces occurring in the group as a whole from the perspective of individual group members. He did this mathematically and topographically, using vectors to describe group forces. Emphasizing the importance of properties of the group that act on the individual member, most field theorists have focused their research efforts on *cohesion*, which they define as the totality of forces acting on individual members to keep them in the group. Studies by field theorists have shown that cohesion is related to agreement on goals and norms, shared understanding, and similar demographic backgrounds of members, as well as to productivity, satisfaction, and cooperative interaction patterns (Cartwright, 1951; Cartwright & Zander, 1968; Lippitt, 1957).

Along with his interest in formulating a theoretical model of group dynamics, Lewin was interested in the effect of groups on individuals' psychological makeup. Before his death in 1947, Lewin developed the t-group as a way to observe the effects of group processes on group members and as a means to help individual group members change their own behavior. Although he was not directly involved, he helped found the first National Training Laboratory in Group Development in 1947. Since then, t-groups have been used extensively at the National Training Laboratories as an experiential means to train group facilitators, to teach individuals about the effects of group dynamics, and to help individuals examine and change their own behavior.

Relying on a principle in Lewin's field theory that suggests individuals will not change their own behavior unless they see their behavior and their attitudes as others see them, the t-group experience attempts to provide participants with extensive feedback about their own behavior. Members are confronted with the effects of their behavior on other group members and on the group's facilitator. Role plays, simulations, and other experiential program activities are often used to illustrate how group processes develop and how they affect members.

Social Exchange Theory

Whereas field theory emphasizes the group as a whole, social exchange theory focuses on the behavior of individual group members. Blau (1964), Homans (1961), and Thibaut and Kelley (1959) are the principal developers of this approach to groups. Deriving their theory from animal psychology, economic analysis, and game theory, social exchange theorists suggest that when people interact in groups, each will attempt to behave in a way that will maximize rewards and minimize punishments. Group members initiate interactions because these social exchanges provide them with something of value, such as approval. According to social exchange theorists, because ordinarily nothing is gained unless something is given in return, there is an exchange implied in all human relationships.

In social exchange theory, group behavior is analyzed by observing how individual members seek rewards while dealing with the sustained social interaction occurring in a group. For an individual in a group, the decision to express a given behavior is based on a comparison of the rewards and punishments that are expected to be derived from the behavior. Group members act to increase positive consequences and decrease negative consequences. Social exchange theory also focuses on the way members influence one another during social interactions. The result of any social exchange is based on the amount of social power and the amount of social dependence in a particular interaction.

Guided Group Interaction (Empey & Erikson, 1972; McCorkle, Elias, & Bixby, 1958) and Positive Peer Culture (Vorrath & Brendtro, 1985) are two specialized group work methods that rely heavily on principles from social exchange theory. They are frequently used with delinquent adolescents in residential and institutional settings. In both approaches, structured groups are used to confront, challenge, and eliminate anti-social peer group norms, and to replace them with pro-social norms through guided peer group interaction.

Social exchange theory has been criticized as being mechanistic because it assumes people are always rational beings who act according to their analysis of rewards and punishments (Shepard, 1964). For the most part, these criticisms are unfounded. Social exchange theorists are aware that cognitive processes affect how people behave in groups (see, for example, Kelley & Stakelski, 1970; Kelley & Thibaut, 1969). Group members' perceptions of rewards and punishments are influenced by cognitive processes such as intentions and expectations. Thus, the work of social exchange theorists in psychology and of symbolic interaction theorists in sociology has helped to account for the role of cognitive processes in the behavior of individuals in groups and other social interactions. The influence of symbolic interaction theory on group work practice can be seen in the work of Balgopal and Vassil (1983).

Systems Theory

Systems theory attempts to understand the group as a system of interacting elements. Although psychodynamic, behavior, field, and social exchange theory are useful in understanding aspects of group functioning, systems theory is probably the most widely used and broadly applied theory of group functioning (Anderson, 1979; Olsen, 1968). Several writers have applied systems theory to group functioning. Each has a somewhat different conception of groups as social systems. Some of the most important concepts used by several systems theorists will be described here to present a view of systems theory from a variety of perspectives.

Talcott Parsons is a leading contributor to our understanding of groups as social systems. To Parsons (1951), groups are social systems with several interdependent members attempting to maintain order and a stable equilibrium while they function as a unified whole. Groups are constantly facing changing demands in their quest to attain goals and to maintain a stable equilibrium. Groups must mobilize their resources and act to meet changing demands if they are to survive. According to Parsons, Bales, and Shils (1953), there are four major functional tasks for systems such as a group: (a) integration—ensuring that members of groups fit together; (b) adaptation—ensuring that groups change to cope with the demands of their environment; (c) pattern maintenance—ensuring that groups define and sustain their basic purposes, identities, and procedures; and (4) goal attainment—ensuring that groups pursue and accomplish their tasks. According to Parsons, groups must accomplish these four functional tasks to remain in equilibrium.

The work of carrying out these four functional tasks is left to the group's leader and its members. The leader and members act to help their group survive so they can be gratified as the group reaches its goal (Mills, 1967). To do this, group members observe and assess the group's progress toward its goals and take action to avoid problems. The likelihood that a group will survive depends on the demands of the environment, the extent to which members identify with group goals, and the degree to which members believe goals are attainable. By overcoming obstacles and successfully handling the functional tasks confronting them, groups strive to remain in a state of equilibrium.

Robert Bales, another important systems theorist, has a somewhat different conception of groups as social systems. Whereas Parsons was interested in developing a generalizable systems model to explain societal as well as group functioning, Bales has concentrated his efforts on observing and theorizing about small task groups in laboratory settings. According to Bales (1950), groups must solve two general types of problems to maintain themselves. These include (a) instrumental problems, such as the group reaching its goals, and (b) socio-emotional problems, which include interpersonal difficulties, problems of coordination, and member satisfaction (Wilson, 1978). Instrumental problems are caused by demands placed on the group by the outside environment, and socio-emotional problems arise from within the group.

The group worker should always be concerned about process and outcome, that is, about members' social and emotional needs and the task accomplishments expected of the group. However, the two types of problems must be balanced if the group is to survive. Attention to instrumental problems alone will lead to dissatisfaction and conflict within the group. Exclusive attention to socio-emotional problems leads to the group's failure to accomplish its objectives and goals. The worker, therefore, is placed in the precarious position of attending to both sets of problems to maintain the group's adequate functioning. Because instrumental and socio-emotional needs often conflict, it is usually impossible to attend to both sets of problems simultaneously. Therefore, workers are forced to work on either instrumental or socio-emotional problems at any one time.

In contrast with Parsons, Bales' systems model emphasizes tension and antagonism rather than harmony and equilibrium. Groups tend to vacillate between adaptation to the outside environment and attention to internal integration. Bales (1950) calls this the group's "dynamic equilibrium." Swings in attention are the result of the functional needs of the group in its struggle to maintain itself. To study this "dynamic equilibrium," Bales observed interactions in several different kinds of task groups such as juries and teams (Bales, 1950, 1954, 1955). Bales found that, to deal with instrumental problems, group members asked for or gave opinions, asked for or gave information, and asked for or made suggestions. To handle socio-emotional problems, group members expressed agreement or disagreement, showed tension or released tension, and showed solidarity or antagonism. Through these interactions group members dealt with problems of communication, evaluation, control, decision making, tension reduction, and integration.

Bales (1950) has developed a scheme for analyzing group interaction, based on his theory about how group members deal with instrumental and expressive tasks. This scheme is called Interaction Process Analysis. It puts members' interactions into 12 categories. Analysis of the distribution of interactions in each category in problem-solving groups suggests that typical task groups emphasize giving and receiving information early in group meetings, giving and asking for opinions in the middle stage, and giving and asking for suggestions in later stages (Shepard, 1964). Bales (1954, 1955) suggests that groups go through a natural process of evolution and development. His research also indicates that in most groups about 25 percent of all members' behaviors are positive reactions, 56 percent are responses to questions, 12 percent are negative reactions, and 7 percent are questions. Therefore, about half of all communications in groups are responses to questions, and the other half are divided among positive reactions, negative reactions, and questions (Shepard, 1964). Bales, Cohen, and Williamson (1979) have continued to develop and refine this system of analyzing group interactions. The new system, known as SYMLOG, is explained in Chapter 7.

The final conception of systems theory relevant to our understanding of group dynamics has been presented in Homans' (1950) early work, *The Human Group*. It is also evident in the writings of Germain and Gitterman (1980) and Siporin (1980a) on ecological systems theory. According to these writers, groups are in constant interaction with their environments. They occupy an ecological niche. Homans suggests that groups have an external system and an internal system. The external system represents a group's way of handling the adaptive problems that result from its relationship with its social and physical environment. The internal system consists of the patterns of activities, interactions, and norms occurring within the group as it attempts to function. Like Bales, Homans notes that the relative dominance of the internal system as compared with the external system varies depending on the demands of the external and the internal environment of the group. Homans, however, denies the homeostatic idea of equilibrium proposed by Parsons and Bales, preferring to conceive of groups as ever-changing entities in which change and the constant struggle for equilibrium are commonplace.

Although they share many of their ideas with Homans (1950) and other systems theorists, the models of practice developed by Germain and Gitterman (1980) and by Siporin (1980a) suggest that attention should be given to the dynamic, ever-changing equilibrium of task and treatment groups. They point out the constant exchange that all social systems have with their environment. They also emphasize the possibilities for growth and change, called *morphogenic properties*, that are a part of all social systems.

The different conceptualizations of systems theory described here may at first appear confusing. However, when considering the vast array of groups in modern society and people's different experiences in them, it becomes easier to understand how different conceptualizations of systems theory have developed. It is important to recognize that each conceptualization represents a unique attempt to understand the processes that occur in all social systems.

Concepts derived from these differing views of systems theory that are particularly relevant for group workers include the following:

- The existence of properties of the group as a whole that arise from the interactions of individual group members.
- The powerful effects of group forces on members' behavior.
- The struggle of groups to maintain themselves as entities when confronted with conflicts.
- The awareness that groups must relate to an external environment as well as attend to their internal functioning.
- The idea that groups are in a constant state of becoming, developing, and changing, which influences their equilibrium and continued existence.
- The notion that groups have a developmental life cycle.

Workers can use these concepts to facilitate the development of group processes that help treatment and task groups achieve their goals and help members satisfy their socio-emotional needs.

SUMMARY

This chapter describes historical developments in the practice of group work and in the social sciences. A historical perspective is presented to help workers develop a broad understanding of the uses of groups in practice settings and develop a knowledge base they can use to practice effectively with different types of groups.

The historical overview of group work practice presented in this chapter suggests that throughout the 20th century, groups have been used for a variety of purposes, including education, recreation, socialization, support, and therapy. The early emphasis on the use of groups for education, recreation, and socialization has waned in recent years in favor of an increased interest in the use of groups for support, mutual aid, and therapy. This trend parallels the gradual transition during the 1930s and 1940s away from group work's amorphous roots in adult education, recreation, and social work to its formal incorporation into the social work profession during the 1950s.

Currently, social group work is being revitalized in schools of social work and in practice settings. As the section on current trends indicates, in recent years there has also been an increased recognition of the roots of social group work, and the multiple purposes group work can serve.

This chapter also briefly explores historical developments in social science research that have relevance for understanding group processes. Findings from these studies emphasize the powerful influence that the group as a whole has on individual group members. The chapter closes with a review of five theories: (a) psychoanalytic theory, (b) learning theory, (c) field theory, (d) social exchange theory, and (e) systems theory, all of which have had an important influence on group work practice.

LEARNING ASSIGNMENTS

1. Read about the lives of two famous group workers in the early history of group work practice. Possible sources are: NASW's *Encyclopedia of Social Work*, K. Reid's *From Character Building to Social Treatment: The History of the Use of Groups in Social Work Practice*, or A. Alissi's *Perspectives on Social Group Work Practice*. Compare and contrast how they practiced with groups. How did their practice differ from your understanding of modern practice?

2. Interview a group worker and ask this individual to describe the theoretical foundation of his or her work. Does the worker draw on theories of group work practice in an eclectic manner, or rely primarily on one theory of practice? Ask the individual to comment on the extent to which theory guides his or her day-to-day practice. Which seems to be more important to him or her: theory, or practice wisdom generated from previous experience?

3. Observe a treatment group, or, if this is not possible, interview a group leader. Using the characteristics described in Table 2–1, determine the extent to which the group leader is practicing within the traditions of the social goals, remedial, and reciprocal models of group work practice. To what extent does the worker blend traditions? What particular tradition is most appealing to you? Why?

CHAPTER 3

Understanding Group Dynamics

A thorough understanding of group dynamics is useful for practicing effectively with any type of group. Although many theories describe group functioning, fundamental to all of them is an understanding of groups as social systems (Anderson, 1979). A system is made up of elements and their interactions. As social systems, therefore, task and treatment groups can be conceptualized as individuals in interaction with each other.

The forces that result from the interactions of group members are often referred to as *group processes* or *group dynamics*. In this text, we use the term *group dynamics* to refer to these forces. Because group dynamics influence the behavior of both individual group members and the group as a whole, they have been of considerable interest to group workers for many years (see, for example, Coyle, 1930, 1937; Elliott, 1928).

One of the worker's most important tasks is to recognize and use the potent dynamics generated in a group as it develops. Northen (1969) and others remind us that this is not an automatic process. Appropriate use of group dynamics can lead to positive outcomes for the group and its members. Inattention to these dynamics, however, can result in a lack of direction and focus, and inappropriate use can have detrimental effects. For example, in an in-depth examination of a variety of encounter groups, Lieberman, Yalom, and Miles (1973) found that many of the groups produced casualties, some of which resulted in severe mental disorders among group participants. Similar findings reported by Galinsky and Schopler (1977) and by Kaul and Bednar (1986) suggest the forces exerted in groups can have a powerful influence on the individual members, as well as the group as a whole.

It is clear that groups can unleash harmful as well as helpful forces (Galinsky & Schopler, 1977). The Hitler youth movement of the 1920s and 1930s, the Ku Klux Klan, the tragedy at Jonestown, and the Branch Davidians at Waco, Texas, are examples of the use of group dynamics for harmful purposes. This chapter seeks to help group workers recognize, understand, and use the dynamics generated through the group process to achieve goals consistent with the humanistic value base of the social work profession. It is our belief that people who are familiar with group dynamics are less likely to be victimized by harmful leaders and groups.

GROUP DYNAMICS

Although there have been several attempts to develop comprehensive schemes for classifying group dynamics, none has proved totally satisfactory. Our discussion focuses on four areas of group dynamics that are of particular importance to group workers in understanding and working effectively with all types of task and treatment groups. These areas include (a) the communication and interaction patterns occurring in groups, (b) group cohesion or the attraction of groups for their members, (c) the social controls exerted in groups, and (d) the culture that develops in groups. A firm grasp of these areas is essential for understanding the social structure of groups and for developing beginning-level skills in group work practice.

Communication and Interaction Patterns

According to Northen (1969), "Social interaction is a term for the dynamic interplay of forces in which contact between persons results in a modification of the behavior and attitudes of the participants" (p. 17). Verbal and nonverbal communications are the components of social interaction. Communication is the process by which people convey meanings to each other, using symbols. Communication entails (a) the encoding of a person's perceptions, thoughts, and feelings into language and other symbols, (b) the transmission of these symbols or language, and (c) the decoding of the transmission by another person. This process is shown in Figure 3–1. As members of a group communicate to one another, a reciprocal pattern of interaction emerges. The interaction patterns that develop can be beneficial or harmful to the group. A group worker who is knowledgeable about helpful communications and interactions can intervene in the patterns that are established in order to help the group achieve desired goals and to ensure the socioemotional satisfaction of members.

FIGURE 3–1
A model of the process of communication

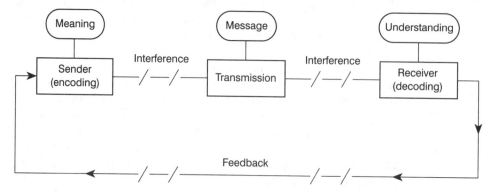

Communication as a Process

The first step in understanding and intervening in interaction patterns is for the worker to be aware that whenever people are together in a group, they are communicating. As shown in Figure 3–1, all communications are intended to convey a message. Silence, for example, can communicate sorrow, thoughtfulness, anger, or lack of interest. In addition, every group member communicates not only to transmit information but also for many other reasons. Kiesler (1978) has suggested that people communicate with such interpersonal concerns as (a) understanding people and finding out where they stand in relation to other people, (b) persuading others, (c) gaining or maintaining power, (d) defending themselves, (e) provoking a reaction from others, (f) making an impression on others, (g) gaining or maintaining relationships, and (h) presenting a unified image to the group. Many other important reasons for communication could be added to this list.

Workers who are aware that group members communicate for many reasons can observe, assess, and understand communication and interaction patterns. Because patterns of communication are often consistent across different situations, group workers can use this information to work with individual members and the group as a whole. For example, a worker observes that one member is consistently unassertive in the group. The worker might help the member practice responding assertively to situations in the group. Because the pattern of a lack of assertiveness is likely to occur in situations outside the group, the worker might also suggest that the member practice the skills in situations encountered between meetings.

In addition to meanings transmitted in every communication, the worker should also be aware that messages are often received selectively. *Selective perception* refers to the screening of messages so they are congruent with one's belief system. As shown in Figure 3–1, messages are decoded and their meanings are received. Individual group members have a unique understanding of communications on the basis of their selective perception. Selected screening sometimes results in blocking of messages so that they are not decoded and received. Napier and Gershenfeld (1981) suggest that the perception of a communication can be influenced by (a) life positions that result from experiences in early childhood, (b) stereotypes, (c) the status and position of the communicator, (d) previous experiences, and (e) assumptions and values. Thus, what might appear to a naive observer as a simple, straightforward, and objective social interaction might have a great deal of hidden meaning, for both the sender and the receiver of a particular communication.

It is not possible, or even desirable, for workers to analyze each interpersonal communication that occurs in a group. However, with a little practice, workers can develop a "third ear," that is, become aware of the meanings behind messages and their effect on a particular group member and on the group as a whole. Group workers are in a much better position to intervene in the group when they have a full understanding of the meanings of the messages being communicated and received by each member.

Communications can also be distorted in transmission. In Figure 3–1, distortion is represented as interference. Among the most common transmission problems are language barriers. Frequently, workers conduct groups with members from different cultural backgrounds, for whom English is a second language. In addition to problems of understanding accents and dialects, the meanings of many words are culturally defined and may not be interpreted as the communicator intended. Special care must be taken in these situations to avoid distorting the meanings intended by the communicator (Draper, 1979; Gitterman & Schaeffer, 1972; Kadushin, 1972).

Noise and other distortions inside or outside the meeting room can interfere with effective communication. Similarly, hearing or eyesight problems can create difficulties in receiving messages. For example, about one third of all elderly men have some hearing impairment (Kart, Metress, & Metress, 1978), and about 1 million older people suffer from severe visual impairment (Kline & Schieber, 1985). Thus, when working with groups, the practitioner should be alert to members' potential difficulties in hearing what other members are saying, and in seeing who is attempting to communicate with them. Some strategies for working with visually impaired and hearing-impaired members of groups are presented in Tables 3–1 and 3–2.

To prevent distortions in communications from causing misunderstandings and conflict, it is important that members receive feedback about their communications. Feedback is a way of checking that the meanings of the communicated messages are understood correctly. For feedback to be used appropriately it should (a) describe the content of the communication or the behavior as it is perceived by the group member, (b) be given to the member who sent the message as soon as the message is received, and (c) be expressed in a tentative manner so that those who send messages understand that the feedback is designed to check for distortions rather than to confront or attack them.

TABLE 3–1
Techniques for communicating with hearing-impaired group members

1. Position yourself so you are in full view of the person and your face is illuminated.
2. Speak in a normal voice.
3. Speak slowly and clearly. Stress key words. Pause between sentences.
4. Make sure no one else is talking when a group member is speaking to a hearing-impaired person or when a hearing-impaired person is speaking to a group member.
5. Make sure the room is free of background noises and has good acoustics.
6. Look for cues, such as facial expressions or inappropriate responses, that indicate the individual has misunderstood.
7. If you suspect that the individual has misunderstood, restate what has been said.
8. Speak to the individual, not about him or her.

Adapted from Blazer (1978).

TABLE 3–2
Techniques for communicating with visually impaired group members

1. Ask the individual if assistance is needed to get to the meeting room. If the reply is yes, offer your elbow. Walk a half step ahead so your body indicates a change in direction, when to stop, and so forth.

2. Introduce yourself and all group members when the meeting begins. Go around the group clockwise or counterclockwise. This will help the group member learn where each member is located.

3. When you accompany a visually impaired person into a new meeting room, describe the layout of the room, the furniture placement, and any obstacles. This will help orient the individual.

4. Try not to disturb the placement of objects in the meeting room. If this is unavoidable, be sure to inform the person about the changes. Similarly, let the individual know if someone leaves or enters the room.

5. When guiding visually impaired individuals to their seat, place their hand on the back of the chair and allow them to seat themselves.

6. Speak directly to the visually impaired person, not through an intermediary.

7. Look at the individual when you speak.

8. Don't be afraid to use words such as "look" and "see."

9. Speak in a normal voice. Do not shout.

10. Visually impaired people value independence just as sighted people do. Do not be overprotective.

11. Give explicit instructions about the location of coffee or snacks, and during program activities. For example, state, "The coffee pot is 10 feet to the left of your chair," rather than, "The coffee pot is right over there on your left."

Adapted from a handout prepared by The Lighthouse, 111 E. 59th St., New York, NY 10222.

Examples of feedback are "John, I understood you to say. . ." or "Mary, if I understand you correctly, you are saying. . . ." When feedback is used correctly and frequently, it can prevent many distortions that arise from faulty encoding, transmission, or decoding of messages. For an extensive discussion about the effects of feedback on task group behavior, see Nadler (1979).

Interaction Patterns

In addition to becoming aware of communication processes, the worker must also consider patterns of interaction that develop in a group. A variety of interaction patterns have been identified in the social work literature (Middleman, 1978) including (a) the maypole, in which the leader is the central figure, and communication occurs from leader to member, or from member to leader, (b) the round robin, in which members take turns talking, (c) the hot seat, in which there is an extended back and forth exchange between the leader and a member as the other members watch, and (d) free floating, in which all members take responsibility for communicating according to what is being said and not said in the group.

The first three patterns are leader-centered, because the leader structures them. The fourth pattern is group-centered, because it emerges from the initiative of group members.

In most situations, workers should strive to facilitate the development of group-centered rather than leader-centered interaction patterns. In group-centered patterns, members freely interact with each other. Communication channels between members of the group are open. In leader-centered patterns, communications are directed from members to the worker, or from the worker to group members, thereby reducing members' opportunities to communicate freely with each other.

Group-centered communication patterns tend to increase social interaction, group morale, and members' commitment to group goals. However, such patterns can be less efficient than leader-centered patterns because communication may be superfluous or extraneous to group tasks (Bavelas, 1950; Shaw, 1964). Sorting out useful communications can take a tremendous amount of group time. Therefore, in task groups that are making routine decisions, when time constraints are important and when there is little need for creative problem solving, the worker may deliberately choose to encourage leader-centered rather than group-centered interaction patterns.

To establish and maintain appropriate interaction patterns, the worker should be familiar with the factors that influence them. Patterns of interaction are affected by (a) the cues and the reinforcements that members receive for specific interactional exchanges, (b) the emotional bonds that develop between group members, (c) the subgroups that develop in the group, (d) the size and physical arrangement of the group, and (e) power and status relationships in the group. Workers can change interaction patterns by modifying these important factors.

CUES AND REINFORCERS.   After discussing changes in interaction patterns that may enhance the group's functioning, workers and members can decide to use verbal and nonverbal behaviors to facilitate modifications in established patterns. Cues such as words or gestures can act as signals to group members to talk more or less frequently to one another or to the worker. Workers and members can also use selective attention and other reinforcers to encourage beneficial interactions. As more appropriate interaction patterns are established, cues and reinforcers can be used intermittently and then be allowed to fade gradually to maintain newly developed patterns (Toseland, Krebs & Vahsen, 1978).

EMOTIONAL BONDS.   Positive emotional bonds such as interpersonal liking and attraction increase interpersonal interaction, and negative emotional bonds reduce solidarity between members and result in decreased interpersonal interaction. Attraction and interpersonal liking between two members may occur because they share common interests, similar values and ideologies, complementary personality characteristics, or similar demographic characteristics (Hare, 1976; Newcomb, 1956).

Bonds may also form because of the emotional or social needs of members. From a social exchange theory perspective, Thibaut and Kelley (1959) propose that interpersonal attraction results from the rewards and satisfactions obtained when needs are met by fellow group members. Sometimes positive emotional bonds between group members form as a result of particular concerns or self-interests. Emotional bonds may also be based on mutual dislike of others in the group, mutual dissatisfaction with the group process, or mutual apathy about the process.

Hartford (1971) calls alignments based on emotional bonds "interest alliances." For example, two members of a planning council might vote the same way on certain issues and they may communicate similar thoughts and feelings to other members of the council on the basis of their common interests in the needs of the business community. Similarly, members of a minority group might form an interest alliance based on similar concerns about the lack of community services for minority groups.

SUBGROUPS.   Subgroups also affect the interaction patterns in a group. Subgroups form from the emotional bonds and interest alliances among subsets of group members. They occur naturally in all groups. They help make the group attractive to its members because individuals look forward to interacting with those to whom they are particularly close. The practitioner should not view subgroups as a threat to the integrity of the group unless the attraction of members within a subgroup becomes greater than their attraction to the group as a whole.

Hartford (1971) discusses a variety of subgroup types including dyads, triads, and cliques—and mentions special forms of the subgroup, such as the individual isolate and the scapegoat, both of whom stand alone. Isolates do not interact with the group, whereas scapegoats receive negative attention and criticism from the group.

In some situations the worker may actively encourage members to form subgroups. This is particularly true in groups that are too large and cumbersome for detailed work to be accomplished. For example, subgroup formation is often useful in large task groups such as committees, delegate councils, and some teams. Members are assigned to a particular subgroup to work on a specific task or subtask. The results of the subgroup's work are then brought back to the larger group for consideration and action.

Whether or not the worker actively encourages members to form subgroups, they occur naturally because not everyone in a group will interact with equal valence. The formation of intense subgroup attraction, however, can be a problem. Subgroup members may challenge the worker's authority. They may substitute their own goals and methods of attaining them for the goals of the larger group. They can disrupt the group by communicating among themselves while others are speaking and by failing to listen to members who are not a part of the subgroup.

When intense subgroup attraction appears to be developing, the worker may want to intervene to prevent it from interfering with the group as a whole. This can be done by changing seating arrangements, asking for certain members to interact more frequently with other members, using program materials and exercises that separate subgroup members, or assigning tasks for members to do outside of the group in subgroups composed of different members.

If intense subgroup loyalties have already formed within a group, the worker should facilitate a discussion of the reasons for them and their effect on the group as a whole. A frank discussion of the reasons for subgroup formation can often benefit the entire group, because it can reveal problems in the group's communication patterns, as well as its goal-setting and decision-making processes. After the discussion, the worker should try to increase the attraction of the group for its members and help them reach out to one another to reopen channels of communication.

In some cases, the worker may wish to use subgroups for therapeutic purposes. For example, Yalom (1985) suggests that the worker can use relationships between members to recapitulate the family group experience. Transference and countertransference reactions among members may be used to help members deal with issues and concerns that are the result of unresolved developmental issues in their early family lives.

SIZE AND PHYSICAL ARRANGEMENTS.   Other factors that influence interaction patterns are the size and physical arrangement of the group. As the size of the group increases, the possibilities for potential relationships increase dramatically. For example, with three people there are six potential combinations of relationships, but in a group with seven people there are 966 possible relationships (Kephart, 1951). Thus, in large groups, each member has more social relationships to be aware of and to maintain, but less opportunity to maintain them (Huff & Prantianida, 1968).

With increased group size there are also fewer opportunities and less time for members to communicate. In some groups, the lack of opportunity to participate might not be much of a problem. It should not be assumed that members who are not actively participating are uninvolved in the group, although this may be true. Commonly, some group members welcome a chance for active involvement and participate only when they have an important contribution that might otherwise be overlooked.

Often, however, a reduced chance to participate leads to dissatisfaction and a lack of commitment to decisions made by the group. Increased group size also tends to lead to subgroup formation, as members strive to get to know those seated near them. In large groups, one or two members often do much of the talking, positioning themselves before the group and maintaining a leader-centered interaction pattern (Zimet & Schneider, 1969). In this way, these individuals attempt to maintain control over the group, reducing the chances for subgroup formation, and decreasing the possibilities for members to communicate with one another.

The physical arrangement of group members also influences interaction patterns. For example, members who sit in circles have an easier time communicating with each other than do members who sit in rows. Even members' positions within a circular pattern influence interaction patterns. Members who sit across from each other, for example, have an easier time communicating than do members on the same side of a circle, who are separated by one or two members.

Because circular seating arrangements promote face-to-face interaction, they are often preferred to other arrangements. There may be times, however, when the group leader prefers a different arrangement. For example, the leader of a task group may wish to sit at the head of a rectangular table to convey his or her status or power. He or she may also wish to seat a particularly important member in close proximity. In an educational group, a leader may choose to stand before a group seated in rows. This arrangement facilitates members' communications with the leader, and tends to minimize interactions among members of the group.

Physical arrangements can also be used to help assess relationships among members, and potential problems in group interaction. For example, members who are fond of each other often sit next to, or near, each other and as far away as possible from members they do not like. Similarly, members who pull chairs out from a circle, or sit behind other members, may be expressing their lack of investment in a group.

POWER AND STATUS.   Two other factors affecting communication and interaction patterns are the relative power and status of the group members. Initially, members are accorded power and status on the basis of their position and prestige in the community, their physical attributes, and their position in the agency sponsoring the group. As a group develops, members' status and power change, depending on how important a member is in helping the group accomplish its tasks, or in helping other members meet their socio-emotional needs. When members carry out roles that are important to the group their power and status increases. Thus, members' performances in the group affect their power and status either positively or negatively.

When a member enjoys high status and power, other members are likely to direct their communications to that member (Napier & Gershenfeld, 1981). Members with high status feel free to talk to all group members, but low-status members may be reluctant to communicate with high-status members because they are fearful of being evaluated by those who have power (Kelley, 1951).

Principles for Practice

With basic information about the nature of communication and interaction patterns in groups, workers can intervene in any group to modify or change the patterns that develop. Workers may find the following principles about communication and interaction patterns helpful:

1. Members of the group are always communicating. Workers should assess communication processes continually, and help members communicate effectively throughout the life of a group.
2. Communication patterns can be changed. Strategies for doing this start with identifying patterns during the group or at the end of group meetings during a brief time set aside to discuss group process. Workers then can reinforce desired interaction patterns, increase or decrease emotional bonds between members, change subgroups, group size, or group structure, or alter the power or status relationships in a group.

3. Members communicate for a purpose. Workers should help members understand each other's intentions by clarifying them through group discussion.
4. There is meaning in all communication. Workers should help members understand and appreciate the meaning of different communications.
5. Messages are often perceived selectively. Workers should help members listen to what others are communicating.
6. Messages may be distorted in transmission. Workers should help members clarify verbal and nonverbal communications that are unclear or ambiguous.
7. Feedback enhances accurate understanding of communications. The worker should educate members about how to give and receive effective feedback, and model these methods in the group.
8. Open, group-centered communications are often, but not always, the preferred pattern of interaction. The worker should encourage communication patterns that are appropriate to the purpose of the group.

Workers who follow these principles can intervene to help groups develop patterns of communication and interaction that meet members' socio-emotional needs while accomplishing group purposes.

Group Cohesion

Group cohesion is the result of all forces acting on members to remain in a group (Festinger, 1950). People are attracted to groups for a variety of reasons. According to Cartwright (1968), four interacting sets of variables determine a member's attraction to a group: (a) the need for affiliation, recognition, and security, (b) incentives and resources available through the group such as the prestige of its members, the group's goals, its program activities, and its style of operation, (c) the subjective expectations of members about the beneficial or detrimental consequences of the group, and (d) a comparison of the group to other group experiences.

Cohesive groups generally satisfy the needs that prompted members to join the group. Some members might have a need to socialize because their relationships outside the group are unsatisfactory or nonexistent. For example, Toseland, Decker, and Bliesner (1979) have shown that group work can be effective in meeting the needs of socially isolated older persons. In other cases, groups provide members with a sense of security. Schachter (1959), for example, has shown that fear and anxiety increase people's needs for affiliation, presumably to reduce their fear and to help them determine the appropriate reactions to anxiety-provoking situations.

The cohesion of a group can also be accounted for by incentives that are sometimes provided for group membership. Many people join groups because of the people they expect to meet and get to know. Opportunities for making new contacts and associating with high-status members are also incentives. In some groups, the tasks to be performed are enjoyable. Other groups might enable a member to accomplish tasks that require the help of others. Prestige may be an incentive for some members. For example, being nominated to a delegate council or other task group may enhance a member's prestige and status in an organization or the community. Another inducement to group membership may be access to services or resources not otherwise available.

Expectations of gratification and favorable comparisons with previous group experiences are two other factors that help make groups cohesive. For example, members with high expectations for a group experience and little hope of attaining similar satisfactions elsewhere will be attracted to a group. Thibaut and Kelley (1959) have found that members' continued attraction to a group depends on the "comparison level for alternatives"—that is, the satisfaction derived from the current group experience compared with that derived from other possible experiences.

Members' reasons for being attracted to a group may affect the group's functioning. Back (1951) found that members who were attracted to a group primarily because they perceived others as similar or as potential friends, related on a personal level in the group, and more frequently engaged in conversations not focused on the group's task. Members attracted by the group's task wanted to complete it quickly and efficiently, and maintained task-relevant conversations. Members attracted by the prestige of group membership were cautious not to risk their status in the group. They initiated few controversial topics and focused on their own actions rather than on those of other group members.

Attraction and cohesion also affect the functioning of groups in other ways. According to Cartwright (1968), cohesive groups tend to maintain their membership. They influence their members more than groups that are less cohesive. Members of cohesive groups are more likely to influence each other. They are also more likely to continue to participate and more likely to persevere in attempts to accomplish the group's goals. In cohesive groups, attendance is higher (Sage, Olmsted, & Atlesk, 1955) and members accept more responsibility for group functioning (Back, 1951; Dion, Miller, & Magnan, 1970).

Cohesive groups have positive effects on task accomplishment. In a meta-analysis of 16 studies focusing on group cohesion and performance, Evans and Dion (1991) found that cohesive groups performed significantly better than noncohesive groups. Cohesive groups have also been found to have positive effects on members' satisfaction and personal adjustment. For example, Pepitone and Reichling (1955) found that members of cohesive groups felt more comfortable in engaging in hostile remarks and more secure when confronted with an "insult."

Seashore (1954) found that members were less likely to feel psychological distress when they participated in cohesive rather than noncohesive industrial work groups. In an extensive look at the effects of cohesiveness on members of therapy groups, Yalom (1985) found that cohesiveness leads to increased self-esteem, more willingness to listen to others, freer expression of feeling, better reality testing, greater self-confidence, and members' effective use of other members' evaluations in enhancing their own development.

Principles for Practice
Because cohesion has many benefits, workers should strive to make groups attractive to members. Workers may find the following principles helpful when trying to enhance a group's cohesiveness:

1. A high level of open interaction promotes cohesiveness. The worker should use group discussions and program activities to encourage interaction among members.

2. Achieving group goals makes the group more attractive to its members. The worker should help members to define and achieve their goals.

3. Noncompetitive intragroup relationships that affirm members' perceptions and points of view increase group cohesion. The worker should help group members to cooperate rather than compete with each other.

4. Competitive intergroup relationships help to define a group's identity and purpose, thereby heightening members' cohesion. The worker should help the group develop pride in its identity and purpose, using naturally occurring intergroup competition to build intragroup bonds.

5. A group that is too large can decrease members' attraction to the group by obstructing their full participation. The worker should compose a group that gives all members the opportunity to be fully involved.

6. When members' needs are met they want to continue participating. Therefore, the worker should help members identify their needs and how they can be met in the group.

7. When members' expectations are understood and addressed, members feel as if they are part of the group. The worker should help members clarify their expectations, and should strive for congruence between members' expectations and the purposes of a group.

8. Groups that offer rewards, resources, status, or prestige that members would not obtain by themselves tend to be attractive. Therefore, workers should help groups to be rewarding experiences for members.

Overall, if the benefits of participating in a group do not exceed the costs of participation in the group, members may stop attending (Thibaut & Kelley, 1954). Although workers cannot ensure that all factors mentioned here are present in every group, they should strive to make sure that the group is as attractive as possible to each member who participates.

Social Control Dynamics

Social control is the term used to describe the processes by which the group as a whole gains sufficient compliance and conformity from its members to enable it to function in an orderly manner. Social controls can be used by workers and members to gain compliance from deviant group members. Without a certain amount of conformity and compliance, social interaction becomes chaotic and unpredictable and the group cannot function effectively. Social order and stability are prerequisites for the formation and maintenance of a cohesive group. Yet social controls that are too stringent can reduce group attraction and lead to intragroup conflict and dissatisfaction.

Social control results from forces generated by several interrelated factors, including the norms that develop in the group and the roles and status of individual group members. The extent of social controls varies from group to group. In groups with strong social controls, members must give up a great deal of their freedom and individuality. In some groups this is necessary for effective functioning. For example, in a delegate council where members are representing the views of their organization, there may be little room for individual preference and viewpoints. In other groups, however, members may have a great deal of freedom within a broad range of acceptable behavior.

Norms

Norms are shared expectations and beliefs about appropriate ways to act in a social situation such as a group. They refer to specific member behaviors and to the overall pattern of behavior that is acceptable in a group. Norms result from what is valued, preferred, and accepted behavior in the group. The opinions of certain members might be given greater consideration than those of others in the development of group norms. For example, the designated leader or a high-status member may be particularly influential in the development of norms. In most groups, however, all members share to a considerable extent in the development of the norms.

Norms develop as the group develops. Members learn about group norms by watching each other behave. As members are rewarded for certain behaviors and punished for other behaviors, norms become clarified. Soon it becomes clear that sanctions and social disapproval result from some behaviors and that praise and social approval result from other behaviors. The emergence of norms reduces the need for personal power and control by the worker. Because norms are developed through the interactions of group members, they also discourage the capricious use of power by one group member or the need for excessive controls to be imposed on the group from outside.

Norms vary in some important ways. Rosenblatt (1962), for example, suggests that norms vary according to the extent that people consider them binding. Some norms are strictly enforced while others are rarely enforced. Some norms are more elastic than others, that is, some permit a great deal of leeway in behavior while others prescribe narrow and specific behaviors. Norms also have various degrees of saliency for group members. For some members, a particular norm may be especially important, while for others it may have little meaning and little effect on their behavior.

Norms stabilize and regulate behavior in groups. By providing clear guidelines for acceptable and appropriate behavior, norms increase predictability and security for members. Norms help groups establish procedures for coordinated action to reach goals. Overall, they are essential for a group's functioning.

Deviations from group norms are not necessarily harmful to a group. Deviation can often help groups move in new directions or challenge old ways of accomplishing tasks that are no longer functional. Despite the positive effects of group norms, norms may be dysfunctional or unethical and it may be beneficial for members to deviate from them. For example, in a treatment group, norms may develop that make it difficult or impossible for members to express intense emotions. A member who deviates from this norm may help the group re-examine its norms and let members deepen their level of communication. The worker should try to understand the meaning of deviant behavior, whether members are aware that it is occurring, and its implications for the group. Because they are so pervasive and powerful, norms are somewhat more difficult to change than role expectations or status hierarchies. Therefore, a worker should strive to ensure that the developing norms are beneficial for the group.

Recognizing the difficulty of changing norms, Lewin (1947) suggested three stages are necessary for changing the equilibrium and the status quo that hold norms constant. According to Lewin, there must first be disequilibrium or unfreezing caused by a crisis or other tension-producing situation. During this period, group members re-examine the current group norms. Sometimes a crisis may be induced by the worker through a discussion or demonstration of how current norms will affect the group in the future. In other cases, dysfunctional norms will lead to a crisis.

In the second stage, members return to equilibrium with new norms replacing previous ones. According to Lewin, the second stage is called freezing. In the third stage, called refreezing, the new equilibrium is stabilized. New norms become the recognized and accepted rules by which the group functions. Napier and Gershenfeld (1981) have suggested ways that norms can be changed, including the following:

1. Discussing, diagnosing, and modifying the group's norms.
2. Having the worker or other high-status member intervene in the group to change a norm.
3. Responding to influences on the group from the external environment.
4. Hiring a consultant to work with the group to change its norms.
5. Having the worker or group members deviate from the group's norms and then helping the group adapt to the new norms resulting from the change.

Roles

Like norms, roles can also be an important influence on group members. Roles are closely related to norms. Whereas norms are shared expectations held, to some extent, by everyone in the group, roles are shared expectations about the functions of individuals in the group. Unlike norms, which define behavior in a wide range of situations, roles define behavior in relation to a specific function or task that the group member is expected to perform.

Roles are important for groups because they allow for division of labor and appropriate use of power. They ensure that someone will be designated to take care of vital group functions. Roles are a means of social control in groups by prescribing how members should behave in certain situations. Performing in a certain role not only prescribes certain behavior but also limits members' freedom to deviate from the expected behavior of someone who performs that role. For example, it would be viewed as inappropriate for a task leader to express feelings and emotional reactions about a personal issue that was not relevant to the group's task.

Changes or modifications of roles are best undertaken by discussing members' roles, clarifying the responsibilities and the privileges of existing roles, asking members to assume new roles, or adding new roles according to preferences expressed during the group's discussion.

Status

Along with norms and role expectations, social controls are also exerted through members' status in a group. Status most often refers to an evaluation and ranking of each member's position in the group relative to all other members (Nixon, 1979; Northen, 1969). The method used to rank members' status varies from group to group. Therefore, the same person may have a different status in different groups. In one group, status may be determined by members' position in the agency sponsoring the group. In another group, status may be determined by how well members are liked by other group members, how much the group relies upon their expertise or how much responsibility they have in the group. A person's status within the group is determined, in part, by his or her prestige, position, and recognized expertise outside of the group. It is also determined by how a person acts once he or she becomes a member of a group. Because status is defined relative to other group members, a person's status in a group is also affected by the other members who compose the group.

Status serves a social control function in a rather complex manner. Low-status members are the least likely to conform to group norms because they have little to lose by deviating. This is less likely if they have hopes of gaining a higher status. Medium-status group members tend to conform to group norms so that they can retain their status and perhaps gain a higher status. High-status members perform many valued services for the group and generally conform to valued group norms when they are establishing their position. However, because of their position, high-status members have more freedom to deviate from accepted norms. They are often expected to do something special and creative when the group is in a crisis situation (Nixon, 1979). If medium- or low-status members consistently deviate from group norms, they are threatened with severe sanctions or forced to leave the group. If high-status members consistently deviate from group norms, their status in the group is diminished but they are rarely threatened with severe sanctions or forced to leave the group.

Status hierarchies are most easily changed by the addition or removal of group members. If this is not possible, group discussion may help members express their opinions and feelings about the effects of the current status hierarchy and how to modify it.

Principles for Practice

Norms, roles, and status are interrelated concepts that affect the social controls exerted on individuals in the group. Because of their powerful influence on group behavior, workers should be familiar with ways to influence social control dynamics. When doing so, workers should be aware of each group member's needs for individuality, freedom, and independence. At the same time, workers should recognize that social controls stabilize and regulate group processes, helping groups function efficiently and effectively. In working with task and treatment groups, workers must balance the needs of individuals and of the group as a whole, managing conformity and deviation, and ensuring that social controls are working to benefit rather than hinder or limit individual members and the whole group. Workers may find the following principles about social control dynamics helpful when facilitating a group:

1. Social control dynamics help regulate and stabilize group processes so that members can accomplish individual and group goals. The worker should help group members assess the extent to which norms, roles, and status are helping the group accomplish its goals.
2. Group structure helps ensure the development of social control dynamics. The worker should provide sufficient structure so that group processes do not become chaotic, disorganized, unsafe, or unduly anxiety provoking.
3. Too much structure can produce social control dynamics that restrict members' ability to exercise their own judgment and free will, and to accomplish agreed-upon goals. The worker should ensure that there is freedom and independence within the range of acceptable behaviors agreed to by the group.
4. Members choose to adhere to social control dynamics in groups that are attractive and cohesive. Workers should help members believe they have an important stake in the group.
5. Members choose to adhere to social control dynamics when they consider the group's goals important and meaningful. Workers should help members make the group attractive to each other.
6. Members choose to adhere to social control dynamics when they desire continued membership because of their own needs, or because of pressure from sources within or outside of the group. Therefore, workers should consider the incentives for members to participate in a group.
7. Rewards and sanctions can help members comply with norms, status, and role expectations. The worker should assess whether rewards and sanctions are being used to help members comply with fair and equitable social control dynamics agreed upon by the group.

By following these principles, workers can ensure that the norms, role expectations, and status hierarchy that develop in a group satisfy members' needs and accomplish goals established for individuals and the group as a whole.

Group Culture

Although it has often been overlooked in discussions of group dynamics, group culture is an important force in the group as a whole. *Group culture* refers to values, beliefs, customs, and traditions held in common by group members (Olmsted, 1959).

When the membership of a group is diverse, group culture emerges slowly. Members contribute unique sets of values that originate from their past experiences as well as from their ethnic, cultural, and racial heritages. These values are blended through group communications and interactions. In early meetings, members explore each other's unique value systems and attempt to find a common ground on which they can relate to each other. By later meetings, members have had a chance to share and understand each other's value systems. As a result, a common set of values develops that becomes the group's culture. The group's culture continues to evolve throughout the life of the group.

Group culture emerges more quickly in groups with a homogeneous membership. When members share common life experiences and similar sets of values, it often takes less time to blend their unique perspectives into a group culture. For example, members of groups sponsored by culturally based organizations, such as the Urban League or Centro Civico, and groups that represent a particular point of view, such as the National Organization for Women (NOW), are more likely to share similar life experiences and similar values than are groups with more diverse memberships. One of the attractions of these homogenous groups is that they provide an affirming and supportive atmosphere.

Culture is also influenced by the environment in which a group functions. As part of the organizational structure of an agency, a community, and a society, groups share the values, traditions, and heritage of these larger social systems. The extent to which these systems influence the group depends on the degree of interaction the group has with them. For example, on one end of the continuum, an administrative team's operational procedures are often greatly influenced by agency policies and practices. On the other end, gangs tend to isolate themselves from the dominant values of society, the community, and local youth organizations. Group workers can learn a great deal about groups by examining how they interact with their environment.

Groups that address community needs often have a great deal of interaction with their environment. When analyzing a change opportunity, building a constituency, or deciding how to implement an action plan, groups that set out to address community needs must carefully consider dominant community values and traditions. The receptivity of powerful individuals within a community will be determined to some extent by how consistent a group's actions are with the values and traditions they hold in high regard. Whenever possible, groups attempting to address community needs should frame their efforts within the context of dominant community values. The practitioner can help by attempting to find the common ground in the values of the community and the group. When a group's actions are perceived to be in conflict with dominant community values, it is unlikely to receive the support of influential community leaders. In these situations the group will have to rely on conflict strategies to achieve its objectives.

Principles for Practice

The culture that a group develops has a powerful influence on its ability to achieve its goals while satisfying members' socio-emotional needs. A culture that emphasizes values of self-determination, openness, fairness, and diversity of opinion can do much to facilitate the achievement of group and individual goals. Sometimes members bring ethnic, cultural or social stereotypes to the group, inhibiting the group's development and effective functioning. Through interaction and discussion, workers can help members confront stereotypes and learn to understand and appreciate those who bring different values and cultural heritages to the group.

In helping the group build a positive culture, the worker should consider the following principles:

1. Group culture emerges from the mix of values that members bring to the group. The worker should help members examine and compare their value systems.

2. Group culture is also affected by the values of the agency, the community, and the society that sponsor and sanction the group. The worker should help members identify and understand these values.

3. Group members and workers can hold stereotypes that interfere with their ability to interact with each other. Workers should help members eliminate stereotypical ways of relating to each other, and develop an awareness of their own stereotypes.

4. Value conflicts can reduce group cohesion and, in extreme cases, lead to the demise of the group. The worker should mediate value conflicts among members, and between members and the larger society.

5. Group culture can exert a powerful influence on members' values. The worker should model values such as openness, self-determination, fairness, and acceptance of difference, which are fundamental to social group work and the social work profession.

6. Groups are most satisfying when they meet members' socio-emotional and instrumental needs. Therefore, the worker should balance members' needs for emotional expressiveness with their needs to accomplish specific goals.

STAGES OF GROUP DEVELOPMENT

According to Northen (1969), "a stage is a differentiable period or a discernible degree in the process of growth and development" (p. 49). The rest of this text is

TABLE 3–3
Stages of group development

Development Stage	Bales (1950)	Tuckman (1963)	Northen (1969)	Hartford (1971)
Beginning	Orientation	Forming	Planning & orientation	Pre-group planning Convening Group formation
Middle	Evaluation	Storming Norming Performing	Exploring & testing Problem solving	Disintegration & conflict Group function & maintenance
End	Decision making		Termination	Pretermination Termination

organized around the skills that workers can use during each stage of a group's development. A group's entire social structure, its communication and interaction patterns, cohesion, social controls, and culture evolve as it develops. Therefore, an in-depth understanding of group development is essential for the effective practice of group work. While the rest of the text elaborates on our model of group development, this section reviews some of the different ways that group development has been conceptualized by other group work theoreticians.

Many attempts have been made to classify stages of group development. Table 3–3 lists some of the models of group development that have appeared in the literature. Most are based on descriptions of groups that the authors of each model have worked with or observed. Most models propose that all groups pass through similar stages of development (see, for example, Hartford, 1971, p. 63). As can be seen in Table 3–3, however, different writers have different ideas about the number and types of stages through which all groups pass. For example, Bales' (1950) model of group development has only three stages, whereas the model presented by Sarri and Galinsky (1985) has seven stages.

Very few empirical studies have been conducted of particular models and little empirical evidence exists to support the notion that any one model accurately describes the stages through which all groups pass. Overall, the studies that have been conducted suggest that groups move through stages, but that the stages are not constant across different groups (Shaw, 1976; Smith, 1978). However, most empirical studies have relied on direct observation or tape recordings of a small number of closed membership groups. Therefore, it is difficult to generalize from these studies to the wide variety of groups that occur in practice settings. Also, in many cases, the reliability and validity of the behaviors being recorded and analyzed have not been adequately established.

Klein (1972)	Trecker (1972)	Sarri & Galinsky (1985)	Garland, Jones, & Kolodny (1976)	Henry (1992)	Toseland & Rivas (1994)
Orientation Resistance	Beginning Emergence of some group feeling	Origin phase Formative phase	Preaffiliation Power & control	Initiating Convening	Planning Beginning Assessing
Negotiation Intimacy	Development of bond, purpose, & cohesion Strong group feeling Decline in group feeling	Intermediate phase I Revision phase Intermediate phase II Maturation phase	Intimacy Differentiation	Conflict Maintenance	Working Evaluating
Termination	Ending	Termination	Separation	Termination	Ending

There is some evidence that stages of group development may be affected by the needs of group members, the type of group, the goals of the group, the setting in which the group meets, and the orientation of the leader (Shaw, 1976; Smith, 1978). For example, a study of open membership groups (Schopler & Galinsky, 1990) revealed that few moved beyond a beginning stage of development. Open membership groups that are able to move beyond a beginning level of development are those that have a membership change less than every two meetings, and those with less than a 50 percent change in membership (Galinsky & Schopler, 1989).

Groups with frequent and extensive membership change almost always remain at a formative stage. Such groups cope with problems in continuity and development by following highly ritualistic and structured procedures for group meetings. For example, a group in a cardiac unit in a large teaching hospital where a patient's typical stay is two weeks is structured to begin with a half-hour educational presentation, followed by a half-hour discussion. The group meets three times a week. Six different topics are presented before they are repeated. Therefore, patients whose typical hospital stay is two weeks can participate in six group meetings, and can begin and end their participation at any time. However, the intimacy that can be achieved during the middle stage of groups with closed memberships is rarely achieved in groups where members are continually entering and leaving the group.

Despite the variable nature of the stages of group development described by different writers, many of the models contain similar stages. As can be seen in Table 3–3, we have divided the various stages of group development into three stages: beginning, middle, and end. Each model of group development is placed in relationship to these three broad stages.

Most writers suggest that the beginning stages of groups are concerned with planning, organizing, and convening a group. The beginnings of groups are characterized by an emergence of group feeling. Group feeling, however, often does not emerge without a struggle. For example, Klein (1972) emphasizes the resistance of members to group pressure, and Garland, Jones, and Kolodny (1976) emphasize the desire of group members to become a part of the group while maintaining their autonomy. Thus, along with the tendency to approach one another, there is also a tendency for members to maintain their distance. Garland, Jones, and Kolodny (1976) have identified this as an approach-avoidance conflict. As the beginning stage progresses and norms and roles are differentiated, members explore and test the roles they are beginning to assume in the group. Conflict may emerge. The leader can help by encouraging members to discuss and resolve the conflict. It is also helpful to point out that this process is a normal part of the development of smooth working relationships in preparation for the intense work to come in the middle stage.

Although some work is accomplished in all stages of a group's development, most occurs in the middle stage. At the beginning of this stage, the conflict over norms, roles, and other group processes found in the later part of the beginning stage gives way to established patterns of interaction. There is a deepening of interpersonal relationships and greater group cohesion. After this occurs, groups concern themselves with the work necessary to accomplish the specific tasks and goals that have been agreed upon. The terms most frequently used to describe this stage are *problem solving, performing, maintenance, intimacy,* and *maturity.* Task accomplishment is preceded by a differentiation of roles and accompanied by the development of feedback and evaluation mechanisms.

The ending of a group is characterized by the completion and evaluation of the group's efforts. Bales' (1950) model of group development suggests that during this stage, task groups make decisions, finish their business, and produce the results of their efforts. Treatment groups, which have emphasized socio-emotional functioning as well as task accomplishment, begin a process of separation, during which group feeling and cohesion decline. Often members mark termination by summarizing the accomplishments of the group and celebrating together.

Models of group development provide a framework to describe worker roles and appropriate interventions during each stage of a group. They also help workers organize and systematize strategies of intervention. For example, in the beginning stage a worker's interventions are directed at helping the group define its purpose and helping members feel comfortable with one another. Models of group development can also prepare the leader for what to expect from a group during each stage of development.

The usefulness of theories of group development for group work practice, however, is limited by the uniqueness of each group experience. The developmental stages of groups vary significantly across the broad range of task and treatment groups that a worker might lead. It should not be assumed that all groups follow the same patterns of development or that an intervention that is effective in one group will automatically be effective in another group that is in the same development stage. Still, we have found that organizing content into specific group developmental stages is a useful heuristic device when teaching students and practitioners how to facilitate a variety of treatment and task groups. Therefore, the rest of this text is organized around the skills, procedures, and techniques that workers use throughout the life of a group.

The model of group development presented in this text includes six distinct stages: (a) planning, (b) beginning, (c) assessing, (d) working, (e) evaluating, and (f) ending. Each stage of group work is presented in detail.

Principles for Practice

The worker should be knowledgeable about the theoretical constructs that have been proposed about the stages of group development. Knowing what is normally expected behavior for members at each stage can help the worker identify dysfunctional behavior as well as problems that are the responsibility of the group as a whole. The following practice principles can be identified:

1. Closed membership groups develop in discernible and predictable stages. The worker should use systematic methods of observing and assessing the development of the group and should teach group members about the predictable stages of group development.

2. The development of open membership groups depends on member turnover. The worker should help open membership groups develop a simple structure and a clear culture to help new members integrate rapidly into the group.

3. Groups generally begin with members exploring the purpose of the group and the roles of the worker and each member. The worker should provide a safe and positive group environment so that members can fully explore the group purpose and the resources available to accomplish the group's goals.

4. After the initial stage of development, groups often experience a period of norm development, role testing, and status awareness that results in expressions of difference among members and the leader. The worker should help members understand that the expression of difference is a normal stage of group development.

5. Tension or conflict sometimes develops from differences among members. The worker should help the group resolve the conflict by mediating the differences and finding a common ground for productive work together.

6. Groups enter a middle stage characterized by norm development, group cohesion, and task accomplishment. The worker should encourage members to stay focused on the purpose of the group, challenge members to develop an appropriate culture for work and task accomplishment, and help the group overcome obstacles to its goals.

7. In the ending stage, the group finishes its work. The worker should help members review and evaluate their work together, highlighting accomplishments and pointing out areas that need further work.

8. Groups sometimes experience strong feelings about endings. The worker should help members recognize these feelings, connect them to what they got out of the group, and help members resolve the feelings by planning for termination.

SUMMARY

Groups are social systems made up of people in interaction. This chapter describes some of the most important forces that result from the interaction of group members. In working with task and treatment groups, it is essential to understand group dynamics and be able to use them to accomplish group goals. Without a thorough understanding of group dynamics, workers will not be able to help members satisfy their needs or help the group accomplish its tasks.

Group workers should be familiar with four types of group dynamics: (a) communication and interaction patterns, (b) the cohesion of the group and its attraction for its members, (c) social controls such as norms, roles, and status, and (d) the group's culture. Communication and interaction patterns are basic to the formation of all groups. Through communication and interaction, properties of the group as a whole develop and the work of the group is accomplished. This chapter presents a model of the communication process.

Groups are maintained because of the attraction they hold for their members. Members join groups for many reasons. The extent to which the group meets members' needs and expectations determines the attraction of the group for its members and the extent to which a group becomes a cohesive unit. As cohesion develops, group structures are elaborated and norms, roles, and status hierarchies form. Norms, roles, and status hierarchies are social controls. They take the form of shared expectations about appropriate behavior in the group. Conformity to expected behavior patterns results in rewards, and deviation results in sanctions. Social controls maintain a group's equilibrium as it confronts internal and external pressure to change during its development, but they can be harmful if they are too stringent.

As the group evolves, it develops a culture derived from the environment in which it functions as well as from the beliefs, customs, and values of its members. The culture of a group has a pervasive effect on its functioning. For example, a group's culture affects the objectives of the group, which task the group decides to work on, how members interact, and what methods the group uses to conduct its business.

Although properties of groups are often discussed as if they were static, they change constantly throughout the life of a group. Many writers have attempted to describe typical stages through which all groups pass. Although no single model of group development is universally accepted, some of the major characteristics that distinguish group process during each stage of group development are discussed in this chapter. These characteristics can be a useful guide for group practitioners in the beginning, middle, and ending stages of work, which are described in later portions of this text.

Overall, this chapter points out the power of group dynamics in influencing group members and in contributing to or detracting from the success of a group. As workers become familiar with properties of groups as a whole, their appreciation of the effects that natural and formed groups have on the lives of their clients is enhanced. In addition, workers can use their understanding of group dynamics to enhance their ability to work effectively with both task and treatment groups.

LEARNING ASSIGNMENTS

1. During a meeting of a group you currently participate in, take notes about the group's communication and interaction patterns. What pattern dominates? Who sends and receives the most communications? Who sends and receives the fewest communications? After the meeting, discuss your observations with another member of the group.

2. Audiotape or videotape a group session, or use one of the case examples in Chapter 14. Review the tape or the case example for the level of cohesion in the group. What circumstances led to the highest and lowest levels of cohesion? What did the leader do to foster cohesion in the group?

3. Choose a film or novel that features a group in its plot, such as *The Breakfast Club, Dead Poets Society, Lord of the Flies,* or *Animal Farm.* Analyze the development of the group over time using one of the models described in Table 3–3. Focus specifically on the development of social control mechanisms. How did norms, roles, status hierarchies, and power develop and evolve in the group? How did this affect the overall culture of the group?

CHAPTER 4

Leadership

Leadership, as a professional role, is the process of guiding the development of the group and its members. A worker acts as leader to help the group and each of its members achieve goals that are consistent with the value base of social work practice. The purpose of this chapter is to help group workers understand the leadership role and work effectively with the members of task and treatment groups.

Although the leadership role is most often associated with the designated leader—that is, the worker—it is important to distinguish between the worker as the designated leader and the indigenous leadership that emerges among members as the group develops. Leadership is rarely exercised solely by the worker. The worker encourages members to exercise their own power, taking responsibility for themselves and for the development of the group as a whole. Thus, leadership can be exercised by members who are encouraged by the worker to take indigenous leadership roles.

Workers share their leadership functions to help members have some influence, control, and stake in the group situation; to divide labor; and to encourage members to exercise their own skills and abilities. Workers should do as much as possible to stimulate and support indigenous leadership in a group to encourage autonomous functioning and ensure that members' existing skills do not atrophy.

Some group work theoreticians eschew the power and influence of the worker in the role of leader, preferring to emphasize the leadership function that members take on as the group develops (see, for example, Klein, 1970, 1972). Others prefer to emphasize the worker's role as leader in structuring the group process and influencing group members (see, for example, Rose, 1989). We believe that both aspects of leadership are essential for effective group work practice. Throughout this chapter, we emphasize both the importance of the worker as group leader and the importance of members' sharing in leadership functions as the group develops.

Leadership and Power

Workers use their influence as leaders within and outside of the group to facilitate group and individual efforts to achieve desired goals. Within the group, the worker intervenes to change the dynamics of the group as a whole or to help individual members change. In exercising leadership outside the group, the worker intervenes to influence the environment in which the group and its members function. For example, the worker might try to change organizational policies that influence the group or obtain additional resources from a sponsor so the group can complete its work. In exerting leadership inside or outside the group, the worker is responsible for the group's processes, actions, and task accomplishments.

Workers who take on the responsibilities inherent in leading a group are rewarded by having attributed to them the power to influence and the ability to lead. Such power is attributed by group members, peers, superiors, the sponsoring agency, and the larger social system. Leaders who are new to the role are sometimes uncomfortable. They sometimes react by denying their power or by trying to take too much control. These strategies are rarely effective. Especially in early group meetings, members look to the leader for guidance about how to proceed. Experienced leaders are comfortable with their power and use it to empower members, gradually enabling them to take increasing responsibility for the group as it develops.

In considering a worker's power, it is helpful to distinguish between attributed power and actual power. *Attributed power* comes from the perception among group members, or others outside the group, of the worker's ability to lead. *Actual power* refers to the worker's resources for changing conditions inside and outside the group. Workers should recognize that attributed leadership ability is as important as actual power in facilitating the development of the group and its members.

Workers can increase the power attributed to them by group members. Studies have shown that members' expectations about the group and its leader influence the group's performance (Kaul & Bednar, 1986; Lieberman, 1976). Preparing members with films, brochures, or personal interviews that offer information about the group, its leader, and the success of previous groups has been shown to be effective in increasing the change-oriented expectations of members (Fish, 1973; Frank, 1961; Garfield, 1986) and in helping individuals and groups accomplish their goals (Frank, 1961). When formal preparation is impossible, informal preparation by word of mouth or reputation can be used.

When attempting to increase their attributed power, workers should keep in mind that their motive is to increase their ability to help group members function independently and at an optimum level. As their attributed power increases, workers are more likely to be regarded with esteem by group members and to be looked to as models of effective coping skills whose behaviors are emulated. Group members give their advice, suggestions, and guidance serious consideration. Workers should not attempt to gain power for its own sake. They should not attempt to control members' behavior or unilaterally impose their own values, standards, and rules concerning conduct inside or outside the group.

The attributed power of the worker comes from a variety of sources. Among these are professional status, organizational position, experience, defined boundaries between worker and group members' roles, fees for service, access to resources, and the commonly held view that a group's success or failure is the result of its leadership.

Gathering people to work in a group can also contribute to the worker's power, because groups are more effective at completing certain tasks than individuals working alone. For example, it has been demonstrated that members are more motivated to carry out decisions made in groups than those made by individuals (Vroom, 1969), that groups can make more creative decisions than individuals (Collins & Guetzkow, 1964), and that certain kinds of groups are more effective than individuals for solving certain problems (Bunker & Dalton, 1972).

Actual power depends upon the sources of a worker's influence. Seven power bases (French & Raven, 1959) that the worker may possess include the following:

1. Connection power—being able to call upon and use influential people or resources.
2. Expert power—having the knowledge or skill to facilitate the work of the group.
3. Information power—possessing information that is valuable to and needed by others.
4. Legitimate power—holding a position of authority and the rights that accrue to that position in the organization or larger social system.
5. Reference power—being liked and admired; the group members want to be identified with the worker.
6. Reward power—being able to offer social or tangible rewards.
7. Coercive power—being able to sanction, punish, or deny access to resources and privileges.

Use of power can have negative as well as positive consequences. For example, coercive power is sometimes used to compel clients to receive treatment. However, coercion can have negative effects such as hostility, anger, rebellion, and absence from group meetings. Therefore, the worker should exercise power judiciously, in a manner consistent with personal, professional, and societal values.

At the same time, the worker's power as leader cannot, and should not, be denied. This is sometimes done by those who suggest that members should take total responsibility for leading the group. We believe groups need leaders to avoid disorganization and chaos, and that leadership and power are inseparable (Etzioni, 1961).

Anyone who has attended the first meeting of a new group recognizes the power the worker has as the designated leader. This power can be illustrated most vividly by examining members' behaviors and feelings during the initial portion of the first group meeting. Members direct most of their communications to the worker or communicate through the worker to other group members. Members are often anxious and inquisitive, wondering what they can expect from the group and its leader. They comply readily with requests made by the worker. Although members may wonder about the worker's ability to help them and the group as a whole, they usually give the worker latitude in choosing methods and procedures to help the group achieve its objectives.

Beginning with the first group meeting, it is essential that workers move as rapidly as possible to share their power with members and the group as a whole. The worker can do this in a variety of ways: (a) encouraging member-to-member rather than member-to-leader communications, (b) asking for members' input into the agenda for the meeting and the direction the group should take in future meetings, (c) supporting indigenous leadership when members make their first, tentative attempts at exerting their own influence in the group, and (d) encouraging attempts at mutual sharing and mutual aid among group members (Shulman, 1992).

Theories of Group Leadership

Early theories about the best method to use in leading a group focused primarily on leadership style. Leadership was considered a trait rather than a cluster of behaviors that could be learned (Halpin, 1961). Three positions on a continuum of leadership behavior—laissez-faire, democratic, and autocratic—were the subject of early investigations (Lewin & Lippitt, 1938; Lewin, Lippitt, & White, 1939). This continuum can be seen in Figure 4-1. Findings from these studies indicated that there was more aggression, hostility, and scapegoating in autocratic groups than in democratic groups. There were no differences in the tasks completed by the groups, although there was some indication that the products of democratic groups were qualitatively superior to those of groups that used autocratic or laissez-faire styles of leadership. Group members also preferred the democratic group's process—that is, they liked the leader better and felt freer and more willing to make suggestions. These early findings seemed to suggest that allowing members to participate in the group's decision-making process was the preferred leadership style. More recent findings have also suggested that a friendly, helpful, and rather permissive leadership style results in more effective groups than an autocratic style (Sherif & Sherif, 1969).

Factors Influencing Group Leadership

As findings began to accumulate, however, it became clear that situational factors help determine what skills and leadership style are most appropriate and effective for a particular group. For example, Hare (1976) has cited several studies indicating that authoritarian leadership is better than democratic or laissez-faire leadership in some situations. Nixon (1979) has suggested that at least seven factors must be assessed before predicting what leadership styles or behaviors are most effective. These include the following:

1. The leadership expectations held by group members.
2. The way leadership has been attained.
3. Whether there is competition between designated leaders and the leaders that emerge as groups develop.
4. The needs, tasks, and goals of the group as a whole.
5. The task and socio-emotional skills of members.
6. The nature of authority within and outside of the group.
7. The environmental demands placed on the group and its leadership.

The growing recognition that group leadership is affected by a variety of interacting factors has resulted from empirical findings in social psychology, sociology, and business administration, as well as from data gathered in evaluating

**FIGURE 4–1
Participation
in decision
making by
leaders and
members in
groups using
three leader-
ship styles**

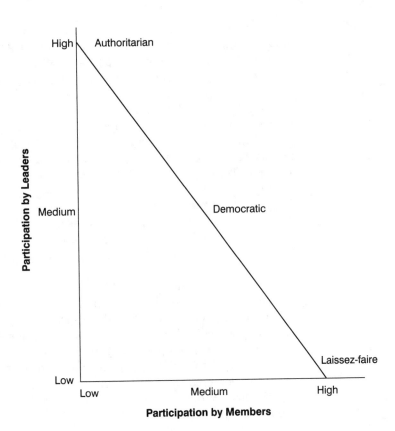

group work practice (see, for example, Fiedler, 1967; Gibb, 1969; Hersey & Blanchard, 1977; Luft, 1984; McClane, 1991; McGrath, 1984; McGrath 1992; Nixon, 1979; Vroom & Yetton, 1973). These investigators found that to understand the dynamics of leadership in diverse treatment and task groups, several factors in addition to the personality and leadership style of the worker must be considered.

For example, in analyzing leadership in task groups, a number of investigators have shown that leaders develop different relationships with different members of a group (Dienesch & Liden, 1986; Graen & Schiemann, 1978; McClane, 1991). Others have demonstrated that the social environment, properties of the group as a whole, the type of problem the group is working on, and the purposes and functions of the group influence the nature of leadership (Gibb, 1969; McGrath, 1984; McGrath, 1992; Nixon, 1979).

The relationship between a leader's power and members' performances has also been examined. These studies suggest that a variety of situational variables affect the type of power used by a leader (Bachman, Bowers, & Marcus, 1968; Ivancevich & Donnelly, 1970; Jamieson & Thomas, 1974; Tannenbaum & Schmidt, 1972). These variables arise from several sources, including the leader, the group members, the group as a whole, and the larger system of which the group is a part (Tannenbaum & Schmidt, 1972).

Several social scientists have attempted to organize all situational factors affecting the group and construct a model of group leadership. For example, Fiedler (1967) and Gibb (1969) have both developed contingency models to explain leadership and decision making in groups. Fiedler considered three dimensions: (a) the degree of structure involved in the task, (b) the amount of power given to the leader because of the leader's position, and (c) the quality of interpersonal relationships between the leader and the members. Vroom and Yetton (1973) have developed a normative model of leadership that considers eight problem attributes that influence the type of leadership that emerges in a given situation. These include the following:

1. The importance of the quality of the decision.
2. The extent to which the leader possesses sufficient information and expertise to make a high-quality decision alone.
3. The extent to which group members have the necessary information to generate a high-quality decision.
4. The extent to which the problem is structured.
5. The extent to which implementation of the decision depends on the acceptance of, or commitment to, the decision.
6. The probability, based on previous experience, that an autocratic decision by the leader will be accepted by group members.
7. The extent to which group members are motivated to attain organizational goals as represented in the objectives of the task.
8. The extent to which group members are likely to disagree on preferred solutions.

Vroom and Yetton's (1973) normative model considers the interaction of all these factors when deciding what type of leadership will be most effective in solving a problem.

Several group work practitioners have also suggested that leadership must be seen as a process within the context of the group and its environment. Tompkins and Gallo (1978) propose a model for goal formulation in social work groups that takes into account environmental forces. Garvin (1987) emphasizes the role of the agency in influencing the work of treatment groups. Vinter and Galinsky (1985) mention several ways workers can help members use relationships and the environment outside of the group to achieve their goals. These methods include interventions with significant others, social systems, and the social environment. For example, a worker might want to intervene with family members to change their attitudes about and behaviors toward a group member who was a former inpatient in a state psychiatric hospital. At the same time, the worker might want to suggest ways the member could change his or her living arrangements so as to be able to cope more effectively with family members. Apart from the group, the worker may want to meet with other professionals in a task force convened to assess and plan for the aftercare needs of former psychiatric inpatients.

In examining group leadership, Heap (1979) suggests that the degree of activity of a worker is directly related to the social health of the group's members.

Thus, a worker should be more active in groups in which members are "out of touch with reality" or "withdrawn or very aggressive" (p. 50). In groups with interested, eager, competent members, the worker should take on a less active, enabler role.

The treatment and task group typologies presented in Chapter 1 also suggest that leadership should vary depending on the purpose and membership of the group. For example, a worker might need to be directive and structured in a remedial group for severely mentally ill inpatients of a state hospital. The worker, as "expert," may work with each member for 10 or 15 minutes. Other members may be asked to offer opinions or provide feedback, but the primary focus is on helping an individual achieve particular treatment goals. Such an approach is similar to individual treatment in a group.

This method of leadership is quite different from a group-centered method, which may be more appropriate for educational or growth groups in which members are eager, competent, and nonimpaired. In using a group-centered method, the worker facilitates communication, interaction, understanding, and mutual aid, and encourages members to help one another rather than to look to the worker as an expert who can solve their concerns or problems.

Overall, one conclusion that can be drawn from social science findings and from data accumulated from group work practice is that one method of leadership is not effective in all situations. Approaches that suggest one method for all circumstances are oversimplified (Davis, Laughlin, & Komorita, 1976; Hersey, Blanchard, & Natemeyer, 1979). In her development of a broad-range model of group leadership, Lang (1972) underscores this point. She demonstrates how workers should vary their leadership depending on the characteristics of the group. The worker's leadership skills and intervention strategies should vary depending on the degree to which the group as a whole and its individual members can function autonomously. The less autonomous the group, the more the worker must play a central role in leading the group. Conversely, the more autonomous the group, the more the worker can facilitate the members' own self-direction and indigenous leadership abilities.

In addition, it is clear that the group has a significant effect on its own success. The worker must learn to recognize and use group forces that lead to effective outcomes. Lieberman (1975) points out five properties of groups that are particularly important to the therapeutic experience of the participant. They include the ability of the group to: (a) develop cohesiveness and a sense of belonging for its members, (b) control, reward, and punish behavior, (c) define reality for the individual, (d) induce and release powerful feelings in its members, and (e) provide a contrast for social comparison and feedback. To these can be added the group's ability to (f) universalize an experience (Yalom, 1985), (g) provide behavior that can be modeled, and (h) provide peers to participate in discussions and re-enactments of previous experiences as well as here-and-now encounters. Although these group properties were obtained from case studies and phenomenological analyses of treatment groups, many of them can be applied to task groups as well. The effective worker helps members facilitate the development of these properties in the group.

Effectiveness of Leaders

Most people assume leaders exert considerable influence on the outcome of task and treatment groups, but what is the empirical evidence to justify this faith in the leader? As Lieberman (1975) notes, "It is quite possible that the leader's behavior, personality, and skill level have taken on mythic proportions as basic causal forces explaining successful . . . change" (p. 357). Most theories emphasize the role of the leader in helping the group achieve its objectives and helping group members feel satisfied with the group's process. Many of these theories, however, are backed by little or no evidence.

Empirical evidence does not fully support the notion that group leadership is central in helping the group attain its objectives. Some evidence supports claims that leaders' behaviors are important to the success of the group (Feldman & Caplinger, 1977; Kaul & Bednar, 1986; Toseland, Rivas, & Chapman, 1984), but other evidence suggests that this may not be so. Lieberman, Yalom, and Miles (1973), for example, found that tape-led (virtually leaderless) groups were more effective than three fourths of the leader-led groups they studied. McLaughlin, White, and Byfield (1974) found that a programmed tape format with the leader present as a member was a better method for achieving group objectives than five other leadership structures, including the traditional leader-led group format.

More recently, in a discussion of the growth of self-help groups during the past several decades, Lieberman (1990) concluded that this type of group, which is often leaderless, provides many benefits to its members. Similarly, in a study of a leaderless women's group that had been meeting for 17 years, Counselman (1991) found that the group performed effectively because functions typically performed by the leader were assumed by members of the group. Therefore, in considering leadership, workers should recognize that other factors in addition to their skills may affect group outcomes. Taken together, these factors may be just as important as the worker's skill in helping a group to achieve its objectives.

LEADERSHIP AS AN EMERGING PHENOMENON

An Interactional Model

Figure 4–2 represents our conception of factors that affect group leadership. The interactional model incorporates the empirical findings of others who have developed comprehensive models of group leadership (Likert, 1967; Tannenbaum & Schmidt, 1972; Vroom & Yetton, 1973). Because this model views leadership as being derived from the interactions of the group, its members, the leader, and the environment, the model is closely related to the ecological systems perspective of social casework proposed by Germain and Gitterman (1980) and Siporin (1980a) as well as the interactional perspective presented by Gitterman and Shulman (1986), and Maluccio (1979). The interactional model represents leadership as a shared function that is not lodged solely in the designated group leader. In addition to the worker's role as designated leader, the model in Figure 4–2 clearly shows that leadership emerges from a variety of interacting factors as the group develops.

FIGURE 4-2
An interactional model of group leadership

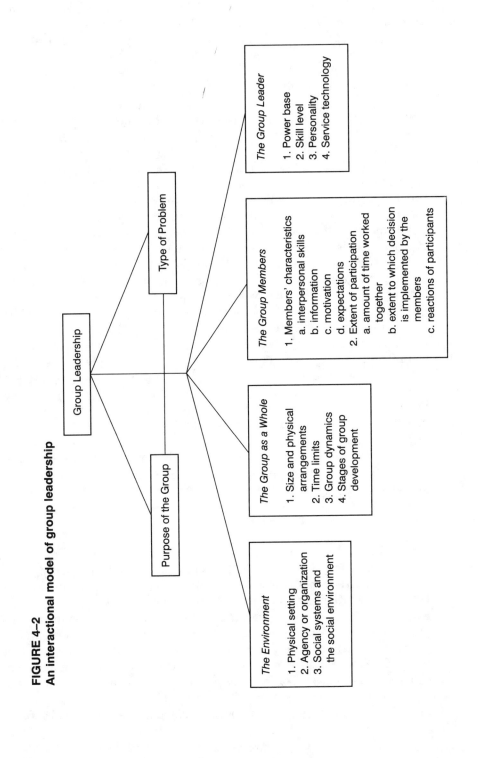

As a heuristic device, the model can be useful in planning effective leadership methods for different types of groups. The model shows six separate but inter-related factors that should be considered when leading a task or treatment group. These factors are (a) the purposes of the group, (b) the type of problem the group is working on, (c) the environment in which the group works, (d) the group as a whole, (e) the members of the group, and (f) the leader of the group.

Purposes of the Group.   When considering how leadership emerges in a group, it is essential to consider the purposes of the group. Purposes are the reasons for bringing group members together. They guide the worker's interventions. According to Browning (1977), a group may be formed (a) to perform tasks that require more than one or two people, (b) to meet individual needs, (c) to bring people together who are involved in the same or similar problems, (d) to represent a larger collection of people, (e) to form the largest collection of people that can be managed together, (f) to help maintain an organization more economically than individuals, (g) to increase motivation, or (e) as a result of physical factors such as working together in the same office. To this list can be added the purpose of using the group to change conditions or situations outside of the group in an organization, a service delivery system, or an entire social system.

A group may have a single purpose or several purposes. The worker should consider how a group's purposes are interpreted by all systems that interact with that group. The worker should ensure that the purpose of the group and the type of problem to be worked on are consistent. For example, if the purpose of a group is to meet the needs of socially isolated individuals, then the types of problems on which the group works should be related to group members' needs for increased social interaction. The group should not be working on problems of housing or finances, for example, unless they are linked to the primary purpose of decreasing isolation.

The purpose of a group helps determine how workers guide group processes. For example, in a group whose purpose is solely to complete a task or solve a problem, a worker might choose to encourage members to structure and focus the interactions more than in a group whose purpose is to have members share common concerns and ideas about an issue.

Type of Problem.   The type of problem or task a group works on has important implications. It has been found that groups do better than individuals on certain types of tasks, but individuals working alone do better on others (Bunker & Dalton, 1972). Generally, groups do better when the task is additive, such as collecting information. Thus, it would be better to form a treatment conference group to collect information about a client from all the professionals working with the client rather than visit each professional separately. Groups also appear to improve on the decisions of individuals working alone in deciding between clearly delineated alternatives. For example, Toseland, Rivas, and Chapman (1984) found that groups improved on the decision-making ability of individuals working alone in deciding on funding priorities for medically underserved counties. Groups also do better on tasks requiring a wide range of responses (Thorndike, 1938). For example, it is preferable to have group members and the leader generate alternative solutions with a woman who is having trouble expressing her anger rather than to have the woman generate the alternatives with one worker. For these kinds of tasks, the worker should promote interaction, input, and feedback from all group members so that a wide range of responses are generated and evaluated.

Individuals working alone solve some problems or accomplish some tasks faster and better than they would working in a group. Individuals working alone more readily solve complex problems requiring many variables to be synthesized into a whole. In these cases, the group's product was no better than the best performance of a member of the group (Thorndike, 1938).

Workers can effectively use the knowledge that individuals may solve some problems better by working alone. For example, in preparing a countywide plan for disseminating emergency energy allocation funds to low-income families, a worker decides to use a nominal group procedure (see Chapter 11), which encourages members to work alone before sharing their ideas with the group (Delbecq, Van de Ven, & Gustafson, 1975). The worker might also help members form subgroups to work on specific ideas generated by the individuals before they are deliberated in the larger group.

Several other aspects of problems should be considered when leading a group. One is whether the problem is of concern to the group as a whole, to a subgroup, or to an individual. All members of the group might not be affected to the same extent by a particular problem or task being considered by a group. For example, when leading a group to teach parenting skills to foster parents, the worker should try to get all members involved in discussing parenting problems that are of interest to everyone in the group. When a member raises a problem unique to his or her particular situation, the worker should try to develop from this information generalized principles of child rearing of interest to all group members. This technique is often called *universalizing*.

Finally, in considering the type of problem confronting a group, workers should be aware of where their legitimate influence ends. It may not be appropriate for the worker to encourage discussion of certain topics. For example, a worker leading a task group planning for an emergency housing shelter should not encourage a group member to talk about his or her family life. In other situations, however, workers may want to encourage discussion of taboo areas. For example, when the problem being discussed is child abuse, it might be helpful for the worker to encourage all members to talk about how they were disciplined during their early childhood.

The Environment. The environment in which the group conducts its work has a profound effect on how leadership emerges in the group. Environmental influences come primarily from three interrelated factors: (a) the immediate physical setting, (b) the agency or organization in which the group functions, and (c) other social systems and the social environment. Each helps create the group's culture, which in turn affects how the worker's actions are perceived by the group.

THE SETTING. The worker should ensure that the setting facilitates the group's work. The decor of the waiting room, the comfort of the meeting area, and the availability of equipment and supplies such as tables, blackboard, or newsprint all influence the group's leadership. It is important for the worker to match group members' needs and preferences to a setting that facilitates the group's work. The worker, for example, may need to meet members of a gang in their own environment before any suggestion can be made about doing an activity in a neighborhood community center. In contrast, a board member may be helped to better understand an issue in the board room before or after a meeting.

THE AGENCY CONTEXT.   In addition to the physical environment, the agency influences the group and its leader in several ways. The worker, for example, must be aware of agency policies, rules, and regulations that govern the group's behavior, its process, and its product. The worker is given legitimate authority by the agency or organization to help the group perform its tasks. The agency's delegation of this authority to the worker often assumes the worker will use the method of service delivery that currently exists in the agency. For example, two group workers trying to help pregnant women stop abusing alcohol may use quite different means, depending on the type of program sponsored by each agency. One group leader might use a reality-therapy group approach, whereas the other may use a group format based on cognitive-behavioral self-control procedures.

A worker's position within an agency or organization can also affect what role the worker plays in a group. For example, in a task group a worker may take four subroles: the meeting head, the administrator, the leader, and the spokesperson (Tropman, 1980). As the meeting head, the worker facilitates group functioning. As administrator, the worker performs maintenance functions that are vital to the group's continuing effectiveness. As leader, the worker sets the climate and direction of the meetings. As a spokesperson, the worker publicizes the official opinions, views, and statements of the group; relates to the administrative hierarchy of the agency; and represents the group at official functions. Workers should be aware of how their position in an agency influences their work in helping members of treatment groups achieve their goals. Some settings encourage the use of particular practice approaches or procedures, whereas others do not.

OTHER SOCIAL SYSTEMS.   The third way the environment influences group leadership is through large social systems, such as the community in which the group operates. The worker's behavior is influenced by norms established by society. For example, in a group for abusive parents, the worker intervenes to help members comply with societal norms and values concerning appropriate parenting behaviors. Smaller social systems can also affect a group's work. For example, an agency committee might hesitate to become involved in a search for additional emergency housing if a delegate council formed by a community planning agency is already looking at ways to develop additional emergency housing resources.

The Group as a Whole.   At least four properties of the group as a whole influence how leadership emerges in the group. These include (a) the size of the group, (b) the time limit in which the group is expected to accomplish its goals, (c) group dynamics, and (d) the stage of a group's development.

GROUP SIZE.   As the size of a group increases, the opportunity for participation among members decreases. Rules may increase as workers use them to maintain order and control in the group. Subgroups are more likely to form. Thus, increases in group size have important implications for how leadership skills should be used in the group. Techniques for leading large groups are discussed in Chapter 11.

Decreases in group size also affect leadership. For example, treatment groups in outpatient settings will often experience a drop in membership after a few sessions. Groups may have 10 participants for the first session and six or seven members after the first three sessions. Reduction in membership can provide the group with an opportunity to build cohesion, because the potential for communication increases when less-motivated members drop out.

TIME LIMITS.   Time limits may be voluntary or mandatory. A treatment group, for example, might decide to use a time-limited method such as a behavioral group approach or a task-centered group approach. A task group, such as a delegate council, might feel responsible for making a speedy decision on an issue for an upcoming statewide meeting. In either case, the time limits affect leadership behavior. They generally lead to greater structuring of interactions and an increase in task-focused behavior so that the group can accomplish its goals within the given deadlines. The way time limits are used depends on the purpose and function of the group, and the need for the group to make a quick decision.

GROUP DYNAMICS.   A third property that can influence leadership is the dynamics that operate in a group. As discussed in Chapter 3, these include communication and interaction patterns, cohesion, social control, and group culture. Workers should use their skills to foster the development of group dynamics that help the group accomplish its tasks and contribute to members' satisfaction. Interventions to change the dynamics of the group as a whole are discussed in Chapter 8.

STAGE OF DEVELOPMENT.   The stage of a group's development is the fourth group-as-a-whole factor that can affect leadership behavior. If the group is to develop successfully, the worker must be aware of the developmental tasks that face the group during each stage. A large portion of this text focuses on the specific skills and methods that workers can use during each stage of a group's development.

Group Members.   Group members influence how leadership emerges in three important ways: (a) through the unique characteristics and life experiences they bring to the group, (b) by the extent to which they participate in the group, and (c) by the extent to which they share in leading the group.

CHARACTERISTICS.   Several characteristics of members affect members' ability to influence the group. These include members' interpersonal skills, access to information, perceived responsibility for the work of the group, motivations, and expectations about the process and outcome of the group. The importance of these characteristics should not be overlooked when considering how leadership develops in a group. It has been shown, for example, that members' expectations influence outcomes in both treatment and task groups (Gibb, 1969; Kaul & Bednar, 1986) and that interpersonal skills and knowledge about a particular problem also help determine how well a group functions (Browning, 1977; Hersey, Blanchard, & Natemeyer, 1979).

Because members' attributes differ, one member who is knowledgeable about a particular topic may become the task leader while that topic is being discussed. Another member may serve as the group's socio-emotional leader by expressing feelings and responding to other members' feelings. The worker should recognize each member's leadership potential when facilitating their efforts to take on leadership roles in the group.

EXTENT OF PARTICIPATION.   The extent of members' participation also influences how a worker leads a group. Some members' lack of interpersonal skills or motivation may prevent them from participating fully. In other cases, the worker may purposefully prevent a group member from making verbal communications, thereby limiting to nonverbal means a member's ability to influence the group. For example, a worker leading a delegate council may decide to limit discussion, thereby effectively stopping some members from speaking out about an issue.

The worker should anticipate members' reactions when they are encouraged or discouraged from active participation in a group. Generally, discouraging or limiting a member's participation in a group leads to the member's dissatisfaction with the group. In some situations, however, members may be more interested in hearing what the worker or a guest speaker has to say than in what other members have to say and may readily accept limits on their participation. This is particularly true in educational groups where members' participation may be limited to a discussion period after a presentation by the worker. In task groups, some members may not have an interest in or a knowledge of certain issues, and the worker may want to encourage more knowledgeable or interested members to express their views. In other cases, the worker may want to limit discussion so the group can come to a speedy decision.

SHARING LEADERSHIP.   The extent of a member's participation in the group and the member's resulting willingness and opportunity to share leadership functions is affected in part by the amount of time the member has been a part of the group. A new group member will often have difficulty exerting leadership in a group in which the relationship among members has been established. Similarly, a member of a street gang that has been together for several years has more influence with the gang than a worker who is just beginning to work with the gang.

The worker should also consider to what extent members will be required to carry out tasks or decisions made by the group. Members are more likely to carry out those they have had a part in shaping, particularly if they agree with the group's decision. For example, when it is suggested by the worker or other members that a member of a parent training group observe her child's behavior at home and report on it during the next meeting, the member should be encouraged to express her feelings about the task. She should also be encouraged to help determine the specifics of the task and help identify any potential obstacles. If she does not agree that the task is feasible or if she thinks it will not help her improve her parenting skills, she should not be encouraged to do it. Similarly, in task groups, it is particularly important to involve members in making decisions when their cooperation is needed for implementing a particular plan of action.

The Group Leader.   The purpose of the group, the type of problem being confronted, the environment, the group as a whole, and the group's members all influence how leadership emerges in the group, but the worker, in the role of designated leader, also has influence over group processes and task accomplishments. As stated earlier, when group leadership was first examined closely in the early part of this century, most studies focused on the personal qualities of the leader and on styles of leadership, such as autocratic, democratic, or laissez-faire (Lewin, Lippitt, & White, 1939). Gradually, the studies broadened to examine how leadership styles interact with the other components of the leadership model shown in Figure 4–2. Although our model is based on findings that suggest leadership is an interactional process among each of these systems of influence, the model would not be complete without considering how qualities of the designated leader influence group leadership.

THE POWER BASE.   Probably the most important factor to consider about a worker is the basis of his or her power. Earlier we indicated that seven types of power can be used to influence a group: coercive, connection, expert, information, legitimate, referent, and reward power bases. Most workers draw on a variety of power bases; workers should realize the power bases at their disposal when they are considering leading a group. With mandated clients, workers may want to use their influence to overcome members' resistance before beginning a group. For example, a worker planning to lead a group of alcoholics who have been referred because of a DWI (driving while intoxicated) offense may influence members by refusing to certify that they are fit to have their licenses returned until they have successfully completed a group treatment program.

SKILL.   The level of skill that workers possess also influences their ability to lead. Experience and training of workers have been correlated with effectiveness in working with individuals and groups (Beutler, Crago, and Arizmendi, 1986). Even when workers have a number of strong power bases they can use to influence group members, unskillful application of their power will often result in members becoming angry and uncooperative or submissive and passive. Through the appropriate use of leadership skills, the worker can more readily achieve objectives and satisfy group members. For this reason, leadership skills are described in greater depth in the next section of this chapter.

PERSONALITY.   A worker's personality, interpersonal style, and preferences for how to lead also influence group leadership. For example, a worker who is shy and sensitive about others' feelings is less likely to use confrontation as a technique when leading a group. Workers should be aware of how their interpersonal style affects their attempts to objectively analyze what the group needs and their attempts to intervene in the group's processes. Some methods for becoming more aware of one's leadership style, and how to modify it, are described later in this chapter.

SERVICE TECHNOLOGY.   The service technology that workers use also affects how they conduct their groups. *Service technology* refers to particular theories or methods of intervention used by a worker. Three leaders of groups for alcoholics, for example, will intervene in quite different ways, using transactional analysis, for example, or behavior therapy or, perhaps, reality therapy. Workers' choice of service technologies may be influenced by their personal preferences, their training, or the ideology of the agency in which they work.

A worker's technological and ideological stance often helps in organizing interventions. Workers may wish to receive specialized instruction in a particular service technology, such as transactional analysis or behavior modification; however, it is essential that they become familiar with basic practice principles of leading groups before they receive specialized training.

GROUP LEADERSHIP SKILLS

Group leadership skills are behaviors or activities that help the group achieve its purpose and accomplish its tasks and help members achieve their personal goals. Both workers and members use leadership skills, although the worker ordinarily uses them more than any other member of the group. Leadership skills are combined when conducting group meetings. For example, in using a problem-solving method, a worker calls upon numerous leadership skills to help a committee arrive at a decision concerning personnel practices in a family service agency. Similarly, in an aftercare treatment group for drug addicts, a worker relies on many different skills to help members remain drug-free.

There has been a longstanding interest in the "skillful use of self" in social work practice (see Goldstein, 1983). Most of the evidence concerning the effect of skill level on desired outcomes has been gathered from the evaluation of work with individuals rather than from work with groups (Brammer, 1979; Orlinsky & Howard, 1986). Reviews of the literature suggest that skills can be learned and that skill level makes a difference in performance (Beutler, Crago, & Arizmendi, 1986; Meltzoff & Kornreich, 1970). There is some evidence that specific skills such as attending intently and responding empathically are directly connected to positive outcomes (Shulman, 1978; Toseland, Rossiter, Peak, & Hill, 1990). Results are tentative, however, because it is difficult to design studies to assess the independent effect of one particular skill.

Group leadership skills are somewhat different from skills used in working with an individual. Both members and the worker have greater choice regarding the level and focus of their interaction. For example, they may choose to be active or passive, and they may decide to interact with some members more than others. There is also a greater possibility for shared leadership and the delegation of various leadership responsibilities. There have been a few attempts to focus on the specific skills necessary to lead groups (see, for example, Bertcher, 1994; Egan, 1976; Middleman, 1978; Middleman & Wood, 1990; Shulman, 1992). Some programs have also been designed to train group workers in specific skills. Evaluations of these programs suggest they can be effective in increasing a worker's skill level (Oxley, Wilson, Anderson, & Wong, 1979; Rivas & Toseland, 1981).

Some of the basic skills necessary for group leadership are categorized in Table 4–1. Skills are listed in three categories: (a) facilitating group processes, (b) data gathering and assessment, and (c) action. Skills are classified on the basis of their most likely functions in the group. However, skills listed under one category may, on occasion, be used in another category, particularly if they are combined with other skills. For example, responding is classified as a skill in facilitating group processes. Although responding to another group member's actions or words facilitates communication, responding may also lead to additional data gathering, assessment, or action.

Facilitating Group Processes Skills

Table 4–1 lists several different skills in the category of facilitating group processes. All these skills can be used by workers differentially, depending on their intentions when attempting to influence various group processes. For example, although some information suggests that a high degree of member-to-member communication leads to better outcomes than minimal peer interaction (Coons, 1957), workers may not always want to increase communication. Instead, they might want to focus group communication, clarify communication, or understand a communication. In general, skills in facilitating group processes con-

TABLE 4–1
A functional classification of group leadership skills

Facilitating Group Processes	Data Gathering and Assessment	Action
1. Involving group members	1. Identifying and describing thoughts, feelings, and behaviors	1. Supporting
2. Attending to others		2. Reframing and redefining
3. Expressing self	2. Requesting information, questioning, and probing	3. Linking members' communications
4. Responding to others		
5. Focusing group communication	3. Summarizing and partializing information	4. Directing
		5. Giving advice, suggestions, or instructions
6. Making group processes explicit	4. Synthesizing thoughts, feelings, and action	6. Providing resources
7. Clarifying content	5. Analyzing information	7. Modeling, role playing, rehearsing, and coaching
8. Guiding group interactions		8. Confronting
		9. Resolving conflicts

tribute to positive group outcome when they improve understanding among group members, build open communication channels, and encourage the development of trust so that all members are willing to contribute as much as they can to the problem on which the group is working (Cabral, Best, & Paton, 1975; Parloff, 1961).

Involving Group Members

Ideally, all members should be involved and interested in what is being discussed in the group. Yalom (1985) has called this universalizing a group member's experience. Involving members who have been silent helps identify commonalities and differences in their life experiences. As members become involved they realize how particular problems affect them and how a solution to one member's problem can directly or indirectly help them. Involving others is also essential for building group cohesiveness, developing a sense of mutual aid, and encouraging shared decision making.

Involving group members also means helping them take on leadership roles within the group. The worker should be cautious about doing too much for members, thereby stifling individual initiative. Instead of jealously guarding the leadership role, workers should encourage members to contribute to the content of group meetings and help shape group dynamic processes. This can be done by providing members with opportunities for leadership roles during program activities, by praising members for their leadership efforts, and by inviting and encouraging members' participation and initiative during group interaction.

Attending Skills

Attending skills are nonverbal behaviors such as eye contact, body position, and verbal behavior that convey empathy, respect, warmth, trust, genuineness, and honesty. Attending skills are useful in establishing rapport as well as a climate of acceptance and cohesiveness among group members. Egan (1990) suggests, in addition to body position and eye contact, skills that indicate that a worker has heard and understood a member are part of effective attending. Such skills include repeating or paraphrasing what a member says and responding empathically and enthusiastically to the meaning behind members' communications. They also include what Middleman (1978) has referred to as "scanning" skills. When scanning the group, the worker makes eye contact with all group members, letting them know that the worker is concerned about them as individuals. Scanning also helps reduce the tendency of workers to focus on one or two group members.

Expressive Skills

Expressive skills are also important for facilitating group processes. Workers should be able to help participants express thoughts and feelings about important problems, tasks, or issues facing the group as well as to reiterate and summarize them when necessary. Members should also be helped to express their thoughts and feelings as freely as possible in an appropriate and goal-oriented manner. Members of task and treatment groups can often benefit from an open discussion of formerly taboo areas that affect the group or its members. Self-disclosure is an expressive skill that can be used effectively for this purpose. Although self-disclosures should be made judiciously, according to their appropriateness for particular situations, they can often be useful in helping the worker promote open communication about difficult subjects.

Responding Skills

Skillful responses help the group as a whole and individual members accomplish tasks. The worker might, for example, amplify subtle messages, or soften over-powering messages (Middleman & Wood, 1990). The worker can also redirect messages that may be more appropriate for a particular member or the group as a whole.

Workers can use responding skills selectively to elicit specific reactions that will affect future group processes. For example, if a worker's response supports a group member's efforts, the member is more likely to continue to work on a task or a concern. If the worker disagrees with a member's statement or action, the member is likely to react either by responding to the worker's statement or remaining silent. The member is not likely to continue to pursue the original statement. Thus, by responding selectively to particular communications, the worker can exert influence over subsequent communication patterns.

Focusing Skills

The worker can facilitate group processes by focusing them in a particular direction. This can be done by clarifying, asking a member to elaborate, repeating a particular communication or sequence of communications, or suggesting that group members limit their discussion to a particular topic. Helping the group maintain its focus can promote efficient work by reducing irrelevant communications and by encouraging a full exploration of issues and problems.

Making Group Processes Explicit

The skill of making group processes explicit helps members to become aware of how they are interacting. For example, a worker may point out implicit group norms, particular member roles, or specific interaction patterns. The worker may ask members if they observed a particular pattern or type of interaction, whether they are comfortable with the interaction, and whether they would like to see changes in the ways members interact. Middleman and Wood (1990) point out that it is important for the worker to verbalize therapeutic group norms, and to encourage the development of traditions and rituals. For example, pointing out that at the beginning of each group meeting members seem to take turns "telling their story" and receiving feedback about how they handled a particular situation encourages members to consider whether they want to continue this pattern of interaction.

Pointing out the here-and-now of group interaction is an underused skill. Sometimes, workers get so caught up in the content of interaction that they forget to pay attention to group processes. Other workers are reluctant to make their observations public. Workers who have difficulty directing the group's attention to group processes should consider practicing this skill by setting aside a few minutes at the beginning or end of each meeting for a discussion of group processes, or by making a conscious effort to point out group processes in brief summary statements at intervals during meetings. Clinical and supervisory experience suggests that the process of pointing out here-and-now group interaction becomes easier with practice.

Clarifying Content

Just as it can be beneficial to make group processes explicit, it can also be beneficial to point out the content of members' interactions. The worker's purpose in clarifying content is to help members communicate effectively. The skill of clarifying content includes checking that a particular message was understood by members of the group and helping members express themselves more clearly. It also includes pointing out when group interaction has become unfocused or has been sidetracked by an irrelevant issue.

The skill of clarifying content can also be used to point out the possible avoidance of taboo subjects. For example, when working with a group of couples, the leader might point out that no mention has been made of the couples' satisfaction with their sex life. Similarly, in a support group for caregivers of the frail elderly, the worker may point out that the subject of nursing home placement has not arisen.

Guiding Group Interactions

The last skill noted in Table 4–1 for facilitating group processes is that of guiding the interactions of group members. To help a group accomplish the goals it has set out for itself, the worker will often find that it is helpful to guide the group's interaction in a particular direction. By limiting or blocking a group member's communications, by encouraging another member to speak, or by linking one group member's communication to those of other group members, the worker can guide the group's interaction patterns. This has been referred to as selecting communications patterns purposely (Middleman & Wood, 1990).

The skill of guiding group interactions has many uses. For example, the worker may want to correct a dysfunctional aspect of the group's process, such as the development of a subgroup that disrupts other members. A worker who can skillfully guide group interaction patterns can limit the communication between subgroup members and increase their communication with other group members. The worker may also want to use guiding skills to explore a particular problem or help members sustain their efforts in solving a problem or completing a task. At other times, the worker may want to encourage open communication. For example, by redirecting a communication, the worker can help members speak to one another. The worker might say, "John, your message is really intended for Jill. Why don't you share your message directly with her rather than through me?"

Data Gathering and Assessment Skills

Data gathering and assessment skills are useful in developing a plan for influencing communication patterns as well as in deciding on the action skills to use to accomplish the group's purposes. These skills provide a bridge between the process-oriented approach of facilitating group processes and the task-oriented approach of using action skills to achieve goals and satisfy members' needs. Without effective data gathering and assessment skills, workers' interventions are not grounded in a complete understanding of the situation. This can result in the use of premature, oversimplified, or previously attempted solutions that have not been carefully analyzed and weighed.

Identifying and Describing Skills

Perhaps the most basic data gathering skill is helping members identify and describe a particular situation. This allows for the elaboration of pertinent factors influencing a problem or task facing the group. In using this skill, workers should attempt to elicit descriptions that specify the problem attributes as clearly and concretely as possible. To understand the problem, it is often useful for the worker to identify or describe historical as well as current aspects of the problem. It may also be helpful to share alternative ways of viewing the situation to obtain diverse frames of reference, alternative interpretations of events, and potential solutions to a problem.

Requesting Information, Questioning, and Probing

The skills of identifying and describing a situation are essential to workers' attempts to gather data by requesting information, questioning, and probing. Using these skills, workers can clarify the problem or concern and broaden the scope of the group's work by obtaining additional information that may be useful to all members. The worker should be careful to ask questions that are clear and answerable. Double questions or value-laden questions may be met with resistance, passivity, anger, or misunderstanding. For some issues and for some group members, questioning or probing may be seen as a confrontation or a challenge to what has already been stated. This is particularly true in areas where the member is reluctant to give additional information because the information is perceived as emotionally charged or potentially damaging to the member's status in the group. The worker should be particularly sensitive to these concerns when seeking additional information from a member. Helping the member explore fears or concerns about the potentially damaging effect of a disclosure can be a helpful intervention. Another is having the member ask for feedback from other members about the realistic basis of his or her fears.

Summarizing and Partializing

When information has been discussed about the problems or concerns facing the group, a worker then can use summarizing or partializing skills. Summarizing skills enable a worker to present the core of what has been said in the group and provide members an opportunity to reflect on the problem. Summarizing skills give members and the worker an opportunity to consider the next steps in solving the problem and allow members to compare their perceptions about what has gone on in the group with the worker's summary. Partializing skills are useful for breaking down a complex problem or issue into manageable bits. Partializing is also helpful in determining group members' motivation to work on various aspects of the problem.

Synthesizing

Another useful data gathering and assessment skill is synthesizing verbal and non-verbal communications. Examples of synthesizing skills include making connections among the meanings behind a member's actions or words, expressing hidden agendas, making implicit feelings or thoughts explicit, and making connections between communications to point out themes and trends in members' actions or words.

Synthesizing skills can be useful in providing feedback to members about how they are perceived by others. Because these skills often involve a considerable amount of judgment and conjecture about the facts available to the worker, they should be used cautiously, and all members should have the opportunity for input into the synthesis. Ideally, when the worker synthesizes a number of interactions or points out similarities in group problem-solving or group communication patterns, all members should be able to give feedback about their perceptions of the situation. For example, during a weekly staff meeting of an adolescent unit in a state mental hospital, a worker mentions the patterns of interactions that have developed among team members. In describing these patterns, the worker asks members for feedback on how they perceived the group's interaction.

Analyzing Skills

Once the data have been gathered and organized, the worker can use analyzing skills to synthesize the information and assess how to proceed. Analyzing skills include pointing out patterns in the data, identifying gaps in the data, and establishing mechanisms or plans for obtaining data to complete an assessment. For example, in a treatment conference at a group home for adolescents, the worker can use analyzing skills to point out patterns used by staff members in previous work with a particular youngster. The group can then explore new methods and techniques for future efforts to work with the youngster. In an educational treatment group for potentially abusive parents, the worker can use analyzing skills to link parents' behavior patterns to the onset of physical abuse of their children.

Action Skills

Supporting Group Members

Action skills are most often used by the worker to help the group accomplish its tasks. Perhaps the most basic skill in this area is supporting group members in their efforts to help themselves and each other. Skills to support group members will not be effective unless members perceive the group to be a safe place where their thoughts and feelings will be accepted. Thus, it is essential to begin by helping the group develop a culture in which all members' experiences and opinions are valued. The worker supports members by encouraging them to express their thoughts and feelings on topics relevant to the group, by providing them the opportunity to ventilate their concerns, by soliciting their opinions, and by responding to their requests and comments.

Support also means helping members respond empathically to each other and validate and affirm shared experiences. Skills in supporting members often involve pointing out their strengths and indicating how their participation in the group can help to resolve their problems. It also means providing hope for continued progress or success.

Ventilation and support are the primary goals of some groups. For example, support groups are often formed for the staff of neonatal intensive-care units and burn units of regional hopsitals. Such groups give staff a chance to talk about, and reflect upon, the emotionally draining situations they frequently face. Medical social workers who form and facilitate these groups encourage staff to ventilate pent-up emotions and provide peer support for one another. Similarly, the therapeutic elements of a treatment group for recently widowed people include the ventilation of feelings about the loss of a loved one, the affirmation of similar feelings and experiences, and the encouragement to cope effectively with the transition despite feelings of grief.

Reframing and Redefining

Often, one of the greatest obstacles to the work of a group or an individual is failure to view a problem from different perspectives to find a creative solution. Thus, a worker may want to reframe and redefine an issue or concern facing the group. For example, in a group where one member is being used as a scapegoat, the worker might help members redefine their relationship to that member. This can be done by having members talk about how they relate to the person who is being scapegoated and how they might improve their relationship with that person. In this case, reframing the problem from one that focuses on the scapegoated member to one that is shared by all members is a useful way to change members' interactions with this particular member. As the problem is redefined and group members change their relationship with the member being scapegoated, the problem often diminishes or disappears. Redefining and reframing the problem can help members examine the problem from a new perspective. Reframing is described in greater detail in Chapter 9.

Linking Members' Communications

The skill of linking members' communications involves asking members to share their reactions to the messages communicated by others in the group. Middleman and Wood (1990) refer to this skill as reaching for a feeling link or an information link. Members have a tendency to communicate with the worker rather than with other members, especially in early group meetings. The worker can prevent this from becoming a pattern by asking members about their reactions to a particular communication. For example, in a group in a psychiatric inpatient setting designed to prepare the members for independent living, the worker might say, "Mary, how do you feel about what Joe just said? I recall that during our last meeting, you expressed feeling anxious about living on your own." Alternatively, the worker might say, "Have any of you had the same feeling?" When members of the group validate and affirm each other's experiences and feelings, they develop a sense of belonging. Members no longer feel isolated or alone with their concerns. They stop questioning and doubting their own interpretations of a situation and their own reactions to it.

The skill of linking members' communications also involves asking members to respond to requests for help by other members. Helping members respond to each other fosters information sharing, mutual aid, and the building of a consensus about how to approach a particular problem. For example, in response to a query from a group member about whether the worker knows of a resource for helping her take care of her frail father while she is at work, the worker might ask if any other members have used adult day care or respite care. Workers will find that members are often more receptive to using a service or a resource when they hear positive reports about it from other members of the group. Particularly when working with mandated and reluctant clients, workers' suggestions to use a particular resource may be viewed with skepticism. Members sometimes believe that the worker has a vested interest in "getting" them to use a particular service. In contrast, the testimonials of one or more group members about the benefits of a particular service are often viewed with less skepticism. Workers should also be aware that once they provide a response, other members will be less likely to provide their own perspective. Thus, although a direct response to a member's communication is often warranted, it is often a good practice for workers to turn to other members of the group for their input before jumping in with their own response.

Directing

Whether the worker is clarifying the group's goal, helping members participate in a particular program activity, leading a discussion, sharing new information, or making an assessment of a particular problem, the worker is directing the group's action. Directing skills are most effective when coupled with efforts to increase members' participation and input (Stogdill, 1974). The worker should not use directing skills without obtaining members' approval or without involving them in decisions about the direction the group should take to accomplish its goals. The worker should be aware of how each member reacts to being directed in a new component of the group's work. For example, in directing a role play in a remedial group designed to help teen-agers learn how to handle angry feelings more effectively, the worker should be aware of how the action will affect each member. Depending on the way they express their anger, some group members may benefit from playing certain roles more than other members. Others may benefit most from observing the action.

Advice, Suggestions, and Instructions

Another cluster of action skills that both workers and members can use include giving advice, suggestions, or instructions. Workers use these skills to help group members acquire new behaviors, understand problems, or change problematic situations. Advice, suggestions, or instructions, however, are infrequently provided by professionals in practice. Studies have revealed, for example, that advice, suggestions, or instructions constitute between 1 percent and 5 percent of all communications made by practitioners (Boatman, 1975; Mullen, 1969; Pinkus, 1968; Smith, Tobin, & Toseland, 1992).

Nonetheless, advice is expected and wanted by many clients, especially those of lower socio-economic status (Aronson & Overall, 1966; Davis, 1975; Mayer & Timms, 1970). Further, these skills appear to have some beneficial effect in helping clients formulate new ideas and approaches to resolving problems (see Davis, 1975; Ewalt & Kutz, 1976; Fortune, 1979; Reid & Shapiro, 1969; and Smith, Tobin, & Toseland, 1992). For example, in a review of studies of various therapeutic mechanisms of change, Emrick, Lassen, and Edwards (1977) reported that advice giving was strongly associated with positive changes in clients.

Advice, suggestions, or instructions should be timed appropriately so that group members are ready to accept them. They must be clear and geared to the comprehension level of the members for whom they are intended. For example, in an educational group for training Department of Social Service workers to lead parenting groups, each group worker should be sure the material is at a level that will be readily understood by the worker's clients. Similarly, a group of teen-age parents who have not completed high school requires a presentation of ideas, advice, suggestions, and instructions quite different from a presentation to a group of highly educated women who have delayed child rearing until their early 30s. Advice or instructions given to children in a group should be simpler than those given to adults.

Workers should also be sensitive to the language and culture of the members of their groups. Certain words in English might not translate appropriately or with the same meaning in another language. Further, the cultural heritage of a population may influence how such individuals receive and decode messages sent from the worker.

The worker should not act alone in giving advice, suggestions, and instructions. This sets the worker off as an expert who may be seen as too directive. The worker should encourage members to share information, advice, and instructions with each other. Middleman (1978) and Shulman (1992) refer to this as the worker reaching for feelings and information that members may be hesitant to disclose.

To encourage members to share information and advice with each other, the worker should facilitate the development of helping networks in which members share their life experiences, information, and resources, as well as their opinions and views. One of the distinct advantages of group work over individual work is the ability of group members to rely on one another for help in solving problems and accomplishing goals. Our experience suggests that well-established helping networks often continue outside the group long after the group experience has ended. For example, a worker who formed a support and parenting skills education group for single parents in an inner city area, later helped the group members form a child-care cooperative that flourished for years after the 12-week parenting skills group ended. Similarly, the members of a support group for family members of patients recently discharged from inpatient settings in the inner city were helped by the worker to form a local chapter of a national welfare rights organization.

Providing Resources

Organizations that sponsor groups have access to a wide variety of resources that the worker can make available to members, such as medical treatment, home health care, financial assistance, job and rehabilitation counseling, family planning, and financial management consultation. Making skillful use of these resources through accurate assessment and referral can be helpful to group members. The worker can also help members to explore resources used by other members of the group. In this way, the cumulative knowledge of all group members can be used to help a member connect to and become familiar with a needed resource.

In task groups as well, workers can provide a variety of resources for members. They can influence the environment in which a group works, either directly or indirectly, to make it easier for the group to accomplish its tasks. Workers may have access to important people or action groups, where the group's work can be given proper consideration. In addition, because task groups are often composed of members with a variety of skills and resources, members can also help one another achieve the group's goals.

Modeling, Role Playing, Rehearsing, and Coaching

The action skills of modeling, role playing, and rehearsing situations in the group can be helpful in both task and treatment groups. *Modeling* refers to the worker or a member demonstrating behaviors in a particular situation so that others in the group can observe what to do and how to do it. For example, the worker in an assertion training group might demonstrate how to respond to a spouse who has become quite angry. In another group, the worker might model caring and concern by going over to a group member who has begun to cry and placing an arm around the member's shoulder.

Role playing refers to having the group members act out a situation with each other's help. The two primary purposes of role playing are to assess a member's skill in responding to an interpersonal situation and to help the member improve particular responses. Responses can be improved through feedback, rehearsal of a new response, and coaching from the worker or other group members during rehearsals (Etcheverry, Siporin, & Toseland, 1987).

Although role plays are commonly used so that members gain experience in the protected environment of the group before attempting a new response outside the group, role playing can also be used to improve responses in future situations.

For example, in a group for couples trying to improve their relationships, the worker asked each couple to role play an argument they had during the past week. During the role play, the worker asked each couple to switch roles so that each partner could experience how the other felt, thought, and acted in the situation. The role play helped members understand their partner's behavior and how their own behavior influenced their partner. The couples used the feedback they received to experiment with new and better ways to communicate during an argument. In this way, the couples learned new communication skills and began to use improved ways of responding to each other during disagreements.

Rehearsing refers to practicing a new behavior or response based on the feedback received after a role play. Because it is difficult to learn new behaviors, or to diminish less adaptive but habituated behavior patterns, a member may have to practice a new response several times.

Coaching is the use of verbal and physical instructions to help members reproduce a particular response. For example, members of a group for the mentally retarded might practice expressing their feelings during interpersonal interactions. As members practice, the worker coaches them by giving instructions and demonstrating how to improve their responses. Additional information about different role-playing techniques is presented in Chapter 9.

Confrontation Skills

Confrontation is a useful action skill for overcoming resistance and motivating members. Confrontation is the ability to clarify, examine, and challenge behaviors so as to help members overcome distortions and discrepancies among behaviors, thoughts, and feelings (Egan, 1990; Toseland & Spielberg, 1982). Confrontation skills should be used only when the worker has carefully assessed the situation and decided that the confrontation will not be rejected by a member. If a member is not ready to examine thoughts, behaviors, or feelings, the member may react negatively to a confrontation by becoming passive, angry, or hostile.

Because confrontations are potent and emotionally charged, workers should be prepared for strong reactions. In certain circumstances, workers may want to make gentle or tentative confrontations to explore a member's reactions before a direct, full-scale confrontation. Although confrontations are often associated with pointing out a member's flaws or weaknesses, they can be used to help members recognize strengths and assets. For example, in a remedial group for psychiatric inpatients, a depressed group member who is self-deprecating might be confronted and challenged to begin to recognize his strengths and assets. Similarly, a member of a growth group might be confronted by pointing out how her words differ from her actions.

Resolving Conflicts

One of the most important action skills is helping resolve conflicts among the members of the group and with individuals and social systems outside the group. Group members may conflict with one another for a variety of reasons. For example, in a delegate council, members may represent constituencies that have quite different concerns, interests, and goals. In a treatment team, group members' responsibilities for different work functions and tasks may cause conflict or competition, particularly if resources for accomplishing a task are limited.

Many of the models of group development described in the previous chapter indicate that conflict may arise among members as the group develops. The worker should help the group view conflict as a healthy process that can clarify the purposes and goals of the group, and the way members can work together.

Although conflicts will inevitably arise, skillful group facilitation can help avoid unnecessary conflicts and resolve disagreements before they turn into hostile disputes. To help avoid unnecessary conflicts, workers can suggest that the group develop and maintain rules for participation. These rules are frequently expressed in early contractual discussions with members. Sometimes these rules, which should be developed with the participation of all group members, are stated in a written agreement that all members sign at the beginning of a new group. An example of such a written agreement is shown in Figure 4–3. We have found that having agreed-upon rules clearly written and displayed on a blackboard or flip chart is particularly helpful in children's groups. Children enjoy setting rules for their group and, with the guidance of a leader, they can help each other follow rules they have made.

When conflicts arise among members, the worker may also use moderating, negotiating, mediating, or arbitrating skills to resolve disagreements before they turn into hostile disputes. Moderating skills refer to keeping meetings within specified bounds so that conflict is avoided. Negotiating skills are used to help members come to an agreement or an understanding when initial opinions differ. Mediating skills are used when two or more members are in conflict and action is necessary to help them reach an agreement and resolve the dispute. Finally, arbitration skills involve having an authoritative third person meet with the group. This person listens to the dispute and binds the members to a settlement. Arbitra-

FIGURE 4–3
Rules for group participation

I, the undersigned, agree to:

1. Attend each group session or call one day before the group meeting to explain my absence.

2. Not talk about anything that occurs in the group to anyone outside the group, unless it applies only to myself and no other group member.

3. Carry out all assignments agreed to in the group between group sessions.

4. Speak in turn so that everyone gets a chance to talk.

5. Give the group two weeks' notice before terminating my participation.

_____   _____
            Name   Date

tion is sometimes used in task groups that have reached an impasse when working on a labor contract. Specific methods that workers can use to help resolve conflicts in groups are described more fully in Chapters 8 and 10 of this book and by Bernstein (1976).

Members may also come into conflict with forces outside the group. The members of therapy groups, for example, often expect workers to provide guidance about how to resolve conflicts with spouses, other family members, friends, fellow workers, and acquaintances. In attempting to be more assertive, a member of a therapy group might receive hostile, angry, or aggressive responses from family members or friends. In such a case, the worker might attempt to reduce the conflict by intervening directly in the situation or by helping the member develop the skills necessary to overcome the conflict on his or her own. When the conflict is an inevitable by-product of a change the member wishes to make outside the group, the worker can help the member feel comfortable with the conflict until a new state of equilibrium is achieved.

Sometimes it is helpful for the worker to meet with people outside the group to resolve a member's conflict. For example, a worker might meet with the parents of an adolescent group member to discuss how the parents set limits and rules for their child. In other cases, workers can prepare members for the reactions they may encounter outside the group. For example, a worker can help members learn how to respond to potential rejection or hostility when they are more assertive than usual with a particular person. Preparing members for what to expect in a wide range of situations and settings also helps ensure their success when they are using newly learned behaviors in unfamiliar settings or situations.

Workers may also need to resolve conflicts between the group as a whole and the larger society. For example, workers may help resolve conflicts between tenants associations and housing authorities, welfare rights groups and county departments of social services, or support groups for individuals with chronic illnesses and health-care providers. Moderating, negotiating, mediating, and arbitrating skills can often be used successfully in these situations. However, in some situations, the mobilization and social action skills described in Chapter 11 may have to be used to resolve a conflict.

Learning Group Leadership Skills

Those who are training to become group workers should begin by becoming thoroughly familiar with the theoretical knowledge about groups as a whole and the way members and leaders function in groups. However, to integrate theoretical knowledge about group dynamics with practical experience, trainees should (a) participate in exercises and role plays illustrating how group dynamics operate, (b) examine their participation as members of natural or formed groups, and (c) lead or co-lead a group in a supervised field practicum.

In the classroom, trainees can learn to lead groups under a variety of conditions and circumstances by combining didactic and experiential methods of learning. Didactic material should expose trainees to the array of groups they may be called upon to lead. Therefore, lectures, discussions, and examples should include groups in several settings with different purposes and clientele. Lecture material can be supplemented with films and videotapes of different social work groups in action. A list of available films is presented in Appendix C.

Cognitive knowledge is, by itself, insufficient for effective social work. Training should include exercises and role plays to illustrate and demonstrate the material presented during lectures. Often lab groups can be formed to help trainees practice the material that has been presented. Lab groups give trainees a sense of what it is like to be a member of a group. Also, leadership can be rotated in a lab group so that all members are responsible for leading a group at least once.

Laboratory group experiences can be enhanced by the use of video and audio equipment. These devices give trainees feedback about their verbal and nonverbal behavior as they participate in or lead a meeting. Tapes made during labs can be reviewed by trainees and the lab leader during supervisory sessions to help members develop their leadership skills.

Trainees can also learn how to lead a group by becoming a member of an existing group in the community. The trainee learns vicariously by observing the leader's behavior. The leader acts as a model of leadership skills for the member.

Learning also occurs through critiques of the group's process. Critiquing the group helps ensure that trainees do not accept all the activities of the group's leader without question. It gives trainees an opportunity to examine the development of a group over time and to observe the effects of leadership skills in action. It is relatively easy to structure lab groups so that part of the group's time is spent analyzing the group process, but trainees may not have this opportunity in community groups. Therefore, to achieve maximum benefit from participation in a community group, trainees should have an opportunity to discuss their experiences as members of a group in supervisory sessions, or in the classroom.

When trainees become familiar with basic skills in leading a group through these experiences, they are ready for a field practicum. The field practicum may include leading several sessions of a group, co-leading a group, or leading an entire group while receiving supervision. For purposes of learning about group leadership skills, group supervision is preferable to individual supervision because the supervisor models group leadership skills while reviewing a trainee's work with a group. Rivas and Toseland (1981) have found that a training group is an effective way to provide supervision. Methods for conducting group supervision are discussed by Rose (1989). If not enough practicum sites are available, trainees can form their own task or treatment groups by providing group services to students or community residents (see, for example, Rivas & Toseland, 1981).

Before leading a group, it is helpful for trainees to discuss their fantasies about the first meeting. Lonergan (1985) reports that fantasies can include (a) unmanageable resistance exhibited by members, such as not talking, (b) losing control of the group because of members' excessive hostility or acting out, (c) inability to deal with specific behaviors such as a member dropping out of the group capriciously, members dating each other, or individuals making sexual advances within the group or between group meetings, (d) overwhelming dependency demands by members, and (e) lack of attendance and the disintegration of the group.

Because trainees react differently to their first group experience, supervisors should explore each individual's fantasies, helping them deal with their anxiety by discussing likely group reactions and reviewing what could be done in the unlikely event that a trainee's worst fantasy is realized.

Leadership Style

It is important to recognize that although leadership skills can be learned, they are not applied in a mechanical, objective fashion. Group work is a subjective encounter among the members of the group, all of whom have distinct personalities, viewpoints, and methods of relating to "objective" reality. Workers and members bring expectations, preferences, and styles of relating with them to the group. While these may be modified during the course of interaction, they continuously color and shape the evolving interaction and the skills that workers use to facilitate the group. As Goldstein (1988) states, "As people enter into a group and take part in shaping its purpose and goals, the underlying premises that they bring to the encounter and their ways of perceiving, thinking and interpreting will inexorably determine how the process unfolds" (p. 25).

The degree to which styles of relating influence what occurs in the group depends on the nature of the group. The more a group is structured, and the more it is focused on impersonal issues that the members have little stake in, the less likely group processes are to be affected by the personalities of the individuals. For example, in a delegate council using parliamentary procedure, the individual personalities of agency representatives are likely to have relatively little influence on group decisions. In contrast, Reid (1991) aptly points out that in therapy groups, "each [person] brings to the [group] experience a history of relating to others, sometimes with success and at other times without. In this therapeutic alliance group members may react to the therapist as if he or she were a significant figure out of their own original family. Similarly, the leader may react in exactly the same way, projecting onto others his or her own unresolved feelings and conflicts" (pp. 105–106).

In the psychoanalytic tradition, projection of feelings by members onto the leader is called *transference*. Projection of feelings onto members by the leader is called *countertransference*.

To become an effective group leader it is not sufficient, therefore, to learn group leadership skills without paying attention to how they are applied. It is essential for leaders to become self-reflective practitioners who consider carefully the meaning of their interactions with all members of the group. One of the hallmarks of an effective leader is the ability and willingness to examine the effect of his or her beliefs, expectations, preferences, personality, style of relating, and subjective experience of reality on a particular group. Effective leaders are not afraid to explore with members, supervisors, or colleagues the possible ramifications of their behavior in a group. They observe carefully and think deeply about the meaning of members' reactions to particular interactions.

A first step in helping leaders become more aware of the effect of their style of interaction is for them to do a self-assessment of their strengths and weaknesses as a leader. In workshops with students and practitioners, we often begin by asking participants to complete the Leadership Comfort Scale (LCS) shown in Figure 4–4. The LCS allows members to rate their degree of comfort with 10 situations that group leaders frequently experience. We also ask participants to write down their responses to a series of open-ended questions, such as:

1. Describe what you perceive to be your major strengths and weaknesses as a leader.
2. What types of group members make you feel uncomfortable?
3. What situations or events during group meetings do you find particularly difficult to deal with?
4. What feedback have you received from others about your leadership skills?
5. What steps have you taken to improve your leadership skills? What steps have you considered but not yet taken?

FIGURE 4–4
Leadership Comfort Scale

Indicate your feelings when the following situations arise in the group. Circle the appropriate feeling.

1. Dealing with silence	Comfortable	Uncomfortable
2. Dealing with negative feelings from members	Comfortable	Uncomfortable
3. Having little structure in a group	Comfortable	Uncomfortable
4. Dealing with ambiguity of purpose	Comfortable	Uncomfortable
5. Having to self-disclose your feelings to the group	Comfortable	Uncomfortable
6. Experiencing high self-disclosure among members	Comfortable	Uncomfortable
7. Dealing with conflict in the group	Comfortable	Uncomfortable
8. Having your leadership authority questioned	Comfortable	Uncomfortable
9. Being evaluated by group members	Comfortable	Uncomfortable
10. Allowing members to take responsibility for the group	Comfortable	Uncomfortable

We tabulate participants' anonymous answers to the LCS and present the aggregate answers on a flip chart or blackboard. We also ask for volunteers to share their answers to the open-ended questions. This inevitably leads to a lively discussion of difficult leadership situations and participants' strengths and weaknesses in dealing with them. It also helps point out the diversity of responses to challenging leadership situations.

Next, we ask participants to complete the Beliefs About Structure Scale (BASS), shown in Figure 4–5. When completing the BASS, participants often say the structure depends on the purpose of the group, the types of group members, and so forth. We acknowledge that leadership is interactive, but point out that individuals have preferences about the degree of structure they are most comfortable with. We ask participants to respond to the inventory in a way that best describes their natural tendencies and preferences.

Participants can be asked to total the number of items they circled in column A and column B of the BASS and to form two groups—one for those who had higher column A scores favoring a higher level of structure, and one for those who had higher column B scores favoring a lower level of structure. Participants in each group are asked to discuss why they preferred a higher or lower level of structure. They may also be asked to prepare for a debate with members of the other group about the benefits of their approach to structuring the work of the group.

FIGURE 4–5
Beliefs About Structure Scale

Circle the statement in Column A or B that best describes your preference when running a group.

Column A	Column B
Time-limited group	Open-ended group
High structure/rules	Low structure/rules
Formal contract	Informal contract
Leader sets group purpose	Members decide purpose
Focus on member goals	Focus on group process
Leader-centered authority	Shared authority
Closed membership	Open membership
Homogeneous membership	Heterogeneous membership
Use of program/exercises	Use of open discussion
Focus on member behavior	Focus on meaning of communication
Directive leadership	Nondirective leadership

Summarize what you have learned about your style from the above choices. What are the major themes that emerge about your preferences for a particular level of structure within a group?

We also ask participants to complete the How Members Achieve Change Scale, which is presented in Figure 4–6. Once this scale is completed, different approaches to helping members change are discussed. For example, the importance of insight in psychoanalytic group psychotherapy is contrasted with the importance of identifying here-and-now feelings in gestalt therapy. Similarly, the importance of cognitions in cognitive therapy is contrasted with the importance of action in behavior therapy. Participants can also be asked to provide examples of the methods they

FIGURE 4–6
How Members Achieve Change Scale

Group leadership style is partly a function of how one believes members achieve change in their lives and how one believes the group should take responsibility for helping members change. Answer the following questions about these dynamics. Avoid using the term *it all depends*. Instead, choose the answer that best expresses your natural preference or inclination.

1. Do people achieve change best through insight or action?

2. Do people achieve change best by focusing on their affect (feelings) or their cognition (thoughts)?

3. When helping a member to achieve change would you concentrate on changing the member's behavior or the member's thoughts?

4. When evaluating whether a member was making progress in the change efforts, would you assess whether the member did what the member wanted, what you wanted, or what society wanted?

5. Is it more important to give your attention to group content or group process?

6. Do you think the responsibility for the functioning of the group rests with the leader or the members?

Choose the statement that best characterizes your opinion. (circle one)

7. The purpose for group work is:
   a. Raising social consciousness, social responsibility, informed citizenship, social and political action.
   b. Restoring and rehabilitating group members who are behaving dysfunctionally.
   c. Forming a mutual aid system among members to achieve maximum adaptation and socialization.

8. The role of the worker is to be a:
   a. Role model and enabler for responsible citizenship.
   b. Change agent, problem solving with members to meet their goals.
   c. Mediator between the needs of the members and the needs of the group and larger society.

9. Which methods would you tend to use in the group:
   a. Discussion, participation, consensus, group task
   b. Structured exercises, direct influence in and out of group
   c. Shared authority, support, building a positive group culture

Based on your responses to the previous nine questions, summarize your preferences for how to help members change.

use to help members change. For example, participants who prefer to help group members change through action strategies might describe role playing or psychodrama procedures that they have found to be particularly effective.

We also discuss preferences for process-oriented vs. outcome-oriented leadership styles, and preferences for member-centered vs. leader-centered styles of leadership. This discussion is not intended to promote a particular style of leadership, or even to help leaders identify what style of leadership they are most comfortable with. Rather, our aim is to encourage leaders to become more self-reflective, to consider their natural tendencies and preferences, and to gain greater insight into how their natural tendencies and preferences affect how they interact with group members.

LEADERSHIP AND DIVERSITY

Group leaders often work with people with a wide range of backgrounds. Diversity within the group can be based on characteristics such as race, ethnicity, culture, national origin, religion, and social class, or based on gender, sexual preference, or disability. When differences exist among members or between the leader and members, leadership can be particularly challenging. It is helpful for leaders to develop a perspective on how to work with people whose experiences may be quite different from their own. Such a perspective has been referred to as ethnic-sensitive practice (Devore & Schlesinger, 1981), minority practice (Lum, 1992), or a cross-cultural approach (Green, 1982, Pinderhughes, 1979, Sue & Sue, 1990). A comprehensive and empirically based approach for working with racial, gender, and class issues in groups is presented by Davis and Proctor (1989).

To work effectively with group members from diverse backgrounds, a group leader should: (a) develop cultural sensitivity, (b) assess cultural influences on group behavior, and (c) intervene with sensitivity to diversity.

Developing Cultural Sensitivity

To develop a perspective from which to work effectively with people of diverse cultural backgrounds, the group leader should engage in a process of self-exploration relative to issues of diversity. Green (1982) describes this process as developing "ethnic competence" (pp. 53–59), and suggests that workers who want to achieve this perspective should have an awareness of their own cultural limitations, be open to cultural differences, and acknowledge the integrity of other cultures.

Leaders can begin the process of becoming more culturally sensitive by exploring feelings about their own culture and ethnicity. Sometimes leaders fail to take into account how they experience their own cultural background and how this might affect their interactions with members from other backgrounds. Among leaders and members alike, there may be little acknowledgment of one's cultural heritage and how it affects one's values, beliefs, and skills.

Leaders also need to acquire knowledge about other cultures. While it is hardly possible for a group leader to know all of the complexities of diverse cultures and backgrounds, it is possible to continually study other cultures. Green (1982) suggests that knowledge can be gained through several methods. For example, the leader can use the research literature, read important information, and develop a personal knowledge base about people from different cultures. When working with a group composed of members from a particular culture, the leader can visit that cultural community, interview key respondents in the community, and become a participant observer.

The leader can also gain knowledge about a particular cultural community through the process of "social mapping," where relationships among members of a community are systematically observed and analyzed. For example, an inexperienced leader assigned to conduct an after-school group that includes several Hispanic members visited the local parish priest serving the Hispanic community. The leader interviewed several members of the parish to gain a better understanding of the needs of young people in the community. In addition, the leader attended several social functions sponsored by the church and met other community members who provided the worker with new insights into the needs of Hispanic youth.

When the leader has little knowledge about a particular culture or background, it is very helpful to become immersed in that culture. Living in or spending a concentrated period of time in a cultural community can help the leader better understand the common values, norms of behavior, and world views held by members of that culture. Understanding these important concepts, and avoiding ethnocentric evaluations of differences in other cultures, is a helpful step in developing cultural sensitivity.

Leaders should be open to the differences exhibited by diverse cultures. It is particularly important for leaders to be accepting and nonjudgmental about the values, lifestyles, beliefs, and behaviors of others, and to recognize the value of difference. The leader can learn a great deal from group members from diverse backgrounds, since they are in the best position to share the realities of how they experience their culture, gender, sexual preference, disability, or other characteristics.

It is also important to acknowledge the effect of societal attitudes on members of minority groups. For example, the leader of an educational group for parents of developmentally disabled children might discuss the effect of societal attitudes toward the disabled, and the effects of discrimination on themselves and their disabled children. As members discuss this issue, the leader might encourage all members to share their experiences of other forms of discrimination based on ethnic/racial background. These experiences can help the whole group more fully understand the dynamics of discrimination. Leaders should keep in mind that members of minority groups continually experience prejudice, stereotyping, and overt and institutional discrimination. The reality of ethnic and racial superiority themes in our society, classism, sexism, and the history of depriving certain groups of rights and resources, all should be considered when attempting to develop a perspective on diversity.

Leaders should honestly explore their prejudices, biases, and stereotypical assumptions in working with people from diverse backgrounds. It is also necessary for the leader to acknowledge such thoughts and feelings and work on correcting them. Attending workshops on cultural sensitivity, doing self-inventories, researching one's own cultural heritage, attending specific cultural activities in the community, and joining cultural associations and organizations can help the leader achieve a fuller sense of cultural self-awareness. These activities can also help leaders gain a sense of their strengths and weaknesses in dealing with diversity. McGrath and Axelson (1993), for example, describe many useful exercises designed to increase leaders' awareness, knowledge, and sensitivity when working with multicultural groups.

Assessing Cultural Influences on Group Behavior

It is important for the group leader to recognize that the cultural backgrounds of members can have a profound effect on how they participate in the group. In planning for the group, the leader should consider how members from differing cultural groups are likely to relate to each other and to the leader. For example, because of their respect for the authority of the leader's status and position in the group, some Asian-Americans may rely heavily on the group leader, especially in the first few sessions. Some groups of Native Americans may consider opinion-giving in the group as impolite. Such behavior could be misinterpreted as resistance by the leader or by non-Native American members.

The group leader should consider how members from differing cultural backgrounds experience the group process. It is wise to keep in mind that members bring preferred patterns of behavior, values, and language to the group (Axelson, 1993). They also bring with them experiences with oppression, and particular feelings about themselves, their group identity, and the larger society. When problems such as member dissatisfaction or conflict among members occur, the leader should keep in mind that they may be due to cultural differences rather than to problems involving an individual member or flaws in the group processes.

A complete assessment of group members should consider the larger cultural context in which the members live, and how that context can influence behavior within the group (Chau, 1992). For example, in a group for resettled refugees, one of the members might have difficulty trusting and self-disclosing in the group. The leader might help that member verbalize what she experienced in her country of origin, which may have included torture, civil disorder, and fear. Through the discussion, the leader can develop a fuller perspective on how the member's behavior in the group has been influenced by the context of her cultural background.

There are many ways to approach learning about how cultural background affects members' behavior in the group, but several factors can interfere with the process. The leader may fail to recognize that cultural differences exist or may diminish their importance. Facing difference is a difficult process, and the leader may think emphasis on difference will cause conflict within the group. The leader may also fail to recognize differences among members of the same cultural group, and may assume that all members have common behavioral characteristics, thereby overgeneralizing and stereotyping members with a common cultural heritage. Among Hispanic-Americans, for example, there are wide differences in life experiences between people from a Mexican-American background and people from Puerto Rico. Similarly, there are differences between African-Americans with ancestry from different regions of Africa, and, for example, African-Americans with ancestry from Jamaica, Puerto Rico and South America. There are also great differences among Native Americans based on tribe, geographic location, and other historical factors.

It is also helpful for the leader to focus on important group dynamics, and assess how these dynamics may be differentially experienced by members with diverse backgrounds. The leader should assess how members' backgrounds are likely to affect the way they experience communication and interaction patterns, cohesion, social controls, and the overall group culture.

To assess communication and interaction patterns, it is important for the leader to understand the language, symbols, and nonverbal communication patterns of people from different cultural backgrounds. For example, in leading her first group with Native American members, a worker learned that group members from this cultural background felt uncomfortable with some of the attending behaviors she had learned in her social work education. Through some gentle probing, she learned that her direct eye contact, forward body position, and open body position were intimidating to some members.

Johnson (1993) suggests that assessing communication and interaction patterns requires language sensitivity, including knowledge of words and expressions that are appropriate and inappropriate in communicating with diverse groups. The leader should also have an awareness of the stylistic elements of communication, which include how members of diverse cultural backgrounds communicate.

The group leader should strive to become aware of the nuances of messages sent by members, including how nonverbal messages differ across various cultures. People from different backgrounds use body language, gestures, and expressions to accompany and define the meaning of the verbal messages they send. In addition, the leader should consider how cultural groups differ in their use of space, whether distance or closeness is the norm, and what other communication norms govern interaction in that culture. It is also helpful for leaders to learn the language of members from diverse cultures. Earnest attempts to learn even rudimentary language skills are often respected by group members. This in turn, can be an important factor in developing a trusting, professional helping relationship with members.

The leader should be aware of differing interaction patterns used by members of diverse cultural groups. Members from some cultural backgrounds may favor a member-to-leader pattern of interaction, while others may easily adapt to a member-to-member pattern that supports mutual aid among members in the group. In task groups, members from diverse groups may have differing views on status hierarchies, and this can affect interaction patterns between members and the leader. For example, in a committee planning a charity fund-raising event, Chinese-American members hesitated to criticize the behavior of a member who was monopolizing the group. The leader learned that the Chinese-American members were hesitant to bring up their feelings because the monopolizing member was a person of advanced age and status in the community. According to their cultural heritage, interactions with older, high-status persons required respect. Criticism was not an acceptable behavior.

When the group has a membership drawn from many cultural groups, the leader should assess how subgrouping patterns will affect the processes of the group. Sociometric patterns can be influenced by cultural background, and this information is useful in assessing the behavior of members in the group as well as the behavior of the group as a whole. In a training group for college peer counselors, some of the members expressed their concerns about why most of the African-American members sat together and communicated among themselves. The leader pointed out that cultural, racial, and ethnic groups often form informal subgroups, based on mutual interests as well as on common characteristics and experiences. The leader helped members to understand how members from minority groups on campus might also have a need for grouping as a protective, security-giving behavior.

The worker should consider how members of diverse groups bring differing expectations and motivations to the group. Group cohesion can be influenced by member expectations, which are often influenced by the cultural background of members. In a support group for caregivers, for example, some members with Hispanic backgrounds may not expect to divulge private family matters, or publicly complain about their role as caregivers, and this may affect how they bond with other group members and experience group cohesion. Where the cultural characteristics of members differ widely, a climate of togetherness and a common sense of group goals may be difficult to achieve, thus affecting the overall cohesion of the group.

The leader should explore how members' cultural characteristics can affect their views of norms, roles, status, and power within the group. Group norms are often the result of the expectations members bring to the group from previous experiences. The leader should assess how members' cultural backgrounds influence the norms that are developed in the group. Members' role expectations, developed within their particular cultural context, will often guide their role behavior within the group. Gender-specific role expectations, for example, may be prominent among some Asian-Americans, Hispanic-Americans, and other particular ethnic groups such as Italian-Americans or Irish-Americans. Thus, the leader should also consider how members' culture influences their role expectations.

The worker should be sensitive to how members from diverse backgrounds experience power and control within the group. Many members from minority groups have had direct experience with oppression, discrimination, and prejudice, and this can affect how members feel about the use of power within the group. The leader should understand that these experiences are likely to influence how some members may deal with power and control. The leader should ensure that patterns of discrimination will not be repeated within the group.

The worker should also assess how the cultural backgrounds of members contribute to the overall group culture. The common ideas, beliefs, and values of the group are, in part, a reflection of what individual members bring to the group experience. The group culture can include, for example, a heightened sense of spirituality when the group is composed of Native Americans or Hispanic-Americans. The strengths of some cultural backgrounds can reinforce other important aspects of group culture. In a caregivers group composed of African-Americans, the cultural strength of the extended family as a natural helping network can help create a group culture of networking and mutual aid among members.

The level of group feeling and the group morale may also be a function of the cultural context of the group's members. In a group composed of Hispanic-Americans, one might expect the expression of a higher level of group feelings and emotions than in a group composed of Asian-Americans. In the latter group, members may believe strong expressions of emotion are not appropriate.

Assessing the cultural influences on group behavior requires constant vigilance throughout the life of a group. Diversity among members from differing cultural backgrounds, as well as among members from the same cultural background, requires careful consideration. Stereotyping members based on preconceived notions of how they will behave is an ineffective approach. Members must be individualized and differentially assessed. As Chau (1992) suggests, cultural sensitivity in assessing members is a prerequisite for becoming an effective group leader.

Intervening with Sensitivity to Diversity

There are many ways for a group leader to intervene with sensitivity to issues of diversity in the group. Such considerations can help the group maximize the advantages of diversity and minimize the disadvantages. These include (a) using social work values and skills, (b) using a strengths perspective, (c) exploring common and different experiences among members, (d) exploring meanings and language, (e) challenging prejudice and discrimination, (f) advocating for members, and (g) using culturally appropriate techniques and program activities.

Using Social Work Values and Skills.   Developing a culturally sensitive approach to group leadership means using social work values to guide interventions. The values of being nonjudgmental, genuine, and accepting can often compensate for wide differences in cultural backgrounds between the leader and member. Effective communication skills can also make a big difference. For example, good questioning skills, which stress open, nonjudgmental questions, can encourage members to respond in their own cultural styles. Similarly, the leader should be aware that for listening skills to be effective, they should be tailored to the cultural background of members. For example, a leader in a group for substance abusers used active listening skills with a Native American member, often paraphrasing and summarizing the content of the member's statements. When the member's participation became less frequent, the leader realized that his frequent paraphrasing was interpreted as being impolite. Recognizing this, the leader used passive listening skills, which conveyed to the member that he was being heard. Depending on the cultural style of the member, the leader may use active listening skills for some members and passive listening skills for others.

Using a Strengths Perspective.   The leader should explore and use the strengths inherent in the cultural backgrounds of members. All cultures have characteristic strengths which can be tapped as a source of empowerment for members. For example, in a group for adults who care for relatives with Alzheimer's disease, the leader discussed the strong natural helping networks of several African-American members, and how these networks might support the efforts of the caregivers. The African-American members were able to recognize these networks as resources, and make use of them for respite care for their relatives. Other members realized that they could explore this arrangement as well, and this contributed to the overall success of the group.

In the same group, a Hispanic member was criticized by one member for passively accepting the sole responsibility for caregiving in the family. The leader intervened, stressing that the role of caregiver was a culturally assigned one, usually given to a female in the household. The leader pointed out that commitment to the care of family members was viewed as a strength in the Hispanic culture. Other group members agreed with the leader's perspective. The Hispanic member became more active in the group as a result of this intervention, because she believed that her cultural heritage had been acknowledged in a positive fashion.

Exploring Common and Different Experiences Among Members.

In working with members from diverse backgrounds it is often useful to acknowledge the differences that exist in the group. There is also value in exploring the experiences that members may have in common. This process can begin by acknowledging diversity in the group and exploring how the cultural backgrounds of members may contribute to that diversity. For example, in a grief therapy group for parents who have experienced the death of a child, the leader began by self-disclosing that she was of Irish-American background. She explained that in her family, death was characteristically dealt with by planning large family gatherings that sometimes took on a festive atmosphere. She also acknowledged that it may be particularly difficult for Irish-American men to verbally express their grief. The members used this opportunity to explore their own cultural reactions to death and grieving, noting how different cultures express their feelings about death. The worker's initial disclosure helped the group deal with difficult issues held in common by the members.

Exploring common and different experiences can also help overcome barriers to member self-disclosure. Members are sometimes reluctant to disclose when they believe others might be judgmental about their cultural values, behavior, and lifestyle. Exploring cultural differences and fostering cultural appreciation can help members feel more secure in disclosing their thoughts and feelings. For example, in a support group for parents, it may be particularly difficult for members from certain backgrounds to share intimate details of their family life. Such matters may be considered private, to be discussed only among close family members. The worker can acknowledge this and help members show sensitivity toward someone who may not self-disclose as readily as others.

The leader can also model the skill of empathy for members, which, in turn, can increase their responsiveness to differences. Helping members develop empathy allows them to more fully comprehend the experiences that result from diverse life-styles.

Exploring Meanings and Language.   Meaning is expressed through language. Many cultures do not attach common meanings to certain phenomena such as social problems or medical diseases. There may be no clear equivalent in the Spanish language, for example, for some psychiatric diagnoses. Likewise, an illness such as Alzheimer's disease may be defined in Spanish using nonmedical terms. The leader should help group members explore the differences in meaning reflected in different languages.

It is also helpful for the leader to help members interpret the significance of certain aspects of their culture to other members. In some instances, members may not understand the reasoning behind a cultural practice or phenomenon, and this can lead to criticism or insensitivity among members. For example, in a rehabilitation group for spine-injured people, a member from Central America noted that he had visited the local Currandero, who has prescribed native herbs and other remedies. The initial reaction of several members was to discount this practice and accuse the member of going outside of the traditional medical establishment. However, the leader and member explained the importance of folk medicine in the member's culture, and how the local healer has contributed to the member's mental and physical well-being. Members learned the importance of this cultural practice and its significance for the member. They also realized that members in the group may have other important sources of folk healing that have gone unrecognized.

Similarly, spirituality may contribute significantly to the well-being of members from diverse cultures. It is important to acknowledge the importance of spirituality for particular members of a group, and explain its significance to other members who may not be aware of its importance. Group workers sometimes ignore spirituality because of the mistaken belief that it is linked to a specific religious denomination. However, spirituality transcends organized religions and can be an important influence on the lives of group members.

Challenging Prejudice and Discrimination.   For members of diverse cultures, the realities of prejudice and discrimination can be heightened in a group. Some members may deny their individual biases, prejudices, or stereotypes, and it is important for the leader to challenge them to more realistically understand how they feel about people who are different from themselves. For example, in a coalition planning a homeless shelter, several of the younger members discounted or ignored the suggestions made by older members. The leader asked all members to discuss how differences in the group might inhibit the group's work. After discussing what she had observed in the group, the leader helped the younger members confront their prejudices about the older members and the group became more cohesive and goal-oriented.

It is also important for the leader to help members understand the discrimination that members from some cultural groups may have experienced in their communities, in employment, or in other circumstances. Experiences with discrimination can shape members' attitudes and behaviors, and the leader can help all members acknowledge this phenomenon and understand how it can affect the group. In a mixed group, the leader can ask each member to identify a situation in which they felt discriminated against and to discuss this with other group members. When nonminority members can identify such experiences, they are more able to appreciate the experiences of others in dealing with discrimination.

Advocating for Members.   In working with people from different backgrounds, the group leader may advocate for members in situations outside the group. Group members may need assistance in negotiating difficult service systems, or may need the provision of benefits and services to be an effective group member. In a parenting skills group, for example, the leader became concerned about the absence of several Hispanic members. In investigating the reasons for their absence, she noted that these group members felt guilty about leaving their child-care duties to attend group sessions. The leader advocated for the members and secured the support of her agency in providing child care at the agency during group meetings. Members felt that they could more regularly attend and their commitment and bond to the parenting group was greatly enhanced. Leaders may also need to consider other advocacy activities for group members, including work with other family members, community support systems, and other organizations that can meet the needs of group members.

Using Culturally Appropriate Techniques and Program Activities.
Developing culturally sensitive skills in intervention can be fostered by reviewing specialized formats reported in the literature for groups composed of members from specific cultures. Chau (1992), for example, suggests that group interventions should be directed at helping members enhance ethnic consciousness and pride, develop ethnic resource bases and sources of power, and develop leadership potential. Pearson (1991) suggests that leadership skills need to reflect a more structured approach for some Asian and Asian-American people. To adopt a traditional Western style, with less structure and reliance on members to take responsibility for group interactions, would cause discomfort for these members. Gutierrez and Ortega (1991) report the success of ethnic identity groups and consciousness-raising groups in empowering Latinos, and Lopez (1991) suggests that structured activity groups, where members work together on tasks, can be helpful for Hispanic youth. Lewis and Ford (1990) describe how group leaders can help African-American group members use social networks, incorporating traditional strengths of African-American families into group work practice. Ashby, Gilchrist, and Miramontez (1987) demonstrate how incorporating traditional Native American "talking circles" into group meetings can be effective in group work with Native American adolescents.

There are numerous special formats that incorporate elements of culture into the group work experience. Leaders can learn some of these specialized, culturally appropriate forms of group work and incorporate them into their practice. A necessary prerequisite for using culturally appropriate interventions is the development of cultural sensitivity and the assessment of members in their cultural context.

CO-LEADERSHIP

Co-leadership presents a dilemma for the practicing group worker (Kolodny, 1980). Do the benefits of co-leadership exceed its potential disadvantages? An entire issue of the journal *Social Work with Groups* has been devoted to this topic.[1] Although there is little empirical evidence to suggest that two leaders are better than one (Yalom, 1985), there are many clinical reports of the benefits of having two leaders (see, for example, Cooper, 1976; Davis & Lohr, 1971; Levine, 1980; MacLennon, 1965; McGee & Schuman, 1970; Schlenoff & Busa, 1981; Starak, 1981).

Among the most frequently cited benefits of co-leadership are the following:

- Leaders have a source of support.
- Leaders have a source of feedback and an opportunity for professional development.
- A leader's objectivity is increased through alternative frames of references.
- Inexperienced leaders can receive training.
- Group members are provided with models for appropriate communication, interaction, and resolution of disputes.
- Leaders have assistance during therapeutic interventions, particularly during role plays, simulations, and program activities.
- Leaders have help setting limits and structuring the group experience.

The above list suggests several ways in which co-leadership can be helpful. For the novice worker, probably the greatest benefit of co-leadership is having a supportive partner who understands how difficult it is to be an effective leader. As Galinsky and Schopler (1980) point out, "The support of a compatible co-leader lessens the strains of dealing with difficult and often complicated group interactions" (p. 54). During group meetings, co-leaders help each other facilitate the work of the group. In between group meetings, they share their feelings about the group and their roles in it. In addition to supporting each other's efforts at group leadership, co-leaders can share feedback with each other about their mutual strengths and weaknesses, thereby fostering each other's professional growth and development.

Co-leadership can also be helpful because it allows workers to share alternative frames of reference regarding the interaction that has taken place in the group. These help fill in gaps in each worker's memory of events and helps each view the interaction from a different perspective. This, in turn, may lead to a more complete and accurate assessment as well as to more adequate planning when preparing for future group meetings.

Another area in which co-leadership has potential benefits is in intervening in a group. Co-leadership provides a group with the benefit of having two experts who can help in problem solving. It provides two models of behavior for members to identify with, and helps in role plays, simulation, and program activities engaged in by the group. Co-leadership can increase workers' abilities to establish and enforce limits as long as they share common goals (Davis & Lohr, 1971).

---

[1] *Social Work with Groups*, Vol. 3, No. 4, is devoted to the topic of co-leadership.

Co-leaders also have the opportunity to structure their roles to meet the needs of members. For example, one worker can focus on members' socio-emotional needs while the other worker can focus on members' task needs.

Despite these benefits co-leadership has some potential disadvantages. Because it requires the time of two leaders, co-leadership is expensive. Leaders must coordinate their actions in planning for the group. Between group sessions, communication can be a problem if workers do not make a concerted effort to find the time to discuss their work together (Herzog, 1980). If leaders do not function well together, they may not serve as therapeutic role models for members (Davis & Lohr, 1971). Yalom (1985) recommends that co-leaders have equal status and experience. He suggests that the apprenticeship format—that is, training new group leaders by placing them in groups with experienced leaders—may create conflict and tension.

Conflict between co-leaders can have detrimental effects on the outcome of a group (Cooper, 1976; Yalom, 1985). Members may be able to play one leader against the other, or avoid working on difficult issues. When co-leaders experience conflict with one another, we have found that it can be helpful to resolve the conflict in the group. This lets members know that the leaders are aware of the conflict and are able to work together to resolve it. Workers also act as models, demonstrating appropriate conflict resolution strategies.

Galinsky and Schopler (1980) caution that, in some situations, it may not be helpful to resolve a conflict between co-leaders in the group. Certainly, members should not be drawn into a conflict. It is not a good idea to express conflict in early group meetings because this may add to the tensions that members are experiencing (Yalom, 1985). The decision about whether to resolve a conflict in a group should depend on its potential effect on members. Because members are usually aware of a conflict, it may be preferable to resolve it within the group, especially if it is not too distressing. When conflict is resolved outside of the group, some members may not be aware that this has occurred. Also, resolving a conflict outside the group does not enhance members' conflict resolution skills. For additional information about conflict resolution see Chapters 8 and 10.

Because of the lack of empirical evidence about its effectiveness, the benefits and drawbacks of co-leadership should be carefully considered before two leaders are used in a group. In situations where it is especially important to have models who represent different points of view, it may be important to have co-leaders. For example, in a group of couples it might be useful to have male and female co-leaders. In other situations, however, the expense of co-leadership, or the incompatibility of potential co-leaders, may negate any potential benefits.

When the decision is reached to co-lead a group, it is essential that co-leaders meet together regularly both to plan for the group and to discuss group process issues that arise as the group develops (Davis & Lohr, 1971). To avoid co-leaders becoming too busy to meet together, it is helpful if they schedule a specific time to meet after each group meeting. During these meetings, co-leaders should review what they did well in working together, what difficulties they experienced, how they plan to work together during the next meeting, and how members and the group as a whole are progressing. Co-leaders should be particularly aware of any attempts to divide their effort so that they are working toward different purposes, or on behalf of two different group factions. We recommend that co-leaders schedule their review meeting soon after a meeting because they are more likely to remember what has occurred, and they have more time to prepare for the next meeting.

To avoid the difficulties that may be associated with co-leadership, it is recommended that co-leaders should feel at ease with one another's leadership style (Yalom, 1985). According to Davis and Lohr (1971), co-leaders should be selected for their complementary characteristics rather than for their similarity. This helps broaden the perspective used to assess the group and its members. It also provides an additional model of ways to handle problematic behaviors and widens the scope of intervention strategies that may be used in the group.

In our experience in leading groups and supervising students who have led groups, we have found that it is worse to have a co-leader with whom you do not agree than to lead a group by yourself. Therefore, group workers should be cautious in choosing a co-leader. Difficulties may arise when workers agree to co-lead a group without carefully considering whether they can work together effectively. Potential co-leaders may want to examine each other's styles while leading a group or during team meetings, before agreeing to co-lead a group. Figure 4–7 presents some issues to discuss before deciding to co-lead a group.

FIGURE 4–7
Some things to talk over with a potential co-leader

1. Describe your leadership style. Discuss whether your style is characteristically nurturing or confrontational, whether you tend to be a high-profile or a low-profile leader, and to what extent you are comfortable with spontaneity as contrasted with sticking with a planned agenda.

2. Describe your strengths and weaknesses as a leader. What makes you feel uncomfortable when leading a group?

3. Describe your beliefs about how people change and grow, and how you will intervene in the group. For example, discuss your favorite interventions, and whether you typically intervene quickly or slowly, waiting for members of the group to engage in mutual aid.

4. Share your expectations for group accomplishments.

5. Discuss your respective roles in the group. Discuss specifically: (a) where you will sit, (b) starting and ending group meetings, (c) how you will divide responsibility for any content you will be presenting, (d) what you will do about talkative and silent members, (e) scapegoating and gatekeeping, and (f) what you will do about lateness and absenteeism.

6. Discuss where, when, and how you will deal with conflict between you, and between either of you and the members of the group.

7. Discuss how you will deal with strong expressions of emotion such as crying and anger.

8. Is there anything that is non-negotiable regarding your co-leadership of a group?

SUMMARY

This chapter focuses on leading task and treatment groups effectively. Although leadership is sometimes viewed as a function exclusively executed by the worker, leadership functions should be shared with group members. In this regard, we distinguish between the worker's role as the designated leader of the group and the leadership roles of group members that emerge as the group develops.

Leadership has been defined as the process of guiding the development of the group and its members to achieve goals that are consistent with the value base of social work practice. A worker's ability to guide group members depends on the power attributed to the worker by group members as well as by the agency or organization and the larger society that sanction the work of the group.

The power bases that can be used to guide the development of the group and its members include: (a) connection power, (b) expert power, (c) information power, (d) legitimate power, (e) referent power, (f) reward power, and (g) coercive power. Leaders vary in the degree to which they have access to each of these power bases and the extent to which they use them to guide the group.

Leadership is affected by a variety of situational factors that act in combination. Thus, there is no one correct way to lead all groups. Rather, leadership methods should vary depending on the particular group a worker is leading. This chapter reviews the remedial, social goals, and reciprocal models of group leadership and examines several variables that affect group leadership.

To help workers examine situational variables, an interactional model of group leadership is described. This model includes (a) the purpose of the group, (b) the type of problem the group is working on, (c) the environment in which the group is working, (d) the group as a whole, (e) the members of the group, and (f) the leader of the group.

It is essential that workers be familiar with a range of leadership skills that can be applied in many different types of groups, and in many different settings. These include skills in (a) facilitating group processes, (b) data gathering and assessment, and (c) action. Together, they form the core skills needed for the effective leadership of task and treatment groups.

It is also essential that workers be aware of their leadership style. A number of exercises are presented to help workers identify their preference for a particular leadership style and how this influences their practice with treatment and task groups.

The issue of leadership and diversity is discussed, with suggestions for how the group leader can develop a perspective on diversity from which to work effectively with members with various backgrounds. The chapter ends with an examination of the benefits and drawbacks of co-leadership.

LEARNING ASSIGNMENTS

1. Observe two leaders. Using Table 4–1, describe these leaders' use of facilitating, data gathering, and action skills. Compare and contrast the skillfulness of each leader.

2. Complete the inventories shown in Figures 4–4, 4–5, and 4–6. Prepare a written description of what you learn about your leadership style.

3. Compare your leadership style with that of a classmate using your responses to Figures 4–4, 4–5, 4–6, and 4–7. How would the similarities and differences in your leadership styles affect your ability to co-lead a group? How would you work together to overcome differences in leadership styles before co-leading a group?

4. Go to the library and find three articles on working with a specific ethnic/racial group. Extract and summarize five practice principles that would help you facilitate a group composed of individuals from this ethnic/racial group.

5. Form a small group. Have each member of the group, in turn, describe his or her ethnic background. Go around the group again and have each member describe how his or her ethnic heritage might influence his or her participation in a group. Ask members of the group who do not strongly identify with a particular ethnic heritage to describe how their psychosocial development influences their behavior in groups.

PART II

The Planning Stage

Chapter 5: The Planning Stage

CHAPTER 5

The Planning Stage

The planning stage of group work marks the beginning of the worker's involvement in the group endeavor. Planning precedes those important first encounters that take place when the worker and group members meet for the first time. This chapter deals with what is referred to in the literature as pre-group planning. Specifically, it considers all the worker's actions directed toward forming the group.

The planning process has two distinct parts. The first is directed at forming the group, the aspect with which this chapter is primarily concerned. The second part of planning includes the ongoing adjustments and forward-looking arrangements that are made by the leader and the members as the group progresses through its beginning, middle, and ending stages.

In forming the group, the worker focuses on the individual member, the group as a whole, and the environment. In focusing on individual members, the worker considers each person's motivations, expectations, and goals for entering the group. The worker focuses on the group as a whole by considering the purpose for the group and how the group may develop as a result of the members' interaction. The worker also focuses on the environment in which the group will function by considering the likely influence on the group of the sponsoring organization, the community, and the larger society.

The second aspect of planning is carried on throughout the life of the group. During the beginning stage, the worker and the members plan in more detail how to accomplish the overall group purpose. The worker carries out detailed assessments of individual members of the group. These assessments lead to additional planning activities in the middle and ending stages of the group. For example, in treatment groups, the worker and the members engage in an ongoing assessment of the extent to which the group is helping members accomplish their goals. This, in turn, leads to the refinement, adjustment, and reformulation of treatment plans and to recontracting with individual members for modified treatment goals.

In task groups, the worker uses data collected during assessments to formulate procedures for accomplishing the group's work, such as developing session agendas, dividing labor and responsibility, and determining methods to be used in making decisions and solving problems. Information about this progressive aspect of the planning process is included in subsequent chapters.

Although this chapter emphasizes the need for pre-group planning, there are many instances in which the worker's ability to plan a group is constrained. It is not uncommon, for example, for the recruitment process to yield a pool of potential group members that is large enough to form only a single group. In this case, a worker faces the choice of accepting all applicants, delaying the group for additional recruitment, or screening out some applicants and beginning a group with few members. It is also not uncommon for workers to inherit leadership of existing groups, or to form a single group from all clients of a particular program or residential setting.

The planning of task groups may also be constrained for a variety of reasons. For example, recruitment may be constrained by organizational bylaws, or dictated by administrative structure. Thus, the members of a delegate council may be selected by the organizations who are represented by the council. Despite constraints, workers still have the responsibility to think carefully about how they will guide the group's development to ensure that it is productive and that it provides a satisfying experience for members. Workers should plan for the group as carefully as possible within any existing constraints. Such planning helps avoid unanticipated difficulties in later group development and helps foster the achievement of positive group and member outcomes.

Elements of Treatment Group Planning

As illustrated in Table 5–1 (pp. 146–147), a number of models for planning treatment groups have been reported in the literature, and several elements of these models are similar. One of the most important is establishing a group's purpose. Almost all the models stress the importance of group purpose. Most models also mention the importance of a group's sponsoring agency and environment, stressing the worker actions needed for a good fit between the group and the agency.

Most writers also mention assessing member characteristics so the group can be composed in a planned fashion. Differences exist among writers about how much emphasis to place on systematic member selection, and some writers emphasize such issues as group procedures, group size, and the number and frequency of meetings, whereas others devote relatively little attention to these elements.

Elements of Task Group Planning

Table 5–2 (p. 148) compares selected planning elements for some of the types of task groups discussed in Chapter 1. One common element is the need for planning group goals. Almost all writers identify this element of planning as important. The emphasis on goals in task groups corresponds to the importance of determining group purposes in treatment group planning. A second element commonly mentioned is planning for task group membership so that the necessary resources and levels of expertise are built into the group. A third element is preparing for meetings. Most writers suggest extensive use of program materials, specific meeting activities and procedures, and the use of a meeting agenda. Pre-meeting planning activities receive more emphasis in task group planning than in treatment group planning.

PLANNING MODEL FOR GROUP WORK

The rest of this chapter is devoted to explicating a model of planning that can be used for both treatment and task groups. This model includes the following:

1. Establishing the group's purpose.
2. Assessing the potential sponsorship and membership of the group.
3. Recruiting members.
4. Composing the group.
5. Orienting members to the group.
6. Contracting.
7. Preparing the group's environment.

The planning model describes an orderly set of procedures to guide workers. In actual practice, however, workers may not plan for the group in a step-by-step fashion. Instead, the worker may find that it is necessary to engage in several aspects of planning at the same time. For example, recruiting, contracting, and preparing the environment can occur simultaneously. Similarly, determining purpose and assessing potential membership can sometimes be done together.

Also, carrying out one step may influence how another step is handled. For example, in assessing the potential membership of a committee, the worker may realize that a budget item for travel is required for certain members of the group. Thus, the information gained in carrying out one procedure (assessing membership) influences action taken in another (preparing the group's environment).

Establishing the Group's Purpose

The first and most important question that can be asked about a proposed group is, "What is the group's purpose?" A statement of the purpose should be broad enough to encompass different individual goals, yet specific enough to define the common nature of the group's purpose. According to Shulman (1992) and Klein (1972), a clear statement of purpose helps members answer the question, "What are we doing here together?" It can help prevent a lack of direction that can be frustrating to group members and lead to an unproductive group experience.

A brief statement of the group's purpose generally includes information on the problems or issues the group is designed to address, the range of individual and group goals to be accomplished, and how individual members and the group as a whole might work together.

Some examples of statements of purpose follow:

- The group will provide a forum for discussing parenting skills, where each member can bring up specific issues about being a parent and receive feedback from other group members.
- The group will study the problem of domestic violence in our community, and each member will contribute to a final task force report on how to address the issue.
- The group will review and assess all proposals for improving services to youth from minority communities and decide what projects to fund.

TABLE 5-1
Models for planning treatment groups

Author	Planning Process	Selected Planning Concerns
Bertcher & Maple (1977)	Group creation and modification	Identify and define common client problems; specify preliminary group objectives; determine critical attributes of potential members and group attributes; obtain information on critical attributes for each potential member; interview client; select tentative group members; obtain members' commitment to group objectives.
Brown (1991)	Pre-group planning	Reasons to form groups; who should be in groups; group composition; dealing with resistance; referrals and recruitment; conditions for group meetings; conditions for preparing group members; leadership preparation.
Garvin (1987)	Pre-group phase	Establishing group purposes; group composition; preparing for group meetings.
Hartford (1971)	Private pre-group phase Public pre-group phase Convening phase	Clarify group's role with sponsoring body; spell out service objectives; justify group work as method of choice; determine composition; assess duration, frequency, and number of meetings; set feasible time limitation; consider location; determine open or closed nature of membership; examine worker's work response in relation to all of these aspects.

Henry (1992)	Initial stage	Initial idea for the group; purpose for the group; composition; pre-group interview.
Kurland (1978, 1982)	Group formation	Need; purpose; composition; structure; content; pre-group contact; agency context.
Reid (1991)	Conception	Idea for the group; recruitment strategies; pre-group interview; the what, why, who, where, and when of the group.
Sarri & Galinsky (1985)	Origin phase	Size of the group; members' characteristics and initial orientations; environmental location of the group.
Schwartz (1976)	Tuning in	Preliminary empathy; anticipating possibilities and rehearsing expectations; generalizing and partializing data; preliminary contracting.
Shulman (1992)	Group formation	Working with staff; group composition, timing and structure; working with prospective members.
Tropp (1976)	Group formation	Organizational auspice; identification of population; type of group and nature of the participants; form of the group—i.e., size of group; number, length, and frequency of sessions; time and place.
Vinter (1985a)	Treatment sequence	Intake, diagnosis, and treatment planning; group composition considerations; preparing for group meetings.
Zastrow (1985)	Intake and selection of members	Viability of group; agreement about goals; group composition.

TABLE 5–2
Models for planning task groups

Author	Planning Process	Selected Planning Concerns
Brilhart (1974)	Preparation (discussion groups)	Planning an agenda; notifying discussants; planning the pattern for guiding the discussion of each problem; making resource materials available; making clear what is expected of each participant; arranging the physical setting.
Brown (1952)	Goal setting and planning (committees)	Selecting group goals; discovering resources; selecting activities; building a general plan.
Ephross & Vassil (1988)	Pre-group phase	Choosing members and having them agree to participate; formulating group purposes; outlining the group's charge; clarifying expectations of members, the staff, and the organization; clarifying benefits of membership; conducting pre-group interviews.
League of Women Voters Education Fund (1977)	Establishing planning committees (conferences, delegate councils)	Arrangements; program content; recruitment; finance; secretary; kits; printing; publicity; follow-up.
Pincus & Minahan (1973)	Forming action systems (action systems, teams)	Determining ideal size of action system; composition; operating procedures.
Trecker (1980)	Planning principles (administrative groups)	Composition and member background; defining and understanding group purpose; achieving group interdependence; balance; organization; planning meetings; evaluation.
Tropman (1977)	Elements of planning (committees)	Goal determination; program development; program implementation; program planning.

Such statements are broad, but they provide information that will help members understand the nature of the group endeavor. As will be seen in Chapter 6, the members of the group will usually discuss and clarify the group's purpose in early group sessions, producing more specific aims and goals through their interaction with each other and with the worker. It is, nonetheless, helpful for the worker to prepare for these early discussions by anticipating questions that members might raise, identifying potential agenda items, clarifying the role that the members and the worker will play in the group, and identifying potential obstacles to effective group functioning.

The purpose of a group can frequently be clarified by considering how the idea for establishing the group was generated. The idea can come from several sources, such as the group worker, agency staff members, potential clients, or the larger community. Frequently, a worker will detect an unmet need for service or a population that might be underserved in an agency. In other cases, the worker collects data to verify a need for service or to identify a particular problem to be solved, and uses this information as a basis for defining the purpose of a group. Staff members can also begin the process of planning for a group by suggesting that certain clients or certain tasks of the agency might best be served in a group. Potential group members can suggest that their personal needs or their need to accomplish certain tasks might best be handled in a group. Similarly, community leaders might identify a need they would like to see addressed. The following examples illustrate how ideas for groups are generated.

Group-Worker Generated

- The worker proposes an educational group for children, based on the worker's perception of the need for adolescent sex education.
- The worker proposes an advising delegate council in a hospital, based on a survey of workers' job satisfaction, which indicates the need for better communication among professional departments.

Agency-Staff Generated

- Several agency caseworkers, concerned with rising rates of family violence, suggest that clients from their caseloads participate in a remedial group for child abusers.
- The chairperson of the agency board of directors requests that a committee be established to study and suggest alternative sources of funding for the agency.

Member Generated

- The parents of children in a day-care center request a series of educational group meetings to discuss concerns about their children's behavior at home.
- Several clients receiving subsidized housing suggest to the director of the agency that a social action group be formed to combat poor housing conditions in a neighborhood.

Community Generated

- A group of Baptist ministers representing community churches approach a community center about developing an after-school program for children of the working poor.
- A coalition of community groups requests a meeting with the administrator of a community center to explore ways to reach out to young people before they are recruited by gangs.

Assessing Potential Sponsorship and Membership

Though assessment of potential sponsorship and membership for the group might be seen as separate, in reality, the agency and its clients are intrinsically linked. The worker must assess both the sponsoring agency and the potential membership base to plan for the group. Agency sponsorship determines the level of support and resources available to the group. The assessment of potential membership helps the worker make an early estimate of the group's potential viability.

Assessing Potential Sponsorship

In Chapter 1, it was noted that group work is carried out in conjunction with a system of service delivery, such as a social service agency. The nature of the sponsoring organization, its mission, objectives, resources, and clientele have a significant effect on the formation of the group. Hartford (1971) suggests that the purpose, focus, goals, and sanctions of the group service are conditioned by the setting and the clientele. Wilson and Ryland (1980) also emphasize the effect of the sponsoring organization, particularly on its task groups, noting that, "whatever is defined as the purpose of the agency has a direct bearing on the decision-making process within the agency's constituent groups" (p. 172). Most group work writers mention the importance of the sponsoring organization, but few discuss this in as great detail as Garvin (1987), who points out how conditions within an organization affect group functioning. For example, treatment groups rely on agency administrators and staff for sanctions, financial support, member referrals, and physical facilities for the group. Similarly, task groups are intrinsically linked to the functioning of their sponsoring agencies and must continually refer to the agency's policies for clarification of their task, charge, and mandate.

In assessing an organization as sponsor for the group, the worker should pay careful attention to the fit between the organization's policies and goals and the purpose of the proposed group. The proposed group should fit within the overall operating goals of the organization. If the group represents a new form of service, or suggests a problem area or a population that has not been the focus of the potential sponsor, the worker will have to be prepared to justify the request to begin a group.

It is important to recognize that the worker's assessment of the sponsoring organization is carried out not only to determine the overall level of support for the proposed group service, but also to garner any additional support that may be needed to begin the group. Abramson (1983) has pointed out that it is essential to identify key areas of interest and perceived need within the entire organizational "community." She suggests that it is often helpful to meet with line staff and program administrators to obtain their ideas about the need for a particular group service. In interdisciplinary settings, it is important to test the idea for a new group service beyond social work staff. The idea for a new group service should be presented to staff from other disciplines, highlighting common perceptions of unmet needs, and pointing out how the new group service could support and enhance the work of other disciplines. This process has the added benefit of breaking down interdisciplinary competition, fostering a sense of mutual mission, and developing a bond with staff on whom the new group program will ultimately depend for referrals.

The worker may also wish to carry out a needs assessment or gather data to document unmet needs. Administrators and boards of directors may be particularly interested in the costs and potential benefits of the proposed group service. A brief review of similar group work efforts can help clarify the possible costs or benefits associated with proposing a particular group program. In other situations, an organization may decide to offer the group service on a trial basis while conducting a cost analysis, such as that described in Chapter 12.

It is also very helpful to gather support for the idea for a new group service from the larger community. This can be done by encouraging consumers within a geographic region to express their interest in a new group service, or by urging community leaders and others who have influence within community social service organizations to express their interest in and support for the new service. At the same time, the relevance of the proposed group program to the sponsoring organization's mission, and the visibility it could bring to the organization should be highlighted.

In some instances, the potential sponsoring organization may decide the proposed group is not central enough to its core mission. In a county-funded rape crisis center, for example, the worker may propose a group service for battered women who have been victims of family violence but who have not been raped. Such an expansion of services, although appropriate and related to the agency's purpose, may be viewed as beyond the scope of the agency's mission, beyond staff resources, or not reimbursable within the agency's current funding sources.

When workers encounter a lack of support or resistance to a proposed group service, they should determine whether the proposal could be modified to increase support and alleviate the concerns that have been expressed, or whether a different sponsor should be sought. For example, with the previously mentioned domestic violence group, the worker might work with supervisors and other administrators within the agency to highlight the need for the group and to seek additional funding for the service. Alternatively, the worker might decide to explore the idea for the group service with a family service agency or a community center that has expressed interest in providing service for domestic violence victims.

When assessing potential sponsorship it is also important to (a) identify the extent to which a resolution of the problem or issue addressed by the group is valued by the sponsor, (b) identify and include staff whose support will be crucial to the implementation of the program in the planning process, (c) identify and resolve any differences in perspective among staff that may lead to hidden agendas, ultimately jeopardizing the new group service, (d) obtain staff consensus about the goals of the program and the group work methods used to achieve them, and (e) assess the willingness of the sponsor to provide external supports, such as transportation, that may be crucial to the development of the group (Abramson, 1983). Overall, garnering support for the idea for a new group service both within and outside the organization helps ensure the success of the group when it is implemented.

Assessing Potential Membership

Along with assessing agency sponsorship and garnering support for a new group work endeavor, the worker should begin to assess the potential membership of a group. Such a beginning assessment does not involve extensive procedures such as arriving at goals for members or agreeing on individual contracts. Rather, in this early assessment the worker is thinking about who should be recruited to participate in a planned group.

When assessing the potential members of a treatment group, the worker can begin by collecting data about the extent of the problem and the need for a new group service. As potential clients are identified, the worker can collect data about them by direct observation, by personal or telephone interview, or by talking with collateral contacts such as family members or agency staff. The worker relates this information to the proposed group's purpose and decides whether the extent of the problem justifies the need for a new group service.

When planning task groups, the worker considers potential members according to their interest in the task, their expertise, and their power and position to help the group accomplish its purposes. Members might also be sought on the basis of their importance to the sponsoring agency, their status in the community, or their political influence.

An important aspect of assessing potential membership is determining whether potential members share the worker's perception of the tasks facing the group. Shared perceptions lead to group cohesion and increase members' satisfaction with group functioning. In addition, the worker spends less time overcoming obstacles and resistance to accomplishing the group's goals when members share similar perceptions of the concerns facing their group.

Information should be gathered about the extent to which potential members recognize the need for the group, its purpose, tasks, and goals. This process helps workers anticipate some issues that might arise during initial group meetings and coalesce divergent views of the purpose of the group and the methods used to accomplish its goals.

It is also important to assess potential members' view of the sponsor. Is there any stigma attached to receiving service from a particular organization? Is the organization known to the potential client group? What is the organization's reputation with the group to be served? The worker should carefully consider what qualities of the potential sponsor are likely to attract clients, and what obstacles may interfere with the successful initiation of a group program.

Often the worker must plan for leading a group of reluctant participants. The extent of reluctance can range from ambivalence about seeking assistance, to active resistance. The term *involuntary* is often applied to individuals who are ordered by the courts to receive treatment. Working with involuntary clients requires special expertise. During the planning stage, the worker should become thoroughly familiar with the legal statutes and ethical issues that apply and the rights of individuals who find themselves in these situations (Rooney, 1992).

More commonly, workers plan groups for reluctant members who are given the choice between treatment and a negative alternative such as incarceration, probation, or the suspension of driving privileges. In these situations, the worker should become thoroughly familiar with the specialized methods and techniques to involve reluctant clients. For example, Brekke (1989) describes the use of five-session orientation groups to engage hard-to-reach clients. As an illustration, he presents an outline for a five-session group designed to prepare men who batter their wives for a more structured and lengthier cognitive behavioral group.

Workers should also become familiar with methods developed to motivate clients to make productive use of the group experience. For example, in a program for motorists convicted of driving while under the influence of alcohol, techniques to confront denial of a drinking problem may be used in combination with powerful incentives such as the return of driving privileges. Similarly, in a residential program for substance abusers, information about the damaging effects of alcohol, peer interaction focused on sobriety, and access to certain privileges may be combined to help members make productive use of a group program.

Workers planning a group for a new population are unlikely to have information at their fingertips about what strategies are most effective for working with individuals who have specialized problems. Identifying experts and information that describe effective techniques to work with a particular client group requires effort. However, experience suggests that this process is invaluable in preparing for the group.

The process of learning more about work with specialized groups is also important when planning groups for people from diverse cultural backgrounds. When workers are significantly different from their group members or when they are less than knowledgeable about the cultural context of group members, it is important for them to learn about the complexities of cross-cultural communication within the group. In addition, workers should recognize their own biases, develop tolerance for their own and others' perceptions, and enhance their abilities to accurately perceive themselves and their clients (Pinderhughes, 1979).

In assessing potential membership, the worker should consider the demographic differences and commonalities of potential members and how such characteristics will affect other steps in the planning process. For example, in assessing potential membership of a support group for Hispanic caregivers of elderly parents, the worker might learn that special recruiting techniques are indicated, such as printing announcements in Spanish, advertising in newspapers for speakers of Spanish, or contacting Hispanic community leaders.

To prepare for recruiting and orienting members in both voluntary and mandatory groups, it can be helpful to list the potential benefits of participating and to share them with potential members. Some workers are reluctant to describe the potential benefits of participating in a group because they fear they will be perceived as boasting about their own skills or because they fear raising the expectation for service among members of vulnerable groups. However, individuals who are considering whether to participate in a group welcome a clear description of the potential benefits of participation. A worker's enthusiasm and optimism can be contagious, increasing members' motivation to participate and their enthusiasm for what might be accomplished. Yalom (1985) refers to this process as the "instillation of hope."

When assessing membership, workers should also identify barriers, obstacles and drawbacks to group participation. In their zest to recruit members, workers sometimes minimize the difficulties individuals might encounter in joining a group. Experience suggests that it is better to acknowledge disadvantages to participation, trying whenever possible to resolve them so they do not prevent individuals from participating. Often, discussing disadvantages with potential members during an orientation interview and planning ways to resolve them can be helpful.

At other times, it may be necessary to find additional resources, or to increase incentives from the sponsoring agency or the larger community. For example, practical barriers may be overcome by the sponsoring agency offering to provide transportation, child care, or a sliding fee schedule. Similarly, an organization in the larger community might offer a meeting site with less stigma, or a group of organizations might lobby with a funding body to provide additional resources for a group program that has wide community support.

Recruiting Members

Recruitment procedures should ensure an adequate number of potential members for the group. In recruiting members, the worker considers sources from which potential members can be identified and referred to the group. Members can be recruited within the worker's agency or in other organizations or the community.

Within a social service agency, potential members can be identified from the caseloads of colleagues, from records, or from mailing lists. In some groups, current members may be able to identify potential members. Potential members might also introduce themselves to the worker, individually or in a group, to suggest that the agency initiate a particular group service. Finally, the worker might consider reviewing the agency's waiting list to determine if any of those waiting for service would benefit from group treatment.

For certain treatment groups, the worker's own agency may not have a large enough potential membership base. In planning for these groups, the worker can contact other social service agencies to obtain referrals. This is particularly true for specialized groups composed of members with particular demographic characteristics, for groups composed around a highly specialized problem area, or groups working on a problem or task that affects a broad segment of the community. In contacting other social service agencies for referrals, the worker should communicate with the administrators of those agencies and inform them of the purpose of the proposed group to elicit their support and, if necessary, gain access to line workers who can identify potential group members.

The worker also can assess the community to locate concentrations of potential members. Census data can be helpful in finding people with certain demographic characteristics (Toseland, 1981). The worker might also talk to community leaders, politicians, police officials, school teachers, or clergy.

For task groups, the type of group and its purpose often suggest excellent sources of recruitment. For example, members of a committee to study an agency's employee benefit package can be recruited from employees of the agency and from the agency's board of directors. A task force to study the problem of refugee resettlement can recruit members from all agencies serving that population in the community.

Occasionally, membership recruitment is determined by the nature of the task group. The members of teams, for example, are selected for their specific expertise and professional background. Boards recruit members from community constituents because the board "stands in" for the community and is accountable to the community for the services the agency provides.

Methods of Recruiting Members

When the worker has identified recruitment sources, decisions must be made about how to reach them. A variety of recruitment techniques will help potential members understand the purpose of the group and help them decide whether to join. The techniques include (a) contacting potential members directly, (b) mailing and posting announcements, (c) preparing television and radio announcements and appearing on television and radio programs, and (d) issuing press releases and making appointments with feature writers of local newspapers.

Some evidence suggests that direct contact with potential clients is the most effective recruitment method (Toseland, 1981). When potential group members can be identified from agency records or from caseloads of colleagues, the worker may wish to set up an initial appointment by letter or by telephone. The worker can then interview the prospective member in the office or at home. Person-to-person contact, particularly in-home contact, can be quite expensive in terms of the worker's time and therefore may not be feasible.

In some situations, the worker may recruit potential group members by contacting key people in the informal networks of a particular population. For example, in recruiting for a group composed of Native Americans, the worker may first discuss the idea with important Native American community elders to gain their acceptance for the group. When recruiting Chinese-Americans, the worker might identify churches or cultural associations that provide support for this population and which could provide the worker with a means for assessing the viability of the group and the potential for recruiting members.

Brief, written announcements also can be an effective recruitment tool. However, care must be taken to ensure that announcements are sent to the correct audience. To be effective, mailed and posted announcements must be seen by potential members, or potential referral sources. Therefore, careful targeting of the pool of potential group members is essential. Too often, workers rely on existing mailing lists developed for other purposes, or post announcements where they will not be noticed by the target group. Computerized record systems are becoming more widely available and are useful in identifying and targeting individuals who may need a particular service.

If the worker has a list of potential members, announcements can be mailed directly to them. The worker may also mail announcements to workers in other social service agencies who are likely to have contact with potential group members. Experience suggests that a follow-up phone call to those who have received announcements increases the probability that referrals will be made. Announcements can also be posted on community bulletin boards, in housing projects, public gathering places, or in local businesses. In rural locations, announcements can be posted at firehouses, church halls, schools, general stores, and post offices. Such locations are usually the best places to post announcements because people gather there to discuss information about their community. The worker also can ask that announcements be read at meetings of community service groups, church groups, business associations, and fraternal organizations.

Appendix D contains two examples of announcements for groups. An announcement should include a clear statement of the group's purpose. The proposed meeting place, dates, times, length and frequency of meetings, and any service fees should also be clearly specified. The sponsoring agency and the group leader's name should be listed along with telephone numbers for potential members to call for more information. It is sometimes helpful to list any special arrangements that are planned, such as child-care services, transportation, or refreshments.

The worker might also want to make information about the group available through public speaking, and through local television or radio stations. Many civic and religious organizations welcome guest speakers. A presentation on the need for the group, its purpose, and how it would operate can be an effective recruitment tool. Commercial television and radio stations broadcast public service announcements deemed to be in the public interest, and the proposed group program might be eligible for inclusion in such broadcasts.

Commercial television and radio stations also frequently produce their own local public interest programs, such as talk shows, public discussions, special news reports, and community news announcements. Although they generally have much smaller audiences, public access cable television channels can also be used by the worker to describe a group service and to invite members to join.

Press releases and newsletter articles are another way to recruit members. Most newspapers publish a calendar of events for a specified week or month, in which brief announcements can be placed. An article in the features section of a newspaper also can reach many potential members. Newspapers frequently publish stories about new group services or particular social problems. The worker should consider whether the group is newsworthy and, if so, contact a local editor and request an interview with a reporter.

Composing the Group

After recruiting potential members, the worker should compose the group. In this process, the worker chooses members according to the individuals' needs and the requirements of the group as a whole. Group composition is also carried out according to a set of established principles that the worker decides upon beforehand. Several important principles of composition require the following:

- A homogeneity of member purposes and certain personal characteristics.
- A heterogeneity of member coping skills, life experiences, and expertise.
- An overall structure that includes a range of member qualities, skills, and expertise.

In addition to these principles, the worker should consider the issues of diversity, group size, and whether the membership will be open or closed.

Homogeneity

The principle of homogeneity suggests that members should have a similar purpose for being in the group and have some personal characteristics in common. This helps facilitate communication and helps members identify with each other's concerns, problems, and tasks. Additionally, commonalities assist members in building relationships with each other.

Members should accept and identify with the major purpose for the group so they can use the meetings to their full advantage. The worker should assess the extent to which members' purposes coincide with one another and with the group as a whole. Without some common purposes for being in the group, members will have little basis for interacting.

Members also should share some personal characteristics, such as age, level of education, cultural background, degree of expertise relative to the group task, communication ability, or type of problem. The worker should determine that all members have enough characteristics in common to facilitate the work of the group. The extent to which members should possess common characteristics varies with the type of group. In an educational group for new parents, it might be important that all members be able to read English at a sixth-grade level to understand program materials recommended for reading at home. In a program-oriented group for youngsters in a treatment center, the most important common characteristic may be their living situation. Groups of alcoholics, drug abusers, and delinquents all have a problem in common.

Heterogeneity

For most groups, there should be some diversity of member coping skills, life experiences, and levels of expertise. It has been noted that the existence of differences in members' coping patterns "opens the eyes of members to options, choices, and alternatives, and makes it possible for them to learn from one another" (Klein, 1972, p.6). In treatment groups, members should be able to hear how others have coped with their problems. Members may also learn by observing different problem-solving approaches carried out by other members.

In some groups, the worker chooses members with differing life experiences or diverse characteristics to foster learning among members. A growth group, for example, might be composed of members from different cultures, social classes, occupations, or geographic areas to expose individuals to the benefits of differing viewpoints, life-styles, and styles of communication. The differences among members can provide multiple opportunities for support, validation, mutual aid, and learning.

Workers should also consider building heterogeneity into the membership of task groups. This practice ensures an adequate range of resources and provides for an efficient division of labor when dealing with complex tasks. For example, agency boards of directors are usually composed of members who represent a variety of professions, agencies, and occupations. They bring different kinds of expertise to the board. Other task groups, such as delegate councils, are also often composed of members who represent differing constituencies with diverse interests and needs. For example, a coalition formed to study the problem of juvenile delinquency might be composed of members from diverse parts of a city, i.e., members from the business district, the inner city, and suburban neighborhoods. Such heterogeneity can be an important asset to the group in accomplishing its tasks.

Group Structure

The worker structures a group so that members will be able to meet their needs and the group will be able to accomplish its purposes. Bertcher and Maple (1977) and Pincus and Minahan (1973), for example, advocate a systematic composition procedure aimed at finding an optimal mix of descriptive and behavioral characteristics of members. Although a highly structured procedure for composing treatment groups is not always appropriate, some guidelines include selecting members who (a) have the ability and desire to communicate with others in the group, (b) can accept each other's behavior, (c) can get along with each other despite differences of opinions, viewpoints, or positions, and (d) have some capacity to understand their own behavior.

Mahler (1969) has suggested that a member who is grossly ineffective in communicating with peers could engender more antagonism than support from fellow members and is best excluded from group treatment. Similarly, people who cannot accept or use feedback are poor candidates for treatment groups.

It is also helpful for the worker to consider the level and source of member motivation when composing a treatment group. Members should be motivated to work on their problems or concerns. Motivation can originate from internal or external sources. Internal motivation may be based on a personal desire to change, grow and develop, or deal with one's problems. External motivation may come from sources such as a spouse, an employer, or the court system.

Guidelines for composing task groups have also been proposed. Likert (1961), for example, suggested that task groups be composed of members who are (a) skilled in various roles of membership and leadership, (b) attracted to the group, (c) highly motivated to abide by the group's values and to achieve group goals, and (d) strongly motivated to communicate fully and frankly all information that is relevant to the group's activity. Put more simply, Scheidel and Crowell (1979) suggest that members of a task group should "together possess all the information necessary to the performance of their task plus the ability to interpret and use it" (p. 122).

The worker should choose members who will be able to put the needs of the group or the requirements of the task before their own personal needs. Klein (1972) notes, for instance, that "committee productivity is curtailed when members use the committee for the meeting of personal needs rather than the fulfillment of group goals" (p. 335).

The worker also should seek members who demonstrate ability to cooperate with one another. No matter what the level of expertise or ability of members, task groups can be hampered by a lack of cooperative effort. Although it is not always possible to predict how people will work together, it is necessary to give this some consideration when composing a group.

Diversity and Demographic Characteristics

Although demographic characteristics alone are not predictive of successful group outcomes (Yalom, 1985), they are important to consider when composing a group. In selecting members, the worker usually considers three major characteristics: age, gender, and sociocultural factors.

It is not sufficient to consider only age when composing a group. The worker should seek members who are similar in their stage of development and their life tasks. The level of maturity, self-insight, and social skills can vary considerably within age groups. Neither children nor adults acquire these characteristics on the basis of age alone, but rather through multiple experiences with their environment, family, peer group, and culture. For example, in composing a children's group, it is helpful to consider the level of member development rather than age alone. Each potential member should be assessed to determine that all have a common basis for interaction and communication.

Research suggests that the behavior of members will vary with the gender composition of the group (Carlock & Martin, 1977). The worker should consider the purpose of the group, along with factors such as age range and level of maturity, to determine the most appropriate gender makeup of the group. In a men's or women's support group, for instance, an atmosphere of support and openness can often be created through homogeneity of composition. In a remedial group for children, a mixed-gender group might interfere with interaction because of the tendency of children at certain ages to either impress or ignore members of the opposite sex.

In other situations, mixed groups are more effective. For example, in a task group such as a teen club planning meeting, a mixed group is most appropriate to help members of the opposite sex learn to relate to one another. Similarly, an assertiveness group might include both men and women so that members can realistically role play training exercises.

Another demographic characteristic that should be considered is the sociocultural background of potential members. The worker should explore the full potential for differences and commonalities among members based on sociocultural factors and should be sensitive to the needs of each member as well as to the overall needs of the group. In general, there should not be wide sociocultural differences among members that would severely interfere with interaction and communication (Klein, 1972).

The level of support and interaction is often increased when members have a common sociocultural background. Support groups for foreign-born students in U.S. colleges, for instance, are frequently based on the similar cultural backgrounds of the members.

In some situations, the worker may decide that similar backgrounds will help members deal with certain problems or issues. For example, a worker may restrict membership in a cultural awareness group to members of a single ethnic group. Similarly, in a support group for parents of terminally ill children, the worker may restrict membership to people from the same cultural background to ensure that members will have similar belief systems and values about death, loss, and grieving.

In other instances, the worker may deliberately plan a group composed of members with diverse sociocultural backgrounds. Diversity can foster mutual understanding and learning among members. Socialization groups in neighborhood centers and youth organizations might be composed by the worker so they encourage members from different ethnic, cultural, and racial groups to interact. Sometimes such differences among members can be a real strength to the group. In planning for a social action group concerned with increasing neighborhood police protection, membership drawn from people of different cultural backgrounds can demonstrate a broad base of support for the group's cause.

Size

There is no optimal size for treatment or task groups. The worker determines the size of the group according to several criteria. Bertcher and Maple (1985) suggest that size "depends on the objectives of the group and the attributes of its members" (p. 190). The group should be small enough to allow it to accomplish its purpose, yet large enough to permit members to have a satisfying experience.

Studies of committees have shown that the most common sizes are five, seven, and nine members (Brilhart, 1974). Bales (1954) suggests that five is the optimum number of members for task groups. For decision-making groups, seven members are desirable (Scheidel & Crowell, 1979). With the exception of larger task groups, such as delegate councils, the optimum range for task groups appears to be between five and seven members.

Similar suggestions appear in the literature for the size of treatment groups. Bertcher and Maple (1985) suggest a range of more than three but less than 15 members. Klein (1972) notes, "Five to seven is often given as ideal . . . developmental groups of fifteen are viable" (p.65). In general, the literature indicates that seven members is ideal (Garvin, 1987; Yalom, 1985). Despite suggestions about the ideal size for treatment groups, little empirical research has been conducted to determine the relationship between group size and group effectiveness (Yalom, 1985).

In determining the size of treatment groups, the worker should consider how the members will be affected. Will members feel satisfied with the attention given to their concerns or problems? This is an issue for the worker, because "as group size increases, the complexity increases rapidly; the number of inter-personal relationships increases geometrically as the number of members increases arithmetically" (Brilhart, 1974, p. 30).

In determining the size of task groups, the worker must consider how many members are needed to accomplish the tasks efficiently and effectively. Although smaller groups are not always best for accomplishing complex tasks, Thelen (1954) suggests that the worker compose the smallest group "in which it is possible to have represented at a functional level all the social and achievement skills required for the particular activity" (p. 187).

The worker should consider the advantages and disadvantages inherent in different group sizes. Larger groups offer more ideas, skills, and resources to members than do smaller groups (Douglas, 1979). In general, larger groups can handle more complex tasks (Bertcher & Maple, 1985). Members have greater potential for learning because of the presence of additional role models. Members have more opportunity for support, feedback, and friendship. There also is less pressure to speak or to perform. Members can engage in what Shulman (1992) refers to as "occasional withdrawal" which all members need to do to reflect on their participation. In larger groups, fewer difficulties arise when one or more members are absent. There is less danger that the group will fall below the size needed for meaningful interaction (Yalom, 1985).

Larger groups also have disadvantages. The larger the group, the less individualized attention each member can receive. Close, face-to-face interaction is more difficult. There is more danger of harmful subgroups forming. Large groups also encourage withdrawal and anonymity by silent members. They create less pressure to attend because members' absence will be less conspicuous than in smaller groups. Larger groups are also more difficult for the worker to manage. They frequently require more formalized procedures to accomplish their meeting agendas. Brilhart (1974) noted that for tasks requiring discussion, larger groups have more difficulty achieving cohesiveness, and Scheidel and Crowell (1979) suggested that large groups have more difficulty reaching consensus.

Overall, decisions about the number of members to include in a treatment or task group should be based on the purpose of the group, the needs of the members and their ability to contribute to the work of the group, practical considerations such as whether a potential member will be able to make meetings, and any constraints imposed by the sponsor.

Open and Closed Membership

During the planning process, the worker should determine if the group will be open or closed to new members. Open groups maintain a constant size by replacing members as they leave (Yalom, 1985). Members enter and terminate throughout the life of the group, ensuring the group's continuance. Closed groups ideally begin and end with the same membership. The closed group "accepts no new members and usually meets for a predetermined number of sessions" (Yalom, 1985, p. 277).

Often the choice between open or closed membership is affected by the purpose of the group, or by practical considerations. A treatment group based in a residential treatment facility, for example, adds members as they become residents. Similarly, a committee formed to study deinstitutionalization of psychiatric patients might discover it needs to add representatives from local community group homes to make more comprehensive recommendations.

In some situations, closed groups may be preferable to open groups. An educational group for those who wish to learn to be more assertive might find it helpful to begin and end with the same membership so that new members will not impede the progress of the original members. A closed group might also be helpful for teen-age mothers learning parenting skills so as to follow a prescribed curriculum that covers the content in a competency-based, step-by-step manner.

In other situations, open group membership is preferable. Many members of Alcoholics Anonymous (AA), report that they are comforted by the knowledge that they can, without notice, attend any open AA meeting in the community. Open membership groups also can provide people who are experiencing crises in their lives with a timely alternative to treatment, so they do not have to wait for a new group to form.

In many situations, open membership is the only practical alternative. Although many group work textbooks are written as if all groups are closed, time-limited groups with distinct beginnings, middles, and endings, there are many settings in which this is not practical. Because of rapid patient turnover in hospitals, for example, workers would find it impractical to form a group and expect the same patients to attend a fixed number of meetings and then be discharged all together.

What modifications should the worker consider when planning an open membership group? If the worker can control when members begin and leave a group, during the planning process the worker should consider when it is optimal to add new members. For example, the worker may decide it is best to add new members during the first few sessions and then close group membership. Alternatively, the worker might plan to add no more than one new member each meeting.

In Chapter 3, it was mentioned that when membership change is frequent and extensive, group development is adversely affected. To cope with the effects of a changing membership, planners of open groups should consider ensuring that there is a well-publicized, fixed structure for every group meeting (Schopler & Galinsky, 1984, 1990; Galinsky & Schopler, 1989). Each meeting, for example, might feature a guest speaker followed by small-group discussion. It is helpful to publicize the topic for each meeting and to stress that meetings are open to new members. In groups with high turnover, each meeting should be independent— that is, an individual should not need to have attended a previous meeting to understand or participate in a current meeting. Also, consideration should be given to rotating a cycle of topics in a fixed period of time so that all clients or patients who have an "average length of stay" in inpatient or outpatient programs can attend a full cycle of meetings before discharge.

When workers have the opportunity to decide whether to form an open or a closed group, they should be guided by reviewing some of the following advantages and disadvantages of each membership option. Open membership allows new ideas and new resources to be brought to the group through new members. Hartford (1971) notes that the "influx of new ideas, beliefs and values" (p. 135) can make open groups more creative than closed groups. New members can change the entire character of the group.

The difficulties involved in adding new members to an already functioning group are not insurmountable. Klein (1972) and Yalom (1985) note the ease with which members can join a group, learn the group norms, and participate in a meaningful way without requiring the group to regress to earlier stages of its development.

There are potential disadvantages to open group membership. Hartford (1971) suggested that "instability is the basic shortcoming of the open group, resulting from loss of leadership, turnover in personnel, exodus of members, loss of group identity" (p. 135). Adding new members can disrupt members' work and delay or arrest the development of the group as a whole (Galinsky & Schopler, 1989, 1990).

Members of closed groups may form a greater sense of cohesion because they have all attended the group since its beginning. There is often a greater stability of roles and norms in closed groups. The benefits of a stable membership include higher group morale, more predictability of role behaviors, and an increased sense of cooperation among members. The stability of membership also makes planning for group sessions easier.

A disadvantage of closed groups is that when members drop out or are absent, the number of members in the group may become too small for meaningful group interaction. Without the benefit of new ideas, viewpoints, and skills from new members, a closed group runs the risk of engaging in what Janis (1972) refers to as "group think," or what Kiesler (1978) calls "the avoidance of minority or outside opinions" (p. 322). Such avoidance can create an extreme form of conformity within the group that can reduce its effectiveness (Janis & Mann, 1977).

Orienting Members

After potential members have been recruited, the worker should screen them for appropriateness and orient them to the group. Orientation is important because the process begins the relationship between the worker and the members. Orientation can also motivate members and clarify their expectations. The primary orientation method for treatment groups is the intake interview (Klein, 1972; Manor, 1986). Generally, intake interviews are conducted individually.

Members of treatment groups also can be oriented by listening to an audiotape of a group meeting, by viewing videotapes of a previous group, through didactic instruction or by rehearsal of membership skills, such as how to effectively communicate one's thoughts and opinions. These role-induction strategies, often referred to as "pretraining," can take a single half-hour session or several sessions lasting several hours. In a review of six studies of pretraining for group psychotherapy, Piper, Debbane, Garant, and Bienvenu (1979) found that it reduced dropout rates and increased members' satisfaction with the subsequent group experience.

Orientation for new members of task groups is sometimes done in small groups. For example, new board members may be asked to participate in a board training program that consists of several small group sessions on governance and the bylaws of the organization, fiduciary responsibilities, fund-raising, and public relations.

Orientations may be designed for many purposes, but three primary ones include (a) explaining the purpose of the group, (b) familiarizing members with group procedures, and (c) screening members for appropriateness.

Explaining the Purpose of the Group

The worker should begin orienting members by stating the group's purpose. The statement should be specific enough to allow members to ask questions about the group and clarify what will be expected of them. At the same time, the statement should be broad enough, and tentative enough, to encourage input and feedback. As Manor (1986) points out, this can help potential members discuss and work through any ambivalence they might have about participating in the group.

Familiarizing Members with Group Procedures

Group members frequently have questions about how the group will work. Through these questions, members try to understand some of the general rules of group functioning. It is helpful for the worker to explain procedures for member participation and for how the group will conduct its business. Shulman (1992) suggests that members be given a job description of the leader, including a statement that the leader will make sure everyone will have a chance to contribute ideas to the group.

Leaders of both treatment and task groups often establish routine procedures for meetings during either the planning stage or the beginning stage of the group. Some treatment group meetings, for example, use a short review period for the first few minutes to discuss the major points of the last session. Time is then allotted for identifying particular member concerns to be discussed during the current session. Some groups use the final few minutes to summarize, to discuss between-meeting assignments, or to talk about the group's progress.

Task groups also frequently follow routine procedures, such as reading the minutes of the previous meeting, discussing old business, and bringing up new business. Many of these procedures are decided upon by the group in its early meetings, but discussion of group procedures during the planning stage helps members see how they can participate in or contribute to the group.

Screening Members for Appropriateness

During the orientation, the worker screens members to ensure that their needs are matched with the purposes of the group. The worker observes members and collects impressions and information about them. Workers also apply any criteria developed for inclusion or exclusion of potential members. Members with impaired functioning can often be recognized during the orientation interview, giving the worker a chance to decide whether their membership in the group is appropriate.

Some factors that may render people inappropriate for group membership include (a) problems with scheduling transportation or other practical considerations, (b) personal qualities, such as level of social skills, that are extremely dissimilar to those of other group members, and (c) needs, expectations, or goals that are not congruent with those of the other group members. Such factors have been linked to members dropping out of treatment prematurely (Yalom, 1985). In considering members' appropriateness for a group, Klein (1972) takes a pragmatic view, suggesting that members should have "the ability to communicate with each other, motivation to work on their problems, no behavior so bizarre as to frighten the others, and no wide differences that are personally or culturally beyond acceptance" (p. 60). Such a view is helpful, because it focuses on behavior that is observed during the orientation process rather than on labels or classifications of disorders that are difficult to observe.

Contracting

During the planning stage, the worker begins the contracting process. Contracts usually result from the dynamic interaction of the worker and the members during the beginning stage of the group, but certain contracting procedures are initiated before the group begins.

Two forms of contracting take place during the planning stage: contracting for group procedures and contracting for individual member goals. The worker should make some preliminary decisions about group procedures before beginning. These decisions include the duration and frequency of group meetings, attendance requirements, procedures to ensure confidentiality, and other considerations such as time, place, and fees for meetings. The worker should also begin the process of contracting for individual member goals although most of this type of contracting takes place during the beginning stage of group work.

A contract is a verbal or written agreement between two or more members of a group. In a legal contract, each party agrees to provide something, although what is provided by each does not have to be equal, and penalties are specified if either party does not fulfill the contract. Recently, interest has increased in the use of contracts in group work practice (Croxton, 1985; Rose, 1989).

In most task and treatment groups, contracts are verbal agreements. For example, the leader of an educational treatment group for foster parents might agree to meet with the group for five two-hour sessions to explain the purposes of the agency. The worker also might agree to explain the help that the agency can offer as well as how the legal rights of foster children can be safeguarded. Members would agree to attend each session and to use the information that is provided to become better foster parents. Similarly, the leader of a treatment conference might verbally agree with group members about the procedures for reviewing cases, the responsibility of each staff member in the review process, and the ways in which the information presented during the meeting will be used in case planning.

At times, a written contract might be more effective for a group. A written contract helps to clarify the group's purpose. It also helps members clarify expectations about the worker and the agency, and allows the worker to specify what is expected of group members (see Figure 5–1). A written contract can be referred to in group meetings if either the members or the worker need to be reminded of the purpose, expectations, or obligations to which they agreed. Generally, written contracts specify ground rules for participation that do not change during the life of the group. However, contracts can be renegotiated by mutual agreement at any time during the group's life.

Written contracts are rarely used in task groups. The meeting agenda and the bylaws or other governance structure under which the task group operates are usually the only written agreements binding group members. Ordinarily, task groups rely on verbal contracts about the tasks to be accomplished, the roles of group members, and the division of labor in the group.

Contracting for Group Procedures

The worker begins to determine group procedures by deciding on the duration and frequency of meetings. These decisions are closely related to the group's purpose and the needs of its members. In treatment groups, the optimal length of time for each meeting varies, with some groups needing one and one-half hours, and others needing as much as three hours. Some groups, such as encounter or sensitivity training groups, use frequent meetings within a short space of time to achieve high communication levels and reduce member defenses. Others, such as marathon groups, meet for long periods of time—for a whole day or for one or more consecutive days.

There is no standard length of time recommended for either treatment or task group meetings. Meeting length should vary according to the needs of members. For example, a worker might limit the duration of meetings of a group for cancer patients because of members' physical limitations and discomfort. Similarly, members of an administrative staff group might hold their meetings to 45 minutes because of their busy schedules.

The frequency of group meetings should also be considered when contracting for group procedures. In general, weekly sessions are recommended for treatment groups, although this does not preclude meeting more often when needed. The frequency of task group meetings depends on the requirements of the task and any time limits or deadlines that need to be considered. The worker must also consider how much time each member can devote to the group.

Numerous other group procedures should be considered. The worker can specify attendance requirements, confidentiality of discussions, or other rules governing behavior in the group, such as how discussions will take place and how decisions will be made. Additional details include the time and place for meetings, the fee involved, and the monitoring and evaluation procedures to be used by the worker.

FIGURE 5–1
Example of a treatment group contract

As a group member I agree to:

1. Attend all group sessions.
2. Arrive on time for each group session.
3. Refrain from repeating anything that is said during group sessions to anyone outside of the group meeting.
4. Complete any readings, exercises, treatment plans, or other obligations that I agree to in the group before the next group session.
5. Participate in exercises, role plays, demonstrations, and other simulations conducted during group meetings.

As the group leader I agree to:

1. Be prepared for each group session.
2. Begin and end all group sessions on time.
3. Provide refreshments and program material needed for each session.
4. Discuss the group only with my colleagues at work and not outside of the work context.
5. Evaluate each group session to ensure that the group is helping all members resolve their problems and is personally satisfying to all group members.
6. Provide members with appropriate agency and community resources to help them resolve their problems.

_____	_____
Group member	Date
_____	_____
Group leader	Date

Contracting for Member Goals

During the planning stage, workers also begin contractual arrangements with individual members. These contracts should be as specific as possible so members will know what is expected of them. Bertcher and Maple (1977) refer to this process as writing behavioral specific objectives for group members. They outline the following basic steps: (a) determining the condition under which the desired behavior will occur, (b) stating the desired behavior in terms of what a person will be able to do, and (c) determining the standards by which results are to be measured. This method can be used when contracting with members of both treatment and task groups and is explained in more detail in Chapter 6.

Preparing the Environment

Three factors should be considered when preparing a group's environment: (a) physical setting, (b) financial support, and (c) special arrangements. The extent to which the worker can control these factors is sometimes limited. However, incorporating them into the planning process will enhance chances for successful group development.

Preparing the Physical Setting

The setting for the group can have a profound effect on the behavior of group members and the conduct of group meetings. Room size, space, seating arrangements, furnishings, and atmosphere should all be considered. Difficulties encountered in early meetings, inappropriate behavior by members, and unanticipated problems in the development of the group can sometimes result from inadequate attention to the group's physical environment.

Room size can influence how active or involved members become with the business of the group. Generally, a small room engenders positive feelings of closeness among members and limits potential distractions. A large room can put too much distance among members, encouraging some members to "tune out." A small group of people meeting in a large room may be distracted by the open space around them and have difficulty concentrating on processes.

On the other hand, a room might be too small and not allow enough space among members. This may lead to discomfort, irritability, anxiety, or acting out. Certain populations are particularly reactive to the size of the meeting room. Young children, for example, often benefit from a large, open area in which to engage in activities. Similarly, disabled older adults benefit from a room with wheelchair access; comfortable, high back chairs that are not difficult to get in and out of; bright glare-free lighting; and good acoustics (Toseland, 1990a).

Comfortable seating should be available. Sometimes group members prefer to sit on the floor to create an informal atmosphere. Carpets, lamps, work tables, and other furnishings should also help create a comfortable atmosphere. A comfortable physical environment conveys a message to group members about the agency's regard for them as clients.

Overall, the worker should consider the total effect of the physical setting on a group's ability to accomplish its tasks. If a group is to engage in informal discussion, the worker can create an informal atmosphere with comfortable couches or pillows for sitting on the floor. If a group is to work on formal tasks, such as reviewing priorities for a five-year plan, the worker should create a more formal atmosphere. For example, a room in which the group can sit around a well-lighted table may be most appropriate.

Securing Financial Support

The worker should be concerned about how the expenses associated with the group will be met. For this reason, the worker should explore the financing arrangements with the group's sponsoring agency, beginning with an assessment of the agency's total financial statement. The costs associated with treatment and task groups vary, but major items include the salary of the worker, the use of the meeting room, and the expense of supervision for the worker. Other expenses may include duplicating, telephone, mailings, refreshments, and transportation.

Expenses such as the worker's salary and the meeting room are often routinely paid for by the agency. For expenses requiring an outlay of cash, the worker should submit a budget request to the sponsoring agency. A petty-cash fund can provide a flexible means to cover expenses incurred by the group.

For some treatment groups, income may be generated by fees collected from members, or it may be produced from outside sources, such as grants or contracts. Although most task groups do not usually generate income, some are formed to generate money for new programs or to raise funds for the agency. Others generate financial savings to an agency through creative problem solving or decision-making. Using information about costs and income, the worker can determine what financial support must be obtained for the proposed group.

Special Arrangements

The worker should be particularly sensitive to any special needs of group members. The worker should be sure that barriers will not prevent particular members from being able to attend meetings. For a group of senior citizens, for example, the worker should consider transportation needs, the safety of the meeting place, the comfort of chairs, and access to the agency and the meeting room (see, for example, Toseland & Coppola, 1984). In working with the physically challenged, the worker should plan a barrier-free location for meetings. If a group for parents is planned, the worker should consider child-care arrangements. For a children's group, the worker should discuss transportation arrangements and obtain parental consent for the children's involvement in the group. In working with a population for whom English is a second language, the worker may need to arrange for the services of an interpreter during meetings or may wish to co-facilitate with a bilingual or bicultural co-leader.

TELEPHONE GROUPS.   In some situations, it is not possible for people who could benefit from social group work to meet face to face. For example, people who suffer from debilitating illnesses, such as the frail elderly and those with terminal illnesses, often are not able to attend group meetings. In other situations, people may find it difficult to avail themselves of a group service because they live a long distance from the organization offering the service. For example, in rural communities, health and social service agencies often serve large geographic areas. Even in urban and suburban communities, some health and social service agencies, such as regional hospitals, serve the needs of special populations dispersed over a large area.

In recent years, technological advances have made it possible to have telephone conversations among a number of individuals. This is often referred to as "teleconferencing" or making a "conference call" (Kelleher & Cross, 1985). Until recently, the use of this technology was largely limited to business meetings. Several pioneering individuals in the social services, however, have begun to use the technology to offer groups to individuals who cannot meet face to face (see, for example, Bertcher, 1990; Evans & Jauregy, 1981; Rounds, Galinsky, & Stevens, 1991).

Galinsky, Rounds, Montague, and Butowsky (1993) and Bertcher (1990) have prepared manuals on how to set up and operate telephone groups. In addition, Bertcher is the editor of *Tell A Group Hotline*, an occasional newsletter published through the School of Social Work at the University of Michigan. Some of the special considerations in setting up a telephone group include (a) teleconferencing capacity in the organization's telephone system, (b) a speaker phone if there will be more than one leader, (c) sufficient funds for teleconferencing, and (d) a willingness to call 15 minutes before the group and stay on the line until all members of the group are connected.

As can be seen in the bibliography on telephone groups in Appendix E, telephone groups are usually planned for people with physical disabilities, and those who live in rural areas. Although research on telephone groups is limited, some clinical evidence suggests that they have certain advantages over in-person interacting groups. Some individuals appear to be more willing to participate in telephone groups than in-person groups. Bertcher (1992) suggests that the anonymity of telephone groups appears to encourage members to discuss issues that were reported to be taboo in in-person groups and that, contrary to expectations, cohesion develops quickly in telephone groups.

Telephone groups also have potential disadvantages. For example, there is no informal time for members to get together with each other before or after the meeting (Rounds, Galinsky, & Stevens, 1991). With members' consent, swapping telephone numbers for between-session contact is one solution. Also, because members lack visual cues, the worker must be particularly attentive to voice tone, inflection, silences, and other cues such as members becoming less responsive or completing dropping out of the discussion over time. Despite these limitations, telephone groups offer a promising, cost-effective alternative to face-to-face interacting groups for frail or isolated individuals.

Writing a Group Proposal

In planning for a group, the worker might find it useful to prepare a written proposal. Such a proposal is sometimes required for obtaining agency sponsorship or for obtaining funding from various sources. A written proposal can also inform potential members about the group. Spending time to organize and write a group proposal can also aid the worker in preparing for meetings.

Sources that explain proposal writing (Lauffer, 1977) can be used when proposing a treatment or task group. Although these sources suggest rather detailed outlines, for most groups, we recommend a brief summary (one to two pages) based on the outline in Appendix F. Two sample proposals, one for a treatment group and one for a task group, are presented in Appendices G and H.

SUMMARY

This chapter stresses the need for planning in group work. Workers consider many variables and exercise control over as many of them as possible. The planning process should be guided by the purposes of the group, the needs of the members, and the requirements of the task.

This chapter presents a model for planning treatment and task groups. Steps in the model include: (a) establishing the group's purpose, (b) assessing the potential sponsorship and membership, (c) recruiting members, (d) composing the group, (e) orienting members, (f) contracting, and (g) preparing the group's environment. This model can be useful in planning for the many different types of groups a worker may lead. All planning models represent an idealized, step-by-step set of procedures that may vary depending on the realities of agency practice, but following a logical planning model can assist workers in helping groups meet members' needs and accomplish established goals.

LEARNING ASSIGNMENTS

1. The local Alzheimer's Disease Association has asked you to convene a committee to advise them on how to reach out to African-American and Hispanic-American caregivers of frail elders with Alzheimer's disease. What issues would you consider when composing the group? What methods would you use to recruit members?
2. In a small group with your classmates, select a population in need of group services. Prepare a brief statement of the purpose of the group. Decide on inclusion and exclusion criteria for group members. Prepare an agenda for a group intake/orientation meeting.
3. Visit an agency that deals exclusively with a distinct population such as the elderly or the disabled. Interview a worker about what physical arrangements and special considerations would be needed to form a group for this population.
4. Your agency director has asked you to prepare a proposal for group services to help students at a local middle school cope with the recent suicides of two of their classmates. Use the outline in Appendix F to help you prepare a written proposal.

PART III

The Beginning Stage

Chapter 6: The Group Begins

Chapter 7: Assessment

CHAPTER 6

The Group Begins

The beginning of a group is often characterized by caution and tentativeness. The members have certain expectations about the group, based on experiences with other groups, previous relationships, and the role expectations and characteristic ways of interacting that they bring to the group (Berne, 1963). Usually, the participants realize that there is an important purpose for their face-to-face contact in the group. They may have met with the worker before the first group meeting or received information on the purpose of the group through other agency workers, from other group members, or from previous group members.

Nevertheless, at the beginning of any group, members are not fully certain about the purposes of the group. As Shulman (1992) has pointed out, members want to know "what are we doing here together?" and "what kind of person will the worker be?" (p. 315). Members also wonder about what will be expected of them and what the other individuals in the group will be like.

From the very first contact, participants assess each other. These assessments are based largely on nonverbal cues such as dress and personal appearance. The first interchanges are often stereotyped conversations in which participants attempt to become familiar with one another through mutual interests in places, people, events, and common experiences (Hartford, 1971).

As the group meeting progresses, an approach-avoidance conflict becomes more evident (Garland, Jones & Kolodny, 1976). Members approach each other in their striving to connect with one another, but they avoid getting too close because they fear the vulnerability that such intimacy implies. Discussion of emotionally charged issues can be detrimental in the beginning of a group. When a member self-discloses emotionally charged issues very early in the group's development, other members sometimes will feel threatened and disclose little personal information for a time. This occurs because few norms have developed about how to behave and members are unsure about how to respond. Members may feel threatened if they think they will be asked to self-disclose at similar levels. They may not be ready to do so, or they may think others will not be receptive or supportive if they disclose personal details they believe reflect poorly on themselves. Members are concerned about the way they present themselves early in a group and often prefer to proceed with caution.

Through their initial interactions, members attempt to find their places within the group. As the group develops norms, members begin to find out what is acceptable and unacceptable behavior. The tentative interactions found at the beginning of most groups are a testing ground for developing relationships. Group members attempt to reach out to find who in the group they can trust with their thoughts and feelings and with whom they can form continuing relationships.

At the beginning of the group, members are cautious about what they reveal. Concerns about their own adequacy are heightened because all interactions occur within the view of the worker and other group members. All members have had experiences in groups of one kind or another, and these past experiences affect their reactions to a new group. Members recall how they were received in other groups and use those experiences as a basis for their behavior in the current group. A useful exercise that can be done early in the group's life is to have each member describe an experience they had in a previous group, emphasizing how that group experience might affect their participation in the current group.

Members react in different ways to the group situation. Some will remain silent, taking a wait-and-see stance toward the other group members. Others will try to reduce their anxiety by engaging in conversation or by asking questions to help them clarify their position in the group. Gradually, a pattern of relating develops within the group. As Hartford (1971) pointed out, this pattern of relating includes affectional acceptances or rejections, alliances and subgroups, status ratings, leader and follower patterns, and characteristic communication patterns. These patterns crystalize as the group develops.

The worker needs to be aware of these patterns of relating as they develop. The worker can point these out to group members and encourage the development of patterns that will help group members accomplish their purpose. For example, open interaction patterns that allow all members to participate can lead to member satisfaction and successful task accomplishment. Open interaction patterns should be modeled and reinforced by the worker.

OBJECTIVES IN THE BEGINNING STAGE

The beginning stage is often considered, by novice and experienced workers alike, to be a difficult stage of group work because members often seek direction about how to proceed but are ambivalent about following the suggestions given. They are struggling to maintain their autonomy and, at the same time, fit in and get along with others in the group. The worker's primary objective is to help members to work together in a cooperative and productive manner while feeling that their unique contribution to the group is respected and appreciated. To accomplish this primary objective in the beginning stage of group work it is helpful to:

- Facilitate member introductions.
- Clarify the purpose and function of the group as it is perceived by the worker, the members, and the sponsoring organization.

- Discuss and clarify the limits of confidentiality within the group.
- Help members feel a part of the group.
- Guide the development of the group.
- Balance task and socio-emotional aspects of the group process.
- Set goals.
- Contract for work.
- Facilitate members' motivation and ability to work in the group.
- Anticipate obstacles to achieving individual and group goals.

In the following pages, these objectives and the corresponding skills necessary to carry them out are presented sequentially. In actual practice, of course, the group worker should be concerned about these objectives simultaneously.

Introducing New Members

When the participants have arrived and the group is ready to begin, the first task of the worker is to introduce members to one another. Introductions help members share their mutual concerns and interests, and develop trust. The worker should decide what information would be important for members to share with the group. Beyond each member's name, the information revealed by each member should depend on the purpose of the group. For example, if the group is an interagency task force to study the problem of battered women, members might be expected to share their position in their agency, their experiences with services to battered women, and their reasons for becoming involved in the task force. If the group is for parents with children who have behavior problems, in addition to information about themselves, parents might briefly describe their children and the behavior problems they are experiencing.

Introductions also can give members a starting point for interaction. Therefore, the information that is shared should attempt to bring out commonalities. The worker can facilitate this process by noting common characteristics and shared concerns disclosed by different members. Rather than proceeding through the introduction mechanically, the worker should encourage members to discuss these commonalities. This helps members feel at ease with one another. It also helps develop group cohesion and demonstrates to members that they are not alone with their problems and concerns.

The fact that members can share common concerns and issues with one another is one of the unique aspects of the group as a practice method. Yalom (1985) has called this phenomenon "universality" (pp. 7–9). People who come to treatment groups often believe that they are alone with their problems, that they are unique, and that no one else faces the same troubles. In reality, while they may have been experiencing their problems in isolation, other people experience similar concerns. The first group meeting provides them with feelings of support and comfort as they realize they are not alone.

A similar process occurs in task groups. For example, workers from different community agencies often experience the same frustrations and problems in serving clients with particular social service needs. Alone, workers may think they can do little to make the system more responsive to clients. But together, in a task force, a treatment conference, or in any of other task groups described previously, workers can share their concerns, coordinate their efforts, and work to change problematic situations.

The Round Robin

The most common method of introducing members to one another is to have them speak in "round robin" fashion. If this method is used, it is helpful for the worker to go first. In the early stages of the group, members take many of their cues from the worker, who can serve as a model by disclosing characteristics about himself or herself. Once members hear the worker's introduction, they are likely to focus on these disclosures as they introduce themselves.

Sometimes, the worker might want members to disclose information about areas of concern that the worker does not share. For example, in a group of parents, the worker may not have children. Workers should note the absence of this characteristic in their own lives, state how it might affect their work in the group, and ask members to mention it in their introductions.

When they introduce themselves, members rarely disclose more than the worker discloses. In fact, they initially tend to disclose to a lesser extent than the worker. Therefore, if workers expect a certain level of self-disclosure or want to foster disclosures in a certain area, their introductions should reflect what is expected. This is not to suggest that the introduction should call on members to reveal in-depth, personal life experiences. Pressing for such disclosures at the beginning of a group is likely to increase rather than decrease barriers to open communication.

This is particularly true for members of specific cultural groups whose communication styles and expectations about self-disclosure are influenced by their cultural backgrounds. Pearson (1991) suggests, for example, that clients who identify with the cultural imperatives in Chinese society may believe that close, personal relationships are usually reserved for family and that high levels of self-disclosure are not as desirable as a "balance and restraint in the experience and expression of emotions" (p. 51).

Variations on the Round Robin

Several variations on the "round robin" may be useful in opening different types of groups. To increase interaction, for example, members can be divided into pairs. One member of each pair interviews the other for five minutes, asking for details specified by the worker. When time is up, members reverse roles and continue for another five minutes. When the group reconvenes, members introduce their partners to the group by recalling the facts learned during their conversation. In addition to helping members develop a relationship with a partner, group workers will find that this method of introduction sometimes leads to a greater depth of self-disclosure than the "round robin" because new group members are likely to reveal more about themselves on a one-to-one basis than when facing the entire group.

A variation on this opening is what Shulman (1992) has called "problem swapping" (p. 320). Members volunteer to discuss their problems or concerns openly before the group. This opening promotes group interaction, leads to the identification of shared problems and concerns, and helps members to consider how they might proceed.

An opening that is useful in growth-oriented groups is known as "top secret." Members are asked to write down one thing about themselves that they have not or would not ordinarily reveal to new acquaintances. The leader collects these "top secrets" and reads them to the group. Members attempt to identify the person who made each revelation, giving a reason for their choice. This exercise can be repeated in a later group session to illustrate the extent to which trust and cohesion have increased in the group. Members will often reveal more intimate or personal "top secrets" after they come to know and feel comfortable with the members of their group.

Another opening exercise that can help members to disclose something about themselves is called "my name." Members can be asked to discuss how they got their name, and what meaning it has for them, and for their family of origin. For example, a member might state that his father felt strongly that he should be named Samuel, after an uncle who had died. The member goes on to discuss the uncle and other facts about his family of origin. He might also mention that he disliked being called Sam by his parents, and decided at age 13 to insist that his parents and friends call him by his middle name, Allen. This exercise can often lead to interesting discussions of members' feelings about themselves now and in the past. It also helps members learn each other's names, which is important for open and personal interaction.

Other openings such as "treasure hunt" can be useful in beginning a children's group. Members are asked to find out two or three facts about each of the other group members. In doing so, there is a great deal of structured, but informal, group interaction that helps members overcome initial anxieties. The facts obtained are shared when the group reconvenes. Another opening is to have members state their name and what they like and dislike about it. This opening often leads to self-disclosures focused on members' feelings about themselves and about their family heritage.

Program activities can also be used in opening a group. Such activities help members share important information about themselves while working on an assigned task or activity. In addition to increasing member self-disclosure, program activities can build cohesion in the group. For example, in children's groups, members may be asked to pick an animal that represents them. When introducing themselves, members can name the animal they have selected and state what characteristics of the animal they identify with. Another program activity for children or adolescent groups is to have members stand in a circle and hold hands with two members who are not next to them. Members are then asked to untangle themselves and form a circle without letting go of each other's hands. For additional program activities that can be used to open a group, see the annual handbook by Pfeiffer and Goodstein (published since 1984) or Middleman (1982).

Variations in Group Beginnings

A number of factors can change the way a worker begins a group. Sometimes workers become involved with groups of people who have known each other since before the group was formed. This can occur when the members are clients of a neighborhood center, a residential treatment facility, or are friends in the community. Similarly, in task groups, members may be familiar with one another as co-workers in the same agency or as co-workers in a network of agencies working with similar clients or a similar social problem. When members know one another, the challenges for the worker are different from those that occur in a group of strangers.

Members who have had previous contact with one another are more likely to relate in ways that are characteristic of their previously established patterns. Roles and relationships established earlier may be carried into the new group, regardless of their functional or dysfunctional nature in the current group situation. In groups where only a few members know one another or where previous relationships between members vary from friendly to neutral or unfriendly, subgroups are more likely to develop than in groups composed of strangers. There is also a natural tendency for friends or acquaintances to interact with one another and exclude strangers.

When it is possible to obtain information about potential group members, the worker should try to find out about any relationships that may exist among them. This will give the worker some indication of what form members' relationships are likely to take as they begin the group. It also gives the worker an opportunity to plan strategies to intervene in dysfunctional relationship patterns. The worker may wish to use information about members' previous relationships to reconsider the composition of the group and to understand members' interactions as the group unfolds. For example, a worker in a group home might use knowledge about the relationships that have developed among residents when deciding how to intervene to change communication patterns in a governance group that has just been established within the facility.

Another common variation in beginning a group occurs when the worker becomes involved in a previously formed group. This can include a worker who (a) reaches out and works with a gang of adolescents, (b) is a consultant for a self-help group, (c) is asked to staff a previously formed committee, or (d) is asked to replace the leader of an intact treatment group. These situations are different from one in which all of the members are new to the group (Northen, 1969). Instead of members looking to the leader for direction, as in a new group, the worker in a previously formed group is the newcomer in a group with established patterns of relating. Members of previously formed groups are concerned with how the worker will affect the group, what they will have to do to accommodate the worker, and what the worker will expect of them. Members may also act on feelings resulting from termination with a previous worker.

In working with previously formed groups, the worker should become familiar with the group's structure and its current functions and processes. It is especially important that the worker become familiar with the formal and informal leadership of the group, with members' relationships with one another, and with the tasks that face the group. Information obtained from a previous leader or from agency records may offer some indication of how to approach the group. In working with gangs or other community groups where little information is available, the worker may find it helpful to gather information about the group. Any information obtained before contact with the group should be considered tentatively, however, because it is difficult to predict how an ongoing group is likely to react to a new worker. The worker may also want to observe the group before attempting to intervene.

Under any circumstances, the worker's presence will cause a need for adjustments in the group. A process of accommodation to the new worker and assimilation of the worker into the culture of the group will occur. In general, cohesive and autonomous groups that have functioned together for some time will find it difficult to accommodate a new worker and will expect the worker to become assimilated into the ongoing process of the group.

Groups that are less cohesive, less autonomous, and have been meeting for a relatively short time will find it easier to adjust to the worker's presence. A worker from a neighborhood center who is interested in working with a closely knit gang of adolescents who grew up together, for example, has to spend a considerable amount of time developing trust and rapport with the group before members will seriously consider participating in a recreational activity at the neighborhood center.

Defining the Purpose of the Group

Opening Statement

After the introduction, the worker should make a brief statement about the group's purpose and the worker's function in the group. When members are not clear about the purpose of the group or the motives of the worker, their anxiety increases and they are less likely to become involved in working on their concerns and problems. Garvin, Reid, and Epstein (1976) found that when objectives are clearly specified, the group is more likely to achieve its goals. Evidence suggests that workers often fail to define the purposes of the group they are leading (Hartford, 1962). Even if the purpose has been explained to members during pre-group intake interviews, the worker should be sure to restate it during the first meeting.

The group's purpose should be presented in as positive a way as possible. Frank (1961) and other cognitive psychologists have pointed out that importance of persuasion, expectancy, and placebo effects in psychotherapy. These factors are also present in group work practice. Presenting a positive, hopeful image of what can be accomplished in the group makes use of the beneficial effects of these cognitive expectancies. Rather than focusing on members' problems or concerns, the worker can express the group's purpose in terms of the goals to be accomplished. Thus, statements that focus on positive objectives and goals such as "Through this group experience you can learn to. . . ." "You can stop. . . ." or "Through all of our efforts in this task force we can. . . ." are preferable to those that focus on the negative aspects of problems or concerns.

If the worker has successfully led a previous group that focused on similar concerns, the worker can mention this success. In treatment groups, such a statement by the leader offers members the hope that the group will help them resolve their own concerns. In task groups, members are more likely to be motivated and to persist in goal achievement. In open-ended treatment groups where new members replace old ones, it is often helpful to have members who have been in the group for some time state how the group has been helpful to them. Professional group workers can learn from the way that self-help groups such as Alcoholics Anonymous and Recovery Incorporated rely on the testimony of successful members as a major component of their group program. In task groups, members who have had some experience in the group can be asked to orient new members.

The opening statement about the group's purpose should include a brief description of the functions of the agency sponsoring the group. In treatment groups, it should define the limits of service so that members will have a clear notion of what services they can expect and what services are beyond the scope of the agency. There is nothing more frustrating for members and workers alike than members' implicit or explicit expectations going unfulfilled. The opening statement should include a brief statement about how the worker intends to function in the group, the worker's role in helping members obtain agency services, and any brokerage or advocacy services the worker will provide if resources or services are unavailable within the agency.

In task groups, relating the agency's function and mission to the group's purpose helps members understand why they were called together to participate in the group. The opening statement allows members to see how the agency's functions are related to the group's task. It is not uncommon, for example, for members of task groups to ask about how and to whom the results of their work will be reported. Task group members may also be interested in the extent that their group can make permanent changes in policies, procedures, and practices through its findings and recommendations.

Involving Members

The opening statement focuses the group on considering the purposes for meeting. It should be presented as a starting point for further discussion rather than an immutable definition that is not open to negotiation, modification, or change. Attempting to impose a definition of the group without input from members tends to reduce members' commitment and motivation, and to increase members suspicions that their autonomy is threatened.

The stated purposes and goals should be broad enough that members can formulate their own purposes and their own goals (Northen, 1969). This does not mean that the worker's opening statement should be so broad that almost any purpose or goal can be contained within it. Statements about improving members' social functioning or coping ability may be too abstract for members to comprehend. Opening statements should be presented in clear, jargon-free language. However, avoid being overly specific. Instead, solicit members' ideas and suggestions about how to operationalize particular purposes and goals.

Open communication, particularly when it may conflict with the purposes or goals articulated by the worker, is often difficult to achieve. In the beginning stage, members are reluctant to risk their own tentative position within the group or to express opinions that may differ from those expressed by the worker or other members. Therefore, in addition to providing members with opportunities to express their opinions and concerns regarding the group's purpose and goals, the worker should reach out for members' input.

This can be done in a variety of ways. First, the worker should state clearly that the group is meant to serve the needs of its members who ultimately determine the group's purpose and goals. Members can then be asked to state their own purposes and goals, as well as to comment on the broad purposes and goals articulated by the worker. During this process workers can encourage feedback by taking their comments seriously and praising them for sharing their feelings and thoughts.

Members can sense if the worker's call for feedback is genuine or perfunctory. If the worker makes a continuous effort to solicit feedback by encouraging all members to express their thoughts and feelings, members are more likely to feel that their input is welcome. Members can be asked to make a statement about how the group's purposes and goals meet their needs and to suggest how the group could be improved.

Confidentiality

In treatment groups and certain task groups, the worker should lead a discussion of issues of confidentiality during the opening portion of the group meeting. In treatment groups, members are often concerned about how information they share with the group will be used outside the group meeting by the worker and other group members. Members cannot be expected to disclose intimate concerns or develop a sense of trust unless they can be assured that discussions within the group will not be shared outside. It is often helpful to remind members about the confidentiality of meetings periodically throughout the life of the group. This is particularly important in residential settings, because frequent interaction outside the group may promote violations of confidentiality. It is also important in children's groups, and in groups for other populations that may have difficulty following confidentiality agreements made during a first meeting.

In some cases, the worker may be obligated to share information discussed in the group with law enforcement officials. Workers are also likely to share information with supervisors and with fellow staff members during treatment conferences. Therefore, workers have an ethical obligation to be clear about the limits of confidentiality, and with whom and under what circumstances data may be shared.

The time set aside for the discussion of confidentiality also provides an ideal opportunity for the worker to bring related value issues to the attention of the group. For example, the worker might engage the group in a discussion of how social group work values such as democratic participation, respect for the individuality of each member, self-determination, cooperation and mutual decision making, and the importance of individual initiative will be operationalized in the group.

We have found that it is helpful for the worker to assist the group in formulating a set of principles—or a code of behavior for its operation—to which each member agrees to adhere. For example, members might agree to listen without interruption when another group member is talking; avoid dominating the group discussion; be respectful of each other's thoughts and feelings; be sincere and honest when communicating their own thoughts and feelings; and make positive, cooperative, helpful, and trustworthy contributions in response to each other's comments.

Confidentiality is also an important issue in many task groups. Members are often unsure about what issues, proposals, and facts can be shared with their colleagues. For example, a state-level task force designed to study ways to improve services to older people trying to be self-sufficient in the community might deliberate for several months on several proposals before issuing press releases and meeting with the governor's staff and members of the legislature in a coordinated effort to have its proposals implemented. Premature or partial release of information can hinder the work of the task force. The worker should make the issue of confidentiality clear from the beginning to avoid premature or unauthorized releases of information.

Helping Members Feel a Part of the Group

When a group begins there is little sense of belonging or cohesion. An important objective for the worker during the beginning stage is to help a diverse collection of individuals, who may be apprehensive and ambivalent, begin to identify themselves as a collectivity of supportive partners in a common enterprise. The worker aims to build cohesion, while respecting individuality. To achieve this objective in early meetings, the worker should begin by helping members feel safe and comfortable in the group. Given a pre-group assessment of each member, the worker is in the best position to ensure that the demands of participating in a group do not exceed members' abilities. Thus, workers may tone down expectations for intimate disclosures suggested by a member, or scale down unrealistic expectations about what can be accomplished in a given time frame.

To help members feel that they are a part of the group, it is a good practice to point out shared interests and common goals among members. Members are comforted by the familiar. Knowing that they are not alone with their concerns or issues helps them to feel closer to other participants in the group.

Pointing out commonalities does not mean the worker should overlook differences, however. The leader can use several techniques to help members acknowledge and begin to appreciate differences in the beginning stage of the group. The leader can point out the contributions that different backgrounds and different perspectives make to the group, and can encourage members to explore differences and welcome new perspectives. The leader can ask nonthreatening, direct questions that help members explore, understand, and appreciate the different perspectives that are presented within the group.

The leader can also use program activities or exercises to help members explore differences in an entertaining and lively fashion. For example, a leader could help the group plan a dinner to which each member would bring a dish representative of their culture, ethnicity, or nationality. Another common activity is for each member to design a coat of arms that represents something about their personal background, and to present the coat of arms to the group for discussion. The leader might also ask each member to create a "self-disclosure collage" that artistically represents elements of themselves not known to other members in the group. Overall, differences among members in their backgrounds and life experiences should neither be magnified nor ignored. Instead, the worker's task is to help members appreciate and respect differences.

The worker also helps members feel that they are a part of the group by protecting them from injury. Thus, misinformation should be corrected, and personal attacks should not be condoned. Also, the worker should continually scan the group to ensure that the content of the group meeting is not having an adverse emotional effect on members.

Guiding the Development of the Group

Different theoretical writings suggest a range of possibilities for guiding the development of a group. Some writers suggest that the worker should provide little or no direction at the beginning of a group, preferring instead an approach that encourages members of the group to struggle with purposes and goals until mutual agreements about them can be achieved (Klein, 1970). Unstructured approaches to group beginnings are often used in t-groups and other growth groups, where the purpose of meeting is to learn about group dynamics, and one's own interpersonal interaction style. The process of struggling to develop purposes and goals without any direction from the leader, however, is often anxiety provoking. Therefore, workers should be cautious about using unstructured approaches with members who are not functioning at optimal levels, where time to achieve particular outcomes is limited, and where exploration of one's interpersonal style is not a primary goal.

Other writers suggest that techniques to guide the development of the group should be used only to empower members to make democratic decisions and to actualize the purposes and goals that members, rather than leaders, have agreed to accomplish. For example, in describing a humanistic approach to group work, Glassman and Kates (1990) suggest that the workers use techniques "in shaping the group members' processes of interaction and self-expression" (p. 121), but take care not to manipulate, coerce, or control members. A humanistic approach to leadership during the beginning stage is especially appropriate in support groups, social action groups, and coalitions where the empowerment of members and the mobilization of their collective energy and wisdom are primary goals. However, elements of a humanistic approach, such as respect for the dignity and individuality of each member and belief in each member's potential for growth and development, are essential in all group work efforts.

Writers within the humanistic tradition point out that techniques such as "directing" and making a "demand for work" can help members develop and implement mutually agreed upon purposes (see, for example, Gitterman & Shulman, 1986; Glassman & Kates, 1990; Shulman, 1992). Yet, few writers within the humanistic tradition spend time addressing issues of limit setting and socialization in groups of severely impaired individuals and in groups with members who have been ordered into treatment because of delinquent or criminal behavior. Clearly, however, there are many practice situations where the sponsoring organization and the larger society expect that workers will use their authority to help members function as more productive members of society. Yalom (1983), for example, points out the need for limit setting and a clear structure when working with psychiatric inpatients. Similarly, Levine and Gallogly (1985) suggest methods for dealing with challenges to the worker's authority when working with groups of alcoholics in inpatient and outpatient settings.

Those who eschew workers' use of expertise and authority to structure the group also rarely address leadership issues in the beginning stage of time-limited treatment groups. In many practice settings, short-term groups such as social skills and life skills training groups for psychiatric inpatients, groups to help new parents learn parenting skills, assertion training groups, and anger control groups are offered because workers have specific information and specific skills they think will benefit members. In these groups, the worker is designated by society and the sponsoring organization as an expert who provides direction and structure so that the members can learn new skills. Of course, even in these groups, members want some opportunity to share their concerns and learn from one another, but they also want specific methods and directions that will help them cope with and alleviate pressing problems and concerns. Thus, other writers have developed methods that are particularly helpful when working with time-limited groups. For example, Rose and colleagues (Rose, 1989; Rose, 1991; Rose & Edleson, 1987; Rose & Lecroy, 1991) propose that workers come to groups with relatively set agendas, concentrating their efforts on time-limited groups focused on specific problem areas rather than on long-term, less structured groups that do not limit the scope of problems dealt with by the group.

An example of a session agenda for a time-limited, structured parenting group is presented in Figure 6–1. The agenda provides the organizing framework for the first meeting. It indicates the goals for the session, the material to be covered during the group meeting, as well as the reading assignments and tasks required of each parent during the following week. Similar session agendas are prepared by the worker for each of the 10 sessions in the time-limited parenting group.

In structured, time-limited groups it is quite common for the agenda to be developed before the group session. As compared with less structured, process-centered approaches, structured group approaches give the worker greater responsibility for group goals and the way the group conducts its work (Papell & Rothman, 1980b). Whereas in process-centered approaches members are encouraged to take informal leadership roles and develop their own goals, agendas, and contracts, in time-limited groups members' input is generally limited to modifying goals, agendas, and contracts that the worker has already developed.

Drum and Knott (1977), Rose (1989), McKay and Paley (1992), and others describe a variety of time-limited, structured groups for acquiring skills, managing anxiety, coping with life transitions, and learning parenting skills. These

FIGURE 6–1
Sample session agenda for a time-limited, structured parenting group

---

AGENDA

Date _____

Session I

Goals
By the end of this session each parent will be able to:
1. Describe the purpose of the group program.
2. State how behavior is learned.
3. Describe specifically one behavior of his/her child.
4. State the behavior he/she will monitor during the next week.
5. Describe how each behavior will be monitored.

Agenda
1. Introduction
   A. Leader introduces self to group
   B. Each member introduces self to group (name, number of children, current problems you would like to work on)

2. Orientation to the group program
   A. Purpose of the group session
      1. Goals
      2. Why should parents be trained in parenting skills?
      3. Who is responsible for what?
   B. Group contracts
      1. Read, modify, sign

3. Introduction to behavior modification—lecture
   A. Behavior is learned
      1. Reinforcement
      2. Extinction
      3. Punishment
   B. Role-play demonstration

4. Break

5. Assessment
   A. Discussion of behavior checklist
   B. Describe one behavior of your child
   C. Develop monitoring plan: what, who, how, when

6. Buddy system
   A. Description
   B. Choose buddy, exchange numbers, arrange calling time

7. Assignment
   A. Monitor chosen behavior and begin to chart it
   B. Call buddy
   C. Read units 1 and 2 (exercises at the end of each chapter are optional)

8. Evaluation

---

groups usually meet for six to 16 meetings. Meetings usually contain a mixture of (a) educational material, (b) exercises, role play, and simulations to help members practice the material, (c) discussion of the material and the problems members are experiencing outside of the group, (d) a brief period to go over weekly assignments for members to do outside the group, and (e) an evaluation of the meeting.

Because they focus on educating members as well as on providing emotional support, these groups are sometimes referred to as "psychoeducational" treatment groups. Psychoeducational groups are an increasingly popular and important source of help for many clients (Papell & Rothman, 1980b). Perhaps the greatest asset of these groups is that they provide a planned framework that can be replicated intact, or modified and adapted to fit different types of client groups. For example, a worker who decides there is a need for a social skills training group in a particular setting can use the framework presented in Rose (1989) to lead this type of time-limited, structured group. Some other agendas for structured, time-limited groups appear in Drum and Knott (1977).

In a series of studies on the efficacy of group work, groups with specific purposes, homogeneous concerns, clear agendas, and structured group meetings were found to be more effective than groups with less structure (Toseland, 1977; Toseland & Rose, 1978; Toseland, Kabat & Kemp, 1983). Members reported appreciating the leader providing specific information and effective strategies to help them with their concerns. Thus, in a group program for patients recovering from bypass surgery, the leader can provide information about nutrition, diet, exercise and other lifestyle changes while providing members with an opportunity to discuss specific concerns and to learn stress reduction and other coping techniques.

At the same time, workers should keep in mind that members' concerns and needs are not always most appropriately served by a time-limited, structured group approach. In support groups, for example, a flexible structure that maximized member input was found to be more effective than a structured approach in helping members to ventilate their concerns, and to give and receive help from fellow group members (Toseland & Hacker, 1982; Toseland, Decker & Bliesner, 1979; Toseland, Sherman & Bliven, 1981). In these groups, members were encouraged to reach out to one another as much as possible. Goals and specific agendas for each meeting were determined on the basis of feedback and mutual agreement among all members during meetings.

It is unfortunate that there is not more dialogue between those who promote short-term, structured, behavioral and task-centered approaches to treatment groups, and those who promote long-term, process-oriented, humanistic approaches. Those who promote one approach over another often fail to acknowledge the value of alternative approaches, actively dismiss important contributions of alternative approaches, and ignore the core skills that form the base of all of group work. It is the thesis of this text that both approaches have much to offer, and that social work practice situations fall along a continuum. At the ends of the continuum "pure" approaches may be effectively applied, but in most practice situations a blending of approaches makes the most sense. In our approach to group work with treatment groups, structure is viewed as a tool that should be used differentially in different practice situations to help members and the group as a whole achieve agreed upon objectives.

Structure in Task Groups

In task groups, feedback is encouraged in several ways. Members might be encouraged to submit formal agenda items before group meetings. These items are then placed on the agenda. When the item is considered by the group, it is often helpful for the member who submitted the item to present it to the group. During meetings, members' feedback is usually limited to a discussion of the specific task or agenda item currently being discussed. Members have a chance to add new agenda items during a meeting but only if the group's predetermined order of business can be concluded in time to discuss any new business.

Written agendas are frequently used in task groups to keep groups focused on the work that is to be accomplished. Figure 6–2 is an example of an agenda for a meeting of a delegate council. It is standard procedure to (a) approve the minutes of the previous meeting, (b) receive reports from standing committees and administrative officers, (c) work on current business, and then (d) discuss any new business that might have been introduced earlier in the group meeting.

Agenda items can be divided into three categories; information, discussion, and action. Often, agendas are accompanied by attachments to explain the agenda items. Agendas with their attachments are usually given to all group members several days before the meeting so they can become familiar with the business that will be discussed during the meeting.

FIGURE 6–2
Sample agenda for a delegate council

Meeting date _____

CYPRUS HILLS DELEGATE COUNCIL

Order of Business	Information	Discussion	Action
1. Call to order			X
2. Approval of the minutes for the previous meeting			X
3. Treasurer's report	X		
4. Program committee's report	X		
5. Director's report	X		
6. Emergency housing proposal		X	
7. Proposed changes in bylaws (see attachment A)			X
8. Election of members of the women's issues task force (see attachment B for slate of candidates)		X	
9. Proposal to develop an ad-hoc committee on community health care		X	
10. New business		X	

Task and Socio-emotional Focus

Another objective of the worker in the beginning stage is to balance the task and socio-emotional aspects of the group process. Through systematic observation of leadership training groups, committees, juries, classes, therapy groups, and labor relations teams, Bales (1950) established a set of 12 categories to describe group interactions. Half of the categories are in problem-solving or task-focused areas, and the other half pertain to socio-emotional areas. Bales' scheme for observing a group is instructive because it points out that in all groups the worker must be conscious of both task and socio-emotional aspects of group process.

In task groups, it has been found that about two thirds of the group interactions are focused on task accomplishment and one third on socio-emotional aspects such as giving support and releasing tension (Bales, 1955). Evidence concerning treatment groups suggests that they may spend considerably more time on socio-emotional than on task-focused discussion (Munzer & Greenwald, 1957).

The evidence presented by Bales (1950, 1955) also suggests that in both task and treatment groups, neither the task nor the socio-emotional aspects of group process can be neglected. An exclusive focus on tasks in any group may lead to members' dissatisfaction with their social and emotional interaction in the group. Focusing exclusively on tasks can lead to conflict among members and may result in a less effective group.

An exclusive focus on the social and emotional aspects of group interaction will lead to a group whose members will be satisfied with their relationships with one another but will be dissatisfied about what has been accomplished. Thus, a balance between the task and the socio-emotional aspects of group process is essential.

No magic formula exists for achieving the appropriate balance between task and socio-emotional aspects of the group. Writers such as Coyle (1930), Klein (1970), Schwartz (1971), Shulman (1992), and Tropp (1968), tend to focus on the socio-emotional side of group interaction. Feldman and Wodarski (1975), Rose (1989), Sarri (1974), and Vinter (1967) are more concerned with group and individual tasks. Through careful assessment of the group needs and the members' needs, the worker can decide on an appropriate balance and help the group achieve it.

Goal Setting in Group Work

In the first few meetings, groups often spend a considerable amount of time discussing goals. When the worker discusses the group's purposes, the process of goal formulation begins. Goals continue to be defined and modified as the functioning of the group and its members are assessed.

Group workers differ in their opinions about who should take responsibility for formulating goals. While Glassman and Kates (1990), Klein (1970), and Tropp (1968) suggest that members should set their own goals, Konopka (1983), Rose (1989), and Vinter (1985a) believe that through diagnosis and assessment the worker formulates goals for the group. Phillips (1951), Schwartz (1971), and Trecker (1972) emphasize that the worker helps formulate goals by finding a common purpose between the individual members' goals and the agency's function and purpose. It is our position that goals in group work practice emerge from the interaction of individual members, the worker, and the system in which the group functions.

As professionals, workers' goals are influenced by the values and aims of the social work profession. As members of social service organizations, workers are aware of the aims and the limitations of the services they provide. Workers should also be cognizant of their function in the larger society, which sanctions and supports their work. Workers' formulation of goals reflect what they believe can be accomplished, given the support, resources, and limitations within which the group operates.

Workers' goals also are affected by what they know about the group members. In treatment groups, workers often have an opportunity to meet each member during the planning stage. Potential members are selected, in part, because of their compatibility with the purposes and goals developed for the group. Workers make preliminary assessments of members' needs and capacities as well as the tasks that face each group member. Goals are formulated on the basis of this assessment process.

In task groups, a similar process occurs. Goals are formulated by the worker in relation to the capacities of members. For example, a worker who is leading a committee to examine problems of interdepartmental coordination would be reluctant to set a goal of changing agency procedures if none of the committee members are in policy-making positions in their departments. However, given the status and role of the members, the worker might help the group formulate a goal that includes making recommendations to respective department heads about steps that could be taken to improve coordination between departments. In this case, goal formulation is affected by the characteristics of the members who compose the group.

Goals are also formulated by individual group members who have their own perspective on the particular concerns, problems, and issues that affect them and their fellow group members. In previously formed or natural groups, members have the advantage of knowing more than the worker does about the concerns of the other group members.

In formed groups where members do not know each other before the first group meeting, members' goals are based on (a) their assessment of their own needs, (b) their previous attempts to accomplish these goals, (c) the environmental, social, and familial demands placed upon them, (d) their assessment of their own capacities and capabilities, and (e) their impressions or experiences of what the social service agency sponsoring the group has to offer.

Goals for the group are formulated through a process of exploration and negotiation in which the worker and the group members share their perspectives. (Schopler, Galinsky, & Alicke, 1985). In this process, members and the worker should communicate openly about the goals they have formulated individually. Evidence suggests that members should share the variables they believe are important in arriving at a decision, and mutually examine and agree upon a common set of criteria before arriving at a decision (Toseland, Rivas & Chapman, 1984). Such a process helps avoid disagreements over solutions, increase group cohesion, and increase members' willingness to implement the decisions.

The extent to which common goals can be developed for all group members varies from group to group. In some groups, members have one overriding concern in common. For example, a group of cigarette smokers suffering from chronic lung disease may be able to move quickly to a discussion of a specific contract to reduce cigarette smoking. In groups that are more diverse, such as outpatients in a mental health setting, it is often more difficult to develop common goals. In these groups, common goals are often formulated on a general level, for example, to improve the interpersonal social skills of members. Goals for individuals in the group are formulated at a more specific level. For example, an individual goal might be to improve my skills when confronting others about behaviors I find unacceptable.

The process of goal setting, therefore, is one in which the goals of the worker and the members are explored and clarified. Three types of goals emerge from this process: (a) group-centered goals that focus on the proper functioning and maintenance of the group, (b) common group goals that focus on the problems, concerns, and tasks faced by all group members, and (c) individual goals that focus on the specific concerns of each group member or the worker. In an educational treatment group for parents of young children, a group-centered goal might be to increase the group's attraction for its members. A common group goal might call for the parents to learn about the normal growth and development patterns of young children. An individual goal might be for a set of parents to reduce their son's temper tantrums.

In task groups, three levels of goals can also be identified. For example, in a committee mandated to review intake procedures in a family service agency, a group-centered goal might be to establish open, member-centered interaction patterns. A common group goal would be to make several recommendations to the program director to improve admission procedures. An individual goal for a committee member might be to interview workers in two other agencies about different approaches to intake procedures that can be shared with the committee at the next meeting.

The worker should help members develop clear, specific goals. Early in the process, members formulate general goals they would like to achieve. Statements such as, "I would like to be less depressed," or "The group should try to reduce the paperwork involved in serving our clients" are common.

After members have stated their goals for the group, workers should help specify and clarify them. This can be done by helping members identify objective and subjective referents of their goals and the criteria that will be used to evaluate goal achievement. For the goal statement "I would like to be less depressed," a member might define the referents of depression as sleeplessness, lack of appetite, and so on, and suggest criteria for improvement, such as sleeping seven hours each night and eating three meals a day.

Defining goals clearly helps workers and members alike focus on what they are attempting to achieve in the group. Developing clear goals is a prerequisite for entering the middle stage of group work. Before goals can be prioritized and a contract between worker and members developed, goals should be stated as clearly as possible. All members of the group should have input into the development of these goals, giving them an opportunity to influence the direction the group will take to accomplish its tasks.

In previously formed groups, which have pre-existing goals, the worker has a different role in goal formulation. In some of these groups, goals may not have been clearly defined and the worker's task is to help members clarify their goals. This is often the case with groups of teen-agers and children who have not carefully considered their goals. In other previously formed groups, clear goals may exist. The worker's task, then, is to become familiar with these goals and help the group achieve those that can be accomplished and modify or abandon those that are not likely to be achieved.

Sometimes a worker is asked to consult with a group when the group is blocked in its attempt to achieve its goals. The worker should help the group reassess its goals to ensure that they are clear and mutually agreed upon by members, that they do not conflict with one another, and that they are achievable.

Achieving consensus about purposes and goals can be particularly difficult with involuntary members who are often pressured into participating in a group. Still, there is usually some common ground in which mutually agreed upon goals can be developed. For example, youthful offenders are sometimes given the choice of participating in group treatment or being sentenced through the usual juvenile court system. The worker can begin by stating the conditions and standards for continued participation and then encourage members to develop their own goals within these minimally acceptable conditions and standards. Trust takes longer to develop in such groups, but if the worker consistently shows interest in the members' goals, concerns, and aspirations, the group can be a useful treatment modality.

Contracting

In the group work context, contracts are mutual agreements that specify expectations, obligations, and duties. Most commonly, a contract is developed between group members and the worker who acts as the representative of the agency. However, as Garvin (1987) indicates, contracts also can be developed between (a) the group as a whole and the agency, (b) the group as a whole and the worker, (c) the group as a whole and a member, (d) a group member and the worker, and (e) two or more group members. Generally, contracts involving the group as a whole are developed around group procedures (see Chapter 5). Individual members' contracts with the agency, the worker, or other members are usually developed around individual treatment goals or individual task assignments.

The most common form of individual member contract is between a member and the worker. For example, a member may contract with the worker to stop smoking, to become more assertive, or to make more friends.

Contracts can also be developed between two or more group members. They help each other achieve particular goals. For example, in an assertiveness training group, one member might decide to practice being assertive in two situations during the group meeting and in one situation during the week. The member may ask another member to praise her if she is assertive in the group and to telephone her during the week to see if she has been assertive in a situation outside the group. In return, she agrees to help the other member achieve a particular goal.

A third form of individual contracting occurs between a member and the group. The member, for example, can agree to obtain information about a resource for the group or can promise to report back to the group about the results of a particular meeting. In an attractive, cohesive group, member-to-group contracts can be quite effective because the member does not want to let other members down by failing to follow through on the contract.

When contracting with individual members for goals or tasks, it is important to be as specific as possible in stating what is to be accomplished, who will be involved in the effort, and how success or failure will be determined. Bertcher and Maple (1977) refer to this process as formulating behaviorally specific outcome goals. Goals specified in a written or verbal contract should state briefly who will do what, under what circumstances, and how it will be measured. The following examples contain outcome goals for a treatment group and a task group:

Treatment Group (To help members stop smoking)

Who:	Mary Jane
Will do what:	will refuse the offer of a cigarette
Under what circumstances:	when it is offered at a social gathering
How will it be measured:	and will report this offer to the group

Who:	John Franks
Will do what:	will smoke less than three cigarettes
Under what circumstances:	at home, during each day of next week
How will it be measured:	as reported by spouse

Task Group (Committee to study juvenile crime)

Who:	Bill Evans
Will do what:	will interview the local family court judge
Under what circumstances:	prior to the next meeting
How will it be measured:	and prepare a written report for the committee

Who:	Ann Murphy
Will do what:	will read five articles on juvenile crime
Under what circumstances:	within the next two weeks
How will it be measured:	and report significant findings to the committee

Facilitating Members' Motivation

After an initial clarification of the broad purpose and goals of the group, the worker then helps members increase their motivation to begin accomplishing the purposes and goals. Motivation is the key to the successful achievement of the group's goals and members' own personal goals. To a large extent, such motivation is determined by members' expectations about (a) the worker's role in the group, (b) the processes that will occur in the group, and (c) what can be accomplished through the work of the group. Members bring a set of expectations to any group experience and those expectations have a powerful influence on the way the members behave in the group. For example, if a member expects the worker to tell him or her how to proceed, it is unlikely that the member will take much initiative in the group. If the member has been involved in a previous group experience where little was accomplished, the member's expectations and motivations to work hard to achieve individual and group goals is likely to be diminished.

As the worker and the members begin to explore how they can work together, the worker should help the members identify their expectations and motivations. The worker can do this by asking members direct questions about what they think they can accomplish in the group and how they expect the group to function. It is surprising how often these questions will uncover ambivalence about giving up old ways of doing things and fear about what new and unknown changes will bring. Ambivalence frequently accompanies members' plans to attain desired goals.

Working Through Ambivalence and Resistance

Sometimes, members will respond evasively to direct questions about their motivations and expectations. This is particularly true when the worker has made an early and clear "demand for work" before assessing members' expectations and motivations (Schwartz, 1971, p. 11). The worker may find members reluctant to state ambivalent feelings about their ability to accomplish the goals for which they have contracted, fearing that the worker will disapprove. Before the worker states his or her expectations about what members need to do to accomplish their goals, the worker should tune in to the overt and covert messages members give about accomplishing the group's work. If the worker picks up signals indicating a lack of motivation to accomplish goals, the worker should check his or her perception of the meaning of the message with the group members.

Ambivalent feelings about change are common and should not be viewed as an obstacle to accomplishing the group's work. It is rare for changes to be proposed and worked on without some ambivalent feelings, and it is often difficult and painful to change problematic areas of one's life. At the very least, it requires giving up the security of old ways of doing things. Rather than ignoring, playing down, or attacking the ambivalence, workers should help members work through it. Acknowledging members' ambivalence is a helpful way to get members to recognize their reactions to change. A frank discussion of a member's ambivalence about change and their perceived ability to achieve a goal will help all members see that this is a common reaction to the changes they are planning to make. Also, a realistic appraisal of the chances for success is much preferred to covering up barriers to task achievement.

One exercise that can help uncover ambivalence is to have each member focus on a goal and list psychological, social, and environmental factors that hinder and promote its achievement. A variation on this exercise done with individual clients has been called "force field analysis" (Egan, 1990). In task groups, all members focus on one group goal. In treatment groups, it is more common for members to focus on one member's goal, but occasionally it is possible to select a common group goal upon which to focus. The exercise can be done by all group members, in pairs, or at home between sessions.

In a force field analysis, the worker helps members list the positive and negative aspects of attaining a goal on paper or a blackboard and display the results before all group members. This facilitates an organized discussion of the factors that can help members achieve goals and those that may hinder them. Such a visual display helps members realize, often with surprise, that despite their verbal assertions about achieving a goal, many factors may be detracting from their motivation.

An example of a list of positive and negative factors that influence a group member's decision about whether or not to separate from her husband is shown in Figure 6–3. The list was made after a lengthy discussion of the member's situation. An examination of a list of factors can help group members decide whether there are sufficient positive motivations for achieving a particular goal.

If a decision is reached to pursue a goal despite numerous factors that reduce motivation, the task of the worker and the members is to suggest ways to

FIGURE 6–3
Analysis of factors that increase and decrease the motivation of a member of a treatment group

Problem: Whether or not to separate from my husband

Factors Increasing Motivation
1. Tom drinks too much.
2. Tom has been physically abusive twice in the last year.
3. There is almost daily verbal conflict between Tom and myself.
4. Staying in the relationship causes me to feel angry and depressed.
5. My relationship is interfering with the quality of my work at my job.
6. Tom and I have infrequent sexual relations.
7. The kids are being affected by our constant fighting.

Factors Decreasing Motivation
1. Concern about what breaking up will do to the kids.
2. Worried about whether I can live on only my salary.
3. Wonder if I can care for three kids and keep working 40 hours a week.
4. Feeling as if I would be breaking my commitment to Tom.
5. I'll have to explain the separation to my parents, friends, etc.

decrease those factors and increase the positive factors. For example, in the situation outlined in Figure 6–3, the member decides to separate from her husband. To help the member change some of the factors that reduce her motivation, the group helps the member (a) overcome her fear about the effects of the separation on her children by suggesting that the children may be harmed more by seeing Mom and Dad constantly fighting than by experiencing their parents' separation, (b) examine her finances, her plans for child care, and other practical needs that she may have as she considers living independently, and (c) build her self-confidence and self-esteem by providing support and positive feedback during the separation process. Through this process, the group helps the member become motivated to achieve her goal with as little ambivalence, fear, and anguish as possible.

In some groups, workers will encounter members who believe they have been coerced or manipulated into coming to the group. Instead of engaging in the work of the group, these members often spend valuable group time complaining about being forced to participate. In an excellent text on dealing with resistant group members, Edelwich and Brodsky (1992) suggest that in such a situation, the worker can point out that the members chose to participate in the group. Although some individuals may have chosen to participate in the group to avoid other less desirable choices, that was an agreement made with a referring agency. For example, in the case of being found guilty of driving while intoxicated, the member may have agreed to participate in a group treatment program instead of losing his driver's license. The worker should acknowledge that the member may not want to be in the group, while noting that he has freely chosen the group over an alternative. The worker should also state that members are free to terminate their participation at any time, but their decision to participate implies that they will adhere to the group norms and contractual obligations that all members agreed to during their intake interview.

As the group progresses, it may be necessary to remind members of the negative consequences of not participating and that the member has the power to make additional choices that have positive consequences. Edelwich and Brodsky (1992) suggest that the worker use "I" statements while making a clear demand for work. For example, the worker might state:

> I have a problem. Some of you don't seem to want to be here. If you don't want to be here, you don't have to be here. I don't want you to get the wrong impression—I'd rather you stay. But if you don't like being in the group, you can take it up with the agency that sent you and deal with the consequences of not continuing your participation. My job is to help you use your time in this group productively. Therefore, I would like those of you who choose to stay, to think now about how you will use the group—what you want to accomplish. Think about the problems and issues in your life and what you'd like to work on in this group. I'll give you a few minutes. Then, let's go around and see what we can do together.

Expectations About Role Performance

In addition to ambivalence about changing a way of doing things, members often are concerned at the beginning of the group that they will not be able to contribute in the way they think is expected of them. For example, members of a committee may think they will be asked to do too much to prepare for group meetings, or they may fear they have nothing to contribute. Similarly, members of educational groups are often apprehensive about their ability to learn new material, and members of support groups are fearful that members will not understand or share their concerns. Because expectations about role performance can interfere with a member's participation in the group, it is helpful for workers to describe their expectations of members, soliciting member feedback and input. This process provides a forum for members to air their fears about the challenges they face. It also helps clarify any mistaken or distorted expectations that members may have, and provides an opportunity for workers to modify or change their own expectations.

Authentic Communication About Purposes and Goals

Ambivalence about changing, and fears about the demands that may be placed on them, may lead members to be less than candid in early group meetings. Shulman (1992) points out that members of treatment groups may begin by sharing "near" problems "that do not bear directly on some of the more difficult and hard-to-talk about issues" (p. 320). In task groups, members may bring up peripheral issues that could potentially sidetrack the group.

To increase authentic communication as the group develops, the worker can take several steps:

- Always treat members' suggestions and ideas about how to proceed with respect. The worker should not dismiss or ignore what a member says, treating it as a "smoke screen" or a "red herring." This will only alienate members and certainly will not encourage them to open up and reveal more meaningful issues. Instead, the worker should strive to understand the deeper issues implied by the member's message.
- Link the member's statements with the larger purposes of the group. The worker can do this by asking members how the suggestions or ideas fit in with the agreed upon purposes of the group.
- Place the relevant parts of the member's message in the context of themes or issues that have been previously discussed in the group.
- Support the initiative the member demonstrated by speaking up, without necessarily endorsing the message. Statements such as "I'm glad to see that you are thinking about what you want to accomplish in the group" or "I'm happy to see that you care enough about the direction of the group to make that suggestion" let members know that their perspectives are welcome and valued without indicating that the worker supports the content of the message.

Anticipating Obstacles

In the beginning stage of group work it is also important for workers to help members anticipate the obstacles they may encounter as they work on specific goals and objectives. It is useful to ask members to describe the obstacles they foresee in accomplishing individual and group goals. Sometimes it is useful to encourage members to engage in a "time projection" program activity. In this exercise, members are asked to imagine what it will be like for them at the end of the group when they have accomplished their goals. Members can be encouraged to discuss how changes brought about in the group will be experienced by those around them, focusing particularly on what might prevent any accomplishments from being implemented, and from persisting over time. As members share potential impediments to long-term, meaningful change, the worker can facilitate a discussion about overcoming these impediments. Experience suggests that when members and the leader are aware of potential obstacles, they can often plan ways to overcome them before the middle or working stage of the group. Chapters 8–11 describe a variety of methods that can be used during the working stage of a group to help members overcome obstacles to accomplishing specific goals.

SUMMARY

Although all aspects of group work are important for the successful functioning of a group, the initial stage sets the tone for its future development. In the beginning stage, the worker's central task is to ensure that a group develops patterns of relating and patterns of task accomplishment that facilitate functioning as the group moves toward its middle stage of development.

To accomplish this, workers should focus on achieving certain objectives in the beginning stage of task and treatment groups. These include (a) introducing members of the group, (b) clarifying the purpose and function of the group as it is perceived by the worker, the members, and the sponsoring organization, (c) clarifying confidentiality issues, (d) helping members feel a part of the group, (e) guiding the development of the group, (f) balancing task and socio-emotional aspects of the group process, (g) setting goals, (h) contracting for work, (i) facilitating members' motivation and ability to work in the group, and (j) anticipating obstacles.

Workers who are able to help their groups achieve these objectives in the initial stage will find themselves in a good position to help the group make a smooth transition to the middle stage of development. Any objectives that are not achieved early in the group's development will have to be reconsidered later as the group and its members encounter difficulties accomplishing agreed upon goals.

LEARNING ASSIGNMENTS

1. If you were asked to lead a group for elementary school children who exhibited acting out behavior in the classroom, what fears would you have about leading the group? How would you overcome these fears? Identify ways that you could structure group meetings to avoid acting out behavior.

2. Form a small classroom group. Select three of the warm-up or introduction exercises described in this chapter. Use each exercise in your group. After you have completed all three, discuss the benefits and drawbacks of each. For what populations would each exercise be most appropriate?

3. Form a small classroom group. Have each member identify a study habit he or she would like to change. Have each member specify a change goal, and the steps to achieve it. Using a format similar to the one shown in Figure 6–3, identify factors that would increase and decrease each group member's motivation for achieving his or her goal.

CHAPTER 7

Assessment

Because of the complexity of human behavior and group dynamics, assessment is one of the most challenging aspects of group work practice. The worker makes assessments to understand particular practice situations and to plan effective interventions. For a complete and thorough assessment, the group worker considers (a) individual group members, (b) the group as a whole, and (c) the group's environment. Workers begin their assessments during the planning stage and continue to assess and reassess until the group ends.

Although assessments are made in all stages of a group's life, the process dominates a worker's time in the beginning phase of group work after the planning tasks discussed in Chapter 5 are completed. It is at this time that the worker is most actively engaged in understanding the functioning of the group and its members.

Assessment Defined

Siporin (1975) has stated, "assessment is both a process and a product upon which the helping process is based" (p. 219). As a process, assessment involves gathering, organizing, and making judgments about information. As a product, assessment is a verbal or written statement of the functioning of the group and its members, which is useful in the development of intervention plans.

There is little agreement in the group work literature about assessment terminology or assessment focus. Some writers use the term *diagnosis* to describe the process of identifying and analyzing problems faced by individual group members (see, for example, Sundel, Radin, & Churchill, 1985; Sarri, Galinsky, Glasser, Siegel, & Vinter, 1967). The term *diagnosis* has also been used to describe the process of analyzing problems in group functioning (Klein, 1970). Other writers use the term *assessment* (Levine, 1979; Rose, 1989), and some prefer not to use either term because both stress problems rather than strengths (see, for example, Schwartz, 1976; Shulman, 1992; Tropp, 1976).

In this text, we use the term *assessment* rather than *diagnosis* because it is more compatible with a generalist approach to social group work practice. *Diagnosis* is a term borrowed from medicine; it refers to the identification of disease processes within an individual. In contrast, a thorough generalist assessment should focus on both the strengths and problems encountered by individual group members and the group as a whole, and should carefully consider the effect of the larger social environment on the group and its members.

As with other aspects of social group work practice, assessment varies according to the type of group being conducted. In a treatment group, for example, the worker frequently focuses assessments on the problems experienced by individual members, whereas a task group leader's assessment is often focused on the ability of members to contribute to the group's productivity.

Despite differences in focus, there are many commonalities in the assessments made by workers leading different types of groups. For example, in both task and treatment groups, most workers assess the strengths and weaknesses of the group as a whole, the members, and the external environment in which the group and its members function. Commonalities also can be found in the assessment of different groups that are at the same stage of development. For example, in the beginning stage, workers make a systematic assessment of the functioning of the group and its members. During the middle stage, workers test the validity of their initial assessments and modify their intervention plans on the basis of the success of early interventions. In the ending stage of the group, the worker makes an assessment of group and member functioning to highlight accomplishments and to focus attention on areas that still need work.

Relationship to Individual Assessment

Many readers of this text are familiar with generalist social work practice approaches to assessing individuals. Generally, these approaches rely on systems theory and take a holistic approach that includes an understanding of the biological, psychological, social, cultural and environmental aspects of an individual's functioning (see, for example, Chess & Norlin, 1991; Longres, 1990; Zastrow and Kirst-Ashman, 1990). What differs about assessment when working with groups is that in addition to assessing individual members, group workers must also assess the functioning of the group as a whole, and the group in relation to its environment.

Still, there is a tendency for group workers to focus on content expressed by individuals in the group rather than on the processes of group interaction. Perhaps this is because many group workers were originally caseworkers, and have more experience working with individuals than with groups. Also, some workers do not have any formal education in group work. In any case, unless an intolerable problem that can't be avoided arises during group interaction, workers rarely make a point of discussing communication and interaction patterns, cohesion, roles, norms, status and the group culture—despite the fact that these dynamics affect the functioning of all members, and the group as a whole. Our clinical and supervisory experience was confirmed by data from an analysis of the content/style of group leaders of peer-led and professionally led caregiver groups (Toseland, Rossiter, Peak, & Hill, 1990). It was also confirmed in a study of more than 200 groups conducted by William Hill during the 1950s and 1960s. His studies revealed that on the average, group leaders spend little time on matters pertaining to group-as-a-whole dynamics (Hill, 1965).

We strongly recommend that group workers be vigilant about spending time during each group meeting discussing group processes. This is most often accomplished by making a conscious effort to point out processes in the here-and-now of group interaction. Sometimes, however, stopping the action to identify, clarify, or discuss group processes can be disruptive to the content being discussed. An effective alternative is to reserve a few minutes at the end of each group meeting for the worker and members to comment on and discuss the group processes. For example, a member might state that there seemed to be a great deal of member-to-member communication during the group meeting, that the discussion included only a few members, or that members did not seem to be considering the points of view of others. Similarly, the worker might comment on the norms developing in the group, or the roles that members were playing. The group can then be encouraged to discuss what changes, if any, they would like to make in the group dynamics during future meetings.

If a separate time is set aside at the ending of the group for "processing the group," care should be taken not to use this time to discuss content. It is easy to slip into discussions of content when group processes are being discussed. For example, during a discussion of group interaction patterns, two members might note that the entire session was spent focused on one member's problem. Another member might say, "John talked a lot because he is having a lot of problems with his wife." The worker should point out that the issue is not John's problem with his wife, but rather whether the group wants to spend an entire session focused on one member's concern. The worker can then guide the group in a discussion of the pros and cons of focusing on one member.

We have also found that, with the exception of social action groups and coalitions, workers also often fail to assess the group's environment. Therefore, we also recommend that periodically throughout the life of a group, workers and members take some time to describe and discuss their perceptions of the relationship of the group to the sponsoring organization and to the larger community that sanctions the group's work.

Overall, then, assessment in group work is more complex than assessment in practice with individuals. In addition to assessing the functioning of individual group members, assessment in group work also means examining the processes that take place in the group as a whole, and the support and opposition the group as a whole is likely to encounter in the larger social environment.

THE ASSESSMENT PROCESS

Fisher (1978) has aptly described assessment as a funneling process. In the early stages, the worker is confronted with amorphous and sketchy data about the group and its members. Initially, the worker fills in gaps by collecting missing data. As information is collected, the worker begins to sort through it, organizing it systematically. The group members should be involved as much as possible in judging the data in order to select goals and decide on targets for intervention.

Gradually, the assessment process narrows as data are collected and organized and judgments are made about how to intervene in, cope with, or alleviate a problem. In a group for people getting a divorce, for example, the worker might ask members to describe their feelings about their spouses. Information gathered from this preliminary assessment will lead the worker to a further assessment of members' feelings of loss and feelings of anger toward their spouses. The worker then facilitates members' discussion of these feelings and helps them to make judgments about what interventions would be most helpful. Results of the assessment process are used to develop an intervention plan, which includes helping members express their feelings, share effective coping skills, and practice using coping skills to help them work through their feelings during and between group meetings.

How Much Information?   Several issues arise when workers assess the functioning of the group and its members. One of the most basic of these is how much information to collect. Although it is often recommended that workers collect as much information as possible (psychosocial histories for members of treatment groups or extensive information-gathering efforts in task groups), increasing information beyond a certain point may not lead to better interventions (see Miller & Tripodi, 1967; Tripodi & Miller, 1966). For example, Wolins (1959) found that beyond a certain point more information reduced rather than increased the reliability of clinical judgments, and Brieland (1959) found that workers tended to formulate judgments before accumulating all available information.

When making an assessment, the worker should balance the need for detailed information with the need for action to relieve a problematic situation. When workers are not faced with urgent situations that require immediate intervention, they should take time to examine all available data about a situation. No matter how much information is collected, workers should suspend their judgments about a problematic situation until they have reflected on all the data they have time to collect. In our experience in practice and in supervising students, we have noticed that a widespread and potentially damaging mistake of novice workers occurs when they make judgments and offer suggestions concerning intervention strategies before they fully understand a problem or have found out what the member has already done to cope with it. When making premature suggestions, the novice is often confronted by a group member who says, "I tried that and it didn't work." The result is that the worker is at a loss as to how to proceed and the member's faith in the worker's ability to help is shaken.

At the same time, workers are sometimes confronted with urgent situations that preclude extensive data collection. The worker should be guided by goals formulated during the planning and the beginning stages of group work. The worker also should be as clear as possible about the relevance of the information being collected. Extensive data collection that has little relation to the group's goals is a violation of members' right to privacy and of dubious value for accomplishing group and individual member goals.

Pincus and Minahan (1973) have suggested some other principles to guide workers in their data collection efforts. These include (a) using more than one mode of data collection whenever possible, (b) distinguishing between the problem, concern, or task about which information is being collected and the source of the information, (c) obtaining relevant samples of data from several sources, (d) structuring data collection so that relevant information can be obtained quickly and efficiently, (e) developing a system that will not place overwhelming demands on those who are collecting information or on those who are asked for information, and (f) avoiding biasing data despite the selectivity and subjectivity that is an inherent part of any data collection and assessment effort. In regard to the last point, involving all group members in the assessment process provides many points of view that can help overcome limitations of the worker's subjectivity. It can also be helpful to discuss assessment data with a co-leader or a supervisor between group meetings.

Diagnostic Labels.   Another issue that often arises when making assessments of the members of treatment groups concerns the use of diagnostic classification systems and labels. Classification systems, such as the Diagnostic and Statistical Manual of Mental Disorders, are used in many mental health settings for assessment and for reimbursement purposes (American Psychiatric Association, 1987). Because diagnostic labels can carry social stigmas, clients may be at risk for harmful stereotyping or may behave in ways that are consistent with the labels ascribed to them (Cone & Hawkins, 1977; Fisher & Gochros, 1975; Hersen & Bellack, 1976).

Previous versions of the manual have been criticized as unreliable and irrelevant in relation to the selection of intervention procedures (see, for example, Hersen & Bellack, 1976). However, the latest version appears to overcome many of those problems. Although group work practitioners should be wary of the indiscriminate use of diagnostic labels in mental health settings because of the social stigma attached to them, diagnostic classification systems can be helpful in making differential assessments and arriving at treatment plans for group members.

While an in-depth examination of the applications of the Diagnostic and Statistical Manual to group treatment is beyond the scope of this text, one example may help illustrate its usefulness. If not diagnosed properly, a confused 71-year-old could conceivably be diagnosed as having organic brain syndrome and be recommended for treatment in reality orientation and program activity groups to prevent further deterioration. Using the criteria stated in the manual, however, the person's confusion may be diagnosed properly as a major depressive episode compounded by isolation and malnutrition. Given this diagnosis, a quite different form of group treatment would be recommended after the person's malnutrition had been treated. For example, the person might be encouraged to attend a remedial group for those suffering from problems of depression and to expand his or her friendship network by becoming involved in an activity group at a senior center or a social group at a church or synagogue.

Assessment Focus.   A third issue that often arises when making an assessment is whether to focus data collection on the present or the past. Fisher (1978), for example, has suggested that assessment should be focused on the present. Others suggest it is important to obtain a developmental perspective that includes historical data (Siporin, 1972). Each of the many different models of social work practice suggests slightly different foci. For example, Germain and Gitterman's (1980) life model focuses on (a) life transitions involving developmental changes, status role changes, and crisis events, (b) the unresponsiveness of social and physical environments, and (c) communication and relationship difficulties. Reid (1978) proposes focusing on the here-and-now problems articulated by clients.

Recommendations about how to focus assessments can help workers become aware of the many approaches available to them for different types of groups. Workers should not become locked into one consistent assessment focus. Premature allegiance to a particular view of a situation can result in workers ignoring important data or attempting to fit all data into a particular conceptualization of the situation (Bieri, 1962; Bieri et al, 1966).

In focusing their assessments, workers should be guided by the unique needs and particular circumstances of specific groups. In one case, for example, it may be important to focus on members' family situations while in another case it may be more beneficial to assess members' problem-solving skills. In other words, the focus of assessment should change with the changing needs of the group and its members.

Although the assessment process should be responsive to each unique situation as it arises, several practice principles can help workers make an accurate assessment of any group and its members. One principle is that workers should strive to obtain facts, not opinions. This can be done by separating subjective impressions from observed events. Inferences about observed events should be based on logic and evidence. Another way for the worker to strive for objectivity is to share observations and inferences with group members. They can confirm the validity of the observations and inferences and give the worker an alternate perspective. Workers can also check the validity of subjective inferences by reviewing the data on which they are based with a supervisor or consultant. Obtaining alternate perspectives in this manner can help the worker make assessments and formulate intervention plans.

ASSESSING THE FUNCTIONING OF GROUP MEMBERS

When making an assessment, workers should examine three broad aspects of members' functioning: (a) the intrapersonal life of the member, (b) the interpersonal interactions of the member, and (c) the environment in which the member functions. Workers should also assess how the personal characteristics of each member interact with their functional abilities. Personal characteristics such as racial and cultural identity, gender, and age have an important influence on how members interact with one another in the group. For example, in working with groups of Native Americans, the worker should be aware of the cultural norm of withholding opinions about other people based on deep respect for the privacy of others and a tradition of noninterference (Good Tracks, J., 1973). When assessing members' behaviors and characteristics in a culturally sensitive way, a characteristic such as noninterference is viewed as a strength rather than as a limitation.

In the assessment process, the worker should consider the current functioning of the members and, whenever possible, also examine members' functioning from a developmental perspective. Acquiring a developmental perspective can help the worker assess whether a member's current functioning manifests itself in a transitory, acute pattern of behavior or a long-term, chronic pattern of behavior. It also helps the worker gain a greater understanding of the meaning of symptoms, and their intensity, duration, and scope. Overall, assessments are more likely to be accurate and complete if they consider the developmental context in which members' problems have developed.

In assessing members' intrapersonal lives, workers rely on their own observations and those of others, as well as members' self-reports. The worker may focus on members' perceived health status; their psychological status and emotional well-being; and their cognitions, beliefs, motivations, and expectations.

As a context for assessment, the group provides a natural laboratory where the worker can observe the functioning of each member as he or she interacts with other group members. It is also helpful to inquire about a member's interpersonal interactions with family and close friends because these relationships often have a significant effect on the member. When assessing interpersonal functioning, workers focus on members' social skills, the extent and quality of their social support networks, and their role performance.

Workers should also examine the environmental context in which members function. Questions such as, "Is the environment supportive or does it hinder members' ability to work on group and individual goals?" and "What resources can members draw on from their environment to help them achieve their goals?" are often pertinent.

In task groups, the worker may also find it useful to assess the intrapersonal, interpersonal, and environmental functioning of members, though in a slightly different way. For example, leaders of task groups generally do not make in-depth assessments of members' physical, psychological or emotional states. However, they are likely to examine a member's motivation for attending and expectations about accomplishing the work of the group. Similarly, a task group leader would be unlikely to assess the extent to which members' families support their work in the group. The leader is more likely to consider what effect a controversial committee report might have on members' day-to-day interactions with their colleagues, or on their interaction with the line staff they supervise.

Methods for Assessing Group Members

A variety of methods exists to help workers assess the functioning of group members. Although some of these methods can be adapted to task groups, they have been developed for use with treatment groups. Among the most commonly used methods for assessing functioning are (a) members' self-observations, (b) worker observations, (c) reports by others who have seen the member function outside of the group, and (d) standardized assessment instruments.

Self-Observation

Self-observation refers to members' examination and assessment of their own behavior. Usually, members simply recall and describe their own behavior, examining and reflecting upon it with the help of the worker and other group members. Hollis and Woods (1981) referred to this both as "exploration-description-ventilation" and as "reflective discussion of the person-situation configuration" (p. 104).

Retrospective self-observation and self-reflection is often very helpful in developing insights about one's behavior, identifying patterns of behavior, and making changes. However, members' recollections may not be accurate. For a variety of reasons, they may be incomplete, vague, or distorted. Therefore, other methods of self-observation have been proposed. Because these methods are more intrusive and require more effort on the part of the member than simply recalling and reflecting upon past behavior, workers should be sure that members are motivated and capable enough to try them, and have sufficient resources to implement them successfully. In addition, workers should be aware that such methods often presume members to be action-oriented, insightful, and sensitive, and may not be useful with all types of members.

SELF-MONITORING.   Rather than relying on memory of past events, members may examine their own behavior outside of the group in a prospective and systematic fashion, collecting data on the frequency, intensity, and duration of a particular behavior, and its antecedents and consequences. This process is often referred to as *self-monitoring.* An assessment of a particular behavior, and its antecedents and consequences can be useful in determining how particular problematic behaviors are maintained. For example, an assessment of the antecedents of the anxiety that a member experiences in social situations might reveal that the statements he tells himself about his lack of anything interesting to say triggers his anxiety.

Some evidence indicates that self-monitoring can be reactive—that is, the act of self-monitoring may by itself increase desired behaviors and decrease undesired behaviors (Stuart, 1977; Thoresen & Mahoney, 1974). Self-monitoring can also have therapeutic benefits by heightening members' awareness of their current behavior patterns. Awareness of a behavior pattern is a prerequisite for changing it.

To begin self-monitoring, the worker should be sure that members are motivated to examine their own behavior and to record it. Then the worker should help members decide exactly what they are going to monitor. It is often helpful to have members monitor behaviors they would like to increase as well as those they would like to decrease. This can help members to replace problematic behaviors with desired ones, rather than merely to reduce problematic behaviors.

In deciding what to monitor, workers should also help members determine what is feasible and realistic, given their life circumstances. We have found, for example, that members often want to collect data about several problematic behaviors at the same time. Our experience has shown, however, that members are rarely able to follow through on such ambitious plans. Therefore, initially, members should be encouraged to develop realistic plans that they can readily accomplish. Later, they may wish to develop more ambitious monitoring plans.

In deciding on a realistic plan, it should be clear where, when, and under what conditions a particular behavior will be monitored. For example, it is unrealistic for a single parent with four children to expect to monitor the behavior of one of the children just before dinner, or in the morning when the children are preparing for school. However, there may be time during the afternoon or evening when she can observe the child's behavior for a short period without being interrupted.

In most groups, members make a mental note of what they have observed by self-monitoring between meetings and share their observations with other members during the next group meeting. Because it is sometimes difficult for members to accurately recall the data they have monitored, methods for recording self-monitored data have been developed. These include charts, logs, diaries, problem cards, and self-anchored rating scales.

CHARTING. Some members find it useful to record monitored data on a chart. This provides members with an organized, visual display of the information. It allows them to see trends in the data—that is, whether a behavior is increasing or decreasing. It also may serve as a reminder for members to perform tasks that they agreed to complete between meetings.

Workers should help members be creative in designing charts. For example, in helping a parent develop a monitoring chart that will be shared with a young child, the worker can suggest using smiling faces, stars, or hearts instead of check marks to signify that a behavior was performed correctly.

The format of a chart depends on the method used to collect self-monitoring data. The simplest format uses a tally to count the frequency of a behavior. More complicated formats are sometimes used to get an accurate assessment of the frequency of a behavior without having to count each occurrence. A chart divided into a number of time intervals can be used to count behaviors. For example, members can count the number of occurrences of a behavior in 10-minute intervals between 6 p.m. and 7 p.m. every evening. Charts can also be made that allow a member to record whether or not a behavior occurred at particular intervals during a designated period, for example, at the beginning of every 30-minute time interval. For further discussion of methods to chart self-monitored data, see Bloom and Fisher (1982) or Thoresen and Mahoney (1974).

Members sometimes fail to follow through on charting self-monitored behaviors. For some, charting may require too much organization. Others find it inconvenient to monitor and record their behavior immediately after it occurs. We have found that members sometimes prefer one of the methods described in the following section.

LOGS AND DIARIES. Logs and diaries are often less accurate than monitoring charts because members rely on their memory of events to record behaviors at some convenient time after they occur rather than as they occur. However, because of their convenience, members sometimes prefer keeping a log or diary to keeping a chart.

Logs and diaries require members to record events in a descriptive fashion and can be a valuable source of qualitative data for the worker, helping the worker gain valuable insights into the world of each member. Logs and diaries can also be used to help the worker understand other data reported in quantitative self-observations. To avoid logs and diaries becoming too idiosyncratic, the worker can give members a clear indication of what data they are to record. For example, a worker may ask members to record problematic situations and their immediate cognitive, affective, and behavioral responses to them. For some examples of logs and diaries and more information about how to use them, see Bloom and Fisher (1982), Gottman and Leiblum (1974), and Rose (1981).

PROBLEM CARD.   A variation on diaries and logs is the problem card (Flowers, 1979; Goodman, 1969; Rose, 1981). Group members are asked to fill in one or more problem cards between meetings. On each card, the member is asked to briefly describe a problem he or she has experienced between sessions that is relevant to the group's theme. The member is also asked to choose a judge or rater from within the group who is willing to assess the member's progress. At intervals throughout the group's life, these judges are asked to rate group members' progress in ameliorating problematic behavior. Because of the evaluation component, the problem card procedure can be used for either assessments or evaluations.

SELF-ANCHORED RATING SCALES.   Members can also record their observations by using a self-anchored rating scale. This is a measurement device made by the worker and a group member specifically for the purpose of recording data about a problematic behavior that has been identified as the target of an intervention. To develop a self-anchored rating scale, the worker helps a group member identify behaviors, feelings, and thoughts that are associated with various levels of the problematic behavior. For example, in developing a scale to measure depression, a member suggests that severe depression occurs when he has suicidal thoughts and does not eat or sleep. Moderate depression occurs when he has thoughts that he is not a good father or husband, when he has little appetite and eats only one meal a day, and when he falls asleep only after lying awake for a long time. The member suggests that he is not depressed when he has a good appetite, can sleep well, and has thoughts that he is a good father and husband. An example of a self-anchored scale to rate depression is shown in Figure 7–1. For further information about developing self-anchored rating scales, see Corcoran and Fisher (1987) and Bloom and Fisher (1982).

Worker Observations

Another method that workers can use to assess the functioning of group members is their own observation of members' behavior during meetings. In most practice situations, workers rely on naturalistic observations. However, specific activities such as simulation tests and program activities to assess members' functioning in a particular area can also be used.

FIGURE 7–1
Example of a
self-anchored
rating scale

| | | | | | | | |

Very
Depressed

1. Does not eat.
2. Does not sleep.
3. Has suicidal
   thoughts.

Moderately
Depressed

1. Eats one meal
   a day.
2. Has difficulty
   in sleeping.
3. Has thoughts
   about not being
   a good father
   or husband.

Not Depressed

1. Has good appetite.
2. Sleeps well.
3. Has thoughts
   about being a
   good father
   and husband.

NATURALISTIC OBSERVATION.   Workers can learn a great deal about members by observing their behavior in the group. Given free interaction within the group, members will often display behaviors similar to behaviors exhibited outside of the group. By scanning the group, the worker can stay aware of the reactions of all group members. The worker observes a member behaving in a certain manner, for example, and makes a mental note. Further observation, over time, helps the worker identify the member's behavior patterns and typical coping styles. Then, the member can be asked to describe his or her behavior. This feedback can be used to determine whether the member's self-perceptions are consistent with the worker's observations. The worker may also solicit other members' observations and reactions. The process of formulating an assessment based on the observations and perceptions of more than one individual is often referred to as *triangulation*. Triangulation can lead to assessments that are more accurate than those made by a single individual.

Although naturalistic observation offers the worker an opportunity to observe members' behavior in an unobtrusive fashion, its chief limitation is that the group interaction may not offer the right opportunities to assess pertinent aspects of a member's behavior. For example, in a parenting skills group, a parent may describe how she sets limits on her child's behavior, but group interaction does not provide the worker with an opportunity to view the parent actually setting limits.

In addition, experience suggests that members may not always give accurate or sufficiently detailed accounts of their behavior. When the worker can actually observe the member engaging in a behavior such as limit setting, for example, the worker may find that the member does not set limits in the way that is stated. For example, the member's tone of voice or nonverbal cues may not match the description of their verbal behavior. Therefore, the worker may find other methods useful when observing members' behavior.

ROLE PLAYING.   Role playing, sociodrama, and psychodrama can be used for assessment as well as for intervention. They allow the worker and the other members of the group to observe a member while acting out a situation. For a discussion of these methods, see Chapter 12.

SIMULATION TESTS.   Simulation tests assess members' functioning in specific role-played situations. The worker asks for one or more volunteers to simulate a real life situation. Members whose behavior is being assessed are asked to respond to the situation created by the volunteers as they would if they were confronted with the situation in their everyday lives. For example, in an assertion training group, three members might volunteer to role play standing in a line at a grocery store. The member whose behavior is being assessed is asked to stand at the end of the line. Then, another group member is asked to try and get ahead of the member at the end of the line. The worker and the remaining group members observe how the unassertive member handles the situation. Similarly, in a parenting group, a simulation test may involve having two members play the role of siblings in an argument about who is to play with a toy truck. The parent whose behavior is being assessed is asked to act as he would if such a situation occurred at home.

Assessments of a member's behavior in a simulation test can be made by all group members. Scales to rate a member's response are designed specifically for the objectives and goals of a particular group. For example, in an assertiveness training group in which all group members are trying to reduce their anxiety and improve their responses, ratings focus on (a) the anxiety level that a member demonstrates while making a response, and (b) the effectiveness of a response in asserting the member's rights in the situation.

Simulation tests have been developed for measuring the skills of several populations, including psychiatric inpatients (Clark, 1971; Goldsmith & McFall, 1975) and outpatients (Schinke & Rose, 1976), women (De Lange, 1977), the elderly (Berger, 1976; Toseland & Rose, 1978), social workers (Rose, Cayner, & Edleson, 1977), adolescents (Freedman, 1974; Rosenthal, 1978), the mentally retarded (Bates, 1978), and parents (Rose & Hanusa, 1980).

These simulation tests were developed using the model described by Goldfried and D'Zurilla (1969), which includes (a) analyzing a problematic situation and developing several realistic situations that members are likely to confront in their daily lives, (b) enumerating possible responses to these situations, (c) evaluating the responses in terms of their efficacy in handling the problematic situation, (d) developing a measurement format, and (e) evaluating the measure's reliability and validity. Workers can use this model to develop simulation tests for populations and problems for which simulation tests have not yet been developed.

Role play simulation tests have the potential limitation that group members know they are acting rather than performing in real-life situations. In most cases, however, members appear to forget that they are acting and perform as they would in real life.

Other simulation tests have been invented to avoid the limitation of role play tests. These tests, which have primarily been used in research projects, involve setting up a situation within or outside the group that assesses a member's skill in a social situation without his or her knowledge. Rose (1989), for example, reported on the use of a Simulated Dating Interaction Test (SDIT), in which a female confederate is asked to interact with a male group member in a waiting room. The interaction is tape recorded and the group member's appropriateness, anxiety, assertiveness, and overall pleasantness are rated. Because of the deception involved in such simulations, the difficulty in designing and setting them up, and their specificity, that is, their ability to assess behavior in only one situation, they have been used infrequently in clinical settings.

PROGRAM ACTIVITIES. Many different types of program activities can be used to assess the functioning of group members. The selection of appropriate activities depends on the type of group the worker is leading. In children's groups, the worker can have members participate in play activities and games. For example, the game Charades can be used to assess how members act out particular situations. Games requiring cooperation can be used to assess the extent to which members are able to negotiate differences.

In adolescent groups, a party, a meal, or a sports activity can often help the worker make an assessment of members' social skills and their level of social development. In adult groups containing moderately or severely impaired members, preparing a meal together or going on an outing can help the worker assess daily living skills. Program activities should be age appropriate and should give members the opportunity to demonstrate behaviors that they would like to improve through their participation in a group.

When using role plays and program activities to assess members' behavior, it is important to keep in mind the influence of cultural heritage on members' performances. Role playing may not be a readily accepted form of group participation. For example, Lewis and Ho (1975) suggest that in group work with Native Americans, the use of certain techniques (for example, role plays) "are highly insensitive to the cultural orientation of Native Americans," and that they can "consider such group behavior to be false; it looks and sounds real but lacks genuineness, depth and real commitment" (p. 381).

With many cultural groups, however, the use of program activities can be a particularly effective means of assessing members during group interaction (Delgado, 1983). For example, Ashby et al. (1987) report the usefulness of cultural activities in reaching sexually abused Native American adolescents, and suggest that program activities and techniques be culturally relevant to the needs of members. For more information about using program materials in groups, see Middleman (1982), and the section on program activities in Chapter 8.

Reports by Others

In addition to members' self-observations and workers' observations, leaders often rely on the reports of people who are familiar with members' behavior outside the group. When considering data reported by others, the worker should assess its reliability and validity, which can vary considerably from person to person and from one report to another. For example, some data may be based on rumors, assumptions, or the statements of unidentified third parties, whereas other data may come from direct observations. Obviously, the worker should place less confidence in rumors than in direct observations.

The worker should also consider the relationship of the person reporting the data to the member about whom data have been collected. Is the person reporting the data interested in the well-being of the group member or is he or she motivated by ill feeling, personal gain, or rivalry? By examining a person's motivation for reporting data about a group member, the worker is in a better position to assess any potential biases in a report.

When a worker has an ongoing relationship with individuals who regularly report data about group members' behavior, such as mental health therapy aides, child-care workers, and teachers, it is often worth the effort to help these individuals use reliable and valid data collection systems. For example, a therapy group leader can offer to help a mental health therapy aide develop a chart to monitor the behavior of a group member at meals or during recreational activities. Similarly, a school social worker can offer an elementary school teacher assistance in using the Walker (1970) or the Devereaux (Spivack & Spotts, 1966) checklists, which are standardized instruments to measure children's social behavior. In this way, the worker can build a relationship with those who have daily contact with group members and, at the same time, ensure that accurate data are reported about members' behaviors outside the group.

Standardized Instruments

A fourth way that workers can assess the functioning of group members is by using standardized assessment instruments. Some instruments require lengthy personal interviews, but others are brief paper-and-pencil measures known as "rapid assessment Instruments." The Beck Depression Inventory (BDI), for example "is a 21-item scale that assesses the presence and severity of affective, cognitive, motivational, vegetative and psychomotor components of depression" (Corcoran & Fisher, 1987, p.107). Levitt and Reid (1981) and Toseland and Reid (1985) found that rapid assessment instruments such as the BDI can be used by clinical social workers who have little training or previous experience in test administration.

Rapid assessment instruments can be used many ways in a group. For example, some members of an outpatient psychiatric group can be asked to spend a few minutes filling out the BDI during a group meeting or at home between meetings. Other members might be asked to fill out the Stait Trait Anxiety Inventory (Spielberger, Gorsuch, Lushene, Vagg, & Jacobs, 1983), or other instruments that assess the particular symptoms individual group members are experiencing.

Despite the usefulness of standardized assessment instruments for understanding the problems and concerns experienced by group members, it should be kept in mind that they may not be appropriate for use with all populations. For example, when administered to members of specific sociocultural groups, or to developmentally disabled persons, such instruments may not be valid or reliable. In fact, they may give the worker a distorted impression of members' strengths. Thus, when considering using a standardized measure with a particular group of individuals, workers should check whether the description of the instrument includes information about its use with particular populations. If no information is available, workers should select another measure that has been found to be valid for use with the population of interest. A measure suspected of being culturally biased should never be used. Even if caution is exercised in interpreting the results, others who have access to the results may draw erroneous conclusions.

Because rapid assessment instruments are focused on particular problem areas, the type of assessment instrument selected depends on the group's focus. Corcoran and Fisher (1987) present a variety of rapid assessment instruments for use with children, adults, couples, and families. They review, for example, nine scales developed by Hudson (1982) that assess (a) depression, (b) self-esteem,

(c) marital discord, (d) sexual discord, (e) parent-child relationships, (f) child's relationship with mother, (g) child's relationship with father, (h) intrafamilial stress, and (i) peer relationships.

Walls, Werner, Bacon, and Zane (1977) briefly describe more than 200 behavior checklists that also can be useful in assessing the problematic behaviors of children and adults. There are also texts that describe measures for specific populations. For example, Kane and Kane (1981) describe measures for assessing older adults; Ollendick and Hersen (1984) and Marsh and Terdal (1981) describe methods for assessing children. For additional information about the wide range of available standardized assessment instruments, see Kramer and Conoley, 1992; Cone and Hawkins, 1977; Hersen and Bellack, 1976; and Robinson and Shaver, 1973.

ASSESSING THE FUNCTIONING OF THE GROUP AS A WHOLE

Methods for assessing the group as a whole have been given less attention in the group work literature than methods for assessing individual members. Klein (1970) proposed a schema for diagnosing and correcting group problems. The many different conceptualizations of group development mentioned in Chapter 3 are also attempts at assessing "normal" group functioning. In recent years, however, the group work literature has tended to emphasize assessing and treating the problems of individual group members within the group context, de-emphasizing methods to assess the functioning of the group as a whole. In assessing the group as a whole, the worker should be guided by the four major areas of group dynamics mentioned in Chapter 3. These are the group's (a) communication and interaction patterns, (b) cohesion, (c) social controls, and (d) culture.

Communication and interaction patterns are established early in the group. Therefore, the worker should be especially concerned about these patterns as they develop during the beginning stage. A careful assessment of communication patterns can alert the worker to potential problems and prevent them from becoming established as a routine part of group functioning. It can also help facilitate member-to-member communication and disclosure of important information that may be helpful in attaining group or individual member goals.

At the beginning of a group, too many member-to-leader interactions and too few member-to-member interactions may be of concern (Toseland, Krebs, & Vahsen, 1978). There is a natural tendency in newly formed groups for members to look to the worker for direction. The worker may feel gratified by this and encourage it. Unfortunately, this pattern may undermine the mutual aid and group problem solving that occurs when members direct their communication to everyone in the group rather than exclusively to the worker.

Other communication patterns can develop in a group that may also alert the worker to potential problems. For example, one member may attempt to dominate group discussion, preventing other members from interacting. Another potential problem is a lack of communication by a member. Although it is not unusual for some members to communicate less frequently than others, the worker should be aware of the potential for isolation when a member says little or nothing during the beginning stage of the group.

It is also important for a worker to understand what attracts members to the group. The worker assesses the group's attraction for its members to maintain and increase these forces and help the group become a cohesive unit in working toward group and individual goals.

The initial attraction of a group for its members may come from a variety of sources. In treatment groups, for example, it may come from members' hopes that the group will help them solve their problems, reduce their emotional distress, or teach them to perform new or more effective roles in their everyday lives. In task groups, it may come from the status or prestige associated with membership, the importance of the task on which the group is working, or a rare chance to share ideas with colleagues.

When workers assess group cohesion, they sometimes find that its development has not progressed satisfactorily. There are many indications that the group is not attractive to one or more of its members. These indicators can include apathy or hostility toward group goals, the failure of members to listen to one another, and the growth of allegiances to other reference groups. By observing these indicators, the worker can gain much information about the attraction of the group for its members. Group cohesion can also be measured by using a sociometric scale, the semantic differential, or the SYMLOG method, or by using scales specifically designed to measure group cohesiveness (see, for example, Budman et al., 1987; Seashore, 1954). Some of these measures are described later in this chapter.

Workers should also assess the social controls, that is, the norms, roles, and status hierarchies that develop in newly formed groups. The norms that develop are extremely important because they define acceptable and unacceptable behavior in a group. Schopler and Galinsky (1981) found that norms have an important influence on members' satisfaction with their group experiences. Both members and observers indicated that inappropriate norms were more important than cohesion, roles, goals, leadership, composition, or extra-group relations in negative group experiences. Workers should help members modify norms that detract from individual and group goals, and promote and protect those that are beneficial for goal achievement.

Members' roles also begin to develop early in the group. According to Levine (1979), initial role taking in a group is a tentative process and may not reflect the roles members will occupy later in the group. Members try out roles and often vacillate among them, such as the socio-emotional leader, task leader, dominator, and so on. During this stage of the group, the worker can point out the functional and dysfunctional characteristics of these roles to members and help them develop role behaviors that will facilitate the group's functioning and their own functioning in the group.

Several typologies of role behavior have been developed to help workers assess member roles. Benne and Sheats (1948), for example, have classified roles into three broad categories: (a) group task roles that are related to helping the group decide on, select, or carry out particular tasks; (b) group building and maintenance roles that help the group function harmoniously, and (c) individual roles that are related to individual members' goals. Group task roles include the instructor, opinion seeker, information giver, elaborator, energizer, evaluator, pro-

cedural technician, and recorder. Group building and maintenance roles include
the encourager, harmonizer, compromiser, gatekeeper, expediter, standard setter,
group observer, and follower. Individual roles include the aggressor, blocker,
recognition seeker, confessor, dominator, and help seeker.

Focusing on problematic roles, Shulman (1992) has identified the scapegoat,
deviant member, gatekeeper, internal leader, defensive member, and quiet member
as common group roles. Most of these roles are not difficult for the worker to identify. The scapegoat, for example, receives much negative attention and criticism
from the group as he or she is blamed for a host of defects and problems. According to Shulman (1992), members attack the portion of a scapegoat's behavior that
they least like about themselves. Although Shulman and others (see, for example,
Garland & Kolodny, 1967) mention that scapegoating is a common role, we have
found it to be relatively rare in the treatment groups we have conducted.

When one or more members of a group assume dysfunctional roles, it is a signal that the group as a whole is not functioning at an optimal level. For example,
when an assessment reveals that a member is functioning as a gatekeeper, that is,
one who does not allow the group to discuss sensitive issues, the worker should
help the group as a whole examine how to change its overall functioning rather
than focus on the member who has assumed the dysfunctional role. The gatekeeper prevents the group as a whole from discussing difficult issues. A quiet
member may signal difficulties in the communication and interaction patterns
established in the group as a whole. It is rare that a problematic group role is an
expression of only individual rather than group dysfunction.

The status of individual group members and the power that the leader and
other group members have at their disposal also affect the development of social
controls within the group. For example, although high-status members are likely
to adhere to group norms and procedures, they are also much more likely to influence the development of a group than are low-status members. Members in the
middle of the status hierarchy are likely to strive for greater status within the
group by adhering to group norms and upholding the status quo (Nixon, 1979).
Low-status members are less likely to conform to group norms than either high-
status or middle-status members (Nixon, 1979). An accurate assessment of the
status hierarchy in the group can help workers understand and anticipate the
actions and reactions of members when the worker intervenes in the group.

An accurate assessment of the power bases that the worker and the members
have at their disposal can also be important in the beginning stages of group work.
Workers who understand the limits of their influence over group members are able
to use their power effectively and avoid trying to use it when it will be ineffective.
An accurate assessment of the sources of members' power can also help the
worker in planning strategies for intervening in the group as a whole and for helping members to form a mutual aid network of shared resources within the group.

A fourth area that workers should assess when examining the functioning of
the group as a whole is the group's culture. Ideas, beliefs, values, and feelings
held in common by group members have a profound effect on the therapeutic
benefits that can be achieved in the group. Just as some societal cultures promote
the public expression of emotion and others do not, groups develop cultures that
value certain ways of behaving.

In the beginning stage, the worker should examine the culture that is developing in a group. Does the culture help the group and its members achieve their goals? Because group culture develops more slowly than the other group dynamics discussed previously, the worker's initial assessment of a group's culture should be viewed as a tentative indication about how it might develop. It is difficult to change a group's culture after it is well established, so the worker may wish to share his or her initial impressions with members early on. For example, in a group where a worker observes that a negative, unsupportive culture is developing, it may be helpful to point out in the first or second meeting that most members' communications are problem-oriented rather than growth-oriented, or that few supportive comments are made within the group. Methods to modify or change a group's culture are described in Chapter 8.

A number of methods to assess the group's culture have been developed. Some methods, such as the Hill Interaction Matrix and SYMLOG, were designed to assess a variety of types of groups along several different dimensions, whereas others, such as the Group Atmosphere Scale (Silbergeld, Koenig, Manderscheid, Meeker, & Hornung, 1975), were designed to assess only the psychosocial environment of therapy groups.

Methods for Assessing the Group as a Whole

In most practice situations, workers reflect on group functioning between meetings and rely on their own subjective observations to assess the functioning of the group as a whole. But it also can be beneficial to involve the group as a whole in a more structured assessment. In addition to helping members become aware of and involved in improving the group's functioning, using one or more of the structured assessment methods described in the following pages can help confirm or disprove a worker's subjective impressions of group functioning.

When choosing an assessment method, it is important to be aware of individuals' strengths and weaknesses. There is no measure of group processes that is perfect for all situations. Therefore, it is important to examine measures carefully, thinking about what group-as-a-whole processes are of greatest interest and what measure is most likely to capture what is occurring in a particular group. In that regard, Fuhriman and Packard's (1986) review of 26 group process measures that were available before 1985 may be helpful.

Measuring Communication and Interaction

There are many ways to measure the meanings that underlie communications in the group. One measure that has been widely used is the semantic differential. Using this method, members are asked to rate the meaning of an object or person on a series of seven-point bipolar attitude scales, such as good/bad, valuable/worthless, and so on. Three dimensions of attitudes that can be assessed by the semantic differential include individual group members' (a) evaluation, (b) perceptions of potency, and (c) perceptions of the activity of objects, concepts, or people being rated (Osgood, Suci, & Tannenbaum, 1957). An example of a semantic differential scale is shown is Figure 7–2.

FIGURE 7-2
Example of a semantic differential scale

INSTRUCTIONS: On each of the scales below please place a check mark in the space that best describes how you feel about _____.

	7 Extremely	6 Quite	5 Slightly	4 Neither or In-between	3 Slightly	2 Quite	1 Extremely		
1. Large								Small	(Potent)
2. Worthless								Valuable	(Evaluative)
3. Fast								Slow	(Active)
4. Cold								Hot	(Active)
5. Happy								Sad	(Evaluative)
6. Weak								Strong	(Potent)
7. Good								Bad	(Evaluative)
8. Tense								Relaxed	(Active)
9. Tough								Soft	(Potent)
10. Active								Passive	(Active)
11. Heavy								Light	(Potent)
12. Fair								Unfair	(Evaluative)

$$A = \frac{3 + 4 + 8}{3} + 10$$

$$P = \frac{}{} + \frac{}{} + \frac{}{} =$$

$$E = \frac{}{} + \frac{}{} + \frac{}{} =$$

By having members use the semantic differential to rate their fellow group members, the worker can begin to understand how members perceive one another. For example, using the activity scale, group members may rate a member as being particularly active and another member as being particularly inactive. Similarly, the scales can be used to obtain members' attitudes about specific concepts that may be relevant to group functioning, such as self-disclosure, communication, or leadership. The method can also be used to assess members' attitudes and perceptions about presenting problems or the group's task.

Sometimes the worker may be less interested in the meaning of members' communications than in the distribution of communication within the group. Rose (1989) suggests that an observer can use a chart such as the one shown in Figure 7–3 to record interactions. A similar procedure has been used by Toseland, Krebs, and Vahsen (1978) to record member-to-member and member-to-leader interactions.

To avoid observer fatigue, a sampling procedure may be used instead of continuous recording. Types of sampling procedures include (a) frequency recording—every time a behavior occurs it is recorded, for example, every communication in the group is recorded; (b) interval recording—behavior is recorded for a specified interval of time, for example, the first two minutes of every five-minute time interval; and (c) time sample recording—behavior is recorded at a particular time, such as every 30 seconds. For ease of rating, and to avoid the intrusiveness of live action ratings, group interaction can be videotaped or audiotaped, and the observations can be made from the tapes.

Measuring Interpersonal Attraction and Cohesion

Sociometry is a widely used method to measure interpersonal attraction. Originally developed by Moreno in the 1930s (see, for example, Moreno, 1934), sociometry refers to the measurement of social preferences, that is, the strengths

FIGURE 7–3
Chart for recording the frequency of group interaction

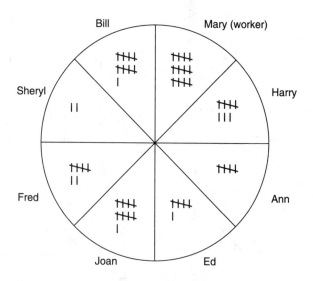

of members' preference or rejection of each other. Sociometric measures are obtained by asking about each member's preference for interacting with other members in relation to a particular activity (Crano & Brewer, 1973; Selltiz, Wrightsman, & Cook, 1976). They can also be obtained by having observers rate members' preferences for one another. Patterns of choices can differ significantly, depending on the activity on which members' preferences are being evaluated (Jennings, 1950). For example, in relation to the activity "playing together" a member of a children's group expressed great willingness to play with a particular member, whereas in relation to the activity "working on a project together" the member expresses less willingness to interact with the same member.

Sociometric ratings can be made concerning any activity of interest to a worker. For example, a worker may want to assess members' preferences for other members in relation to socializing between group meetings or choosing a partner to complete a task.

To obtain sociometric ratings, members are usually asked to write the names of the other members on one side of a sheet of paper next to a preference scale, for example, 1 = most preferred to 5 = least preferred. Members are than asked to rate everyone in the group except themselves in relation to a particular activity. For example, children in a residential treatment center might be asked, "If we were going on a day trip together, who would you like to sit next to during the bus trip?" and "Who would be your second choice?"

An index of preferences can be calculated for each member by dividing the total score a member receives from all group members by the highest possible score the member could receive. Members of attractive, cohesive groups have higher mean preference scores than members of groups that are less cohesive and attractive.

Another way of presenting sociometric data is through a sociogram. As shown in Figure 7–4, solid lines represent attraction, dotted lines represent indifference, broken lines represent repulsion, and arrows represent the direction of preferences that are not reciprocal. For research purposes, sociometric data can be analyzed by more complicated methods, such as multidimensional scaling (see, for example, Gazda & Mobley, 1981).

Several other measures of the relationships between individual group members, and of overall group cohesion have been developed. Cox (1973), for example, has developed the Group Therapy Interaction Chronogram, a graphic representation of interactions and relationships among group members that is similar to a sociogram but more complex. For assessments of the psychometric properties and utility of the Chronogram, see Fuhriman and Packard (1986) and Reder (1978). For industrial work groups, Seashore (1954) developed a measure of cohesion that assesses the degree to which members (a) perceive themselves to be a part of the group, (b) prefer to remain in the group rather than to leave it, and (c) perceive their group to be better than other groups with respect to the way members get along together, the way they help each other, and the way they stick together. More recently, Budman et al. (1987, 1993) developed The Harvard Community Health Plan Group Cohesiveness Scale, which can be used by trained clinical raters viewing half-hour videotaped segments of psychotherapy groups.

FIGURE 7–4
A sociogram

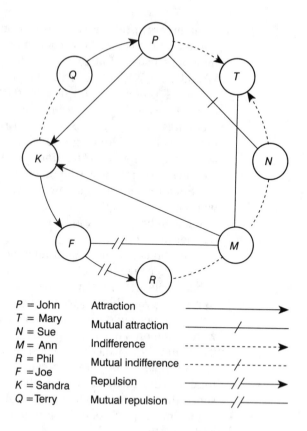

P = John	Attraction
T = Mary	Mutual attraction
N = Sue	
M = Ann	Indifference
R = Phil	Mutual indifference
F = Joe	
K = Sandra	Repulsion
Q = Terry	Mutual repulsion

Measuring Social Controls and Group Culture

The most fully developed method for assessing norms, roles and other dimensions of a group as a whole is Bales' Systematic Multiple Level Observation of Groups (SYMLOG). Although it has received little attention since its development (Bales, 1980; Bales, Cohen, & Williamson, 1979), SYMLOG is the most comprehensive method now available to assess the functioning of groups. It is useful in the training of novice group workers in connection with processing lab group experiences. SYMLOG can be used as a self-report method in which members rate each other in relation to 26 behavioral descriptors, such as, "dominant, talks a lot." Each descriptor is used to rate each member on a three-point scale from 0 = not often, to 2 = often, or it can be used as an observational measure in which independent raters assess group functioning. The product of a SYMLOG analysis of group functioning is a three-dimensional pictorial representation of group members' relationships to one another, called a SYMLOG field diagram.

Figure 7–5 is a SYMLOG field diagram made by Sharon, a member of an educational group for students learning how to lead treatment groups. The horizontal axis of Figure 7–5 represents the dimension friendly vs. unfriendly, and the vertical axis represents the dimension instrumental vs. emotionally expressive. The third dimension, dominant vs. submissive, is represented by the size of the circles. Larger circles represent greater dominance and smaller circles represent greater submissiveness. For example, in Figure 7–5 Sharon perceives that Ann is the most dominant group member and Ed is the most friendly and emotionally expressive member.

Each member rates all other members as well as themselves in relation to the three-dimensional SYMLOG space. In addition to rating overt behaviors, members can rate their values by evaluating which behavior they would avoid, reject, wish to perform, and think they ought to perform (see the circles marked "avoid," "reject," "wish," and "ought" in Figure 7–5).

SYMLOG field diagrams can be used for assessment in a variety of ways. One of the most basic ways is for members to compare their field diagrams. Are members' perceptions of the relationships among group members similar? Do individual members place themselves in the same position that other members place them?

A composite of group field diagrams can be made from the field diagrams of individual members. The composite can be used to analyze the functioning of the group as a whole. For example, who are the most dominant group members? Which members are included in the dominant subgroup (in Bales' terminology, "dominant triangle" as illustrated in Figure 7–5)? Which members are similar (spatially close), and which members appear to be dissimilar (spatially distant)? Who is the task (instrumental) leader and who is the socio-emotional (emotionally expressive) leader? In this way, the SYMLOG procedure can be used to help members gain an understanding of how they are perceived within the group.

Particular roles of individual group members can also be identified. For example, Figure 7–5 shows Bill isolated in the unfriendly, instrumental quadrant of the

**FIGURE 7–5
Sharon's
SYMLOG
diagram of
the group**

field diagram. Is he an isolate or perhaps a scapegoat? Several more complicated and more sophisticated ways of interpreting field diagrams have been developed. For a detailed discussion of these methods, see Bales, Cohen, and Williamson (1979) and Bales (1980).

The SYMLOG method has two major limitations. First, the method is complex and takes several hours to learn before it can be used effectively. A more serious limitation is that a SYMLOG self-study takes about three hours to complete. Although this amount of time may be warranted for a team that functions together on a daily basis over a long period of time, it may not be justifiable for a short-term treatment group.

Other Methods of Assessing the Group as a Whole

Several other methods, including the Hemphill Index of Group Dimensions (Hemphill, 1956), the Hill Interaction Matrix (Hill, 1965, 1977), and the Group Rating Scale (Cooper, 1977) have been developed to rate dimensions of the group as a whole. For example, the Hill Interaction Matrix employs a 16-cell matrix to assess the content and style of group interaction. It has been used in a large number of published and unpublished studies to assess therapeutic processes in a wide range of therapy and support groups (see, for example, Toseland, Rossiter, Peak, & Hill, 1990). Still, because these measures have been more frequently used by researchers than by clinicians, they will not be described in detail in this text.

ASSESSING THE GROUP'S ENVIRONMENT

The worker's assessment of the environment's influence on the functioning of the entire group should be distinguished from the assessment of environmental factors that affect individual group members. In both cases, however, the environment in which group members and the group as a whole function has an important effect on group work practice. When assessing the influence of the environment on the group, the worker focuses on (a) the organization that sponsors and sanctions the group work effect, (b) the interorganizational environment, and (c) the community environment. The emphasis on the influence of the environment is a distinctive aspect of social work practice and is not found to any great extent in the writing of group workers from other professional disciplines (see, for example, Corey & Corey, 1992; Dinkmeyer & Muro, 1979; Yalom, 1985).

Assessing the Sponsoring Organization

When assessing the influence of the sponsoring organization on the group, the worker examines how the group's purposes are influenced by the agency, what resources are allocated for the group's efforts, what status the worker has in relation to others who work for the agency, and how the agency's attitudes about service delivery influence the group work endeavor. Taken together, these factors can have a profound influence on the way the group functions.

As Garvin (1987) points out, an organization always has a purpose for sanctioning a group work effort. An organization's purpose may be stated explicitly or may be implied in the overall program objectives. The organization administration's purpose for encouraging the development of a group may not correspond to the worker's or the group members' ideas about a group's purpose. The extent to which the organization, the worker, and the group members can agree on a common purpose for the group will determine, in part, the extent to which the group will receive the support it needs to function effectively and the extent to which the group experience will be judged as beneficial by all concerned.

It is helpful for the worker to clarify the organization's purpose for sponsoring the group. A written group proposal, such as the one described in Chapter 5, can clarify the worker's intentions and provide the organization's administration with an opportunity to react to a written document.

During the process of clarifying the organization's purposes for the group, the worker can help shape the purposes proposed for the group. For example, a nursing home administrator decides to sponsor a group to help the residents "fit in better" with the nursing home's rigid schedule of bathing, feeding and housekeeping. The worker could help the nursing home staff and residents reformulate the group's purpose, considering the needs of both the group members and the organization. The purpose might be reformulated to improving the relationship between residents and staff, and working together to find a way to meet staff's busy schedules while accommodating residents' needs for autonomy and individual preference.

An organization can also influence a group by its allocation of resources (Wolfe & Proshansky, 1974). As mentioned in the planning chapter, the worker should identify as early as possible the resources the group will need to function effectively. Once this is done, the worker can assess the likelihood that the organization will be able to allocate sufficient resources, and plan the best strategy to obtain any that may be needed. The worker's assessment may also include the extent to which resources, for example, a meeting room or some refreshments, can be obtained from alternative sponsors.

The worker's status in the sponsoring organization can also influence the group. If a worker is a low-status member of the sponsoring organization, he or she is likely to have difficulty obtaining resources for the group, convincing the sponsor that the endeavor is a good use of his or her time, and demonstrating that the group's purposes are consistent with the overall objectives of the organization. In this situation, the worker may want to consult with trusted colleagues who can give the worker some feedback about the feasibility of the proposed group. The worker might also ask these colleagues for their support for the development of the new group service.

The attitudes and practices of the sponsoring organization in regard to service delivery can also influence the group work endeavor. The worker should assess whether the organization stresses individual or group work services. Where individual services are given priority, the worker may have to spend considerable time developing the rationale for the group and convincing the organization it is important to undertake such an endeavor (Hasenfeld, 1985).

The organization's policies regarding recruitment and intake of potential members also can affect a group. The worker should assess whether the clients are receiving services voluntarily or whether they have been ordered to attend the group. Mandated clients are likely to be hostile or apathetic about becoming members of the group. It is also helpful to gather information about the extent to which individuals are prepared by intake workers to receive group work services.

The organization's commitment to a particular service technology, such as practice theories, ideologies, and intervention techniques, may also influence the group work endeavor. For example, if the organization is committed to a long-term psychodynamic treatment model, it may oppose the development of a short-term, behaviorally oriented group. When the service technology planned for a particular group runs counter to an organization's preferred service technology, the worker should develop a convincing rationale for the particular service technology he or she plans to use. For a treatment group, the rationale might include the effectiveness and efficiency of a particular method for treating a problem. In the case of a task group, the rationale might include the effectiveness or efficiency of a particular method for generating ideas or making decisions about alternative proposals.

Assessing the Interorganizational Environment

In assessing the group's environment, the worker should also pay attention to anything happening in other organizations that may be relevant to the group. The worker can make an assessment of the interorganizational environment by asking several questions: Are other organizations offering similar groups? Do workers in other organizations perceive needs similar to those that formed the basis for the worker's own group? Do other organizations offer services or programs that may be useful to members of the group? Would any benefit be gained by linking with groups in other organizations to lobby for changes in social service benefits?

Unless the worker or others in the organization are already familiar with what is being offered by all other organizations in the community, the worker's primary task in making an interorganizational assessment is to contact other organizations to let them know about the group offering. In addition to generating referrals and making other organizations aware of the group, the assessment may uncover needless duplication of service or, conversely, a widespread need that is either not being met or is being met by uncoordinated individual efforts within separate organizations.

An example of a recent practice experience illustrates the importance of interorganizational assessments. An executive director of a small organization decided to do an interorganizational assessment after problems encountered in serving homeless people had been raised several times in monthly staff meetings. The director discovered a lack of sufficient space in shelters and a general lack of community interest in the welfare of the homeless. The worker called a meeting of professionals from several organizations to see what could be done. This interorganizational group contacted a local planning organization. In cooperation with the planning organization, the interorganizational group sought federal, state, local, and private funding to address the needs of the homeless. After much work, a social service program for the homeless was founded with a combination of federal, state, and local funding, and a new community shelter was opened.

Assessing the Community Environment

The worker should also assess the effect of the community environment on the group, and the extent of support for the group from other community groups and the community as a whole. When assessing the effect of the community on a group, the worker focuses on the attitude of the community concerning the problems or issues being addressed by the group. Within Hispanic and African-American communities, for example, support groups for people with Alzheimer's disease are difficult to organize because of the stigma attached to the disease. These communities also attach great significance to handling such matters in private, through family caregiving (Cox & Monk, 1990).

In treatment groups, if the problem is one that violates basic community values, members of the group are likely to be stigmatized. Lack of community acceptance and the resulting stigma attached to the problem may have other consequences, such as discouraging potential members from reaching out for help. It may also increase the level of confidentiality of group meetings and may affect procedures used to recruit new members. For example, because of the stigma attached to those who abuse their children, Parents Anonymous groups generally have confidential meetings, and the recruitment process occurs on a first-name basis to protect members from people who may be more interested in finding out their identity than in attending meetings. Similar recruitment procedures are used in other groups that deal with socially stigmatized problems, such as spouse abuse, alcoholism, and compulsive gambling.

The worker should also make an assessment of the support for the group from other community groups, and the community as a whole. For example, ministers, priests, and rabbis might be receptive to a group for abusive or neglecting parents, alcoholics, or spouse abusers. The worker can get referrals from them or obtain a meeting room such as a church basement. Similarly, a worker in a family service agency may find that several community groups—such as a women's civic organization, a battered women's shelter, a victim's compensation board, a council of churches, or a dispute resolution center—would welcome the development of a support group program for domestic violence victims. Workers who assess support from community groups are often in a better position to obtain new funding for a proposed group work service.

Group workers interested in building social action groups and coalitions need to be good at finding out what problems are important to individuals in a community, which individuals have the capacity to make a change in a particular problem, and which individuals have the capacity to prevent change or delay change. Information may be gathered from those affected by the problem and those who have the capacity to affect it through a variety of means, such as (a) focused individual interviews, (b) focus groups, (c) community needs assessments, and (d) state and national survey data and reports.

However, the importance of unsolicited and unfocused information gathered while interacting with and forming alliances with community members, community leaders, politicians, and community activists, should not be overlooked. It is essential for group workers who are interested in building social action groups and coalitions to get to know a community. To understand competing factions, uncover hidden problems, and form alliances often takes a considerable amount of time and commitment. Still, when the intent is to mobilize social action groups and coalitions, there is no substitute for taking the time necessary to get to know a community and establish trusting relationships with as many different representatives of the community as possible.

A worker's assessment of the community environment may lead to a coalition of community forces to resolve a concern. According to Rubin and Rubin (1992) when assessing a community there "is the systematic gathering of information by people who are both affected by a problem and who want to solve that problem" (p. 156). At the same time there is "a fact-gathering endeavor as people learn about the problem, a mobilization endeavor as people learn to share the problem, and a capacity-building endeavor as people work to solve the problem" (p. 156). For example, a community assessment might indicate that police officers have been asked increasingly to handle family disturbances. With the cooperation of the police force and local community leaders, a community organization might decide to reach out to those experiencing family disturbances. In addition to casework service, these efforts could result in the development of several treatment groups, such as a couples communication group, a parenting group, and a recreational group for adolescents. It also might result in a task force of community leaders to work on issues of concern to families in the community. For additional methods for assessing community environments, see Cox, Erlich, Rothman, and Tropman (1977, 1987), Lauffer (1978), Rubin and Rubin (1992), and Warren (1977).

LINKING ASSESSMENT TO INTERVENTION

In preparation for the middle stage of treatment groups, which will be discussed in Chapter 8, workers should consider how they will use their assessment data to plan effective interventions. This chapter has suggested that the worker assess three areas of the functioning of individual group members, four areas of the functioning of the group as a whole, and three areas of the environment is which the group functions. Chapters 8 through 11 describe a variety of interventions that the worker can use when assessment indicates an intervention is warranted.

Few texts in group work or casework practice have addressed the way assessments are linked to intervention methods and treatment plans. This may, in part, account for findings from practice studies suggesting there is little correlation between workers' assessments or diagnoses and the interventions that are selected (see, for example, Mullen, 1969; Stuart, 1970). Without guidelines about the interventions that are most appropriate for particular problems, workers will rely on interventions with which they are most familiar, regardless of their assessment of the group or its members.

Figure 7–6 illustrates a framework for developing treatment plans that result from an assessment of the individual group member, the group as a whole, and the group environment. Because problems are often multidimensional, several different interventions may be selected to become part of a comprehensive treatment plan. For example, in a couples group, the worker and each member select specific interventions to meet individual needs. One member decides to use a

FIGURE 7–6

Linking assessment and intervention in treatment groups

Selected Intervention Methods

1. Cognitive restructuring
2. Cognitive self-instruction
3. Thought stopping
4. Reframing

1. Modeling
2. Role playing
3. Coaching
4. Cueing

1. Connecting members to resources and services
2. Intervening in members' social networks
3. Managing contingent rewards and punishments
4. Changing physical environments

1. Identifying and discussing patterns
2. Cueing and prompting
3. Selective attention
4. Confronting

1. Clarifying the group's common goal
2. Increasing interaction around the common goal
3. Promoting noncompetitiveness in the group
4. Reinforcing the importance of the group's work and the group's ability to succeed

1. Clarifying norms and roles
2. Discussing dysfunctional norms and roles and seeking group consensus to alter these
3. Increasing normative and functional integration of members
4. Insuring that status differentials do not inhibit members' self-disclosures

1. Clarifying values
2. Discussing dominant features of the group culture
3. Pointing out taboo areas
4. Developing a contingency contract to change specific aspects of the group culture

1. Clarifying group needs to agency administrators
2. Understanding agency purposes
3. Overcoming resistance by developing support
4. Negotiating for additional resources

1. Establishing contact persons in other agencies
2. Making linkages
3. Promoting collaboration
4. Joining in social action

1. Surveying community needs
2. Increasing community awareness of available services
3. Lobbying for needed services
4. Organizing for social action

Individual Group Member

Group as a Whole

Group Environment

Level of Assessment

1. Individual Group Member
   a. Intrapersonal
   b. Interpersonal
   c. Environmental

2. Group as a Whole
   a. Communication and interaction patterns
   b. Group attraction
   c. Social controls
   d. Group culture

3. Group Environment
   a. Agency
   b. Interagency
   c. Community

Treatment Plan

Steps:

1. _____
2. _____
3. _____
4. _____

cognitive restructuring intervention to help her stop getting defensive when confronted by her husband. As part of his treatment plan, another member decides to join Alcoholics Anonymous. At the same time, the worker helps the first member change her interaction patterns in the group and helps the second member stop avoiding confrontation in the group.

To help ensure continued organizational support for the group, between meetings, the worker discusses the group's progress with a clinical supervisor. This provides an opportunity for the worker to discuss needed organizational support. For example, a worker leading a parenting group discusses the progress made by members but notes that problems in attendance could be reduced if the agency provided baby-sitting services during group meetings. In the following chapters, guidelines are presented for choosing interventions and formulating treatment plans based on the needs of members and the group as a whole.

SUMMARY

This chapter examines the process of assessment. Although assessments are made throughout all stages of a group's development, they are often concentrated in the latter portions of the beginning stage and the initial portions of the middle stage. These are when the worker and the group members are planning intervention strategies to achieve the goals they have agreed upon in the planning and beginning stages of the group.

In making assessments, the worker examines the functioning of individual group members, the group as a whole, and the group's environment. When assessing individual members, the worker examines intrapersonal, interpersonal and environmental areas of each member's functioning. In addition, the worker examines each member's functioning in relation to what they can contribute to the group, what needs they bring to the group, and what intervention plans are most likely to be successful in helping them alleviate their concerns and problems. A number of methods that can be used separately or in combination for assessing the functioning of individual members are presented in this chapter.

To assess the group as a whole, the worker focuses on the four areas of group dynamics described in Chapter 3. These include (a) interaction and communication patterns, (b) the attraction of the group for its members, (c) social controls such as roles, norms, and status hierarchies, and (d) the group's culture. Several methods for assessing the group as a whole are described.

Because group work practice occurs within the context of a larger service delivery system, it is important to consider the effect of the group's environment on its functioning. To make a thorough assessment of the group's environment, it is suggested that the worker assess the sponsoring organization, the interorganizational environment, and the larger community environment in which the group functions. After a brief discussion of the potential effects of each of these aspects of the environment on the group, the chapter describes the linkage between assessment and intervention.

LEARNING ASSIGNMENTS

1. Imagine you are leading a group of parents of young children. Three of the parents mention they are having difficulty handling their children's temper tantrums. What steps would you take to help the parents develop a chart to monitor their children's behavior? How would encourage other group members to assist in this process? Prepare a monitoring chart that you could use as an example in the group.

2. Using Figure 7–3, observe a committee meeting or other task group and record the frequency of interaction among members. Were you able to identify distinct subgroups? Did your observations help you identify task and socio-emotional leaders within the group? Was there a scapegoat? Based on your observations, speculate about why some members spoke more frequently than others.

3. Interview the executive director of a social service agency. Inquire about the mission and goals of the agency and the types of group services offered to the agency's clients. How do the group work services that are offered reflect the mission and goals of the agency? Ask the director what types of group services he or she would consider to be outside the mission and goals of the agency. Ask about the extent of influence of the agency's board of directors on the group work services that are offered. Also, inquire about the effect of any formal or informal interagency service arrangements, and the influence of the larger community on group work services in the agency.

4. Choose a group in which you are currently involved. Prepare a written assessment focusing on a problem experienced by (a) one member of the group, (b) the group as a whole, and (c) the group in interaction with its environment. Using Figure 7–6, select appropriate interventions to address each of these levels of problems and prepare a treatment plan.

PART IV

The Working Stage

CHAPTER 8

Treatment Groups: Foundation Methods

This chapter focuses on the common foundation of methods, activities, and skills needed to lead treatment groups during the middle stage of their development. It is also designed to illustrate commonalities in group work practice across different types of treatment groups. The typology of treatment groups in Chapter 1 and the history of group work presented in Chapter 2 both suggest that treatment groups can be used for many purposes.

Treatment groups are often associated with remediating social and psychological impairments. However, they often have other purposes. For example, group treatment can be used to educate members, to promote psychological and social growth and development, to maintain and enhance coping skills, to offer support during difficult experiences, or for socialization. A narrow conception of group work focused solely on therapy unnecessarily limits the scope of a very versatile treatment modality.

During the working stage, the group is focused on accomplishing the objectives, goals, and tasks developed in the planning, beginning, and assessment stages. It is assumed that by this stage, workers have already discussed the group's purposes; developed a group contract concerning confidentiality, attendance, and number of sessions; and developed individual contracts with particular treatment goals for each member. It is also assumed that the group as a whole has developed an initial set of dynamic processes, including a pattern of communication and interaction; a beginning level of interpersonal attraction and group cohesion, norms, roles and other social control mechanisms; and a group culture. The primary task of the worker is to help members accomplish the goals they have contracted to achieve. This is accomplished by (a) helping members overcome obstacles to goal achievement in their own lives, (b) facilitating group dynamics that support members' efforts, and (c) helping the organization and larger community respond to members' efforts.

LEADING TREATMENT GROUPS

The working stage of treatment groups is characterized by an initial period of testing, conflict, and adjustment as members work out their relationships with one another and the larger group. Contracts are negotiated and renegotiated, members establish their positions in relation to one another, and the group develops a niche within the sponsoring organization.

After the initial period of adjustment, the middle stage focuses on goal achievement. Members work together to achieve the goals expressed in the contracts they have made with the group's leader, other group members, and the group as a whole. The worker is aware of how the group has been planned and what has been accomplished during the beginning stage. During the middle stage, the worker makes modifications in relation to the assessment of the group's development, the changing needs of members, and the changing demands of the social environment in which the group functions.

Although every group has a unique developmental pattern that calls for different leadership skills, workers are often expected to perform six broad activities during the working stage of all treatment groups. These activities include the following:

1. Preparing for group meetings.
2. Structuring the group's work.
3. Involving and empowering group members.
4. Helping members achieve their goals.
5. Working with reluctant and resistant group members.
6. Monitoring and evaluating the group's progress.

Preparing for Group Meetings

During the working stage, the worker should continuously assess the needs of the group and its members and plan to meet identified needs in subsequent meetings. The cycle of assessment, modification, and reassessment is the method by which the leader ensures continued progress toward contract goals.

In structured, time-limited groups, the worker spends a considerable amount of time between meetings preparing the agenda for the next group meeting. For example, for the fourth session of an educational group for prospective foster parents, a worker prepares (a) material on helping children develop values, (b) a brief handout on value clarification, (c) an exercise to illustrate some concepts about helping children develop their own value system, and (d) questions that will help to organize the group's discussion of values. In preparing for the meeting, the worker selects material that will lead to a stimulating and interesting discussion. The worker also estimates the time needed to cover the material in relation to the time available for the meeting.

Less structured process-oriented groups also require preparation. A worker leading a group for residents of an adolescent treatment center prepares for the next meeting according to her assessment of the efficacy of previous group meetings and the current functioning of each group member discussed in weekly treatment review meetings. After discussion with members, the worker decides to focus the next meeting on helping members improve how they express anger. In preparing for the group, the worker gathers examples of how anger has been expressed in the past by residents, and uses these examples to prepare role play exercises designed to improve their expression of anger. The worker models more appropriate methods of expressing anger and helps members practice the new methods.

Preparation is also required when workers use program materials to achieve group goals. Middleman (1980) pointed out that the use of program materials has had an important place in the history of group work. *Program materials* are activities, games, and exercises designed to provide fun-filled, interesting experiences for members while achieving particular goals. Workers sometimes make the mistake of thinking that program activities such as arts and crafts or preparing for a dance are not appropriate group work activities because they are not solely focused on therapeutic verbal interactions. However, when carefully selected, program activities can be very therapeutic.

Program activities provide a medium through which the functioning of members can be assessed in such areas as interpersonal skills, ability to perform daily living activities, motor coordination, attention span, and ability to work cooperatively. Program activities can also be used as a part of specific treatment interventions. In addition to achieving specific goals such as improving skills in interpersonal functioning, leadership, problem solving, and activities of daily living, program activities help build group cohesion, prosocial group norms, and a group culture that fosters continued member participation. Program activities can also be used to make the group more attractive for its members. For example, in a children's group, the worker may place a program activity, such as Charades, in-between group discussions to maintain members' interest.

Choosing appropriate program activities can be a demanding task that requires a careful assessment of the needs of group members. Characteristics of members should be matched with the characteristics of potential program activities. Vinter (1985b) has developed a scheme for rating program activities on their prescriptiveness, control, movement, rewards, competence, and interaction. Similarly, Middleman (1982) has attempted to point out some of the particular benefits of more than 100 program activities, and Henry (1992) has attempted to categorize program media that are especially useful for members at different stages of a group's development.

Because of the great number of possible program activities for children, adolescents, adults, and the elderly, workers should keep a resource file of catalogued activities to draw on as they are called upon to work with different types of groups. Such a resource file can be an asset in selecting specific program activities during the life of a group. Appendix I lists a variety of sources that contain program activities for children, adolescents, and older adults that workers may find useful.

Figure 8–1 presents a procedure for evaluating program activities for specific group needs. The selection should be based on (a) the objectives of the program activity, (b) the purposes and goals of the group, (c) the facilities, resources, and time available for the activity, (d) the characteristics of the group members, and (e) the characteristics of particular program activities.

FIGURE 8–1
A procedure for selecting
program activities

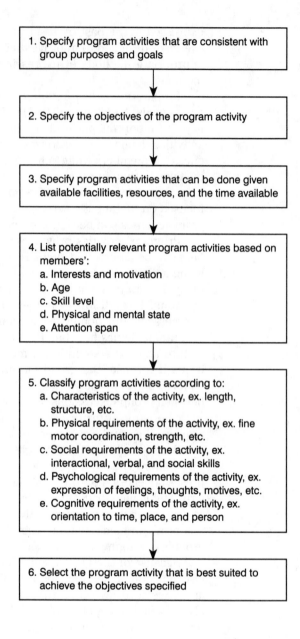

1. Specify program activities that are consistent with group purposes and goals

2. Specify the objectives of the program activity

3. Specify program activities that can be done given available facilities, resources, and the time available

4. List potentially relevant program activities based on members':
   a. Interests and motivation
   b. Age
   c. Skill level
   d. Physical and mental state
   e. Attention span

5. Classify program activities according to:
   a. Characteristics of the activity, ex. length, structure, etc.
   b. Physical requirements of the activity, ex. fine motor coordination, strength, etc.
   c. Social requirements of the activity, ex. interactional, verbal, and social skills
   d. Psychological requirements of the activity, ex. expression of feelings, thoughts, motives, etc.
   e. Cognitive requirements of the activity, ex. orientation to time, place, and person

6. Select the program activity that is best suited to achieve the objectives specified

The procedure suggested in Figure 8–1 can be used to help workers select program activities for any type of treatment group. For example, when choosing activities for an inpatient group whose purpose is to help prepare members for community living, the worker should consider activities that stimulate members' interest in the outside world. In addition to the group's purpose and the objectives of particular program activities, the worker should consider the other factors shown in Figure 8–1. For example, the inpatient group meets in an occupational therapy room, equipped with kitchen facilities, tables, blackboards, arts and crafts, and toys. All members are more than 70 years old and their physical and mental health is poor. Their interests include gardening, nature, travel, and cooking. The worker wants to select a program activity that stimulates members physically as well as socially to prepare them for living in a community residence.

Using Figure 8–1 as a guide, the worker ruled out activities such as a bus trip or a discussion of current events in foreign countries, and selected an activity in which each member helped prepare a meal to be shared by all. Afterward, the worker reconvened the group around the meal and asked members to share their feelings. Questions such as "Did the activity remind you of when you lived at home?" and "How do you feel about living on your own and having to prepare meals?" were used to stimulate a therapeutic discussion based on the program activity.

The therapeutic benefit of any program activity depends on how it is used by the worker. Activities provide little benefit if careful attention is not given to making sure they are directed toward therapeutic purposes. For example, the program activity of preparing the meal stimulated the sensory awareness of members. During the activity, the worker encouraged social and physical interactions among members. At the end of the meal, a discussion of the thoughts, feelings, and behaviors that members experienced during the activity was used to stimulate members' interest and desire to return to the community.

To prepare for meetings, workers should also review recordings of previous meetings and data from other monitoring devices. Making effective use of feedback about the progress of a group is essential during the working stage. The worker can use observations collected in summary recordings, for example, as the basis for determining that the interaction pattern of the previously described inpatient group should be changed to encourage participation from several members who have not been active in group discussions. In another case, data about members' satisfaction with the previous meeting of a single parents support group suggested that information about educational opportunities for adult students should be included in future meetings.

Preparation for the next group meeting may also include visualizing how it will be conducted and, if necessary, rehearsing intervention procedures or techniques. This is particularly important when a worker is using a new or unfamiliar procedure or exercise in the next meeting. Co-leaders can be particularly valuable when discussing future group meetings or rehearsing new procedures.

Workers must be fully cognizant of the history of the group's development and needs when preparing for meetings during the middle stage. Preparing agendas, developing role play exercises, selecting program activities, reviewing and assessing the last group meeting, and visualizing and rehearsing aspects of future meetings are some of the many ways effective workers prepare for meetings. In recent years, an increased awareness of the benefits of clear contracts and specific goal statements has highlighted the need for careful preparation between meetings.

For example, Rose (1989) has suggested that specific written agendas be distributed at the beginning of each meeting. Such agendas are appropriate for structured short-term groups that are focused on a single concern or problem. Other treatment groups may have broader concerns that are not easily anticipated or addressed by a written agenda for each meeting. However, whether or not a written agenda is used, workers should be sufficiently prepared so they are clear about their objectives for each meeting and their plans for achieving those objectives.

Structuring the Group's Work

Structuring the work of treatment groups has been recognized as a necessary ingredient of social work treatment for many years (see, especially, Perlman, 1970; Reid, 1978, 1992; Reid & Epstein, 1972; Ryder, 1976), but in recent years it has been given increasing attention. *Structure* refers to the planned, systematic, time-limited interventions used to help clients change in desired directions. Highly structured interventions rely on the guidance and direction of the worker, whereas less structured approaches encourage members to take full responsibility for the purpose, goals, and interventions used in the group. A worker may structure group processes to enable the group as a whole to help members change. Structure may be used by intervening with individual members to help them plan how to achieve their goals, or by intervening in the group and its environment to help all members achieve their goals.

In general, structure encourages the rapid learning of new responses. Therefore, one of the advantages of structured groups is that they provide an efficient means for members to learn new skills. The appeal of the Minnesota Couples Communication Program (Miller, Nunnally, & Wackman, 1972), Parent Effectiveness Training (Gordon, 1975), Positive Peer Culture (Vorrath & Brendtro, 1985), Systematic Training in Effective Parenting (Dinkmeyer & McKay, 1982), and similar approaches testifies to the popularity of structured group programming for certain types of problems.

Structure is essential in multicomponent treatment programs, sometimes referred to as "psychoeducational" groups. For example, an assertion training group may include a brief lecture and group discussion about what it means to be assertive, followed by role playing, modeling, rehearsal, reinforcement, and cognitive interventions—all designed to help members practice becoming more assertive. As the number of treatment components grows, the need for careful structuring of the entire intervention program increases.

During the middle stage of treatment groups, the worker can perform a variety of activities to structure the group's work. One of the most basic activities is to let members know that each meeting will begin and end on time. Except for the first meeting, openings should not be delayed in anticipation of late members. Starting meetings late only reinforces members' tardiness in the future.

The worker should also structure the end of a meeting to summarize and conclude interactions rather than to begin new agenda items. New items should not be introduced near the end of a session. Sometimes a group member will wait until the end of the meeting to disclose an important piece of information or to voice an important concern. These "door knob" communications (Shulman, 1992) can't be dealt with adequately in the short time remaining, so the worker should ask the member to hold the new material until the next meeting. If the member's concerns cannot wait until the next group meeting, the worker may want to schedule an individual meeting.

One of the best ways a worker can structure a group's time is by setting agendas (Rose, 1989; Shulman, 1992). Whether verbal or written, a clear agenda helps focus attention on what will be covered during the meeting and make members aware of how much time is available for exercises, role plays, presentations, and discussions. When preparing and presenting agendas, workers should encourage members to share their ideas about what direction the group should take.

The worker also can structure a group by establishing and maintaining orderly communication and interaction patterns. The structure of the interaction process should give all members an opportunity to participate. Some members, however, may receive more attention in one meeting and less in others. For example, in a remedial group where members have individualized treatment contracts, the worker may decide to focus on one member at a time, helping each one work on his or her treatment contract for an extended period. In other situations, such as an educational group, the worker may decide to present some didactic material and then encourage all members to discuss the material. The worker might decide to structure the discussion so that each member is encouraged to participate and no member is allowed to talk for longer than several minutes at one time. In either case, the worker will have made a planned effort to structure the group's use of communication and interaction patterns.

The worker structures a group's communication and interaction patterns by helping the group determine how much time should be spent on a particular issue or problem and by guiding their participation in role plays, exercises, and other group activities. In these efforts, the worker balances the socio-emotional needs of individual members and the needs of the group as a whole to accomplish specific goals. The worker also should strive to foster members' initiative and leadership, while at the same time prevent the group from being dominated by a single individual or a subgroup.

Sometimes workers are reluctant to assert themselves, for example, by guiding the group from a discussion of one issue to another or directing role plays or program activities. Workers should be aware, however, that group members expect them to provide guidance and leadership, particularly when the group is having trouble staying focused on its stated objectives. Workers are expected to use their professional knowledge and skills to guide members' progress toward the goals they have set without dominating or suppressing member initiative. When the worker is unsure about whether or not the group needs more time to work on an issue or an exercise, the worker should ask members a direct question about their needs. When guiding group activities, the worker should ensure that the transition from one activity to another is as smooth as possible. This can be done by summarizing what has been said, recommending how the group might pursue unresolved issues, and suggesting that the group move on to remaining issues.

Time is an important factor in structuring the work of a group. Time-limited, structured group work methods have been shown to be effective for children, adolescents and adults experiencing a variety of problems (see, for example, Drum & Knott, 1977; McKay & Paleg, 1992; Rose & Edleson, 1987; Rose, 1989). Despite the evidence for the effectiveness of time-limited approaches to group work, some needs are clearly better served in long-term groups. For example, although Drum and Knott (1977) suggest that short-term structured group treatment can be helpful for facilitating members' growth and development, the popularity of self-help groups indicates that support through life transitions and life crises is best provided in long-term support groups (Powell, 1987). It may also be preferable to address other needs in groups that do not emphasize a time-limited structured format. For example, when members seek help in changing established personality characteristics, long-term rather than short-term group treatment approaches are often recommended (Frances, Clarkin, & Perry, 1984).

Focusing is another way to structure the work of a group. In any treatment group, the focus of an intervention, sometimes referred to as the level of an intervention, can be either the individual member, the group itself, or the group's external environment. The focus of the group should change with the changing needs of the group. For example, a worker leading a group for men who have battered their wives might make an assessment that the group has failed to encourage members to express feelings of anger—and that this is inhibiting the group from achieving its objective of preventing further domestic violence. The worker might decide to select the group as the target of an intervention designed to help members talk about feelings. In such a situation, the worker has each member express two feelings about being a member of the group. Other exercises used in later group sessions help members learn to identify their feelings of anger and intervene before they escalate into violent outbursts (see, for example, Edleson, Miller, & Stone, 1983; Novaco, 1975; Rahaim, Lefebvre, & Jenkins, 1980). At the end of the first exercise, the group leader might change the focus of the group and concentrate on helping members work on individualized treatment plans. In a subsequent group meeting, the leader might again suggest a change of focus by asking group members if they would like to invite their partners to a meeting. The leader might explain that this will help members appreciate the devastating effect that domestic violence has had on their partners. By suggesting changes of focus, the leader helps the group to obtain new perspectives on problems, and to tackle problems in multidimensional ways that add variety to the type of work that is done in the group.

Degree of Structure

Reviews of the effectiveness of social work interventions (Fisher, 1978; Mullen, 1981; Reid & Hanrahan, 1982; Rubin, 1985) indicate that structured interventions are effective in helping clients to achieve treatment goals. Fisher (1978), for example, suggests that the use of structure is a critical element of social work practice. Melnick (1974) suggests that lack of structure tends to increase members' fears and anxieties. Similarly, Goldstein (1973), Kanfer and Goldstein (1975), and Reid and Shyne (1969) all indicate that structured interventions are more effective than unstructured ones.

Considerable controversy exists, however, about how *much* structure is useful for treatment groups. It has been argued, for example, that a great deal of structure may not be beneficial because it prevents members from exercising their own initiative (Egan, 1976; Glassman & Kates, 1990). Too much structure may decrease members' commitment to the group because they may feel structure has been imposed on them rather than selected by them to help them achieve their own self-monitored goals. Lieberman, Yalom, and Miles (1973) found that structured exercises did not facilitate group development or successful outcomes in the groups they observed.

Although much of the available evidence indicates that structured, short-term interventions are at least as effective as less structured, longer-term interventions (Fisher, 1978; Koss & Butcher, 1986; Lazarus, 1971; Mullen, 1981), highly structured interventions may be more appropriate for some problems than for others. For example, although a highly structured, multicomponent group treatment program was found to be more effective than a less structured program for helping older people increase their social skills (Toseland & Rose, 1978), a less structured, process-oriented approach that was focused on facilitating group members' determination of their own purposes and goals was found to be more effective than a structured approach in developing mutual support groups for older people (Toseland, Sherman, & Bliven, 1981).

Similarly, short-term, highly structured approaches may not be best for clients who are mandated to attend group treatment. These clients take time to develop relationships and to build trust in workers' efforts to help them. On the other hand, clients who are "in crisis" may need less time to build relationships with the worker and other members and therefore can profit from short-term treatment.

The nature of clients' problems and needs should be carefully considered when deciding how to structure a group. For example, work with antisocial adolescents, clients in residential treatment centers, severely impaired psychiatric patients and street gangs often occurs in long-term groups. This is because these groups focus on specific, narrowly defined concerns and objectives only in the context of broader, long-term objectives and goals. For example, a short-term goal for a group of psychiatric inpatients might be for them to learn specific social skills. This may be accomplished in a short-term social skills group. However, the long-term goal for each member to live independently in the community may best be accomplished through a program that includes a series of short-term groups focused on specific skills, and a long-term group integrating what is learned in the brief, focused groups. Short-term structured approaches such as the task-centered approach seem to recognize long-term treatment needs when suggesting that successive short-term contracts can be developed for certain clients, such as antisocial adolescents, who may need long-term treatment (Larsen & Mitchell, 1980; Reid, 1978).

In some situations, it may be best to strive for a group structure that encourages members to use their own resources when carrying out intervention plans. A group for parents of children with Down syndrome, for example, may be most successful if members are encouraged to share their mutual concerns and diverse efforts at being effective parents for their disabled children. Such a structure encourages the formation of a mutual support network among the parents.

In other cases, it may be best if interventions are highly structured by the worker. For example, a worker leading a group to teach children to resolve conflict may have a specific outline for each group session that includes didactic material about resolving conflict, reviewing homework assignments, role playing, observing and recording observations about the role play, making suggestions and giving feedback about the role play, modeling a new response, reviewing the new response, and assigning tasks to be done before the next session (see, for example, Edleson, 1981; Rose & Edleson, 1987).

In both the parents' group and the children's group, the worker is clear about how the structure of the group has contributed to goal achievement. The worker has selected an intervention method by assessing the specific problems facing members and the needs of the group as a whole. The worker has not simply applied a familiar intervention plan regardless of the situation. Overall, then, no simple guidelines can be provided about the "right" amount of structure for a group. Instead, workers should carefully assess the needs and desires of members before deciding on how to structure a particular group.

Involving and Empowering Group Members

Another important activity in the work stage of treatment groups is to help members become fully involved in the work of the group. The ultimate goal of this process is to empower members so they can take charge of their lives both inside and outside the group. Workers who are insecure about their position often make the mistake of being overly directive or even manipulative. Instead of doing their utmost to help members take as much responsibility as they are able to for the direction of the group, insecure workers often think they have to be in control at all times. This often is counterproductive, leading members to become rebellious or passive-aggressive.

An important first step in the process of involving and empowering group members is for workers to show their belief in members' strengths. Statements that express confidence in members' motivation and tenacity, point out their abilities, and describe their previous accomplishments help to foster members' resolve to accomplish particular goals.

Expressing belief in members' strengths does not mean that the worker should be unrealistic, ignoring impediments to goal achievement. Thus, a second step in the process of empowering group members is to acknowledge the difficulties and obstacles members encounter as they attempt to reach particular goals and objectives while at the same time recognizing their efforts. Statements such as, "Ann, I really admire that you're not giving up—that you continue to confront this difficult issue with your daughter" or "Expressing yourself about this painful issue really shows your courage, Charlie" affirm and validate members' efforts to take charge of their own lives, even when the work is difficult.

A third way to empower group members is to help them know that they have a stake in the content and direction of the group. Statements such as, "This is your group—what do you want to see happen in it?" help members overcome a tendency to expect the worker to take responsibility for group content and process.

A fourth step to encourage involvement and empowerment is to praise members for reaching out to help each other. Statements such as, "I really liked the way you shared how you felt about Ann's situation" or "This group is really making progress—it's wonderful to see how supportive you are of each other" demonstrate support of members self-help efforts. They also foster the continued development of cohesion in the group as a whole. Vannicelli (1992) has found similar statements help foster cohesion in groups for substance abusers and their families.

A fifth way to empower group members is to encourage them to try out new behaviors and actions both within and outside of the group. Members should be encouraged to begin by taking small action steps and carefully observing the results. Members can then report the results of their efforts to the group. They should be encouraged to acknowledge each other's accomplishments, and to support each other when obstacles are encountered.

Program activities can also be used to involve and empower group members. Activities should involve as many members as possible, and members should be encouraged to take leadership roles and support each other's efforts. Members also should be encouraged to adapt program activities to suit their needs. Rigid adherence to particular ways of conducting program activities should be deemphasized.

Involving and empowering members does not mean that the worker stops providing direction and guidance. However, when guiding group interaction, workers should solicit members' input and feedback, and make sure their suggestions are given serious consideration. For example, the worker might state, "Jane, I'm glad you expressed your feeling that we may be moving too fast. How about others in the group? What is your opinion about how fast we have been moving today?"

Helping Members Achieve Their Goals

During the working stage of the group, workers should concentrate on helping members achieve the goals they have agreed to accomplish. Contracting for treatment goals is an evolving process. A tentative agreement or contract is usually discussed while interviewing potential members during the planning stage of a group. It is reaffirmed and made more concrete and specific during the beginning stage of the group as members interact with one another for the first time. Although much of a treatment group's work during the middle stage is devoted to carrying out contracts developed during the beginning stage of a group, contracts continue to evolve as the group progresses during the middle stage.

Croxton (1985) notes that secondary contracts may be developed to refine initial contracts. For example, a member of a group for recently separated people might contract to reduce her angry feelings and violent outbursts toward her former spouse when he picks up their children. A secondary contract might involve the member in discussing her feelings of anger with another member outside of the group and reporting back to the group what she has learned about how to handle angry feelings. A variety of different secondary contracts could be used to help this member achieve the goals specified in her primary contract. Thus, secondary contracts evolve as group members progress toward their treatment goals.

Although a portion of a treatment group's work should be devoted to maintaining a group's optimal functioning, most of an effective group's time during the middle stage should be focused on helping members achieve their goals. This can be accomplished by helping members (a) maintain their awareness of their goals, (b) develop specific treatment plans, (c) work on treatment plans, and (d) carry out treatment plans.

Awareness of Goals

The first step in helping members to achieve their goals is to maintain their awareness of the goals they identified and agreed to work on in earlier group meetings. Workers should not assume that members continue to be aware of these goals as the group progresses. Reconfirming members' commitment to the goals they decided to achieve in earlier meetings serves several purposes. It lets members know the worker remains interested in their progress. It checks for a continued mutual understanding of the contract. It helps ensure that the worker and members remain focused on the same issues. Confirming goals also helps avoid confusion and promotes members' organized and systematic efforts to work on contracts.

In treatment groups where a group contract for all members is emphasized, and individualized treatment contracts are de-emphasized, periodically confirming goals gives the worker an opportunity to check if any changes need to be made as the group develops. It also gives members a chance to share their feelings and thoughts about how to improve their treatment contract. For example, the contract for a group of parents waiting to adopt children might include attending group meetings on (a) child development, (b) legal proceedings for adoption, (c) special issues and concerns of adopted children, and (d) supportive resources and services available for adoptive parents and their children. During each meeting the worker might ask members if the content of the meeting is useful. Members can be given the opportunity to express their reactions to what has occurred, making suggestions for improving future meetings or continuing them as planned.

Maintaining members' awareness of, and commitment to, contract goals is also essential in treatment groups that focus their work on individual contracts. Garvin, Reid, and Epstein (1976) have recommended that during each meeting the worker go around the group helping each member in turn. At times, the worker may spend a considerable amount of time helping one member work toward a particular goal. For example, in a group for alcoholics, the worker might spend 40 minutes working with one member in relation to a secondary contract to help the member improve his methods of expressing anger. As a result, during the two-hour group meeting, only three members have an opportunity to work intensively on their treatment goals. When this occurs, it is particularly important to generalize work with an individual to other members so that everyone feels involved in the group. For example, members can be asked if they use similar ways of coping with stressful situations to those described by the member being given the group's attention. The worker can also encourage other members to share experiences that may be helpful to the member. Such interventions help to establish a norm for mutual helping among members.

If extensive time is spent with only a few members during one meeting, the worker should spend a brief period of time checking on other members' progress. Members who did not have an extensive opportunity to participate in a meeting should be encouraged to do so during the next one. This helps prevent repeated and prolonged attention to a few members and reduces the possibilities that some members will avoid working on their contracts.

During the middle stage, the worker should also help members to develop a process for reviewing their treatment goals and contracts. Although the review process may be idiosyncratic to the needs of a particular group, the worker should avoid haphazard or constantly changing review procedures. Without a clearly defined process that all members can expect, there is the danger that some members' progress will be carefully monitored and others' will not. When monitoring is haphazard, those who are assertive and highly involved will be more likely to be monitored, whereas those who are less assertive and those who are resistant will not receive the attention they require.

With unsystematic monitoring procedures, tasks that are to be completed between meetings do not receive proper follow-up. There is nothing more frustrating and disconcerting for members than to complete a task between meetings and then not be given the opportunity to report the results during the next meeting. In addition to creating an ambiguous demand for work, failure to follow up on tasks often gives members the impression that the worker is disorganized and that there is little continuity from one meeting to the next.

Once a systematic procedure for monitoring is established, the worker rarely needs to remind members to report their progress to the group. The expectation of weekly progress reports helps maintain members' motivation to work toward contract goals between sessions and reduces the need to remind members of their contract agreements. It also helps members gain a sense of independence and accomplishment as they assume responsibility for reporting their own progress.

Developing Treatment Plans

A second way to help members achieve contract goals is by facilitating the development of specific, goal-oriented treatment plans. When all members are working on the same contract goal, the worker develops and implements plans with the group as a whole. For example, in a weight-loss group, a medical social worker might help members prepare a method for monitoring their daily caloric intake, present material on good nutrition, and introduce methods for modifying eating habits. The worker may then help individual members discuss their special needs, helping them modify what has been presented to fit their specific circumstances.

When helping a member develop and implement an individual treatment plan, the worker should enlist the support of all group members. The worker should use every available opportunity to make connections among members, to point out parallel issues and concerns among members' situations, and to encourage all members to participate. As members become involved as helpers, the group's cohesion increases and members feel satisfied that they have something to contribute. Known as the helper-therapy principle (Lieberman & Borman, 1979), this strategy works in such a way that members who help others often benefit as much as those who are helped.

Before deciding on a treatment plan, the worker helps members explore and gather facts about their situations. A guided group discussion on the specifics of a situation, the alternatives that have been tried, and the possibilities that have not been explored is often sufficient to help members develop intervention plans. Sometimes, however, members will try to grab at potential solutions without exploring alternatives. This is particularly true when members are experiencing a great deal of stress or psychic pain from their problems. The worker should encourage members to explore alternatives thoroughly before deciding on an action plan.

An exploration of the situation may reveal a need for additional information. The member, with or without the help of the worker, might be asked to spend time between sessions gathering data. The process of members' monitoring their own behavior and gathering additional facts about their situation is essential to effective treatment plans. Effective action plans can not be developed without sufficient information. When a member is severely impaired, or unwilling or unable to collect needed information, the worker may have to share the responsibility for collecting additional information about a member's situation to use in treatment planning during the next meeting.

A treatment plan may become apparent as the group explores a particular situation. For example, information gathered by a depressed member of an outpatient psychotherapy group might suggest that negative and self-deprecating thoughts and self-statements are maintaining his depression. These thoughts and self-statements persist despite the member's adequate performance in job-and family-related responsibilities.

The treatment plan focuses on helping the member replace negative thoughts and self-deprecating statements with realistic thoughts and self-statements about his abilities, accomplishments, and positive qualities. This is done by having the member contract with the group to make a list of positive self-statements to be repeated each time an obtrusive, negative, self-statement occurs. Secondary contracts, such as having the member ask other group members to describe how they perceive him during interactions in the group and having the member get positive feedback from significant others, are also used to help him overcome his depression.

Sometimes, exploration of the problem may not immediately lead to a clear plan of action. The worker should help members consider alternatives before deciding on a final plan of action. Because of workers' professional training and knowledge, they are often the primary generators of alternative intervention plans. Although the intervention plan that is selected may have been originally generated by the worker or another group member, members should be encouraged to refine alternatives and select the most appropriate plans for their own needs. They should not look upon a plan as imposed on them by someone else. Members who experience their action plans as self-selected are more likely to follow through on them.

A treatment plan can be quite complex. It may involve a sequence of actions suggested by different members of the group. These different sequences of actions occur simultaneously. A complex plan should be divided into a series of discrete steps that are defined as clearly and specifically as possible. For example, to become more assertive, a member might (a) clarify the difference between aggressiveness and assertiveness through group discussion and reading a book on assertiveness, (b) decide in which situations to become more assertive, (c) practice being more assertive in the group during role plays and group discussion, (d) practice being assertive outside of the group with family members or a friend, and (e) practice being assertive in a real-life situation.

Ideally, each step of the treatment plan should specify (a) who, (b) does what, (c) when, (d) where, (e) how often, and (f) under what conditions (Maple, 1977). It is especially important to be clear and specific when there are several people responsible for different aspects of a comprehensive treatment plan. Treatment plans often require the involvement of the worker, the client, other agency personnel, and the client's family. The effective worker should make sure that all those who are a part of the treatment plan are clear about their roles, their responsibilities, and their expected contributions.

In some groups, all work is completed during meetings, but we have found that it is often helpful to encourage members to complete tasks between meetings. Many different tasks can be developed to help accomplish treatment plans between meetings. According to Wells (1982), there are (a) observational or monitoring tasks to gather information or to increase awareness of behaviors, emotions, or beliefs; (b) experiential tasks to arouse emotion, to challenge beliefs or attitudes; and (c) incremental change tasks to stimulate change step by step. Other types of tasks include mental or cognitive tasks to help group members change cognition and belief systems (Reid, 1978, 1992) and paradoxical or two-sided tasks that result in changes no matter how they are carried out. For example, the treatment plan of a nonassertive group member includes the paradoxical task of having the member assert her right in a situation where she would normally remain passive. If the member does the task, she is learning to be more assertive. If she does not do it, then she is showing that she can assert herself in reference to her treatment plan.

According to Reid (1978), tasks can be individual, reciprocal, or shared. For example, an individual task for a member in a smoking cessation group may be to keep a log of the number of cigarettes smoked each day. Workers may also agree to perform individual tasks. A worker in a rural county welfare agency, for example, agrees to find out if there are any transportation services available to enable teen-age parents to attend a parenting skills group.

In a reciprocal task, if one person does something, another person will also do something. For example, if a member of an adolescent group does his assigned chore in his community residence each day for one week, the worker will help the member to obtain a pass to see his parents the next weekend.

A third type of task is shared by two or more people. For example, members of the group may form a buddy system (Rose, 1989), also referred to as consulting pairs (Garvin, Reid, & Epstein, 1976), in which each member is expected to remind his or her buddy to work on a specific task between group meetings.

In developing treatment plans and specific tasks, the worker should proceed by making sure that members are able to carry out each step successfully. It is especially important for members to have a successful experience in carrying out the first task they agree to accomplish. If they are successful with their first task, they are much more likely to successfully complete a second task (D'Zurilla and Goldfried, 1971; Stotland, 1969). Successfully completing an initial task gives members a sense that their goals are reachable. It also helps build self-confidence, feelings of self-efficacy, and a sense of control and mastery over the problem the member is attempting to alleviate. As members begin to feel self-confident, they are more likely to persist in their attempts at solving problems and concerns and are therefore more likely to be successful than when feelings of inadequacy limit their attempts to solve problems (Bandura, 1977b).

In developing treatment plans, the worker should assess a member's competencies and work with the member to plan an initial task that can be accomplished without an extraordinary amount of effort. Novice workers often develop treatment plans with too few steps. Members may agree to tasks to please a worker, or another group member, only to find that they are not prepared to undertake such involved tasks. The worker should also attempt to ensure that tasks are paced appropriately so that they become progressively more difficult as the member gains confidence and skill.

The worker can intervene to reduce the possibility that a member might have a great deal of difficulty completing a task. Simulations, role plays, and other exercises can be performed in the group before the member tries the task at home, in the community, or in any other less hospitable environment. Rose (1989) suggests that members can be prepared for unreceptive or hostile environments by simulating these conditions in the group. One of the advantages of group treatment is that members can practice with other members of the group before they attempt to perform a task in the natural environment. Acting out roles also helps members become more aware of their own roles in a situation. An entire treatment method known as *psychodrama* is based on the benefits of acting out life experiences with others (Blatner, 1973).

Members should be encouraged to tackle one task at a time. In treatment planning, it is surprising to find how many underorganized, multiproblem clients will suggest working on several different problems and their resulting tasks simultaneously. Although members often have good intentions in the group session, when they return home they have less motivation to follow through on the multiple tasks they have agreed to accomplish. It is better to start with one or two concrete, carefully planned tasks than to encourage a member to work on a variety of tasks simultaneously. When a member has completed the initial tasks, he or she can then take on more difficult ones. If a member does not perform a task satisfactorily, the worker should help the member to view this as a learning experience rather than as a failure experience. A task can then be planned that can be completed on the basis of the information and feedback gained from the initial experience.

At the end of a session, the worker should ask members to review the tasks that were agreed upon during the session. It is not uncommon for members or the worker to forget tasks that were agreed to one or two hours earlier in the midst of an active and interesting group session. A review can eliminate confusion, misconceptions, or discrepancies about specific tasks. At this time, members should also be encouraged to remind each other of any tasks or portions of tasks that have not been mentioned. This ensures that everyone leaves the group with a clear notion of what has to be done before the next meeting. A recording form such as that shown in Figure 8–2 can also be used to help the worker and the group members keep track of the tasks they have agreed to complete.

FIGURE 8–2
A group task recording form

Date: _____

Session #: _____

Group: _____

Member's Name	Task	When	Where	How Often	Under What Circumstances

Helping Members Work

A third way to help members achieve their goals is by increasing their willingness to work on the concerns, problems, and issues that confront them. Members need help to work on their goals because they often find it difficult to make changes in their lives. For example, a member of a psychotherapy group who has contracted to stop drinking alcohol might begin drinking again after only two days of abstinence. In a different group, a member, who has contracted to become independent of her parents, might make excuses about why she has not had time to explore alternative living arrangements.

In both cases, members have encountered obstacles to achieving their goals. First, the worker should check with the member to find out if the member also acknowledges that he or she has encountered an obstacle. Shulman (1992) suggests that the worker should also make a clear and specific "demand for work." The initial demand for work is a gentle reminder to the member that the worker and the other group members are interested in helping that member achieve his or her goals. The demand for work should be accompanied by an offer to help the member overcome obstacles.

With a member's agreement, the worker can take several steps to facilitate a return to goal-directed work. The first step is to encourage a member to explore what has been happening to prevent or block him or her from working on treatment goals. The worker can involve the group as a whole by having members participate in the analysis of the factors that may be inhibiting a member's goal achievement. This can help both the member who is having difficulty following through on a treatment contract and other members, who can practice overcoming ambivalence and resistance in their own change efforts.

In helping members overcome obstacles, workers should not ask "why" questions because these have been found to be unproductive in helping members work toward treatment goals (Flowers, 1979). Group members often do not have the answers to "why" questions, and if they do, their explanation may attribute causes to incorrect sources, further complicating their problem. The worker instead should ask members "how" or "what" questions that encourage them to describe cognitive, affective, behavioral, or environmental circumstances that may be diminishing their ability to work on treatment goals.

"How" questions and "what" questions keep members focused on current behaviors that lead to or exacerbate existing problems. Thus, for example, the worker might ask, "What occurred just before you became angry?" or "How did you feel when _____ happened?" Such questions tend to elicit actual behavior and events, whereas "why" questions tend to elicit the opinion or judgments of members on the basis of their interpretations of information. This makes it difficult for the worker and other members to form their own opinions. It also makes it more difficult for the worker to suggest ways in which a member's current thoughts, feelings, behaviors, and environmental situation could be changed to alleviate a particular problem.

For example, in response to a "why" question, a member who is depressed indicates that her depression is a result of her low self-esteem, which she attributes to her relationship with her now-deceased mother. In response to a "how" question, the member says she constantly repeats phrases to herself, such as, "You can't do that," which she first heard from her mother when she was a young girl. Although the response to the "why" question may produce some insight into the origins of the member's depression, insight by itself often produces little behavior change. The response to the "how" question, however, leads directly to helping the member change her cognitive self-statements that are maintaining her depression. Thus, "how" questions are more likely than "why" questions to elicit information that will help members make active behavior changes and achieve their treatment goals.

Obstacles interfering with members' ability to work toward treatment goals may be the result of an inappropriate contract. A careful analysis of the contract may indicate that it was poorly designed and should be renegotiated. A contract can be inappropriate for several reasons, including the following:

- Goals in the contract are vaguely defined or too global to be achieved.
- Goals are too difficult to achieve at the current stage of treatment.
- The worker and the member focused on long-term goals rather than on more immediate, short-term goals that have a higher probability of being accomplished in a shorter period of time.
- There is a misunderstanding between the member and the worker about the nature of specific contract goals.
- Inappropriate goals were set without careful assessment of the member's situation.
- Changing problems and situations necessitate modifications in the treatment goals developed for a contract made earlier in the group's development.

For all these reasons, helping members work toward treatment goals often means helping them clarify, redefine, or renegotiate contracts.

Working toward goals also involves increasing members' motivation to take action to overcome the obstacles they have encountered. If a member agrees that action is important, the worker's task is to help the member believe that change is possible. Many group members are willing to act, but refuse to do so because they do not believe in their own ability to change their situation. In such cases, self-instructional training (Meichenbaum, 1977), described in the next chapter, may be useful in increasing a member's willingness to attempt a new behavior. When the lack of motivation is severe, the worker should consider renegotiating a contract, focusing the new contract on helping the member increase his or her motivation to work on a specific issue or concern rather than to work on the concern itself. Such a contract may involve helping the member examine factors that affect his or her motivation to work on a particular goal and to examine any potential consequences of not working toward the goal.

The final step is to help members decide what actions to take to overcome obstacles and renew their progress toward treatment goals. In making the plan, the worker helps members to get support for their efforts from as many sources as possible. For example, the worker instructs the member who returned to drinking after two days to go around the group and tell each of the other group members that he will not drink until the next group meeting. Members are encouraged to support this member by making replies such as, "I'm happy for you—I admire your determination to work on your problem." Group members can also help by suggesting interventions such as changing his cognitive self-statements and modifying his home environment by removing all liquor from his house. The worker asks several members to give the member a call during the week to help him follow through on his verbal commitment. To enlist the help of his family and friends, the worker asks the members' permission to contact them to gain their support and encouragement for the member's decision not to drink. To provide continued support during evening hours, the member is referred to an Alcoholics Anonymous group. In this way, the member receives support for working toward contract goals from a variety of sources within and outside of the group.

In summary, helping members work toward treatment goals is an important activity for any worker who plans to lead effective treatment groups. All treatment groups require effort from members if they are to be successful in achieving their goals. The worker's task is to help members mobilize their resources and maximize their use of the group to help them accomplish their goals. The worker should be constantly vigilant, pointing out inertia, ambivalence, and other psychological, social, and environmental barriers that block members' progress in the group.

Helping Members Carry Out Treatment Plans

Workers can use five intervention roles to help members carry out their treatment plans. These include the roles of (a) enabler, (b) broker, (c) mediator, (d) advocate, and (e) educator. Although other roles have been identified as appropriate for helping members carry out their treatment plans, these five roles are the most important and most frequently assumed by workers leading various types of treatment groups.

ENABLER ROLE.   The enabler role is the most basic of all intervention roles. As Shulman (1992) points out, the enabler reaches out to members, letting them know that their ideas, opinions, and feelings are valued. The worker encourages members to express their concerns and feelings regarding their treatment plans. The worker monitors members' reactions to the work occurring in the group and encourages those who appear to have something to contribute to share their thoughts with the group. As obstacles are encountered, the difficulty of making changes in established behavior patterns is acknowledged. In this way, the worker shows empathy for members who are confronted with difficult life situations. At the same time, the worker helps members use their own skills to identify, confront, and remove obstacles that detract from their ability to carry out treatment plans.

As the group progresses, members are praised for their contributions and encouraged to continue their participation. The worker helps the group develop a supportive culture in which members can count on one another for mutual aid in overcoming difficult problems. As an enabler, the worker helps members revitalize and mobilize their own strengths and resources to cope with difficult problems (Compton & Galaway, 1989).

BROKER ROLE.   In the broker role, the worker identifies community resources that may help clients carry out their treatment plans. In most communities throughout the United States, there is a complex and often confusing network of community services and resources that group members may know little about. As a broker, the worker helps members become aware of appropriate services, eligibility criteria, and other conditions for using a service. For example, a member of a group is experiencing great distress in caring for her elderly mother. As part of a plan to help reduce this distress, the worker suggests that the member contact a local home health-care agency. First, though, the worker discusses eligibility criteria for receiving home health aid, the availability of third-party reimbursement, the duration and extent to which services can be expected, and whether services are available 24 hours a day. After this discussion, the worker refers the member to a specific contact person in the home health-care agency. To avoid frustration, disappointment, and unmet expectations, the worker also prepares the member for barriers that may be encountered, such as a one-month delay in processing reimbursement claims for home health-care services.

To help workers perform broker functions adequately, agencies should keep an up-to-date listing of community resources, with brief, pertinent information about contact people, access points, eligibility requirements, and other requirements for receiving services. In some communities, directories are prepared by a planning agency and made available. Workers who may not be thoroughly familiar with all community services available in their area can refer to a community resource directory for information.

MEDIATOR ROLE.   As a mediator, the worker helps resolve disputes, conflicts, or opposing points of view within the group or between a member and some other person or organization. For example, in a group for adolescents in a residential treatment center, the worker might help two members resolve a conflict about their participation in a recreational activity. In another group, the worker might help a member resolve a conflict with a child-care worker.

To be an effective mediator, Compton and Galaway (1989) suggest that a worker should help members in conflict recognize the legitimacy of each other's interests. The worker identifies and works toward common values and interests, helps the members avoid a situation in which winning and losing are paramount, attempts to get at the specifics of the conflict, and helps the members recognize that their ongoing relationship is more important than winning or losing a specific conflict.

As a mediator, the worker resolves disputes by helping members arrive at a settlement or an agreement that is mutually acceptable. It is essential for workers to avoid taking sides or favoring one of the parties in a dispute. Workers should also avoid making judgments about disputes based on their own positions or values. The mediator role is based on an assumption of neutrality and on the ability of disputing parties to work together through constructive, open communication.

ADVOCATE ROLE.   In some cases, a worker's efforts to act as a broker and refer members to needed services and resources may not succeed. The referral source may not be sympathetic to members' needs or there may be no appropriate services or resources available. In these situations, the worker advocates on behalf of group members to help them obtain services or resources. As an advocate, the worker represents members' interests and needs.

The worker can negotiate to obtain needed services on behalf of one or more group members. For example, in negotiating with a community service center to plan more activities for adolescents, a worker might offer to supervise the youth worker or volunteer who is to lead one of the new activities. In other cases, the worker might use persuasion to obtain voluntary acceptance of a change. According to Pincus and Minahan (1973), voluntary acceptance of a change comes about because the target of the change realizes that the worker's request is correct, just, and legitimate and recognizes and accepts the worker's professional expertise and judgment.

In attempting to gain what is needed for members of a group, the worker may also assume an adversarial role. As an adversary, the worker challenges the validity of the status quo. The worker may appeal a ruling, lobby for a change in rules, organize a rally, or in countless other ways work for changes in systems that affect members of the group. For example, in a group for nursing home residents, one member's treatment plan included having him take part in a regularly scheduled activities program. But in this case, the member missed the program several times because the clock in his room had been stolen, and the activities director had a policy that residents must be responsible for getting to the program by themselves. The worker advocated for the member by speaking to the activities director, explaining the situation, and working out a plan whereby the member was notified by the director one hour before the program began. In the same group, the worker also advocated for members by requesting that nurses' aides change their order of serving dinner so that residents who took part in the group did not have to eat cold food.

When services or resources to address particular needs are not available, advocacy efforts include making others aware of the unmet needs and establishing services to address them. For example, in an activities group in a board-and-care facility for older adults, members expressed a variety of concerns about their lack of control over their living conditions. The worker met with the director of the facility to advocate for patients' rights to self-determination. Through these efforts, the worker obtained the permission of the director to form a residents' council to advise the administrative staff on issues affecting residents. Members of the activity group served as the nucleus for the residents' council, which continued after the 12-week group ended.

The worker's advocacy efforts may, therefore, also include helping develop new services and resources. The worker acts as an advocate by helping others understand the importance, intensity, and extent of a particular problem. By demonstrating how a need is relevant to the objectives and goals of an agency and by making their own expertise and knowledge available, workers can actively participate in developing new services for group members.

EDUCATOR ROLE.   One of the most important roles assumed by workers in helping members achieve their treatment goals is that of the educator. As an educator, the worker presents new information to help resolve members' concerns; demonstrates and models new or improved behaviors; and suggests role plays, simulations, and in-vivo activities to help members practice new or different ways of behaving in problematic situations. Unlike the enabler role, in which the worker helps members use their own resources, the educator draws on professional knowledge about changing or modifying behavior patterns and adds to members' existing knowledge and skills.

In educating group members, it is often helpful to use visual and motor modes of teaching, as well as the more common didactic mode. Learning can often be enhanced, for example, by visual displays on newsprint and by graphs, charts, or other media. Videotape and audiotape recordings can provide members with feedback about their behavior in a group.

Motor modes of learning are best suited for teaching new skills (Bandura, 1977a). Novice workers sometimes assume that simply mentioning a new piece of information or discussing how to perform a new behavior is sufficient to help members learn it. Our experience suggests that members are frequently unable to perform behaviors described verbally. Therefore, it is important to have members practice new behaviors before trying to perform them in real-life situations. This is particularly true with complex skills. Sometimes a series of steps involving modeling the new behavior, practice, feedback, coaching, and additional practice is necessary to help a member perfect a new skill.

Working with Reluctant and Resistant Group Members

In some situations, workers will be called upon to work with members who do not want to be in the group. These individuals resist goal setting because they do not acknowledge that they have a problem that they need to work on in the group. When working with resistant clients, it can be helpful to dramatize natural consequences (Edelwich & Brodsky, 1992). Avoid talking about abstract consequences. Instead, focus on the natural consequences that have occurred because members failed to confront their problems. For example, "You almost lost your license for driving while you were drunk. What would you do if they took away your license? How would you get to work? In what other ways would not being able to drive affect you?"

Encourage resistant members to make "I" statements. Instead of allowing them to project blame onto someone else, "I" statements help members take responsibility for their feelings, thoughts, and actions.

Confrontation is often necessary to help members overcome their resistance. Edelwich and Brodsky (1992) point out that it is best for members to confront each other. Because they are based on members' experiences, members' confrontations are often more powerful than workers' confrontations. In the working stage, the leader should strive to build a group culture that encourages confrontation of members' motivation to work in the group. However, because resistant members avoid taking responsibility for their actions, it is unrealistic to expect them to confront each other initially. The leader has to set the climate by modeling constructive confrontation.

According to Edelwich and Brodsky (1992) constructive confrontations should be (a) solicited rather than imposed, (b) done gently and with caring, (c) descriptive rather than evaluative, (d) specific and concrete, (e) presented in an atmosphere of trust, and (f) timed so that the member is able to hear and experience the full effect of the interaction. Constructive confrontations should include a descriptive statement, an "I" statement, and a reference to natural consequences (Edelwich & Brodsky, 1992). For example, "You say that you didn't do anything, and you can't understand why you're being singled out. But if I had been caught driving with a blood alcohol level as high as yours, I would have been given the same choice as you: Lose my license or come here. And if I kept avoiding the consequences of my behavior, I'd probably also have problems on the job and at home—as you are having. Avoiding problems doesn't help. When you decide to face up to them, then you can start to do something about them."

Even though constructive confrontations can help overcome members' resistance to working in the group, it is important to remember that reluctant and resistant members will continue to experience obstacles to goal achievement as they attempt to develop and implement treatment plans. These obstacles can reduce their motivation, making them reluctant to continue to work to accomplish specific goals. Reid (1992), for example, points out that beliefs about change and obstacles encountered in the external environment reduce members' motivation to engage in tasks to resolve particular problems. Methods designed to help members change their beliefs and to make the external environment more responsive are described in the next chapter.

Monitoring and Evaluating the Group's Progress

Monitoring and evaluating progress provides feedback for workers and members, which is useful in developing, modifying, and changing treatment plans. It also is helpful in maintaining the functioning of the group as a whole. Monitoring and evaluating are important ongoing processes that should occur throughout the life of a group.

One of the most common methods of obtaining feedback from members during the middle stage of a group's development is to give members a session evaluation form, such as that shown in Chapter 12 (Figure 12–3), at the end of each group session. Although the format of session evaluation questions (closed-ended Likert-type questions and open-ended questions) remains fairly standard from group to group, the content of questions varies. Changing the content of questions provides workers with the specific information they need about a particular group's work.

How frequently should session evaluation forms be administered? In some groups, they can be used at the end of each session. Workers who are not familiar with using session evaluation forms sometimes wonder how they will be received by members, but brief forms that take only a few minutes to fill out are not a burden for members to complete. In fact, members often enjoy the chance to let the worker know what they like and don't like about the group.

In other groups, workers may prefer to evaluate the group's progress after every second or third session. The exact frequency of monitoring and evaluating ultimately depends on the need for ongoing feedback about the group's development. Verbal evaluations are often used as a substitute for written evaluations, but anonymous written evaluations may offer better quality feedback because they can offer a measure of confidentiality not available through verbal evaluations.

Other frequently used methods of monitoring and evaluating include having members self-monitor their own behaviors and having others who are familiar with members' concerns (such as other workers or family members) report progress to the worker. These and other monitoring and evaluation methods are described in Chapters 7 and 12. The actual methods used for obtaining feedback are, however, not as important as whether the feedback is systematically solicited, collected, and acted upon. Obtaining feedback allows workers to fine-tune a group as it progresses through the working stage. It also is a signal to members that their opinions are valued and that their ideas and concerns will be analyzed and acted upon. For these reasons, monitoring and evaluating a group's progress is an essential worker activity during the working stage of group development.

SUMMARY

The working stage of treatment groups is the period in which members focus on the goals they have contracted to achieve in the group. This chapter focuses on six foundation activities that all workers perform while leading treatment groups during their working stage. The section about preparing for group meetings includes a discussion of how to select program activities. The section on structuring the group's work includes a discussion of the optimal amount of structure to meet members' needs. The section about involving and empowering group members includes building on members' strengths and their commitment to the group as a whole. The section on helping members achieve contract goals includes techniques for (a) keeping members aware of goals they have contracted for, (b) developing treatment plans, (c) motivating members to work on their treatment plans, and (d) helping members carry out their treatment plans. The section about working with reluctant and resistant group members includes a discussion of constructive uses of confrontation. The chapter concludes with the foundation activity of monitoring and evaluating the group's progress.

LEARNING ASSIGNMENTS

1. You are preparing to lead a socialization group in an after-school program for third- and fourth-graders. Develop three program activities that are age appropriate. Prepare a list of materials that you would need to have on-hand to conduct these activities. Write a paragraph describing the benefits of each of these activities for members. Describe a *variation* on one of these activities (or an additional program activity) that would help members develop problem solving skills. Describe a *variation* that would help members develop expressive skills.

2. Develop a written session agenda for an educational group for individuals who want to be foster parents. Develop a written agenda for the meeting of a task group in which you participate.

3. Identify a social action group in your community. Observe the extent to which members are involved and active. To what extent do the leaders and other active participants help all members feel empowered to work toward a particular group goal? If you were the leader, how would you have run the meeting differently to help empower members?

4. Using the principles described in this chapter, describe how you would work with a newly formed group of teen-agers who were court-referred through a juvenile diversion program.

5. Develop a written group contract for outpatients meeting in a community mental health center. In addition, give an example of a contract that one of the members might make with (a) the group as a whole, (b) the group's leader, and (c) another member.

CHAPTER 9

Treatment Groups: Specialized Methods

This chapter focuses on specialized intervention methods for planned change efforts involving individual group members, the group as a whole, and the group's external environment. The selection of intervention methods is based on the changing needs of the group and its members throughout the working stage. For example, in the fourth session of a therapy group, the worker focuses on a member who is in crisis. During the processing of group interaction at the end of the meeting, the worker notes that because of the time spent on the individual's concerns, member-to-member interaction was somewhat limited. Before the next group meeting the worker plans several program activities to ensure a high level of member-to-member interaction in the group as a whole. At the next meeting, while engaging in these program activities, it becomes clear that the institution where the members live does not foster peer interaction. During a team meeting with staff, the worker shares her perceptions, and the team discusses how the institutional environment could be changed to promote peer interaction.

Even though this chapter sequentially presents interventions for the individual group member, the group as a whole, and the group's environment, in actual practice, interventions at one level often affect other levels (Garvin, 1987). The skilled worker moves easily among all the levels as the group unfolds, combining interventions for the individual member, the group as a whole, and the group's environment to help members reach their treatment goals.

INTERVENING WITH GROUP MEMBERS

When intervening with individual group members, the worker may select from (a) intrapersonal, (b) interpersonal, or (c) environmental interventions. Intrapersonal interventions are focused on members' cognitions and affects—that is, their thoughts, beliefs, values, feelings, sensations, and emotions. These interventions are particularly appropriate when an assessment has determined that a member's psychosocial development may have helped to contribute to dysfunctional or irrational belief systems.

Interpersonal interventions focus on members' relationships with others within and outside the group. These are particularly useful when an assessment has determined that members need further development of their skills in relating to others.

Environmental interventions seek to change or modify the psychosocial and physical space in which members function to help them achieve their treatment goals. They are particularly useful when an assessment determines that a member lacks material resources to ameliorate a problem.

In keeping with the eclectic approach of this text, the interventions included in this section were drawn from several practice perspectives. Workers using some approaches rely exclusively on the skills mentioned in Chapter 4, but we have included specialized intervention methods in this chapter because we have found them to be effective for particular types of problems that we have encountered in leading treatment groups. Many specialized intervention methods have not been included. We encourage readers to add to the methods described here as they become familiar with those that are grounded in practice models and theories that they find particularly useful.

Intrapersonal Interventions

Since the beginnings of group work practice, workers with psychodynamic orientations have focused most of their interventions in treatment groups on the intrapersonal aspects of group members' behavior. In recent years, there has also been a growing interest in techniques to intervene in the covert, intrapersonal lives of group members based on cognitive-behavioral approaches to practice. Perhaps this is the result of the accumulating evidence suggesting that what people think and feel has a direct bearing on how they behave (Mahoney, 1974; Meichenbaum, 1977). Increased interest in covert, intrapersonal events has led to an explosion in the number of techniques designed to alter cognitive and affective development.

Before using specific techniques, group workers should be aware of the overall process of helping members make intrapersonal changes. This process includes helping members (a) identify and discriminate among thoughts, feelings, and behaviors; (b) recognize associations between specific thoughts, feelings, and behaviors; (c) analyze the rationality of thoughts and beliefs; and (d) change distorted or irrational thoughts and beliefs.

Identifying and Discriminating

The first step in any intrapersonal intervention is to help members accurately identify thoughts, feelings, and behaviors and to discriminate among them. Some members have great difficulty putting their subjective thoughts and feelings into words. But without clearly identifying a member's thoughts and feelings for the rest of the group, it is not possible to help members cope with or change these covert processes.

In helping members identify and discriminate behavior from thoughts and feelings, members should describe their behavior as if a camera were taking a picture of the event and the member were a bystander observing the behavior (see, for example, Maultsby, 1975; Maultsby & Carpenter, 1980). This technique also helps members describe events in specific, observable terms.

Some people have a difficult time describing feelings. It is common for group members to respond to a question about what they are feeling with a description of a behavior or a thought. This is particularly true of men, who are taught as they are growing up that expressing feelings is a feminine, not a masculine, trait. For example, in response to a question about what he was feeling, an obviously angry group member stated, "I'm not feeling anything." When the worker said we are always feeling something, no matter how slight, the member said, "I'm feeling that your interpretation of my behavior is not correct." This statement, of course, is a thought, not a feeling, and such responses were quite common from this group member.

To help members who have difficulty discriminating feelings from thoughts, the worker can have the member get feedback from the group. In the previously described situation, for example, the member went around the group asking the others if they had an idea of how he was feeling. As the members expressed that he appeared to be angry, the member gradually became aware that he was not in touch with his feelings. Sometimes it is necessary to have members practice discriminating thoughts from feelings in several situations inside and outside the group before they are able to correctly identify and separate them.

Recognizing Associations

The second step in intrapersonal interventions is to help members recognize that there is an association among thoughts, feelings, and behaviors. For example, if a man thinks someone is deliberately following him as he walks home one evening, he is likely to feel apprehensive and to behave accordingly. He may look over his shoulder or walk on the well-lighted side of a street. Similarly, if a woman thinks she is not skillful at a particular task, she is likely to feel incompetent and is less likely to continue to work on the task if she encounters difficulty than if she thinks that she can perform the task adequately.

For members to alter associations among thoughts, feelings, and behaviors, they must be aware of their existence. Awareness can be accomplished through a self-monitoring process. Members are asked to monitor particular thoughts as well as the feelings and behaviors that occur immediately following them. The group helps members look for patterns of association among particular thoughts, feelings, and behaviors. Sometimes members may clearly remember specific thoughts and their associated feelings and behaviors, and it may not be necessary to spend time monitoring them before reporting them to the group. This is often the case with automatic thoughts that constantly reoccur to members (Beck, 1976; Beck, Freeman, & Associates, 1990).

Data about thoughts, feelings, and behaviors collected either prospectively or retrospectively are discussed in the group. Such a discussion usually reveals that specific thoughts are exacerbating or maintaining unwanted feeling states and behavior patterns. For example, the anxious group member found that her thoughts were focused on her "inability to do anything right" and that she "would not be able to complete her work assignments on time." As her thoughts were discussed in the group, it became clear that they led to her fears and her anxiety about her performance on the job. These feelings, in turn, tended to distract her from her work and often led to migraine headaches. Both of these consequences reinforced her beliefs that she would not be able to complete her assignments, that she couldn't do anything right, and that she was a failure.

The previous example suggests that thoughts lead to feelings and behavior, but it is also possible that particular cues or signals can lead to thoughts, which can, in turn, lead to feelings and behavior. For example, a cue for an anxiety-producing thought might be the approach of a person of the opposite sex in a singles bar. The approach cues or signals the person who begins to think anxiety-producing thoughts, such as, "I hope he doesn't come over here" and "I won't know what to say." These thoughts can then lead to feelings of anxiety and to avoidance behavior. Such a sequence of events can become habituated, and a particular cue, or even the thought of the particular cue, can lead to the entire sequence of dysfunctional thoughts, feelings, and behaviors.

The second step in the process of intrapersonal interventions, therefore, also includes helping members become aware of internal cues such as muscle tension or "butterflies" in the stomach and external cues, such as the approach of a person, that trigger a sequence of events. In long-term treatment focused on personality change, workers may want to help members gain insight into the historical determinants of these cues. Once members are aware of the cues that trigger an association between thoughts, feelings, and behavior, they are ready to move on to the next step in the process.

Analyzing the Rationality of Thoughts and Beliefs

The third step in intrapersonal intervention is to help members analyze the rationality of the thoughts and beliefs that maintain or exacerbate dysfunctional feelings and behavior patterns. Epictetus wrote in *The Enchiridion:* "Men are not disturbed by things but by the views taken of them." According to many cognitive psychologists, dysfunctional and irrational thoughts and beliefs arise from erroneous or misleading interpretations of events (Beck, Rush, Shaw, & Emery, 1979; Ellis, 1962; Freeman, Fleming, Simmons, & Pretzer, 1990; Mahoney, 1974; Meichenbaum, 1977; Stern & Drummond, 1991). Group members may (a) overgeneralize from an event, (b) selectively focus on portions of an event, (c) take too much responsibility for events that are beyond their control, (d) think of the worst possible consequence of future events, (e) engage in either/or dichotomous thinking, and (f) assume that because certain events have led to particular consequences in the past they will automatically lead to the same consequences if they occur in the future.

Sometimes corrective information and feedback are sufficient to change thoughts and beliefs based on incomplete or incorrect information. For example, some teen-age girls believe that they won't get pregnant if they have sexual intercourse only once or twice. With proper information, however, beliefs about the result of sexual activity can be changed.

Ellis (1962) and others (Beck et al., 1990; Stern & Drummond, 1991; Yost, Beutler, Corbishley, and Allender, 1985) have suggested that faulty interpretations occur because of irrational beliefs and ideas people have about the way things should operate in their world. For example, members may believe that they must be thoroughly "competent, adequate, and achieving in all possible respects if they are to consider themselves worthwhile" (p. 63). Ellis lists 11 common irrational ideas that affect members' interpretations of events. These beliefs are usually based on absolutist thinking rather than on well-reasoned, logical interpretations or elaborations from factual evidence. Words such as *should, ought,* and *must* are cues to the existence of absolutist thinking which may lead to irrational or erroneous interpretations of events. For example, a group member might believe that to consider himself worthwhile he must be competent in all possible respects. When his performance falls short of his unrealistically high standards, he becomes depressed.

Changing Thoughts, Beliefs, and Feeling States

The fourth step in intrapersonal interventions is to help members change irrational or distorted thoughts and beliefs and associated feeling states. Several techniques that have been developed for this purpose are listed here along with a brief description of their use in group treatment.

COGNITIVE RESTRUCTURING.   Cognitive restructuring is a term used by Mahoney (1974) to refer to a group of techniques such as rational emotive therapy and misattribution therapy. These techniques are designed to expose faulty logic in group members' thought patterns and to help them replace these irrational thought processes with logical, rational patterns of thought. Yost et al. (1985), for example, report using cognitive restructuring techniques effectively when working with groups of depressed older adults.

The worker can help members change faulty logic by doing the following:

1. Having members examine the assumptions on which thoughts and beliefs are based.
2. Helping members generate alternative assumptions.
3. Helping members test assumptions by taking actions to verify them in situations outside of the group.
4. Helping members get feedback from others in the group about the logic of their assumptions.

Through a combination of group discussion, rational analysis, and action, members help each other change their attributions concerning previous events and replace the cognition that results from these attributions with thoughts and beliefs that are more functional for coping with events in their daily lives.

COGNITIVE SELF-INSTRUCTION.   The cognitive self-instruction technique, described by Beck (1990), Meichenbaum (1977), and Stern and Drummond (1991), refer to helping members use internal dialogues and covert self-statements for solving problems and coping with difficult life events. Children and adults can use the technique to replace dysfunctional internal dialogues with self-statements that help them to solve a problem. For example, instead of a member saying to herself, "I can't do this," she can be trained to say, "I'll try to do it the best I can" or "I'll bet my answer is as good or better than anyone else's," and "First I'll examine all the data and then I'll think of the possible solutions."

Cognitive self-instructions can be used to prepare for a particular situation or to help a member perform effectively during a situation. For example, to prepare for a situation, a member might say, "When I talk to Sally, I'll tell her directly that I can't do it. If she tries to persuade me I'll just repeat that I've decided not to do it." While in a particular situation, a member might say, "I'm in control" or "I can do this."

It has been found by D'Zurilla and Goldfried (1971) and Meichenbaum (1977) that internal dialogues are important mediators of effective problem solving. Poor problem solvers tend to repeat dysfunctional self-statements, which make them give up more quickly and get blocked more easily in problem-solving efforts than those whose self-statements encourage active problem-solving efforts. Research evidence presented by Mahoney (1974) and Meichenbaum (1977) confirms that this procedure is an effective intrapersonal intervention for members who engage in dysfunctional internal dialogues.

THOUGHT STOPPING.   Some group members have difficulty controlling maladaptive or self-defeating thoughts and internal dialogues. The thought-stopping technique is a way to help them reduce these thoughts (Upper & Cautela, 1982; Wolpe, 1973). While the member is concentrating on a thought, the worker suddenly and emphatically says, "Stop." This procedure is repeated several times. The member gradually begins to think "Stop" and to remember the worker's voice saying "Stop" whenever the obtrusive thought occurs. Variations of the technique include having members pinch themselves when obtrusive thoughts occur, having them replace obtrusive thoughts with covert dialogues and images that are not self-defeating, and having members meditate on a particular scene or phrase when obtrusive thoughts occur.

REFRAMING.   Reframing is a cognitive technique used to help group members see situations or problems from another point of view. It "means to change the conceptual and/or emotional setting or viewpoint in relation to which the situation is experienced and to place it in another frame which fits the facts of the same concrete situation equally well or even better, and thereby changes its entire meaning" (Watzlawick, Weakland, & Fisch, 1974, p. 95).

For example, a member who complains that he is afraid to ask a co-worker to dinner might be helped to reframe the situation as one in which he is sparing himself and his co-worker from possible romantic entanglements that may interfere with job performance. In another case, a single parent who is angry at her former husband for encouraging their child to fight back when teased may be helped to reframe the situation as one in which her former husband is helping the child develop and maintain a male identity.

Once a member experiences a problem from a new perspective, the positive aspects of the situation are highlighted and the negative aspects of the situation have a better chance of being changed. The woman, for example, thanked her former husband for staying involved with their child and suggested some other ways that the husband might help the child, such as how to settle disputes without fighting. The male group member developed a platonic friendship with his co-worker.

Reframing can also be used to help a member experience a problem or concern as an asset (Beck, 1990; Haley, 1973; Stern & Drummond, 1991; Yost et al., 1985). For example, in a situation in which a member's spouse does not want to have sexual relations, the problem can be viewed as a helpful sign that something is wrong in their relationship.

COGNITIVE IMAGERY TECHNIQUES. Flooding and implosion are two cognitive imagery techniques used to extinguish excessive and unproductive reactions to feared or anxiety-provoking events (Rimm & Masters, 1974; Shipley & Boudewyns, 1980). In implosion, the member is asked to imagine the most extreme version of a feared event or stimulus within the protected environment of the group. Thus, if a group member experiences anxiety when thinking about asking someone for a date, the member would be asked to imagine that person saying no and making a disparaging remark such as, "I wouldn't go out with someone like you" or "You're not sophisticated enough for me." Because the member will not experience any horrible consequences from such a rebuff, he or she will overcome the fear associated with the possible consequences of asking for a date. Members often react to this technique with comments such as "That wasn't so bad" or "I didn't like the reaction I received, but I learned that I could live with it. I won't be so afraid of the consequences the next time."

Flooding is a procedure similar to implosion except that the member is asked to imagine the actual feared event rather than an extreme or exaggerated version of it. Feedback from other group members can be used to help the member see that although reactions may, at times, be unpleasant, they can be handled without great difficulty. The member learns how others cope with unpleasant reactions and develops his or her own methods for coping.

Research evidence on flooding and implosion suggests that in-vivo exposure to the situation or event is more successful than imagined exposure (Rimm & Masters, 1974). In group treatment, a role play exercise may be used to expose a member to the feared situation. When the member practices handling the situation in the group, the member can then be assigned the task of experiencing the situation outside the group. Because duration of exposure is also associated with treatment outcome, the member should be encouraged to practice coping with the situation several times inside and outside the group.

A variety of other cognitive imagery techniques can be used effectively in groups. Lazarus (1971) suggests that rational imagery can be used effectively to help members challenge irrational beliefs and assumptions and to act effectively in anxiety-producing situations. For example, in practicing to be more effective in a situation in which a member would routinely begin irrational self-talk, the member could use rational imagery that includes a covert dialogue challenging irrational self-talk and replacing it with rational statements. Other cognitive imagery techniques include imagining pleasant events during anxiety-producing, feared situations. For example, in a group for agoraphobics, members could be asked to imagine themselves walking in a beautiful outdoor setting on a sunny, autumn day.

When using imagery techniques, the worker should ensure that members remain in a relaxed state and that they are able to vividly imagine the situation.

Members should be instructed to signal the worker immediately if their anxiety increases or if the cognitive image they are visualizing fades. To help produce vivid imagery, the worker should recite a richly detailed image while members are in a relaxed state with their eyes closed.

PROGRESSIVE MUSCLE RELAXATION. This technique combines cognitive instructions with physical activities to relieve stress and help group members overcome anxiety. The premise is that muscle tension is related to anxiety and stress. Helping members reduce muscle tension, therefore, will help relieve anxiety.

With members either seated in comfortable chairs or reclining on the floor, the worker explains the entire procedure to them. Members should be as comfortable as possible throughout the procedure. In a calm, hypnotic voice, the worker (or an audiotaped voice) repeats the relaxation instructions, which include tensing and relaxing each of the major muscle groups in the body. For example, the worker might say, "Stretch your arms out next to you (or on your lap, if seated). Make a fist with both hands as hard as you can. Feel the tension and tightness in your hand. Keep your hands clenched (10 seconds). Now relax. Just let your hand rest against the floor (or on your lap, if seated). Notice how the tension and tightness are leaving your hands. Notice how the feelings of tension are being replaced by warm feelings of relaxation and comfort. Notice how your hands feel now compared with when you were tensing them."

Each of the muscle groups are tensed and relaxed in this manner. Instructions for the entire relaxation procedure will not be given here because several excellent sources exist (Bernstein & Borkovec, 1973; Rimm & Masters, 1974; Wolpe, 1973). Records and audiotape cassettes are also available with complete instructions (Bernstein & Borkovec, 1973).

Although progressive muscle relaxation is most often conducted in individual treatment, it can be used effectively in group treatment (Rose, 1989; Wolpe, 1973). The major drawback in using this technique in group treatment is that it requires cooperation from every member. A single member who distracts the group can ruin the effect of the procedure for everyone else. Sometimes the distraction may be unintentional such as when a member falls asleep and begins to snore. In other situations, the distraction may be intentional. For example, a member who is not motivated may laugh or joke during the first tension release cycle, thereby distracting other group members.

To use relaxation effectively, the entire procedure should be explained before beginning. To reduce intentional distractions, members should have the opportunity to voice any questions or any reluctance about using the procedure before beginning. To reduce unintentional distractions, members should be given a signal to let the group leader know if they are having a problem. For example, a member might not be able to relax or, in rare cases, may become more tense. The member can signal the worker and the worker can give that member individual attention.

The relaxing nature of the procedure, dim lights, and comfortable position sometimes cause members to fall asleep. However, the regular breathing or snoring of a sleeping member can be distracting to other group members. Such unintentional distractions can be reduced if the worker explains that sleeping members will be awakened by a touch on the hand or arm.

Other relaxation procedures can be used as a substitute for progressive muscle relaxation. Some workers prefer meditation, bioenergetics, hypnosis, rolfing (deep muscle massage), or jogging. Although each of these procedures was developed from differing theoretical orientations, they all can achieve a similar result: a relaxed group member.

SYSTEMATIC DESENSITIZATION.   The technique of systematic desensitization can be particularly effective for treatment groups composed of members with phobias. With this technique, the worker helps members construct a hierarchy of situations or scenes that are feared. Starting with the least feared situations and progressing to the most feared situation, members are asked to imagine each situation while they are in a state of deep relaxation induced by progressive muscle relaxation.

A hierarchy of situations should consist of at least 10 scenes in which the member experiences gradually increasing levels of anxiety. For example, a hierarchy for a member who has been too fearful to date consists of (a) thinking about a prospective dating partner, (b) considering asking that person for a date, (c) planning where to go on the date, (d) planning how to ask the person for a date, (e) approaching the person to ask for a date, (f) starting a conversation, (g) asking the person for a date, (h) driving to the person's house, (i) walking up to the person's home, and (j) going out together.

Depending on the extent and the intensity of the anxiety, hierarchies may contain many more scenes. Scenes should not jump too quickly from a low to a high level of anxiety. For very fearful members, it is often necessary to construct hierarchies with as many as 20 or 30 scenes.

Once the members are helped to construct their own hierarchies (even if each member has the same phobia, individual hierarchies will differ), the progressive muscle relaxation technique is used to induce a state of relaxation. The members are then asked to imagine the first scene on their hierarchy as if they were actually involved in it for about 10 seconds (Wolpe, 1973). If members experience anxiety, they are instructed to signal by raising a finger. Members experiencing anxiety are told to stop imagining the scene and helped to return to their former state of relaxation. When they are fully relaxed, they can imagine the scene again.

At this point, desensitization proceeds at the pace of the slowest group member (Fisher, 1978), unless some provision is made for members to complete their hierarchies at their own pace. One method to overcome this problem is to have members work in pairs, helping each other work through the hierarchy each has developed (Rose, 1989). The worker should not allow members to work on their hierarchies for more than 30 minutes, because the desensitization procedure is quite demanding, both in terms of continuously visualizing scenes and in remaining in a deeply relaxed state. If members do not complete their hierarchies during one meeting, they can begin the next meeting with the next to last scene they completed successfully in the previous meeting.

Interpersonal Interventions

Group work is an especially appropriate modality for dealing with interpersonal problems. Used effectively, the group can become a natural laboratory for examining and improving the relationships members have with one another. Unlike individual treatment, a group offers members the opportunity to demonstrate their interpersonal skills and to receive feedback from a variety of people. Members can serve as models of particular interpersonal skills and can play various roles in situations acted out in the group.

Interpersonal behaviors can be learned indirectly, by listening to others describe how to behave in a situation. But behaviors are more effectively learned (a) vicariously, by watching what other people do or say, and (b) directly, by repeating and practicing new behaviors. When learned directly, a new behavior is usually performed on a trial-and-error basis until it is performed appropriately.

Learning a new behavior by hearing it described is often imprecise and fraught with potential misinterpretation. Therefore, teaching behavior is most adequately accomplished by having a member watch someone else perform a behavior correctly and having the member practice the new behavior in a role play exercise.

Many workers tend to allow the group to spend too much time discussing how to behave without actually helping members practice new behaviors. Perhaps this is because of the contrived nature of role play situations, the initial resistance of some members to role playing, and the extra instructions and direction the worker must provide to make a role play successful. The learning that occurs from watching a model and rehearsing a new behavior, compared with merely talking about how to perform a new behavior, suggests that both modeling and role play techniques should be used more frequently by workers when helping members learn new or improved interpersonal behaviors.

Learning by Observing Models

Several factors affect the extent to which behaviors are learned by observing others (Bandura, 1977b). Workers should understand the process underlying observational learning so that they can use modeling to help members solve interpersonal problems and learn new interpersonal skills.

Figure 9–1 illustrates the major components of observational learning. As can be seen, performance of the modeled behavior depends on (a) the level of attention or awareness of the observer, (b) the extent to which the observer retains what is seen, (c) the observer's abilities to perform the observed behavior, and (d) the extent to which the observer is motivated to perform the behavior (Bandura, 1977b).

The attention of a member who observes a model is important, because, although behavior may be learned without one's awareness, attention is always selective and it is greatly facilitated by focusing on what is being observed. The worker can help focus awareness by calling members' attention to particular aspects of a model's behavior. For example, a member who is learning to be more assertive may be asked to pay particular attention to the facial expressions, body positions, and voice tones of a member who is modeling an assertive response.

FIGURE 9-1
The process of
observational learning

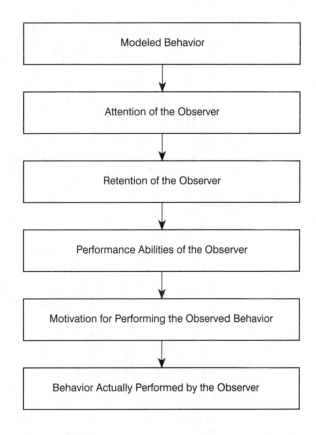

Attentional processes are also enhanced by the attractiveness of the model. For example, a member is more likely to pay attention to a group member who is held in high regard than to a member who has little status in the group. Members find models most attractive when they are similar to themselves. Thus, workers should try to match the demographic characteristics of models to the members who are observing them.

Retentional processes are also important in learning an observed behavior. In addition to developing images of the behavior that can be easily retrieved from a member's memory, retention is often facilitated if the model explains the covert and overt processes he or she goes through before performing a behavior. These explanations help the member develop a cognitive structure in which to organize perceptual images. When modeling an assertive behavior, the worker may, for example, explain the cognitive process occurring before the assertive response. Internal dialogues such as, "I say to myself, 'I have a right to tell that person . . .'" can be helpful to members observing someone modeling a behavior.

The model may also explain general principles. For example, in making an assertive response, the member modeling the behavior might explain, "In general, I am always direct—I explain my needs to the person and I make a direct request for him or her to change his behavior." Explaining general principles also provides an organizing framework that the member can use in different situations encountered in the future.

The member's ability to perform the modeled response is a critical component of observational learning. The member may pay careful attention to the way a model performs a behavior and retain details of the performance but may not be able to respond in a similar fashion. The best way to ensure that a member is able to perform a behavior correctly is to have the member perform the behavior in the group and receive feedback about the performance. If it is available, videotape feedback of the member's performance can also be effective in teaching new interpersonal behaviors.

Group members may know how to behave in interpersonal situations but may not be motivated to do so. What factors increase motivation? According to Bandura (1977b), behaviors are more likely to occur if the observer sees others being rewarded for similar performances. Conversely, if an observer sees others being sanctioned for a given behavior, the observer is less likely to behave in a way that may result in similar sanctions.

A member, however, may not have to observe someone being sanctioned to not perform a new behavior. New behaviors are often difficult to perform until they are well-learned. Difficulties associated with learning a new behavior, along with the absence of strong incentives, are frequently a sufficient disincentive for members considering performing new behaviors. Therefore, observational learning is selective. In daily living, for example, we often do not repeat a new behavior that we see performed by someone else.

To ensure that group members learn new behaviors by observing the worker or other members, several factors should be present. Members' attention should be carefully focused on how the behavior is being performed. Members should be helped to retain cognitive images of observed behavior by developing a set of organizing principles—a cognitive framework—that explains why a model responded in a particular manner. To build their capacity to respond, members should practice responses and receive feedback about the quality of their performances. Members' motivation for performing observed behaviors can be increased by demonstrating to them that the incentives sufficiently outweigh the disincentives for performing a particular behavior.

Learning by Role Playing

Role playing has been defined as a realistic enactment of a social role in an imagined social situation (Shaw 1980). It is frequently used in group work. The first reported therapeutic use of role playing was by Moreno (1946), who developed psychodrama and sociodrama procedures in the 1930s. Kelly (1955) also reported early uses of role playing procedures in the development of fixed role and exaggerated role therapies. Since that time, many books have been written about role playing from a variety of theoretical orientations (see, for example, Blatner, 1973; Corsini, 1966; Klein, 1956; Maier, Solem, & Maier, 1975; Shaw, 1980).

Role playing has at least five functions in group work, including (a) assessment, (b) simulation, (c) understanding, (d) decision making, and (e) behavior change (Etcheverry, Siporin, and Toseland, 1987). Role playing is a powerful tool for any of these purposes. As shown in Table 9–1, role playing techniques increase members' awareness and understanding of their interpersonal skills, and produce behavior changes by providing members with corrective feedback and the opportunity to practice improved responses in the sheltered environment of the group.

Different role playing techniques available for use by group workers can be divided into structured and unstructured procedures. Structured procedures use predetermined scripts or vignettes developed by the leader. Members are called upon to act out prescribed roles and in this way learn to handle specific situations believed to be important by the leader. For example, in an assertiveness training program group members may be asked to role play a number of common situations requiring assertive responses such as dealing with someone who has cut into a line, returning damaged merchandise, or turning down a request to borrow an item. Structured role plays are not spontaneous, but they have the advantage of ensuring that the worker is ready with an effective response.

Different unstructured role play procedures are listed in Table 9–1. These procedures are developmental and open-ended (Shaw, 1980). They allow for spontaneous, emerging processes of learning and problem solving. Unstructured role play procedures can be further divided into primary and secondary procedures. Primary role play procedures can be used alone to accomplish particular purposes, whereas secondary procedures are used in conjunction with primary procedures to extend their effect and widen their scope (Etcheverry, Siporin, & Toseland, 1987).

Primary Role Play Procedures

OWN ROLE.   In the own role procedure, a member uses his or her experiences and plays the protagonist. Other roles are played by the worker or other group members. These auxiliaries may represent people, feeling states, thoughts, or objects. The own role technique is particularly useful in assessing a member's interpersonal skills, because it allows the worker and other group members to observe how the protagonist acts in a particular situation. The own role procedure is also helpful as a means for members to practice new behaviors. Supportive procedures such as the soliloquy, on-the-spot interview, or doubling can be used to increase a member's awareness of his or her behavior while performing the role of protagonist.

ROLE REVERSAL.   In role reversal, a group member acts as the protagonist by taking on the role of another person. For example, a husband may act in the role of his spouse. The procedure enables a member to experience a situation from another's point of view. It is particularly useful for teaching empathy, especially if it is used with doubling or soliloquy. It helps clarify situations and it increases members' self-awareness. As Shaw (1980) points out, role reversal also increases spontaneity, flexibility, and openness of the member playing the protagonist's role. Variations of this procedure include substitute role playing (playing a symbolic, substitute role) and role distance (playing an emotionally distant role).

TABLE 9–1
Uses of unstructured role play procedures

Procedure	Awareness/Understanding	Behavior Change
A. Primary Role Play Procedures		
1. Own role	Demonstrates and clarifies members' behavior, their role in interpersonal interactions, and their concerns and problems Facilitates members' insight into their own feelings, thoughts, and behaviors Identifies situational cues to facilitate differential responses Identifies members' problems and concerns	Allows members to practice new behaviors Reduces members' performance anxiety Prepares members for obstacles and set-backs
2. Role reversal	Stimulates empathy for another person whose role is being enacted by the protagonist Increases members' awareness of cognitive and affective aspects of other people Objectifies and clarifies the situational context of members' own behaviors	Encourages spontaneity and participation Facilitates changes in members' expectations of others Facilitates change in members' behavior Improves empathic skills
3. Autodrama/ monodrama/ chairing	Same as for own role and role reversal procedures Identifies and clarifies members' own feelings at deeper levels than own role or role reversal procedures Increases members' awareness of their own "self-talk"	Same as for own role and role reversal procedures Facilitates learning of adaptive "self-talk" Enables changes on deeper, more complex levels than own role or role reversal procedures
4. Sculpting/ choreography (Action sociogram)	Stimulates members' awareness and discussion of their own behavior and the group's interaction patterns	Facilitates changes in members' attitudes, behaviors, and interaction patterns

B. Supportive Role Play Procedures

Procedure	
1. On-the-spot interview	Identifies and clarifies members' thoughts and feelings while they are in a role Connects thinking and feeling to behaviors in a role Provides practice in self-awareness and self-talk
2. Soliloquy	Same as on-the-spot interview procedure but less structured Same as on-the-spot interview procedure
3. Doubling	Helps members verbalize and express covert thoughts, feelings, and behaviors Same as on-the-spot interview procedure Identifies new behaviors for acquisition Same as on-the-spot interview procedure Gives permission and support for members' "owning" their own thoughts, feelings, and behaviors Facilitates expression of feelings Promotes members' skill in using feelings as cues for appropriate responses Allows members to practice their self-expression skills
4. Mirror	Promotes members' knowledge of the consequences of their own behavior upon others Enables self-confrontation Provides members the opportunity to practice new behaviors Enables feedback and reinforcement when learning new behaviors
5. Sharing	Universalizes members' experiences Models self-disclosure Provides support and confirmation of members' experiences, abilities, etc. Facilitates learning of self-disclosure skills

AUTODRAMA, MONODRAMA, AND CHAIRING. A procedure in which a group member plays multiple roles is variously called autodrama, monodrama, and chairing (Blatner, 1973). The multiple roles represent the different ways the member views himself or herself or the different ways others view the member. The procedure is usually conducted using one or more empty chairs, each representing a role, a character part, or a personality aspect. The member switches from one chair to another as he or she changes roles. When occupying each chair, the person initiates and maintains a dialogue with the other chairs, which represent other aspects of the person's self.

The technique is particularly useful in helping members become aware of the various roles they play and their effect on each other. It is also useful in helping members assess internal dialogues and self-talk, including irrational beliefs and devaluating self-statements. Therefore, the procedure can be used effectively in cooperation with cognitive restructuring procedures to practice adaptive self-statements and self-instructions that aid effective problem solving. Self-role and double chairing are other names for this procedure.

SCULPTING AND CHOREOGRAPHY. Also called action sociogram, variations of the sculpting and choreography technique are psychodrama and sociodrama (Blatner, 1973; Moreno, 1946). In this procedure, a member, as protagonist, is directed to sculpt or position himself or herself and other group members in a drama that represents a symbolic or real situation in the member's life. The protagonist explains each person's role and the worker directs the action, which can last for an extended period of time.

The dramatic enactment is designed to expose intense feelings and conflicts in a member's life. Because of this, it can be used as an assessment device by the worker. Another benefit of the technique is that it immerses the whole group in intense participatory involvement leading to in-depth self-disclosure and enactment of crucial concerns and issues. In addition to the self-awareness this produces, the procedure helps the protagonist understand the importance of others in his or her own life situations. Although there is little empirical evidence for the efficacy of the technique, clinical reports and our own experience suggest that the cathartic experience and heightened awareness that result from participating in a dramatic enactment can lead to changes in members' thoughts, feelings, behaviors, attitudes, and interaction patterns.

The psychodrama variation of the technique focuses on the internal, psychological status of the actors. The sociodrama variation emphasizes the social and environmental aspects of the protagonist's situation. For an excellent, in-depth explanation of these procedures, see Blatner (1973).

Supplementary Role Play Procedures

ON-THE-SPOT INTERVIEW. This involves stopping the role play action before it is finished and interviewing one or more of the actors. The worker asks specific, detailed questions designed to elicit particular thoughts and feelings at that point in the role play. The procedure is designed to increase an actor's awareness of cognitive, affective, and behavioral aspects of a role performance. It identifies self-statements and self-talk that is dysfunctional and self-devaluating. It also teaches self-observation and enhances self-awareness.

SOLILOQUY.   The soliloquy procedure involves stopping the role play action and asking an actor to disclose what he or she is thinking or feeling. Unlike the on-the-spot interview, in which the actor is asked specific, closed-ended questions, soliloquy questions are open-ended, encouraging the member to engage in a monologue that discloses in-depth thoughts and feelings. The procedure is particularly useful for increasing a member's self-awareness.

DOUBLING.   The doubling procedure uses an auxiliary group member to act as the alter-ego or inner voice of the protagonist. To emphasize identification with the protagonist, the double is required to speak in the first person, for example, saying, "I feel . . ." or "I think. . . ." Variations on the procedure are the "divided double" and the "multiple double." In the divided double, the alter ego speaks for different parts of the protagonist's inner self. The multiple double calls for two or more actors to speak for different aspects of the protagonist's self. To validate the truth of a double's statements in offering inferences, interpretations, or alternative reactions, the protagonist is sometimes asked to repeat and accept or reject the double's statements.

The doubling procedure can serve several important functions. It helps make role plays more dramatic and in-depth experiences. It facilitates understanding and self-awareness of the protagonist's behavior. In addition to fostering insight, it gives permission for the protagonist to acknowledge repressed or taboo thoughts and feelings. It also increases the emotional sensitivity and self-expression of the protagonist. The procedure is often used in conjunction with own role, chairing, and sculpting procedures.

MIRROR.   In the mirror procedure, a group member re-enacts a role-played performance for the protagonist. Other members can verify the accuracy of the replay. The procedure may also be used in an exaggerated, amplified, and stereotypical manner to emphasize particular aspects of the protagonist's behavior.

The procedure is useful as a confrontational technique to help the protagonist gain awareness of his or her behavior. It is an excellent substitute for videotape feedback when videotape equipment is unavailable. The procedure is particularly useful in conjunction with modeling, coaching, and prompting to provide feedback to a member attempting to learn a new behavior. It is also a way of involving other group members in a member's situation, facilitating their empathy and their skills in self-expression.

SHARING.   The sharing procedure is often used at the close of role play action. Group members give the protagonist and the other actors feedback about their performances. They may also share similar experiences and self-disclose their own reactions and feelings regarding the role play. The procedure is designed to provide supportive feedback to the member who risked himself or herself in revealing a difficult situation by acting as the protagonist in the role play. It also facilitates the learning of self-disclosure skills.

Environmental Interventions

A third way for workers to intervene is by helping members to modify or change the psychosocial and physical situations in which they live. Environmental modification is an important but often neglected aspect of social work practice (Grinnell, 1973). Environmental interventions consist of (a) connecting members to concrete resources, (b) expanding members' social networks, (c) modifying the contingencies that result when members perform desired behaviors, and (d) planning physical environments to facilitate members' goal achievement. The roles of enabler, broker, and advocate—discussed previously—are particularly useful when making environmental interventions.

Connecting Members to Concrete Resources

To connect clients to concrete resources, the worker first identifies the member's need and then assesses the member's ability and motivation to follow through and obtain the resource. For highly motivated, well-functioning group members, the worker may be able to act as a broker, identifying a contact person at the appropriate resource and giving the member general information about what to expect when contacting the resource. The worker verifies that the member has obtained the needed resource at the next group session.

In some treatment groups—such as those composed of severely impaired psychiatric patients or older people with organic brain disorders—workers may have to take additional steps to ensure that members obtain the resources they need. For example, it may take some time to prepare members for a referral because of their lack of motivation or their failure to recognize their need for services. It may also be necessary to contact family members or guardians to help prepare them for a referral. In addition, medical impairments may limit or prevent members from contacting resources without assistance. Transportation may have to be arranged and the worker, an aide, or a volunteer may have to accompany the member to the resource. It may also be necessary to teach members the skills necessary to obtain a needed resource. For example, an unemployed group member might need to learn interviewing and resume-writing skills before renewing her search for a job.

Expanding Members' Social Networks

Another type of environmental intervention consists of helping socially isolated members expand their social networks by gaining needed support from others (see, for example, Collins & Pancoast, 1970; Toseland, Decker, & Bliesner, 1979). The first step in expanding a member's social network is to analyze the member's current social relationships. Figure 9-2 illustrates the social network of Tom, a socially isolated member of a support group for people who have recently been separated. The diagram indicates that Tom has only two active social relationships. Tom's other network relationships are inactive. He no longer plays with the softball team. He no longer sees Jean or Bob, with whom he used to be friendly. His brother lives nearly 1,000 miles away, and they rarely see one another.

FIGURE 9–2
**A social network
chart**

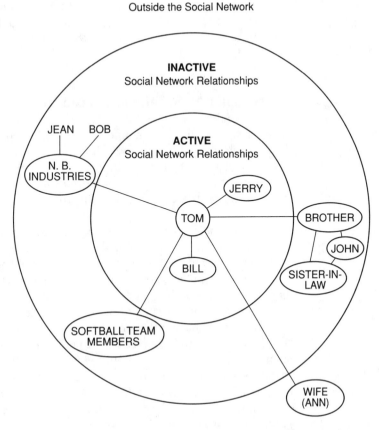

Diagramming a member's social network on a flip chart or blackboard can stimulate group discussion about ways to expand it. For example, after examining the chart in Figure 9–2, several group members suggested that Tom renew former network relationships that lapsed after he got married three years ago. To do this, Tom rejoined the softball team and renewed his friendships with Jean and Bob. Tom also was encouraged to join Parents Without Partners, a self-help group that sponsors many social, recreational, and educational events in his community.

Analyzing one group member's social network can stimulate other members to consider their own networks. In the group described previously, several other members became aware that they could also benefit from expanding their own social relationships. After confirming that group members wanted to become more involved with one another, the worker suggested that members exchange telephone numbers and choose one person to call during the week. By scheduling one meeting at a member's home and supporting members' suggestions that they get together informally after the meeting, the worker encouraged them to form a supportive social network for one another.

As the members began to meet regularly, it became apparent that child-care responsibilities limited many of the members' abilities to socialize, so members with children decided to help each other with child-care, thereby freeing each other to engage in social activities. Thus, through a worker's intervention efforts and the mutual aid properties of the group, members' social networks were expanded.

Contingency Management Procedures

So that members can maintain their successes between group sessions, it is often necessary to modify or change the rewards and punishments they receive for behaving in ways that are not consistent with their treatment goals. This procedure is sometimes called contingency management, because the rewards or punishments that are contingent on the performance of a behavior are modified to increase or decrease the probability that a behavior will be performed in the future.

Contingencies that increase the probability that a member will perform a behavior are called *reinforcers*. Typical positive reinforcers include social rewards that are verbal, such as praise, and nonverbal, such as a smile, a pat on the back, and similar signs of approval. They also include tangible rewards such as money and food.

Negative reinforcers also increase behaviors. But unlike positive reinforcers that increase behavior through rewards, negative reinforcers increase behavior through aversive means. Negative reinforcers include yelling, nagging, and "the silent treatment." Workers should emphasize the use of positive reinforcers that members enjoy receiving rather than negative reinforcers that are unpleasant and often result in deleterious side effects such as anger.

Unless a behavior is self-reinforcing, it will decrease if rewards are not received for performing it. Therefore, ignoring a behavior will tend to extinguish it if the behavior is not self-reinforcing to the member. Social disapproval, confiscation of tangible rewards, and physical punishment will also decrease behaviors.

In general, workers should encourage the use of positive reinforcers and extinction procedures rather than negative reinforcers or punishment procedures. Often, it is sufficient to reward a desired behavior and ignore an undesirable behavior. Although positive reinforcers are preferred whenever possible, in some circumstances punishments may be imposed for failure to comply with group rules. For example, the members of a children's group decided that those who came late to group meetings would clean up after snacks were served.

Rose (1989) points out that the undesirable side effects of punishment procedures are avoided when members impose their own punishments, sometimes referred to as "response costs." Thus, punishment procedures should not be imposed unilaterally by the worker. The group as a whole should decide on a policy—that is, the type of punishment (social disapproval or removal from the group), and the circumstances in which sanctions will be applied. The resulting policy should be applied uniformly.

The worker should help the group develop a realistic policy that is not too severe. Sometimes members develop unrealistically harsh rules to govern behavior in the group. William Golding's novel *Lord of the Flies* is an excellent literary example of how groups can decide on punishments that are too severe. It is common, for example, for members of children's groups to develop group rules which, left unchallenged, would lead to severe punishment. For example, in one group, members decided that anyone caught laughing should be thrown out of the group. In such cases, the worker should intervene and help the group develop less severe sanctions for misbehavior.

When using contingency management procedures, the worker should begin by helping members identify the rewards and punishments they receive for performing desired and undesired behaviors. These contingencies are identified by monitoring the consequences resulting from the performance of a particular behavior. If contingencies do not act to increase desired behavior and decrease undesired behavior, the worker can help the member modify them. Sometimes members may be able to administer their own rewards and punishments. For example, members may be encouraged to praise themselves for performing a certain behavior—to take themselves out for a good meal or buy a new piece of clothing. Such self-reinforcement procedures have been shown to be effective in helping members control their own behaviors and feel better about themselves (Beck, 1990; Stuart, 1977; Thoresen & Mahoney, 1974; Yost et al., 1985).

It can also be helpful to involve other group members or significant others in members' lives in modifying the contingent rewards and punishments members receive for performing desired and undesired behaviors. Family members and friends can help provide an environment that promotes therapeutic goals. For example, a wife or husband may compliment his or her spouse for positive changes. A mother or father may praise their daughter for helping her little brother with his homework.

To formalize an agreement about what behaviors to reinforce, a verbal or written contingency contract can be developed. Such a contract specifies (a) what specific behaviors will be performed, (b) who will perform the behavior, (c) how the behaviors will be reinforced, and (d) who will administer the reinforcement. For example, the father of an adolescent group member may agree to take his son on a fishing trip if his son agrees to attend classes without misbehaving for two weeks. Although developing a written contingency contract may strike some individuals as too rigid or formal, it should be recognized that written agreements have the advantage of avoiding confusion later when individuals may have different recollections of the nature of an agreement.

There are many different types of contingency contracts. As mentioned, members may administer their own rewards and punishments in self-administered contingency contracts. Contracts may be made between the group member and significant others, between two group members, or between all group members and the worker. Contracts may also be reciprocal, that is, parties to the contract reward each other for performing desired behaviors. Reciprocal contracts are particularly useful in couples groups where spouses can reinforce each other for performing desired behaviors.

By using contingency management procedures, the worker helps members perform desired behaviors by changing the environmental consequences that result when a behavior is performed. Too often, workers intervene effectively in the group to help members reach desired goals but fail to pay any attention to what will happen when members try to perform desired behaviors outside the group. Contingency management procedures are a useful way to extend therapeutic interventions beyond the boundaries of group sessions. Yost et al. (1985), for example, describe how contingency management procedures can be used to help group members who are depressed.

Some individuals react negatively to contingency contracts because they perceive them as manipulative, artificial, or as relying exclusively on extrinsic rather than intrinsic motivation. It is important to remember that contingency contracts are *voluntary* and *explicit* agreements between two or more parties. Coercive, exploitative, and underhanded attempts to control behavior have no place in the design or the execution of contingency contracts. While it is true that contingency contracts specify artificial arrangements of rewards and punishments, they should be prepared while considering what naturally occurring consequences will sustain the behavior over the long-term. For example, although father will not be able to take son on a fishing trip each time he behaves well for a two-week period in school, it is anticipated that by behaving well, son will stop receiving negative feedback from teachers, administrators, and peers and will start enjoying school. Therefore, the artificial arrangement of contingencies will be replaced with naturally occurring contingencies, such as praise from the teacher and good report cards. The extrinsic rewards for behaving well will be replaced, over the long-term, by intrinsic rewards such as feeling competent, well liked or self-confident.

Planning Physical Environments

Helping members modify their physical environments is another type of environmental intervention. Although it is often given little consideration, the physical environment has a profound effect on the problems and concerns members experience. Environmental stimuli can make it easier or more difficult for a member to accomplish treatment goals. For example, members of a weight-loss group find that it is more difficult to lose weight if their refrigerators are stocked with fattening foods than if their refrigerators contain only those items that are a part of the diet that members agreed upon. Similarly, it is difficult for a member of an inpatient psychotherapy group who is about to be discharged to learn independent living skills in an institutional environment that does not allow him or her to cook, clean, or shop.

To the extent possible, workers should help members modify physical environments so they promote goal achievement. In general, physical environments should give members the opportunity to practice the skills they are learning in the group. For example, members who are learning skills for independent living should have the opportunity to practice as many of these skills as feasible in the institutional setting in which they live. Physical environments should reduce barriers that are likely to impede a member's attempts to accomplish a goal. For example, a member who is attempting to stop drinking should remove all alcohol from her home.

Environmental interventions should be proactive as well as reactive. That is, in addition to ensuring that an environment does not provide unwanted stimuli, the worker should help members modify environments so that they encourage goal-directed behavior. A member who is attempting to lose weight may, for example, place a calorie chart on his refrigerator door to help him plan meals. A member of a parenting group may place a monitoring chart in her child's room. Each time the child behaves correctly, gold stars are placed on the chart. When a certain number of stars accumulate, they can be redeemed for a trip to the zoo or extra play time with Mom or Dad. In both cases, modifications of the environment stimulate efforts toward goal achievement.

In inpatient settings, environmental modifications can include a restructuring of the entire milieu. Wright, Thase, Beck, and Ludgate (1993), for example, describe how cognitive therapy with inpatients can be enhanced by developing a cognitive milieu that permeates the entire residential unit.

INTERVENING IN THE GROUP AS A WHOLE

Workers select the group as a whole as the focus of interventions when they decide that the group process should be altered to help members achieve their goals. In this way, the group becomes the means as well as the context of treatment. As discussed in Chapter 3, four areas are critical to the effective functioning of any group, including (a) communication and interaction patterns, (b) attraction, (c) social controls, and (d) culture. These are the primary areas in which the worker intervenes when selecting the group as a whole as the focus of interventions.

Group dynamics have developed before the middle stage of a treatment group's development. The worker's task in the middle stages is to maintain and enhance dynamics that are contributing to the group's success and intervene to change those dynamics that are interfering with the group's development.

Experienced workers realize the power that group dynamics have in leading to successful group outcomes. In comparing 10 different methods of leading encounter groups, Lieberman, Yalom, and Miles (1973) found that "group characteristics" such as norms, cohesiveness, and climate had an important effect both on members' satisfaction with their experience in different groups and on the overall outcomes achieved by the groups. In a study comparing methods of working with antisocial boys in groups, Feldman, Caplinger, and Wodarski (1983) also found that group dynamics had a powerful mediating effect on outcome, regardless of the type of treatment modality used.

With these notable exceptions, studies about how specific group dynamics influence the outcome of treatment groups are rare. Evaluation of the effects of group processes on treatment outcomes is difficult to conduct because one must sort out the separate effects of such factors as norms and cohesiveness from the effects of leadership and specific intervention procedures. A review of process studies in group treatment suggests that most are methodologically flawed (Bednar & Kaul, 1978). Therefore, recommendations about what dynamics workers should try to increase or decrease in particular situations should be viewed cautiously. They are based largely on clinical, impressionistic data and data from secondary analyses of studies designed for other purposes.

Changing Communication and Interaction Patterns

The worker may intervene to change the frequency, duration, distribution, or content of the communication and interaction patterns occurring in a treatment group. The frequency of interactions a member initiates in a group is important because it is difficult, if not impossible, to assess and treat a member who remains relatively silent throughout the group. Members must actively participate if they are to benefit from group treatment.

Usually, two relatively simple methods can be used to increase a member's participation. One is to point out that a member is communicating infrequently. Although members usually respond well to such feedback, sometimes it is helpful for the worker or the member to use one of the instruments discussed in Chapter 7 to obtain objective feedback about the frequency of a member's participation. Shulman (1992) points out that what silent members really fear is being confronted with their silence. Therefore, in some cases, it may be more helpful to prompt such members to speak with statements like, "What do you think about what _____ is saying?" or "You have some experience with this _____, what do you think?" rather than to confront them with data that suggest they are not participating frequently enough.

Another way to increase participation is to praise members when they add to the group's discussion. Positive comments such as, "That was really helpful" or "I see that you understand what _____ is saying" can be used to show quiet group members that their contributions are valued. Positive reinforcement procedures have been demonstrated to be effective in several studies that have examined methods to increase members' participation in groups (Rose, 1989). Other techniques to increase the frequency of communication include asking members to lead the group discussion on a certain topic or going around the group and eliciting members' thoughts and comments on a particular topic.

Workers also may wish to change the duration of a member's communications in the group. This is particularly true with verbose members who dominate the group's discussions. Sometimes simply pointing out that other members of the group need time to participate is sufficient to limit the member's communications. For others, it is necessary to develop a contingency contract in which members agree to ignore the talkative member when he or she talks for more than a specified length of time. Alternatives to this procedure include interrupting the member after he or she talks for a certain amount of time or reminding the member with a nonverbal cue that he or she is talking too much.

Workers may also want to change the distribution of communication and interaction patterns. Ideally, each member of the group should have an opportunity to participate. Although some group members may be more involved in a particular discussion than other members, communications should be distributed fairly evenly among all members over the course of several meetings. Workers should prevent situations in which they are doing most of the communicating or situations in which members direct most of their comments to the worker rather than to each other. Workers may also want to intervene when members of subgroups interact primarily with one another rather than with everyone.

As in efforts to change the frequency and duration of members' communication patterns, the most successful interventions for changing the distribution of communication patterns include cues to help members remain aware of their inappropriate communications, accompanied by prompts and positive reinforcement to help them change these patterns. For example, Toseland, Krebs, and Vahsen (1978) reported that an intervention consisting of cues, verbal prompts, and reinforcement was successful in reducing the number of member-to-leader communications and increasing the number of member-to-member communications.

The content of the messages sent and received in the group is just as important as the frequency, duration, and distribution of group members' communications. Workers should be particularly concerned about the task orientation and the tone of the messages communicated in the group. Workers should intervene when most communications are not task-relevant or when they are excessively negative.

Of course, some group discussion will not be task-relevant. Joking, small talk, and interesting but irrelevant stories often make the group more attractive. Members have a need to express their own identity in the group. However, task-irrelevant discussions should not be allowed to take a great deal of the group's time. Members come to treatment groups for particular purposes and too much irrelevant conversation interferes with their ability to achieve goals, ultimately leading to their dissatisfaction with the group.

Usually, it is sufficient to point out excessive digressions to the group, call the group's attention back to the session agenda and the goals that should have been briefly mentioned at the beginning of the meeting. In some cases, however, such an intervention may not be sufficient to help the group return to a task-centered discussion. The group's digression may signify a test or a challenge to the worker's authority, dissatisfaction with the content outlined in the session agenda, or an indication that group members are too fearful or anxious to discuss a particular topic. In such cases, it is helpful for the worker to point out his or her hypothesis about the reasons for the group's digression. Through discussion and feedback, the worker can help members to decide on how best to renew their focus on the group's goals. This may make members aware that they are avoiding a difficult issue that they need to discuss. In other cases, it may lead to changes in the worker's style or the session agenda.

Workers should also be concerned about the tone of the messages conveyed in the group. Frequent put downs; excessive negative comments without suggestions for improvement; and infrequent supportive, warm, or reinforcing comments make the group unattractive for its members. To change the tone of messages being communicated in the group, workers can act as models, making supportive comments whenever possible. Workers can also show their disapproval of negative comments by ignoring them or by suggesting that the member who makes the negative comment accompany it with a positive comment. Exercises designed to help members give positive feedback can also be helpful. For example, a worker might say, "I've noticed we make a lot of comments about what a person does wrong during our role plays. How about for the next role play, each member identify at least one thing that the person does well."

Changing the Group's Attraction for Its Members

There is a consensus in the group work literature that workers should help their groups become cohesive and attractive units. In his classic text on group psychotherapy, Yalom (1985) points out the benefits that cohesive groups have on members' self-esteem, their willingness to listen to and be influenced by others, and their continued attendance and participation in group meetings.

Group cohesion is built in a warm, caring, and empathic group environment. The worker can foster the development of this type of environment by actively listening to members, validating their experiences, and affirming their attempts to cope with the situations confronting them. By modeling genuine concern and interest in each member's experiences, the leader encourages members to tune in to each other's needs, and to reach out in supportive, mutual helping interactions.

Lieberman (1971) and Rose (1989) both suggest that cohesion and interpersonal attraction can be stimulated by acknowledging members' efforts to support each other, and by praising members for their active and constructive participation in the group. Thus, in addition to modeling concern and interest, the leader should take an active stance in guiding the group to increased cohesion and intimacy. Appropriate self-disclosures and revelations that deepen the group experience, making it more meaningful and more profound, should be encouraged. Similarly, gentle and caring confrontations that encourage members to get in touch with their strengths, or realize overlooked possibilities and alternative perspectives, should be invited.

Physical arrangements can also make a difference in building group cohesion. Groups tend to be more cohesive and attractive when they are relatively small and there is plenty of interaction that is distributed fairly evenly throughout the group. In small groups where there is a good deal of interaction, members have the feeling that their ideas are being heard and considered, whereas in large groups and groups with poorly distributed communication patterns, members who are not a part of the "inner circle" of decision makers often feel that their ideas and suggestions are not being given sufficient attention. Suggestions made in the previous section for redistributing communication patterns can be used to help make a group more attractive. For large groups, procedures such as Phillips 66 (described in Chapter 11) can also be useful in maintaining the group's attractiveness for its members.

Simple creature comforts can also make a difference in the attractiveness of the group. Refreshments such as coffee and doughnuts can be offered, and socializing over coffee during a break in a long session or immediately after a short session helps reduce the exclusive problem focus of groups and allows members to get to know each other as "ordinary people" rather than as "clients." In addition, for some group members, refreshments and snacks can be strong incentives for participating in a group. This is particularly true for children and psychiatric inpatients, because their access to snacks is often limited.

Other ways to increase the attractiveness of groups include dispensing rewards such as a weekend pass as an incentive for participation in a group, planning interesting program activities and outings for the agenda of future group meetings, encouraging members to select topics for group discussion, and ensuring that members continue to make progress toward their treatment goals.

As the group becomes more cohesive, some members may fear becoming overly dependent on the group. The leader should encourage members to talk about these feelings and ease their concerns by indicating that they are commonly experienced in groups when cohesion and intimacy increases. Acknowledging the support and security that the group provides, while at the same time acknowledging members' efforts to maintain their autonomy and their ability to function independently can also help allay members' fears.

Fears about becoming overly dependent sometimes have their roots in problems with members' ability to develop intimate relationships. Intimacy implies vulnerability. When members disclose personal, emotionally charged issues that they may not have been able to talk about with others, they are exposing their vulnerability to the group. Members may have had previous unsatisfactory experiences in revealing emotionally charged issues with those whom they felt intimate. Thus, it is natural for members to feel ambivalent about sharing personal issues with the group. It is helpful for the leader to point this out so that all members of the group will be more likely to respond in a sensitive and caring way to fledgling attempts to self-disclose personal issues. Leaders should also make it clear that they will protect members by blocking critical, insensitive comments and by encouraging supportive and caring interactions.

There are times when a worker does not want to increase a group's cohesion. For example, cohesion should not be increased in groups in which anti-therapeutic norms have been established. Research by Feldman, Caplinger, and Wodarski (1983), for example, has found that in groups composed solely of antisocial boys, interpersonal integration, defined as the reciprocal liking of the boys in a group for one another, was negatively associated with treatment outcomes. In these groups, cohesion apparently resulted in peer pressure to conform to anti-therapeutic group norms. Thus, antisocial behaviors were reinforced rather than extinguished by group treatment. Similarly, in work with street gangs, the more cohesive a gang is, the more difficult it is for the worker to influence the group.

Using Social Controls Effectively

The social controls exerted in a group can enhance the functioning of the group as a whole or they can lead to the demise of the group. Social controls exerted through norms, roles, status hierarchies, and the various power bases from which the leader draws authority are important forces within the group. As mentioned in Chapter 3, without social controls, group interaction would become chaotic and unpredictable, and the group would soon cease functioning. But in groups in which social controls are too strong, members soon feel restricted and coerced. They tend to rebel against the control or refuse to attend future meetings.

During the middle stage of treatment groups, the effective worker helps the group develop social controls to integrate members' activities for goal achievement. Both normative integration (members' acceptance of group norms) and functional integration (members' assuming roles and activities that contribute to the group's work) are positively associated with beneficial group outcomes (see, for example, Feldman, Caplinger, & Wodarski, 1983).

Workers should help members become normatively and functionally integrated into a group. They should prevent the domination of a group by one or more members who have a great deal of social power. It has been found that group members who are socially powerful (able to exert a great deal of influence over the group) are likely to resist change efforts (Feldman, Caplinger, & Wodarski, 1983).

Effective workers are potent leaders who command the respect and admiration of group members. Their interventions have considerable influence over how a group conducts its business. Strong, effective workers exert social control over the group without dominating it and without the need to apply social sanctions to control deviant members.

Potent leaders share many of the same characteristics: They are self-confident, but able to admit mistakes. They have the knowledge and the practical experience to help members with their problems and concerns. They are emphatic, yet able to remain calm and collected in difficult situations. They tend to ignore rather than sanction deviant behavior exhibited by group members, preferring to praise and encourage members for positive contributions to the group. In general, potent workers possess characteristics that members would like to develop.

In facilitating the development of social controls that will help the group function effectively, potent workers help members adhere to therapeutic group norms and change norms that are interfering with the group accomplishing its goals. In groups that have developed therapeutic norms, the worker should help members become normatively integrated in the group by helping those who are deviating from group norms to accept and abide by them. For example, in a group that has developed a norm that members are not to be verbally abusive with one another, a member who becomes verbally abusive may be asked to leave the group until he or she can regain control.

In other cases, the worker may encourage and protect members who are deviating from anti-therapeutic group norms. For example, a worker supports and encourages a member of a couples group who begins to describe problems in the couple's sexual relations, a topic that has not been previously discussed by group members. In another group, the worker encourages a member to talk about the scapegoating of a member who is intensely disliked by other group members.

Workers should also help members become functionally integrated in the group. As mentioned in Chapter 7, some members take on deviant group roles such as the "group jester" or the "isolate." It is the worker's responsibility to either help the member assume a more functional role or, in some cases, help the group modify its processes to find a useful role for the member. For example, the jester might be encouraged to take on a more functional role, such as helping members express feelings and concerns about a particular problem.

Changing Group Culture

Another aspect of group dynamics that workers should consider during the middle stage of treatment groups is the culture that has developed in the group. Does the culture help the group achieve its goals? If not, one way to change the group's culture is to challenge commonly accepted beliefs and ideas held by members. For example, in a group for abusive parents, the worker wanted to change a group culture that discouraged the expression of intense feelings and emotions. First, the worker pointed out that feelings were rarely expressed during group sessions. Next, the worker invited the group to discuss this observation. Several members indicated if they showed their feelings they were afraid they might lose control of their actions. To help members learn that they could express feelings without losing control, the worker suggested a series of role play exercises designed to help the members gradually express more intense emotions. The exercises taught members new ways to express emotions and at the same time helped them realize they could express their emotions without losing control. As the group progressed, members acknowledged that allowing feelings to build up inside until they explode is much less healthful for themselves and their families than learning to express their feelings appropriately as they experience them.

Another way workers can change the existing group culture is to point out its dominant features as well as areas that appear to be taboo or not able to be discussed. When this is done, members often indicate that they had wanted to discuss taboo areas in previous group meetings but feared the group would not be receptive. These members can then be encouraged to express their thoughts and feelings on the taboo subject. In other instances role play exercises can be used to stimulate the group's consideration of an area that was formerly taboo.

A third way to change the culture established in a group is for the worker to develop a contingency contract with members. This procedure was used successfully in working with adolescents in a group home. The contract specified that if a member was supportive and helpful to other members who disclosed personal problems and concerns during three out of five group meetings each week, the member would have access to special rewards such as a trip to a sports event or tickets to a movie. The contract helped change the group culture from one in which members were ridiculed for expressing personal issues to one in which members supported and encouraged personal disclosures.

A similar procedure was used in a children's group. Peer pressure had created an environment in which members were teased for participating in role play and program activities. The worker developed a contingency contract using a point system. Points accumulated for participating in role plays could be used at the end of the group meeting to obtain special refreshments, games, or small toys. The incentive system was effective in encouraging the children to participate in role play exercises designed to teach them problem-solving skills.

CHANGING THE GROUP ENVIRONMENT

Groups do not exist in a vacuum. Usually, group treatment is offered as one component of the clinical services of a social service agency. Hasenfeld (1985) points out the tremendous influence that agencies have on the groups they sponsor. In addition to the material resources provided for group work services, the types of clients treated by an agency and the service technologies and ideologies endorsed by the agency all have a bearing on the services the group worker offers.

Group services are also influenced by interagency linkages and by the community's response to the problems and concerns of those who seek group treatment. Despite the effect of agency, interagency, and community environments on group work services, relatively little has been written about this subject. Those writers who have pointed out the influence of the environment in which groups function have made few suggestions about how workers might intervene to improve support for group work services (see, for example, Hasenfeld, 1985; Hirschowitz, 1974; Peterson, 1974; Shulman, 1992). In this section, suggestions are made about ways to (a) increase social service agency support for group work services, (b) develop links to interagency networks, and (c) increase community awareness of social problems that could be treated through group work services.

Increasing Agency Support for Group Work Services

Before intervening to increase support for group work services, workers must first have a thorough understanding of their agencies. Like people, agencies have unique histories that influence their continued growth and development. It is often helpful to trace the development of clinical services within an agency, learning about the changes and innovations that have taken place over time. This can help the worker understand the rationale for current clinical services, the agency's responsiveness to proposals for change, and the ways in which previous proposals for change were incorporated into the agency's structure.

A historical perspective helps the worker avoid making a proposal for increased support for group work services based on a rationale that has been rejected in the past. It also helps to give the worker an understanding of the long-term development of the agency, an understanding that is likely to be shared by administrators whose support for innovations in clinical programming is essential.

Before proposing an increase in support for group work services, the worker also should have a sound grasp of the current needs and future development plans of the agency. A proposal for group work services should be structured in such a way that it clearly shows how new or increased services will meet the current needs and future developments anticipated by the agency's administrators and board members. The proposal should emphasize the distinct advantages of group work services. For example, it may be possible to show that treatment groups are a cost-effective alternative to individual treatment services (see, for example, the cost-benefit analysis example in Chapter 12). Because most agencies want to get the most out of their resources by serving as many clients as possible for as little cost as possible, group treatment services may be an attractive alternative to individual treatment services.

A well-developed proposal alone is not enough to guarantee that an agency will increase its support for group work services. Workers also should know how to proceed within their agencies to get proposed changes accepted. Patti (1974) suggests that workers be aware of several organizational factors that help to predict the degree of resistance that can be expected to a change proposal. These include (a) the extent of the proposed change, (b) the value orientation and decision-making style of the administrator responsible for deciding whether to accept the proposal, (c) the administrative distance between the practitioner and the decision maker, and (d) the agency's investment in the status quo.

The worker can, for example, expect greater resistance to a proposal for a basic change in the agency's services, such as a change from individual treatment to group treatment in all clinical programs, than to a modest proposal for group services to a specific client group.

The rationale for a proposal is also important in terms of the resistance it will encounter. An administrator who is concerned about saving money will probably be less inclined to accept a proposal that requires new funding than a proposal that is expected to reduce costs. Whenever possible, workers should try to present multiple rationales for group work services, including at least one that is likely to gain the support of the decision maker. For example, the worker might help overcome resistance to the group service by citing relevant research about the type of group being proposed or by suggesting how desired individual and group outcomes might be achieved.

The more levels of approval—that is, the further a proposal must go from the originator to final administrative approval—the greater the likelihood of resistance. If a group worker's proposal requires approval from administrators who are at a much higher level in the bureaucratic structure, he or she will have to elicit the support of supervisors who can argue for the proposal when it reaches higher levels of review. Even with support from supervisors, proposals are more likely to be altered the higher up they go in the bureaucracy.

Resistance may also be encountered if the worker is proposing changes that reverse or negate program components or services that have received a great deal of support in the past. Agencies are not likely to abandon funded commitments in favor of a new proposal unless it can be proved to be quite exceptional.

Once the worker has anticipated the resistance a proposal may encounter, he or she is ready to develop support to overcome this resistance. Brager and Holloway (1978) suggest involving resistant co-workers in the proposal's development. Because they have had a hand in shaping the proposal, initially reluctant co-workers can usually be counted on for support in later negotiations. It is especially important to allow administrators who will be deciding whether to accept the proposal and those who will be responsible for carrying out the proposal to have input into its development. During its development, a proposal may be revised several times to gain the support of those who have reservations about the proposed changes. By the time it is ready for final consideration, the proposal should have gone through several levels of review, in which important participants have become sensitized to its benefits and their own questions or concerns have been addressed. See Chapter 5 for more information about developing a written proposal for a group.

Links with Interagency Networks

Interventions in a group's environment also include establishing links between agencies. Interagency links can be established by identifying and contacting workers in other agencies who work with similar populations or deal with similar social service problems. After informal telephone discussions are initiated, a planning meeting should be scheduled. Because workers are often extremely busy, meetings do not have to occur frequently (monthly or quarterly is usually sufficient). However, they should be scheduled regularly so that time can be set aside before workers' schedules become filled with other appointments.

Interagency links can have several benefits. When other agencies are aware of particular types of group services offered by an agency, they may refer clients for treatment. For example, if a worker at a community agency is aware that a battered women's shelter offers support groups for women, the worker can refer women, who would otherwise not receive services, to this agency.

Agency networks help identify needs for particular services. In a meeting of workers from several agencies, for example, it became apparent to a group worker from a family service agency that no services existed for treating men who battered their wives. After carefully documenting the need in other agencies, a group work service was established for this population by the family service agency.

Interagency networks also help avoid duplication of services. Competition between agencies can be avoided by preventing the development of duplicate services existing elsewhere in the community and by facilitating the development of services when gaps in service delivery exist. Workers who cultivate interagency links can share the knowledge and practice experience they have gained from working with specific client groups and learn from the experiences of group workers in other agencies. In this way, knowledge can be pooled and mistakes made by one worker can be avoided by others.

Interagency networks are also useful in lobbying for new group work services. For example, in a meeting of workers from a number of community agencies, it became apparent that additional services were needed to prevent criminal activity among unemployed youths. Although none of the workers was able to do anything about this problem alone, together they put enough pressure on the city's youth services program to obtain funding for a half-time group worker for the local community center.

Increasing Community Awareness

Ultimately, group work services depend on the support of local community residents. Their awareness of the social problems that exist in their communities and their belief that group work services can help maintain adequate social functioning and alleviate social problems are essential. Group workers have a responsibility to bring community problems to the attention of local officials and civic organizations and to make them aware of how group work services can help to alleviate their problems.

A variety of methods can be used to raise a community's awareness of social problems and increase its commitment to group work services. Needs assessments (see Chapter 12) are especially effective for documenting the need for additional services. Agency statistics about the number of clients not served because of a lack of resources or a lack of available services can also be useful. To call attention to community problems, workers can testify at legislative hearings. They can become members of local planning bodies or they can help to elect local officials who are supportive of the community's social service needs. Only through such efforts will group work services remain available to those who need them.

A group worker's skills can also be used to organize clients so that they can lobby for needed services on their own behalf. For example, an outpatient group in community mental health center in a poor urban area was composed entirely of women who were receiving AFDC benefits. It became apparent that many of these women's problems were tied to the subsistence level benefits they received, as well as to the environmental conditions in which they lived. The worker informed these women of a national welfare rights coalition and helped them form a local rights group. Although this effort did not make a tremendous or immediate change in their life circumstances, it did give the women a constructive way to voice their complaints and lobby for changes in their community. It helped them to overcome what Seligman (1975) has called "learned helplessness."

SUMMARY

This chapter focuses on some of the specialized intervention methods that can be used during the working stage of treatment groups. These methods are commonly used to intervene at the level of (a) the group member, (b) the group as a whole, and (c) the environment in which the group functions. Because of the extent to which the group treatment literature has focused on individual change in small groups, much of the chapter is devoted to interventions at the level of the individual member. These interventions are subdivided into those that deal with (a) intrapersonal, (b) interpersonal, and (c) environmental concerns.

Interventions in the group as a whole are divided into those that focus on each of the four major areas of group dynamics described in Chapter 3. These include changing the group's (a) communication and interaction patterns, (b) attraction for its members, (c) social control mechanisms, and (d) culture.

The chapter concludes with an examination of interventions to change the environment in which a group functions. This is an important, but often neglected, area of group work practice. Discussion of interventions in this portion of the chapter includes ways to (a) increase agency support for group work services, (b) develop links to interagency networks, and (c) increase community awareness of social service problems that can be alleviated by group treatment.

LEARNING ASSIGNMENTS

1. Form a small group and choose a leader. Have each member identify one situation that makes them anxious. Have the leader help each member construct a hierarchy of situations relating to his or her source of anxiety. Using the progressive muscle relaxation technique mentioned in this chapter, have the members achieve a relaxed state. Then have them visualize each item in the

hierarchies they have created. Encourage members to go at their own pace, and to return to a less anxiety-provoking item as soon as they become anxious.

2. Design and make your own audiotape or videotape to help you and other group members achieve positive cognitive imagery and a relaxed state. Choose relaxing music, sounds, or scenes from nature that you think would help someone relax. Play your tape for members of the group. What images did your composition evoke?

3. How would you design a session for the middle phase of a social skills group for children? What interventions or program activities would you use to increase the quantity and quality of social interactions among the members?

4. Form a small group of members who are willing to experiment with role playing. Have each member spend a few moments independently writing a short case scenario which illustrates a client problem. Choose some of the scenarios, assign roles to members of the group, and role play the situations. Have members discuss how they felt about playing the roles.

5. Assume you are leading a support group for women who have recently been widowed. Describe three ways you would help the members develop new social relationships. Refer to Figure 9–2, and diagram an example of a social network for one of the members. How could you help this member expand her social network? How could you encourage the group to assist in this process?

6. For a group of your choice, design three activities/interventions to increase group cohesion.

7. You are leading a structured educational group with a lot of content to be covered. During the sessions, you note that there is a great deal of leader-to-member interaction, but little member-to-member interaction. How could you increase member-to-member interaction in the group?

8. Describe three strategies for working with a too-talkative male member in a mixed group for recently separated people.

9. Assume you have been running an open group in an agency of your choice. The group has had some difficulties getting referrals, and you are concerned that you will not have enough members to run a viable group. What interventions could you carry out to increase agency support for the group? What interventions could you carry out to increase support for the group in other organizations or in the community?

CHAPTER 10

Task Groups:
Foundation Methods

This chapter focuses on the foundation skills, procedures, and methods used in task groups during their working stage. After a brief discussion of the importance of task groups in social service and health agencies, the first section of the chapter describes nine activities that workers commonly engage in during the working stage of task group development.

The second section of this chapter describes a six-step model for effective problem solving in groups. The model includes a discussion of the practice skills workers use during each step of the process. Chapter 11 describes specialized procedures that workers can use to help task groups achieve particular goals and objectives.

The Ubiquitous Task Group

It has been said that Americans are involved in committees and other task groups more than any other people (Tropman, Johnson, & Tropman, 1979). Participation in the decisions that affect our lives is characteristic of our democratic society. Every day millions of meetings take place throughout the United States. Social service agencies could not function without committees, treatment conferences, teams, boards, and other work groups.

Social workers and other helping professionals are often called upon to chair committees, teams, and other task groups. For example, social workers are frequently designated team leaders in interdisciplinary health-care settings, because social work functions include coordination, case management, and concern for the bio-psycho-social-cultural functioning of the whole person (Kane, 1975a, 1975b, 1976; Siporin, 1980a; Wise, 1974). Workers also are asked to "staff" task groups (Tropman, Johnson, & Tropman, 1979). In general, the staff person plays a supportive role, helping the group clarify its goals and carry out its work. Acting under the direction of the task group's leader, the staff person reports directly to the group. The duties and roles of a staff person are quite varied and can include serving as a resource person, consultant, enabler, analyst, implementer, tactician, catalyst, and technical adviser (Tropman, Johnson, & Tropman, 1979).

Despite the importance and widespread use of task groups in social service agencies, relatively little has been written about how to lead or staff them. Brill (1976) and Trecker (1946) point out that teams and other task groups have great potential for helping clients receive effective services. Yet, with a few notable exceptions (see, for example, Bradford, 1976; Brill, 1976; Ephross & Vassil, 1988; Toseland & Ephross, 1987), the human services have paid little attention to how task groups work.

Although task groups can be useful, they can be a source of frustration for their participants when they function ineffectively. For example, Napier and Gershenfeld (1981) describe the "incredible meeting trap" in which little is accomplished and members leave feeling frustrated by the group process. In one of the few articles published in a social work journal about leading task groups, Edson (1977) suggests unorthodox methods that can be used to guard against the irrational and manipulative strategies used by "narrowminded, pigheaded, sly, opinionated, bigoted manipulators" who often dominate committee meetings (p. 224).

Edson's (1977) comments are rather strongly stated, but they make the important point that many workers are dissatisfied with task group meetings and indifferent to or suspicious about their outcomes. Meetings that are not well-run are boring and unsatisfying. They suffer from a lack of participation and corrective feedback from members, who lose interest.

Although task group meetings are often seen as a chore to be endured by members for the good of the organization, well-run meetings can be a positive experience. They help draw people together, creating effective teamwork in which ideas are shared, feelings are expressed, and support is developed for group members, as well as for the decisions made by the group. There are few experiences in the work place that equal the feelings of cohesion, commitment, and satisfaction that members feel when their ideas have been heard, appreciated, and used in resolving a difficult issue and arriving at a decision.[1] The next sections of this chapter describe methods that can help workers lead task groups effectively.

LEADING TASK GROUPS

Workers perform many similar activities in task and treatment groups during the working stage. Nonetheless, the differing foci of task and treatment groups are evident in the respective activities the worker is expected to perform. Task groups, for example, are more concerned with creating new ideas, developing plans and programs, solving problems that are external to the group, and making decisions about the organizational environment.

To lead task groups effectively during their working stage, it is important to stay focused on what purposes and functions the group is expected to accomplish. In his classic text on leading task groups, Maier (1963) suggests that the

---

[1] See the film *Meeting in Progress*, Round Table Films, 113 N. San Vincente Blvd., Beverly Hills, CA 90211, for a vivid example of task group members who are ready to end a meeting as soon as a decision is reached.

primary purposes of task groups are problem solving and decision making. He goes on to describe methods designed to increase task groups' problem-solving and decision-making abilities.

Although problem solving and decision making are important, several other functions of task groups have been identified in the literature (see, for example, Bradford, 1976; Napier & Gershenfeld, 1981; Scheidel & Crowell, 1979). Sometimes, task groups perform only one function, but usually they attempt to perform several functions simultaneously. Task groups often develop primary and secondary functions. For example, in a community agency serving homebound older people, para-professional outreach workers might meet weekly with their supervisor to discuss common problems in obtaining psychological, social and medical services for their clients. Because they spend so much time out of the office, a secondary function of the group is to help workers identify with the organization for which they work. To accomplish primary and secondary objectives during the working stage of task groups, workers are called upon to help with a variety of activities including the following:

1. Preparing for group meetings.
2. Sharing information, thoughts, and feelings about concerns and issues facing the group.
3. Involving members and helping them feel committed to the group and the agency in which they work.
4. Facilitating fact finding about issues and concerns facing the group.
5. Dealing with conflict.
6. Making effective decisions.
7. Understanding the political ramifications of the group.
8. Monitoring and evaluating the work of the group.
9. Problem solving.

Preparing for Group Meetings

During Meetings.   At the beginning of a meeting, the worker is responsible for several tasks. The worker begins by introducing new members and distributing handouts not included with the material distributed before the meeting. Before working on agenda items, the worker should make a brief opening statement about the purpose of the meeting. In this statement, the worker may want to call members' attention to previous meetings and to the mandate of the group as a way to indicate that the meeting will undertake a necessary and important function. Making members aware of the salience of the agenda items they will consider is important for maintaining members' interest and willingness to work during the meeting.

The worker should seek members' approval of written minutes that were distributed before the meeting and request that members raise any questions, changes or amendments they would like to enter into the minutes. After the minutes are approved, the worker makes announcements and calls upon group members to make designated reports. Reports should be brief and to the point. Members should verbally summarize written reports that have been circulated with the agenda rather than reading them verbatim. Reading lengthy reports can be boring and can result in the loss of interest and attention of other members.

During the middle portion of the meeting, the worker's task is to help the group follow its agenda. Whatever the purpose of a specific meeting, the middle portion is the time when the group accomplishes much of its most difficult work. To avoid getting stuck on one item of business in meetings that have extensive agendas, details of particular items should be worked out before the meeting. If this is not possible, Tropman (1980) points out, the group can agree "in principle" on overall objectives and goals about a particular task and a subcommittee or an individual group member can be charged with working out the details and bringing them back to the group later.

The worker should model the behavior that is expected of all members. A worker who shows respect, interest, integrity, and responsibility will convey these feelings to members. By encouraging equitable participation, the expression of minority group opinions, and an appreciation of all sincere contributions to the group's work, the worker sets a positive example for group members to follow.

Jay (1977) suggests that the worker should act more as a servant of the interests of the group as a whole rather than as a master who imposes his or her will upon the group. According to Jay, the worker's self-indulgence is the "greatest single barrier to the success of a meeting" (p. 263). By demonstrating that he or she has the good of the group as a whole in mind in conducting the group's business, the worker gains the respect of members. Authority, control, and discipline should be used only to reduce threats to the group's effective functioning rather than to impose the worker's wishes on the group. As members perceive that the worker is committed to accomplishing the group's common objective, he or she will gain the cooperation and the admiration of group members.

The worker should ensure that the pace of the meeting leaves enough time to accomplish the items specified in the agenda. Workers should not rush through important decisions because they are pressed for time at the end of a meeting. Members also become frustrated when they are expected to present or discuss ideas but have no time to do so because the group has spent too much time on earlier agenda items. Part of the responsibility of an effective worker in preparing for a meeting is making sure that the number of agenda items is manageable. Items sometimes take longer to discuss than anticipated, so it is a good practice to plan some extra time into an agenda. When too many agenda items are submitted for a meeting, the worker should rank the items for importance. Items that are assigned a low priority should be postponed to a later meeting.

Before adjourning, the worker should summarize the meeting's accomplishments, identity issues and agenda items that need further attention, and mention major topics for the next group meeting. When the group is working on a large task, the worker should also mention where the meeting has placed the group in terms of its overall schedule. At this time, the worker should also summarize as clearly as possible the tasks that members agreed to accomplish before the next meeting. This avoids confusion, clarifies responsibilities and reduces the possibility that members might forget assignments that were agreed to during earlier portions of the group's discussion. For more information about ending meetings, see Chapter 13.

Between Meetings.   Two major tasks to accomplish between meetings are (a) seeing that decisions and tasks decided upon at the previous meetings are carried out, and (b) preparing for the next meeting. The worker can do the first task by reading the minutes of previous meetings. Properly kept minutes include a summary of actions taken, tasks that were assigned, and the time frame for reporting back to the group. It is also helpful for the worker to make brief notes during a meeting or soon after the meeting ends about any decisions made that need to be followed up before the next meeting.

In seeing that the decisions decided upon by the group are carried out between meetings, Tropman (1980) suggests that a worker should ensure that members work on and complete reports and other assignments that are necessary for the next group meeting. This does not mean that the worker takes over these tasks, but rather encourages and facilitates the progress of those assigned to carry out a task. This might include, for example, meeting with subcommittees of the larger group to provide information or guidance as they carry out their functions.

Between meetings, the worker should also develop and maintain close contacts with administrative staff, governing bodies, and the constituencies that may be affected by the group's work. As spokesperson for the group, a worker should keep in mind that he or she represents the group's public image. A worker should express the officially accepted opinions of the committee rather than his or her own personal views. The worker should not enter into private agreements, or commit to decisions or positions that have not been discussed and accepted by the group. In all but emergency situations, the worker should convene the group and consult with it before making decisions. The only exception is when the group, the agency, or a regulatory body has empowered the worker to act independently without first consulting with the group.

The second major task of the worker between meetings is to prepare for the next group meeting. When there is a written agenda for each meeting, the worker or the member designated as the group's secretary should send a memo to each group member soon after a meeting to request agenda items well ahead of the next meeting. This allows enough time for the agenda and background or position papers to be completed and sent to members so they can be read before the next meeting. Meeting agendas should be established to facilitate discussion. One effective framework is the following:

1. Examine and approve (with any corrections) brief, relevant minutes from the last meeting.
2. Make information announcements.
3. Vote to include special agenda items.
4. Work on less controversial, easier items.
5. Work on difficult items.
6. Break.
7. Work on "for discussion only" items.
8. Consider any special agenda items if there is sufficient time.
9. Summarize.
10. Adjourn.

In preparing for the next meeting, the worker should also organize opening remarks and administrative summaries to be presented during the meeting. Special care should be taken in preparing for meetings that do not have a written agenda. In such instances, the worker should be clear about how to direct the meeting, what tasks the group will work on, and what goals are to be achieved.

Part of the worker's responsibility in preparing for a meeting is assessing the group's functioning. Questions such as "What is the group's relationship with its outside environment?", "Has the group been functioning smoothly?", "What norms, roles, and interaction patterns have developed in the group?" can stimulate the worker to consider how to best prepare for the next meeting.

In many task groups, the worker acts as both the leader and staff person. However, if a separate staff person is available to a task group, he or she can prepare background reports and memos that analyze the group's options, develop resources, set up the meeting arrangements, and attend to other group needs.

Sharing Information

Another important activity of the leader during the working stage is to help members share information, thoughts, and feelings with one another. For example, medical social workers from different community hospitals organize into an informal support group. Once each month, the leader and the group meet to share information about their work and new techniques for working with people in medical settings.

Teams, committees, delegate councils, and boards use group meetings as a means for members to share their concerns, their experiences, their perspectives, and their expertise. This is an important activity because, as a result of highly differentiated work roles, there is infrequent contact among workers in many agencies. Job assignments such as individual treatment sessions and home visits limit opportunities for communication among workers.

Social issues and problems often affect several agencies, and task groups can bring workers from different agencies together. A group meeting is a convenient way for them to share unique viewpoints and differing perspectives on issues, problems, or concerns they face in their own agencies. By providing a forum for sharing knowledge and resources, interagency task groups encourage cooperative and coordinated problem solving.

Open communication and unimpeded sharing of information are prerequisites for task groups to accomplish their objectives. Brill (1976) suggests that a group's established communication network is the key to effective work in teams and other task groups. Empirical findings regarding group productivity and group process confirm that how information is communicated and used in a group has an important effect on the quality and the quantity of a group's productivity (Hackman & Morris, 1975; Steiner, 1972).

Task group participants make differential use of the information and resources possessed by various group members, depending on how their expertise relates to the issues and tasks facing the group. During the middle stage of group work, the worker should be helping the group develop open channels of communication that can be used appropriately as members have contributions to make during the meeting.

The first step in aiding effective communication and sharing information is to ensure that all members have a clear understanding of the topic being discussed and the task facing the group. To stimulate all members' participation in the discussion, the topic must be relevant. If members have little interest in the topic and no stake in the outcome, there is little reason for them to participate. In many groups, members become bored, disinterested, and dissatisfied because they do not understand the importance of a particular topic. The leader should help each member see the relevance and importance of issues as they are brought before the group. When it is clear that a discussion topic is relevant to only a few members of a task group, the worker should consider forming a subgroup to meet separately from the larger group. The subgroup can provide a brief report of its deliberations and recommendations at a later meeting of the entire group.

To focus interest, promote task-relevant discussions, and reduce confusion among members, Huber (1980), Steiner (1972), and Zander (1977) suggest developing clear procedural steps that can be followed during the discussion. Maier (1963) refers to discussions that follow clear procedural steps as "developmental discussions." Later in this chapter, a six-step problem-solving model for conducting task group discussions is presented.

Workers also can use their leadership skills during the group meeting by summarizing frequently and helping the group remain focused on the task. Summarizing can be used to check understanding, to review previously discussed subjects, to go back to items that were not fully discussed, to help separate a problem or issue into several parts, and to bring members' attention to a particularly important aspect of the discussion.

Focusing can be accomplished by suggesting that the group discuss one issue at a time, pointing out that the group has digressed from the discussion topic, and making task-relevant statements. Jay (1977) points out that effective workers often have self-imposed rules limiting their communications early in group meetings to allow members the maximum opportunity to participate in the discussion. A few brief summaries and comments that focus the discussion are all that is often needed early in the group's work.

Another method of establishing open communication channels and promoting information sharing among all group members is to ensure equitable participation in the group. Domination by a few members who have high status or who are very expressive leads to less felt freedom to participate among all members and to a reduction in the quality of group decisions (Chung & Ferris, 1971; Delbecq, Van de Ven & Gustafson, 1975; Torrance, 1957). Workers should help task groups develop mechanisms that ensure equitable participation. According to Huber (1980), equitable participation "is the level of participation that is in keeping with the individual's information, knowledge, or other contribution to the group's effort" (p. 185). Inequitable participation occurs when members participate more frequently or less frequently than their potential contribution to the group warrants.

The worker should help the group develop a standard of fairness in participation (Huber, 1980). This can be done by helping the group develop rules for participation. Members may agree to keep their comments brief, be attentive to the communication of others when they are speaking, and to encourage silent members to participate. In addition to modeling appropriate behavior, the worker can help members follow the rules that are established. For example, the worker can interrupt long speeches, ask members to summarize their comments briefly, or suggest that members give others a chance to reply. When a member presents an idea, the worker can invite participation by asking other members for feedback about the proposal. In some cases, it is helpful to structure the discussion by using a round robin procedure or the rules of parliamentary procedure.

In a round robin procedure, each member is asked to present one idea or one piece of information. Going around the group, members take turns presenting one piece of data. This procedure is continued and each member takes as many turns as needed. Members who do not have any additional ideas or information simply pass during their turn. The cycle is completed when all ideas have been shared by all members.

The round robin procedure has several advantages over unstructured, interacting communication procedures: It does not force members to participate equally although all members have an equal opportunity to participate. Because only one idea is presented at a time, the procedure avoids the boredom that often results when one member enumerates several ideas at the same time. By continuing to go around the group until all ideas are heard and by asking members to pass if they do not have any new information to present, a norm is established for sharing as many ideas as possible.

In large task groups, however, round robin procedures are often too time-consuming. Unless the group is divided into subgroups, the procedure is not useful. To facilitate equitable participation in large groups, the worker should consider using parliamentary procedures (Gulley, 1968; Maier, 1963; Scheidel & Crowell, 1979) following *Robert's Rules of Order* (Robert, 1970). These procedures, which have been developed over the past 600 years in meetings in business, industry, and political bodies in Britain and the United States, provide for orderly and structured participation in large group meetings. Group workers should be aware that parliamentary procedures are subject to manipulation by members who are familiar with its complexities. Maier (1963) and Strauss and Strauss (1952) claim that parliamentary procedures have been used for years by a small minority of members to control large meetings. By trading favors for votes before a meeting and calling for votes with few members present, parliamentary procedure can be used to subvert majority rule. Despite these disadvantages, *Robert's Rules of Order* can be helpful in ensuring equitable participation in large meetings. A brief description of parliamentary procedures is included in Chapter 11.

Enhancing Involvement and Commitment

A third important activity during the work stage of task groups is to help members feel that they are a vital part of the organization for which they work. Because much of any organization's work is done by individuals, there is a danger that staff can become isolated and alienated from an organization. Task groups provide support for their members and a sense of belonging that reduces alienation. For example, an individual worker in an agency for disabled children spends much of her time helping new parents with the trauma associated with giving birth to physically and mentally challenged children. Weekly team meetings with other professionals who work with the infants in a preschool program provide support and recognition for the worker who is faced with the difficult, often emotionally charged, task of helping parents adjust to having disabled children.

Helping members become involved through their participation in a task group benefits the organization as well as individuals. Task groups provide an organized means of developing, implementing, and getting members to follow policies, procedures, and goals of the agency. They allow members an opportunity to influence the policies and procedures developed by their agency. This process helps to make the agency responsive to the needs of its workers. At the same time, by clearly delineating how a task group fits into the overall structure of an agency—that is, to whom the group reports and what authority and power the group has to develop or change agency policies—members' input can be organized and channeled appropriately. This helps coordinate the efforts of workers performing a variety of tasks within an agency.

Several steps can be taken to help task group members feel their input is vital to the agency's sound functioning. First, workers should make sure members understand the importance of the group's work, its relationship to the agency's purpose, and how the group fits into the agency's administrative structure. This can be accomplished by clearly stating the group's purpose, using flow charts to explain how the group fits into the agency's administrative and decision-making structure, and clarifying the duties, responsibilities, authority and power that result from membership in the group. At first, this explanation might mean little to members. However, as work is accomplished within the group and recommendations and reports are prepared for the larger agency, members gain more personal, firsthand experience of the governance structure of their agency.

Assigning members specific roles can also help them become actively involved in their agency. Roles that encourage members to depend on one another for task accomplishment and roles that place them in the position of representing the group to a larger constituency increase the attractiveness and cohesion of the group, and help members feel that they are part of a collective effort that is of vital importance for effective agency functioning (Deutsch, 1973).

A third method of enhancing members' involvement and commitment is to invite their input into the agenda and the decision-making processes of the group. This can be done by encouraging members to develop and submit agenda items for future group meetings. Circulating the agenda and any background papers before a meeting can help members prepare their thoughts and concerns before a meeting and increase the chances that they will participate by sharing them during the meeting. It has been shown that the greater a member's effort and sacrifice in preparing for and working on a task, the more likely the member is to stay involved and committed to the group (Kiesler, 1978). Therefore, asking members to prepare for a meeting by reading background papers, collecting information, and submitting agenda items will tend to increase involvement and commitment to the group and the larger organization.

A fourth method of helping members become involved is to encourage them to participate in the decision-making process to the extent possible (Scheidel & Crowell, 1979). Shared decision making has been found to increase motivation (Kiesler, 1978), increase acceptance and understanding of decisions (Bradford, 1976), increase the information available for decision making (Huber, 1980), and help in processing complex information (Carnes, 1980).

Although some writers suggest that decision making should always be shared among members (Bradford, 1976), there are potential disadvantages to giving members decision-making authority. According to Huber (1980), these include (a) the great amount of personnel time spent in group decision making, (b) the tendency for groups to produce decisions that are not acceptable to management, (c) expectations that future decisions will also be made through group participation, (d) the tendency for groups to take longer than individuals to reach decisions, and (e) the possibility that group decision making could cause conflict among group members who may have to work together every day. Thus, the decision to delegate decision making to groups should be made only after carefully considering both its advantages and disadvantages in a particular situation. When the advantages of group decision making are questionable, it is often possible to have the group make several recommendations but leave the final decision to one person.

Developing Information

A fourth activity of the worker during the working stage of task groups is to help members generate information and develop creative alternatives for responding to difficult issues and problems facing the group. Although task groups are often thought to be particularly effective for sharing information and developing creative ideas, the available evidence suggests that ordinary interacting group discussions inhibit rather than increase the disclosure of information, ideas, and creative solutions (see, for example, Delbecq, 1967; Miner, 1979; Van de Ven, 1974; Van de Ven & Delbecq, 1971).

Reasons that group processes may inhibit information sharing and the development of creative ideas include the following:

- Status-conscious group members feel intimidated by those with higher status (Torrance, 1957). Lower-status members will tend to share less information and avoid making suggestions that will offend higher-status members.
- Norms and social pressures for conformity tend to limit the expression of new and creative ideas (Van de Ven, 1974; Vroom, Grant, & Cotton, 1969).
- Groups have the advantage of the variety of opinions and knowledge offered by all members, but group members may censor controversial opinions.
- Covert judgments are often made but not expressed openly in groups (Collaros & Anderson, 1969). Members, therefore, become concerned about the effects their self-disclosures will have on future interactions with group members.
- Interacting groups tend to reach premature solutions without considering all the available evidence (Maier & Hoffman, 1960; Van de Ven, 1974).

To reduce or eliminate the difficulties associated with generating information and developing creative solutions in interacting groups, several methods have been suggested, such as brainstorming, the nominal group technique, and social judgment analysis. These methods will be described in Chapter 11. However, because interacting group discussions are commonly used in task groups, workers should be aware of procedures that can help overcome the limitations often associated with them. For example, an agency director forms an ad-hoc group of staff to design the agency's policy on racial and sexual harassment. The group leader chooses the brainstorming procedure to develop creative ideas that can be incorporated into the contents of the new policy. In selecting among the creative ideas for inclusion in the policy, the leader uses the nominal group technique to organize and rank members' choices.

The worker can help in several ways to improve group members' opportunities to present new ideas, combine information, and generate creative solutions in interacting groups. First, the worker must clearly indicate to all members that their input is welcome. This means that the worker must be able to address the members' concerns about sanctions that may result from expressing sensitive or controversial ideas in the group. If the worker cannot guarantee freedom from sanctions, he or she should try to be as clear as possible about the boundaries of the discussion. For example, it might be possible for committee members to discuss new policies regarding service delivery, but it might not be acceptable for them to criticize existing supervisory staff who have to follow current policy guidelines. When sanctions are possible from individuals outside the group, the worker can encourage the group to consider keeping their discussions confidential. If lower-status members fear reprisals from higher-status members, the worker can discuss the use of sanctions with higher-status members before the group meeting and gain their cooperation in refraining from applying them. The worker can also suggest that higher-status and lower-status members discuss this issue in the group.

Feedback can both help and hinder the group's development of information and creative solutions. It is commonly thought that all feedback is useful because it helps group members detect and correct errors in information processing (see, for example, Argyris, 1977; Bowers & Franklin, 1976; Nadler, 1977). This is not true in all circumstances. In the early phase of developing information and forming creative solutions, evaluative feedback can have the effect of suppressing further suggestions (Nadler, 1979; Van de Ven, 1974). Members fear their ideas may be evaluated negatively and that this will reflect on their competence and their status in the agency. Under these circumstances, few members will risk making suggestions, giving opinions, or volunteering information that will not be readily accepted. To encourage free discussion, creative ideas, and new insights about a problem or issue, the worker should ask members to refrain from evaluating ideas early in the group's discussion.

Several other steps can also be taken to help the group develop information and creative ideas to solve a problem. The worker can encourage the group to develop norms that promote free discussion of ideas. As the meeting progresses, it is often helpful to point out group pressures that inhibit members' free discussion. By presenting creative, controversial, and thought-provoking ideas, the worker can act as a model for the group. Workers can also encourage members to continue to share unique ideas by praising those who present innovative suggestions. Because it is more difficult for lower status members to present their ideas after higher status members have expressed their opinions, lower status members should be encouraged to share their ideas as early as possible in the group's discussion. To avoid premature solutions during group discussions, the worker should help the group separate information and idea-generating steps from decision-making steps. When these suggestions are implemented, interacting groups can develop more creative solutions than they would under ordinary conditions.

Dealing with Conflict

It is unlikely that all members of a task group will immediately agree on all aspects of the work of the group. Thus, it is important for workers to realize that conflicts occur even in effective task groups (Napier & Gershenfeld, 1981; Scheidel & Crowell, 1979). Conflict often emerges in the work stage of the group—in earlier stages, members are just getting to know one another and are less likely to express conflicting viewpoints. Conflicts often occur over control of resources, values, beliefs, preferences, and the nature of the relationship between members (Deutsch, 1973). Filley (1974) and Maier (1963) suggest that disagreement among members can lead to either increased conflict and failure to accomplish a task or the development of creative solutions. The outcome of a disagreement depends on how the worker and the members handle it (Lowe & Herranen, 1978). For example, the worker leading a treatment conference in a mental health center might notice that a subgroup of members are not participating as expected. The worker comments on this and discovers that subgroup members are quiet because they disagree with the opinions of a very vocal, controlling member. The worker helps the subgroup and the individual member resolve their differences by pointing out the conflict and helping the members confront it. The worker also acts as a mediator, helping the subgroup and the member negotiate differences.

Unfortunately, many workers have difficulty dealing with conflict. They tend to avoid, ignore, or minimize it, hoping it will go away. When conflict is avoided and remains unresolved, the group may (a) decide not to decide, (b) delegate its decision-making responsibilities to others, or (c) decide on a solution that is not substantiated by accurate information (Kiesler, 1978). However, these strategies are generally counterproductive. Avoiding conflict rarely leads to satisfying and meaningful dialogue about the issues facing the group. Most often, when conflicts are avoided, members get the message that they should not express their true feelings, and that an honest sharing of information and opinions should be sacrificed so that the group can function "harmoniously." Sometimes, however, when conflicts are ignored they grow more intense. At other times, conflicts subside, but one or more group members are left feeling they have "lost the battle." None of these outcomes is desirable.

How can the worker handle conflict in a productive and satisfying manner? Burke (1970) and Guetzkow and Gyr (1954) suggest that substantive and affective conflicts can be reduced by the following procedures:

- Help members recognize the conflict.
- Help members express the reasoning behind conflicting opinions and alternatives.
- Develop facts and seek expert judgments to help resolve the conflict.
- Emphasize those factors in the group discussion that promote consensus.
- Follow orderly, pre-planned steps for considering alternatives and deciding on a solution.
- Use decision criteria that are mutually agreed upon by group members.
- Clarify and summarize the discussion frequently so that all members have a similar understanding of what is being discussed and the decision criteria that will be used.
- Be sensitive to members' personal concerns and needs in developing solutions and arriving at a decision.
- Remain neutral in the conflict, asking questions that seek clarification whenever possible.

In the classic text *Getting to Yes*, Fisher and Ury (1981) suggest that the worker should help members (a) separate the person from the issue or problem being addressed, (b) focus on interests or attributes of the problem rather than on members' position on the issue, (c) generate a variety of possible options before deciding what to do, and (d) insist that the decision about how to proceed be based on some objective standard.

In their analyses of hundreds of decision-making groups, Guetzkow and Gyr (1954) distinguished between two types of conflict, substantive and affective. Affective conflict is based on the emotional and interpersonal relationships among members within and outside of the group. Substantive conflict is based on members' differing opinions about ideas, information, and facts presented during the task group's work. In general, affective conflict is more difficult to resolve than substantive conflict because it is resistant to persuasive reasoning.

Probably the single most important step in dealing with affective and substantive conflicts in a group is to help members view disagreements as opportunities to gather information and to share views and opinions, rather than as personal attacks or as threats to one's authority or position. Ephross and Vassil (1988) suggest that cooperative processes involve recognizing the legitimacy of others' interests. Thus, it is important for the leader to welcome differing viewpoints and to encourage the members to do the same. Also, it is helpful to (a) ask members to elaborate on the thinking that led to their viewpoints, (b) suggest that other members listen carefully and ask questions before they react, and (c) highlight points of consensus and mutual interest as they arise.

Another step in dealing with conflict involves helping members to avoid turning conflicts into personal attacks. Ask members to keep their comments focused on the issues rather than on members' personal characteristics. Encourage members to make "I" statements and to avoid "you" statements which attack other members, or subscribe motives to their behavior. Do not react to outbursts, and do not encourage members to defend their position. Instead, help each party in a conflict to describe their interests, values, fears, and their goals or objectives.

Notice how this method of dealing with conflicts makes a difference in the next two statements. In the first statement the member attempts to defend a position. "I don't want my staff to take on this new program because they are already overworked. We were asked to take on more work last meeting. I don't think it's fair to ask us again. What about Joe's department? Why can't they handle this?" In the second statement, however, the member expresses her interests, fears, and objectives using "I" statements whenever possible. "My interests are in ensuring that the workers in my department don't get too overloaded with work. I appreciate your faith in my department, but I fear that my already overworked staff will become overwhelmed. My objective is to ensure that the workers in my department don't get so overloaded that they can't do a good job, and also that they don't get so burned out that they just throw up their hands and stop trying to do a quality job." The second statement lends itself to negotiation. For example, the leader might ask the member to describe the workload of his or her department, and any changes in it over the past year. If the workload has increased, and concerns about an overload are warranted, then the leader might help the group to explore options for getting the work accomplished.

Another useful procedure for dealing with conflict is to help members look beyond their particular position on an issue, and to understand what others hope to accomplish. Encourage members who are having a conflict to state their concerns and their priorities as concretely as possible. However, discourage them from defending their position. Instead, encourage members to ask questions of each other and to put themselves in each other's positions. Point out shared interests and mutual gains. For example, the worker might point out that all department heads have a stake in ensuring that the members of one department don't get so overloaded that they can't do a good job. Next, help members to reach consensus by agreeing in principle to mutually acceptable goals. Generate as many solutions as possible for achieving the goals. Ask members to express their preferences for particular options. If a single option is not preferred by all parties, negotiate a solution by combining options that include some gains and some sacrifices on the part of all parties to the conflict.

Making Effective Decisions

Facilitators of task groups are often called upon to help members make effective decisions. For example, a board president helps the board of directors decide whether to expand their agency's geographic service area. A community organizer helps a neighborhood association decide whether to establish a "neighborhood watch" group to address the crime rate in the community. The leader of an executive council helps the group determine who will be promoted within the organization.

Although groups are often used to make decisions, the evidence as to their effectiveness is mixed. Groups are better than individuals in influencing opinions and obtaining commitments from members (Kelley & Thibaut, 1969; Lewin, 1948). Napier (1967) found that groups are better at integrating complex perceptual and intellectual tasks, because members can rely on one another for assistance. However, for other types of problems, groups may not be any more effective than individuals and sometimes may be less efficient than individuals working alone (Campbell, 1968; Rotter & Portugal, 1969). In summarizing the literature that has compared the problem-solving activities of task groups with those of individuals, Hare (1976) has drawn the following conclusions:

- Groups are superior to individuals in solving manual problems such as puzzles. This is particularly true when the problem can be subdivided so that each person can use his or her own expertise to work on a problem component. The superiority of groups has been less consistently documented when the task to be accomplished is of a more intellectual nature, such as a logic problem.
- While groups are better than the average individual, they are not better than the best individual. Therefore, a group of novices may perform worse than one expert.
- Groups have the advantage of the variety of opinions and knowledge offered by the members, but group members may censor controversial opinions.
- Part of the superiority of group problem solving is due to the pooling of individual judgments to converge on a group norm. For some problems, similar accuracy may be achieved by averaging the decisions of noninteracting individuals.
- When groups solve intellectual tasks, members' rational information-processing orientation may be impeded by socio-emotional concerns.
- Because task groups require members to deliberate until they reach a decision, the decisions made in task groups may be more costly than those made by one or more individuals working alone.

To improve group decision making, workers should help members avoid the phenomenon known as "group think" (Janis, 1972). Group think occurs when group contagion takes over and members fail to express their own thoughts and feelings. Instead, they go along with the predominant sentiment of the group. This phenomenon has been recognized for years by those who have written about groups. For example, more than 80 years ago LeBon (1910) referred to "group mind," where members allow an emotional state generated from their participation in a group to dominate their intellectual powers. Similiarly, more than 70 years ago, Freud (1922) wrote about the power that the group has over an individual's ego.

Before 1960, it was generally thought that problem-solving groups make more conservative decisions than individuals. Experiments by Stoner (1961) and Ziller (1957), however, indicated that groups make riskier decisions than individuals. Stoner (1961) called this phenomenon the "risky shift." As evidence began to accumulate, it became clear that this shift may be toward either greater or lesser risk. Riskier decisions are made when a group's members approve of risk taking (Teger & Pruitt, 1967; Wallach & Wing, 1968), when persuasive information is presented (Ebbesen & Bowers, 1974), when the responsibility for the decision is shared among group members (Myers & Arenson, 1972; Zajonc, Wolosin, &

Wolosin, 1972), or when the leader approves of a risky decision (Myers & Arenson, 1972). On the other hand, risk taking is discouraged in some groups, and members are rewarded for developing conservative solutions (Stoner, 1968).

Several steps can be taken to help members avoid "group think" and "risky shifts." Norms and a group climate that encourages free and open discussion of ideas tend to discourage conformity and to decrease "group think." Procedures that clarify how a group will use information and arrive at a decision also tend to reduce conformity. Early in the decision-making process, the group should decide how to use the information it possesses in making a decision. For example, in a family service agency, a personnel committee deciding between many qualified applicants for a clinical position develops decision criteria. They are the rules and the standards that govern rational choices between alternative candidates. Criteria for making decisions should include all the factors that group members consider to be essential in making a good judgment. The personnel committee developed decision criteria calling for an applicant who has clinical experience and supervisory skills, speaks Spanish, and is familiar with the use of psychotropic medications in outpatient mental health settings.

To avoid disagreements later, the worker should allow the group to discuss the rationale behind each decision criterion. To avoid confusion, it is often helpful to ask members about their understanding of each criteria and to use examples to illustrate how each criteria would be applied in rating alternative solutions. After developing and clarifying the criteria, the group should rate their relative importance so that the group can decide between alternative solutions. In the previous example, group members decided that clinical competency and supervisory experience were twice as important as the other criteria for this particular position. They then used the criteria to review each job applicant's folder to select the best candidate. A more detailed explanation of developing and using decision criteria in task groups is presented in the section on social judgment analysis in Chapter 11.

To arrive at a final group decision, a procedure for choosing among alternatives is needed. Most groups make their final decisions using one of the following procedures: consensus, compromise, or majority rule (Gulley, 1968). In certain situations, each of these procedures can result in quite different decisions. To avoid the suspicion that a particular decision-making procedure is being chosen to influence a decision about a particular issue, a method of choosing among alternatives should be agreed upon as early as possible in a task group's deliberations.

Consensus is often considered the ideal way to select among alternatives because all group members commit themselves to the decision. When reviewing conditions for effective work with groups, Whitaker (1975) suggests that helping a group achieve consensus reduces conflict within the group and makes the group more effective. Consensus does not, however, necessarily imply agreement on the part of all group members. Napier and Gershenfeld (1981) point out that consensus "simply requires that individuals must be willing to go along with the group's predominant view and carry out the implications of the decision in good faith" (p. 402).

Consensus is sometimes difficult to achieve in groups. It can be time-consuming and tension-provoking because each alternative must be discussed thoroughly along with dissenting viewpoints. Also, there is the danger that members will acquiesce and decision quality will be sacrificed to arrive at a solution that is acceptable to all group members (Napier & Gershenfeld, 1981). Although other decision-making procedures are quicker, reaching consensus often brings considerable support for a decision because members are more likely to cooperate in implementing decisions that they have thoroughly discussed and agreed upon.

When issues are controversial and there is much dissenting opinion, it is often possible to reach a decision by modifying original proposals. To develop amendments to proposals that are acceptable to all group members, the discussion of each alternative should focus on the reasoning behind members' objections to the alternative. This process helps all group members identify the acceptable and unacceptable parts of each alternative. After a discussion of all the alternatives, the acceptable parts of several alternatives can often be combined into one solution that is acceptable to most, if not all, members.

Majority rule is a frequently used procedure to decide between alternatives in task groups. It is less time-consuming than consensus or compromise procedures and when the vote is done by secret ballot it protects the confidentiality of members. Majority rule is an excellent procedure for deciding routine and relatively minor questions. However, because a significant minority may not agree with the final outcome, majority rule is a less appealing procedure when the issue is important and when the support and cooperation of the entire group is needed for successful implementation. For important decisions, a two-thirds majority vote is an alternative to simple majority rule. A two-thirds majority vote ensures at least substantial support for a decision made by the group.

In recent years, simple mathematical procedures have also been recommended to achieve majority rule (Delbecq, Van de Ven Gustafson, 1975; Huber, 1980). For example, each member of a task group can be asked to rate alternative solutions on a five-point scale from 5 = best alternative to 1 = worst alternative. The group's leader or staff person tabulates the vote on each alternative solution. Because this procedure is easily done without identifying member's individual ratings, it also preserves their anonymity during the decision-making process. Another mathematical procedure is to have all members rank order alternative solutions. Ranks are tallied, and the mean of the ranks is calculated for each alternative. The nominal group technique discussed in Chapter 11 uses this procedure for selecting among alternatives.

Understanding Task Groups' Political Ramifications

Although much of this chapter and the next are focused on problem solving and decision making, task groups also have political functions that are frequently overlooked or ignored by group workers. They often overlook these functions because they are uncomfortable with the notion of behaving in a political fashion. Levinson and Klerman (1973) recognized this when they said the cultivation of power is viewed by many professions, including social work, "as vulgar, as a sign of character defect, as something an upstanding professional would not be interested in or stoop to engage in" (p. 66). Yet, politics are an important part of the dynamics that govern the functioning of task groups during the working stage.

An essential step in becoming more aware of the political functions of task groups is to develop an orientation that views political behavior as an essential ingredient of all task groups. Gummer (1987) points out that rather than viewing political behavior as symptomatic of a character defect, it may be better viewed "as the quest of the mature personality for the resources needed to effect increasingly larger areas of one's world" (p. 36).

Gummer says task groups should be analyzed and understood in terms of how they are used to exercise and enhance the power of those who participate in them. While the overt exercise of power is generally frowned on in our society, there are many symbolic ways that task groups help managers exercise their power and position within an organization. In a power-oriented analysis of task groups, Gummer (1987) focused on four elements: (a) the physical setting, (b) membership, (c) the agenda, and (d) procedural rules.

In regard to the physical setting, Gummer suggests considering the symbolic meaning of the meeting location. For example, is the meeting taking place in a "neutral" place, or one that is "owned" by the leader or a particular member? Is the meeting taking place in a symbolic setting such as an outreach office or a new building to symbolize the importance of the setting? Gummer also suggests analyzing the symbolism attached to how the meeting room is arranged. For example, does the setting promote work or comfort? Are chairs set up around a table with paper, pencils, overhead projectors and other work-oriented aides? Or is the setting filled with couches, soft chairs, food, and other items that convey a relaxed, informal atmosphere?

Who is invited to participate in a meeting is also important from a political perspective. Participation in meetings is the organizational equivalent of enfranchisement. Gummer (1987) says "whether an organization is run along autocratic, oligarchic, or democratic lines, whatever rights members are entitled to are accorded by their inclusion in certain organizational groups. Conversely, limits on one's organizational position are established by exclusion from certain groups" (p. 30).

Determining who can participate is an important source of power because it "organizes into attention" the interests and positions associated with the included individuals (Forester, 1981). For example, the character of a task group might be changed when consumers are included on advisory boards. Similarly, the substantive deliberations of a committee examining staffing ratios and workloads will almost certainly change when nonprofessional and professional staff are included in the meetings.

Meeting agendas can also be used for political purposes. Bachrach and Baratz (1962) suggested that power can be exercised by confining the scope of decision making to relatively "safe" issues. The ordering of items on the agenda may also be used for political purposes. For example, the leader or certain members may take a long time to discuss several trivial issues at the beginning of a meeting, leaving little time to work on issues that they would rather not address. Similarly, how agenda items are presented often has political ramifications. Gummer (1987) suggests that politically oriented individuals who want certain items tabled, defeated, or changed encourage their proponents to present their issues in the broadest terms possible so that the specifics of the issue are not discussed, and the issue becomes confused or obfuscated by a general discussion of the philosophical principles of the organization. Conversely, items that these members would like to see acted upon and accepted by the group are presented as specifically and noncontroversially as possible.

Procedures governing how the group conducts its business can also be developed with political purposes in mind. In democratic organizations it is expected that, at a minimum, procedural rules should (a) provide task group members with sufficient time to deliberate about the issues the group is charged to address and (b) provide for adequate representation of minority opinions. However, procedural rules can be manipulated by politically minded individuals. For example, important decisions may be deferred to the executive committee of a board, rather than being taken up during a full board meeting. Similarly, the membership of a nominating subcommittee or a finance subcommittee may be stacked to favor the wishes of the leader or a certain subgroup of powerful members.

Monitoring and Evaluating

The worker is also often called upon to help task groups structure monitoring and evaluation efforts. Task groups may monitor and evaluate their own functioning or be called upon to monitor and evaluate other systems. For example, the board of a social service agency is responsible for monitoring and evaluating the functioning of the agency. Because boards are ultimately responsible and legally liable for the proper conduct of social service agencies, monitoring and evaluating functions are a critical component of an effective board's work (Houle, 1960; Swanson, 1978). Other groups, like alcoholism treatment teams, monitor and evaluate their own performances by reviewing recidivism data on all former clients at three-month "progress review" meetings.

For effective monitoring and evaluation during the middle stage, task groups must be clear about their mandate from the agency and their ethical, moral, and legal obligations, as expressed by regulatory agencies, professional societies, legislative bodies, and the larger society. At times these are clear but it is often the responsibility of the task group to develop a set of standards, rules, or guidelines that can be used to monitor and evaluate performance. For example, a large, private social service agency decided to encourage evaluations of several of its service programs. To ensure that the research would serve a useful purpose, protect the rights and the confidentiality of their clients, and meet state and federal rules and regulations, an institutional research review board was formed. The first meeting of this group focused on reviewing the procedures of similar review boards at other agencies and examining state and federal regulations. The group then prepared guidelines governing its own operation and guidelines for researchers to use when preparing proposals to be reviewed by the board.

To fulfill their monitoring and evaluating functions adequately, task groups develop feedback mechanisms to help them obtain information about the results of a decision and take corrective actions when necessary (Nadler, 1979). The type of feedback useful to a task group depends to a great extent on the group's mandate and the monitoring and evaluating required in the particular situation. A board, for example, may require periodic reports from the agency director, the director of clinical services, the agency executive, and the coordinator of volunteer services. In addition, the board may review program statistics, quarterly financial statements from a certified accountant and reports from funding sources about the performance of the agency. In other cases, a task group may use formal data gathering procedures to perform its monitoring and evaluation functions. For a discussion of these methods, see Chapter 12.

Problem Solving

Problem solving has been given more consideration in the group work literature than any of the other functions of task groups. Task groups spend a great deal of time performing other functions, but problem solving is often seen as a task group's major function. Although it is separate from sharing information, involving others, or making decisions, problem solving incorporates many of these functions of task groups. Thus, problem solving is best viewed as a complex set of functions that vary with the type of problem facing the group. The next section describes a generic, six-step problem-solving model that can be used effectively in a variety of task groups.

A MODEL FOR EFFECTIVE PROBLEM SOLVING

Problem solving can take as little as 5 or 10 minutes or as long as several months. The length of any problem-solving process depends on the nature of the problem, the structure and function of the group, and the capabilities and willingness of the group members and group leader to solve the problem. The effectiveness of any problem-solving effort depends on the extent to which an optimal solution is developed and implemented. It also depends on how satisfied the members of the group are with the problem-solving process and the extent to which they support the decision made by the group. It is important for task group leaders to become thoroughly familiar with the problem-solving model presented here so they can apply it in a manner that will satisfy group members and gain necessary cooperation and support. Problems solving involves six steps:

1. Identifying a problem.
2. Developing goals.
3. Collecting data.
4. Developing plans.
5. Selecting the best plan.
6. Implementing the plan.

FIGURE 10–1
The problem-solving process in task groups

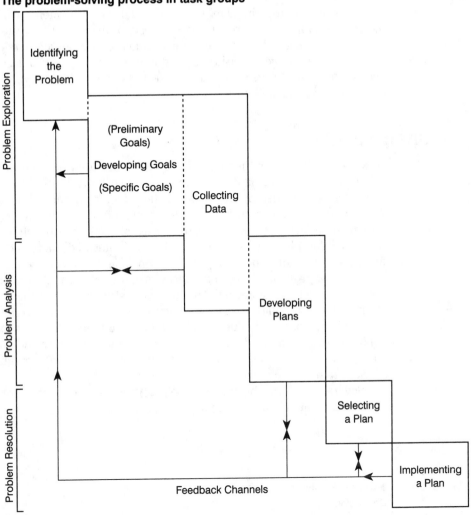

As can be seen in Figure 10–1, these steps are not discrete. In practice they often tend to overlap. For example, preliminary goals are often discussed during problem identification. Goals are modified and refined as data collection continues. Similarly, data collection often continues as the group begins to develop plans for problem resolution.

Problem-solving processes are often described as if they occur once. This may be true in groups convened to solve a single problem, but it is not always the case. Problem-solving processes are generally used repeatedly by groups as they conduct their business. A task group may have to use two or more cycles of a problem-solving process to accomplish a single task. This process is represented in Figure 10–2. An adult protective service team, for example, spends three meetings developing a plan for emergency evening coverage for all clients on team members' caseloads. The plan is implemented for a two-month trial period. After the trial period, the team reconsiders aspects of the plan. Using the problem-solving process a second time, the team decides on a modified version of the plan that proves effective in assuring adequate emergency evening coverage. Thus, over the course of several months the team is involved with two problem-solving cycles to accomplish its task.

Identifying a Problem

How a problem is identified and defined is crucial to effective problem solving. It affects what data will be collected, who will work on the problem, what alternatives will be considered, and who will be affected by the problem's resolution. When they are first identified, problems are often unclear and muddled. They appear to be unsolvable, complicated mazes of tangled or disjointed components. Even when problems appear to be fairly well delineated, there is often a need for further clarification. For example, the staff of a social service agency perceives that it has a problem in serving a large group of Mexican-Americans who live in the area served by the agency. Although at first glance this appears to be a fairly clear problem, it could be defined in several ways, including (a) not having Spanish-speaking workers, (b) not conducting any outreach efforts to this population, (c) having a poor public image with Mexican-Americans in the community, (d) not having the financial resources to develop programs, or (e) providing the wrong services to meet the needs of the population.

Several steps can be taken to help a group define a problem and promote rather than hinder problem solving:

FIGURE 10–2
Two cycles of a problem-solving process

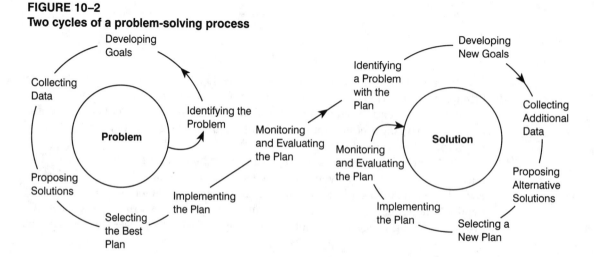

1. Clarify the boundaries of the problem.
2. Seek out members' perceptions of the problem and their expectations about how it will be solved.
3. Develop a problem-solving orientation.
4. Define a solvable problem.
5. Specify the problem as clearly as possible.

Clarifying Boundaries.   The first issue that confronts workers and members as they define the boundaries of a problem is how to handle large problems that may have several interrelated components. Groups are often confronted with large problems that seem to be unmanageable and unsolvable. In other cases, a vague concern or problem expressed by a group member may emerge as a large problem as members begin to discuss the issues. One method of handling large problems is to partialize them. Several manageable, solvable problems, for example, can be developed from a large problem that at first seems unsolvable, unmanageable, or overwhelming.

When the group partializes a problem, it must decide on which aspect of the large problem to work on first. Some guidelines suggest that groups should first work on a problem that:

- Is clearly under the group's legitimate authority.
- Is a pressing problem.
- Is potentially under the group's control.
- Will have far-reaching, beneficial effects when solved.
- Is meaningful enough so that a solution is important to group members and to others outside the group.
- Has a good chance of being resolved successfully.

Boundaries refer to the extent and scope of a problem or issue facing the group. Defining clear boundaries helps problem solvers focus and clarify their thoughts and suggestions about a problem, leading to more effective solutions (D'Zurilla & Goldfried, 1971). When setting boundaries the worker is in a delicate position. On the one hand, an effective worker does not want to hamper the group's creative problem-solving ability. The worker would like to encourage the group to consider all the relevant options for problem resolution. On the other hand, the worker is often in a better position than any other group member to recognize what is politically, economically, and organizationally feasible. For example, in a group working on ways to increase services for Mexican-Americans, it would be helpful to inform members that solutions to the problem should not commit the agency to new services that require additional funding because no new money is available during the current fiscal year. The worker could explain that although the solution should not require new funds, the group might consider making recommendations to the agency's administrative staff about seeking additional funding during the next fiscal year.

Whenever possible, the boundaries of the problem solving process should be as broad and as flexible as possible so as not to stifle creative problem solutions. The worker should point out members' freedom within these boundaries and the importance of accomplishing the task within specified limits. The group should be given a convincing rationale for limiting the scope of a problem and the scope of the efforts used to resolve it. Without guidelines, the group may arrive at a solution that is unacceptable to those who must implement it. Members who spend their time and energy developing a solution that is not feasible will feel frustrated and disappointed when they realize their recommended solution was not implemented.

An example of the delicate balance the worker should strike in suggesting boundaries for problem solving occurs in the following statement by the leader of the task group addressing the needs of Mexican-Americans:

> The needs assessment we have just completed confirms our suspicions—we are not doing enough to serve Mexican-Americans in our catchment area. As we discuss the problem and decide about what to do, we should keep in mind that we have just entered a new fiscal year and the agency's budget does not allow for new programming that requires additional funding. The executive director has informed me that within this constraint she will actively pursue any solutions that you suggest for improving service to this population. She is ultimately responsible for presenting solutions we suggest to the board and getting the solutions implemented in the entire agency. In discussing the problem, we should consider ways that existing services could be redirected or applied differently to the clients we serve. Eligibility requirements and other issues related to access might also be explored. We may also want to consider using regularly scheduled in-service training and supervision to increase our awareness of the problem and to enhance our skills in dealing with this population. What are your thoughts about tackling this problem?

This example illustrates that the worker has set some broad guidelines for problem solving and has made some tentative suggestions to the group about what aspects of the problem might be worth exploring. The worker has given the group some indication of what is feasible within the budget constraints of the agency and has clarified who is responsible for implementing potential solutions. By asking for members' thoughts about the problem the worker is inviting them to define the boundaries of the problem within these broad guidelines.

Members' Perceptions and Experiences.   Members' perceptions of problematic situations and their expectations about how they should be resolved determine the way they will approach a problem. If the members of a group are to be satisfied with the group's problem-solving process and committed to the solution that is reached, the members' views about problems facing the group must be respected. There is no better way to show respect than to solicit their views and ensure that they are given a fair hearing by all members. Failure to clarify members' expectations and perceptions about a problem often leads to difficulties later in the group's problem-solving process. Hidden agendas can develop, in part, because unclarified expectations are acted on by members.

Clarifying boundaries and helping members express their perceptions and expectations of the problem-solving situation can be helpful techniques in arriving at a common understanding of the problem. An open discussion usually causes a modification of all group members' perceptions and expectations. Common perceptions and expectations form the basis for mutually agreed upon goals.

Careful consideration of the views of individual group members does not mean that every opinion or bit of information should be treated as equally correct or important. Although there is a tendency to equate equality of ideas with equal treatment of group members, these concepts should not be confused (Kiesler, 1978). Members should be treated equitably in the group process, but the importance of their contribution changes as the work of the group changes.

Sometimes, one or more members may hold tenaciously to initial perceptions of a problem or to initial expectations about how a problem should be resolved. Group members should be invited to discuss the logic of their assessments as a means of arriving at a shared view of the problem.

When the majority of the group's members agree with the leader's assessment and ideological differences separate one or two members from the rest of the group, workers can acknowledge the conflict and help members to express minority opinions while continuing to carry out decisions made by the majority.

Problem-Solving Orientation.   During the process of identifying a problem it is important for the worker to help members develop a problem-solving orientation (D'Zurilla & Goldfried, 1971). Such an orientation includes:

- Minimizing irrational beliefs about problematic situations.
- Recognizing and being willing to work on problems as they occur.
- Inhibiting tendencies to either respond prematurely on the first impulse or do nothing.

Irrational beliefs about "how the world should be" can inhibit members from recognizing problematic situations and can also interfere with problem resolution (Ellis, 1962). Irrational beliefs can lead to primitive solutions that can have detrimental consequences for the group as a whole. It is important for the worker to encourage all members to challenge irrational beliefs and to encourage rational approaches to problem solving. Members should be helped to use evidence, logic, and sound reasoning as they identify and define a problematic situation (see, for example, Barker, 1979; Gouran, 1982; Harnack & Fest, 1964; Stattler & Miller, 1968).

An effective problem-solving orientation includes recognizing problems that need attention and being willing to work on them. It is sometimes difficult for task groups to confront and work on problems facing them. For example, a team in a psychiatric hospital avoids discussing problems in its own functioning for fear that the discussion will be viewed as an attack on individual members. In this case, the team leader helps by facilitating the development of a group climate that encourages problems to be viewed as shared concerns whose resolution will benefit all team members.

In developing a problem-solving orientation within the group, it is important to help members reduce their tendency to make immediate and automatic responses (Toseland, 1977). Frequently, members will suggest solutions without carefully considering the problem. It has been found that less effective problem solvers are impulsive, impatient, and quick to give up (Bloom & Broder, 1950). Therefore the workers should encourage members to stop and think about the problem, collect data, and analyze alternative solutions before deciding what to do (Dollard & Miller, 1950).

There should be sufficient time during a meeting agenda to grapple with difficult problems. According to Tropman (1980), difficult items should be placed in the middle third of the agenda. This is when members are at the peak of their (a) psychological focus, (b) physiological awareness, (c) attention, and (d) attendance. Easier items should be placed earlier in the agenda. Items for discussion only can be placed at the end, because they require less energy at a time when members have little energy for problem solving.

Defining a Solvable Problem.   Groups are sometimes blocked in their problem-solving ability because they fail to locate the problem correctly (Maier, 1963). Group members may fail to identify the correct actors, the correct systems, or the correct obstacles that constitute the problem situation. In the early stages of problem solving, the group should be tentative and flexible with its problem definition so that it can be modified when new data are collected.

How problems are stated can effect the entire problem-solving process. The worker can use several techniques to improve the group's ability to define a solvable problem. Maier (1963) suggests that whenever possible, problems should be stated in institutional rather than personal terms. For example, a definition that attributes the problem of lack of services to Mexican-Americans to an inept director of clinical services will tend to alienate the director of clinical services, making the problem more difficult to solve. However, identifying the problem as a lack of service hours for Mexican-Americans opens possibilities for modifying service delivery patterns. Similarly, defining the problem as a lack of knowledge and expertise about Mexican-American clients suggests that the committee should consider assessing members' willingness to learn more about this population.

To help the group obtain a new perspective on a problem, the worker can use the reframing technique described in Chapter 9. An exercise that can help members reframe a problem is to ask them to imagine themselves experiencing it as another might experience it. For example, members of a program committee who have reservations about making efforts to improve services for Mexican-Americans are asked to imagine themselves going to an agency where no one speaks English and where most clients and all workers have a different cultural and ethnic background from their own. The exercise encourages members to reconsider their stand on the question of whether something should be done to improve services for the Mexican-American population.

Reframing may also be done by focusing on the positive aspects of a problem. For example, a problem that is experienced as anxiety-provoking may be reframed as one that motivates the group to improve a situation. In these ways, members' motivation to solve problems can be increased.

Specifying the Problem.   Having a clearly defined and mutually understood problem is essential if members are to work effectively together. When problems are first expressed in a meeting, they are often stated as partially formulated concerns. For example, a committee member might say, "I get a sense that some of our staff may be having difficulty with the new record-keeping system." Many of the terms in this statement are vaguely defined. Terms such as "get a sense," "some of our staff," and "difficulty" can have different meanings for each member of the group.

As concerns are raised by members, the worker should help them clarify vague or ambiguous terms. The statement mentioned previously, for example, could be clarified to indicate that three members of the community team and one member of the day treatment team expressed concerns that the new record-keeping forms took too long to fill out. Further, the phrase "took too long to fill out" should be clarified so that it becomes clear what it is the group is being asked to consider. For example "took too long to fill out" might mean "cannot complete the case record in the 15 minutes allocated for that purpose," or it might mean "being asked to collect data which is not needed to work with clients." Sometimes members of the task group may find that they cannot specify the problem further without collecting additional information.

After the group has clarified the problem, the worker should summarize it in a clear, brief statement. Ideally, the problem should be defined in objective terms that have similar meanings for all members. Objective terms with clear, observable referents help members arrive at a common understanding of the situation. When summarizing, the worker should restate the boundaries of the problem and the group's authority and responsibility so that members will have a clear idea of their role in resolving it.

Developing Goals

The second step in the problem-solving process is goal setting. Goal setting does not occur just once in the problem-solving process. Tentative goals are formulated soon after the problem has been identified. These tentative goals aid in data collection because they help shape the scope of the information that is to be collected. Goals are often modified and specified as information is accumulated. Initial goals may sometimes be abandoned altogether and new goals may be developed on the basis of the data accumulated.

The procedures for developing goals for specific problems are similar to goal-setting procedures described in beginning a group. Through a process of exploration and negotiation, the worker and the members share their perspectives about what goals the group should achieve related to a particular problem. The emphasis should be on formulating goals that are mutually acceptable.

Like problem statements, goal statements should be as clear and specific as possible. Desired changes in problem situations should be stated as objective tasks. For example, goals to increase services to Mexican-Americans might include (a) providing eight hours of training for each outreach worker during the next six months, (b) increasing the number of Mexican-Americans served by the agency from an average of three a month to 15 a month by the next fiscal year, (c) translating program brochures into Spanish within three months, and

(d) printing 400 bilingual Spanish-English brochures at the beginning of the next fiscal year. Each of these goals is specific and easily understood.

Group workers can use several other principles for developing effective goals, including the following:

- Goals should be directed at the mutual concerns of all members.
- Goals should be consistent with the group's mandate, its overall objectives, and the values which have been agreed upon by the group as a whole.
- Goals should be attractive enough to gain the commitment, cooperation, and investment of all group members.
- Goals should be realistic and attainable through the resources available to the group and its members.
- Goals should be time-limited.
- The goal-setting process should set a supportive, encouraging climate for goal attainment.

At the end of the goal-setting process, members should be clear about the tasks they must perform to achieve the goals. It is important for the worker to summarize the goals that have been decided upon by the group and review each member's role in their achievement. This avoids misunderstandings about who is responsible for what during a specified time period. Members should be clear about the time frame for accomplishing goals and about the mechanisms for reporting their achievements to the group.

It is often helpful to partialize large goals into a series of smaller ones that can be accomplished in a short time period. This is particularly true in newly organized groups, whose members may be overwhelmed by the enormity of a task and unsure about the group's ability to accomplish it. Partializing goals gives members a sense of accomplishment as they reach subgoals. This sense of accomplishment increases the attractiveness of the group, helping ensure highly motivated members for future problem-solving efforts.

Collecting Data

Data collection is the third step in the problem-solving process. It begins as soon as a problem is identified by a group and continues as broad goals are defined and refined and as plans are developed. As a process, data collection is concerned with the generation of ideas. It should be kept separate from analyzing facts and generating solutions. Data collection relies on creative, imaginative thinking, whereas data analysis relies on evaluative thinking. Groups sometimes arrive at hasty, ill-conceived solutions because they rush to implement initial ideas without carefully exploring the situation, the obstacles to problem resolution, and the ramifications of a proposed solution.

Areas of information that are important for the group to obtain when attempting to solve any problem include (a) the history of the problem; (b) previous attempts to resolve the problem; (c) facts about the situation, such as who is involved and where, how, and when the problem occurred; (d) characteristics of the problem, such as its duration, intensity, scope, and importance; (e) the psychosocial context of the problem; and (f) organizational and societal rules and regulations that impinge on the problem. The group should have as much information as possible about the problem as it analyzes data and prepares alternative solutions.

Knowing the history of the problem helps the group develop a longitudinal perspective on its development and its course. Comparing the state of affairs before and after a problem has occurred can often point to potential causes and possible solutions. While gathering data about the history of the problem, the group should become familiar with previous attempts to solve it. This can help the group avoid repeating past failures.

The worker should help members pinpoint as many facts about the situation as possible. To help members separate facts from opinions and feelings, the worker should encourage members to describe the situation. After the facts of the situation are described, members should be encouraged to share their unique perspectives about the problem. Scheidel and Crowell (1979) list five conditions that help to create a group climate that encourages members to share their unique perspectives. These include (a) maintaining the group's openness to speculation, (b) encouraging an open search for all pertinent data, (c) encouraging all group members to present their ideas, (d) demonstrating genuine appreciation of differences, and (e) refraining from evaluation (Scheidel & Crowell, 1979).

A supportive group climate reduces the need for members to defend their positions. Gibb (1961) points out that communications should be expressed (a) nonjudgmentally, (b) genuinely, (c) without the intent of controlling others, (d) with tentativeness rather than certainty, and (e) as an equal rather than as a superior. Facilitating this type of communication in a group increases problem exploration and contributes to high-quality solutions.

Members occasionally can become "stuck" in the ways they explore and review a problem (Napier & Gershenfeld, 1981). To develop new approaches, members should be encouraged to (a) view problems flexibly rather than rigidly, (b) expand rather than restrict the way information is collected and combined, (c) recognize and fill gaps in available information, (d) generate new ideas by viewing situations from alternative perspectives, and (e) use lateral as well as vertical thinking processes.

Vertical thinking processes are often associated with rational problem-solving strategies. Vertical thinking relies on inductive and deductive reasoning. Evidence and reason are used in a logical fashion until a solution is reached. Solutions are grounded in facts that are built one upon another in an orderly, systematic, and linear fashion.

Lateral thinking processes are particularly useful when vertical thinking processes have not yielded a creative solution. Lateral thinking helps free ideas that have been blocked by stale, routine ways of conceptualizing a problem and its potential solutions. Instead of relying on an orderly, linear combination of facts, lateral thinking is characterized by the use of analogies, metaphors, similarities, contrasts, and paradoxes. Seemingly disparate facts, thoughts, and ideas are put together in new and creative ways. Analogies, for example, help bring out similarities between objects or situations that were previously considered to be different. Solutions found to be helpful in analogous situations might, for example, be tried in the current situation. For further information about the lateral thinking process, see De Bono (1968, 1971, 1972).

Developing Plans

Whereas data collection encourages divergent thinking processes, preparing plans for problem resolution encourages convergent thinking processes (Scheidel & Crowell, 1979). The worker calls on members to organize, analyze, and synthesize facts, ideas, and perspectives generated during problem exploration. Figure 10–1 (p. 315) shows that plans should be developed during the analysis portion of problem-solving efforts.

The first step in analyzing the information generated during data collection is to display it so that all members can see it. It is difficult for members to keep a great deal of information in mind as they attempt to develop alternative solutions. Displaying information on newsprint or a blackboard helps to ensure that all members are aware of the full range of information shared during a discussion.

The next step is to order and clarify the information generated by the group. Useful techniques include (a) separating relevant from irrelevant facts, (b) combining similar facts, (c) identifying discrepancies, (d) looking for patterns across different facts, and (e) ranking facts from most important to least important. During the process of organizing data, members should be encouraged to discuss the logic behind their reasoning rather than to discuss their particular ordering of information. Members should be encouraged to give each other a chance to explain why they see things the way they do, rather than to defend their own choices. Defending choices often entrenches group members' opinions, whereas discussion of how members think information should be used often brings out commonalities and similarities in their views of the situation.

After the information is ordered, it is helpful to redefine the problem, specifying, refining, and, if necessary, reframing it in view of the facts, ideas, and perspectives that have been discussed. It is also helpful to re-examine the group's goals by comparing the problem situation with the outcomes the group would like to achieve by resolving the problem. Once a common definition of the problem is reached and a valued end state is specified, the group should have little trouble developing a plan to solve the problem.

Before making a decision, members should be encouraged to develop as many alternative solutions as possible. Because critical and evaluative comments tend to inhibit the production of creative ideas, workers should caution members not to criticize each other's solutions as they are presented. When members generate alternative solutions, they should also keep in mind that their strategies and plans must begin to specify the action system and the tasks, as well as the time, energy, and resources necessary for implementing the solution.

Selecting the Best Plan

After all members have presented their alternatives, the group should review each one. This review has several purposes. It helps ensure that all members understand each alternative. Misunderstandings at this point can cause conflict and reduce the chances for achieving closure in the problem-solving process. Reviews can be used to clarify the objectives and goals described in each alternative plan. Objectives should clearly indicate who will be involved in problem resolution efforts and what they will be doing. Objectives should be developed in a way that allows them to be evaluated. When reviewing each alternative, members can discuss how they would overcome obstacles and challenges likely to be encountered if the alternative were implemented. For large or costly decisions, task groups sometimes recommend that one or more alternatives be tested in a pilot program before full-scale implementation.

Once this is done, members are ready to choose among alternative plans. When selecting among alternatives, members should be encouraged to consider the overall likelihood that a plan will resolve the problem in a manner that is valued by all group members (Edwards, 1961). For this purpose, it is helpful for members to develop criteria that can be used to judge each plan. Rational decision-making methods based on utility theory have been developed to help members develop judgment criteria. Although much has been written about these methods (see, for example, Becker & McClintock, 1967; Edwards, Lindman, & Phillips, 1965; Shelly & Bryan, 1964), until recently they have not been widely applied in the human services (Huber, 1980; Jessup & Valacich, 1993; Rohrbaugh, 1979, 1981; Toseland, Rivas & Chapman, 1985).

To select among alternatives, groups sometimes rely on decision criteria developed by experts. For example, a task group formed by the U.S. Department of Health and Human Services was charged with distributing funds for health maintenance organizations in "medically underserved" areas. By using panels of experts, the committee developed four criteria for deciding among programs that applied for funds in "medically underserved" areas. These included (a) the number of physicians per 1,000 people, (b) the percentage of families in the area with less than $5,000 annual income, (c) the infant mortality rate in the area, and (d) the percentage of the area's population over age 65 (Health Services Research Group, 1975).

At other times, groups rely on the expertise of their own members to develop decision criteria. This is frequently done by having members rate the advantages and the disadvantages of each alternative. Alternatives may be combined or modified to maximize advantages and minimize disadvantages. As members decide among alternatives, they should keep in mind the group's mandate, its goals, and the ideal situation they would like to see result if the problem were resolved successfully. Members may also want to consider other factors, such as the benefits and costs of implementing alternative solutions, the comfort and ease with which particular solutions are likely to be implemented, and the political ramifications of alternative solutions. The most effective solution to a problem may not be the most desirable solution if it is too costly or likely to offend, inconvenience, or otherwise upset those who will be asked to implement it.

Implementing the Plan

Excellent decisions can be worthless if they are not implemented properly. Effective problem solving requires that a task group actively oversee the implementation of its plan.

Input from those who will be influential in implementing the plan should be solicited as early as possible in the problem-solving process. Once a solution is decided upon, members should begin to gain support for the decision from constituencies outside the group. Members should seek the support of those with authority to implement the decision and those who will be accountable for the decision. For example, the committee that decided to improve outreach efforts to Mexican-Americans by training staff and publicizing agency programs in the community sought the cooperation of the board of directors, the agency's executive director, the directors of programs responsible for implementing staff training and publicity campaigns, all direct service staff who were going to be involved in the program, and leaders of the Mexican-American community.

When seeking the support of others, members may have to educate people about the value of a new approach to a problem. Motivating people to cooperate with the implementation of a decision is not an easy task. However, motivation is important because passivity during the implementation stage of problem solving can mean the demise of a promising solution. In gaining cooperation, individual members or the group as a whole may also have to use some leverage to gain the support of others (Cox, Erlich, Rothman, & Tropman, 1974). This leverage may include persuasion by those with prestige and power or lobbying by those who will benefit by the solution.

Once the receptivity of those responsible for implementing the decision is ensured, the group can begin to organize and supervise the plan's implementation. With a large plan, a division of labor is often helpful, where each member may be assigned specific responsibilities. There may also be a need for training to educate those who will implement the plan.

It is often helpful to delineate steps in the implementation sequence. Objectives can be specified for each step, allowing the group to obtain periodic feedback about the plan's implementation. A time line can be attached to the implementation sequence. This helps to clarify how much time is available for each step during the implementation stage. During this process, members often experience surprise and even shock at how long a plan will take to become fully operational.

Implementing the proposed solution also includes identifying, contacting, and utilizing available resources. A heterogeneous group can be advantageous in the process because of the diversity of available resources. Members can also help the group prepare for opposition. Obstacles might include inertia, passive resistance, and perceived or actual conflicts of interest that can lead to attempts to block implementation of a plan.

As Figure 10–1 shows, feedback is essential in the problem-solving process. When planning for the implementation of a decision, group members should establish feedback channels, which can keep the group apprised of a solution's utility in terms of its expected outcome. Feedback can be used to overcome obstacles, stabilize change, and meet the challenges of a continually changing environment.

SUMMARY

This chapter focuses on the foundation skills, procedures and methods needed to work effectively with task groups. Task groups have an important place in all human service organizations. Each day, meetings take place that have an important effect on what services are provided and how they are delivered. Social workers and other helping professionals are frequently called upon to chair or staff committees, teams, and other task groups. When meetings are well run, members become a satisfied and cohesive team that is committed to achieving its objectives. Poorly run meetings, however, often lead to boredom and frustration.

During the work stage of task groups, the worker often is called upon to engage in the following activities: (a) preparing for group meetings, (b) helping members share information, (c) helping all members get involved in the work of the group, (d) helping members develop ideas and information, (e) dealing with conflict, (f) helping members make effective decisions, (g) understanding the political ramifications of task groups, (h) monitoring and evaluating, and (i) problem solving.

Although some of the activities in which workers engage in task groups and treatment groups overlap, task and treatment groups can be distinguished by their primary focus. Task groups are concerned with the results produced by the group as a whole, whereas treatment groups are concerned with the functioning of individual group members.

Problem solving is probably the single most important function of task groups. Six major steps in problem solving include (a) identifying a problem, (b) developing goals, (c) collecting data, (d) developing plans, (e) selecting the best plan, and (f) implementing the plan. In practice, these steps overlap and they are interconnected by feedback channels. Task groups repeat variations of problem-solving processes as they perform their functions and work on the tasks that confront them.

LEARNING ASSIGNMENTS

1. You have been asked to chair a committee charged with the task of making recommendations about whether it would be feasible for the large social service agency in which you work to provide child care for employees. Describe how you would prepare for the first meeting of the committee. Prepare a written agenda.

2. Observe a task group meeting. After the meeting, evaluate the effectiveness of the leader. What are the strengths and weaknesses of this individual's leadership style? Did he or she appear to be well-prepared for the meeting? What changes would have helped make the meeting more productive?

3. You are leading an organizational decision-making group charged with deciding how to expand its services to an underserved minority community. As the deliberations of the group proceed, there appear to be wide differences of opinion and conflict among the members. As the group's leader, what strategies could you employ to help the members of the group resolve their conflicts and decide on a plan?

4. Conduct separate interviews with the leader and a member of an interdisciplinary team. Ask them to describe how well members of the team get along with each other. Ask specifically about role boundaries and role ambiguity among the members of the team. Also ask about how conflicts and professional rivalries are handled. Compare and contrast the responses of the two individuals you interviewed.

5. Observe a meeting of a community group or organization. How did the group problem solve? How did the group make decisions? How did the leader involve the members in group problem-solving procedures? When faced with alternative solutions, what procedures were used to decide among alternatives?

CHAPTER 11

Task Groups: Specialized Methods

This chapter describes specialized methods for helping organizational and community groups accomplish their goals. The first section is divided into two parts describing methods for helping small and large organizational groups accomplish their objectives during the working stage. A brief introduction to each method is followed by descriptions of the procedures necessary to implement the method, recommended uses of the method, and evidence for the effectiveness of the method.

Most of the methods described in this chapter have been used successfully in social service organizations, as well as in business. However, methods such as quality circles, focus groups, and social judgment analysis have received wider attention in business and industry and are only now being widely adopted in social service organizations. For a comprehensive review of these and other structured problem solving techniques see VanGundy (1988).

The second section of this chapter describes specialized methods for helping community groups accomplish their objectives during the working stage. Although many of the methods described throughout this book may be used to help community groups, this section will emphasize methods that have not been previously described in this text.

SMALL ORGANIZATIONAL GROUPS

Brainstorming

Brainstorming is probably the best known of the specialized methods presented in this chapter. The primary purpose of brainstorming is to increase the generation of ideas and to inhibit critical, judgmental responses that stifle members' willingness to take risks by sharing controversial or socially unacceptable solutions. Elements of brainstorming, such as suspending judgment, have long been recognized as effective techniques, but Osborn (1963) was the first to develop a systematic set of rules for generating creative ideas, which he called *brainstorming*.

During brainstorming, total effort is directed toward creative thinking rather than analytical or evaluative thinking. Analytical and evaluative thinking can reduce ability to generate creative ideas. Members are concerned about their status in a group, and if they expect critical judgments about their thoughts and ideas they are not likely to express them. Analytical and evaluative thinking can also serve as a social control mechanism. Members who continue to present ideas that are viewed critically are likely to be sanctioned. Members may also screen out potentially creative, but controversial, ideas before they are ever expressed. By attempting to reduce analytical and evaluative thinking, brainstorming encourages a "free" disclosure of ideas.

Four rules are used to manage the group's interaction during brainstorming:

1. "Freewheeling" is welcomed. Members are encouraged to express all their ideas no matter what they might be. Members should not hold back on ideas that might be considered wild, repetitious, or obvious.
2. Criticism is ruled out. Members are asked to withhold analyses, judgments, and evaluations about any ideas presented during the idea-generating process. Members should not try to defend or explain their ideas.
3. Quantity is wanted. According to Osborn (1963) and Clark (1958), the more ideas suggested in the allotted time, the better the quality of ideas. Quality will occur by itself if enough ideas are generated.
4. Combining, rearranging, and improving ideas are encouraged. Often called "hitchhiking," this technique calls upon group members to build upon ideas that have already been expressed. Members can combine or modify ideas and suggest how other members' ideas can be improved.

Procedures.   Brainstorming can be conducted in any size of group, although large groups may inhibit idea generation and reduce a member's ability to participate in the allotted time. Because brainstorming encourages the generation of creative and unique ideas, a heterogeneous membership representing many points of view will facilitate the process. The procedure can be conducted in a short period of time (15 minutes) but longer meetings may produce more quality ideas. This occurs because ideas presented in the last third of a group's meeting are often of a higher quality than ideas produced during the first two thirds of the meeting (Stattler & Miller, 1968).

At the beginning of the meeting, the worker explains the problem to be brainstormed and the four basic rules of brainstorming. A warm-up period of 10 to 15 minutes can be used to familiarize members with the procedure and to help them learn to express and hear ideas without criticizing them. During this time, the worker can model appropriate behavior and make some suggestions about procedures, such as lateral thinking, that may increase creativity. Even when some members of the group have used brainstorming procedures previously, the warm-up time gives all members an opportunity to prepare to change routine patterns of analyzing and evaluating ideas. It also allows them to become acclimated to freewheeling idea generation.

During the brainstorming procedure, the leader or co-leader writes the members' ideas on a flip chart or a blackboard. Having a co-leader record ideas is particularly helpful during warm-up sessions, because it is difficult for the leader to train members, record ideas, and model appropriate behavior at the same time. Ideas should be recorded, using the words of the speaker as much as possible.

Key words should be abstracted to reduce suggestions to fit on a sheet of newsprint or a blackboard.

The interaction pattern in the group should encourage the free flow of ideas. Members are asked to offer one idea at a time and to allow everyone to have a turn presenting ideas. Occasionally, it is necessary to limit talkative members by encouraging those who have not contributed extensively to express their ideas. In large groups (more than 15), it has been recommended that members raise their hands before they begin to speak (Scheidel & Crowell, 1979). This procedure also makes it easier to record, because ideas can be clarified more quickly when the recorder's attention is focused on the speaker.

Sometimes groups run out of ideas or repeat similar ideas without pursuing new or alternative thinking patterns. At this point, instead of closing a session, the worker should read ideas from the list to stimulate thinking, focus the group's attention on unexplored areas of the problem, or pick out one or two ideas around which the group may want to generate additional ideas. Throughout the process, the worker should (a) express interest in the ideas as they are presented, (b) urge members to continue to produce creative ideas, and (c) help the group elaborate on ideas that have already been presented.

The worker should not try to have the group evaluate ideas immediately after the brainstorming procedure. Waiting a day or more allows members to think of new ideas to add to the list and allows time for them to return to an analytical way of evaluating ideas. Once the meeting has ended, the worker should ensure that members are not blamed or sanctioned for the ideas they have expressed. If they are, brainstorming will not succeed in future meetings.

Uses.   Brainstorming procedures are very useful under certain conditions. Brainstorming should be done in groups that have already defined a problem. In many respects, brainstorming can be used as a substitute for the methods described in the "developing plans" portion of the problem-solving model described previously. Brainstorming procedures are particularly appropriate if the problem the group is working on is specific and limited in range (Scheidel & Crowell, 1979). It has been shown that the quality of solutions improves in groups that have been instructed to focus on specifically defined problems rather than on broadly defined problems (Davis, Manske, & Train, 1966). Parnes (1967) suggests using "limited critical thinking" rather than "free associating" as recommended by Osborn (1963). This ensures that group members focus their ideas, making them relevant to a specific situation being examined by the group.

Brainstorming can be used in both groups and organizational settings. For example, for a board of directors of a social services agency to begin a search for a new executive director, the board president decides to involve line staff in the hiring process. The president convenes a diverse group of agency staff members to brainstorm ideas about what qualities a new executive director should demonstrate. Members of the brainstorming group are encouraged to think of as many positive qualities as they can, and each is asked to contribute creative ideas. The board president, acting as group leader, prepares a list of ideal qualities or attributes the staff have contributed and presents these to the board of directors for consideration during the search for the new executive director.

Brainstorming methods are useful when the group wants to generate as many ideas as possible. Brainstorming, therefore, should not be used when the group faces a technical problem that requires systematic, organized thinking. Implicit in the brainstorming approach is the notion that the problem can have many solutions (Scheidel & Crowell, 1979). In many situations, groups confront problems that can be solved several ways, but sometimes problems have only one right answer. In these situations, brainstorming is not appropriate, and other rational, structured problem-solving methods such as social judgment analysis or the nominal group technique are more likely to help a group produce the best solution (Toseland & Rivas, 1984).

Effectiveness.   Most of the evidence for the effectiveness of brainstorming is based on anecdotal accounts of its use in business meetings (see, for example, Clark, 1958; Osborn, 1963), but the method has been investigated through empirical research (see, for example, Bayless, 1967; Maltzman, Simon, Raskin, & Licht, 1960; Taylor, Berry, & Block, 1958). Although the Taylor study is often cited to disclaim the effectiveness of brainstorming, this study did not compare brainstorming and nonbrainstorming conditions. Taylor et al. (1958) found that brainstorming produced better results when it was done by individuals working alone than by individuals in a group. Findings from the study suggest that nominal group brainstorming is better than interacting group brainstorming but do not suggest whether group brainstorming is better than a group meeting without brainstorming. Other studies show that when brainstorming is used in a group context, the results are positive (Maltzman et al., 1960; Bayless, 1967). Groups that use brainstorming produce more ideas of a higher quality than groups that do not use this approach (D'Zurilla & Goldfried, 1971). Nominal brainstorming, in which members generate as many ideas as possible without interacting, may be even more effective than brainstorming in interactive groups.

Brainstorming generates ideas from a wide base because it encourages all group members to fully participate. The method also tends to establish members' commitment to the idea that is ultimately decided upon because members have helped shape the idea that is selected. Napier and Gershenfeld (1981) have listed other benefits of brainstorming in groups, including the following:

- Dependence on a single authority figure is reduced.
- Open sharing of ideas is encouraged.
- Members of highly competitive groups can feel safe.
- A maximum output of ideas occurs in a short period of time.
- Members' ideas are posted immediately for everyone to see.
- Ideas are generated internally rather than imposed from outside the group, increasing the feeling of accountability.
- Brainstorming is enjoyable and self-stimulating.

Despite its benefits, brainstorming is not without its drawbacks. It is not easy to achieve an atmosphere in which ideas are generated freely. Brainstorming can initially cause discomfort to those who are not used to freely sharing their ideas (Collaros & Anderson, 1969; Hammond & Goldman, 1961; Vroom, Grant, & Cotton, 1969). The brainstorming procedure breaks norms that ordinarily protect members from making suggestions that may result in overt or covert sanctions (Bouchard, 1972b).

Other factors also may reduce the efficacy of brainstorming procedures. For example, although the warm-up period is essential for optimum performance during brainstorming, warm-ups require time, which may not be available. Inertia may also interfere with brainstorming because the technique requires a change from ordinary group procedures. The worker may not feel justified in imposing the procedure on reluctant or skeptical members who are unaware of its benefits. Although brainstorming has many potentially beneficial effects, if it is to be used effectively, members must be made aware of its usefulness and workers must apply it correctly.

Variations on Brainstorming

Reverse Brainstorming

First proposed by Richards (1974), reverse brainstorming is a procedure that can be used to list the negative consequences of actions quickly and thoroughly. Group members are asked "what might go wrong with this idea?" Reverse brainstorming is useful after a variety of ideas have been generated. Members should first use a scanning procedure such as the one suggested by Etzioni (1968) to reduce a long list of ideas to several alternatives. Members then brainstorm about the consequences of carrying out each alternative. When the group is aware of potential obstacles to solving the problem, the worker then can ask members to suggest ideas for overcoming these obstacles.

Trigger Groups

The trigger group procedure uses the findings of Taylor et al. (1958) and Dunnette, Campbell, and Joastad (1963), who discovered that brainstorming is more effective when it is done by individuals working alone than by individuals interacting in groups. In a trigger group, each individual works alone for five to 10 minutes, developing a list of ideas and suggestions (Richards, 1974). Each member then reads his or her entire list of ideas to the group. The group takes about 10 minutes to clarify, add to, or combine ideas that each member has presented. As in brainstorming, these suggestions are made without criticism. After all members have presented their ideas, the group decides together on criteria for evaluating the ideas. Ideas are then screened by the group, one at a time, to arrive at a single solution to a problem.

Among the benefits of this approach is that it allows members to work independently, developing ideas without verbal or nonverbal evaluative comments from other group members. This avoids some of the difficulties group members may have with presenting their ideas freely in brainstorming groups. At the same time, it focuses the attention of the entire group on the ideas of one individual. This gives members a feeling that their ideas are heard, understood, and carefully examined and gives each member an opportunity to receive constructive comments from all group members. Trigger groups are best when conducted with five to eight members, because the time necessary to develop ideas, to brainstorm, and to critically evaluate each individual's ideas can be prohibitive in larger groups.

Synectics

Synectics is a method for generating creative ideas during problem solving. *Synectics* is a Greek word that means the joining of different and seemingly irrelevant elements. Gordon (1961) developed synectics after years of exploring methods to increase creativity. Prince (1970) added to Gordon's ideas and expanded the method for use in group problem solving.

A synectics meeting lasts about three hours and includes five to eight members with diverse interests and experiences. Much of the meeting follows an ordinary problem-solving sequence. A problem is introduced by the worker and members are encouraged to present their ideas about it. To avoid coercion and intimidation, the worker should not be someone with influence or power over other group members. The worker also should have a neutral view of the problem. A major goal of synectics is to develop a climate of trust in which all ideas are valued. During the preliminary discussion the problem is clarified and specified. The worker's job is to help members reframe the problem by separating it from its usual context, help members present unique ideas without criticism, and help the group refrain from making premature decisions.

As the problem-solving process continues, the worker may notice that members are making predictable noncreative responses to a problem. At a timely point during this discussion, the worker can suggest that the group go on an excursion (Napier & Gershenfeld, 1981). An *excursion* is a method of using analogies to stimulate new ideas. For members who have not participated in synectics meetings before, the worker should begin with a direct analogy that is easy to develop.

A direct analogy is an analogy to something in the environment, and the worker might ask a question such as, "What is there about this problem that's like what is often found in nature?" Other types of analogies include the following:

- Personal analogy: "How would you feel if you were this problem?"
- Symbolic analogy: "What object or thing do you associate with this problem?"
- Fantasy analogy: "Imagine that you could control time—how would you use time to help resolve this problem?"

Such questions can help members develop creative ideas about a problem (Gordon, 1961).

Synectics is an interesting alternative to rational problem-solving approaches, such as social judgment analysis. Although there have been several anecdotal accounts of the effectiveness of synectics (see, for example, Prince, 1970), only one study confirms assertions that groups using this method develop more creative ideas than they would if they used ordinary problem-solving or brainstorming approaches (Bouchard, 1972a).

Others have attempted to discover the processes that encourage creative thinking (see, for example, Parnes & Harding, 1962). They have found that reducing criticism and encouraging the free expression of ideas are useful methods in generating creative ideas. It is unclear, however, whether using analogies during "excursions" further increases the problem-solving ability of task groups. More research should be conducted on synectics and other creative problem-solving methods, such as lateral thinking, to ascertain whether they are viable alternatives for generating creative ideas and effective solutions to problems.

Focus Groups

Focus groups are designed to collect in-depth, qualitative information about a particular service or topic of interest to the managers of an organization. The emphasis is on facilitating members' discussion of a subject until points of agreement and disagreement become clear. The strength of focus groups is their ability to explore topics and generate hypotheses through the explicit use of group interaction (Morgan, 1988). Focus groups are often associated with marketing research where they are used to solicit opinions and reactions to new or existing products. However, within the social sciences, they were used as early as World War II to examine the effectiveness of wartime propaganda (Merton & Kendall, 1946). Since that time, focus groups have been used by health and social service organizations as a qualitative research method to collect information about a variety of topics, but, especially, to assess clients' satisfaction and opinions about particular services.

Procedures.   Focus group meetings consist of a semistructured group interview and discussion with six to 12 group members. Meetings typically last between one and two hours. The worker's task is to gently direct the group to discuss items of interest to the sponsor of the group, probing superficial answers, and encouraging the group to move on when a particular topic appears to be exhausted.

Aaker and Day (1990) have presented four key elements to the success of a focus group: (a) planning a specific agenda, (b) recruiting and screening appropriate participants, (c) effective moderation during meetings, and (d) clear and detailed analysis and interpretation of the results. Planning the agenda begins by carefully considering the purpose for the group and the topics to be covered. Because focus groups are meant to encourage in-depth discussion, it is important to maintain the focus by not exploring too many topics. Next, the worker should develop a series of relevant questions for which responses are sought. From these questions, a discussion guide is prepared. The guide is an outline that helps ensure that specific issues are covered. The discussion guide should proceed in a logical order from general to specific areas of inquiry. Although all topics should be covered, the guide is not meant to be a rigid template for the conduct of group meetings. If a question does not generate useful, nonrepetitive information, the facilitator should move on to the next question or probe. Similarly, new or interesting ideas that emerge from the interaction between members should be pursued.

Careful screening of participants is crucial to the success of a focus group. Focus group participants should be interested in, and have opinions about, the topic to be discussed. They should have enough characteristics in common so that they will feel comfortable interacting. At the same time, to get a broad and in-depth understanding of a subject, it is important to select individuals with a wide range of experience and diverse opinions. Because individuals who have participated in previous focus groups may dominate the discussion, they are generally excluded from participation. Also, it is preferable to recruit individuals who do not know one another. Relatives, friends, and neighbors tend to talk to each other rather than to the whole group, and, because of the presence of individuals they know, they are sometimes less open about their true opinions.

Because positive, freewheeling group interaction can help reticent participants express in-depth opinions and discuss all aspects of a particular topic, effective leadership is essential in focus groups. Aaker and Day (1990) suggest that focus group leaders should have the ability to (a) establish rapport quickly, (b) listen carefully to each member's opinions, (c) demonstrate a genuine interest in each member's views, (d) avoid jargon and sophisticated terminology that may turn off members, (e) flexibly implement the discussion guide, (f) sense when a topic is exhausted or when it is becoming threatening, (g) know what topic to introduce to maintain a smooth flow of the discussion, and (h) facilitate group dynamics that encourage the full participation of all members and avoid domination by talkative members.

Focus groups often yield a wealth of disparate comments and opinions. To prepare reports, and to do qualitative analyses of the data derived from a focus group meeting, it is useful to have an audiotape or videotape of group meetings. Reports of focus group meetings should capture the diverse opinions that are expressed as well as any consensus that is achieved. It also useful to categorize members' comments in a manner that relates them to the specific hypotheses or questions that the focus group was intended to provide data about.

Uses.   Focus groups are often used for (a) generating hypotheses about the way individuals think or behave that may be tested quantitatively at a later point, (b) generating information to help develop client-satisfaction questionnaires, (c) generating or evaluating impressions and opinions about the services an organization offers or plans to offer, (d) overcoming reticence about responding in-depth to a particular topic, and (e) interpreting the results of previous studies (Kinnear & Taylor, 1991; Lehmann, 1989).

Overall, focus groups are particularly well-suited for gathering in-depth data about the attitudes and cognitions of participants (Morgan, 1988). For example, a community mental health agency might be concerned about its effectiveness in reaching Native Americans within its service area. It was decided that one of the agency outreach workers would recruit a focus group composed of local Native American community leaders and explore community perceptions of the mental health center and its services. Following a carefully planned agenda and using a structured interview guide, the group leader helps the focus group members identify their perceptions of the agency and its strengths and weaknesses. The group leader uses information gained during the focus group meeting to design a larger needs assessment research project and to make preliminary recommendations to the agency director for improvements in service delivery procedures.

Because a limited number of participants can be included in focus groups, the data derived may not be as representative of a larger population as data derived from a well-designed survey. Thus, while they are excellent for developing hypotheses, and for exploring issues in-depth, focus groups should not be used as the sole basis for making important decisions effecting a large group of individuals.

Effectiveness.   Much of the data about the effectiveness of focus groups is based on case examples and anecdotal data (Dillon, Madden, & Firtle, 1994). According to Kinnear and Taylor (1991), compared with other procedures for soliciting attitudes and cognitions, focus groups have the following advantages: (a) synergism resulting from interacting group members who produce a wider range of information insight and ideas than individuals who are interviewed alone, (b) snowballing resulting from group members stimulating each other to share their ideas and opinions and express their feelings, (c) security resulting from having others express similar opinions and feelings, and (d) speed resulting from interviewing several individuals together.

Swenson, Griswold, and Kleiber (1992) also indicate that focus groups can have a positive effect on participants. For example, 67 percent of the participants of the focus groups in their study reported continuing to think about the topics raised in the meetings, 67 percent reported that the discussion during the groups affected their thinking, and about 27 percent reported discussing and following up on the issues raised in the focus groups after the meetings had ended. At the same time, Fern (1982) found that individual interviews produced more ideas than focus groups. Byers and Wilcox (1991) and Lederman (1989) found that focus groups were not suitable to many types of data collection, although they did generate rich qualitative data and hypotheses for future exploration.

Most experts agree that the effectiveness of focus groups depends heavily on the moderator's ability to facilitate the discussion. As with any group, the effectiveness of a focus group can be limited by group think, domination by a talkative member, and a host of other problems with group dynamics described in Chapter 3. The interpretation of data from focus groups can also present problems because the small sample of individuals makes it unclear whether the opinions expressed are representative. Also it can be difficult to interpret any sharp discrepancies in group members' views of a particular situation.

Despite these limitations, with adequate preparation and a skillful moderator, focus group interviews can provide an effective and efficient method for collecting in-depth, qualitative data about the thoughts and opinions of consumers of health and social services. For more information about conducting focus groups see Krueger (1988) or Stewart and Shamdasani (1990), and for more information about using focus groups as a qualitative research method see Morgan (1988).

Nominal Group Technique

The nominal group technique (NGT) is different from traditional interacting approaches to solving problems in task groups. The technique was developed by Andre Delbecq and Andrew Van de Ven as they studied program planning groups in social service agencies and the operation of committees and other idea-aggre-gating and decision-making groups in business and industry (Delbecq, Van de Ven, & Gustafson, 1975). The technique has been used extensively since its devel-opment in the late 1960s in health, social service, industrial, educational, and governmental agencies as an aid in planning and managing programs.

Procedures.   An NGT meeting should have between six and nine group mem-bers. Larger groups should be separated into two or more smaller groups. Because participants are required to write, and because ideas are presented on a flip chart, group members should be seated around a table in the shape of a "U." A flip chart with newsprint should be placed at the open end of the "U." Supplies that are needed include a flip chart, a felt-tip pen, a roll of tape, index cards, work sheets, and pencils.

Before an NGT meeting, the worker should develop a clear statement of the problem. According to Delbecq, Van de Ven, and Gustafson (1975), the agency is responsible for deciding on the group's purpose and the problem to be addressed before the meeting. At the beginning of the group, the worker states the purpose of the meeting. Then the worker hands out work sheets (lined paper) with the problem statement written at the top, reads the problem statement and asks all members to take five minutes to list their ideas or responses to the problem. Ideas and responses should be written in brief phrases, without verbal or nonverbal communications with other group members. To give the members some notion of what type of responses are being asked for, workers may want to prepare some sample ideas or responses as models. While group members are working, the leader writes his or her ideas in silence and ensures that members of the group do not interact with one another.

The next step is a round-robin recording of ideas generated by each group member. The ideas are listed on a flip chart that is visible to all group members. The worker asks one member for an idea and writes it on the flip chart. The worker goes around the group, asking each person in turn for one idea. Members are encouraged to "hitchhike," that is, they can use ideas already on the chart to stimulate their thinking, writing ideas on their work sheet that they did not think of during the silent period. When a member has no new ideas, he or she passes and allows the next group member to present an idea until everyone is finished.

The ideas should be recorded as rapidly as possible in the words members use. During the round robin, members should not critique, elaborate on, or defend ideas. Completed sheets from a flip chart should be taped to a flat surface in view of all group members.

The third step is a serial discussion to clarify the ideas that have been pre-sented. Items from the flip chart are taken in order and discussed for two or three minutes. Members who expressed each idea are encouraged to explain briefly the evidence and the logic used in arriving at the idea. At this point, members are free to express their agreement or their disagreement with the idea and to discuss its relative importance. Although evaluative comments are welcome, the group should not be allowed to focus on any one idea for a long period of time or to get into a debate over the merits of a particular idea.

The fourth step is a preliminary ordering of the importance of the ideas that have been listed. Each member is asked to work independently in selecting a predetermined number of highest priority ideas from the list. The number of items selected varies, depending on the length of the list, but should include about one quarter to one half of the original ideas on the list. Each member writes his or her choices on index cards and hands them to the worker. The number of votes that each idea receives from all members is recorded next to that item. This process helps individual members obtain feedback about ideas that are highly regarded by their fellow members.

Each member is then asked to choose five highest priority ideas from the narrowed-down list. The members rank order these ideas from 5 = highest priority to 1 = lowest priority. The idea and its rank order are then placed on an index card. One index card is used for each idea. The cards are collected and the rank orders are tallied by writing them next to their corresponding idea on the flip chart. After all ranks have been tallied, the mean rank for each idea is determined by adding the numbers (ranks) next to each item and dividing by the number of group members.

Delbecq, Van de Ven, and Gustafson (1975) suggest that the group may want to discuss the ranks when (a) there are large discrepancies among members' rating patterns or (b) items that are obviously rated too high or low (in the worker's opinion) appear when the items are tallied. Delbecq, Van de Ven, and Gustafson (1975) claim the resulting discussion and second vote often increase the judgmental accuracy of the group. It is usually the worker or a powerful group member who calls aspects of preliminary votes into question. This may be viewed by less powerful group members as a way to manipulate the group process. Therefore, it is recommended that before beginning NGT, the group as a whole should decide under what circumstances a second vote should be taken.

Uses.   NGT was created to "increase rationality, creativity, and participation in problem-solving meetings associated with program planning" (Delbecq, Van de Ven, & Gustafson, 1975, p. 1). In a brief review of the literature on small groups, Van de Ven and Delbecq (1971) identified eight inhibiting influences on the performance of interacting groups:

1. A focus effect in which interacting groups pursue a single thought pattern for long periods.
2. Members participate only to the extent that they feel equally competent as other members.
3. Covert judgments are made but not expressed as overt criticism.
4. The inhibiting effect of status differentials within a group.
5. Group pressure for conformity resulting from sanctions by "expert" group members.
6. Influence of dominant personalities upon the group.
7. Too much time and energy spent on maintaining the interacting group rather than to work on the task.
8. Members' tendencies to reach quick decisions without fully exploring the problem.

By combining the positive aspects of noninteracting nominal groups and interacting problem-solving groups, Delbecq, Van de Ven, and Gustafson (1975) developed NGT. According to Van de Ven and Delbecq (1971), NGT does the following:

- Stimulates activity through the presence of others and by everyone working in silence.
- Avoids evaluative comments when the problem dimensions are being formed.
- Provides each member an opportunity to search his or her own thought processes.
- Avoids dominance by strong personalities.
- Prevents premature decision making.
- Encourages all members to participate.
- Allows minority opinions to be expressed.
- Tolerates conflicting and incompatible ideas that are written in silence before they are presented to the entire group.
- Eliminates hidden agendas.
- Gains members' cooperation in achieving a solution.
- Structures the process so that members feel obligated to work on the problem.

As an example of the effective use of NGT, consider the case of a multiservice agency facing financial crisis. The executive council charged with tightening the budget uses NGT to generate ideas for saving money. The executive director leads her executive council in this effort by first asking that each member work alone and write down his or her creative ideas for saving money in the budget. In round-robin fashion, each member presents one idea at a time to the group until all ideas are presented and recorded on a flip chart. Next, the executive director leads a limited discussion of the suggested savings measures, discussing the pros and cons of each suggestion. After this process, she asks each member to again work independently to rank each item in order of its value to the savings effort. Selecting the most frequently mentioned suggestions she asks members to choose the five best alternatives. She computes the five highest priority suggestions and uses these to initiate plans for budget savings at the agency.

NGT can be used to create a long list of ideas or alternative solutions to a problem. Scheidel and Crowell (1979) suggest that it produces more ideas than any of the other idea-generating and problem-solving techniques they reviewed. NGT can also be used as a consensus-building technique because each group member is given an equal opportunity to express ideas and participate in reaching a decision. By structuring the interaction, NGT reduces the domination of a few members and makes full use of the creative capabilities and pooled wisdom of all group members. This, in turn, helps to ensure a broad base of support for any decision made by the group.

Effectiveness.   The NGT procedure is based on social science findings about task groups that have been accumulated over decades of research. Each step is designed to make use of these findings. Delbecq, Van de Ven, and Gustafson (1975) report that research findings indicate the following procedures increase judgmental accuracy in decision making:

1. Having members make independent judgments.
2. Expressing judgments mathematically by rank ordering or rating items.
3. Using the arithmetic mean of independent judgments to form the group's decision.
4. Having members make decisions anonymously.
5. Using feedback about preliminary judgments for final voting.

NGT uses these research findings in its decision-making step by taking the mean rating of independent rank order judgments that have been placed on anonymous index cards. Similarly, scientific evidence is the basis for each step in the NGT procedure. Reliance on scientific evidence in developing NGT has apparently worked. Overall, the empirical evidence supports contentions that NGT is more effective than interacting group methods for idea generation, problem solving and consensus building (see, for example, Toseland, Rivas, & Chapman, 1984; Van de Ven, 1974). Some recent evidence indicates that social judgment analysis may be as good as NGT in problem resolution and better than NGT in producing group consensus (Rohrbaugh, 1981), but other evidence (Toseland, Rivas, & Chapman, 1984) does not confirm these findings.

NGT does have some drawbacks. The method is cumbersome. It takes a considerable amount of time (at least one and one half hours), which may not be available to a task group that must complete its work in a short time. This is especially true for routine decisions that may not require the precision afforded by this method. Also, the worker has to be trained in the method and equipped with the necessary supplies to conduct an NGT meeting.

A seemingly inconsequential, though often important, drawback of NGT is that the group process is highly structured, which members may find unpleasant. One study found that members of NGT groups were less satisfied than members of less structured discussion groups (Toseland, Rivas, & Chapman, 1984). Initially members may be suspicious that they are being manipulated. Aspects of NGT tend to exacerbate rather than quell these fears. For example, having the worker rather than group members define the problem, and having the worker or a powerful group member influence voting procedures by calling for a second vote both can undermine members' feeling of freedom in solving a problem. Despite these drawbacks, NGT can help task groups generate ideas and solve difficult problems effectively. Some evidence, however, suggests there is no clearly superior solution to task group problem solving under all problem circumstances (Fischer, 1981; Hackman & Morris, 1975). If this finding is correct, then the shorter and more familiar generic problem-solving model may be preferred over NGT in some situations.

Social Judgment Analysis

Whereas NGT structures the method used in problem-solving groups to maximize beneficial group dynamics, social judgment analysis (SJA) focuses on the content of the interactions in a group. SJA structures the group only to the extent that participants are given a method for using information about a problem. SJA uses decision rules to specify the relationship between attributes of a problem. These decision rules, often called multi-attribute utility models, are used to maximize the utility of decisions made by task groups.

SJA is based on the cognitive social judgment theory of Tolman (1932) and Brunswick (1943). Tolman and Brunswick (1935) suggest that to integrate information and come up with a decision individuals will (a) place a certain amount of importance on each piece of information (a weight), (b) develop a specific functional relationship (functional form) for each piece of information, and (c) use an organizing principle to interpret all pieces of information about a problem. A similar process for making judgments has been pointed out more recently by Hammond, McClelland, and Mumpower (1980). They suggest that group members (a) obtain whatever pieces of information they can find, (b) weight each piece of information in terms of its importance or value, and (c) organize the weighted information in some way to arrive at a decision. SJA uses these findings in its approach to decision making in task groups.

Procedures.   SJA begins by having each member work alone. This can be done either in individual meetings between each member and the worker or in a nominal group meeting where all members work separately on instructions given by the worker. During this time, the problem and its alternative solutions are explained to members. For example, members are informed that their group has been appointed to decide among applicants for the position of assistant program director. The worker helps group members clarify their thinking about the problem. Specifically, the worker helps each member determine the attributes that are thought to be relevant to making a decision, the "levels" of each attribute, and how attributes are weighted in relationship to one another. A member decides that the attributes she considers important for the position of assistant program director include (a) amount of supervisory experience, (b) amount of clinical experience, (c) level of management skills, and (d) extent that the candidate likes to develop new and innovative service programs.

The worker also helps each member specify the levels of each attribute that members have identified. This is done by specifying minimal criteria for the solution, any constraints on the solution, and the functional form of each attribute. For example, members decide that minimal criteria for the assistant program director's position include three years of supervisory experience and five years of clinical experience. The members also decide that the candidate must have an MSW or an MPA degree.

The functional form of an attribute specifies the attribute's relationship to the overall solution—that is, how levels of an attribute are related to the choice of a particular solution. Figure 11–1 gives one member's functional forms for the four attributes mentioned previously. The functional forms indicate that as the amount of supervisory experience increases, satisfaction with the candidate (the utility of choosing a particular candidate) increases until the candidate has more than 10 years of experience, at which time the member's satisfaction with the candidate declines. At this point, the member thinks a candidate may have too much supervisory experience for the position.

FIGURE 11–1
A group member's decision rules for choosing among applicants for assistant program director

Constraints = MSW or MPA degree
Minimum Criteria = 3 years of supervisory experience, 5 years of clinical experience

Weight

30

Satisfaction with Candidate

Supervisory Experience

Weight

10

Satisfaction with Candidate

Clinical Experience

Weight

40

Satisfaction with Candidate

Management Skills

Weight

20

Satisfaction with Candidate

Interest in Innovation

For the clinical experience attribute, a similar functional form occurs except that satisfaction with a candidate increases until the candidate has more than 15 years of clinical experience. For the management skills attribute, a straight linear relationship exists, suggesting that the higher the score on a management skills test and interview, the higher the satisfaction with the candidate. In the case of developing innovative programs, a curvilinear relationship is present, that is, candidates who are either low or high on this attribute are less preferred than candidates who have moderate inclination to develop new programs.

Figure 11–1 also shows the weight that a group member gave to each attribute. Weights can be assigned by dividing 100 points among all attributes in a manner that reflects the relative importance of each in relation to the others. In Figure 11–1 the management skills attribute is assigned a weight of 40, making it four times as important as clinical experience, which has been assigned a weight of 10.

The procedure of establishing minimal criteria, constraints, and attributes with their weights and functional forms is the basis of a member's decision rule, that is, how a group member will use information about a problem to make a judgment. Each member develops his or her own decision rules. When all members have completed this task, they share their decision rules with each other. It is helpful for the worker to post each member's decision rules side by side on a flip chart or blackboard so that all members can see how their decision rules compare.

The next step in SJA is to have members discuss the logic behind their decision rules. During this unstructured discussion, the only rule is to focus on the reasoning behind the choice of attributes, weights, and functional forms (Edwards, 1977; Harmon & Rohrbaugh, 1990; Huber, 1980; Rohrbaugh, 1979, 1981). For example, members would not be allowed to discuss individual candidates for the position, but would be encouraged to discuss why a member gave management skills four times the weight of clinical experience when considering candidates for this particular job.

Members discuss the decision rules until they agree on a common group rule that satisfies all members. Consensus is usually not difficult to reach because members find it easier to agree on how information will be used than about specific alternatives. Once a group decision rule has been decided upon, it is a routine procedure to see how each alternative is ranked on the basis of the decision rule. First, alternatives that do not meet the criteria or the constraints set up by the decision rule are eliminated. The next step is to calculate each alternative's score on the decision rule. Each score is multiplied by that attribute's weight, and the total score is summed across each attribute. A total score on each alternative is calculated. The alternative (in this case, a candidate) that is rated the highest based on the decision rule is the one selected by the group as its final decision.

Uses.   SJA has been used in a variety of settings including business, industry, urban planning, health, and mental health (see, for example, Edwards, 1977; Huber, 1980; Rohrbaugh, 1984; Rohrbaugh & Harmon, 1981). SJA is used primarily as a decision-making technique for choosing among distinct alternatives and should not be used for generating ideas.

Although Rohrbaugh (1979, 1981) has shown that SJA is better than other group methods in achieving consensus, other evidence does not confirm these findings (see, for example, Toseland, Rivas, & Chapman, 1984). SJA tends to enhance commitment and support for decisions made by the group. This is particularly important in groups that face difficult choices between alternatives. By providing for a thorough discussion of each individual's decision rules, rather than the more traditional discussion of alternative choices, the group achieves consensus about how information will be used to make a decision. This type of discussion also helps eliminate the polarization that often takes place when members try to defend their choices of alternative solutions. Once the group decides on a decision rule, all alternatives are rated according to that rule. Because members have had a chance to influence the decision rule, the choice that is made by the group reflects the input of all members and, therefore, is likely to have the cooperation and commitment of all members when it is implemented.

Effectiveness.   SJA is the most rational and technical method discussed in this chapter for leading task groups. It attempts to order and systematize information by assigning each piece of information a weight and a functional relationship to the overall decision. Empirical evidence about this approach (Edwards, 1977; Harmon & Rohrbaugh, 1990; Huber, 1980; Rohrbaugh, 1979, 1981) suggests that it can be helpful as an analytical tool in making decisions based on the information available in a problematic situation. Rohrbaugh (1979, 1981) also found that SJA is more effective than both interacting group methods and NGT in developing group consensus and commitment to a decision. Recent research by Toseland, Rivas, and Chapman (1985) suggests that SJA is better than NGT or problem solving in producing consistent high-quality decisions.

The primary drawback to SJA is that it is a complicated method limited to making decisions between clear, established alternatives. When decisions between clearly delineated alternatives are crucial and consensus is important, SJA should be considered the method of choice for problem-solving groups. SJA should be used only by a trained worker who has some conceptual as well as practical experiences in developing decision rules. SJA is not useful for generating ideas or alternative solutions, but can be used once alternatives have been developed by other methods (see, for example, Rohrbaugh, 1984). For further information about this relatively recent approach to decision making in problem-solving groups, see Huber (1980, especially, Chapter 5), or write Executive Decision Services Inc., P.O. Box 9102, Albany, N.Y. 12209-0102.

Quality Circles and Quality Improvement Teams

Although quality circles (QCs) and quality improvement teams (QITs) are associated with business and industry, they are now used widely in social service and health organizations. QCs are small groups of line employees from the same department who get together voluntarily, elect a leader, and identify and solve problems they have in completing their work assignments. In the United States, the idea behind QCs is to encourage line workers to get together and use their brains as well as their hands to produce a quality product (Robson, 1982). Management intent, however, was not only to improve quality, but also to prevent workers from becoming alienated from the process and place of their work.

QIT is a newer concept that has evolved from Total Quality Management. In contrast to QCs, QITs frequently consist of employees from different organizational levels and a variety of departments or functions within the organization. Members are often selected by management, and membership on the team is required. Also, the project the team works on is often selected, and almost always approved, by management (Berry, 1991).

There are frequent misconceptions about the origins of quality circles, and their original purposes. Although they are often associated with Japanese business, the American quality control expert Dr. W. E. Deming taught statistical quality control techniques and the value of cooperation to workers during World War II (Walton, 1990). The concept was not received well in the United States. However, after World War II, Japanese business became increasingly interested in statistical quality control, and found Dr. Deming's ideas appealing. Later, when his ideas were reintroduced in the United States during the 1970s, less emphasis was placed on statistical quality control, and more emphasis was placed on the socio-emotional and participatory aspects of QC (see, for example, Cole & Tachiki, 1983; Seely & Sween, 1983). Today, however, QCs and QITs are encouraged to rely on data from statistical quality control procedures (see, for example, Kinlaw, 1992; Shuster, 1990).

Procedures.   An organization generally has a coordinator for all QC activities. This individual's role is to ensure that (a) training is provided, (b) there is coverage when facilitators are sick or take personal leave, (c) each circle has a way of communicating their suggestions about problem solving to top level management.

Each QC consists of six to eight employees who meet for about one hour each week with the purpose of identifying and solving problems facing their department or work group. A facilitator is selected by the membership. Often this individual is a mid-level manager who serves as the link between the QC and upper management. To ensure that QCs run smoothly and effectively, facilitators should be trained in group dynamics and leadership skills. During meetings, the facilitator uses group dynamics, as well as problem solving, brainstorming, and other procedures previously described in this text to facilitate an in-depth discussion and analysis of the topic or issue being addressed by the group.

There are few specific "procedures" for the operation of QCs. Rather, they operate on the basis of core principles, including (a) commitment from top-level management to the process, (b) a commitment to providing training for staff in QC process, problem-solving and statistical control procedures, (c) voluntary membership in QC groups, (d) a focus on problems identified by workers, not management, (e) the selection of leadership and the ownership of the QC process by line staff, (f) a focus on data-based problem solving, and (g) a focus on solving problems in ways that benefit both line workers and management.

According to Kinlaw (1992), QITs use the following steps for quality improvement: (a) understanding the opportunity or problem, (b) defining the specific improvement target, (c) designing strategies to reach the target, (d) designing data-acquiring strategies, (e) designing a process to use the data, and (f) determining how the project will be managed. Whereas QCs are often used for idea generation and for improving the work environment, QITs place more emphasis on systematic data-based problem-solving strategies for improving the quality of services delivered by an organization.

Uses.   The primary purpose of QCs and QITs is to improve the quality of the service or product delivered to consumers. Thus, QCs and QITs are one way for management and line staff to demonstrate their commitment to delivering health and social services in the most effective manner. For example, in a multiservice agency serving developmentally disabled adults, members of the nursing staff form a QIT to monitor the health-care program for their clients who live in community group residences. The nursing director asks the group to study the rate of medication errors made in the residences and to make suggestions for reducing the error rate. The QIT leader helps the group design a research study to determine the error rate and the group helps design a new system for medication distribution which significantly reduces error. After three months, the QIT notes that medication errors have been reduced by 50 percent.

QCs and QITs have several other benefits. They encourage workers to solve problems that interfere with job satisfaction and their performance. They help workers gain a greater sense of control and autonomy. In turn, workers may have more of a sense of responsibility and commitment to their work.

Effectiveness.   Many writers have claimed that QCs improve productivity, quality, and employee attitudes. For example, Goldstein (1985) suggests that in addition to quality improvements, QCs have been reported to have:

> . . . increased productivity, raised level of morale, increased employee motivation, improved communication, changed the emphasis from fire fighting to prevention, enhanced the commitment to job and organization, reduced reliance on authority to get things done, reduced costs, reduced delivery times, developed people, trained leaders and supervisors, introduced an orientation toward learning, enhanced the coordination of work, and reduced vertical and horizontal demarcations over ownership of problems. (p. 514)

Despite these assertions, findings about the effectiveness of QCs and QITs are equivocal. While some studies have found a strong correlation between participatory management systems and the quality and quantity of the work produced, other studies have found little correlation (Gummer, 1988). In reviews of studies of QC performance, Adam (1991) and Barrick and Alexander (1987) found that most studies revealed that quality circle programs result in improved quality and efficiency of services, and the reduction of production costs and unpleasant working conditions. However, with some noticeable exceptions (see, Marks, Mirvis, Hackett, & Grady, 1986), QCs were not effective in improving employee's attitudes, or reducing staff turnover, absenteeism, or tardiness. Overall, therefore, Adam (1991) tentatively concluded that QCs are effective in improving services, but are not effective in improving worker attitudes and morale.

Despite positive findings about the improved efficiency of services, Lawler and Mohrman (1985) report that managers' initial enthusiasm for quality circles is often dampened when they try to document savings from early quality circle ideas. To avoid QCs and QITs becoming fads that end after initial enthusiasm wanes, Lawler and Mohrman (1985) suggest they might best be viewed as part of a larger organizational effort to move toward a more participatory management system.

Also, for QCs and QITs to have a lasting effect on an organization there must be a commitment to them from all levels of management, and they must be compatible with the organization's work culture. For example, in a study of the use of QCs in state government, Denhardt, Pyle and Bluedorn (1987) concluded that in many departments employees had never been asked to consider how their work processes might be improved. Smith and Doeing (1985) point out that as contrasted to American managers, Japanese managers often also take a longer-term perspective on the development of employees. Thus, making a meaningful shift to participatory management styles that include QCs or QITs is a slow process that takes a long-term and concerted commitment at all levels of an organization.

LARGE ORGANIZATIONAL GROUPS

Parliamentary Procedure

Parliamentary procedure is a framework for guiding decision making and problem solving in large task groups. It has been developed over time in many different settings to meet the needs of a variety of task groups. Although there are some commonly accepted rules, there is no single body of laws that is universally accepted as parliamentary procedure.

Parliamentary procedure originated in 1321 in the English Parliament as a set of rules called "modus tenedia Parlia-mentarium" (Gray, 1964). From these roots, Thomas Jefferson developed a *Manual of Parliamentary Practice* in 1801 for use in Congress, and Luther Cushing formulated a manual for use in lay, as well as legislative, assemblies in 1845 (Robert, 1970). *Robert's Rules of Order* was initially published in 1876 and has had many subsequent revisions and printings. Today, Robert's rules are the set of parliamentary procedures most frequently followed by task groups.

Procedures.   In parliamentary meetings, the activity of the group is determined by motions brought by group members. Motions fall into one of four classes:

1. **Privileged motions** deal with the agenda of the group meeting as a whole. They do not have a relationship with the business before the group and include motions such as adjournment and recess.

2. **Incidental motions** are concerned with procedural questions relating to issues "on the floor." Some examples include a "point of order" or a "point of information."
3. **Subsidiary motions** assist in the handling and disposal of motions on the floor. Motions to table, postpone, or amend are subsidiary motions.
4. **Main motions** introduce the central, substantive issues for group consideration. There can be no pending motions when a main motion is proposed. Examples of main motions include reconsideration of an issue previously disposed of and resuming consideration of a tabled motion.

All motions made from the floor follow procedures governing the introduction of that type of motion. It is the chairperson's job to ensure that these rules and procedures are followed. Although the chairperson is supposed to remain neutral during group deliberations, he or she can influence the group's work in a variety of ways. Group members must be recognized by the chair before they can make a motion. The chairperson rules on questions of procedure that arise during a meeting and also organizes the meeting by ordering the agenda items and specifying the amount of time available to discuss each item.

Although the rules of parliamentary procedure are not universally standardized, that is, groups often modify a set of procedures such as *Robert's Rules of Order*, there is a method of prioritizing motions that is adhered to by most groups conducting parliamentary meetings. Table 11–1 shows the priority that each motion takes during a meeting. Although main motions contain the essential business of the parliamentary meeting, they receive the lowest priority. This is because privileged motions govern how all agenda items are considered, and incidental and subsidiary motions are always made in reference to a main motion. Therefore, these motions are given a higher priority than main motions. For further information about parliamentary meetings, see *Robert's Rules of Order* (Robert, 1970).

Uses.   Parliamentary procedure is often used in large groups because it provides a well-defined structure to guide group process. The rules of parliamentary procedure help ensure a high level of order and efficiency in task group meetings when many agenda items are discussed. Order and efficiency are achieved through rules that demand consideration of one issue at a time. They prescribe the way in which issues are brought before the group, processed by the group, and disposed of by the group. In a meeting of a delegate council composed of representatives from many social service agencies, for example, parliamentary procedure can be used to lend order to how representatives interact. Thus, with many members representing the diverse interests of several agencies, meetings are run in a formal manner and members are generally guaranteed a structured means by which they can bring their interests, motions and agenda items to the large group.

Parliamentary procedure is especially useful for considering well-developed agenda items that need some discussion and debate and a relatively speedy decision by an entire task group (Gulley, 1968). Parliamentary procedure is of limited value, however, when a problem or issue facing the group has not been clearly

TABLE 11–1
Procedures for acting on motions during a parliamentary meeting

Type of Motion	Priority of the Motion	Can the Speaker Be Interrupted?	Does the Motion Need a Second?	Is the Motion Debatable?	Can the Motion Be Amended?	Vote Needed to Adopt the Motion
Privileged Motions						
Set the time of adjournment	1	N	Y	N	Y	Majority
Call for adjournment	2	N	Y	N	N	Majority
Call for recess	3	N	Y	N	Y	Majority
Question of privilege	4	Y	N	N	N	Chair's decision
Call for pre-scheduled items of business	5	Y	N	N	N	No vote
Incidental Motions						
Point of order	6	Y	N	N	N	Chair's decision
Request for information	6	Y	N	N	N	No vote
Call for a re-vote	6	N	N	N	N	No vote
Appeal the chair's decision	6	Y	Y	N	N	Majority
Object to consideration of a motion	6	Y	N	N	N	2/3
Call to suspend the rules	6	N	Y	N	N	2/3
Request to withdraw a motion	6	Y	Y	N	N	Majority

Subsidiary Motions						
Table a motion	7	N	Y	N	N	Majority
Call for immediate vote	8	N	Y	N	N	2/3
Limit/extend debate	9	N	Y	N	N	2/3
Postpone the motion	10	N	Y	Y	Y	Majority
Refer the motion to a subcommittee	11	N	Y	Y	Y	Majority
Amend the motion	12	N	Y	Y	Y	Majority
Postpone the motion indefinitely	13	N	Y	Y	N	Majority
Main Motions						
General main motion	14	N	Y	Y	Y	Majority
Reconsider a motion already voted on	14	Y	Y	Y	Y	2/3
Rescind a motion under consideration	14	N	Y	Y	Y	2/3
Resume consideration of a tabled motion	14	N	Y	N	N	Majority
Set a special order of business	14	N	Y	Y	Y	2/3

defined, when sufficient data have not been gathered about the problem, or when alternative solutions have not been explored and developed for consideration during decision making. Thus, these procedures should not be used as a substitute for problem solving done by subcommittees of the larger task group.

Effectiveness.   The long history of using parliamentary procedure in important decision-making bodies throughout the Western world testifies to its usefulness in providing a structure for task group meetings. By limiting and focusing the deliberations of a task group to one solution at a time, discussion and debate are facilitated and motions are dealt with expeditiously. Clearly specified rules lead to an orderly and systematic consideration of each agenda item. Rules that remain consistent throughout the life of a group assure members that there is an established order that they can rely on for fair and equitable treatment when sensitive or controversial issues are presented.

Parliamentary procedure also protects the rights of the minority. For example, it takes only two members to introduce a main motion, one to state the motion and another to second the motion. Some motions can be made by a single member. Every group member is given an equal opportunity to participate. Majority rights are also protected because a quorum is needed to conduct a meeting and majority rule is relied upon for all decisions.

Parliamentary meetings have several disadvantages. Meetings are subject to manipulation by those who are familiar with parliamentary procedures. Members who are less familiar with the procedures may be reluctant to speak or unsure of when or how to raise an objection to a motion. Another limitation is that private deals may be made outside of a meeting to gain a member's support for an agenda item in a forthcoming meeting. Private deals circumvent the intent of parliamentary procedure, which is based on openly debating the merits of a proposal. Private deals also tend to enforce the will of powerful members who offer attractive incentives to members who support their position on particular agenda items.

Parliamentary meetings have other limitations. The procedure encourages debate, which can lead to polarization of members' opinions. Also, members often try to defend their positions rather than understand the logic behind opposing viewpoints. Perhaps the most important limitation of parliamentary procedure is that it is not well suited for problem solving, especially when the problem is complex, muddled, or not fully understood. A large task group using parliamentary procedure does not usually attain the level of interaction, the depth of communication, or the flexibility necessary to explore alternative solutions that may be necessary to resolve difficult problems. Large task groups should conduct most of their problem-solving efforts in subcommittees which report back to the larger group. The larger group can then debate the merits of a proposed solution and reach a decision based on majority rule.

Phillips' 66

Phillips' 66, or "buzz group," as the method is often called, was developed to facilitate discussion in large groups (Phillips, 1948). Originally, Phillips' 66 referred to a technique of dividing a large group or audience into groups of six and having each group spend six minutes formulating one question for the speaker. The method has been expanded to include many different ways to facilitate communication in large groups. For example, Maier and Zerfoss (1952) suggest using multiple role-playing strategies for training staff in large groups. Members of the larger group are asked to form smaller groups and role play the same or similar situations. Each group designates a recorder who reports a summary of group members' experiences when the large group reconvenes.

Other variations have also been developed. Bradford and Corey (1951) have suggested organizing audience listening teams in which each team is asked to listen to, discuss, and report back to the larger group about an aspect of the speaker's presentation. They have also suggested selecting individuals from the audience to serve on an "audience representational panel" to react to the speaker. All of these techniques are modifications and expansions of the basic principles of Phillips' 66.

Procedures.   In our experiences in facilitating large group meetings, we have found that Phillips' 66 should only be used after clear instructions are given to members about what they will be doing during the procedure. This is especially important because once the large group has broken down into smaller groups, the sudden change from the structure and control of a large group meeting can cause confusion. If the groups are not clear about their direction, they may flounder or begin to work on something other than what was assigned by the leader.

To reduce the chances for confusion, the worker should ensure that each group is clear about the problem or task they are facing. Problem statements, tasks, and goals should be specific. When they are broad and nonspecific, the small groups will have to spend time refining them. Further, this refinement may lead to work that is quite different from what the worker had intended. Members should also be clear about their assignments. They should understand what subgroup they belong to, what the group is supposed to do, what should be contained in the recorder's report, how much time they have, and where and when they are supposed to meet.

The size of the subgroups and the amount of time each subgroup spends together depends on the situation. The original design for Phillips' 66, six member groups meeting for six minutes, may be appropriate in some situations but not in others. Generally, at least 20 to 30 minutes are required for a large group to break down into smaller groups and accomplish any meaningful work. Subgroups should be separated so members can hear each other and conduct their work. However, in a large meeting room it is not necessary to ask members to talk quietly. The noise and activity of other groups can be contagious, spurring all groups to work harder (Maier, 1963).

In very large meetings, having each subgroup report back to the larger group may be monotonous and time consuming. Alternatives include limiting the reporting time to a few minutes for each subgroup, having each subgroup report on a portion of the discussion, or developing a brief written report prepared by each subgroup that can be shared after the meeting.

Uses. Although most problem-solving activities take place in small task groups, occasionally there is a need for large groups such as members of a social agency or a delegate assembly to engage in problem-solving discussions. Parliamentary procedure, in which the chair must recognize individual speakers from the floor, is not designed for large problem-solving discussions. It is designed for debating the merits of proposals and voting on alternatives that are already well developed. Phillips' 66 can be used as an alternative method for problem solving in large task groups. For example, during an in-service training program covering management skills, the group trainer asks the large group to divide into smaller groups and answer the question "What makes a good manager?" Members of the small groups work to develop a short list of answers to this question within a limited period of time. When the large group reconvenes, each group reports its answers, and this material is used by the trainer in the didactic presentation and in group discussion following the presentation.

Although Maier (1963) suggests that a skillful, self-confident worker can conduct large problem-solving discussions by using techniques such as summarizing and posting alternatives, the obstacles to large group interaction tend to make such discussions difficult. For example, it may be difficult for the worker to maintain order and encourage participation while helping the larger group work on a problem. It is also difficult to encourage shy members to express themselves, particularly if they have minority opinions.

Using Phillips' 66, the worker can involve all members in a group discussion. The small size of individual buzz groups makes it easier for shy members to express themselves. Reporting ideas generated by individual buzz groups back to the larger assembly ensures that input from all members is considered in the problem-solving process. Overall, Phillips' 66 is a useful method that overcomes the limitations of parliamentary procedure when large groups are called upon to solve problems.

Effectiveness. Phillips' 66 is a practical, common-sense procedure for facilitating discussion and problem solving in large groups. Its effective use has been reported in a variety of sources (see, for example, Gulley, 1968; Maier, 1963; Stattler & Miller, 1968). When it is applied correctly, it can be used in a variety of situations. However, poor planning, confused or nonspecific instructions, or a muddled explanation of the goals of the procedure can turn a large task group meeting into disorganization and chaos.

METHODS FOR WORKING WITH COMMUNITY GROUPS

Work with community groups such as social action groups, coalitions, and delegate councils involves many of the methods and skills described throughout this text. For example, community groups frequently use brainstorming and other problem-solving methods to generate ideas and address issues during meetings. Work with community groups is distinguished from other forms of group work practice by special emphasis on the following: (a) mobilizing individuals to engage in collective action, (b) building the capacity of the group and its members to effect community change, and (c) planning and organizing social action strategies. The remainder of this chapter focuses on these three aspects of practice with community groups.

Mobilization Strategies

Whether working with social action groups, coalitions, or delegate councils, a primary task of the worker is to mobilize individual members to action. The worker is a catalyst, stimulating interest in community problems and motivating members to work together. When engaging in mobilization efforts, the worker identifies and works with several constituencies including the individuals who are experiencing the problem, community leaders, informal and formal community groups and organizations, and larger social institutions. For example, to mobilize a coalition to prevent domestic violence a worker meets with victims of domestic violence, women's groups, the staff of domestic violence shelters, dispute resolution centers, police departments, family courts, and departments of social services, as well as with ministers, priests, rabbis, and local politicians.

An important initial step in any mobilization effort is to become familiar with the perceptions of community members concerning the issues the community group will attempt to address. It is often helpful to begin by meeting with civic and religious leaders, and community activists. These individuals can provide a helpful overview of the community's past responses to the issue, and to similar issues. However, it is also essential to meet with as many community residents as possible.

Kahn (1982) notes that person-to-person contact with community residents helps build community groups and organizations in which each member feels valued. When meeting with community residents, the worker should avoid telling them why they should be concerned about a particular issue or problem. A more effective strategy is to ask them to describe their problems and concerns, validating and affirming the issues they raise by mentioning how they are consistent with those of other community residents. In this way, community residents will begin to get a sense that it is their issues, not the worker's issues, that will be addressed through collective action.

As the worker becomes familiar with the community, he or she should identify individuals, community groups, and organizations who might be willing to help with mobilization efforts. To determine the extent to which individuals, groups, and organizations can help, the worker should evaluate their position within the power structure of the community. The worker should then consider how forming a partnership with particular individuals and groups may help or hinder mobilization efforts. Often, the worker will decide to form partnerships with a wide range of individuals, community leaders, and organizations. However, the worker should also be careful about involving individuals or organizations who do not share compatible goals, or who have such a negative reputation in the community that they might damage the group's effort.

Mobilization involves consciousness raising. Working with individual citizens, community leaders, and formal and informal organizations, the worker attempts to bring a single issue, or a group of related issues, to greater public awareness. This may be done several ways, including (a) meeting with community residents; (b) making presentations to civic and religious organizations; (c) testifying at public hearings; (d) publicizing the issue through local newspapers and radio and television stations; and (e) demonstrating, picketing, and boycotting. The goal of these consciousness-raising efforts is to encourage community members to gain a renewed sense of individual and community pride, and to join forces to improve their community.

Mobilization to action involves helping members understand the power of collective action against injustices and inequities. Helping individuals vent their frustration and anger "through public declarations, and by acting against those causing the problem" (Rubin & Rubin, 1992, p. 69) can sometimes resolve individual problems. However, individual actions are easily ignored, dismissed, or punished by those in power. Therefore, the goal of the worker should be to help individuals understand the value of pooling their efforts so they can exert sufficient influence to effect change.

One way to accomplish this is to highlight the incentives for collective action. Individuals will become actively involved in a community group if they think they have something to gain, if they think they can contribute, and if they believe in the goals of the group. According to Rubin and Rubin (1992), the worker can highlight a variety of incentives, including "material incentives like improved income or better housing, solidarity incentives such as the enjoyment of belonging to the group, and expressive incentives including the excitement and satisfaction of articulating opinions and values" (p. 211).

Mobilization to action also involves "bootstrapping," that is, engaging in action projects that build interest and commitment in a community (Rubin & Rubin, 1992). A good way to begin bootstrapping is to identify a project or activity that is relatively easy to accomplish and leads to an immediate success. For example, a social action group, a coalition, or even a delegate council might sponsor a community forum to which they invite local politicians and the news media. Similarly, a "community education day" might be planned at a shopping mall, a "teach in" might be scheduled at a school, or a rally might be organized in a public square. Later, when members have experienced the initial successful completion of a project, they can be encouraged to tackle larger projects, such as a community survey or an extensive lobbying effort, that require more effort and resources.

Capacity Building Strategies

Capacity building means helping community groups develop the ability and the resources to successfully tackle an issue, or a set of issues. The worker plays the role of a coordinator, helping members gather data and build resources. A first step in capacity building is to help group members become as knowledgeable as possible about the issues they are addressing. Workers should facilitate exchanges of information among members about the issues facing the group and about ways to accomplish particular objectives.

In many instances, the worker and the members will not have enough information about a problem. In these situations, the worker should encourage the group to gather data before proceeding. Original data can be gathered through community surveys or focused interviews with key informants. The worker might also help members gain access to public records and reports. For example, in helping to organize a neighborhood association, (a) city building department files could be used to gather data on building-code violations, (b) police department records could be used to collect data on the number and type of crimes in a particular neighborhood, (c) the county clerk's office could be used to gather data on property ownership, and (d) the department of public welfare or the local community development agency could be used to obtain estimates of poverty rates.

A second step in capacity building involves helping the group become familiar with the structures within a community that can aid change efforts. It is important to identify individuals with the power to bring about needed changes within a community and determine to whom these individuals report. The worker also can help the group identify and contact religious and civic organizations that may be interested in joining forces to work on a particular issue, or analyze the strengths and weaknesses of opponents to change and what tactics might be used to change their minds. For example, would a landlord be most vulnerable to a rent strike, to moral pressure from a church group, or to having housing code violations strictly enforced?

A third step is to help the group learn how to influence local government. The worker can help group members identify policy makers and bureaucrats who might support group efforts to have existing laws enforced, or introduce new legislation to address a particular issue. The worker can help the group develop a clear position on the issues with as much supporting documentation as possible. To the extent possible, the group might form a partnership with legislators and bureaucrats so they can collaborate on the change effort. Rubin and Rubin (1992) note that legislators are receptive to ideas that make them look active, creative, and effective. The worker can help legislators and bureaucrats get the issue on the agenda by testifying at public hearings, and through lobbying efforts.

A fourth step in capacity building is to help the group make an inventory of its existing resources and identify resources needed to accomplish particular goals. For example, the group may find it needs legal advice. Can a lawyer be identified who would be willing to work with the group? Similarly, the group may want to publish a fact sheet or a brochure for a lobbying effort. Can a business or community organization be identified that would be willing to help the group design or print the brochure? An important role of the worker is to help the group locate resources to accomplish its objectives.

Social Action Strategies

A variety of social action strategies can be used to help community groups accomplish their objectives during the working stage. These include political action strategies, legal strategies, and direct action strategies (Rubin & Rubin, 1992). Many forms of political activity are available to community groups, such as (a) organizing voter registration drives; (b) nominating and working on the campaigns of public officials; (c) developing and supporting referendums, propositions, and other grass-roots efforts to bypass legislators and get proposals directly onto the ballot; (d) lobbying and advocating political issues; (e) participating in community advisory boards' testimony at public hearings; (f) helping bureaucrats prepare regulations; (g) helping politicians prepare legislation; and (h) monitoring compliance with laws by bureaucratic and regulatory agencies.

Whereas political action strategies are designed to get those in power to pay attention to the goals of a community group, legal action strategies are designed to force politicians and bureaucrats to take action on issues supported by a community group or a coalition of community groups. While political action strategies can have sweeping and binding effects, they are often expensive and time consuming. Sometimes, the threat of legal action by a single counsel on retainer can create some action. More often, however, legal action requires a professional staff, a large budget, and a great deal of patience. While coalitions of community groups and community groups affiliated with national organizations can use legal strategies effectively, political action strategies and direct action strategies are often preferred.

Direct action strategies include rallies, demonstrations, marches, picketing, sit-ins, vigils, blockades, boycotts, slowdowns, strikes and many other forms of nonviolent and violent protest. While direct action strategies allow members to ventilate frustration and anger, they can be counterproductive. Negative publicity, fines, physical injury, and time lost at work are just a few of the possible consequences. Thus, direct action strategies should not be undertaken without careful thought and preparation, and then only if it is clear that safer political and legal strategies are unlikely to achieve the desired objective. It is also important to keep in mind that the threat of direct action is often as terrifying as the action itself. Therefore, if a community group is serious about engaging in a direct action strategy, it is often wise to publicize the group's intent and the specific steps that an opponent can take to avoid the action.

In his text *Rules For Radicals*, Alinsky (1971) developed a number of pragmatic rules for selecting among different action strategies. For example, he suggested picking a direct action strategy that enjoys wide support among members. He also suggested picking a strategy that emphasizes the weaknesses of the opponent. Thus, a rally that gets widespread news coverage might be particularly effective against an opponent concerned about negative publicity, whereas an economic boycott might be more effective against a corporation under pressure from shareholders to increase profits.

In choosing a social action strategy, there is a generally accepted protocol which social work and other professions should adhere to when carrying out their work with community groups. Less intrusive and more cooperative strategies should be tried before disruptive or conflict-oriented strategies are engaged. It has been suggested that when considering a social action strategy, collaboration or negotiation be employed before conflict (Pincus & Minahan, 1973). Collaboration simply means that in attempting to effect some change in a target system, the worker tries to convince the target system that change is in the best interest of all involved. In negotiation, the worker and the target system both give and get something in the process of change. The process of bargaining involves a good faith "quid pro quo" arrangement and assumes that each party will make some change desired by the other.

Should collaboration and negotiation fail to achieve a desired change, the group may be forced to engage in conflict strategies. In any case, the worker should always help group members use each of the three strategies in a constructive and an ethical fashion. The worker should carefully guard against a group choosing conflict as an initial strategy because of the perception that the strategy will result in change more quickly and easily, because members may be used to solving problems through conflict, or because members wish to carry out personal retribution against a target system.

SUMMARY

A variety of methods have been developed in industry, business administration, and human service organizations to help task groups accomplish their goals during the working stage. This chapter examines some of the most widely used methods. Brainstorming procedures, for example, can be used to help generate new and creative ideas, alternative plans, and problem solutions. Variations such as reverse brainstorming, trigger groups, and synectics also can be used for creative problem solving.

Focus groups are designed to collect qualitative, in-depth information. Within the group, members' discussion of a subject is facilitated until points of agreement and disagreement become clear. The strength of focus groups is their ability to explore topics and generate ideas and hypotheses. They should not be used to gather data that is intended to be truly representative of the attitudes and opinions of a larger population.

NGT breaks with the tradition of problem solving in interacting groups. By combining nominal group and interacting group procedures in a highly structured format, NGT has proved to be successful in generating ideas and solving problems.

Social judgment analysis is a rational decision-making method. It provides a way to use information to make decisions. SJA helps members specify the relationships between attributes of a problem and the problem's solution. The resulting decision rule is used to sort through alternative solutions. SJA has proved to be especially effective in encouraging group consensus when members must choose between distinct alternatives.

Quality circles and quality improvement teams are focused on improving the work environment and the quality of services offered by health and social service organizations. QCs are composed of small groups of employees from the same department who get together voluntarily to identify and solve problems they have in completing their work assignments. In contrast to QCs, QITs tend to rely, to a greater extent, on systematic data-based problem solving strategies. Also, they frequently consist of employees from different organizational levels and a variety of departments within the organization who are mandated to participate by management. There is a greater emphasis in QCs on improving the quality of the work environment, and a greater emphasis in QITs on improving the quality of services.

Although large task groups often use modified and streamlined versions of parliamentary procedures, *Robert's Rules of Order* is still the major source for the conduct of parliamentary meetings. Phillips' 66 is presented as an alternative method for working with large task groups. It can be used to reduce the inhibiting effects of size on communication and interaction in large problem-solving groups.

The second section of this chapter describes specialized methods for helping community groups accomplish their objectives during the working stage. This section focuses on three methods for helping community groups achieve their objectives: (a) mobilizing individuals to engage in collective action, (b) building the capacity of the group and its members to effect community change, and (c) social action strategies.

LEARNING ASSIGNMENTS

1. Form a small group. Using the brainstorming procedures described in this chapter, come up with as many creative ways as possible to learn group leadership skills.

2. You have been asked by the Director of Catholic Charities in your area to help the Committee on Children and Youth plan a series of focus groups in several parishes in the Diocese. The focus groups are designed to gain a better understanding of parishioners' views of the most pressing problems and needs of teen-agers in the Diocese. Develop an agenda and a specific series of questions that might be used during focus group meetings. What suggestions would you make to the committee to help ensure that appropriate participants are recruited? How would you help the committee ensure that there was effective moderation during meetings?

3. Locate and interview a manager of a for-profit private sector organization. For example, select a production or service industry, a large corporation, or a small business. How does the organization involve its employees in organizational decision making? Are there group formats for employees to contribute to the management of the company? To what extent are managers, supervisors, or line employees expected to be group leaders?

4. A family shelter for victims of domestic violence has recently received a large grant to be used to expand its services. The board of directors has suggested three discrete ways that the money could be used: (a) initiate a group services program for men who abuse their wives, (b) expand the shelter's services, or (c) begin a new program to provide treatment to children who live in abusive homes. Form a small group. Use the nominal group technique or the social judgment analysis procedure described in this chapter to decide on one alternative for how the money should be spent.

5. Seek permission to attend a board meeting or the meeting of some other group that uses parliamentary procedure. How knowledgeable did the chairperson appear to be about the rules of parliamentary procedure? To what

extent were parliamentary procedures used? Do you think that a different level of adherence to the rules of parliamentary procedure would have affected the meeting? Why?

6. Identify a social action group or organization in your community. Interview a leader of the group. Ask the leader to describe how the group originally formed. How were individuals mobilized to engage in collective action? What obstacles had to be overcome? What strategies were used to build the capacity of the group and its members to effect community change? What types of social action strategies have been used by the group? What types of strategies would not be used by the group? Why?

PART V

The Ending Stage

Chapter 12: Evaluation

Chapter 13: Ending the Group's Work

Chapter 14: Case Examples

CHAPTER 12

Evaluation

Evaluation is the process of obtaining information about the effects of a single intervention or the effect of the total group experience. Workers can use either informal or formal measures to obtain such information. In conducting an informal evaluation, a worker might ask the members of a group to evaluate how the group is progressing. To complete a formal evaluation, a worker might collect information systematically using preplanned measurement devices before, during, or after the group has met. In either case, the worker uses the information to evaluate the group. The purposes of this chapter are to explore the many ways to obtain information about a group and to guide the worker in deciding what evaluation methods will be most useful in various situations.

The Practitioner's Dilemma

Increasingly in social work and allied disciplines, there has been a push toward accountability and empirically validated practice. Workers have been urged to become practitioner-researchers to improve their work as they practice (Browning & Stover, 1971; Jayaratne & Levy, 1979; Thomas, 1975). The push for evaluating practice has occurred even though group workers sometimes fail to keep adequate records, let alone perform systematic evaluations of their practice (Garvin, 1987).

The dilemma for many practicing group workers is that other demands of practice seem to be more pressing than evaluations, which require valuable time and energy. Further, many practitioners find it difficult to understand the logic of evaluation methods or their day-to-day usefulness. It has been proposed that practitioners (a) leave most research to the researchers, (b) become consumers of research, and (c) concentrate on developing experience and expertise as group leaders (Trotzer, 1977). However, Trotzer and most others urge group workers to evaluate their own practice whenever possible.

The push toward accountability and empirically validated group work practice has made a difference. In a review of the literature in 1986, Feldman (1986) found that compared with a review completed 20 years before (Silverman, 1966), the number of research studies had more than doubled. However, Feldman noted that the number of research studies was still very small, and that much needed to be done before group workers could claim that their practice is well-grounded in scientific research.

Why Evaluate? The Group Worker's View

When considering whether or not to evaluate their work with a particular group, workers will need to (a) determine their reasons for conducting an evaluation, (b) assess the ability of their agencies to provide the encouragement and resources necessary for evaluating their own practice, (c) determine the time they have available for an evaluation, and (d) match their information needs and available time with an appropriate method for evaluating their practice.

Reasons for Conducting Evaluations. Workers' reasons for wanting information about a group depend on how they believe they can use the information. Some of the benefits of evaluation for group workers include the following:

- Evaluations can satisfy workers' curiosity and professional concerns about the effects of specific interventions they perform while working with a group.
- Information from evaluations can help workers improve their leadership skills.
- Evaluations can demonstrate the usefulness of a specific group or a specific group work method to an agency, a funding source, or society.
- Workers can assess the progress of group members and see whether the group as a whole is accomplishing agreed upon purposes.
- Evaluations allow group members and others who may be affected to express their satisfactions and dissatisfactions with a group.
- Workers can gather knowledge that can be shared with others who are using group methods for similar purposes and in similar situations.
- Workers can systematize and make overt the covert hypothesis-generating and hypothesis-testing processes they routinely engage in as they work with individual group members and the group as a whole (Anderson, 1987).

Organizational Encouragement and Support. To evaluate their practice with a group, workers should begin by assessing the willingness of the organization for whom they work to provide the resources to conduct an evaluation. Some organizations do little or nothing to encourage evaluations and may even penalize the worker for attempting one. Agency norms, peer pressure, or administrative directions may suggest to workers that other tasks are more important than evaluating their practice. In other cases, requirements to serve many clients may inhibit workers' abilities to evaluate their practice.

Without active encouragement by an organization's administrators, workers are left to rely on their own motivations for evaluating their work with a group. Organizations can increase workers' opportunities for evaluation by including evaluation tasks as a part of workers' practice responsibilities, by providing the time for practice evaluations, and by encouraging workers to discuss evaluations during regularly scheduled staff meetings. Rather than requiring workers to fill out forms and records that they do not use and often do not see again after administrative processing, organizations can also help by developing and implementing information systems that can also be used by workers to evaluate their practice. A well-designed information and evaluation system can provide feedback for group work practitioners as well as for agency administrators.

Time Considerations.   Workers should consider how much time they have available to conduct an evaluation. Most workers collect some information about the groups they lead, and this information can often be the basis for an evaluation if it is collected appropriately. Little additional time is needed for evaluation beyond the time necessary to make modifications in the original data collection system. In other instances, workers may want information that is not routinely collected. They should estimate the amount of time it will take them to collect, process, and analyze the additional information. They can then compare the time needed for the evaluation with the time they have available and decide whether the evaluation is feasible. When workers have valid reasons for evaluating their practice, they may be able to persuade their organization to allow them sufficient time to conduct the evaluation. This is particularly true when a worker is developing a new, innovative program to achieve the goals the organization has set as a priority for service delivery.

Selecting an Evaluation Method.   After determining how much time is available for evaluation, workers should consider how to match their information needs and available time to an appropriate evaluation method. This chapter will review the major types of evaluations. Each evaluation method will be discussed in terms of its strengths and weaknesses, time requirements, and flexibility.

Workers must also decide what data collection instruments they will use in conjunction with a particular evaluation method. Some of the major types of data collection instruments used by group workers include the following:

- Progress notes.
- Self-reports or personal interview data from workers, members, and observers.
- Questionnaires.
- Analysis of reports or other group products.
- Review of audiotapes and videotapes of group meetings.
- Observational coding schemes.
- Role play or in-vivo performance tests.
- Reliable and valid scales.

These data collection instruments can be used with any of the major types of evaluation methods. Some measures, however, are frequently associated with one type of evaluation. For example, progress notes are often used in monitoring evaluation methods and reliable and valid scales are more frequently used in effectiveness and efficiency evaluations. As each type of evaluation method is reviewed, the methods of collecting data that are often associated with each method will be described.

EVALUATION METHODS

Workers can use four broad types of evaluation methods to obtain data. These include evaluations for (a) planning a group, (b) monitoring a group, (c) developing a group, and (d) testing the effectiveness and efficiency of a group method. Workers can use any of these evaluation methods to obtain information about the process or the outcome of a group. Process evaluations focus on the interaction in a group; properties of a group such as cohesion, norms, roles, and communication patterns; how the group is being conducted; or other aspects of the functioning of a group. Outcome evaluations focus on the products or tasks achieved by individual members or the group as a whole.

Regardless of the type of evaluation employed, or whether the evaluation focuses on processes or outcomes, workers should be able to use evaluations to receive feedback about their practice. Instead of viewing practice evaluations as useless administrative requirements, workers should see them as a way to help them become more effective, and as a way to develop new knowledge that can be shared with other group workers. Evaluations can be used to test new interventions that may prove more effective in helping clients achieve their objectives. They can also be useful as a means for workers to begin to understand what interventions work under what conditions.

EVALUATIONS FOR PLANNING THE GROUP

Evaluations used for planning a group are seldom mentioned in the group work literature. This section will discuss two important evaluation methods for planning: (a) obtaining program information, technical data, and materials for specific groups that the worker is planning to lead and (b) conducting needs assessments to determine the feasibility of organizing a proposed group.

Obtaining Program Information

The worker can often benefit from information about previous methods used in working with similar groups. Workers may be able to obtain some information from colleagues or from workers in other agencies where similar groups have been conducted. Workers may also find it useful to (a) examine records from previous groups that focused on similar concerns, (b) review relevant journals[1] or texts using computerized or manual search procedures, and (c) attend workshops and conferences where group workers share recent developments in the field.

For planning task groups, helpful information often includes (a) the minutes of previous group meetings, (b) the operating procedures of previous groups, (c)

---

[1] Some of the most important journals that focus on specific groups and specific group work methods include *Group and Organization Studies, Group Psychotherapy, Psychodrama and Sociometry, International Journal of Group Psychotherapy, Small Group Research,* and *Social Work with Groups.*

the charges and responsibilities of previous groups, and (d) information about how similar objectives and goals were accomplished in other organizations, and by other task groups. Also, it can be helpful to attend meetings of groups working on similar concerns.

Library literature searches have been made much easier and much less time-consuming in recent years by the availability of on-line CD-ROM computerized databases. Two databases that are particularly relevant to social group workers are Social Work Abstracts Plus and PSYCLIT (psychology). Also, group workers in health settings may find MEDLINE (medicine) useful; group workers in school settings may find ERIC (education) useful; and group workers in forensic settings may find NCJRS (National Criminal Justice Reference Service) useful.

Needs Assessment

Workers might also find it useful to have some information about potential members of a proposed group. This information might include (a) potential members' willingness to attend the group, (b) their motivations for attending, and (c) their capabilities for helping the group achieve its purposes. In treatment groups, workers may want to conduct a needs assessment by asking other workers if clients with whom they work might be appropriate for the group or if workers have received requests for a particular group service they have been unable to meet.

Data from community needs assessments designed for multiple purposes can be useful in obtaining information about potential group members. Contacting people or organizations in the community may also provide access to potential members. When workers have identified these clients, they can contact them directly by a personal interview, a telephone call, or a letter. Toseland (1981) has described these methods of reaching out to clients in more detail.

In some task groups, membership may result from elections, appointments, or the person's position in an organization. A planning evaluation can familiarize a worker with rules and regulations governing a task group's composition and operation. Planning evaluations can also help a worker collect information and assess the potential contributions that members can make in helping the group achieve its objectives (Rothman, 1974). For more information about conducting planning evaluations, see Polansky (1960), or Rossi, Freeman, and Wright (1979).

EVALUATIONS FOR MONITORING A GROUP

Monitoring refers to collecting information about group members and group processes. Monitoring has already been discussed in Chapter 7 as an assessment device, but it can also be used to evaluate group work practice. Monitoring is the least demanding and most flexible of the evaluation procedures described in this chapter. It can be useful for obtaining information for process or outcome evaluations.

Monitoring Methods

The first step in the monitoring process is to decide what information to collect. For example, those who work with remedial groups designed for clients with psychological disorders may be interested in monitoring changes in individual members over the course of the group on the five axes presented in the Diagnostic and Statistical Manual of Mental Disorders. A worker asked to lead an interdepartmental committee of a large public welfare agency may be interested in monitoring the extent to which individual committee members complete assigned tasks.

Whatever information group workers decide to collect, they must be clear about how they define it, so it can be monitored using appropriate measures. Concepts that are ambiguous, obscure, or unspecified cannot be measured accurately.

The next step in monitoring is to decide how the needed information will be collected. Data can be collected by administering questionnaires; asking for verbal feedback about the group; or by recording information about the group through written records, tape recordings, or video recordings of group sessions.

In treatment groups, members may be asked to record information about their own behavior or the behavior of other group members. Both Garvin (1987) and Rose (1989) describe a variety of procedures group members can use to monitor their own behavior. These include (a) counting discrete behaviors; (b) keeping a checklist, a log, or a journal of events that occur before, during, and after a behavior or a task that is being monitored; and (3) recording ratings of feeling states on self-anchored rating scales. Monitoring methods such as these have been described in Chapter 7 because they are often used for assessment. As illustrated in the following sections, in the monitoring process, collecting data can be the task of either the worker or the group members.

Monitoring by the Group Worker

One of the easiest methods of monitoring a group's progress is to record activities that occur during or after each meeting. This form of record keeping involves writing or dictating notes after a meeting (Wilson, 1980). The worker may use a process recording method of monitoring or a summary recording method. Process recordings are narrative, step-by-step descriptions of a group's development. Wilson and Ryland (1949) note that process recordings can help a worker analyze the interactions that occur during a group meeting. However, process recordings are time-consuming and therefore rarely used by experienced group workers. They are, however, useful in the training and supervision of beginning group workers because they provide rich detail and give trainees an opportunity to reflect on what occurs during group meetings.

A method of recording that is less time-consuming, more selective, and more focused than processed recording is called summary recording. Summary recording focuses on critical incidents that occur in a group, and involves using a series of open-ended questions. The questions are most frequently used for monitoring a group's progress after each group session, although they may be used at less frequent intervals during a group's development. Figure 12–1 is an example of a summary recording form used to record a meeting of a family life education group for foster parents.

FIGURE 12–1
Group recording form

Group name: _____   Beginning date: _____

Worker's name: _____   Termination date: _____

Session number: _____   Date of session: _____

Members present: _____

_____

_____

_____

Members absent: _____

_____

_____

Purpose of the group: _____

_____

Goals for this meeting: _____

_____

Activities to meet these goals: _____

_____

_____

_____

Worker's analysis of the meeting: _____

_____

_____

_____

_____

Plan for future meetings: _____

_____

When using either summary or process recordings, it is important for the worker to record the information as soon as possible after the meeting so that events are remembered as accurately as possible. The meaning of the open-ended summary recording questions should be as clear as possible so that workers' recordings are consistent from group to group. Ambiguous questions open to several interpretations should be avoided. The amount of time required for summary recordings depends on the number of questions to which the worker responds and the amount of analysis each question requires.

The open-ended questions of summary recording devices sometimes fail to focus or define the recorded information sufficiently, especially when the worker wants similar information about all clients. Summary recording devices are usually not designed to connect the group worker's activities to specific goals and outcomes. Some recording systems, such as the problem-oriented record (Kane, 1974), have been designed to overcome such problems in summary recording systems. In the problem-oriented record keeping system (Weed, 1969), problems to be worked on by the group are clearly defined, goals are established, and data are collected and recorded in relation to each of the specified problems. Specific interventions are also entered in the record under each problem. This system enables workers to show how group work interventions designed to accomplish a certain goal are connected to a specific assessment of a problem. Periodic entries are made in the problem-oriented record, assessing progress toward established goals. A final entry is made when the goals for a particular problem have been reached.

In task groups, the minutes of a meeting serve as the record of the group's business. They are often the official record of the proceedings of a group. Minutes are prepared from notes taken during the meeting by a person designated by the worker or elected by the group's membership. A staff person, the secretary of the group, or another person may take notes regularly. Sometimes, members rotate the task. The minutes of each meeting are usually distributed to members before the next meeting and are approved by members, with any revisions, during the first part of the next meeting.

Workers may also want to use audiotape or videotape recorders to obtain information about a group. Such recordings have the advantage of providing an accurate, unedited record of the meeting. In remedial groups, audiotapes provide immediate feedback about members' verbal behavior. Members may want to replay a segment of the tape if there is a discrepancy about what was said during some portion of the meeting.

In educational groups, videotapes can be used to demonstrate appropriate behavior and critique inappropriate behavior. Videotaping is especially useful during program activities, such as role playing, that are designed to increase skills or change behavior patterns. Video feedback helps members review their behavior during role play practices to discuss alternative ways of behaving. For example, members of an assertion training group might watch videotapes of themselves in a situation requiring an assertive response. They may analyze voice tone, facial expressions, and body posture, as well as the verbal interactions that occurred. Audiotapes and videotapes provide the worker with a permanent record that can be shared with the group, with supervisors, or in educational workshops.

There are some disadvantages to taping a group. Because of its absolute quality, group members are not able to make statements "off the record," which may inhibit the development of trust in the group. The worker may not find it necessary or even desirable to have the level of detail provided by a tape. The worker may have to spend too much time reviewing irrelevant portions of a tape to find information that could have been obtained quickly if brief, summary recordings had been used instead. However, if a worker is interested in monitoring the group's interaction patterns in a thorough and precise fashion, or if an entire transcript of the group session is needed, then audio or video recordings may be the best method.

Sometimes, it is desirable to use specialized coding systems to obtain reliable and valid data from tape-recorded group sessions. This is particularly true when the worker wishes to obtain a detailed and accurate picture of group processes for research. Coding systems can be used by one or more raters of the tapes to determine the frequency and content of a group's interactions. Coding systems described by Bales (1950), Bales, Cohen, and Williamson (1979), Budman et al. (1987), Hill (1977), and Rose (1989) are examples of methods that can be used to analyze specific group interactions. Other coding systems are described in a comprehensive review of group process instruments prepared by Fuhriman and Packard (1986).

Monitoring by Group Members

Members, as well as the group worker, can monitor their own behavior or the behavior of the group. Self-monitoring members provide an important source of information about the effects of the group and of the worker's interventions. At the same time, members may not be as accurate or as consistent as the group worker in collecting information. Workers should ensure that members understand and are able to carry out data collection procedures when monitoring their own behavior or the behavior of the group. Training is often necessary for accurate monitoring.

The most common use of monitoring by group members occurs in treatment groups where individual members keep a record of their behavior between group meetings and report back on these behaviors during the next meeting. An illustration of the steps in the self-monitoring procedure appears in Figure 12–2. During this procedure, the worker and the group members together decide (a) what data to collect, (b) when to collect the data, (c) how much data to collect, (d) how to collect the data, and (5) when the information collected by members should be analyzed by the group. As these questions are discussed and answered, the worker reviews each member's monitoring plan. Members can also monitor a group's progress at the end of each meeting or at intervals during the life of the group. Members may use a short questionnaire devised for such purposes or they can discuss the group's performance orally with the worker. Monitoring allows members to share their feelings with one another and with the worker as the group progresses. Workers can use the data to modify their leadership to reflect members' concerns. Shulman (1992) has called the process of using feedback to change the way the worker interacts with members "tuning in." It is most notable in the early stages of a group's development but the effective worker solicits feedback from members throughout the development of a group.

FIGURE 12–2
The self-monitoring process

Group members also benefit from self-monitoring procedures. Members can share ideas about the group's performance and how it might be improved. This gives them a sense of control and influence over the group's progress and increases their identification with the group's purposes. Also, members who believe their ideas are valued, respected, and listened to are more likely to feel satisfied with their participation in the group.

Verbal evaluations of a group's performance do not provide a permanent record. An evaluation form, consisting of closed-ended, fixed-category responses and open-ended items, can be used if the worker, group members, or the agency wants written feedback about the group. Figure 12–3 shows a session evaluation form developed by a worker leading a group for single parents. The form contains several easily understood closed- and open-ended questions. The closed-ended questions are Likert-type scales that require respondents to record their opinions on an ordered scale. Because the same scale values are used for all group members, responses made by each member can be compared with one another. Open-ended items are designed to allow each member to reply in a unique manner with responses that may vary considerably from member to member.

In task groups, members often make oral reports of their progress. Although they are often not considered to be evaluation devices, they are an important means by which the worker and the members monitor the group's work. At the

FIGURE 12–3
Session evaluation form

Was the information presented about child development helpful to you in understanding your child's behavior?

4	3	2	1
Very Helpful	Somewhat Helpful	A Little Helpful	Not at All Helpful

What information did you find most helpful? _____

_____

_____

Rate the effectiveness of the leader in this group session.

4	3	2	1
Very Helpful	Somewhat Helpful	A Little Helpful	Not at All Helpful

What did you find most helpful about the group during this session? _____

_____

_____

_____

What did you find least helpful about the group? _____

_____

_____

Overall, rate your satisfaction with today's group meeting.

4	3	2	1
Very Helpful	Somewhat Helpful	A Little Helpful	Not at All Helpful

Additional comments: _____

_____

_____

---

completion of a task group, the products or final reports that result from the group's efforts can also be used to evaluate the success of the group.

In treatment groups, an important indicator of the group's performance is the completion of contracts, which individual members make with the group or the worker about tasks to be done during the week to resolve a problem or change a particular behavior. Rose (1989) calls the completion of tasks or assignments the "products of group interaction." He suggests that the rate of completion of assigned tasks is an important indicator of the success of the group.

Monitoring methods have received more attention in the group work literature than other types of evaluation methods. Process recordings, summary recordings, automated recording devices, oral evaluations, written evaluation forms, and products of group interaction can all be used to monitor a group's progress. Information collected from monitoring a group can serve a variety of purposes in helping workers improve their practice methods and their skills in working with groups. For additional information about evaluation methods used for monitoring a group, refer to Epstein and Tripodi (1977); Patton (1989); and Rossi, Freeman, and Wright (1979).

EVALUATIONS FOR DEVELOPING A GROUP

A third method of evaluating group work practice, developmental evaluation, is useful for the worker who is interested in preparing new group work programs, developing new group work methods, or improving existing group programs. Developmental research, as it has been called by Thomas (1978), is similar to research and development in business and industry. It allows practicing group workers to create and test new group work programs. For example, Rose, Tallant, Tolman and Subramanian (1986) described a five-year developmental research approach to creating groups to address a variety of problems including chronic stress, pain management, and spouse abuse that was still ongoing at the time the report was prepared.

The process of developmental evaluation includes developing, testing, evaluating, modifying, and re-evaluating intervention methods as new groups are offered. Developmental evaluations are especially appealing for workers who offer the same or similar group programs repeatedly, because they require workers to evaluate group programs in a sequential manner. A developmental evaluation occurs as successive group programs are offered.

Unlike monitoring evaluations, which are relatively easy for group workers to conduct, developmental evaluations are rather complex. They require careful thought, planning, and design by the worker. The process of conducting a developmental evaluation consists of (a) identifying a need or problem, (b) gathering and analyzing relevant data, (c) developing a new group program or method, (d) evaluating the new program or method, and (e) modifying the program or method on the basis of the data obtained. As shown in Figure 12–4, this process may be conducted several times as new group programs are offered and evaluated by the worker. Although developmental research requires careful thought as well as time and energy, it yields improvements in programs and methods that can make group work practice more effective and more satisfying.

In developing and evaluating a new group program or a new group method, the worker can select from a variety of research designs, depending on the type of program or method being developed and the context in which the evaluation will occur. Single system methods and case study methods are particularly useful for developmental evaluations. Although quasi-experimental design methods are also frequently used in developmental research, these methods will be described in relation to effectiveness and efficiency evaluations, because they are also fre-

FIGURE 12–4
Steps in the developmental research process

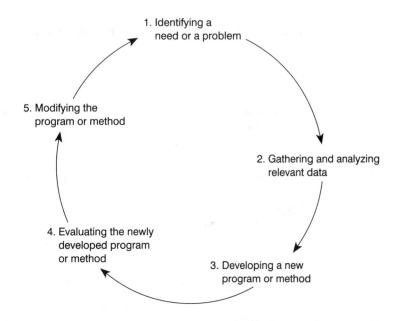

1. Identifying a need or a problem

2. Gathering and analyzing relevant data

3. Developing a new program or method

4. Evaluating the newly developed program or method

5. Modifying the program or method

quently used in evaluations of group outcomes. For a more thorough discussion of the issues involved in choosing an appropriate method for developmental research, see Fairweather (1967), Rothman (1974), Thomas (1978, 1990), or Toseland (1993).

Single System Methods

Single system methods (often called single subject designs) have been developed to evaluate data collected over time from a single system such as a group. The data obtained by using single system designs may include information about a single group member or the group as a whole. Single system methods compare baseline data to data collected when an intervention is made in the group. The baseline period occurs before the intervention period. Data collected during the preintervention or baseline period are intended to represent the functioning of the group as a whole or a group member on a particular variable. After the baseline period, an intervention occurs that may cause a change in the data collected during the baseline period.

As shown in Figure 12–5, there may be a change in level or in slope of the data collected after the intervention. Observations before and after the intervention are compared to see how the change has affected what the group worker is measuring. For example, after collecting baseline data and finding that members of a group were talking almost exclusively to the worker rather than to each other, the worker intervened by discussing the issue with the group, prompting members to talk with one another more frequently, and praising them when they initiate conversation with one another.

FIGURE 12–5
Changes in baseline data after an intervention in a group

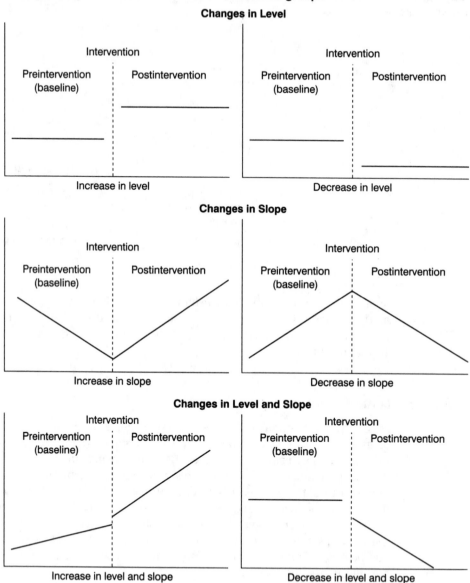

After the intervention, communications between members and the worker decrease and communications between members increase. Figure 12–6 is a graph of the results of such an intervention. The single system method illustrated in Figure 12–6 is often called an AB design, in which A is the baseline period before intervention and B is the postintervention data collection period.

Various single system designs include multiple baseline, withdrawal, reversal, and changing criterion designs. These single system designs are more compli-

FIGURE 12–6
Graphed data from a single
system evaluation

● = member–worker communications
× = member–member communications

cated to apply for the practicing group worker than the AB, baseline-intervention design, but they are also more effective than the AB design in reliably evaluating practice outcomes. They are especially useful when workers have the time, energy, interest, and resources to test the efficacy of a new or alternative intervention to improve practice with future groups working on similar problems. For additional information about single system methods, see Bloom and Fisher (1982); Jayaratne and Levy (1979); Rose (1989); and Toseland, Krebs, and Vahsen (1978).

Case Study Methods

Case studies rely on precise descriptions, accurate observations, and detailed analyses of a single example or case. They were developed by researchers interested in qualitative research methods. Because group workers are used to keeping records and analyzing their work in detail, these methods may have more appeal for some group workers than the quantitatively oriented single system research methods previously described.

As with single system methods, case study methods are based on intensive analysis of a single case. Therefore, the data collected may not be as internally or externally valid as data collected using classic control group designs. Despite this, the strengths of case studies are that they can provide a clear, detailed, vivid description of the processes and procedures of a group in action and are often more feasible to apply in practice settings than control group designs.

Case study methods include participant and nonparticipant observation (Johnson, 1975; Patton, 1989), case comparison methods (Butler, Davis, & Kukkonen, 1979), ethnographic methods (Watts, 1981), and focus group interviews (Greenbaum, 1987; Higginbotham & Cox, 1979; Krueger, 1988; Merton, Fiske, & Kendall, 1956; Morgan, 1988). For example, a group worker who is considering leading a preventive health group for cardiac patients may find it useful to observe a group being conducted at another hospital or to have the group recorded for playback and analysis. The worker could use case study methods to analyze the content of the tape recordings or notes made from observing the group and use the information obtained to change group work methods or develop new group programs in the worker's own setting.

Using a case comparison method, a worker who has developed a group program for alcoholics may want to compare his or her program with similar programs offered by Alcoholics Anonymous and a county alcoholism program. A comparison of the three programs along pre-specified dimensions created by the worker to answer his or her specific information needs could lead to innovations in the worker's program. The worker may also want to conduct focus group interviews with individuals who have participated in each program to determine the most and least valued features of each program. These innovations could then be evaluated for their efficacy, as described in the process shown in Figure 12–4.

Group workers might also want to use case study methods in working with task groups. For example, a worker might want to use nonparticipant observation to compare the methods that other day treatment mental health agencies use when reviewing clients in treatment team meetings.

Taken together, both single system methods and case study methods offer workers the opportunity to continually develop and improve their practice. Rigorous application of these methods requires that workers spend time designing and implementing evaluation methods and collecting data that are not routinely available. The worker must decide whether the extra effort spent in organizing and carrying out a developmental evaluation is worth the new or improved programs that can result.

EVALUATIONS FOR DETERMINING EFFECTIVENESS AND EFFICIENCY

Effectiveness evaluations focus on the extent to which a group accomplishes its objectives. They give workers the opportunity to gain objective feedback about the helpfulness of the methods being used. Efficiency evaluations compare the benefits of a group program with its cost. They attempt to place a monetary value on the outcomes of a group and to compare this with the costs incurred by conducting a group.

Effectiveness and efficiency evaluations rely on experimental and quasi-experimental designs, reliable and valid measures, and statistical procedures to determine the significance of an intervention on the outcome of task or treatment groups. Compared with the other types of evaluations mentioned in this chapter, effectiveness and efficiency evaluations are less flexible, more technically complex, and more difficult to conduct. Because of the nature of the methods employed and the precision and rigor necessary to apply them, a flexible and cooperative setting is needed to conduct effectiveness and efficiency evaluations. The sponsoring agency must be willing to supply the needed resources and the technical assistance necessary for conducting such evaluations.

One method for evaluating outcomes, which is less difficult to apply than many other effectiveness evaluation methods, is called goal attainment scaling (Kiresuk & Sherman, 1968). Using this method, the worker can obtain information about the achievement of goals by individual group members or the group as a whole. An example of goal attainment scaling is shown in Figure 12–7, in which each of several problem areas is listed on a five-point scale from most unfavorable outcome to most favorable outcome. The third scale point represents the expected outcome.

Members and the group leader can work together to develop outcome measures for each scale level. For example, the group decided that the most unfavorable outcome for the problem of depression is suicide. Similarly, the group decided that the most favorable outcome for loss of appetite is to eat three meals a day and to snack between meals. After work on the problem areas is completed, goal attainment can be measured by using the scales that have been developed for

FIGURE 12–7
Example of goal attainment scaling

Scale Levels	Problem Areas		
	Anxiety	Depression	Loss of Appetite
1. Most unfavorable expected outcome	Four or more self-rated occurrences of feeling anxious each day.	Suicide.	Refuses to eat any daily meals.
2. Less than expected outcome	Three self-rated occurrences of feeling anxious each day.	One or more attempts at suicide.	Eats one meal each day.
3. Expected outcome	Two self-rated occurrences of feeling anxious each day.	No attempts at suicide, discusses feelings of depression.	Eats two meals each day.
4. More than expected outcome	One self-rated occurrence of feeling anxious each day.	No attempts at suicide, discusses possible causes of depression.	Eats three meals each day.
5. Most favorable expected outcome	No self-rated occurrence of feeling anxious each day.	No attempts at suicide, identifies two causes for depression.	Eats three meals a day and snacks between meals.
Weight	5	25	5
Goal Attainment Score	4	3	3
Weighted Goal Attainment Score	20	75	15

each problem area. In the example in Figure 12–7, goal attainment is indicated by a box around the actual outcome. For the problem of anxiety, the outcome was one self-rated occurrence of feeling anxious each day. This outcome was given a score of 4.

As shown in Figure 12–7, it is possible to weight each scale differentially so that attaining more important goals receives greater emphasis in the overall evaluation than attaining less important goals. Thus, the goal attainment score of 4 obtained for the problem of anxiety is multiplied by its weight of 5, yielding a goal attainment score of 20. Even though the goal attainment score on the problem area of depression is a 3, after it is multiplied by its weight (25), the weighted goal attainment score for the problem of depression (75) is much greater than that obtained on the problem of anxiety (20). Goal attainment scores on each scale can be added together to form a composite score for individual or group goal attainment.

Statistical procedures have been developed to compare goal attainment scores across individual group members and across groups (Garwick, 1974). Although goal attainment scaling has received some methodological criticism (Seaberg & Gillespie, 1977), the procedure remains an important tool for group workers to consider when conducting effectiveness evaluations.

A variation on goal attainment scaling that has been used successfully in several group research problems is the pressing problem index (see, for example, Toseland, 1990b; Toseland, Labrecque, Goebel, & Whitney, 1992; Toseland, Rossiter, & Labrecque, 1989). In this procedure, during the intake interview, potential group members are asked to describe several problems they would like to work on in the group. An inventory of these problems, plus any other problems known to commonly affect the individuals targeted for the intervention, are listed in an inventory of pressing problems. Before meeting, and at the end of the group, participants are asked to rate the stress caused by each pressing problem and their efficacy in coping with it. Change in stress, and efficacy in coping with the pressing problems are assessed by adding up the responses to all pressing problems at each time of measurement.

Effectiveness evaluations rely on experimental and quasi-experimental designs to determine whether a group accomplishes its objectives. A true experimental design employs random assignment of participants to treatment and control groups. It compares the treatment and control groups on specific outcome variables to measure differences between treatment and control group subjects. Quasi-experimental designs are those in which participants cannot be randomly assigned to treatment and control groups. It is often difficult to randomly assign subjects to treatment and control groups in practice settings. Therefore, quasi-experimental designs are often used in effectiveness evaluations even though they are subject to possible biases because nonrandomly assigned subjects may not be equivalent on important variables that may affect the outcome variables being measured (see, for example, Toseland, Kabat, & Kemp, 1983).

It is especially difficult to conduct adequate effectiveness evaluations in group research projects. To do valid statistical analyses of data from experimental designs, the observations or measures on each unit of analysis must be independent. Researchers testing the effectiveness of group treatment sometimes assume that individual group members are the unit of analysis. However, individual members are not independent of one another in a group setting because they are affected by other members of the group. For example, while members are taking a questionnaire, a lawn mower might go past the window and disturb all members of the group. Members' scores are not totally independent of one another; that is, the lawn mower has affected all members in a similar manner. One way to overcome this problem is to ensure that all evaluations instruments are given to group members on a one-to-one basis outside of the group meeting.

The requirement for independent observations is also violated by researchers interested in group level phenomenon such as cohesion and leadership. Glisson (1986) has pointed out that statistical procedures such as analysis of variance (ANOVA) are not robust to this violation. This can lead to serious overestimates of the effectiveness of group procedures (Eisenhart, 1972). Because there must be a relatively large number of units of analysis to obtain valid statistical comparisons of group level phenomenon, effectiveness evaluations of group work practice require that a relatively large number of groups be conducted in both treatment and control conditions. This is often difficult to do in practice settings because of the limitations on resources, group participants, and competent group leaders.

Efficiency evaluations can also be complex and time-consuming, but they can be useful to those who want to assess whether their programs are cost-effective. For example, a nonprofit health agency employs a group worker to conduct a smoking cessation group program. The worker conducts an effectiveness evaluation and finds that 60 percent of the group members become nonsmokers after the group program. The worker also collects data about the costs of the program and the costs to employers who have employees who smoke. This provides the basis for the worker's efficiency evaluation.

Figure 12–8 shows the worker's calculations and illustrates that at a 50 percent success rate the smoking cessation group program saves the employer $220.00 each year, beginning one year after the program ends. Savings to the employer last for as long as the employee remains with the company as a nonsmoker. Because the smoking cessation program has a success rate of 50 percent, employers who have long-term employees are likely to save more than $220.00 each year for each employee who participates in the smoking cessation program. This information is helpful to the nonprofit health agency in motivating a number of large employers, whose workers' average length of employment exceeds one year, to offer smoking cessation group programs to their employees.

A complete description of the methodology for effectiveness and efficiency evaluations is given in Campbell and Cook (1979) and Rossi, Freeman, and Wright (1979). Group workers should have a basic understanding of these methods to be able to assess the efficacy of their own practice and to be able to critically evaluate methodologies used in published reports about the effectiveness and efficiency of group work methods and group programs.

FIGURE 12–8

An efficiency evaluation of a group program for smoking cessation

Costs of Smoking to the Employer Per Employee Per Year*	
Insurance:	
Health	$220.00
Fire	10.00
Workers' Compensation and other accidents	40.00
Life and disability	30.00
Other:	
Productivity	166.00
Absenteeism	100.00
Smoking effects on nonsmokers	110.00
Total cost of smoking	$660.00
Per Employee Cost of the Smoking Cessation Program	
Smoking cessation program	$120.00
Employee time to take the program	100.00
Total Cost for Each Employee	$220.00
Total Cost of Achieving One Nonsmoker	
(based on a projected success rate of 50%)	$440.00
Savings to Employers	
Total cost of smoking	$660.00
Total cost of the smoking cessation program	– 440.00
	$220.00

*Cost figures taken from Marvin Kristein, "How Much Can Business Expect to Earn from Smoking Cessation," presented at a Conference of the National Interagency Council on Smoking and Health, Chicago, Illinois, January 9, 1980, 1–11.

EVALUATION MEASURES

The four broad types of evaluation methods described provide a framework that workers can use to collect information for planning, monitoring, developing, or assessing the efficacy or efficiency of their practice with a group. In applying these methods, workers can choose from a variety of measures to collect the necessary information for an effective evaluation. Numerous measures have been developed for evaluating group work practice. These include some that specifically focus on properties of the group as a whole and others that may be useful to the worker in evaluating changes in members of specific groups. Decisions about which measures to use depend on (a) the objectives of the evaluation, (b) properties of the measures being considered for use, (c) the form in which the data will be collected, and (d) what constructs will be measured.

Choosing Measures

The first and most essential step in choosing appropriate measures is to decide on the objectives of the evaluation. Clarifying the information that is needed, what the information collected will be used for, and who will use the information can help the worker choose the appropriate measures for the evaluation. For example, if the worker is interested in obtaining feedback from members about their satisfaction with a particular group, the worker may be less concerned about the reliability and validity of a measure than about the difficulties group members might experience in responding to the measure. The worker may also be concerned about members' reactions to the measures and the time it will take to administer them. This is particularly true if the worker has a limited amount of group time available for conducting an evaluation.

The worker should be familiar with two properties of measures that govern the quality of the data to be collected. *Reliability* refers to the extent to which an instrument measures the same phenomenon the same way each time it is used. A reliable measure is consistent. When measuring the same variable, it yields the same score each time it is administered. *Validity* refers to the extent to which a data collection instrument measures what it purports to be measuring. A valid measure is one that yields a true or actual representation of the variable being measured. The ideal situation is for a group worker to use a reliable and valid measure that has already been constructed. When such measures exist, they are generally superior to measures developed quickly by the worker without regard to reliability or validity. Reliable and valid measures that can be quickly and easily administered are becoming more widely available (Corcoran & Fisher, 1987; Levitt & Reid, 1981; Toseland & Reid, 1985), but there are many concepts for which no reliable and valid measures exist.

Constructing reliable and valid measures takes a considerable amount of time. Workers should decide what level of measurement precision and objectivity is needed when deciding how much time to spend constructing and validating measures. For additional information about constructing reliable and valid measures, see Nunnally (1978), Spilker (1990), or Stanley and Hopkins (1972).

Another consideration in choosing appropriate evaluation measures is what form of data collection would be most useful to the group worker and most convenient for group members. Data can be collected by interviewing members, by written response to a questionnaire, or by audio or video recordings. The data collection form that will be most helpful to the worker depends on how the data will be used and the extent to which group members are willing and able to cooperate with the data collection procedures used. In evaluating group work with children, older people, and disabled people, for example, audiotaped responses can often overcome any difficulties they might have making written responses.

Finally, the worker must decide how a particular property or concept will be measured. For example, after deciding that the objective of an evaluation is to test the effectiveness of a particular group, the worker must decide whether information is sought about changes in the behavior, cognition, or the affect of individual group members. In task groups, the worker may want to measure the extent to which a group completes its tasks, as well as the quality and the quantity of the products or tasks achieved. In conducting evaluations, it is often helpful to have multiple measures of the property being measured. When measuring the effectiveness of a group program for drug abusers, for example, the worker might want to measure reductions in drug intake, changes in self-concept, and changes in beliefs about the effects of drug abuse. Multiple measures including a blood test, an attitude scale, and a questionnaire concerning information about drug use might all be useful in assessing the group's effectiveness in helping members become drug free.

Types of Measures

A wide array of reliable and valid measures is available for group workers to use when they are evaluating interventions with specific groups (see, for example, Buros, 1966; Corcoran & Fisher, 1987; and Robinson & Shaver, 1973). These include self-report measures, observational measures, and measures of the products of group interaction. In describing each of these measures we will mention particular ones that have often been used in evaluations of group work.

Self-Report Measures.   Perhaps the most widely used evaluation measures are written and oral self-reports, in which group members are asked to respond to questions about a particular phenomenon. Although they may focus on any phenomenon, self-report measures are particularly useful in measuring intrapersonal phenomena such as beliefs or attitudes that cannot be measured directly using observational measures. There are a variety of published self-report measures available, including measures of anxiety, depression, assertiveness, self-concept, and locus of control. Group workers can also construct their own self-report measures for specialized situations in which no published self-report measures exist. Three published self-report measures that may be of particular interest to group workers include Hemphill's Index of Group Dimensions (Hemphill, 1956), the Hill Interaction Matrix (HIM-A, HIM-B, HIM-G) (Hill, 1977), and Seashore's Group Cohesiveness Index (Seashore, 1954). Hemphill's Index of Group Dimensions measures 13 properties of groups: autonomy, control, flexibility, hedonic tone, homogeneity, intimacy, participation, permeability, polarization, potency, stability, stratification, and viscidity. The measure consists of 150 items to which group members respond on a five-point scale from definitely true to mostly false.

The Hill Interaction Matrix is a self-report measure in which a group leader, a group member, or an observer responds to 72 items about group process. The measure is designed to discriminate between types of group interactions on two dimensions: the content discussed and the level and type of work occurring in the group.

Seashore's Group Cohesiveness Index is a measure of group cohesiveness, defined as members' attraction to the group. It is especially designed for task groups and has been used with industrial work groups. Hemphill's Index of Group Dimensions, Hill's Interaction Matrix, and Seashore's Group Cohesiveness Index have all proved to be reliable and valid measures in several evaluations of group work.

Observational Measures.   Unlike self-report measures that rely on the accuracy of a respondent's memory, observational measures use independent, objective observers to collect data while they occur or as they are replayed using video or audio recordings. Although observational measures are less susceptible to biases and distortions than self-report measures, they are used less frequently than self-report measures because they require the availability of one or more trained observers to collect the data. The observers code discrete group interactions into categories that are mutually exclusive and exhaustive; that is, during each observation period, one observation is recorded and it can be recorded in one, and only one, category.

The most well-known observational measure for groups is called Bales' Interaction Process Analysis (Bales, 1950). This observational index consists of 12 categories. Interactions are coded by assigning each person a number and, for example, marking a 1–4 or a 3–1 in the appropriate category when an interaction occurs from member one to member four or member three to member one. With well-trained observers, Bales' Interaction Process Analysis can be a useful tool for the evaluation of group interactions.

More recently, Bales (1980) and Bales, Cohen, and Williamson (1979) have developed a new measure called SYMLOG (Systematic Multiple Level Observation of Groups). As explained in Chapter 7, SYMLOG is a method for analyzing the overt and covert behaviors of group members. With SYMLOG, a three-dimensional graphic presentation or field diagram of the interaction of group members is made. Through the field diagram, group members can analyze the way they interact with one another and improve the ability of the group to accomplish its tasks. An example of the use of SYMLOG for assessing group functioning can be found in Chapter 7. As an evaluation tool, SYMLOG can be used to measure several variables affecting both the socio-emotional and the task aspects of members' behavior in groups.

Other observational measures have also been used for evaluating changes in a group over time. For example, Moreno's (1934) scales of sociometric choice and sociometric preference, described more fully in Chapter 7, assess relationships among members of a group. This is done by having each member rank order other members on certain dimensions such as their preference for working with other group members or their liking for other group members.

Products of Group Interaction.   A worker may be able to measure the products of group interaction in a simple and straightforward manner. In task groups, products of the group's work are often tangible. For example, a team may develop a written document that governs how services will be delivered to clients. The work of a delegate council may be evaluated by the number of agenda items it acts on during its monthly meeting. In both instances, group products can be used for purposes of evaluation. In treatment groups, products of group interaction may also be useful measures. Rose (1989) suggests that measurable products of group interaction include behavior change, the number of between-meeting tasks generated at a group meeting, and the number of tasks actually completed.

Evaluation measures from which workers can choose when evaluating their practice with a group range from those consisting of a few open-ended questions made by a worker who wants to get some feedback from group members to sophisticated observational measures requiring highly trained observers. Workers develop or select measures in relation to the evaluation design they are going to use and ultimately to the information they hope to obtain. While selecting appropriate measures and implementing effective evaluations is time-consuming for the practicing group worker, it is often well worth the effort because it may result in improved service and in new and innovative group programs.

SUMMARY

Evaluation is the method by which practitioners obtain information and feedback about their work with a group. In the current age of accountability and fiscal constraints where difficult program choices are made, evaluation methodologies are useful tools for practitioners. This chapter discusses some of the reasons group workers may choose to use evaluation methods in their practice.

Practitioners are often faced with a dilemma when considering whether or not to evaluate their practice. They must decide whether the demands of serving clients are compatible with developing and conducting evaluations. This chapter describes the strengths and weaknesses of a number of evaluation methods that may be used in differing practice situations and settings.

Four broad types of evaluation methods include evaluations for (a) planning a group, (b) monitoring a group, (c) developing a group, and (d) testing the effectiveness and efficiency of a group. These methods are used with a variety of evaluation measures to help practitioners develop, test, and implement more effective group work methods. Evaluation methods can also be combined with knowledge accumulated from practice experiences, sometimes referred to as "practice wisdom," to improve the methods used by group workers to meet a variety of needs in diverse practice settings.

LEARNING ASSIGNMENTS

1. Schedule an interview with an administrator in a social service agency and ask him or her the following questions: What requirements do funding agencies have for evaluating the group work services offered by the agency? Have these requirements changed in recent years? What additional efforts, if any, are made to evaluate the quality of the services offered by the agency? What incentives and disincentives do workers have for evaluating their practice?
2. Form a classroom group and identify a population that you think may be in need of group work services. Prepare a questionnaire that could be used to assess the needs of this population. Make sure to include items that assess the barriers that may interfere with this particular population's use of existing group work services.
3. Locate a social service agency offering group work services. How are group work services monitored? Is there a standardized format for recording infor-

mation on each group session? Is a summary form used periodically or at the end of a group? Are clients asked to provide any feedback about their satisfaction with the group work services that are offered? If you were called in as a consultant to this agency, how would you change the way services are monitored?

4. Select a target population or problem for a group work service. Conduct a literature search using a computerized on-line database such as Social Work Research and Abstracts. Find the articles that appear to be most relevant. How helpful was the computer search in planning for the group?

5. If you are the leader or a member of a task or treatment group, ask members to fill out the Session Evaluation Form presented in Figure 12–3 at the end of a meeting. Prepare a written analysis of the responses of the group members to each question. What conclusions can you reach about the helpfulness of the meeting, the satisfaction of the members, and the effectiveness of the leader? How could the group be more helpful and satisfying to the members? How helpful was the measure in providing feedback about the effectiveness of the group?

6. Locate a published assessment instrument that could be used to evaluate the effectiveness of a treatment group of your choosing. Review the items in the assessment instrument and comment on the extent to which you think they would help you assess the effectiveness of your work. Prepare six additional items that might be particularly pertinent when assessing the effectiveness of a group work service for this population.

CHAPTER 13

Ending the Group's Work

Although it has not received as much attention in the practice literature as the beginning or working stage, the ending stage is an important part of group work practice (Fox, Nelson, & Bolman, 1969; Mayadas & Glasser, 1981). The skills workers use in the ending stage determine, in part, the success of the entire group experience. In this stage, workers and members form their lasting impressions of the group. An otherwise satisfying and effective group can be ruined by a worker who is not skillful in closing the group.

During the ending stage, the group's work is consolidated. In task groups, the decisions, reports, recommendations, and other products of the group as a whole are completed, and consideration is given to how the results of the work can best be implemented. In treatment groups, the changes made by individual group members are stabilized, and plans are made for maintaining these gains after the group ends. In groups where member self-disclosure has been high, it is necessary to help members work through their feelings about terminating their relationships with the worker and with each other. It is also a time when workers confront their own feelings regarding ending their work with a particular group.

Planned and Unplanned Termination

At the beginning of closed, time-limited groups, workers and members decide how many times the group will meet. Northen (1969) points out, "Ideally, termination occurs when a person or a group no longer needs the professional services" (p. 223). Fortune and colleagues (Fortune, 1985; Fortune, Pearlingi, & Rochelle, 1991) found that few social workers considered terminating with a client unless they considered that their work together had been successful. The most important criteria for termination included improved coping in the environment, improved intrapsychic functioning, the client's wish to terminate, meeting initial goals, and changes in therapeutic content (Fortune, Pearlingi, & Rochelle, 1991).

Sometimes members stop attending before the planned ending date. Unplanned termination of membership is a relatively common experience. Yalom (1985), for example, reported unplanned termination rates ranging from a high of 51 percent to a low of 25 percent. Others have reported unplanned termination rates of between 5 percent and 20 percent (Labrecque, Peak, & Toseland, 1992; Toseland, 1990b; Toseland, Labrecque, Goebel, & Whitney, 1992). Still others have reported dropout rates of 30 percent (Connelly & Piper, 1984; Connelly, Piper, DeCarufel, & Debbane, 1986).

In treatment groups in which participation is voluntary, a reduction in membership sometimes occurs after the first and second meeting of a group. After this initial drop, groups generally develop a stable core of members who continue until the group ends.

Unplanned termination occurs in many forms of service. For example, in a study of family service agencies, Beck and Jones (1973) report that only 57 percent of the terminations were planned. In 43 percent of the cases, clients decided not to continue treatment even though service had not been completed.

In leading groups, workers sometimes find themselves asking rhetorically, "What have I done to cause members to fail to return to the group?" In follow-up contacts with members who terminated prematurely, many workers find they have done nothing to cause premature termination. For example, in a group for separated and divorced persons, three people did not return to the second group meeting. When they were contacted, it was found that one person lived 40 miles from where the group met and decided not to return after driving home on foggy rural roads after the first group meeting. Another member's job had unexpectedly changed, requiring the person to be at work during the group's meeting. It was learned from the third person's employer that one of his children had a serious accident. The member called two weeks later to explain that, "I have been running between the hospital and my responsibilities to the other two (children)."

Similarly, in evaluating a smoking cessation group treatment program, it was found that members left treatment prematurely for a variety of reasons (Toseland, Kabat, & Kemp, 1983). Several were dissatisfied with their group or their group's leader, but others left for reasons unrelated to their treatment experience. Although it is commonly assumed that dropouts are treatment failures, in evaluating eight smoking cessation groups, it was found that one of seven dropouts left treatment prematurely because he had stopped smoking and believed he no longer needed treatment. Another dropout quit smoking before a follow-up evaluation. Thus, it is important to realize that unplanned termination of members may be the result of their lack of interest or motivation, particular life circumstances, or other factors beyond the control of the worker that have little or nothing to do with a worker's leadership skills.

Yalom (1985) lists nine factors that may cause group members to drop out of treatment prematurely. Yalom states that some of these arise out of faulty selection of members for the group. Those factors include the following:

1. External factors, such as scheduling conflicts and changes in geographic location.
2. Group deviancy, such as being the richest group member, the only unmarried member, and the like.
3. Problems developing intimate relationships.
4. Fear of emotional contagion.

Other premature terminations are the result of "faulty therapeutic technique" (Yalom, 1985, p. 243). These include the following:

5. Inability to share the worker.
6. Complications of concurrent individual and group therapy.
7. Early provocateurs.
8. Inadequate orientation to therapy.
9. Complications arising from subgrouping.

Workers should not, however, assume that members' decisions to terminate prematurely have nothing to do with the group's process or its leadership. Some members drop out as a result of their dissatisfaction with the group or its leader. For example, in therapy and growth-oriented groups where confrontation is used as a therapeutic technique, members occasionally become so angry when confronted with an emotionally charged issue that they threaten to terminate. To prevent premature termination resulting from anger, some workers specify in the initial contract that members must give two weeks' notice before leaving the group. This gives members a chance to rethink the decision.

Pre-group training has also been found to be an effective way to prevent premature dropouts from therapy groups (Budman, Clifford, Bader, & Bader, 1981; Connelly, Debbane, De Carufel, & Piper, 1986; Piper, Debbane, Bienvenu, & Garant, 1982; Piper, Debbane, Garant, & Bienvenu, 1979). For example, Piper et al. (1982) found a 13 percent to 30 percent reduction in the dropout rate that was attributed to the successful management of anxiety and the development of interpersonal bonds that resulted from a pre-group training program.

When workers take the time to explore members' reasons for terminating, the data they gather can help them reduce premature terminations in subsequent groups. Sometimes, for example, workers learn that simply arranging for child care while the group is in session helps reduce the number of dropouts. Arranging transportation to and from the group may also help. At other times, workers may find that there are ways they can improve their own skills and prevent members from dropping out of the group. For example, they may learn to be more gentle or tentative when they use confrontation as a leadership skill.

Occasionally, an entire group may end prematurely. Just as there are many reasons for the premature termination of individuals, there are also many reasons for the premature termination of groups. A group that begins with a small number of members may lose several of them and may no longer be able to continue functioning effectively (Hartford, 1971). Groups may not receive sufficient support from their sponsoring agency to continue functioning, or they may be unable or unwilling to respond to external pressure to change their functioning.

Groups may also end prematurely as a result of internal dysfunction. For example, communication and interaction patterns may be maldistributed, causing subgrouping, scapegoating, or domination by a few members. The group may lack sufficient attraction for its members and, therefore, may fail to coalesce or function as a cohesive unit (Northen, 1969). Social controls such as norms, roles, status hierarchies, and power may cause severe tension and conflict as some members revolt against the control of the worker or other members. A lack of appropriate social controls may cause chaos or an aimless drift that eventually leads to dissolution of the group as a whole. Members may also have great difficulty deciding on common values, preferences, ways of working together, or other aspects of the group's culture.

Whenever workers confront the possibility of a group ending prematurely, they should carefully examine what factors are contributing to the problem. It is often possible to trace a group's dysfunction back to the planning stage. A careful examination of the factors that contributed to a group's demise can help workers avoid such pitfalls in future groups.

Worker Termination

Although it is rarely mentioned in the literature, there are many instances in which workers have to terminate their work with a group. Students leaving at the end of their field placements are probably the most common reason for worker termination, but change of employment or shifting job responsibilities also lead to worker termination. In a study of two groups where workers terminated their participation, Long, Pendleton, & Winter (1988) found that the termination of the worker led to testing of the new worker, and to a reorganization of the former group processes and group structures.

Several steps can be taken to reduce the disruption that can be caused by worker termination in an ongoing group:

- The worker might consider co-leading the group so there will be continuity of leadership.
- Group members should be told as early as possible when termination will occur.
- The reasons for termination should be shared with the group and members should be encouraged to frankly discuss their feelings about it.
- Any unfinished business should be completed.
- The new worker should be introduced to the group. If possible, the new worker should co-lead the group for a while with the terminating worker.

Variations in Endings

The process of ending varies considerably from group to group (Lewis, 1978). For example, in therapy, support, and growth groups, termination may be accompanied by strong emotional reactions. However, in educational and socialization groups, termination rarely results in the expression of strong emotional reactions.

What are some of the factors that influence group endings? Endings vary depending on whether a group has an open or closed membership policy. In closed groups, unless there are unplanned terminations, all members end at the same time. In these groups, the worker can help all members to deal with common issues and feelings that arise as the group draws to a close. Open groups present a more difficult challenge for the worker. Some members may be experiencing reactions to termination at the same time that others are experiencing reactions common to the beginning or working stages of the group. In open groups, the worker should individualize his or her work with each member. However, because each member will eventually experience disengagement from the group, the worker can use the reactions of members who are terminating to help those who will be experiencing similar reactions in the future.

Endings also vary depending on the attraction of the group for its members. In groups that members find attractive, ending may not be viewed as a positive event. Conversely, if group meetings are viewed as something to be endured, news of the last meeting may be received with relief.

Endings also vary depending on whether the group is a treatment group or a task group. In many therapy groups and support groups, for example, members reveal intimate details of their personal lives. They let down their defenses and become vulnerable as they share concerns and issues that are important to them. In these types of groups, mutual aid and support develop as members deepen relationships with one another and the worker. They come to trust each other and to rely on the therapeutic advice and suggestions given by the worker and fellow group members.

Terminating the relationships that may have influenced the members of treatment groups is quite different from terminating the relationships formed in task groups. In task groups, members' self-disclosure is generally at a relatively low level. Because the focus of these groups is on a product, such as a report or the development of a plan of action, members often look forward to the end of a group with a sense of accomplishment or with relief that their work is finished. Because they have not let down their defenses or shared their personal concerns to any great extent, there is rarely an intense emotional reaction to ending. Also, members of task groups may work together again on other committees, teams, or councils. Therefore, the endings of task groups do not have the same sense of finality as is often the case with treatment groups.

In the task group literature, the focus is on what skills the leader can use to end individual group meetings rather than on how a leader ends the entire group experience (see, for example, Scheidel & Crowell, 1979; Tropman, 1980). This contrasts sharply to the treatment group literature, which generally focuses on ending work with the group rather than ending work in a particular meeting (see, for example, Hartford, 1971; Mayadas & Glasser, 1981; Northen, 1969; Shulman, 1992). This chapter will examine the tasks and skills involved in ending individual group meetings and will then consider the tasks and skills involved in effectively closing the work of the group as a whole.

ENDING GROUP MEETINGS

Scheidel and Crowell (1979) list four generic worker tasks in ending group meetings: (a) closing the group's work, (b) arranging another meeting, (c) preparing a summary or report of the group's work, and (d) planning future group actions. In preparing to close, the worker should help the group keep to its agenda. The worker should ensure that all items of business and all members' concerns are given sufficient attention, but the group should not be allowed to spend too much time discussing one item of business or one member's concerns. To move the group along the worker can do the following:

- Keep members focused on the topic of discussion.
- Limit the time that each member has to discuss an issue.
- Summarize what has been said.
- Obtain closure on each issue or concern as it is discussed.

In closing the group's work, the worker should not bring up new issues, concerns, or items of business. Despite efforts to use structure to reduce discussion of important issues at the end of a meeting, Shulman (1992) points out that members will occasionally raise "door-knob issues" just before ending. If consideration of these issues can be postponed, they are best handled during the next meeting when they can be given fuller consideration. When discussion of an important issue cannot be postponed, the worker should ask group members if they would like to continue the discussion for a brief period. If not, the issue may be taken up outside of the group by the worker and any interested members.

In closing the group's work, the worker should also help members to resolve any remaining conflicts. Resolving conflicts will help members to work in harmony for the decisions reached by the group as a whole. In addition, the worker may want to discuss the strengths and weaknesses of the working relationship that has developed among members during the group meeting, particularly if the group will work together in the future.

During the ending minutes, the worker should help the group plan for future meetings. When considering whether to meet again, it is helpful to review and summarize the group's work. A summary of the group's activities during the meeting clarifies issues that have been resolved and points out other issues that remain unresolved. A clear summary of the group's progress is a prerequisite for arranging another meeting. Summaries also remind members of the activities or tasks they have agreed to work on between meetings, and they help the worker become aware of items that should be included in the agenda for the next meeting.

If a group has completed action on a particular task, the final minutes can also be used to ensure that all members understand and agree to the oral or written information that will be presented at the conclusion of a group's work. Some task forces may prepare extensive written reports of their findings and conclusions. In these groups, it is not productive to prepare the report during the group meeting. The closing minutes can be used to formulate and highlight the major conclusions to be enumerated in the report, to assign members responsibility for preparing major sections of the report, and to develop a mechanism for obtaining approval from members before disseminating the report.

Scheidel and Crowell (1979) also suggest that the endings of group meetings be used to plan future group actions. However, because planning action steps is time consuming, plans are usually developed during the middle of a group meeting. At the ending of a meeting, plans are summarized and members select or are assigned roles to carry out.

The worker should help members maintain their motivation, commitment, and responsibility to implement plans and carry out tasks they have agreed to complete between meetings. To help members maintain their motivation, the worker should praise them for their work in the group and for their willingness to commit themselves to tasks outside of the meeting. The worker may also want to mention any benefits that will accrue to members for maintaining their commitment to the plans and activities they have agreed to complete.

ENDING THE GROUP

A variety of tasks are associated with ending a group including the following:

- Maintaining and generalizing change efforts.
- Reducing group attraction and promoting the independent functioning of individual members.
- Helping members deal with their feelings about ending.
- Planning for the future.
- Making referrals.
- Evaluating the work of a group.

With the exception of evaluating the work of a group, which has been discussed in Chapter 12, the remaining portion of this chapter will examine each of these tasks and indicate the skills and techniques the worker can use to facilitate the effective ending of a group. Many of these tasks may be carried out simultaneously. The specific order in which each task is completed depends on the specific group the worker is leading.

Maintaining and Generalizing Change Efforts

After treatment plans have been developed and carried out, workers should ensure that the changes that have been achieved are maintained and generalized to other important aspects of members' lives. Evaluations of the results of therapeutic interventions suggest that positive changes are often difficult to maintain over time. For example, in an evaluation of two different group intervention programs for caregivers of the frail elderly, it was found that some of the positive changes found immediately after group intervention were not sustained at one year (Labrecque, Peak, & Toseland, 1992; Toseland, 1990b).

Positive changes are even harder to maintain in group treatment programs that are focused on individuals with addictive disorders. For example, in an evaluation of a group treatment program for smokers, it was found that although more than 60 percent of those who attended the program initially stopped smoking, after three months the cessation rate had dropped to 36 percent (Toseland, Kabat, & Kemp, 1983). Results obtained for a variety of other addictive disorders, such as narcotics use, alcohol use, and overeating, show similar relapse rates (see, for example, Hunt, Barnett, & Branch, 1971). Maintenance is also difficult to achieve when working with antisocial group members such as juvenile delinquents and when working with group members who have severe psychological disorders.

Both novice and experienced workers often mistakenly believe that changes in specific behaviors can be taken as a sign of generalized improvement in a member's level of functioning. These workers do little to ensure that specific behavior changes generalize to related, but untreated, behaviors. Results of a variety of different treatment programs have shown, however, that therapeutic changes occurring in specific behaviors do not always generalize to similar behaviors performed by a member in other contexts (Goldstein, Keller, & Sechrest, 1966; Stokes & Baer, 1977). For example, an unassertive group member may learn to be assertive in a particular situation but may continue to be nonassertive in other situations. Similarly, a parent may learn how to reduce a child's temper tantrums, but this success may not affect the parent's ability to help the child play cooperatively with other children.

Although some people seek group treatment only for changes in specific behaviors, most people enter group treatment with the expectation that there will be a generalized improvement in their life situation. For example, educational, growth, and program-oriented groups often provide benefits in a number of areas of a member's life. Therefore, it is important for workers to help members generalize changes achieved in specific behaviors and performed in particular situations to related behaviors performed in other contexts.

With the notable exception of Rose and colleagues (Rose, 1989; Rose & Edleson, 1987), little has been written about these topics in group work. Almost all the theoretical and clinical work on maintenance and generalization of change has come from the literature on behavior modification and learning theory (Stokes and Baer, 1977). This literature suggests several things workers can do to help members maintain and generalize the changes they have achieved, including the following:

- Helping members work on relevant situations.
- Helping members develop confidence in their abilities.
- Using a variety of different situations and settings when helping members learn new behaviors.
- Using a variety of naturally occurring consequences.
- Extending treatment through follow-up sessions.
- Preventing setbacks in an unsympathetic environment.
- Helping members solve problems independently by providing a framework for organizing data and solving problems that can be used in many different situations.

Relevant Situations.   To achieve long-lasting changes that will generalize to similar situations in members' lives, the concerns and issues worked on in the group should be a relevant and realistic sample of those experienced by members in their daily lives. Sometimes members become distracted by issues that are not central to their concerns. This may be a sign that they are avoiding difficult issues and the changes they necessitate. The worker can help by drawing members' attention back to the central concerns that brought them together as a group.

In other cases, the situations discussed may be highly specific and individual. Although it is important to be as specific and concrete as possible when developing treatment plans, it is also important to ensure that situations that are relevant to all group members are included in the group's work. This helps to ensure that members are prepared for situations they are likely to encounter in the future.

Although group meetings should provide a protected environment where members receive support, encouragement, and understanding, the group should also be a place where members can get honest feedback about how their behavior is likely to be seen outside the group. Members should be encouraged to try out new behaviors in the group, but they should not be misled into thinking they will receive the same level of support and encouragement for trying new behaviors outside the group. In short, although the group should provide a supportive and caring atmosphere in which to work, the group should help members to understand, cope with, and prepare for reactions likely to be experienced outside the group.

Helping Members Develop Confidence.   Many treatment groups spend much of their time discussing members' problems and concerns as well as their inappropriate ways of handling situations. Although ventilating thoughts and feelings may be therapeutic, as Goldstein, Keller, and Sechrest (1966) point out, perhaps too much time in treatment is spent on the negative aspects of members' concerns, issues, and problems. They suggest that the emphasis on negative thoughts, feelings, and experiences only reinforces the members' tendency to continue to express them outside the group.

As the group progresses, workers should encourage members to focus on adaptive alternatives to the problematic situations they are experiencing. If members dwell on poor performances and inhibiting thoughts in the group, they are less likely to feel confident about their abilities to cope with or resolve the problems they experience in their daily lives. Although it is not possible or desirable to avoid discussions of problems in treatment groups, workers should help members become more aware of their abilities. Members should be encouraged to use their abilities and their resources to resolve the problematic situations that they encounter as they prepare for leaving the group. Program activities, role plays and exercises are particularly useful in helping members become more aware of their strengths and to build confidence in their ability to solve problems. This, in turn, will help members gain confidence in their ability to continue to function adaptively after they leave the group.

Using a Variety of Situations and Settings.   Another aspect of maintaining and generalizing change is preparing members for different situations that may interfere with their ability to maintain the changes they have made. Although preparations for maintaining changes are emphasized during ending stage meetings, they should be given attention throughout members' participation in a group. Issues and concerns brought to group treatment are rarely, if ever, confined to one situation or setting in a member's life. A member who experiences communication difficulties, for example, often experiences them in many situations with different people. Therefore, in treatment groups it is often helpful to have members practice responses with different members in a variety of situations. Because of the availability of group members who will respond differently from one another, group treatment is ideally suited for this purpose. Bandura's research (1969) confirms that the use of multiple models (group members) promotes generalization of treatment effects.

As mentioned in Chapter 9, it is helpful to structure practice so that easier situations are practiced before more difficult ones. What constitutes an easy or a difficult situation varies from person to person, so the worker should assess each person's needs when developing a hierarchy of situations to work on in the group. Once a member demonstrates ability to handle a variety of situations in the group, he or she should be encouraged to get additional practice by trying new ways of behaving between meetings.

Program activities can also be used to simulate situations that may be encountered outside the group. For example, children referred to a group because they have difficulty playing with classmates can be encouraged to participate in a team sport where cooperative play is essential. Long-term chronic psychiatric patients may be encouraged to prepare and participate in a group dinner as a way of practicing skills that will help them when they are placed in a community residence.

Using Naturally Occurring Consequences.   Although it is often difficult to make changes initially, changes are maintained and generalized by the resulting positive consequences. For example, although losing weight is initially uncomfortable, it soon results in positive compliments from peers and feeling better about oneself. To maintain and generalize behavior changes, the worker should help group members experience the positive consequences of changes as soon as possible and maintain the positive consequences for as long as possible.

One method for doing this is to help members focus on positive consequences while reducing their attention to negative consequences. For example, a member who decides to stop smoking should be encouraged to seek out the reactions of family members, friends, and group members who no longer have to put up with the smell of stale cigarettes and smoke-filled rooms. At the same time, the member should be encouraged to replace urges to smoke with thoughts about the soon to be experienced positive effects of not smoking, such as increased lung capacity and greater vitality and endurance. The worker can also contact significant others in the member's life and ask that they continue to reinforce the ex-smoker's resolve to not smoke after the treatment program has ended.

Another way to enhance naturally occurring contingencies is to help members modify environmental consequences so that behavior change is more readily maintained and generalized. For example, a buddy system may be established so that group members receive positive feedback for changes between group sessions. Group members may be asked to modify friendship patterns, social activities, or their home environment so as to provide them with positive consequences for changes they have made through their efforts in the group. By enhancing and highlighting naturally occurring positive consequences and by reducing negative consequences, initial changes can be maintained and generalized.

Follow-Up Sessions.   Another way to help ensure that treatment results are maintained and generalized is to provide members the opportunity to meet together for follow-up sessions after the completion of a formal group treatment program. For example, a time-limited outpatient psychotherapy group meets for

12 weekly sessions and then meets for six follow-up sessions at one-month intervals. After this time, two quarterly meetings during the rest of the year complete the treatment contract.

Although follow-up sessions are infrequently used by professionals, they make self-help groups appealing to participants. The popularity of self-help groups can, in part, be attributed to the flexible, open-ended, long-term membership that is encouraged in many of these groups. Self-help groups often have a small group of members who regularly attend meetings, along with many other members who attend occasionally "as needed" (Toseland & Hacker, 1982). For self-help group participants who have attended sessions regularly in the past, occasional attendance at future meetings can maintain treatment gains and gradually reduce their dependency on the group.

Follow-up sessions have several advantages (Toseland, Kabat, & Kemp, 1983). They review members' commitment to maintaining changes. They remind members of the changes that have taken place in their lives since they began treatment. Members can share similar experiences about their difficulties in maintaining changes and trying to generalize changes to new situations and new life experiences.

Follow-up sessions are generally not used to introduce members to new material. Instead, they are used as an opportunity for members to share their experiences since last meeting together. Members are encouraged to discuss any new problem situations they have encountered and to describe how they have handled them. The emphasis is on helping members identify the coping skills they have used to maintain changes achieved during treatment.

Follow-up sessions are particularly helpful for members who have difficulty maintaining treatment gains. Members can discuss the circumstances surrounding particular relapses, consulting the group worker and the other members about how to best handle these occurrences. The additional support provided by follow-up sessions is often sufficient to help members overcome brief relapses that might otherwise turn into treatment failures.

Preventing Setbacks in Unsympathetic Environments.   Even when careful attention has been given to the environment that a member faces outside the group, the support, trust, and sharing found in well-functioning treatment groups is rarely duplicated in the members' home or community environments. Members should be prepared to face possible setbacks in the unsympathetic environment they are likely to experience outside the group. Rose (1989) suggests that the experiences of the worker in leading previous groups, as well as the experiences of former group members, are useful in developing vignettes that describe realistic and typical situations group members are likely to encounter outside the group. During the final few group sessions, members discuss how to respond to these situations and practice responses with one another, using modeling, role play, rehearsal, and coaching.

Because members are likely to experience situations that threaten their treatment gains soon after changes are initiated, members should be encouraged to describe these situations in the group. In this way, all group members become exposed to a variety of situations and reactions to changes that they can learn to handle before they occur in their own life situations. Meichenbaum (1977), for example, reports that a stress inoculation treatment program in which members are taught to anticipate negative reactions and ways to cope with them can be effective in helping to maintain treatment gains.

Members may encounter difficult situations any time of the day or night. Often, the group worker may not be available to members, so the worker should inform members about how to contact on-call workers, emergency hot lines, and other 24-hour services.

The pervasive nature of some members' problems suggests that they may respond best to intensive and extensive treatment. For such problems, group treatment with a professional worker may be supplemented by linkages with self-help organizations. Alcoholics Anonymous groups, for example, often meet each evening, or at least several times each week, providing members with an alternative to spending their evenings in a neighborhood bar or drinking alone at home. They also encourage recovering alcoholics to form close relationships with new members. This provides new members with models of sobriety and encourages the development of a network of supportive relationships. Similarly, organizations such as Recovery, Inc., Parents Without Partners, Parents Anonymous, and Gamblers Anonymous help members with all types of problems and concerns become involved with a network of people to whom they can turn at particularly difficult times.

Members of task groups can also benefit from preparing for an unsympathetic environment. Plans, reports, and other products of a task group's work may encounter resistance as they are considered by others outside the group. Resistance is especially likely when the products of a task group are controversial or have negative implications for a particular program, an entire organization or a social service delivery system. Also, resistance is more likely to be encountered when proposals must go through several levels of review before they are approved (Brager & Holloway, 1978). Therefore, it is important for task group members to anticipate resistance to implementing the group's work and to plan strategies to counteract this resistance.

Helping Members Solve Problems Independently.   No matter how many different situations are discussed and practiced within a group, it is not possible to cover the full range of situations that members may experience outside a group. Therefore, during the group, members should be learning how to solve their own problems independently, gradually lessening the need for continued treatment. This process should begin as early as possible in the group experience and be given particular emphasis in the last few meetings of the group.

Workers can support independent functioning by building members' confidence in their existing coping skills and by helping them develop and rely on new coping skills throughout the group treatment process. Workers should also teach members the principles underlying the intervention methods used in the group. Workers sometimes fail to teach members the underlying therapeutic principles of an intervention because they think professional knowledge should not be shared with clients. Others fear that group members may not be able to understand these principles or may misuse the information they receive. Most group members who enter treatment voluntarily are eager to learn more about ways to cope with their concerns. For example, having members of an assertion training group read *Your Perfect Right* (Alberti & Emmons, 1974), or members of a parent training group read *Parents Are Teachers* (Becker, 1971), or members of a weight-loss group read *Slim Chance in a Fat World* (Stuart & Davis, 1972) helps them to learn some basic principles that can help them as they encounter new situations not discussed in the group. Some treatment approaches, such as Eric Berne's *Transactional Analysis* (see Berne, 1961) and Albert Ellis's *Rational-Emotive Therapy* (see Ellis, 1962), encourage workers to help members understand the basic principles underlying their treatment approaches. Workers using other treatment approaches should spend more time teaching members the basic principles underlying therapeutic interventions.

When teaching members, technical terms should be translated into jargon-free explanations. This is an especially important consideration when English is a second language for members.

Having members summarize what they have learned in the group and deducing general principles from these summaries is also effective in helping them see how they can be applied to other situations. For example, in summarizing what they have learned, members of a couples group became aware of some general principles regarding communication, including maintaining eye contact to show that they are listening, summarizing core content of messages to ensure understanding, and using "I" messages to communicate their feelings and thoughts.

Reducing Group Attraction

In addition to helping members maintain and generalize the changes they have made in a group, the ending stage should help members become less dependent on the group. This can be done by helping them rely on their own skills and resources as well as on sources of support outside the group. Planning for termination should begin with workers' awareness of their own feelings about terminating with individual members and the group as a whole. Particularly in support groups and therapy groups, it is not uncommon for workers to become emotionally attached to individual members or the group as a whole. Workers should be careful not to foster dependence. They should carefully assess whether they are being overly protective of members or covertly or overtly undermining their efforts to function without the group. Supervision can be very useful in helping workers examine their feelings about terminating.

To ensure that members are prepared for ending, it is a good practice to begin discussions of termination at least four sessions before the planned termination date. Members should be fully involved in planning for termination. Just as program activities can be useful in simulating situations that may be encountered outside the group, they can also be useful in helping to reduce the group's attraction for its members (Henry, 1992; Mayadas & Glasser, 1981; Wayne & Avery, 1979). Thus, workers should share ideas they have about program activities for ending the group, soliciting members' feedback, and asking for additional suggestions.

Appropriate program activities for ending a group include those that (a) demonstrate or encourage reflection about the skills members have learned in the group, (b) allow members to express their feelings about the group and its members, (c) focus on future activities, and (d) encourage individual as well as group participation. For example, getting together for a dinner is a program activity that is commonly used at the ending of a group. Planning for a dinner encourages individual as well as group-oriented participation. During the dinner, members often discuss the things they have learned in the group, their feelings about ending, and their plans for the future.

Endings are often marked by ceremonies (Garvin, 1981). Program activities, such as having a party or a potluck dinner, awarding certificates of merit, or having each member say or write something special about other members, can be viewed as ceremonies that signify the end of the group. When they are used creatively, ceremonies can also help maintain and generalize changes made by members. For example, in the next-to-last session of a weight-loss group, members were asked to write themselves two letters containing (a) their feelings about being overweight, (b) how good it felt to be losing weight, and (c) reiterating their commitment to continue losing weight. These self-addressed letters were mailed by the worker at three-week intervals after the group ended as a reminder to members of their commitment to losing weight and maintaining weight losses.

Group attraction can be reduced in other ways. Members can be encouraged to summarize their accomplishments and discuss why they no longer need the group. Meetings can be scheduled less frequently or for shorter periods of time to reduce the importance of the group for members. Workers can encourage members to become involved in outside activities that will compete with the group for members' time and energy. Such activities also can support members and maintain changes.

Feelings About Ending

The feelings that members and workers have about ending are related to the relationships that have developed in the group. Germain and Gitterman (1980) point out, "the intensity of feeling associated with a relationship and with its ending depends upon its duration and its quality of mutual regard, respect, and reciprocity" (p. 258). Group work literature often suggests that the endings of groups are painful times during which members experience a variety of feelings such as denial, anger, sadness, rejection, and hostility. But the ending of a group can also be a positive, growth-promoting experience. In fact, although endings are frequently characterized by members' ambivalence as they vacillate between positive and negative feelings about terminating their relationship with the people in the group (Lewis, 1978), others have found that clients' strongest reactions were positive affect, positive flight to constructive outside activities, and objective evaluations of treatment goals and processes (Fortune, 1987; Fortune, Pearlingi, & Rochelle, 1992).

Many positive feelings can result from a skillfully facilitated group ending. One of the most important is a feeling of potency as members realize they are capable of accomplishing goals. A closely related feeling of independence results from being in control of their own lives rather than feeling their lives are controlled by their environment. Members also can feel a sense of satisfaction and pride in accomplishing treatment goals and successfully completing the group experience. Another feeling is that of usefulness in being able to help others by providing feedback, support, suggestions, information, and alternative frames of reference (Lieberman & Borman, 1979). Another is that of confidence, as members learn how to cope with termination, an experience they will encounter in other aspects of their lives.

At the same time, members may experience negative feelings about the ending of a group. A common reaction is denial (Levine, 1979). Not wanting to show that they will miss the worker or others in the group, members sometimes ignore workers' attempts to prepare them for ending by changing the topic of discussion or by indicating that they are looking forward to ending. Another common reaction is feeling abandoned or rejected. Members may express the rejection they are feeling by becoming angry or hostile. In other cases, they may engage in regressive behavior that exhibits the symptoms or problems they had when they first entered the group. Other reactions to feeling rejected can include clinging to the worker, acting out, and devaluing the group experience or the skill of the worker (Levinson, 1977).

More often, members may wish they could continue with the warm, supportive relationships they have found in the group. Therefore, they may experience a sense of loss and accompanying sadness at the ending of the group. Members may also question their ability to maintain changes without the help of the group.

As mentioned earlier, workers are not immune to reactions to ending a group. In a study of practitioners' reactions to termination of individual treatment, Fortune, Pearlingi, & Rochelle (1992) report that the practitioners' strongest reactions are (a) pride and accomplishment in the client's success, (b) pride in their own therapeutic skill, (c) a renewed sense of therapeutic process, (d) sadness, sense of loss or ambivalence about no longer working with the client, (e) doubt or disappointment about the client's progress or ability to function independently, (f) re-experience of their own losses, and (g) relief, doubt, or guilt about their therapeutic effectiveness. Although this study was focused on termination of individual treatment, it is clear in the clinical group work literature that therapeutic pride, doubt about their effectiveness and a sense of loss are the three primary types of emotions experienced by group workers.

According to Levine (1979), workers should be aware of their own reactions to ending to fully appreciate the difficulties that members may be experiencing. If workers are not aware of their own feelings, they may withdraw emotionally or they may encourage the dependence of members and prolong treatment beyond what is needed. Workers also may want to share their reactions as a way of helping members identify and express their own feelings and reactions.

It is helpful to begin the ending process several meetings before the final group. As members begin to react to ending, the worker can point out that conflicting or ambivalent feelings during this stage are common. Members should be encouraged to discuss their ambivalent and conflicting feelings.

Workers can reduce members' negative emotional reactions to ending by helping them realize their strengths and the gains they have made as a result of being in the group (Lacoursiere, 1980; Northen, 1969). The worker can prepare members for ending by clarifying what the role of the worker and the sponsoring agency will be in helping members maintain gains after the group ends.

The worker should plan for the future with each member. Plans should include the support systems and resources that will be available after the group ends. Workers should also encourage members to use their own skills, resources, and strengths to meet their needs. This can be done by expressing confidence in members' abilities, encouraging them to try new skills outside the group (Feldman & Wodarski, 1975), and repeating successful skill-building activities and role plays so members develop feelings of mastery and self-confidence.

Planning for the Future

In time-limited groups, some members may wish to contract for additional services. When considering new services, the worker should help members clarify (a) their continuing needs, (b) the goals they hope to achieve, (c) the duration of the new service period, and (d) any appropriate modifications of the original contract. Recontracting should occur when there is a clear need for additional services and when members are highly motivated to achieve additional goals or to continue work on original goals that they have only partially achieved. Occasionally, all members of a group may express interest in continuing to meet. In such cases, the worker may recontract for additional meetings with all members or may encourage members to meet on their own without the worker.

When workers encourage members to continue to meet on their own, they are participating in the development of a self-help group. The worker helps groups continue to meet by developing natural leadership and by helping with any resources that may be needed (Toseland & Coppola, 1985). Rather than total independence, many new self-help groups prefer continuing contact, guidance, and leadership from the worker until the new group has been firmly established. Many existing self-help groups have been started by professional workers in this manner (Toseland & Hacker, 1982). The worker can continue to assist self-help groups after they have developed by (a) providing material support to maintain a group, (b) referring clients to a group, and (c) acting as a consultant to a group.

In some instances, the members of a group may wish to continue meeting because they are unable to terminate the group in a positive and responsible fashion. The group may develop a culture that supports members' dependency rather than preparing them for independent functioning in the environment outside the group. When this occurs, the worker should explore this with the group and, in a supportive manner, help the members end the group experience by using the activities discussed in this chapter. Klein (1972) has referred to this process as a worker's skill in letting go of the group.

Sometimes the ending of a group may result in no further contact with members. However, workers are rarely sure that members will not need services in the future. Changing life situations, new crises, or relapses may cause members to seek help again. The worker should discuss how they can seek additional services if they are needed. In some agencies, the worker may explain that he or she has an open-door policy, so that members who need additional services can contact the worker directly. In other agencies, the policy may be for former clients to apply for services in the same manner that other clients apply. This clarifies the position of the worker and the agency with regard to how members can obtain any additional services that may be needed.

In some situations, preparation for the future may involve planning with others for continuing treatment for members. For example, in preparing for the ending of the children's group, the worker should contact the children's parents to review each child's progress and to plan for additional services. In groups where members are participating in other agency services such as individual counseling, the worker should contact the member's case manager or primary worker to evaluate the member's progress in the group and to plan for additional services. Similarly, in residential and inpatient settings, the ending of a group may not signify the end of service. The worker should meet with other staff, perhaps in a case conference or team meeting, to report progress and to plan for the future needs of members.

Those who prematurely terminate from groups should not be forgotten when planning for future service needs. Without follow-up contact, dropouts may feel abandoned. Their failure to continue with a particular group may signify to them that their situation is hopeless. Therefore, dropouts from treatment should be contacted whenever possible. One of the primary objectives of a follow-up contact is to motivate those who terminate prematurely to seek further treatment if it is needed. The worker can inquire about difficulties they may be having in continuing to attend group meetings, and may suggest ways to overcome these impediments. During this process, the worker should identify any needs that former group members have for continuing service and refer them to appropriate resources and services whenever possible.

Making Referrals

During the ending stage of group work, workers frequently connect members to other services or resources. In some cases, members may be transferred to workers in the same agency. In other cases, referrals may be made to workers in other agencies.

A referral should be made only after the worker and the member have appraised the member's need for additional services or resources. If the member is motivated to seek additional services, the referral can proceed. If the member is not motivated to seek additional services, but the worker's assessment suggests that they may be beneficial, the worker should proceed by helping the member explore his or her resistance.

Whenever possible, the member should be helped to use informal, natural helping systems. If these are unavailable, or are judged to be inadequate, then the member should be referred to professional helping resources. Before making a referral, the worker should discuss the reasons for the referral with the member, answering any questions he or she may have. It is often helpful to find out if the member has had any prior contact with the referral source or has heard anything about it. Members' impressions and previous experiences with particular referral sources can be influential in determining whether or not they follow through and use the resources to which they are referred.

In preparing to make effective referrals, workers should become familiar with available community resources. If possible, workers should get to know a particular contact person in frequently used referral sources. It is also helpful to be familiar with some basic information about referral sources to share with members who are being referred. This includes information about eligibility requirements, the waiting time for service, the business hours of the agency, and the type of service provided. Such information will prepare the member for what to expect when contacting the referral source and will avoid members' developing expectations that will not be met. Because it may be difficult for workers to be familiar with all community resources that are available in an area, agencies should maintain up-to-date files with basic information about such resources and services.

When making a referral, the worker should write the name of the agency, the contact person, and the agency's address on a card to give to the member. In some cases, referral sources may have forms that have to be filled out before a member can be seen. Often, release forms need to be signed by the member so that information in a member's file can be sent to the referral source. Because many people never reach the resources or services to which they were referred (see, for example, Craig, Huffine & Brooks, 1974; Weissman, 1976), it is helpful for the worker to call the contact person while the member is there to emphasize that the member is expected at the referral source for a particular appointment. The worker should also ensure that the member (a) knows how to get to the agency to which he or she was referred, (b) has a means of transportation, and (c) is capable of getting to the referral source independently. Members who are severely impaired may need help in getting to referral sources. The worker, a volunteer, or a case aide may have to accompany the member during the first visit.

The worker should check to ensure that members have reached the referral resource and have received the needed service. In addition, members should be instructed to contact the worker if they fail to get what they need from the referral source. A referral may fail for a number of reasons, including the following: (a) The referral source has had a change in policy—for example, eligibility requirements have become more stringent; (b) the member lacks motivation; (c) the member lacks the skill necessary to obtain the needed resources; or (d) the worker has given the member incorrect information or insufficient help to contact the referral resource. Follow-up contacts allow workers to assess why members did not obtain needed services or resources. They also allow workers to plan with members about how to obtain needed resources and services in the future.

██████ **SUMMARY**

The ending stage is a critical time in the life of a group. During the ending stage, the work of the group is consolidated, and lasting impressions are made about the efficacy of the entire group experience. Endings can either be planned or unplanned. Unfortunately, in many voluntary groups, unplanned terminations are fairly common. This chapter makes suggestions about how to facilitate planned endings and what to do when members terminate before the planned ending of a group.

Procedures for facilitating endings vary, depending on the type of group being led. In task groups and treatment groups where members have not been encouraged to self-disclose or form supportive relationships, endings are less emotionally charged than in groups where a great deal of self-disclosure has taken place and where members depend on one another for help with their personal concerns and problems.

Other variations in group endings depend on whether the group has an open or closed membership policy, is short-term or long-term, and is attractive or unattractive to its members. This chapter examines how these factors influence the use of worker skills during the ending stage.

This chapter also examines the tasks that workers are often called upon to perform in ending meetings and in ending the group as a whole. Major tasks in ending a meeting of a group include (a) closing the work, (b) arranging another meeting, (c) preparing a summary or a report of the group's work, and (d) planning for future group actions. Major tasks in ending the group as a whole include (a) maintaining and generalizing change efforts, (b) evaluating the work of the group, (c) reducing group attraction and promoting independent member functioning, (d) helping members with their feelings about ending, (e) planning for the future, and (f) making effective referrals.

LEARNING ASSIGNMENTS   ██████████████████████████████

1. Interview an experienced group worker. Ask the respondent to discuss his or her experiences with members who drop out of treatment groups. Make a list and rank order the reasons for unplanned termination of members. What might the group worker have done to reduce the number of unplanned terminations?

2. You have been leading a short-term social skills group designed to help psychiatric inpatients live independently in the community. In preparing for ending the group, describe four strategies that you could use to help members maintain their newly acquired skills.

3. How would you assist a member of a group in a residential setting who started acting out when she learned that she will be leaving the facility for a foster placement after a one-and-a-half year stay? What effects might her acting out behavior have on other members of the residence? How would you help the residents deal with these effects?

4. Imagine that you work in an intensive outpatient alcoholism rehabilitation program that relies on group treatment as the primary therapeutic modality. How would you help prepare the members of the group you are leading to maintain sobriety after they leave the program?

5. Design three program activities that would be useful for the ending stage of a treatment group. Describe the purpose of each activity. How would each activity help members end their group experience on a positive note? How would each activity help group members resolve their feelings about ending?

CHAPTER 14

Case Examples

Although case examples are very useful in the teaching and learning of group work practice, there is a dearth of examples illustrating practice with treatment and task groups. This chapter presents two case examples. The first example of a caregiver support group illustrates work with a treatment group. The second case example, of a community coalition helping people with AIDS, illustrates work with a task group.

A CAREGIVER SUPPORT GROUP

The case example selected to illustrate practice with treatment groups describes a support group for family members who are providing care for frail elderly relatives. It illustrates the blending of supportive, educational and psychotherapeutic interventions in a single group. It also illustrates a blending of a relatively structured group format with relatively unstructured follow-up meetings.

The leader of the group is a professional social worker who has had extensive clinical experience working with individuals and family members with chronic disabilities. The group met for eight weekly two-hour sessions, followed by 10 monthly meetings. During the first eight meetings, the group agreed to use a structured approach that included support, education, coping skills, and problem solving. Monthly follow-up meetings were less structured, with members reporting in turn what had transpired since the last meeting, and seeking support and assistance as needed.

The Support Component

Whereas specific time was set aside during each meeting for the educational component and the problem-solving/coping-skills component, support interventions were used throughout each group meeting. Supportive interventions included (a) ventilation of stressful experiences in an understanding and supportive environment, (b) validation and confirmation of similar caregiving experiences, (c) affirmation of members' ability to cope with their situations, (d) praise for providing high quality care, (e) support and understanding during difficult situations, (f) hopefulness about the future, and (g) mutual aid. The worker took the lead in modeling supportive interventions, encouraging members to be supportive of each other.

The Educational Component

The educational component usually occurred during the first 30 to 40 minutes of each of the initial eight meetings. A different topic was covered each week:

- Session 1 provided an introduction to the support group.
- Session 2 focused on caregivers' emotions and feelings.
- Session 3 focused on care receivers' reactions to illness.
- Session 4 focused on the caregivers taking care of themselves and doing positive things with their frail parent.
- Session 5 focused on communication between the caregiver and care receiver, and between the caregiver and other family members.
- Session 6 focused on community resources.
- Session 7 focused on medical needs, pharmacology issues and the nursing home placement process.
- Session 8 focused on home management techniques and strategies, and on resources for environmental modifications and specialized home-care appliances and devices.[1]

After a brief presentation by the leader or a guest speaker, members were encouraged to ask questions, share information, and discuss issues related to the weekly topic presented by the leader.

The Coping-Skills Component

This part of the program was conceptually linked to Lazarus and Folkman's (1984) model of stress and coping and is based on the Stress Inoculation Training (SIT) developed by Meichenbaum and his colleagues (Meichenbaum, 1977, 1985; Meichenbaum & Cameron, 1983). SIT involves multiple strategies such as didactic teaching, relaxation training, cognitive restructuring, self-monitoring, and self-instruction. Instead of teaching a single stress-management technique, members were introduced to several techniques and encouraged to use those that worked best for them. Although the leader's goal was to cover specific coping skills during each meeting, the contents of the coping skills component were incorporated flexibly into the first eight sessions depending on the needs of the members, and the pressing problems they expressed during discussions in the educational component and during the problem-solving component (Everly, 1989).

---

[1] A number of manuals are available that describe topics for caregiver support group meetings and provide useful background material. Three of these include: *Caregiver's Support Group Facilitator's Manual,* which can be obtained by writing to the Department of Veteran's Affairs, Central Office, Social Work Service (122), 810 Vermont Avenue NW, Washington, D.C. 20420; Montgomery, R. (Ed.). (1985). *Helping Families Help.* Washington: University of Washington Press; and *Practical Help: Guide for Course Leaders,* which can be obtained by writing to the New York State Office for the Aging, 2 Empire State Plaza, Albany, NY 12223.

Session 1 of the coping-skills component was focused on assuring caregivers that their reactions to their family members' health problems were normal. It was also focused on acquainting members with the concept of stress, appraisal, and coping (Lazarus & Folkman, 1984). At the end of the session, members were given the opportunity to discuss their reactions to their family members' illness, their illness-related appraisals, and the coping strategies they had been using to deal with these reactions.

Session 2 focused on helping members identify and label their emotional and bodily coping responses to their spouses' physical and mental condition, and to their role as a caregiver. The leader reinforced effective coping skills and encouraged members to work toward changing ineffective coping skills. As in previous successful group intervention programs for caregivers of the chronically ill (see McCallion, Toseland, & Diehl, 1994; Toseland, 1990b; Toseland, Labrecque, Goebel, & Whitney, 1992; Toseland & Rossiter, 1989), members were encouraged to recognize their own specific emotional and bodily reactions to stress, and to identify situations that provoke stress and characteristic coping responses. They were also taught to better recognize early signs of stress and their typical cognitive appraisals and coping reactions. To facilitate this learning process, members were asked to keep a diary between group meetings of the stressors they experienced during the week, and their cognitive and behavioral responses to those stressors. Practice in recognizing stressors and identifying typical appraisals and coping reactions continued in the remaining sessions.

During Sessions 3 and 4, two relaxation techniques were introduced and practiced by members as a means to creatively counteract the negative effects of strain associated with caregiving, and to cope with other, unavoidable life stresses. First, a deep breathing technique was introduced and practiced (Toseland, Labrecque, Goebel, & Whitney, 1992). This technique, which is easily learned, provides members with an effective strategy to moderate their typical reactions to stress by interrupting their habituated responses and slowing down their cognitive processes, thereby increasing the likelihood that more planned and effective coping reactions will be chosen. Second, progressive muscle relaxation (Jacobson, 1978) was introduced and practiced. Members were given an audiotape containing muscle relaxation instructions and encouraged to practice at home between sessions. Members' experiences with the relaxation tape were reviewed during subsequent sessions. The tape contained two sets of instructions, a full 45-minute set of instructions on Side 1, and a shorter version of the same instructions on Side 2 for individuals who had mastered Side 1.

Sessions 5 through 8 focused on cognitive restructuring strategies including self-talk, perspective-taking, and cognitive self-instruction strategies (see Meichenbaum, 1985; Meichenbaum & Cameron, 1983). Building on exercises presented in Session 2, members were taught how to use early stress cues as signals to activate more effective appraisals and coping strategies. In particular, members were taught how to use the method of "inner dialogue" or coping self-talk to slow down their "hot" cognitive processes and to plan their coping reactions in a way that is more effective and gratifying for them. Members were asked to identify their typical and preferred coping self-talk phrases and to reflect on their usefulness.

In addition, members were introduced to the concept of coping imagery and asked to identify coping images they preferred. Between meetings, members were asked to continue to note stressful events in their log, and also what self-talk and cognitive imagery strategies they used to cope with the stressful event. Entries in their log were discussed during each group meeting. During Session 8, members' use of the cognitive restructuring strategies were reviewed and potential problems were addressed.

The Problem-Solving Component

A problem-solving model similar to the one described in Chapter 10 was introduced during the first group session as a device to help members move beyond ventilation of experiences and emotional reactions to using methods for improving their coping skills. Each week, members were encouraged to take turns working on their individual concerns using the problem-solving model displayed on two flip charts for easy viewing. Frequently, the problem-solving component was combined with the coping-skills component. Sometimes, members learned a new skill and then practiced it on a pressing problem that they were experiencing. At other times, members shared a problem they were having and the group leader or another member suggested a coping skill that might help.

It should be noted that because the members of the caregiver support group had a tremendous need to ventilate pent-up emotions and to share their experiences and concerns with each other, the problem-solving model was not always carried out in a linear, step-by-step fashion. Still, by using it, the leader was able to help all the members address at least one pressing problem during the eight-week group, and many members addressed several problems.

Session 1

During the first session, members shared information about themselves. The leader, Mrs. S., spoke first. She modeled the level of self-disclosure she hoped members would engage in when they introduced themselves. She described her professional experience, her own caregiving experience, some of the positive experiences she had in previous caregiver groups, and what she hoped would be some of the beneficial outcomes of participating in the support group. Next, she asked members to introduce themselves one by one. They shared the following information about themselves and the person for whom they were caring:

Mrs. Z: Mrs. Z has four children and is 54 years old. Because she married late in life, two of her four children are teen-agers and living at home. Mrs. Z's mother, age 81, lives alone, has diabetes, is extremely overweight, has been widowed twice, and is depressed. Although married and working full time, Mrs. Z still manages to see her mother almost every day. She does her mother's shopping and supervises her mother's medication.

Mrs. B: Mrs. B. is a 61-year-old widow with one child who lives in another state. Mrs. B cares for her mother-in-law, age 86, who came to live in her home seven years ago after suffering a stroke. Three years ago, Mrs. B's husband died. Since his death, her mother-in-law, who is also a diabetic, has been totally dependent on Mrs. B and is home alone all day while Mrs. B works as a legal secretary.

Mrs. A: Mrs. A is caring for her bedridden mother, who has heart disease and Parkinson's disease, and has lived with Mrs. A and her husband for five years. She has also been recently diagnosed with cancer. An aide comes in three times a week for four hours a day but the remaining burden of care is left to Mrs. A.

Miss G: Miss G is 28 and works part time as a clerk in a neighborhood store. Miss G's 76-year-old mother, Bertha, a fiercely independent woman, lived alone until she suffered a stroke six months before the first group meeting. She now lives next door to Miss G in a duplex that Miss G bought with her mother's help.

Mrs. H: Mrs. H's father, age 87, has lived with her for 10 years. Mrs. H is an only child, divorced, with no children. Her father has a heart condition, arthritis, wears a hearing aid, and is argumentative. Mrs. H finds it difficult to live with him and wants to learn how to cope with her impatience with him.

Mrs. L: Mrs. L's mother, age 83, has Alzheimer's disease and diabetes. Mrs. L's husband resents his mother-in-law's presence and would like Mrs. L to place her in a nursing home.

Miss O: Miss O has been taking care of her mother for 13 years since her father died. Her mother, age 74, lives next door. Miss O's own health is poor due to arthritis and open heart surgery three years ago.

Mrs. M: Mrs. M's mother, age 77, lived alone until four years ago when she had a series of strokes. Her physician did not think she should be home alone when released from the hospital. She has been living with Mrs. M since then.

Mrs. T: Mrs. T is a 36-year-old married woman with three children ages 4, 7, and 12. Mrs. T. had planned to go back to work when her youngest child entered first grade, but she is not sure that she can manage this now that her mother has come to live with them. Mrs. T is caring for her 71-year-old mother who is suffering from manic depression and high blood pressure. Mrs. T's mother has been in this country for 45 years and has lived with Mrs. T since being released from a state psychiatric institution three and a half years ago. Mrs. T's mother worked as a cleaning lady and is now retired. She has had mental health problems for many years and has been in and out of the psychiatric units of local hospitals. She takes medication to control her psychiatric symptoms and her high blood pressure.

Notice that all members of the group are women and that all are caring for parents or parents-in-law. Having done some research before leading her first caregiver group, the leader, Mrs. S, was aware that the two most common groups of caregivers of the frail elderly are spouses and adult children. In a previous group she had conducted for caregivers, Mrs. S found that adult children caring for their parents had different concerns and issues than did spouses. For example, she found that adult children were more concerned about the effect of caregiving on their relationships with their husbands and their children. They were also more concerned about work-related issues, and about the responsibilities and duties of a child to a parent.

Mrs. S also found that women and men react differently to caregiving and have different concerns and issues. She observed, for example, that women were less comfortable discussing their relationships with their husbands and their roles as wives, mothers, and caregivers when men were present in the group. She also realized that many daughters-in-law shared the same concerns as daughters. Therefore, she decided to limit participation in this particular group to daughters and daughters-in-law.

After the introductions, norms for group participation were discussed and agreed to by all members. Emphasis was placed upon the confidential nature of the group discussions. Because problem solving was a major focus of the group, the previously described eight-step problem solving model was presented in some detail by Mrs. S. She also tried to incorporate problem solving into each of the weekly educational topics. For example, when discussing feelings that caregivers typically experienced, the focus was not just on group sharing of emotions such as anger or guilt, but also on problem-solving techniques that could help members to cope better with these feelings outside of the group.

Session 2

By the second session, members were beginning to feel comfortable with each other. Cohesion and trust were beginning to build. The following dialogue occurred during the problem-solving component of the session:

Mrs. T: My husband really has a hard time dealing with my mother. I can understand his feelings. She is hard to live with. But I'm caught in the middle—I'm the only daughter she has.

Mrs. L: I know what you mean. You know, my mother has Alzheimer's disease. In the past two years it's gotten a lot worse. My husband says its about time that I think about putting Mom in a nursing home. I *do* think about it, but I just can't bring myself to do it.

Mrs. T: (looking at Mrs. S) What should I do? I feel like I'm trapped.

Mrs S: Both of you are in a difficult situation. (She looks at Mrs. T.) Is there one thing that your mother does that is particularly bothersome?

Mrs. T: (pause) When Mom refuses to take her medication her mood swings really get out of hand. At that point, even I have trouble with her.

Mrs S: Is there any pattern to your mom's refusal to take her medication?

Mrs. T: It seems she does it when we try to get away. We have a summer camp on Lake Jones. (pause) We've been going up there on weekends for years. It's only been the past few years when Mom has gotten so frail that it (going to camp) has become a real problem. We have a neighbor that we met at church look after her when we go now, but I think she resents us leaving her alone.

Mrs. S asks Mrs. T to elaborate on her relationship with her mother. After gathering additional information, several possible solutions to the problem are suggested by members.

Mrs. L: Why don't you take her when you go?

Mrs. T: We've tried that. The trip is too much for her. She gets exhausted. Besides she really doesn't like it up there. You know, it's a pretty primitive camp. TV and radio reception isn't very good, and the place is small, only three rooms. That's the way they were built years ago.

Mrs. H: Maybe you could put the medication in her favorite beverage and leave it for her in individual containers in the refrigerator.

Mrs. T: I don't think that will work. My mother insists on taking her own medication.

Miss G: How about using that respite service up at St. Peter's. We used it and it was good. They could give her medications.

Mrs. T: Mother would never go for that.

Mrs. S: Remember about Step 2 of the problem-solving model (pointing to the flip chart and turning to Mrs. T). Don't judge the solutions before hearing what everyone has to say. Okay?

Mrs. T: Oh, right. I forgot.

Miss G: What does her psychiatrist say? Why don't you ask him what to do?

Mrs. M: What about having a home health aide come in when you're gone?

Mrs. S: Anybody else have any suggestions?

Miss O: You have a brother, don't you?

Mrs. T: Yes, I do.

Miss O: Does he live in town?

Mrs. T: Yes he does. We've always been close.

Miss O: What about asking him to take your mother or to sit with her when you want to go away?

Mrs. S: Anybody else? (She scans the group for suggestions). Okay, then, let me go over what has been suggested.

Mrs. S recaps the suggestions. Mrs. T says that asking the psychiatrist is the suggestion she is most comfortable with. Mrs. T describes what she will ask the psychiatrist, and the group helps her figure out how she will respond if he does not address her questions appropriately. Mrs. S suggests that Mrs. T role play the situation, but Mrs. T is reluctant. Mrs. S. models a response with Mrs. Z playing the psychiatrist. The group laughs as Mrs. Z pretends she has a Viennese accent and introduces herself as Dr. Freud. Next, Mrs T practices her response. At the end of the role play, Mrs. T also says she might ask her brother to help out. She explains that she has not wanted to trouble him because "he is very busy with his own family." She also explains that he has offered to help out in the past. During subsequent sessions, Mrs. S tries to reinforce problem-solving skills and to focus group discussion in that direction.

The following dialogue which occurred at the end of the group meeting illustrates how Mrs. S tries to help group members become more aware of group processes, and how she encourages members' input.

Mrs. S: Gee, I don't know where the time goes, but we're almost out of time. As you know, I like to spend a few minutes at the end of each meeting talking about what I've observed and getting some feedback from you. I noticed today that you are really becoming comfortable with each other. I like the way you're connecting with each other, the way you share with each other and support each other.

Miss G: You mean you can't get a word in! (laughter from the group)

Mrs. S: It's good to see. What about the rest of you? What are your feelings about the group? (She scans the group.)

Mrs. T: So far, it's been great. I really look forward to coming.

Miss O: I wish I had joined a group a long time ago. It's really helping me to see how others are managing.

Mrs. A: I really like it, too. If I had one suggestion, I guess it would be that I'd like to get a little more specific information.

Mrs. S: Specific information?

Mrs. A: Well, my mother's doctor really didn't tell me much about what I should expect. I mean, I'd like to find out more about Parkinson's disease.

Mrs. S: I see. I won't be able to get too specific during meetings because of all the different problems you're coping with (scanning the group). But what I can do is to identify resources where you can find out more information. How would that be?

Mrs. A: I'd really appreciate that.

Mrs. L: If it's possible, I'd like to find out more about Alzheimer's disease.

Mrs. A: Okay, on the way out write down what illnesses, or what things, you'd like more information about. During the week, I'll do a little investigating and see if I can't find out where you can get more information.

Session 3

The following dialogue from the third session illustrates how the coping-skills component was implemented.

Mrs. B: I feel really sorry for my mother-in-law. I have to work and she's home alone all day. She really misses Tom (her son). She keeps saying she can't understand why he died and she's still alive. She says she wants to die.

Mrs. S: That's really hard.

Mrs. B: The thing is, there's nothing I can do. She just keeps repeating the same things. Sometimes, you know, I get really frustrated. Then I feel guilty because I know she can't help it.

Mrs. S: What's the feeling like?

Mrs. B: I can feel myself getting tense just before I get home. I think I'm anticipating hearing her say how much she misses Tom and that she wishes she was with him. Sometimes, I feel like pulling out of the driveway and not walking in. But I know that's not realistic.

Mrs. S: What about the deep breathing exercise we just practiced? Do you think that might help calm you down? You could practice that while you're still out in the car before you come in.

Mrs. B: Yes, I could try that. I'll try anything at this point. Sometimes, my stomach really starts to churn when I start driving down my street. Maybe if I take a few deep breaths and remind myself that I'm doing the best I can for her, then it won't get to me so much.

Miss G: Yeah, I know that when mother drives me crazy it helps me to disappear into another room for a few minutes. Anything that will get me to stop and think before I snap at her might help. Maybe the deep breathing will help me not to lose it—if you know what I mean.

Mrs. H: I sure do. Sometimes, I could strangle my father. You know, it's funny. I would never say that in front of anybody else. They'd think I was a terrible person, a terrible daughter.

Miss O: I think we all feel like that sometimes. (Several group members nod.) How can you help it! I love her (Miss O's mother) but sometimes it just gets to me, it's so constant.

Mrs. S: (looking at Miss G, Mrs. H, and Miss O) It's a real struggle but you can really be proud of how much you are doing. Well, maybe the deep breathing will help. Try it and let me know what you think next week. Okay?

During the third session a brief sample of dialogue also illustrates how the support component of the group has a positive effect.

Mrs. L: I feel better than I did before coming here. The situation hasn't become any easier but I've begun thinking about various alternatives (for her mother). You (looking at Mrs. S. and then around the group) really understand what I'm going through deciding if it's time to put her in a home. I think that somehow that has given me the courage to really begin to explore options. I feel like I'm not an awful person.

Mrs. Z and others: Of course you're not! You've done so much for her, more than what a lot of others would have done. But, sometimes it's time. It may be better for her and for you.

Mrs. L: Before I came here I really felt like I was going crazy. Like I was the only one in this kind of a situation. But I'm not. Some of you have it a lot worse than me.

Miss O: Jean (Mrs. L.) I just wanted you to know that you're an inspiration to me. Sometimes, when I'm down and I think about giving up, I think of you. I'm sure whatever you decide about your mom, it will be for the best.

Mrs. Z: We're all trying our best, it's just so hard!

Session 4

The following dialogue taken from a discussion after the educational component of the fourth group session illustrates that it is possible for more than one member of a group to derive benefit from the discussion of a particular topic.

Mrs. H: Does anybody feel that their parent is manipulative in their caregiving situation?

Mrs. A: I think manipulation gains advantage.

Mrs. S: I don't understand quite what you mean, why don't you give us an example?

Mrs. H: When my father says he really doesn't feel good, I think he is really telling me that I shouldn't go out and leave him (alone). I feel like my life is out of my control—that I'm being manipulated by him. If I leave him, and something happens while I'm out, I'd feel terribly guilty for not being there. But when I stay home, I really resent having to give up my plans, my life.

Mrs. S: Maybe he needs to be reassured that he's still as important to you as you are to him.

Mrs. T: You know the need to be reassured could explain my mother's behavior, too.

Mrs. S: Do you see a connection between your mother's medication problem and feeling manipulated?

Mrs. T: Well yes, when she doesn't take her medicine she becomes the center of attention. It's almost like she believes it will distract us from going to our camp without her on weekends.

Mrs. H: Your mother won't take her pills just to feel that you still love her and will not abandon her?

Mrs. T: It sounds like that could be, don't you think so? (She looks at Mrs. S.)

Mrs. S: (scanning the group) What do you think?

Mrs. L: Even if it's true, what can she do about it?

Mrs. S: You know, I've found it helps to let them know you know they are manipulating you. Sometimes if you lay your cards on the table you can be in a better position to prevent the manipulation.

Mrs. B: That's fine, but it's not easy to do. My mother-in-law would just say I was overreacting.

Miss O: You have to remember that you have rights, too, you have to stand up for yourself. Remember the topic for today's meeting, taking care of yourself.

Mrs. S asks Mrs. T if she has any other thoughts. Mrs. T brings up her worries about vacation plans for the upcoming summer season.

Mrs. T: If my husband and I can't handle her intrusion into our weekend trips, what would she do if we tried to go on a longer vacation? I thought I was going to enjoy myself once he (her husband) retired. Even having company over is a problem. Mental illness is not like physical illness.

The group members respond with empathy. They agree that mental illness is potentially more embarrassing because of the unpredictable nature of some psychiatric symptoms.

Mrs. T: And you know, I'm darn tired of hearing, "I don't know how you do it" from family and friends. I'm not looking for meaningless praise.

Mrs. Y: I know exactly what you mean. Occasionally, I'd like to hear an offer of help, rather than being praised for what I'm doing all by myself!

Miss G: What's the use? I have four brothers and they expect me to do everything. It's always been that way. When I complain to my mother, all she does is stick up for them. She makes excuses for them. She says they are busy with their own families, that if they could help out they would. But, what about me? What about my life? Don't I deserve a break?

Mrs. S: It's frustrating isn't it?

Miss G: It sure is. But at least I can share some of my feelings here. Before, I had no one I could talk to.

Mrs. S: Well, I tell you what. Why don't we take a break? When we come back I'll go over a strategy that may help you cope with your frustration, and then during problem solving we can think of ways that may help us get family more involved.

Miss. G: Sounds good to me.

Mrs. Y: Me too.

Session 6

The original group contract was for members to meet for eight weekly sessions (no monthly follow-up meetings), so during Session 6, Mrs. S brings up the issue of group termination. She mentions that another group she conducted had continued to meet. She also mentions that group members could be a resource for each other by keeping in regular phone contact. This leads to a general discussion by group members about the benefits of the support group.

Miss O: On the way over here tonight I was worrying about what I would do when the group ended. You know, friends don't really understand. They mean well, but unless they are doing it too, they just don't know what it's like to be tied down like this and not know when it's going to end. Sometimes, I think my mother will go on forever and I will die first.

Mrs. S: You're right, how many friends can you discuss the differences between Depends and Attends (different brands of adult diapers), which ones to use, and what store has the best prices?

Mrs. M: Yeah, even if you have a good friend, you might drive her away if you talk about what's really on your mind. Can you tell your friend you think about what it would be like if your mother died? Your friend will think you're a monster and tell you should be grateful your mother is still alive. I don't know what I would do without the group.

Mrs. T: You know, ever since I started coming here I've been more patient with my mother. I think it's because I know I can let it all out here. I really look forward to coming here because I know you all understand what I'm going through.

Mrs. S: I take it, then, from all your comments that you're not sure if you want to end. Why don't you all give it some thought. We'll discuss this again next week. Okay?

Session 7

During the problem-solving component, Mrs. T admits to still feeling manipulated.

Mrs. T: I'm playing her game, playing into her hands, and I can't take it anymore. I finally got a chance to speak to Dr. L about my mother's medication. He mentioned an apartment where they have staff 24 hours a day, run by the county mental health center. I think he called it the Supportive Living Program.

Mrs. S: How do you feel about the suggestion from the doctor?

Mrs. T: Terrible, I can't even bring myself to dial the phone numbers to find out more about it. I want to, but I feel like I'd be abandoning her.

Mrs. Z and Mrs. H both say that even if she feels uncomfortable considering this move, that Mrs. T has still come a long way from the first session. However, other members confront Mrs. T and remind her it takes two to continue the manipulative pattern.

Mrs. B: Nobody can manipulate you unless you let them.

Mrs. M: That's right, it takes two, you know. You must be letting her do this to you or she wouldn't be able to do it.

Mrs. S: By not going (on weekends) you give your mother a tremendous sense of power and control.

Mrs. T: But even her psychiatrist says he never dealt with someone like her before.

Mrs. M: Do you find that reassuring?

Mrs. T: Yeah, wouldn't you?

Mrs. S: Just remember, you are the one who is responsible for your own happiness, not Anna (Mrs. T's mother). It's up to you to take control of this situation, and you can do it.

Mrs. T: I know I have to do it, I have to do something.

During the seventh group session the following dialogue occurred:

Mrs. T: I have some good news. I finally got up the courage to ask my brother. He spoke to his wife and they agreed to team up and help out. They said they would take care of Mom anytime we went away, as long as we let them know in advance, and that's not a problem. Jack (her husband) was real happy about that, so he hasn't bothered me one bit about Mom being in our house recently. In fact, he's been a big help lately.

Mrs. S: That's wonderful. (Other members nod and there is a pause.)

Mrs. L: I've been thinking maybe it's time to find a place (nursing home) for Mom. But, every time I do, I get to feeling so guilty.

Mrs. S: (speaking to Mrs. L and the entire group) Remember the self-talk coping skills we learned earlier, part of guilt is what you tell yourself. Give yourself credit for time served, look at what you have done, and have tried to do already.

During the seventh group meeting, the members also decided to continue to meet once a month, and to stay in contact with each other by telephone between meetings.

A Follow-Up Session

During a follow-up meeting almost one year after the eight weekly group meetings, Mrs L reported the following news.

Mrs. L: As some of you already know, Mom is now at Eaton Park (a skilled nursing facility). She took a turn for the worse about a month ago. She had to be sent to St. Peter's (hospital) for over a week. I didn't know what to do (pause) about taking her back, I mean. I still wanted her home. I know that's what she would have wanted. But she was so bad she didn't even recognize me anymore. I thought about what you had said to me (during the meetings), how I shouldn't feel guilty when it was time to have her go to a home, how much I had done for her over the years. It meant a lot to me.

Mrs. S: You've meant a lot to us.

Mrs. L: I just couldn't keep taking care of her. I had to watch her every minute, afraid she'd walk out of the house and get lost—or worse, burn down the house or something. I had lunch with Beatrice (Mrs. M) while my mother was in the hospital, and Mary and Sarah (Mrs. W and Mrs. Z) called. That helped give me the courage to go ahead with what I had to do. You know, without the support of the group, I think I would have fallen apart.

A COMMUNITY COALITION

This case example describes a group work effort to bring together representatives of several community service agencies to help establish a community residence for people with AIDS. The case was selected because it portrays how the group worker plans and implements a strategy for community change using a range of group work skills during several sessions of the group. The case also illustrates that members of coalitions have varied special interests and political concerns, requiring the worker to assess and intervene both within the group and within larger systems outside of the group, such as the community.

The group worker, Ms. C, is an experienced social worker employed by the United Services Association (USA), a small, multiservice agency in River Falls, a city of about 250,000. River Falls has a well-developed social service system, several hospitals and health facilities, and a number of community residences for the mentally Ill and the developmentally disabled. However, there are no community residences for people with AIDS, perhaps because the AIDS crisis has never been fully acknowledged by community residents and leaders. This might be because of the conservative nature of the community, or because most cases of AIDS in the state have been diagnosed in the state's largest city more than 200 miles away.

The chief executive of USA asked Ms. C to compose a group to help the agency establish a community residence for people with AIDS. The executive had recently been contacted by two of the local hospitals urging him to involve the agency in community residence programming for people with AIDS. The hospitals were getting more AIDS cases, but few had discharge planning options for patients who no longer required hospitalization but were unable to return home.

The state had recently announced funding for community residences for people with AIDS, and the executive director had completed the agency's grant application for the project. The agency expected a response to its application in about two months. Meanwhile, the executive director thought the coalition group could begin to discuss how they could assist in establishing the residence and its services. The cooperative effort of these agency representatives was an important factor in establishing the community residence because it would provide a wider resource base in support of such an effort, and might help overcome the anticipated negative reaction to the residence from members and leaders of this conservative community.

The Planning Stage

Several planning considerations needed resolution before the coalition could be established:

1. Ms. C was assured of the support of the USA organization in planning for and financing the new residence, but was concerned about how other social service agencies would perceive the organization's intentions. In establishing other community residences for the developmentally disabled, the agency had encountered some resistance from other agencies, which USA assessed as "turf issues." It would be necessary to involve these agencies early in the planning effort to help avoid similar resistance.

2. On the positive side, Ms. C noted that she had several important contacts in local social service and community organizations, and these people could probably be counted on to support the plan and work together.

3. Ms. C would need to identify potential members and assess their organizations' willingness to align with the purpose of the coalition (planning and supporting the community residence). In addition, she would need to assess potential differences of opinion and inform potential coalition group members about how the coalition could help USA in its efforts.

4. In recruiting for the coalition, a diverse group of members would be sought, representing a variety of service issues relevant to people with AIDS. Ms. C would seek coalition members who displayed a homogeneity of attitude about support for people with AIDS, but who had heterogenous talents and resources that were needed for the group to achieve its purpose.

5. While the coalition could start out as a small group, it would probably be necessary to add members, as other agencies important to the project were identified. Thus, the coalition would function as an open group.

6. Because of the potential for interagency "turf issues," and because of the likelihood of community resistance to the proposed residence, the coalition would need to meet in a neutral community setting. The setting would also have to accommodate larger numbers of community people when public testimony and discussion would be sought by the coalition.

It was arranged for meetings to take place every other week in the meeting room of the local Episcopal church. The church had adequate space, and outreach workers from the church's volunteer service committee had a strong history of serving people with AIDS in River Falls. Ms. C made a list of potential members, visiting several of them, and telephoning others. Briefly orienting them to the purpose of the group, she was able to secure promises of weekly attendance from the following people, who would represent their organizations:

The Rev. and Mrs. W: Co-directors, River Falls Episcopal Street Ministry

Mr. S: Manager, River Falls City Housing Authority

Ms. P: Director, The Fallsview Homeless Shelter

Mr. L: Outreach worker, The Gay and Lesbian Community Center

The Rev. G: Pastor, Our Lady Star of the Sea, Roman Catholic Church

Mr. A: AIDS educator, Aids Council of River Falls

Dr. J: Chief of staff, River Falls General Hospital

Mrs. B: Social worker, St. Mary's Hospital of River Falls

Mr. Z: Support group coordinator, Families of PWA

Ms. T: Director of social services, River County

Mr. R: Professor of Social Work, River College

The Beginning Stage

Ms. C arranged a mutually agreeable time for all potential members to meet in the Episcopal Church Meeting Room. Before the first session, she reviewed the purpose of the coalition as she envisioned it. To help members fully identify with the goals of the group, the short statement she prepared included a recognition that the members might want to discuss the group's purpose in the early sessions.

> The purpose of this group is to discuss the need for community residence planning for people with AIDS in River Falls. The USA organization is prepared to sponsor a community residence for people with AIDS, and is interested in securing planning assistance and support from this coalition. Of particular importance is how to secure community acceptance for this new type of community residence. As a group, I think it would be really helpful for us to discuss how we might attempt to gain community acceptance and support for the residence.

The First Session

Members arrived on time and appeared to be enthusiastic. Ms. C noted that members greeted each other eagerly, breaking into dyads and triads to discuss topics of mutual interest and exchange small talk. For several of the members who knew each other from telephone conversations or who had heard of each other before, this was their first face-to-face contact, so the mood of the group took on a festive tone. Ms. C called the group to order, and members gathered chairs in a circle. The following dialogue occurred:

Ms. C: I want to thank all of you for coming today. I noticed that several of you have finally seen faces of people you have only known from the telephone. This is a great way to start this group, and it suggests that we need to find other ways of getting together more often. (She pauses.) As I discussed with each of you, the USA organization is interested in exploring the possibility of starting a community residence for persons with AIDS. I have been asked to convene a coalition group of experts in this work, to assist in this project. Your initial reaction to our proposal has been quite positive, and the next step is for us to meet and discuss the project. I am distributing a statement which I envision as a beginning purpose for this group. (She hands out a copy of the statement of purpose.) I would appreciate it if you would take a minute and read this. (Members read silently.) Having read the statement, perhaps this would be a good time to introduce ourselves. Would each of you introduce yourself, and give the group some feedback about the statement of purpose?

The Rev. W: I'll start, since it is our pleasure to host all of you today in our community meeting room. My wife and I have long been supporters of services to people with AIDS, and we have a special program in our street ministry that offers support and emergency assistance to people with AIDS and their families. We see the need for housing for these folks, and we are pleased to offer any support we can.

Mr. S: I agree. The Housing Authority supports the idea of community residences for people with AIDS, although I would add that many of our elected officials would rather see them treated in larger facilities in other communities. There is a housing shortage in River Falls, and I don't see it getting any better. I would suggest that we proceed carefully so we can overcome some of the stereotypes about people with AIDS and convince other community leaders that this project is a worthy one.

Ms. P: I believe there are several people with AIDS residing on a temporary basis in our homeless shelter. We have been offering shelter to several people who are in the process of testing and treatment for AIDS, but can offer little help other than our shelter, which is not particularly well-equipped for dealing with people who have difficult health problems. Our organization recognizes the need for a more specialized facility, but we are skeptical about whether such a residence would be accepted in any of River Falls' neighborhoods.

Mr. L: The Gay and Lesbian Community Center has offered some support to people with AIDS, but we are not equipped for dealing with some of their difficult health concerns. It would seem to us that any community residence for people with AIDS should have a strong health or medical services orientation. We see the major issue here as overcoming the strong homophobic reaction of community leaders and residents, even though many persons with AIDS are heterosexual.

Mr. A: The AIDS Council is prepared to contract with the USA organization to provide health and medical services for residents of the proposed residence. We also think we can be valuable in educating the public about AIDS, as this is part of our mission. Any proposal such as this would need to have a strong component of community education; this is the only way to overcome the usual resistance to dealing with AIDS.

The Rev. G: It is a shame that our community would have such narrow ideas about people with AIDS. I agree with what has been said so far. I can't speak for our parish, but our priests recognize the need to minister to people with AIDS—we need assistance in learning more about how to be helpful. This is why I am here.

Dr. J: The River Falls General Hospital has been seeing more patients who have been diagnosed as HIV positive, and has been treating increasing numbers of people with serious opportunistic infections related to AIDS. While some of these people remain in the hospital for extended periods, when they are ready to be discharged they find that they have no place to go. Many lose their housing because they can't afford to keep up mortgage or rent payments. Many lose their jobs, and as you know this means they lose their health insurance. It is a very difficult situation, and I'm not sure that the County Social Services Department is doing its share to help these people.

Mrs. B: Our experience in the social services department of St. Mary's Hospital is very similar. I agree with Dr. J.

Ms. T: I don't think that last statement is an accurate one. The county has emergency funds to help people with some of the costs for temporary housing, but we are not equipped to serve the increasing numbers of homeless people in this county. I'm not sure that the hospitals are taking enough responsibility in these matters.

Mr. Z: The support groups we run for families of people with AIDS have many similar themes. We think a community residence would assist people in transition from hospital to more permanent housing. In some cases, people with AIDS will never return to a place they call "home."

Mr. R: I am here because River College, particularly the social work program, is interested in lending support and perhaps student assistance to this effort to plan for people with AIDS. Last semester, my students and I did a preliminary needs assessment in cooperation with the department of health, and what we found may surprise you. I brought copies of our report today and I will gladly discuss our findings with this group.

Ms. C noted that all members had spoken and contributed their organization's initial reaction to the USA proposal. While there appeared to be support expressed for the idea of a community residence, she noted some tension between the director of the County Social Services Department and representatives of the local hospitals. She decided not to address the tension at this time. Instead, she decided to summarize some of the major points of the previous discussion.

Ms. C: I appreciate your candid comments. Several themes have emerged; let me try to summarize them. The problem of housing for people with AIDS seems to be verified based on most of your comments. Another important issue identified by some of you is the potential reaction of community residents to housing for individuals who are HIV positive. Several of you commented on local reaction in general to the AIDS crisis. In addition, some of you suggested services for people with AIDS, as well as health and medical services, and the need for community education about AIDS. How does that summary sound to you? Is it a fair portrayal of our first conversation together?

This summary of the initial comments helped the group review some of the overt agendas of the individual members and their agencies. Ms. C thought it important to let the group know that the USA organization was in the process of applying for state funding and was prepared to take action on establishing the community residence within the next few months if funding was received. The agency also wanted to make it clear at the first meeting that it would be the actual service provider, with autonomy and control over the operation of the residence. Ms. C stated USA's agenda and solicited feedback from the group:

Ms. C: I need to speak briefly on behalf of my own agency. My executive has asked me to make clear our intentions to carry out this project. While we intend to do most of the work of establishing funding, finding a location, and applying for housing permits and other regulatory requirements, we need your help in two ways. First, we recognize the collective expertise in this room today. We hope to use many of the services your organizations offer. We may contract for services with some of you and ask others for guidance in this effort to provide services to people with AIDS. Second, we recognize that, as many of you have suggested, there is potential for a great deal of community resistance to this project. We hope that you will assist us in challenging potential resistance and help us mediate conflicts that could occur. I'd like to get some feedback from you about our intentions and how we can cooperate in this important endeavor.

Dr. J: I appreciate your openness, and I think my organization can support your intentions.

Mr. Z: I'm not sure how I can help, but perhaps we can find that out as we go along.

Ms. C: Thank you. Are there other comments from members? (She scans the group.)

Mr. R: I have discussed the need for community residence programming with students at River College and they are interested in helping. Could a student representative of the Social Work Club attend our meetings?

Ms. C: How would everyone feel about that? (Members nod in agreement.)

The Rev. W: It looks to me as if most of us here think this is a good idea. It also appears that most of us support the idea of USA taking the lead in this project.

Ms. C: Can I ask if there are concerns about the project that any of you have.

Ms. T: I personally support this project. However, I think it's important to recognize that many of our local leaders and politicians in River Falls might not feel the same way. They may also think the Department of Social Services should not be involved. Since our funding is somewhat controlled by our community leaders, our agency may have some difficulty in participating.

The Rev. W: I appreciate what you are saying, and you might count on some of us talking to our politicians about the project if you think it will help.

Mr. L: We can't forget politics here. Many of our political leaders are not in favor of services that make them or their constituents uncomfortable.

Ms. C: Can you elaborate on this for us?

> **Mr. L:**   I just think there is a lot of resistance to acknowledging that our community has a problem with AIDS. I think we should start discussing this and how we can overcome the resistance. (Members verbalize agreement.)
>
> **Ms. C:**   It is easy to see, from all of your reactions to (Mr. L's) comment, that you think River Falls should acknowledge the AIDS crisis. This seems to be a recurring theme in our discussions so far. Do others want to comment on this?
>
> **Ms. P:**   I would suggest that this group concentrate on helping the community learn about AIDS. This would allow the USA to do what it does best—namely, work on establishing community residences.
>
> **Mr. L:**   This seems reasonable.
>
> **The Rev. G:**   You're suggesting we establish some sort of educational effort to get information about AIDS to the community?
>
> **Ms. P:**   Yes, that's a possibility. If the public could see us working together to do this, they might take this information more seriously.
>
> **Mr. L:**   Then perhaps community residence programming might go more smoothly.
>
> **Ms. P:**   Exactly!

This interaction demonstrates how group discussion helped the group come to a fuller understanding of the group's purpose. While Ms. C stated the general purpose for the group (assisting in establishment of a community residence), the group started to define and modify the purpose through its initial discussions. Ms. C realized that modifying the group purpose was an important step to building group cohesion and was necessary before the group could be productive.

In the next interaction, Ms. C probed the group for potential obstacles to group consensus on purpose, including differences of opinion about the work of the group. She recognized that groups often mask their differences in the beginning stage, and the illusion of unanimity among members can hide obstacles to productive work.

> **Ms. C:**   While most of us appear to be in favor of helping the community accept the AIDS crisis, I wonder if we all mean the same thing? How do you think the group might approach this task of community education?
>
> **Mr. S:**   I hope this doesn't mean that we want to have a demonstration or picket the city offices! I could lose my job.
>
> **Ms. C:**   Could you elaborate on that?
>
> **Mr. S:**   Well, you might have read last week in the papers, there was an organization called ACT-UP demonstrating at the Center City Commissioner's office. They were trying to get the attention of some local politicians and were hoping to get them to appropriate money for support of persons with AIDS. They made the commissioner and themselves look bad.

Mr. L: ACT-UP demonstrations are only one way to educate the public, but sometimes that type of strategy is necessary.

Mr. S: I can't be part of something like that, I'm a city employee.

Mr. L: I can understand that and maybe there are other ways you can contribute.

Mr. Z: Most of the members of our support group for families do not agree with ACT-UP's philosophy and tactics. Many of our members have a need for anonymity and confidentiality. I doubt they would support that kind of experience.

Ms. C: Perhaps we need to consider some ideas about how to go about our task. Planning a demonstration or using conflict as a strategy are only two ways to approach our task; let's discuss other ways.

Two members expressed their mutual concern about how the group would achieve its goals. While Ms. C encountered potential obstacles to the group working together, she recognized that these concerns were part of a normal functioning group in its beginning stage. She facilitated work on how the group would achieve its goals. During this first session, the group agreed to consider possible strategies for carrying out a "community education" project to help USA in its efforts to establish a community residence.

The Second Session
The second session focused on the content of the planned educational presentation, how group members could gather general information about AIDS and specific information about its prevalence in River Falls. The group decided to divide into two subcommittees, one to collect resources such as videotapes, written material and names of possible speakers, and the other to collect specific information on how many cases of AIDS have been diagnosed in River Falls. Each member volunteered for a particular subcommittee depending on what expertise was needed. Each subcommittee was to bring its information back to the next meeting.

The Third Session
In the third session, each subcommittee presented its findings, and the session was educational for all. Discussions centered on how the group would use this material to teach members of the community about AIDS. The group discussed how to design the educational effort. Ms. C led the group in a brainstorming exercise to generate as many ideas about how to teach members of the community about AIDS. The group then had a freewheeling discussion of all of the options, and members were asked to rank their top three choices. The choices with the most votes were listed on a flip chart, and members were again asked to discuss the top few choices. Although the group was asked to vote one more time to choose the best options, it decided to try to reach consensus without a formal vote. The following dialogue took place:

Mr. R: It appears that we have a few good ideas about how to inform the public about AIDS. I prefer a general educational meeting, open to the public.

Ms. C: (scanning the group) What are other members' preferences?

Mrs. B: I have been impressed with the work done by Mr. A and the AIDS Council. I wonder if the council would take major responsibility for presenting a program open to the public?

Mr. R: I was wondering the same thing. It seems this type of educational program should be done by experts, who have the most up-to-date information.

Mr. A: Our agency would be glad to take the lead.

Ms. C: How would other members feel about that?

Ms. P: This seems like a logical choice. Still, we should be involved in the effort to provide support and to suggest that we are all in this together.

Mr. R: I suggest we all be available to be discussion leaders, perhaps divide into smaller groups to discuss questions.

Ms. P: I agree, we need to be part of all of the strategies to get this information to the public. Let's decide where and when.

Ms. C: I just want to make sure that we are all in agreement. Can I ask all of you if an open educational presentation is your first choice? (All members indicate their support.) Then we have reached consensus on this issue.

The Working Stage

The group met for a fourth and fifth session to plan the details of the educational meeting with the public. Room and space arrangements were made, refreshments were purchased, and members of the group took responsibility for advertising and encouraging community leaders to attend. One day before the presentation, the local television news ran a story about the coalition and its work, giving much needed publicity to the educational effort. Overall the presentation was interesting, and community residents had opportunities to ask questions in small group discussions.

The coalition had a "debriefing" session at a local restaurant, where Ms. C announced that the community residence proposal had received the grant and the project was ready to proceed. The next step was to find a suitable location with room to house five to eight people with AIDS. She reported that a house had been found in a neighborhood near a hospital, and that discussions were taking place between the owners of the house and the USA agency. Ms. C asked the group to convene again to discuss further planning for the project.

The Sixth Session

The sixth session of the group was supposed to focus on plans to open the community residence. While the USA agency was taking the responsibility for many of the details involved in opening the residence, the executive director wanted the group to help plan how some of the health, counseling, transportation and other services could be provided.

However, as news of the proposed residence spread throughout the community, opposition to the chosen location began to grow. Community political leaders, responding to pressures from residents, were threatening to pass zoning legislation which could exclude the USA from opening the residence in the chosen area. Ms. C convened the group to discuss this new development. After Ms. C's opening remarks, the group started a discussion of a newspaper feature story about local reaction to the idea of opening a community residence for people with AIDS, and the threatened zoning change by the River Falls City Council.

Ms. C: As we all know, our plans for a community residence are well under way, and we need to consider what steps the group can take to make this residence a reality. But I have some bad news to announce: It now appears that some members of the River Falls City Council are opposing our efforts. I have been informed by my agency's director that soon, the City Council will attempt to rezone the area we have chosen for the residence, to prevent us from opening a multiple-resident dwelling. Our agency is prepared to go to court to prevent this, but I was wondering if the group had some suggestions for a different strategy?

Ms. P: I think the coalition can do several things. For one thing, we all know some of our City Council members—we could meet with them individually and try to persuade them to change their minds.

Ms. C: How do you suggest we go about that?

Ms. P: There are any number of ways, but I wonder if some of us could make individual appointments with some of them, perhaps to discuss the proposal, and find out what their objections are.

The Rev. G: I agree, at least we could show up, identify ourselves, and ask for a public meeting or hearing to discuss the residence.

Ms. C: This strategy sounds very good. We have an important perspective to offer here. Any other ideas?

Dr. J: I can provide all of us with our latest figures on new cases of AIDS among River Falls residents. Some of this information might suggest that our City Council members need to start making plans for these people rather than ignore them.

Ms. C: I think we can all agree that we have more information than the council members do, and we need to get the information to them before they vote to rezone.

Mr. L: I think they would lose a case in court. They are clearly discriminating against people with AIDS, which is against federal and state anti-discrimination laws.

Mr. S: I share that opinion, but I wonder if an adversarial position is the first strategy we should use?

> **Mr. R:**   I'm afraid they're the ones taking the adversarial position. However, I'm in favor of working with them rather than against them.
>
> **Mr. S:**   I don't like this whole idea of going against the City Council. I have to remind you again that I am a city employee, and it would look pretty bad if I were involved in a group that supported a court action against the city.
>
> **Mr. L:**   I'm sorry to hear you say this, because I think eventually we will have to take sides here.

In addition to dealing with the crisis precipitated by the threatened actions of the City Council, Ms. C is now facing conflict within the group. The opposing viewpoints of two of the members pose a threat to the cohesiveness of the group. While the outside threat—represented by the possible actions of the City Council—brought the group together, the internal conflict threatened to split the group into opposing sides.

> **Ms. C:**   I think it is good that we are open and honest about our reactions here. I appreciate your position, Mr. S, and I wonder if others wish to comment on what you have said?
>
> **Mr. Z:**   I support taking the more conservative approach. As I mentioned before, many of the members of the support groups my agency sponsors wish to keep their anonymity, and others are not inclined to challenge their City Council members.
>
> **Mr. L:**   I respect what you are saying, but eventually, when things can't be worked out, we will have to challenge them. Perhaps we need to discuss this possibility.
>
> **Ms. C:**   The group seems to be struggling here. I suggest we discuss how we can work out our differences before they interfere with our important efforts to make the residence a reality. Each of you has a valid point. How can we come together on this?
>
> **Mrs. B:**   I think we should consider taking it one step at a time. I was always taught to consider collaboration before conflict. It seems to be more effective for some situations.
>
> **Mr. L:**   Our agency is often forced into conflict with public officials around their continuing homophobia. As you remember, the City Council recently failed to pass anti-discrimination legislation for gay men and lesbian women. I am becoming accustomed to having to fight for the rights of our organization's members.
>
> **Ms. C:**   And you think their opposition to the residence is a similar problem?
>
> **Mr. L:**   Well, no. I guess there are some similar issues here, but I think the City Council might respond positively if we contacted them and discussed the residence and the incidence of new cases of AIDS in our hospitals.

Ms. C: Do others feel the same way? (The group members appear to agree.) So if we agree that our first strategy should be talking and collaborating, can the group work together to accomplish this?

Mr. S: I have no problem with this. I just want us all to agree as a group before we try any other strategy.

Ms. C: You're suggesting that we discuss and reach a consensus on each strategy before we try it?

Mr. S: Yes, this will guarantee we all work together.

Mr. L: We should present a united front, and work together whenever we can.

Ms. C: Can the group agree on a "rule of consensus" when deciding which strategies to employ? (The group orally indicates agreement.)

In this interaction, Ms. C attempted to mediate differences among the members. She remained neutral in the discussion, recognizing the validity of opposing viewpoints, and using the resources of the group to support a solution. In addition, Ms. C recognized the necessity of processing group dynamics with the members, when the group appeared to be struggling. This had the eventual effect of helping members agree on the "rule of consensus," which became a norm for the group's future deliberations.

The Seventh Session

The strategy of meeting individually with City Council members was successful. Members divided into subgroups of three and met with council members to share information and make recommendations. The concerted effort of the coalition helped persuade the council to support the project. Two members of the council who were particularly supportive of the community residence were invited to join the group and help implement the project.

The following excerpt is from a group discussion on how to obtain some of the necessary support services for the community residence. Ms. C told the group members they could help USA by suggesting how services could be arranged and financed. The climate of the group was positive, having resolved the crisis posed by the threat of rezoning and having added new members who supported the purpose of the group.

Ms. C: I wanted to let you know that progress is being made on the community residence. We have a signed contract with the seller, and we are planning renovations. Our time line is about four weeks. We have also begun to identify potential staff for the residence. Do any of you have suggestions about how to find additional staff who might be interested in working in the residence?

The Rev. G: I wanted to know if volunteers would be used. Some of our parishioners are interested in donating items, cooking meals, being companions.

Mr. R: I'm also proud of the fact that some of our social work students are interested in volunteering to work at the residence.

Ms. C: The USA organization briefly discussed the use of volunteers, but we didn't reach any conclusions. Are other members in touch with possible sources of volunteers?

Mr. A: The AIDS council has a Buddy Program, where a volunteer is paired with a person with AIDS. We could also provide volunteers to help with shopping and transportation and to provide companionship.

Mrs. W: Our church has a volunteer committee, and if some of the group members could make a short presentation to them, they might be helpful in providing volunteers as well.

Ms. C: Are there any suggestions about how to proceed on the volunteer possibility?

Mr. R: I would be glad to take responsibility for studying the volunteer idea, talking to those of you who are interested in helping provide volunteers. Would that be agreeable? (Mr. R looks around at the other members.)

Ms. C: It looks like we have some support for this idea. (She looks at Mr. R.) Can you form a subcommittee and get back to us at our next meeting?

Mr. R: Sounds good!

Ms. C: Any other ideas about staffing?

Ms. P: We have several applications for employment in our shelter, and we don't have any openings right now.

Ms. C: I don't think we could have access to those without violating confidentiality and informed consent, could we?

Ms. P: No problem. If you develop a short employment announcement, we can send it to people whose applications we have. Just don't read it to any of our current staff. (The group laughs.)

Ms. C: I promise!

This excerpt illustrates how the members developed a system of mutual aid during the working stage of the group's development. Frequent intervention on the part of the group leader was not as necessary as it was in earlier sessions when the group processes included organizing, norm development, and conflict resolution. Members took more responsibility for the business of the group, playing important leadership and task accomplishment roles.

The work of the group continued, supporting the eventual opening of the USA community residence for people with AIDS. Several members of the coalition helped develop a service plan for the residence. The AIDS Council provided educational services for families of the residents. Visiting social workers from the two hospitals were assigned to the residence as part of the discharge planning process for some of the residents. A volunteer program was initiated with the cooperation of several agencies, and oversight of the program was assigned to Mr. Z, the support group coordinator of the Families of PWA organization. Eventually, the coalition changed its focus from providing support for the community residence to carrying out a community needs assessment for further community residences for people with AIDS.

The Ending Stage

The coalition continued to meet during the implementation phase of the new community residence. The residence had a waiting list of many potential residents, and this troubled the coalition. This following excerpt illustrates how the coalition agreed to change its focus and reformulate its goals.

> **Ms. C:**   It has been several months since we started this group. I think we have accomplished quite a bit. This might be a good time to evaluate what we have done as a group. How do you feel about this?
>
> **Mr. Z:**   It seems to me we have achieved our initial goals. I think there is more work to be done in establishing other community residences.
>
> **Dr. J:**   I think we have learned a lot about community residence programming. We have helped educate the community about AIDS and we have gained support from some important community leaders. We should continue to meet and think about what other tasks we can accomplish.
>
> **Ms. C:**   Do other members feel this way?
>
> **Mr. R:**   I agree. It might be possible for the group to continue, but change its focus slightly.
>
> **Ms. T:**   What do you have in mind?
>
> **Mr. R:**   I have been doing some research on the number of new cases of AIDS treated at the local hospitals. I am concerned that the residence only serves a few people, and many more need this service. Perhaps we should study this problem, and try to come up with some recommendations to solve it.
>
> **Ms. C:**   I agree with your observations. Would other members be interested in continuing?
>
> **Mrs. B:**   I would be very interested in continuing, especially if we can develop some additional resources for people with AIDS. At the hospital, we are very concerned about developing new discharge planning options.
>
> **Ms. C:**   I notice that many of you appear receptive to the idea of continuing the group. If we agree to continue meeting, we should reformulate our goals. Perhaps we can brainstorm for a while and try to develop some new ideas.
>
> **Mr. A:**   This is a good strategy. We have worked well together and accomplished a lot. I think we should discuss this further.

In its ending stage, the group attempted to evaluate its effectiveness in accomplishing its goals. Although the community residence was operational and other important tasks had been accomplished by the group, several members identified additional possible tasks. Members felt that it was important to continue the work of the group by doing additional research on the needs of people with AIDS in River Falls.

SUMMARY

This chapter presents two cases that illustrate group work practice in a treatment group and a task group. The first case deals with a support group for family members who are providing care for frail elderly relatives. The case illustrates four different components of the group: support, education, developing coping skills, and problem solving. The dialogue concentrates on how members support each other, and how they solve problems by developing a system of mutual aid.

The second case illustrates a coalition of community organizations who work together to open a community residence for people with AIDS. The case illustrates how task groups are used in the community and how members with different interests and approaches can work together to accomplish the group's goals.

These two case examples do not necessarily illustrate the ideal processes or outcomes for such groups. They were developed to help the readers of this book improve their ability to analyze group work, and to apply group work theory to practice situations. It is hoped that these case examples will encourage the readers of this book to develop and analyze their own case material.

LEARNING ASSIGNMENTS

Caregiver Support Group

1. Consider the information shared by the group members during the first session of the group. Construct a chart that illustrates the heterogeneous as well as the homogeneous characteristics of the members. Using this chart, write a summary statement of what members have in common and how they are different. If you were the worker, what other member characteristics would you have sought during the group's composition?

2. Prepare a session agenda addressing one of the topics listed in the educational component of this group. How would you foster member discussion during the educational component of the session?

3. Prepare a short statement of purpose which could be used to orient members during the first meeting. What rules of group behavior would you suggest for members? How would you introduce norms to the members?

4. Choose two of the sessions illustrated in the case example. Write a statement that Mrs. S could have used to summarize the work that had been done in each of those sessions.

5. If you were asked to lead this type of support group, how would you handle the following situations that might surface in the group?
    a. One of the members continually shows up late for meetings.
    b. One of the members monopolizes the conversation.
    c. One of the members violates the norm of confidentiality by talking to a neighbor about someone in the group.

    d. One of the members refuses to allow the group to move into deeper and more sensitive areas of discussion.

    e. The group uses one of its quiet members as a scapegoat.

    f. The group appears sluggish and does not want to discuss difficult issues common to members.

    g. The group develops two subgroups which dominate the session discussions.

    h. The group wants to become independent from the leader, holding meetings at the homes of different members, and inviting new members to participate.

6. The agency director has asked you to evaluate the effect of this group on the individual members and on the larger community. Design evaluation strategies for each purpose.

7. What else could Mrs. S have done to plan for the termination of the group? How could she have helped ensure that the gains members made during the group were maintained?

LEARNING ASSIGNMENTS

Community Coalition

1. Although six planning considerations are listed in this case, what other planning issues might be involved in forming this coalition? How would you use homogeneity and heterogeneity of member characteristics in composing the group? What special community/environmental considerations would you consider if you were the worker?

2. Choose five situations, issues, or social problems for which a community coalition might be an effective means of gaining community support. Choose one of these issues and identify five to 10 organizations in your community that might be particularly important to include in the coalition. Write a short statement of purpose which could be used to begin the first session of the group.

3. During the first and sixth sessions of the group, Mr. S and Mr. Z expressed concern about how the group might carry out its purpose. If you were the worker, how would you have handled this potential source of conflict within the group? What techniques would you have used to increase group cohesion?

4. The purpose of the coalition was tested when the community political leaders threatened to pass legislation to preclude the opening of the community residence. How would you have handled this situation? How would you have used the coalition to achieve the desired support from community political leaders?

5. In the working stage of the group, several members engage in a process of mutual aid, which assists the group in achieving its purpose and helps the members get their own needs met. Identify three situations in which members worked together to achieve the goals of the group. How could the worker have increased mutual aid among the members?

6. Identify the bond that helped members continue the community coalition after the group had accomplished its goals. If you were the worker, what actions would you suggest to help the group change its goals?

7. How would you have arranged for a systematic evaluation of the process and outcomes of this group? Construct a follow-up questionnaire which could be used to obtain data about the effectiveness of the group.

APPENDIX A

Guidelines for Ethics
American Group Psychotherapy Association, Inc.[1]

INTRODUCTION

The American Group Psychotherapy Association is a professional multidisciplinary organization whose purpose is to: "... provide a forum for the exchange of ideas among qualified professional persons interested in group psychotherapy and to publish and to make publications available on all subjects relating to group psychotherapy; to encourage the development of sound training programs in group psychotherapy for qualified mental health professionals; to encourage and promote research on group psychotherapy and to establish and maintain high standards of ethical, professional group psychotherapy practice."

Membership in the American Group Psychotherapy Association presumes strict adherence to standards of ethical practice. As a specialty organization, AGPA supports the ethical codes of the primary professional organizations to which our members belong. Providing guidelines for the ethical behavior of group psychotherapists serves to inform both the group psychotherapist and public of the American Group Psychotherapy Association's expectations in the practice of group psychotherapy.

GENERAL GUIDELINES

Ethics complaints about AGPA members will be directed to the primary professional organization of the members. AGPA's response as to sanctions will parallel that of the primary organization. For example, if the primary organization concludes that an individual's membership should be suspended for one year, AGPA will suspend membership for one year. Should an ethical complaint be received regarding a member of AGPA who does not belong to a primary professional organization, the complainant will be directed to the state licensing board and/or the state or federal legal system. If the member is found guilty, AGPA's sanctions will parallel the sanctions of the state licensing board, other governmental agencies or courts of law as to the person's ability to practice; the AGPA cannot parallel such sanctions as fines, penalties or imprisonment.

For those members of the American Group Psychotherapy Association who are psychiatrists, the principles of ethics as applied by the American Psychiatric Association shall govern their behavior; those members who are clinical psychologists shall be expected to comply with the principles of ethics laid down by the American

[1] Reprinted with the permission of the American Group Psychotherapy Association, Inc., 25 East 21st Street, 6th Floor, New York, NY 10010, Telephone: (212) 477-2677.

Psychological Association; those members who are clinical social workers shall be expected to comply with the ethical standards established by the National Federation of Societies for Clinical Social Work; those members who are clinical specialists in nursing shall be expected to comply with the principles of ethics of the American Nurses' Association; those members who are pastoral counselors shall be expected to comply with the ethical standards of the American Association of Pastoral Care; and those members of other professional disciplines having published principles of ethics shall follow those principles. Members of the Association who do not belong to one of the above professional groups having a published standard of ethics shall follow the principles of ethics laid down by the American Psychological Association.

GUIDELINES OF GROUP PSYCHOTHERAPY PRACTICE

The following guidelines of group psychotherapy practice shall serve as models for group therapists' ethical behavior.

Responsibility to Patient/Client

1. The group psychotherapist provides services with respect for the dignity and uniqueness of each patient/client as well as the rights and autonomy of the individual patient/client.

   1.1 The group psychotherapist shall provide the potential group patient/client with information about the nature of group psychotherapy and apprise them of the risks, rights and obligations as members of a therapy group.

   1.2 The group psychotherapist shall encourage the patient/client's participation in group psychotherapy only so long as it is appropriate to the patient/client's needs.

   1.3 The group psychotherapist shall not practice or condone any form of discrimination on the basis of race, color, sex, sexual orientation, age, religion, national origin or physical handicap, except that this guideline shall not prohibit group therapy practice with population specific or problem specific groups.

2. The group psychotherapist safeguards the patient/client's right to privacy by judiciously protecting information of a confidential nature.

   2.1 The group shall agree that the patient/client as well as the psychotherapist shall protect the identity of its members.

   2.2 The group psychotherapist shall not use identifiable information about the group or its members for teaching purposes, publication or professional presentations unless permission has been obtained and all measures have been taken to preserve patient/client anonymity.

3. The group psychotherapist acts to safeguard the patient/client and the public from the incompetent, unethical, illegal practice of any group psychotherapist.

   3.1 The group psychotherapist must be aware of her/his own individual competencies, and when the needs of the patient/client are beyond the competencies of the psychotherapist, consultation must be sought from other qualified professionals or other appropriate sources.

   3.2 The group psychotherapist shall not use her/his professional relationship to advance personal or business interests.

   3.3 Sexual intimacy with patients/clients is unethical.

   3.4 The group psychotherapist shall protect the patient/client and the public from misinformation and misrepresentation. She/he shall not use false or misleading advertising regarding her/his qualifications or skills as a group psychotherapist.

Professional Standards

The group psychotherapist shall maintain the integrity of the practice of group psychotherapy.

1. It is the personal responsibility of the group psychotherapist to maintain competence in the practice of group psychotherapy through formal education activities and informal learning experiences.

2. The group psychotherapist has a responsibility to contribute to the ongoing development of the body of knowledge pertaining to group psychotherapy whether involved as an investigator, participant, or user of research results.

3. The group psychotherapist shall accept the obligation to attempt to inform and alert other group psychotherapists who are violating ethical principles or to bring those violations to the attention of appropriate professional authorities.

Revised February, 1991

Ethical Guidelines
for Group Counselors[1]
Association for Specialists in Group Work[2]

ETHICAL GUIDELINES

1. Orientation and Providing Information: Group counselors adequately prepare prospective or new group members by providing as much information about the existing or proposed group as necessary.

   Minimally, information related to each of the following areas should be provided:

   (a) Entrance procedures, time parameters of the group experience, group participation expectations, methods of payment (where appropriate), and termination procedures are explained by the group counselor as appropriate to the level of maturity of group members and the nature and purpose(s) of the group.

   (b) Group counselors have available for distribution a professional disclosure statement that includes information on the group counselor's qualifications and group services that can be provided, particularly as related to the nature and purpose(s) of the specific group.

   (c) Group counselors communicate the role expectations, rights, and responsibilities of group members and group counselor(s).

   (d) The group goals are stated as concisely as possible by the group counselor including "whose" goal it is (the group counselor's, the institution's, the parent's, the law's, society's, etc.) and the role of group members in influencing or determining the group's goal(s).

   (e) Group counselors explore with group members the risks of potential life changes that may occur because of the group experience and help members explore their readiness to face these possibilities.

   (f) Group members are informed by the group counselor of unusual or experimental procedures that might be expected in their group experience.

   (g) Group counselors explain, realistically as possible, what services can and cannot be provided within the particular group structure offered.

[1] Permission to reproduce granted by the Association for Specialists in Group Work, a Division of the American Counseling Association, 5999 Stevenson Avenue, Alexandria, VA 22304.

[2] These guidelines were approved by the Association for Specialists in Group Work (ASGW) Executive Board, June 1, 1989.

(h) Group counselors emphasize the need to promote full psychological functioning and presence among group members. They inquire from prospective group members whether they are using any kind of drug or medication that may affect functioning in the group. They do not permit any use of alcohol and/or illegal drugs during group sessions and they discourage the use of alcohol and/or drugs (legal or illegal) prior to group meetings which may affect the physical or emotional presence of the member or other group members.

(i) Group counselors inquire from prospective group members whether they have ever been a client in counseling or psychotherapy. If a prospective group member is already in a counseling relationship with another professional person, the group counselor advises the prospective group member to notify the other professional of their participation in the group.

(j) Group counselors clearly inform group members about the policies pertaining to the group counselor's willingness to consult with them between group sessions.

(k) In establishing fees for group counseling services, group counselors consider the financial status and the locality of prospective group members. Group members are not charged fees for group sessions where the group counselor is not present and the policy of charging for sessions missed by a group member is clearly communicated. Fees for participating as a group member are contracted between group counselor and group member for a specified period of time. Group counselors do not increase fees for group counseling services until the existing contracted fee structure has expired. In the event that the established fee structure is inappropriate for a prospective member, group counselors assist in finding comparable services of acceptable cost.

2. Screening of Members: The group counselor screens prospective group members (when appropriate to their theoretical orientation). Insofar as possible, the counselor selects group members whose needs and goals are compatible with the goals of the group, who will not impede the group process, and whose well-being will not be jeopardized by the group experience. An orientation to the group (i.e., ASGW Ethical Guideline #1), is included during the screening process.

Screening may be accomplished in one or more ways, such as the following:

(a) Individual interview.

(b) Group interview of prospective group members.

(c) Interview as part of a team staffing, and,

(d) Completion of a written questionnaire by prospective group members.

3. Confidentiality: Group counselors protect members by defining clearly what confidentiality means, why it is important, and the difficulties involved in enforcement.

(a) Group counselors take steps to protect members by defining confidentiality and the limits of confidentiality (i.e., when a group member's condition indicates that there is clear and imminent danger to the member, others, or physical property the group counselor takes reasonable personal action and/or informs responsible authorities).

(b) Group counselors stress the importance of confidentiality and set a norm of confidentiality regarding all group participants' disclosures. The importance of maintaining confidentiality is emphasized before the group begins and at various times in the group. The fact that confidentiality cannot be guaranteed is clearly stated.

(c) Members are made aware of the difficulties involved in enforcing and ensuring confidentiality in group setting. The counselor provides examples of how confidentiality can nonmaliciously be broken to increase members' awareness, and help to lessen the likelihood that this breach of confidence will occur. Group counselors inform group members about the potential consequences of intentionally breaching confidentiality.

(d) Group counselors can only ensure confidentiality on their part and not on the part of the members.

(e) Group counselors video- or audiotape a group session only with the prior consent, and the members' knowledge of how the tape will be used.

(f) When working with minors, the group counselor specified the limit of confidentiality.

(g) Participants in a mandatory group are made aware of any reporting procedures required of the group counselor.

(h) Group counselors store or dispose of group member records (written audio, video, etc.) in ways that maintain confidentiality.

(i) Instructors of group counseling courses maintain the anonymity of group members whenever discussing group counseling cases.

4. Voluntary/Involuntary Participation: Group counselors inform members whether participation is voluntary or involuntary.

(a) Group counselors take steps to ensure informed consent procedures in both voluntary and involuntary groups.

(b) When working with minors in a group counselors are expected to follow the procedures specified by the institution in which they are practicing.

(c) With involuntary groups, every attempt is made to enlist the cooperation of the members and their continuance in the group on a voluntary basis.

(d) Group counselors do not certify that group treatment has been received by members who merely attend sessions, but did not meet the defined group expectations. Group members are informed about the consequences for failing to participate in a group.

5. Leaving a Group: Provisions are made to assist a group member to terminate in an effective way.

(a) Procedures to be followed for a group member who chooses to exit a group prematurely are discussed by the counselor with all group members either before the group begins, during a pre-screening interview, or during the initial group session.

(b) In the case of legally mandated group counseling, group counselors inform members of the possible consequences for premature self-termination.

(c) Ideally, both the group counselor and the member can work cooperatively to determine the degree to which a group experience is productive or counterproductive for that individual.

(d) Members ultimately have a right to discontinue membership in the group, at a designated time, if the predetermined trial period proves to be unsatisfactory.

(e) Members have the right to exit a group, but it is important that they be made aware of the importance of informing the counselor and the group members prior to deciding to leave. The counselor discusses the possible risks of leaving the group prematurely with a member who is considering this option.

(f) Before leaving a group, the group counselor encourages members (if appropriate) to discuss their reasons for wanting to discontinue membership in the group. Counselors intervene if other members use undue pressure to force a member to remain in the group.

6. Coercion and Pressure: Group counselors protect member rights against physical threats, intimidation, coercion, and undue peer pressure insofar as is reasonably possible.

(a) It is essential to differentiate between "therapeutic pressure" that is part of any group and "undue pressure," which is not therapeutic.

(b) The purpose of a group is to help participants find their own answer, not to pressure them into doing what the group thinks is appropriate.

(c) Counselors exert care not to coerce participants to change in directions which they clearly state they do not choose.

(d) Counselors have a responsibility to intervene when others use undue pressure or attempt to persuade members against their will.

(e) Counselors intervene when any member attempts to act out aggression in a physical way that might harm another member or themselves.

(f) Counselors intervene when a member is verbally abusive or inappropriately confrontive to another member.

7. Imposing Counselor Values: Group counselors develop an awareness of their own values and needs and the potential effect they have on the interventions likely to be made.

(a) Although group counselors take care to avoid imposing their values on members, it is appropriate that they expose their own beliefs, decisions, needs, and values, when concealing them would create problems for the members.

(b) There are values implicit in any group, and these are made clear to potential members before they join the group. (Examples of certain values include expressing feelings, being direct and honest, sharing personal material with others, learning how to trust, improving interpersonal communication, and deciding for oneself.)

(c) Personal and professional needs of group counselors are not met at the members' expense.

(d) Group counselors avoid using the group for their own therapy.

(e) Group counselors are aware of their own values and assumptions and how these apply in a multicultural context.

(f) Group counselors take steps to increase their awareness of ways that their personal reactions to members might inhibit the group process and they monitor their countertransference. Through an awareness of the effect of stereotyping and discrimination (i.e., biases based on age, disability, ethnicity, gender, race, religion, or sexual preference), group counselors guard the individual rights and personal dignity of all group members.

8. Equitable Treatment: Group counselors make every reasonable effort to treat each member individually and equally.

(a) Group counselors recognize and respect differences (e.g., cultural, racial, religious, lifestyle, age, disability, gender) among group members.

(b) Group counselors maintain an awareness of their behavior toward individual group members and are alert to the potential detrimental effects of favoritism or partiality toward any particular group member to the exclusion or detriment of any other member(s). It is likely that group counselors will favor some members over others, yet all group members deserve to be treated equally.

(c) Group counselors ensure equitable use of group time for each member by inviting silent members to become involved, acknowledging nonverbal attempts to communicate, and discouraging rambling and monopolizing of time by members.

(d) If a large group is planned, counselors consider enlisting another qualified professional to serve as a co-leader for the group sessions.

9. Dual Relationships: Group counselors avoid dual relationships with group members that might impair their objectivity and professional judgment, as well as those which are likely to compromise a group member's ability to participate fully in the group.

(a) Group counselors do not misuse their professional role and power as group leader to advance personal or social contacts with members throughout the duration of the group.

(b) Group counselors do not use their professional relationship with group members to further their own interest either during the group or after the termination of the group.

(c) Sexual intimacies between group counselors and members are unethical.

(d) Group counselors do not barter (exchange) professional services with group members for services.

(e) Group counselors do not admit their own family members, relatives, employees, or personal friends as members to their groups.

(f) Group counselors discuss with group members the potential detrimental effects of group members engaging in intimate inter-member relationships outside of the group.

(g) Students who participate in a group as a partial course requirement for a group course are not evaluated for an academic grade based upon their degree of participation as a member in a group. Instructors of group counseling courses take steps to minimize the possible negative effect on students when they participate in a group course by separating course grades from participation in the group and by allowing students to decide what issues to explore and when to stop.

(h) It is inappropriate to solicit members from a class (or institutional affiliation) for one's private counseling or therapeutic groups.

10. Use of Techniques: Group counselors do not attempt any technique unless trained in its use or under supervision by a counselor familiar with the intervention.

(a) Group counselors are able to articulate a theoretical orientation that guides their practice, and they are able to provide a rationale for their interventions.

(b) Depending upon the type of an intervention, group counselors have training commensurate with the potential effect of a technique.

(c) Group counselors are aware of the necessity to modify their techniques to fit the unique needs of various cultural ethnic groups.

(d) Group counselors assist members in translating in-group learnings to daily life.

11. Goal Development: Group counselors make every effort to assist members in developing their personal goals.

(a) Group counselors use their skills to assist members in making their goals specific so that others present in the group will understand the nature of the goals.

(b) Throughout the course of a group, group counselors assist members in assessing the degree to which personal goals are being met, and assist in revising any goals when it is appropriate.

(c) Group counselors help members clarify the degree to which the goals can be met within the context of a particular group.

12. Consultation: Group counselors develop and explain policies about between-session consultation to group members.

(a) Group counselors take care to make certain that members do not use between-session consultations to avoid dealing with issues pertaining to the group that would be dealt with best in the group.

(b) Group counselors urge members to bring the issues discussed during between-session consultations into the group if they pertain to the group.

(c) Group counselors seek out consultation and/or supervision regarding ethical concerns or when encountering difficulties which interfere with their effective functioning as group leaders.

(d) Group counselors seek appropriate professional assistance for their own personal problems or conflicts that are likely to impair their professional judgment and work performance.

(e) Group counselors discuss their group cases only for professional consultation and educational purposes.

(f) Group counselors inform members about policies regarding whether consultation will be held confidential.

13. Termination from the Group: Depending upon the purpose of participation in the group, counselors promote termination of members from the group in the most efficient period of time.

   (a) Group counselors maintain a constant awareness of the progress made by each group member and periodically invite the group members to explore and re-evaluate their experiences in the group. It is the responsibility of group counselors to help promote the independence of members from the group in a timely manner.

14. Evaluation and Follow-Up: Group counselors make every attempt to engage in ongoing assessment and to design follow-up procedures for their groups.

   (a) Group counselors recognize the importance of ongoing assessment of a group, and they assist members in evaluating their own progress.

   (b) Group counselors conduct evaluation of the total group experience at the final meeting (or before termination), as well as ongoing evaluation.

   (c) Group counselors monitor their own behavior and become aware of what they are modeling in the group.

   (d) Follow-up meetings might be with individuals, or groups or both to determine the degree to which: (i) members have reached their goals, (ii) the group had a positive or negative effect on the participants, (iii) members could profit from some type of referral, and (iv) as information for possible modification of future groups. If there is no follow-up meeting, provisions are made available for individual follow-up meetings to any member who needs or requests such a contact.

15. Referrals: If the needs of a particular member cannot be met within the type of group being offered, the group counselor suggests other appropriate professional referrals.

   (a) Group counselors are knowledgeable of local community resources for assisting group members regarding professional referrals.

   (b) Group counselors help members seek further professional assistance, if needed.

16. Professional Development: Group counselors recognize that professional growth is a continuous, ongoing, developmental process throughout their career.

   (a) Group counselors maintain and upgrade their knowledge and skill competencies through educational activities, clinical experiences, and participation in professional development activities.

   (b) Group counselors keep abreast of research findings and new developments as applied to groups.

APPENDIX B

Suggested Readings: Treatment and Task Groups

TREATMENT GROUPS

Support Groups

Gartner, A., & Riessman, F. (Eds.). (1984). *The self-help revolution.* New York: Human Science Press.

Gidron, B., Guterman, N. B., & Hartman, H. (1990). Stress and coping patterns of participants and non-participants in self-help groups for parents of mentally ill. *Community Mental Health Journal, 26*(6), 483–496.

Gitterman, A., & Shulman, L. (Eds.). (1986). *Mutual aid groups and the life cycle.* Itasca, IL: F. E. Peacock.

Glassman, U., & Kates, L. (1990). *Group work: A humanistic approach.* Newbury Park, CA: Sage Publications.

Gonyea, J. G. (1989). Alzheimer's disease support groups: An analysis of their structure, format and perceived benefits. *Social Work in Health Care, 14*(1), 61–72.

Katz, A. H., & Bender, E. I. (1987). *The strength in us: Self-help groups in the modern world.* Oakland, CA: Third Party Associates.

Land, H., & Harangody, G. (1990). A support group for partners of persons with AIDS. *Families in Society, 71*(8), 471–481.

Lieberman, M., & Borman, L. (1979). *Self-help groups for coping with crisis.* San Francisco: Jossey-Bass.

Nahmani, N., Neeman, E., & Nir, C. (1989). Parental bereavement: The motivation to participate in support groups and its conse-quences. *Social Work with Groups, 12*(2), 89–98.

O'Rourke, K. (1990). Recapturing hope: Elementary school support groups for children of alcoholics. *Elementary School Guidance and Counseling, 25*(2), 107–115.

Powell, T. (1987). *Self-help organizations and professional practice.* Silver Springs, MD: National Association of Social Workers Press.

Stewart, M. J. (1990). Expanding theoretical conceptualizations of self-help groups. *Social Science and Medicine, 31*(9), 1057–1066.

Toseland, R. W. (1990). *Group Work with Older Adults.* New York: New York University Press.

Toseland, R., & Hacker, L. (1982). Self-help groups and professional involvement. *Social Work, 27*(4), 341–347.

Toseland, R., Rossiter, C., Peak, T., & Smith, G. (1990). Comparative effectiveness of individual and group interventions to support family caregivers. *Social Work, 35*(3), 209–217.

Winton, M. A. (1990). An evaluation of a support group for parents who have a sexually abused child. *Child Abuse and Neglect, 14*(3), 397–405.

Education

Antonuccio, D. O. (1984). An exploratory study: The psychoeducational group treatment of drug-refractory unipolar depression. *Journal of Behavior Therapy and Experimental Psychiatry, 15*(4), 309–313.

Cohen, M., & Irwin, C. E. (1983). Parent-time: Psychoeducational groups for parents of adolescents. *Health and Social Work*, *8*(3), 196–202.

Daley, D. C. (1989). A psychoeducational approach to relapse prevention. *Journal of Chemical Dependency Treatment*, *2*(2), 105–124.

Dow, M. G., Verdi, M. B., & Sacco, W. O. (1991). Training psychiatric patients to discuss medication issues: Effects on patient communication and knowledge of medications. *Behavior Modification*, *15*(1), 3–21.

Drum, D., & Knott, J. (1977). *Structured groups for facilitating development: Acquiring life skills, resolving life themes and making life transitions*. New York: Human Science Press.

Ettin, M. F., Heiman, M. L., & Kopel, S. A. (1988). Group building: Developing protocols for psychoeducational groups. *Group*, *12*(4), 205–225.

Greene, V. L., & Monahan, D. J. (1989). The effect of a support and education program on stress and burden among family caregivers to frail elderly persons. *The Gerontologist*, *29*(4), 472–477.

Leclerc, G. J. (1985). Understanding the educational needs of older adults: A new approach. *Educational Gerontology*, *11*(2–3), 137–144.

Sternbach, J. (1990). The men's seminar: An educational and support group for men. *Social Work with Groups*, *13*(2), 23–39.

Wallace, B. C. (1989). Relapse prevention in psychoeducational groups for compulsive crack cocaine smokers. *Journal of Substance Abuse Treatment*, *6*(4), 229–239.

Growth

Anderson, J. (1975). Human relations training and group work. *Social Work*, *20*(3), 195–199.

Back, K. W. (1987). *Beyond words: The story of sensitivity training and the encounter movement* (2nd ed.). New Brunswick, NJ: Transaction Books.

Bennis, W., & Schein, E. (Eds). (1965). *Personal and organizational change through group methods: The laboratory approach*. New York: Wiley.

Bradford, L., Gibb, J., & Benne, K. (Eds.). (1964). *T-group theory and laboratory method: An innovation in re-education*. New York: Wiley.

Burton, A. (Ed.). (1969). *Encounter: The theory and practice of encounter groups*. San Francisco: Jossey-Bass.

Campbell, J. P., & Dunnette, M. D. (1973). Effectiveness of T-group experiences in managerial training and development. In D. W. Johnson (Ed.), *Contemporary social psychology*. Philadelphia: J. B. Lippincott.

Cohen, A. M., & Smith, D. (1976). *The critical incident in growth groups, theory and technique*. La Jolla, CA: University Associates.

Gustaitis, R. (1969). *Turning On*. New York: Macmillan.

Hawes, E. C. (1985). Personal growth groups for women: An Adlerian approach. *Journal for Specialists in Group Work*, *10*(1), 19–27.

Howard, J. (1970). *Please touch*. Toronto: McGraw-Hill.

Lakin, M. (1972). *Experiential groups: The uses of interpersonal encounter, psychotherapy groups and sensitivity training*. Morristown: General Learning Press.

Levinson, C. P. (1986). Patient drawings and growth toward mature object relations: Observations of an art therapy group in a psychiatric ward. *Arts in Psychotherapy*, *13*(2), 101–106.

Otto, H., & Mann, J. (Eds.). (1968). *Ways of growth: Approaches to expanding awareness*. New York: Grossman.

Rogers, C. (1970). *On encounter groups*. New York: Harper and Row.

Schutz, W. (1967). *Joy*. New York: Grove.

Shepard, M., & Marjorie, L. (1970). *Marathon*. New York: Putnam's.

Solomon, L., & Berzon, B. (Eds.). (1970). *The encounter group: Issues and application*. Pacific Grove, CA: Brooks/Cole.

Swan, L. A. (1988). Grounded encounter therapy: Its characteristics and process. *Clinical Sociology Review*, *6*, 76–87.

Therapy

Berns, E. (1966). *Principals in group treatment*. New York: Oxford University Press.

Corey, M., & Corey, G. (1992). *Groups: Process and practice* (4th ed.). Pacific Grove, CA: Brooks/Cole.

Jacobs, A., & Spradlin, W. (Eds.). (1974). *The group as agent of change: Treatment, prevention, personal growth in the family, the school, the mental hospital, and the community.* New York: Behavioral Publications.

Levine, B. (1979). *Group psychotherapy: Practice and development.* Englewood Cliffs, NJ: Prentice-Hall.

Levine, B., & Gallogly, V. (1985). *Group therapy with alcoholics: Outpatient and inpatient approaches.* Newbury Park, CA: Sage Publications.

Longergan, E. C. (1982). *Group intervention: How to begin and maintain groups in medical and psychiatric settings.* New York: Jason Aronson.

MacLennan, B. W., & Felsenfeld, N. (1968). *Group counseling and psychotherapy with adolescents.* New York: Columbia University Press.

Rose, S. D. (1977). *Group therapy: A behavioral approach.* Englewood Cliffs, NJ: Prentice-Hall.

Rose, S. D. (1989). *Working with adults in groups: Integrating cognitive-behavioral and small group strategies, a multimethod approach.* San Francisco: Jossey-Bass.

Rose, S. D., & Edleson, J. C. (1987). *Working with children and adolescents in groups.* San Francisco: Jossey-Bass.

Shaffer, J., & Galinsky, M. (1989). *Models of group therapy* (2nd ed.). Englewood Cliffs, NJ: Prentice-Hall.

Sundel, M., Glasser, P., Sarri, R., & Vinter, R. (Eds.). (1985). *Individual change through small groups* (2nd ed.). New York: Free Press.

Yalom, I. D. (1985). *The theory and practice of group psychotherapy* (3rd ed.). New York: Basic Books.

Yost, E. B., Butler, L. E., Corbishley, M. A., & Allender, J. R. (1986). *Group cognitive psychotherapy: A treatment approach for depressed older adults.* New York: Pergamon Press.

Socialization

Douglas, M. S., & Mueser, K. T. (1990). Teaching conflict resolution skills to the chronically mentally ill: Social skills training groups for briefly hospitalized patients. *Behavior Modification, 14*(4), 519–547.

Dow, M. G. (1985). Peer validation and idiographic analysis of social skill deficits. *Behavior Therapy, 16*(1), 76–86.

Englander-Golden, P., Jackson, J. E., Schwarzkopf, A. B., & Lyle, P. S. (1989). Communication skills and self-esteem in prevention of destructive behaviors. *Adolescence, 24,* 495–502.

Eriksen, L., Bjornstad, S., & Gotestam, G. (1986). Social skills training in groups for alcoholics: One-year treatment outcome for groups and individuals. *Addictive Behaviors, 11*(3), 309–329.

Fingeret, A. L., Monti, P. M., & Paxson, M. A. (1985). Social perception, social performance, and self-perception: A study with psychiatric and nonpsychiatric groups. *Behavior Modification, 9*(3), 345–356.

Kelley, J. A., Urey, J. R., & Patterson, J. (1981). Small group job interview skills training in the mental health center setting. *Journal of Behavioral Counseling Quarterly, 1*(3), 202–212.

Kindness, K., & Newton, A. (1984). Patients and social skills groups: Is social skills training enough? *Behavioural-Psychotherapy, 12*(3), 212–222.

Kolko, D. J., Loar, L. L., & Sturnick, D. (1990). Inpatient social-cognitive skills training groups with conduct disordered and attention deficit disordered children. *Journal of Child Psychology and Psychiatry and Allied Disciplines, 31*(5), 737–748.

Long, S. J., & Sherer, M. (1984). Social skills training with juvenile offenders. *Child and Family Behavior Therapy, 6*(4), 1–11.

Manderino, M. A., & Bzdek, V. M. (1987). Social skill building with chronic patients. *Journal of Psychosocial Nursing and Mental Health Services, 25*(9), 18–23.

McKenna, J. G., & Gaffney, L. R. (1982). An evaluation of group therapy for adolescents using social skills training. *Current Psychological Research, 2*(3), 151–159.

Miller, I. W., Norman, W. H., Keitner, G. I., Bishop, S. B., & Dow, M. G. (1989). Cognitive-behavioral treatment of depressed inpatients. *Behavior-Therapy, 20*(1), 25–47.

Oei, T. P., & Jackson, P. R. (1982). Social skills and cognitive behavioral approaches to the treatment of problem drinking. *Journal of Studies on Alcohol, 43*(5), 532–547.

Parsons, R. J. (1988). Empowerment for role alternatives for low income minority girls: A group work approach. *Social Work with Groups, 11*, 27–45.

Rose, S. D. (1989). *Working with adults in groups: A multi-method approach.* San Francisco: Jossey-Bass.

Tanner, V. L., & Holliman, W. B. (1988). Effectiveness of assertiveness training in modifying aggressive behaviors of young children. *Psychological Reports, 62*(1), 39–46.

Thomas, A. P., Bax, M. C., & Smyth, D. P. (1988). The social skill difficulties of young adults with physical disabilities. *Child Care, Health and Development, 14*(4), 255–264.

Toseland, R., & Rose, S. (1978). Evaluating social skills training for older adults in groups. *Social Work Research and Abstracts, 14*(1), 25–33.

TASK GROUPS

Teams

Abramson, J. (1989). Making teams work. *Social Work with Groups, 12*(4), 45–63.

Brill, N. (1976). *Teamwork: Working together in the human services.* Philadelphia: J. B. Lippincott.

Browning, L. D. (1977). Diagnosing teams in organizational settings. *Group and Organizational Studies, 2*(2), 187–197.

Compton, B. R., & Galaway, B. (1979). *Social work processes* (rev. ed.). Belmont, CA: Wadsworth.

Connaway, R. S. (1975). Teamwork and social work advocacy: Conflicts and possibilities. *Community Mental Health Journal, 11*(4), 381–388.

Halstead, L. (1976). Team care in chronic illness: A critical review of the literature of the past 25 years. *Archives of Physical Medicine and Rehabilitation, 57*, 507–511.

Horwitz, J. J. (1969). Dimension of rehabilitative teamwork. *Rehabilitative Record, 10*, 37–40.

Horwitz, J. (1970). *Team practice and the specialist: An introduction to interdisciplinary teamwork.* Springfield, IL: Charles C. Thomas.

Kane, R. A. (1975). The interprofessional team as a small group. *Social Work in Health Care, 1*(1), 19–32.

Kane, R. A. (1975). *Interprofessional teamwork.* Syracuse: Syracuse Vocational School of Social Work.

Kramer, R. M. (1956). Dynamics of teamwork in the agency, community and neighborhood. *Social Work, 1*(3), 56–62.

Lonsdale, S., Webb, A., & Briggs, T. (1980). *Teamwork in the personal social services and health care.* London: Croom Helm.

Lowe, J. (1981). Understanding teamwork: Another look at the concepts. *Social Work in Health Care, 7*(2), 1–11.

Lowe, J., & Herranen, M. (1978). Conflict in teamwork: Understanding roles and relationships. *Social Work in Health Care, 3*(3), 323–330.

Nagi, S. Z. (1975). Teamwork in health care in the U.S.: A sociological perspective. *The Millbank Memorial Fund Quarterly, 53*, 79–91.

Nason, F. (1983). Diagnosing the hospital team. *Social Work in Health Care, 9*(2), 25–45.

New, K. M. (1968). An analysis of the concept of teamwork. *Community Mental Health Journal, 4*(4), 326–333.

Odhner, F. (1970). Group dynamics of the interdisciplinary team. *The American Journal of Occupational Therapy, 24*, 484–487.

Rae-Grant, Q. A., & Marcuse, D. F. (1968). The hazards of teamwork. *American Journal of Orthopsychiatry, 38*(1), 4–9.

Regenburg, J. (1974). A venture in interprofessional discussion. In H. Rehr (Ed.), *Medicine and Social Work* (pp. 35–73). New York: Prodist.

Rothberg, J. S. (1981). The rehabilitation team: Future direction. *Archives of Physical and Medical Rehabilitation, 62*, 407–410.

Rubin, I. (1978). Factors influencing the effectiveness of health teams. In I. Rubin et al. (Eds.),

Managing human resources in health care organizations: An applied approach (pp. 251–262). Reston: Reston Publishing Co.

Stevenson, O. (1981). *Specialization in social service teams*. London: George Allen and Unwin, Ltd.

Wise, H. (1974). *Making health teams work*. Cambridge: Ballinger Publishing Co.

Treatment Conferences

Baglow, L. J. (1990). A multidimensional model for treatment of child abuse: A framework for cooperation. *Child Abuse and Neglect: The International Journal, 14*(3), 387–395.

Buckholdt, D. R., & Gubrium, J. F. (1979). Doing staffing. *Human Organization, 38*(3), 255–264.

Carter, R. M. (1966). It is respectfully recommended. *Federal Probation, 30*(2), 28–42.

Clarke, T. R., Distasi, W. L., & Wallace, C. J. (1978). Developing a multidisciplinary conference. *Health and Social Work, 3*(1), 166–174.

Overs, R. P. (1967). The staffing conference. *Rehabilitation Literature, 28*(4), 110–112.

Toseland, R., Ivanoff, A., & Rose, S. (1987). Treatment conferences: Task groups in action. *Social Work with Groups, 10*(2), 79–94.

Weinstein, B. (1968). The parent counseling conference. *Rehabilitation Literature, 29*, 233–236.

Staff Development

Aronson, M. L. (1990). A group therapist's perspectives on the use of supervisory groups in the training of psychotherapists. *Psychoanalysis and Psychotherapy, 8*(1), 88–4.

Austin, M. J. (1981). *Supervisory management for the human services*. Englewood Cliffs, NJ: Prentice-Hall.

Bass, R., & Vaughan, J. (1966). *Training in industry: The management of learning*. Belmont, CA: Wadsworth.

Bertcher, H. (1988). *Staff development in human service organizations*. Englewood Cliffs, NJ: Prentice-Hall.

Borders, L. D. (1991). A systematic approach to peer group supervisor. *Journal of Counseling and Development, 69*(3), 248–252.

Danto, E. A., & Mazzella, A. J. (1988). Peer supervision in occupational social work. *Employee Assistance Quarterly, 4*(1), 29–44.

Epstein, L. (1986). Collusive selective inattention to the negative impact of the supervisory interaction. *Contemporary Psychoanalysis, 22*(3), 389–409.

Freudenberger, H. (1974). Staff burn-out. *Journal of Social Issues, 30*, 159–165.

Hayes, R. L. (1990). Developmental group supervision. *Journal for Specialists in Group Work, 15*(4), 225–238.

Holloway, E., & Johnston, R. (1985). Group supervision: Widely practiced but poorly understood. *Counselor Education and Supervision, 24*(4), 332–340.

Joelson, J. (1982). Friday afternoon at the board: Group supervision in school practice. *Social Work in Education, 4*(4), 26–34.

Kaslow, F. W. (1972). Group supervision. In Kaslow & Associates (Eds.), *Issues in Human Services*. San Francisco: Jossey-Bass.

Keller, J. F., & Protinsky, H. O. (1985–86). Family therapy supervision: An integrative model. *Journal of Psychotherapy and the Family, 1*(4), 83–90.

Kruger, L. J., Cherniss, C., Maher, C. A., & Leichtman, H. M. (1988). Group supervision of paraprofessional counselors. *Professional Psychology Research and Practice, 19*(6), 609–616.

Lauffer, A. (1978). *Doing continuing education and staff development*. New York: McGraw-Hill.

List, D. (1986). Bringing it all back home: Individual and group supervision in family therapy training. *Australian and New Zealand Journal of Family Therapy, 7*(1), 7–12.

Loucks, S., & Melle, M. (1982). Evaluation of staff development: How do they know it took? *The Journal of Staff Development, 13*(4), 102–117.

Marks, J. L. (1986). Training agency staff through peer group supervisor. *Social Casework, 67*(7), 418–423.

Maslach, C. (1976). Burned out. *Human Behavior, 3*, 16–32.

Maslach, C. (1982). *Burnout: The cost of caring*. Englewood Cliffs, NJ: Prentice-Hall.

Paihar, B. (1983). Group supervision: A naturalistic field study in a specialty unit. *The Clinical Supervisor, 1,* 3–14.

Pawlak, E. (1976). Organizational tinkering. *Social Work, 21,* 376–380.

Pfeiffer, J., & Jones, J. (1965–75). *Structured experiences for human relations training.* La Jolla, CA: University Associates.

Quinn, W. H., Atkinson, B. J., & Hood, C. J. (1985). The stuck-case clinic as a group supervision model. *Journal of Marital and Family Therapy, 11*(1), 67–73.

Rabi, J. S., Lehr, M. L., & Hayner, M. L. (1984). Study group II: The peer consultation team: An alternative. *Journal of Strategic and Systemic Therapies, 3*(2), 66–71.

Schecter, D., & O'Farrell, T. (1970). *Training and continuing education: A handbook for health care institutions.* Chicago: Hospital Research and Educational Trust.

Schneider, S., & Berman, M. H. (1991). The supervision group as a transitional object. *Group Analysis, 24*(1), 65–72.

Schreiber, P., & Frank, E. (1983). The use of a peer supervision group by social work clinicians. *Clinical Supervisor, 1*(1), 29–36.

Valle, S. K. (1984). Supervision in alcoholism counseling. *Journal of Alcoholism Treatment Quarterly, 1*(1), 101–114.

Westwood, J. J. (1989). Group supervision for counselors in training. *Canadian Journal of Counselling, 23*(4), 348–353.

Wilbur, M. P., Roberts-Wilbur, J., Morris, J. R., Betz, R. L., & Hart, G. M. (1991). Structured group supervision: Theory into practice. *Journal for Specialists in Group Work, 16*(2), 91–100.

Committees

Benson, P. G., & Hornsby, J. S. (1988). The politics of pay: The use of influence tactics in job evaluation committees. *Group and Organization Studies, 13*(2), 208–224.

Bradford, L. P. (1976). *Making meetings work: A guide for leaders and group members.* La Jolla, CA: University Associates.

Carnes, W. T. (1980). *Effective meetings for busy people: Let's decide it and go home.* New York: McGraw-Hill.

Edson, J. B. (1977). How to survive on a committee. *Social Work, 10*(3), 224–226.

Gummer, B. (1987). Groups as substance and symbol: Group processes and organizational politics. *Social Work with Groups, 22*(2), 25–39.

Imber, M., Neidt, W. A., & Reyes, P. (1990). Factors contributing to teacher satisfaction with participative decision making. *Journal of Research and Development in Education, 23*(4), 216–225.

Jay, A. (1976). How to run a meeting. *Harvard Business Review, 54,* 43–57.

Magura, S., Goldsmith, D. S., Casriel, C., Lipton, D. S., Goldstein, P. J., Spunt, B. J., & Strug, D. L. (1988). Patient-staff governance in methadone maintenance treatment: A study in participative decision making. *International Journal of the Addictions, 23*(3), 253–278.

Napier, R., & Gershenfeld, M. (1981). *Groups: Theory and experience* (2nd ed.). Boston: Houghton Mifflin.

O'Neill, P., & Leiter, M. P. (1986). Shared assumptions: A citizen action group simulation. *Canadian Journal of Behavioural Science, 18*(2), 115–125.

Sundstrom, E., De Meuse, K. P., & Futrell, D. (1990). Work teams: Applications and effectiveness. *American Psychologist, 45*(2), 120–133.

Tropman, J. (1980). *Effective meetings: Improving group decision making.* Newbury Park, CA: Sage Publications.

Tropman, J., Johnson, H., & Tropman, E. (1979). *The essentials of committee management.* Chicago: Nelson-Hall.

Cabinets

Ephross, P. H., & Vassil, T. B. (1988). *Groups that work: Structure and process.* New York: Columbia University Press.

Gouran, D. S. (1982). *Making decisions in groups: Choices and consequences.* Glenview, IL: Scott, Foresman.

Scheidel, T. M., & Crowell, L. (1979). *Discussing and deciding: A deskbook for group leaders and group members.* New York: Macmillan.

Boards

Chait, R. P., Holland, T. P., & Taylor, B. E. (1991). *The effective board of trustees*. New York: Macmillan.

Clark, M. L. (1988). The board of directors as a small dynamic group: A review. *Administration and Policy in Mental Health, 16*(2), 89–98.

Conrad, W. R., & Glenn, W. R. (1976). *The effective voluntary board of directors: What it is and how it works*. Chicago: Swallow Press.

Hartogs, N., & Weber, J. (1974). *Boards of directors: A study in board management and board operations in voluntary hospital, health and welfare organizations*. Dobbs Ferry, NY: Oceana Publications.

Herman, R. D., & Tulipana, F. P. (1985). Board-staff relations and perceived effectiveness in nonprofit organizations. *Journal of Voluntary Action Research, 14*(4), 48–59.

Houle, C. O. (1960). *The effective board*. New York: Association Press.

Koontz, H. (1967). *The board of directors and effective management*. New York: McGraw-Hill.

Louden, J. K. (1975). *The effective director in action*. New York: Amacon Books.

Mathias, T. A. (1986). Composition and effectiveness of the board of directors—Part II. *Management and Labour Studies, 11*(4), 235–246.

Mathias, T. A. (1987). The chief executive and the board of directors—Part I. *Management and Labour Studies, 12*(2), 89–96.

Miller, L. E., Weiss, R. M., & MacLeod, B. V. (1988). Boards of directors in nonprofit organizations: Composition, activities, and organizational outcomes. *Journal of Voluntary Action Research, 17*, 81–89.

Mueller, R. K. (1974). *Board life: Realities of being a corporate director*. New York: Amacon Books.

Puckey, W. (1969). *The board room: A guide to the role and function of directors*. London: Hutchinson Publishing Group.

Sorenson, R. (1962). *How to be a board or committee member*. New York: Association Press.

Swanson, A. (1978). *The determined team: A handbook for board members of voluntary organizations*. New York: Exposition Press.

Taylor, B. E., Chait, R. P., & Holland, T. P. (1991). Trustee motivation and board effectiveness. *Non-Profit and Voluntary Sector Quarterly, 20*(2), 207–224.

Trecker, H. B. (1970). *Citizen boards at work: New challenges to effective action*. New York: Association Press.

Waldo, C. N. (1986). *A working guide for directors of not-for-profit organizations*. New York: Quorum Books.

Coalitions

Black, T. F. (1983). Coalition building—some suggestions. *Child Welfare, LXII*(3), 263–268.

Cox, E. (1988). Empowerment of the low income elderly through group work. *Social Work with Groups, 11*(4), 111–119.

Gamson, W. A. (1961). Theory of coalition formation. *American Sociological Review, 26*, 373–382.

Gentry, M. E. (1987). Coalition formation and processes. *Social Work with Groups, 10*(3), 39–54.

Greeley, A. M. (1974). *Building coalitions: American politics in the 1970s*. New York: New Viewpoints.

Humphreys, N. A. (1979). Competing for revenue-sharing funds: A coalition approach. *Social Work, 24*(1), 14–18.

Joyner, N. D. (1982). Coalition politics: A case study of an organization's approach to a single issue. *Women & Politics, 2*, 57–70.

Kahn, S. (1982). *Organizing, a guide for grassroots leaders*. New York: McGraw-Hill.

Kronus, C. L. (1977). Mobilizing voluntary associations into a social movement: The case of environmental quality. *The Sociological Quarterly, 18*, 267–283.

Lawler, E. J., & Youngs, G. A., Jr. (1975). Coalition formation: An integration model. *Sociometry, 38*(1), 1–17.

Newstetter, W. I. (1948). *Proceedings of the National Conference of Social Work* (pp. 205–217). New York: Columbia University Press.

Pernell, R. (1986). Empowerment and social group work. In M. Parnes (Ed.), *Innovations in social group work* (pp. 107–118). New York: Haworth Press.

Prigmore, C. S. (1974). Use of the coalition in legislative action. *Social Work, 19*(1), 96–102.

Riker, W. H. (1962). *The theory of political coalitions.* New Haven: Yale University Press.

Ross, E. C. (1985). Coalition development in legislative advocacy. *Exceptional Children, 51*(4), 342–344.

Rubin, H. J., & Rubin, I. S. (1992). *Community organizing and development* (2nd ed.). New York: Macmillan.

Staggenborg, S. (1986). Coalition work in the pro-choice movement: Organizational and environmental opportunities and obstacles. *Social Problems, 33*(5), 374–390.

Tanguay, M. C. (1987). Citizen advocacy: Strategies for addressing human service needs in the community. *Canada's Mental Health, (35)*1, 10–12.

Weisner, S. (1983). Fighting back: A critical analysis of coalition building in the human services. *Social Service Review, 57*(2), 291–306.

Social Action Groups

Abels, P. (1980). Instructed advocacy and community group work. In A. Alissi (Ed.), *Perspective on social group work practice* (pp. 326–331). New York: The Free Press.

Bakalinsky, R. (1984). The small group in community organization practice. *Social Work with Groups, 7*(2), 87–96.

Cox, F., Erlich, J., Rothman, J., & Tropman, J. (1977). *Tactics and techniques of community practice.* Itasca, IL: F. E. Peacock.

Cox, F., Erlich, J., Rothman, J., & Tropman, J. (Eds.). (1987). *Strategies of community organization* (4th ed.). Itasca, IL: F. E. Peacock.

Curtis, R., Jr., & Zurcher, L., Jr. (1973). Stable resources of protest movements: The multi-organizational field. *Social Forces, 52,* 53–61.

Delgado, G. (1986). *Organizing the movement: The roots and growth of ACORN.* Philadelphia: Temple University Press.

Gamson, W. (1975). *The strategy of social protest.* Homewood: Dorsey Press.

Gerlach, L., & Hine, V. (1970). *People, power, change: Movements of social transformation.* Indianapolis: Bobs-Merrill.

Henderson, P., & Thomas, D. N. (1980). *Skills in neighborhood work.* London: Allen and Unwin.

Huenefeld, J. (1970). *The community activist's handbook.* Boston: Beacon Press.

Lee, J. A. (Ed.). (1988). Group work with the poor and the oppressed [Special issue]. *Social Work with Groups, 11*(4), 1–132.

McCarthy, J. D., & Mayer, N. Z. (1977). Resource mobilization and social movements: A partial theory. *American Journal of Sociology, 82,* 1212–1241.

Pearlman, M., & Edwards, M. (1982). Enabling in the eighties: The client advocacy group. *Social Casework, 63*(9), 532–539.

Pincus, A., & Minahan, A. (1973). *Social work practice: Model and method.* Itasca, IL: F. E. Peacock.

Rubin, H. J., & Rubin, I. S. (1992). *Community organizing and development* (2nd ed.). New York: Macmillan.

Shapiro, T. M. (1985). *Population control politics: Women, sterilization, and reproductive choice.* Philadelphia: Temple University Press.

Smith, U. (1979). How interest groups influence legislators. *Social Work, 24*(3), 234–240.

Thursz, D. (1971). The arsenal of social action strategies: Options for social workers. *Social Work, 16*(1), 27–34.

Tilly, C. (1978). *From mobilization to revolution.* Reading: Addison-Wesley.

Delegate Councils

Gulley, H. (1968). *Discussion, conference and group process* (2nd ed.). New York: Holt, Rinehart and Winston.

Maier, N. R. (1963). *Problem solving discussion and conference: Leadership methods and skills.* New York: McGraw-Hill.

Sattler, W. M., & Miller, N. E. (1968). *Discussion and conference* (2nd ed.). Englewood Cliffs, NJ: Prentice-Hall.

APPENDIX C

Films and Videotapes

Ed Berkowitz & Alex Gitterman. *Social Work with a Group of Developmentally Disabled Young Adults.* Columbia University, School of Social Work, 622 West 113th Street, New York, NY 10025.

Len Brown. *Problem Solving.* Rutgers University, School of Social Work, 536 George Street, New Brunswick, NJ 08903.

Len Brown. *Termination.* Rutgers University, School of Social Work, 536 George Street, New Brunswick, NJ 08903.

Tom Casciato. *Circle of Recovery, with Bill Moyers.* Circle of Recovery, Box 2284, South Burlington, VT 05407.

Naomi Feil. *Looking for Yesterday.* Edward Feil Productions, 4614 Prospect Avenue, Cleveland, OH 44103.

Naomi Feil. *The More We Get Together: How to Form a Validation Group.* Edward Feil Productions, 4614 Prospect Avenue, Cleveland, OH 44103.

Mel Goldstein. *Reflections on Group Work: The Video Curriculum to Teach Social Group Work.* School of Social Work, State University of New York at Stony Brook, Health Sciences Center, Stony Brook, NY 11794.

Insight Media. *Groups and Group Dynamics.* Insight Media, 121 West 85th Street, New York, NY 10024.

William Lauzon. *Staff Groups: Wellness in the Workplace.* Office of Television and Radio, Building 4048–Kilmeer, Rutgers University, New Brunswick, NJ 08903.

Walter Lifton. *Just Like a Family.* University Film Service, University at Albany, State University of New York, 1400 Washington Avenue, Albany, NY 12222.

Edward Mason. *Chrysalis '86: The Development of a Therapeutic Group.* Penn State Audio-Visual Services, 1127 Fox Hill Road, University Park, PA 16803.

Public Broadcasting Video. *Frontline: The Color of Your Skin.* PBS Video, 1320 Braddock Place, Alexandria, VA 22314. #Fron-9211K. (This is not a film about group work, but rather a film showing group dynamics at the U.S. Army's Defense Equal Opportunity Management Institute. This film can be used to discuss sensitivity training or race relations in groups.)

Sheldon Rose. *The Best of the Children's Groups.* School of Social Work, University of Wisconsin–Madison, 425 Henry Mall, Madison, WI 53706.

Sheldon Rose. *Common Problems in Parent Training Groups.* School of Social Work, University of Wisconsin–Madison, 425 Henry Mall, Madison, WI 53706.

Sheldon Rose. *The Golden Eagles.* School of Social Work, University of Wisconsin–Madison, 425 Henry Mall, Madison, WI 53706.

Sheldon Rose. *Problem Solving in Groups.* School of Social Work, University of Wisconsin–Madison, 425 Henry Mall, Madison, WI 53706.

Round Table Films. *Meeting in Progress.* Round Table Films, 113 North San Vincente Boulevard, Beverly Hills, CA 90211.

Lawrence Shulman. *Skills of Helping: Leading a First Group Session.* Instructional Communication Center, McGill University, Montreal, Quebec, Canada H3A2K6.

OTHER FILM RESOURCES

Interviews of *Saul Bernstein, Giesela Konopka, Helen Northen, Helen Phillips, Mary Lou Sommers, Gertrude Wilson* and other films available in VHS format available from David Klaassen, Social Welfare History Archives, University of Minnesota, 1012 Walter Library, 117 Pleasant Street, SE, Minneapolis, MN 55455.

APPENDIX D

Group Announcements

SUPPORT GROUP FOR NEW PARENTS

You are invited to join a support group of parents who have children between 6 months and 2 years. The group will discuss concerns identified by its members including such possible issues as infant care, sharing household responsibilities, disciplining your child, toilet training, and child-care resources.

Sponsor
Greenwich Community Mental Health Center
49 Cambridge Avenue
Greenwich, NY
(212) 246-2468

Group Leaders
George Oxley, ACSW, clinic director
Marybeth Carol, BSW, clinic social worker

Membership
Open to all parents with children between the ages of 6 months and 2 years

Dates and Times
March–April–May, Thursday evenings from 7:30 to 9:30 p.m.

Child Care
Parents are encouraged to bring their children to the center. Child care will be available from human service interns of Hudson Center Community College.

Cost
Enrollment fee for the three-month group, total $90.00 per couple, payable monthly.

For further information, call Mr. Oxley or Ms. Carol at (212) 246-2468.

YOUTH CENTER INTEREST MEETING

The residents of the Johnsonville, Pittstown, and Valley Falls area are invited to discuss the proposed establishment of a youth center for these communities. Issues to be discussed include cost of service, fund-raising, need for service, and support for such a service.

Sponsor
Rensselaer Council of Community Services

Meeting Place
Johnsonville Firehouse

Date and Time
Thursday, March 25, from 7 to 9 p.m.

Further Information
Call Jim Kesser, ACSW
241-2412

Refreshments will be served.

APPENDIX E

Bibliography-Tell-A-Group
Prepared by Harvey Bertcher

Davis, D. (1985). Evaluation and comparison to teleconference training with face-to-face training and the effects on attitude and learning. *Dissertation Abstracts International, 46,* 130.

Evans, R., Fox, H., Pritzl, D., & Halar, E. (1984). Group treatment of physically disabled adults by telephone. *Social Work in Health Care, 9,* 77–85.

Evans, R., & Jaureguy, B. (1981). Group therapy by phone: A cognitive behavioral program for visually impaired elderly. *Social Work in Health Care, 7,* 79–91.

Evans, R., Kleinman, L., & Halar, E. (1984, August). Predicting outcomes of group counseling for the physically disabled. *VA Practitioner,* 49–53.

Evans, R., Smith, K., Werkhaven, W., Fox, H., & Pritzl, D. (1986). Cognitive telephone group therapy with physically disabled elderly persons. *The Gerontologist, 26,* 8–11.

Galinsky, M., Rounds, K., Montague, A., & Butowsky, E. (1993). *Leading a telephone support group for persons with HIV disease.* Chapel Hill: University of North Carolina.

Goodman, C., & Pynoos, J. (1988). Telephone networks connect caregiving families of Alzheimer's victims. *The Gerontologist, 28,* 602–605.

Ingersall, B., & Goodman, L. (1980). History comes alive: Facilitating reminiscence in a group of institutionalized elderly. *Journal of Gerontological Social Work, 2,* 305–317.

Kelleher, K., & Cross, T. (1985). *Teleconferencing: Linking people together electronically.* Englewood Cliffs, NJ: Prentice-Hall.

Lewis, M., & Butler, R. (1974, November). Life-review therapy—putting memories to work in individual and group psychotherapy. *Geriatrics,* 165–168.

Rounds, K., Galinsky, M., & Stevens, S. L. (1991). Linking people with AIDS in rural communities: The telephone group. *Social Work, 36,* 13–18.

Shaddock, A., & Batchler, M. (1986). An analysis of the use of teleconferencing to support a rural early intervention program. *Exceptional Child, 33,* 215–219.

Shepard, P. (1987). Telephone therapy: An alternate to isolation. *Clinical Social Work Journal, 15,* 56–65.

Smeltzer, L., & Davy, J. (1987). Teleconferencing: Reach out to train someone. *Personnel Administrator, 32,* 211–219.

Stein, D., & Lambert, M. (1984). Telephone counseling and crisis intervention: A review. *American Journal of Community Psychology, 12,* 101–126.

Strickland, L., Guild, P., Barefoot, J., & Paterson, S. (1978). Teleconferencing and leadership emergence. *Human Relations, 31,* 583–596.

APPENDIX F

Outline for a Group Proposal
Treatment/Task

Abstract
Short statement summarizing major points of group.

Purpose
Brief statement of purpose.
How the group will conduct its work.
Job description of the worker.

Agency Sponsorship
Agency name and mission.
Agency resources (physical facilities, financial, staff).
Geographic, demographic data on agency.

Membership
Specific population for the group.
Why population was chosen.

Recruitment
Methods to be used.

Composition
Criteria for member inclusion/exclusion.
Size, open or closed group, demographic characteristics.

Orientation
Specific procedures to be used.

Contact
Number, frequency, length, and time of meeting.

Environment
Physical arrangements (room, space, materials).
Financial arrangements (budget, expense, income).
Special arrangements (child care, transportation).

APPENDIX G

An Example of a Treatment Group Proposal

ADOLESCENT DISCHARGE GROUP

The Children's Refuge Home

Abstract
This is a proposal for a social skills training group for adolescents who are about to be released into the community from the children's refuge home.

Purpose
The group will discuss what each member will expect to be doing upon release to the community. The group will reinforce social learning that hås taken place during the residential placement and will help members learn new social skills that will be needed to successfully relate to parents, siblings, teachers, and employers. Role playing, behavior rehearsal modeling, and reinforcement will be employed as methods of teaching social skills.

Agency Sponsorship
The Children's Refuge Home, a residential treatment facility for delinquent youth, serves teenage boys who cannot live at home because of lawbreaking activities. About 200 boys reside here in 15 cottages. The agency has a 200-acre campus with an on-campus school. Staff ratio is about one staff per four boys, and direct-care staff include child-care workers, social workers, nursing staff, psychologists, psychiatrists, and clergy.

Membership
Approximately 10 boys are released to the community each month. The discharge group will be composed from a population of boys for whom discharge is planned within the next three months.

Recruitment
Because this group represents a new service for the institution, members will be recruited by asking cottage parents for volunteers from their respective cottages. An announcement will be printed and delivered to the senior cottage parents for all cottages. Additionally, teachers and social workers will be contacted to suggest possible candidates for the group.

Composition
The group will be composed of six to eight boys between 12 and 14 years old who anticipate discharge from CRH within the next three months. Additionally, this first group will include only children who will be returning to natural parents or relatives rather than to foster care or group homes. The group will be closed and will not add new members because it is important that social skills be learned in a gradual and cumulative fashion.

Orientation
Each member will be interviewed by the leaders. During this interview, the members will view a tape on group treatment for children, and the details of the tape will be discussed to demonstrate how group meetings will be conducted.

Environment
The ideal location for this group is the diagnostic classroom within the campus school. Proximity to

videotaping equipment is necessary so group members can tape and view role plays. A small budget is required ($120) for proposed field trips, charts, and materials for listing skills and posting individual and group progress, and for refreshments after meetings. Additional expenses include two color videotapes ($60). Special arrangements will have to be made so that each member's after-school recreation schedule is free for Monday afternoon meeting times.

APPENDIX H

An Example of a Task Group Proposal

TASK FORCE ON RESEARCH UTILIZATION IN PROBATION

Abstract
This is a proposal for establishing an interagency task force to study how research and research procedures are used in three county probation offices. The group will issue a report with recommendations for increasing research use in probation settings.

Purpose
This group will be formed to study the use of research in county probation offices. The group will meet to discuss the results of surveys taken on each probation office regarding the extent to which probation workers use published research to inform their practice and the extent to which they conduct research in conjunction with their practice. The group will be convened by Robert Rivas, ACSW, at Siena College.

Agency Sponsorship
The task force will be sponsored by the tri-county consortium of probation agencies. The Rockwell County agency will provide physical facilities for meetings. Financial costs will be shared by all county agencies.

Membership
Each county agency will nominate three representatives to attend meetings to ensure equal representation among agencies.

Recruitment
Mailings will be sent to all agency directors. Members of the tri-county association will be informed by an announcement in the newsletter. Each agency director will be requested by letter to appoint three representatives to the task force.

Composition
The task force will require that each agency appoint one representative from each of the following categories: probation administrator, probation supervisor (or senior officer), and probation officer. The task force will include nine representatives from agencies and two research consultants from local colleges. All members of the task force should have some knowledge about research methods. This will be a closed group, although interested people may attend specific meetings after obtaining permission from the group's leader.

Orientation
The group will be given several research reports to read to prepare them for discussions. The group leader will contact each member individually to get ideas for composing an agenda.

Contact
The task force will meet once a month for six sessions. Meetings will last for three hours and will take place every fourth Monday of the month from 9 a.m. to noon. The group will be required to compose and issue a preliminary report on research use within one month after the final meeting.

Environment

The Rockwell County agency will provide the use of its staff meeting room, which is equipped with tables and blackboards for the group's work. Copying facilities will be provided by Rockwell County, and each county will be billed for one third of these expenses (limit $30.00 per county).

About $100 will be required to prepare and distribute the task force's final report and recommendations (contributed by the county association). Agency directors for each county have been requested to provide travel allowance (25 cents a mile) for all travel in conjunction with the work of the task force.

APPENDIX I

Suggested Readings on Program Activities

PROGRAM ACTIVITIES FOR GROUPS OF CHILDREN AND ADOLESCENTS

Borba, M., and Borba, C. (1978). *Self-esteem: A classroom affair.* Minneapolis: Winston Press.

Carrell, S. (1993). *Group exercises for adolescents: A manual for therapists.* Newbury Park, CA: Sage Publications.

Cartlege, G., and Milbrun, J. F. (Eds.). (1980). *Teaching social skills to children.* Elmsford, NY: Pergamon Press.

Dinkmeyer, C. D., and Muro, J. J. (1979). *Group counseling* (2nd ed.). Itasca, IL: F. E. Peacock.

Duncan, T., and Gumaer, J. (1980). *Developmental group for children.* Springfield, IL: Charles C. Thomas.

Ehly, S., and Dustin, R. (1989). *Individual and group counseling in the schools.* New York: Guilford Press.

Ferrara, M. (1992). *Group counseling with juvenile delinquents: The limit and lead approach.* Newbury Park, CA: Sage Publications.

Hazel, J. S., et al. (1981). *A social skills program for adolescents.* Chicago: Research Press.

Mandell, G., and Damon, L. (1989). *Group treatment for sexually abused children.* New York: Guilford Press

Middleman, R. (1982). *The non-verbal method in working with groups: The use of activity in teaching, counseling, and therapy.* An enlarged edition. Hebron, CT: Practitioners Press.

Morganett, R. (1990). *Skills for living: Group counseling activities for young adolescents.* Champaign, IL: Research Press.

Norem-Hebeisen, A. A. (1976). *Exploring self-esteem.* New York: National Humanities Education Center.

Pfeiffer, J. W., and Goodstein, L. (Eds.). (1984–1994). *The annual: Developing human resources.* San Diego: University Associates Inc.

Rathjen, D. P., and Foreyt, J. P. (Eds.). (1980). *Social competence: Interventions for children and adults.* Elmsford, NY: Pergamon Press.

Rose, S., & Edleson, J. (1987). *Working with children and adolescents in groups.* San Francisco: Jossey-Bass

Smith, M. A. (1977). *A practical guide to value clarification.* La Jolla, CA: University Associates.

Wells, H. C., and Canfield, J. (1976). *One hundred ways to enhance self-concept in the classroom.* Englewood Cliffs, NJ: Prentice-Hall.

PROGRAM ACTIVITIES FOR GROUPS OF OLDER PEOPLE

Beisgon, B. (1989). *Life enhancing activities for the mentally impaired elderly.* New York: Springer.

Birren, J., & Deutchman, D. (1991). *Guiding autobiography groups for older adults.* Baltimore: John Hopkins Press.

471

Booth, H. (1986). Dance/movement therapy. In I. Burnside (Ed.), *Working with the elderly: Group processes and techniques* (2nd ed., pp. 211–224). Boston: Jones and Bartlett.

Clark, P., & Osgood, N. J. (1985). *Seniors on stage: The impact of applied theater techniques on the elderly.* New York: Praeger.

Fisher, P. (1989). *Creative movement for older adults.* New York: Human Sciences Press.

Flatten, K., Wilhite, B., & Reyes-Watson, E. (1987). *Exercise activities for the elderly.* New York: Springer.

Flatten, K., Wilhite, B., & Reyes-Watson, E. (1987). *Recreation activities for the elderly.* New York: Springer.

Foster, J., & Foster, R. (1983). Group psychotherapy with the old and aged. In H. Kaplan & B. Sadock (Eds.), *Comprehensive group psychotherapy* (pp. 269–277). Baltimore, MD: Williams & Wilkins.

Foster, P. (Ed.). (1983). *Activities and the "well elderly."* New York: Haworth Press.

Fry, P. (1983). Structured and unstructured reminiscence training and depression among the elderly. *Clinical Gerontologist, 1*(13), 15–37.

Helgeson, E., & Willis, S. (Eds.). (1987). *Handbook of group activities for impaired older adults.* New York: Haworth Press.

Hennessey, M. (1986). Music therapy. In I. Burnside (Ed.), *Working with the elderly: Group processes and techniques* (2nd ed., pp. 198–210). Boston: Jones and Bartlett.

Hurley, O. (1987). *Safe therapeutic exercise for the frail elderly: An introduction.* Albany, NY: Center for the Study of Aging.

Ingersoll, B., & Goodman, L. (1983). A reminiscence group for institutionalized elderly. In M. Rosenbaum (Ed.), *Handbook of short-term therapy groups* (pp. 247–269). New York: McGraw-Hill.

Ingersoll, B., & Silverman, A. (1978). Comparative group psychotherapy for the aged. *The Gerontologist, 18*(2), 201–206.

Kamin, J. (1984). How older adults use books and the public library: A review of the literature. Occasional papers number 165 (Eric Document Reproduction Service No. ED 247954).

Killeffer, E., Bennett, R., & Gruen, G. (1985). *Handbook of innovative programs for the impaired elderly.* New York: Haworth Press.

King, K. (1982) Reminiscing psychotherapy with aging people. *Journal of Psychosocial Nursing and Mental Health Services, 20*(2), 21–25.

Lesser, J., Lazarus, L., Frankel, R., & Havasy, S. (1981). Reminiscence group therapy with psychotic geriatric in-patients. *The Gerontologist, 21*(3), 291–296.

Lewis, M., & Butler, R. (1974). Life review therapy: Putting memories to work in individual and group psychotherapy. *Geriatrics, 29*(11), 165–173.

Lowman, E. (1992). *Arts & crafts for the elderly.* New York: Springer.

McMorde, W., & Blom, S. (1979). Life review therapy: Psychotherapy for the elderly. *Perspectives In Psychiatric Care, 17,* 292–298.

Piper, W., McCallum M., & Azim, H. (1992). *Adaptation to loss through short-term group psychotherapy.* New York: Guilford Press.

Schlenger, G. (1988). *Come and sit by me: Discussion programs for activity specialists.* Owings Mills, MD: National Health Publishing.

Sherman, E. (1987). Reminiscence groups for the community elderly. *Gerontologist, 27*(5), 569–572.

Sherman, E. (1990). Experiential reminiscence and life review therapy. In G. Lietaer, J. Rombauts, & R. Van Balen (Eds.), *Client-centered and experiential psychotherapy in the nineties.* Leuven, Belgium: Leuven University Press.

Thurman, J., & Piggins, C. (1982). *Drama activities with older adults.* New York: Haworth Press.

Toseland, R. (1990). *Group work with older adults.* New York: New York University.

Wilson, M. (1977). Enhancing the lives of aged in a retirement center through a program of reading. *Educational Gerontology, 4*(3), 245–251.

Bibliography

Aaker, D., & Day, G. (1990). *Marketing research* (4th ed.). New York: John Wiley & Sons.

Abels, P. (1980). Instructed advocacy and community group work. In A. Alissi (Ed.), *Perspectives on social group work practice* (pp. 326–331). New York: The Free Press.

Abramson, J. (1983). A non-client-centered approach to program development in a medical setting. In H. Weissman, I. Epstein, & A. Savage (Eds.), *Agency-based social work* (pp. 178–187). Philadelphia: Temple University Press.

Abramson, J. (1989). Making teams work. *Social Work with Groups, 12*(4), 45–63.

Adam, E. (1991). Quality circle performance. *Journal of Management, 17*(1), 25–39.

Addams, J. (1909). *The spirit of youth and the city streets.* New York: Macmillan.

Addams, J. (1926). *Twenty years at Hull House.* New York: Macmillan.

Alberti, R., & Emmons, M. (1974). *Your perfect right* (2nd ed.). San Luis Obispo, CA: Impact Press.

Alinsky, S. (1971). *Rules for radicals.* New York: Random House.

Alissi, A. (1980a). Section A: The nature of social group work. In *Perspectives on social group work practice* (pp. 3–5). New York: The Free Press.

Alissi, A. (Ed.). (1980b). *Perspectives on social group work practice.* New York: The Free Press.

Allport, F. (1924). *Social psychology.* Boston: Houghton Mifflin.

American Association of Group Workers. (1947). *Toward professional standards.* New York: Association Press.

American Psychiatric Association. (1987). *Diagnostic and statistical manual of mental disorders* (3rd ed. rev.). Washington, D.C.

Anderson, J. (1979). Social work practice with groups in the generic base of social work practice. *Social Work with Groups, 2*(4), 281–293.

Anderson, J. (1981). *Social work methods and processes.* Belmont, CA: Wadsworth.

Anderson, J. (1987). Integrating research and practice in social work with groups. *Social Work with Groups, 9*(3), 111–124.

Argyris, C. (1977). Organizational learning and management information systems. *Accounting, Organizations and Society, 2,* 113–123.

Aronson, H., & Overall, B. (1966). Therapeutic expectations of patients in two social classes. *Social Work, 11,* 35–41.

Asch, P. (1957). An experimental investigation of group influences. In Walter Reed Army Institute of Research, *Symposium on preventive and social psychiatry.* Washington, D.C.: Walter Reed Army Institute of Research.

Ashby, M., Gilchrist, L., & Miramontez, A. (1987). Group treatment for sexually abused Indian adolescents. *Social Work with Groups, 10*(4), 21–32.

Axelson, J. A. (1993). *Counseling and development in a multicultural society.* Pacific Grove, CA: Brooks/Cole.

Bachman, J., Bowers, D., & Marcus, P. (1968). Bases of supervisory power: A comparative study in five organizational settings. In S. Tannenbaum (Ed.), *Control in organization* (pp. 229–240). New York: McGraw-Hill.

Bachrach, P., & Baratz, M. S. (1962). Two faces of power. *American Political Science Review, 56*, 947–952.

Back, K. (1951). Influence through social communication. *Journal of Abnormal and Social Psychology, 46*, 9–23.

Bales, R. (1950). *Interaction process analysis: A method for the study of small groups.* Redding, MA: Addison-Wesley.

Bales, R. (1954). In conference. *Harvard Business Review, 32*, 44–50.

Bales, R. (1955). How people interact in conference. *Scientific American, 192*, 31–35.

Bales, R. (1980). *SYMLOG: Case study kit.* New York: The Free Press.

Bales, R., Cohen, S., & Williamson, S. (1979). *SYMLOG: A system for the multiple level observations of groups.* New York: The Free Press.

Balgopal, P., & Vassil, T. (1983). *Groups in social work: An ecological perspective.* New York: Macmillan.

Bandura, A. (1969). *Principles of behavior modification.* New York: Holt, Rinehart and Winston.

Bandura, A. (1977a). Self-efficacy: Toward a unifying theory of behavioral change. *Psychological Review, 84*(2), 191–215.

Bandura, A. (1977b). *Social Learning Theory.* Englewood Cliffs, NJ: Prentice-Hall.

Barker, L. (1979). *Groups in process: An introduction to small group communication.* Englewood Cliffs, NJ: Prentice-Hall.

Barrick, M., & Alexander, R. (1987). A review of quality circle efficacy and the existence of positive-findings bias. *Personnel Psychology, 40*, 579–593.

Bates, P. (1978). *The effects of interpersonal skills training on the acquisition and generalization of interpersonal communication behaviors by moderately mildly retarded adults.* Unpublished doctoral dissertation, University of Wisconsin, Madison.

Bavelas, A. (1950). Communications patterns in task oriented groups. *Journal of the Acoustical Society of America, 22*, 725–730.

Bayless, O. (1967). An alternative pattern for problem solving discussion. *Journal of Communication, 17*, 188–197.

Beck, A. (1976). *Cognitive therapy and the emotional disorders.* New York: International Universities Press.

Beck, A., Freeman, A., & Associates. (1990). *Cognitive therapy of personality.* New York: Guilford Press.

Beck, A., Rush, A., Shaw, B., & Emery, G. (1979). *Cognitive therapy of depression.* New York: Guilford Press.

Beck, D., & Jones, M. (1973). *Progress on family problems.* New York: Family Service Association of America.

Becker, G., & McClintock, G. (1967). Value: Behavioral decision theory. *Annual Review of Psychology, 18*, 239–286.

Becker, W. (1971). *Parents are teachers.* Champaign, IL: Research Press.

Bednar, K., & Kaul, T. (1978). Experimental group research: Current perspectives. In A. Garfield & A. Berger (Eds.), *Handbook of psychotherapy and behavior change* (2nd ed., pp. 769–816). New York: John Wiley & Sons.

Bell, J. (1975). *Family therapy.* New York: Jason Aronson.

Bell, J. (1981). The small group perspective: Family group-therapy. In E. Tolson & W. Reid (Eds.), *Models of family treatment* (pp. 33–51). New York: Columbia University Press.

Benne, K., & Sheats, P. (1948). Functional roles of group members. *Journal of Social Issues, 4*(2), 41–49.

Bennis, W., Benne, K., & Chin, R. (Eds.). (1969). *The planning of change.* New York: Holt, Rinehart and Winston.

Berger, R. (1976). *Interpersonal skill training with institutionalized elderly patients.* Unpublished doctoral dissertation, University of Wisconsin, Madison.

Berne, E. (1961). *Transactional analysis in psychotherapy.* New York: Ballantine Books.

Berne, E. (1963). *The structure and dynamics of organization and groups.* Philadelphia: J. B. Lippincott Company.

Bernstein, D., & Borkovec, T. (1973). *Progressive relaxation training: A manual for the helping professions.* Champaign, IL: Research Press.

Bernstein, S. (1976). Conflict in group work. In S. Bernstein (Ed.), *Explorations in group work* (pp. 72–106). Boston: Charles River Books.

Berry, T. (1991). *Managing the total transformation.* New York: McGraw-Hill.

Bertcher, H. (1990). *Tell-a-group: How to set up and operate group work by telephone.* Unpublished manuscript, University of Michigan, School of Social Work, Ann Arbor.

Bertcher, H. (Ed.). (1992, January). Anonymity. In *Tell-a-Group Hotline* (a manual published and distributed by Harvey Bertcher, DSW, University of Michigan, School of Social Work, Ann Arbor, MI 48109–1285).

Bertcher, H. (1994). *Group participation: Techniques for leaders and members* (2nd ed.). Newbury Park, CA: Sage Publications.

Bertcher, H., & Maple, F. (1977). *Creating groups.* Newbury Park, CA: Sage Publications.

Bertcher, H., & Maple, F. (1985). Elements and issues in group composition. In M. Sundel, P. Glasser, R. Sarri, & R. Vinter (Eds.), *Individual change through small groups* (2nd ed., pp. 180–203). New York: The Free Press.

Beutler, L., Crago, M., Arizmendi, T. Research on therapist variables in psychotherapy. In S. Garfield & A. Bergin (Eds.), *Handbook of psychotherapy and behavior change* (pp. 257–310). New York: John Wiley & Sons.

Bieri, J. (1962). Analyzing stimulus information in social judgments. In S. Messick & J. Ross (Eds.), *Measurement in personality and cognition* (pp. 229–240). New York: John Wiley & Sons.

Bieri, J., Atkins, A., Briar, S., Leanan, R., Miller H., & Tripodi, T. (1966). *Clinical and social judgment.* New York: John Wiley & Sons.

Bion, W. (1959). *Experiences in groups and other papers.* New York: Basic Books.

Blatner, H. (1973). *Acting-in.* New York: Springer Publishing.

Blau, P. (1964). *Exchange and power in social life.* New York: John Wiley & Sons.

Blazer, D. (1978). Techniques for communicating with your elderly patient. *Geriatrics, 33*(11), 79–84.

Bloom, B., & Broder, L. (1950). *Problem-solving processes of college students.* Chicago: University of Chicago Press.

Bloom, M., & Fisher, J. (1982). *Evaluating practice: Guidelines for the accountable professional.* Englewood Cliffs, NJ: Prentice-Hall.

Boatman, F. (1975). *Caseworkers' judgments of clients' hope: Some correlates among client-situation characteristics and among workers' communication patterns.* Unpublished doctoral dissertation, Columbia University, New York.

Bouchard, T. (1972a). A comparison of two group brainstorming procedures. *Journal of Applied Psychology, 56,* 418–421.

Bouchard, T. (1972b). Training, motivation and personality as determinants of the effectiveness of brainstorming groups and individuals. *Journal of Applied Psychology, 56,* 324–331.

Bowers, D., & Franklin, J. (1976). *Survey-guided development: Data-based organizational change.* Ann Arbor, MI: Institute for Social Research.

Bowman, L. (1935). Dictatorship, democracy, and group work in America. In *Proceedings of the National Conference of Social Work* (p. 382). Chicago: University of Chicago Press.

Boyd, N. (1935). Group work experiments in state institutions in Illinois. In *Proceedings of the National Conference of Social Work* (p. 344). Chicago: University of Chicago Press.

Boyd, N. (1938). Play as a means of social adjustment. In J. Lieberman (Ed.), *New trends in group work* (pp. 210–220). New York: Association Press.

Brackett, J. (1895). The charity organization movement: Its tendency and its duty. In *Proceedings of the 22nd National Conference of Charities and Corrections.* Boston: Geo. H. Ellis.

Bradford, L. (1976). *Making meetings work: A guide for leaders and group members.* La Jolla, CA: University Associates.

Bradford, L., & Corey, S. (1951). Improving large group meetings. *Adult Education, 1,* 122–137.

Bradford, L., Stock, D., & Horowitz, M. (1953). How to diagnose group problems. *Adult Leadership, 2*(7), 12–19.

Brager, G., & Holloway, A. (1978). *Changing human service organizations: Politics and practice.* New York: The Free Press.

Brammer, L. (1979). *The helping relationship: Process and skills*. Englewood Cliffs, NJ: Prentice-Hall.

Brekke, J. (1989). The use of orientation groups to engage hard-to-reach clients: Model, method and evaluation. *Social Work with Groups, 12*(2), 75–88.

Breton, M. (1989). Liberation theology, group work, and the right of the poor and oppressed to participate in the life of the community. *Social Work with Groups, 12*(3), 5–18.

Brieland, D. (1959). *An experimental study of the selection of adoptive parents at intake*. New York: Child Welfare League of America.

Brilhart, J. (1974). *Effective group discussion* (2nd ed.). Dubuque, IA: William C. Brown.

Brill, N. (1976). *Team-work: Working together in the human services*. Philadelphia: J. B. Lippincott.

Brill, N. (1990). *Working with people: The helping process* (4th ed.). New York: Longman.

Brown, I. (1952). Working towards goals. *Adult Leadership, 1*(4), 13–20.

Brown, L. (1991). *Groups for growth and change*. New York: Longman.

Browning, L. (1977). Diagnosing teams in organizational settings. *Group and Organization Studies, 2*(2), 187–197.

Browning, R., & Stover, D. (1971). *Behavior modification in child treatment*. Chicago: Aldine Publishing.

Brunswick, E. (1943). Organismic achievement and environmental probability. *Psychological Review, 50*, 255–272.

Budman, S., Clifford, M., Bader, B., & Bader, L. (1981). Experiential pregroup preparation and screening. *Group, 5*, 19–26.

Budman, S., Demby, A., Feldstein, M., Redondo, J., Scherz, B., Bennett, M., Koppenall, G., Daley, B., Hunter, M., & Ellis, J. (1987). Preliminary findings on a new instrument to measure cohesion in group psychotherapy. *International Journal of Group Psychotherapy, 37*(1), 75–94.

Budman, S., Soldz, S., Demby, A., Davis, M., & Merry, J. (1993). What is cohesiveness? An empirical examination. *Small Group Research, 24*(2), 199–216.

Bunker, D., & Dalton, G. (1972). The comparative effectiveness of groups and individuals in solving problems. In J. Lorsch & P. Lawrence (Eds.), *Managing group and intergroup relations*. Homewood, CA: Dorsey Press.

Burke, R. (1970). Methods of resolving superior-subordinate conflict: The constructive use of subordinate differences and disagreements. *Organizational Behavior and Human Performance, 5*, 393–411.

Butler, H., Davis, I., & Kukkonen, R. (1979). The logic of case comparison. *Social Work Research and Abstracts, 15*(3), 3–11.

Byers, P. Y., & Wilcox, J. R. (1991, Winter). Focus groups: A qualitative opportunity for researchers. *The Journal of Business Communication, 28*(1), 63–77.

Cabral, R., Best, J., & Paton, A. (1975). Patients and observer's assessments of process and outcome in group therapy: A follow-up study. *The American Journal of Psychiatry, 132*, 1052–1054.

Campbell, D., & Cook, T. (1979). *Quasi-experimentation: Design and analysis for field settings*. Skokie, IL: Rand McNally.

Campbell, J. (1968). Individual versus group problem solving in an industrial sample. *Journal of Applied Psychology, 52*, 205–210.

Carlock, C., & Martin, P. (1977). Sex composition and the intensive group experience. *Social Work, 22*(1), 27–32.

Carnes, W. (1980). *Effective meetings for busy people*. New York: McGraw-Hill. Cartwright, D. (1951). Achieving change in people. *Human Relations, 4*, 381–392.

Cartwright, D. (1968). The nature of group cohesiveness. In D. Cartwright & A. Zander (Eds.), *Group dynamics: Research and theory* (3rd ed., pp. 91–109). New York: Harper & Row.

Cartwright, D., & Zander, A. (Eds.). (1968). *Group dynamics: Research and theory* (3rd ed.). New York: Harper & Row.

Chau, K. (1992). Needs assessment for group work with people of color: A conceptual formulation. *Social Work with Groups, 15*(2/3), 53–66.

Chess, W., & Norlin, J. (1991). *Human behavior and the social environment: A social systems model* (2nd ed.). Boston: Allyn & Bacon.

Chung, K., & Ferris, M. (1971). An inquiry of the nominal group process. *Academy of Management Journal, 14*, 520–524.

Clark, C. H. (1958). *Brainstorming.* New York: Doubleday & Company.

Clark, K. (1971). *Evaluation of a group social skills training program with psychiatric inpatients: Training Vietnam era veterans in assertion, heterosexual dating, and job interview skills.* Unpublished doctoral dissertation, University of Wisconsin, Madison.

Cole, R., & Tachiki, D. (1983, June). A look at U.S. and Japanese quality circles: Preliminary comparisons. *Quality Circles Journal, 6*, 10–16.

Collaros, R., & Anderson, L. (1969). Effects of perceived expertness upon creativity of members of brainstorming groups. *Journal of Applied Psychology, 53*(2), 159–164.

Collins, A., & Pancoast, D. (1970). *Natural helping networks: A strategy for prevention.* Washington, D.C.: National Association of Social Workers.

Collins, B. & Guetzkow, H. (1964). *A social psychology of group processes for decision making.* New York: John Wiley & Sons.

Compton, B., & Galaway, B. (1989). *Social work processes* (4th ed.). Homewood, CA: Dorsey Press.

Cone, J., & Hawkins, R. (Eds.). (1977). *Behavioral assessment: New directions in clinical psychology.* New York: Brunner/Mazel.

Connelly, J. L., & Piper, W. E. (1984). *Pretraining behavior as a predictor of process and outcome in group psychotherapy.* Paper presented at the 15th Annual Meeting of the Society for Psychotherapy Research, Lake Louise, Alberta.

Connelly, J. L., Piper, W. E., DeCarufel, F., & Debbane, E. (1986). Premature termination in group psychotherapy: Pretherapy and early therapy predictors. *International Journal of Group Psychotherapy, 36*(1), 145–152.

Conrad, W., & Glenn, W. (1976). *The effective voluntary board of directors: What it is and how it works.* Chicago: Swallow Press.

Cooley, D. (1909). *Social organization.* New York: Charles Scribner's Sons.

Coons, W. (1957). Interactions and insight in group psychotherapy. *Canadian Journal of Psychology, 11*, 1–8.

Cooper, C. (1977). Adverse and growthful effects of experimental learning groups: The role of the trainer, participant, and group characteristics. *Human Relations, 30*, 1103–1129.

Cooper, L. (1976). Co-therapy relationships in groups. *Small Group Behavior, 7*(4), 473–498.

Corcoran, K., & Fisher, J. (1987). *Measures for clinical practice: A sourcebook.* New York: Free Press.

Corey, M., & Corey, G. (1992). *Groups: Process and practice* (4th ed.). Pacific Grove, CA: Brooks/Cole.

Corsini, R. (1966). *Roleplaying in psychotherapy.* Chicago: Aldine Publishing Company.

Counselman, E. F. (1991). Leadership in a long-term leaderless women's group. *Small Group Research, 22*, 240–257.

Cowger, C. (1980). Social group work educators: Factors associated with literature preferences. *Social Work with Groups, 3*, 87–94.

Cox, C., & Monk, A. (1990). Minority caregivers of dementia victims: A comparison of black and Hispanic families. *Journal of Applied Gerontology, 9*(3), 340–354.

Cox, E. (1988). Empowerment of the low income elderly through group work. *Social Work with Groups, 11*(4), 111–119.

Cox, F., Erlich, J., Rothman, J., & Tropman, J. (Eds.). (1977). *Tactics and techniques of community practice.* Itasca, IL: F. E. Peacock.

Cox, F., Erlich, J., Rothman, J., & Tropman, J. (Eds.). (1987). *Strategies of community organization* (4th ed.). Itasca, IL: F. E. Peacock.

Cox, M. (1973). The group therapy interaction chronogram. *British Journal of Social Work, 3*, 243–256.

Coyle, G. (1930). *Social process in organized groups.* New York: Richard Smith.

Coyle, G. (1935). Group work and social change. In *Proceedings of the National Conference of Social Work* (p. 393). Chicago: University of Chicago Press.

Coyle, G. (1937). *Studies in group behavior.* New York: Harper & Row.

Craig, T., Huffine, C., & Brooks, M. (1974). Completion of referral to psychiatric services by inner-city residents. *Archives of General Psychiatry, 31*(3), 353–357.

Crano, W., & Brewer, M. (1973). *Principles of research in social psychology.* New York: McGraw-Hill.

Croxton, T. (1985). The therapeutic contract in social treatment. In M. Sundel, P. Glasser, R. Sarri, & R. Vinter (Eds.), *Individual change through small groups* (2nd ed., pp. 159–179). New York: The Free Press.

Davis, F., & Lohr, N. (1971). Special problems with the use of co-therapists in group psychotherapy. *International Journal of Group Psychotherapy, 21*, 143–158.

Davis, G., Manske, M., & Train, A. (1966). An instructional method of increasing originality. *Psychonomic Science, 6*, 73–74.

Davis, I. (1975). Advice-giving in parent counseling. *Social Casework, 56*, 343–347.

Davis, J., Laughlin, P., & Komorita, S. (1976). The social psychology of small groups: Cooperative and mixed-motive interaction. *Annual Review of Psychology, 27*, 501–541.

Davis, L., & Proctor, E. (1989). *Race, gender & class: Guidelines for practice with individuals, families and groups.* Englewood Cliffs, NJ: Prentice-Hall.

Davis, L., & Toseland, R. (1987). Group versus individual decision making. *Social Work with Groups, 10*(2), 95–105.

De Bono, E. (1968). *New think: The use of lateral thinking in generation of new ideas.* New York: Basic.

De Bono, E. (1971). *Lateral thinking for management.* New York: American Management Associations.

De Bono, E. (1972). *Lateral thinking: Productivity step by step.* New York: Harper & Row.

De Lange, J. (1977). *Effectiveness of systematic desensitization and assertive training with women.* Unpublished doctoral dissertation, University of Wisconsin, Madison.

Delbecq, A. (1967). The management of decision making within the firm: Three strategies for three types of decision making. *Academy of Management Journal, 10*, 329–339.

Delbecq, A., Van de Ven, A., & Gustafson, D. (1975). *Group techniques for program planning: A guide to nominal group and delphi processes.* Glenview, IL: Scott, Foresman.

Delgado, M. (1983). Activities and Hispanic groups. *Social Work with Groups, 6*, 85–96.

Denhardt, R., Pyle, J., & Bluedorn, A. (1987). Implementing quality circles in state government. *Public Administrative Review, 47*(4), 304–309.

Deutsch, M. (1973). *The resolution of conflict.* New Haven: Yale University Press.

Devore, W., & Schlesinger, E. (1981). *Ethnic-sensitive social work practice.* St. Louis, MO: C. V. Mosby.

Dienesch, R. M., & Liden, R. C. (1986). Leader-member exchange model of leadership: A critique and further development. *Academy of Management Review, 11*, 618–634.

Dillon, W., Madden, T., & Firtle, N. (1994). *Marketing research in a marketing environment* (3rd ed.). Burr Ridge, IL: Irwin.

Dinkmeyer, D., & McKay, G. (1982). *Systematic training for effective parenting.* Circle Pine, MN: American Guidance Service.

Dinkmeyer, D., & Muro, J. (1979). *Group counseling: Theory and practice* (2nd ed.). Itasca, IL: F. E. Peacock.

Dion, K., Miller, N., & Magnan, M. (1970). Cohesiveness and social responsibility as determinants of risk taking. *Proceedings of the American Psychological Association, 5*(1), 335–336.

Dollard, J., & Miller, N. (1950). *Personality and psychotherapy.* New York: McGraw-Hill.

Douglas, T. (1979). *Group process in social work: A theoretical synthesis.* New York: John Wiley & Sons.

Draper, B. (1979). Black language as an adaptive response to the hostile environment. In C. Germain (Ed.), *Social work practice* (pp. 267–281). New York: Columbia University Press.

Drum, D., & Knott, J. (1977). *Structured groups for facilitating development: Acquiring life skills, resolving life themes and making life transitions.* New York: Human Science Press.

Dunnette, M., Campbell, J., & Joastad, K. (1963). The effect of group participation on brainstorming effectiveness for two industrial samples. *Journal of Applied Psychology, 47*, 30–37.

D'Zurilla, T., & Goldfried, M. (1971). Problem solving and behavior modification. *Journal of Abnormal Psychology, 78*, 107–126.

Ebbesen, E., & Bowers, R. (1974). Proportion of risky to conservative arguments in a group discussion and choice shift. *Journal of Personality and Social Psychology, 29*, 316–327.

Edelwich, J., & Brodsky, A. (1992). *Group counseling for the resistent client: A practical guide to group process.* New York: Lexington.

Edleson, J. (1981). Teaching children to resolve conflict: A group approach. *Social Work, 26*(6), 488–494.

Edleson, J., Miller, D., & Stone, G. (1983). *Counseling men who batter: Group leader's handbook.* Albany, NY: School of Social Welfare.

Edleson, J., & Syers, M. (1990). The relative effectiveness of group treatments for men who batter. *Social Work Research & Abstracts, 26*, 10–17.

Edson, J. (1977). How to survive on a committee. *Social Work, 22*, 224–226.

Edwards, W. (1961). Behavioral decision theory. *Annual Review of Psychology, 1*, 473–498.

Edwards, W. (1977). How to use multiattribute utility measurement for social decision making. *IEEE Transactions on Systems, Man and Cybernetics, 7*, 326–340.

Edwards, W., Lindman, H., & Phillips, L. (1965). Emerging technologies for decision making. In T. Newcomb (Ed.), *New directions in psychology II* (pp. 259–326). New York: Holt, Rinehart and Winston.

Egan, G. (1976). *Interpersonal living.* Belmont, CA: Wadsworth.

Egan, G. (1990). *The skilled helper* (4th ed.). Pacific Grove, CA: Brooks/Cole.

Eisenhart, C. (1972). The assumptions underlying the analysis of variance. In R. Kirk (Ed.), *Statistical Issues* (pp. 226–240). Pacific Grove, CA: Brooks/Cole.

Elliott, H. (1928). *Process of group thinking.* New York: Association Press.

Ellis, A. (1962). *Reason and emotion in psychotherapy.* Secaucus, NJ: Lyle Stuart Publishers.

Empey, L., & Erikson, M. (1972). *The Provo experiment: Impact and death of an innovation.* Lexington, MA: Lexington Books.

Emrick, C. D., Lassen, C. L., & Edwards, M. T. (1977). Nonprofessional peers as therapeutic agents. In A. Gurman & A. Razin (Eds.), *Effective psychotherapy: A handbook of research* (pp. 120–161). New York: Pergamon Press.

Ephross, P. H., & Vassil, T. V. (1988). *Groups that work.* New York: Columbia University Press.

Epstein, I., & Tripodi, T. (1977). *Research techniques for program planning, monitoring & evaluation.* New York: Columbia University Press.

Etcheverry, R., Siporin, M., & Toseland, R. (1987). The uses and abuses of role playing. In P. Glasser and N. Mayadas (Eds.), *Group workers at work: Theory and practice in the 1980s* (pp. 116–130). Lanham, MD: Littlefield, Adams & Company.

Etzioni, A. (1961). *A comparative analysis of complex organizations on power, involvement and their correlates.* New York: The Free Press.

Etzioni, A. (1968). *The active society: A theory of societal and political processes.* New York: The Free Press.

Evans, C., & Dion, K. (1991). Group cohesion and performance. *Small Group Research, 22*(2), 175–186.

Evans, R., & Jaureguy, B. (1981, Winter). Group therapy by phone: A cognitive behavior program for visually impaired elderly. *Social Work in Health Care, 7*, 79–91.

Everly, G. S. (1989). *A clinical guide to the treatment of the human stress response.* New York: Plenum.

Ewalt, P., & Kutz, J. (1976). An examination of advice giving as a therapeutic intervention. *Smith College Studies in Social Work, 47*, 3–19.

Fairweather, R. (1967). *Methods for experimental social intervention.* New York: John Wiley & Sons.

Falck, H. (1988). *Social work: The membership perspective.* New York: Springer.

Feldman, R. (1986). Group work knowledge and research: A two-decade comparison. *Social Work with Groups, 9*(3), 7–14.

Feldman, R., & Caplinger, T. (1977). Social work experience and client behavior change: A multivariate analysis of process and outcome.

Journal of Social Service Research, 1(1), 5–33.

Feldman, R., Caplinger, T., & Wodarski, J. (1983). *The St. Louis conundrum: The effective treatment of antisocial youth.* Englewood Cliffs, NJ: Prentice-Hall.

Feldman, R., & Wodarski, J. (1975). *Contemporary approaches to group treatment: Traditional, behavior modification and group-centered.* San Francisco: Jossey-Bass.

Fern, E. (1982). The use of focus groups for idea generation: The effects of group size, acquaintanceship, and moderator on response quantity and quality. *Journal of Marketing Research, 19*, 1–13.

Festinger, L. (1950). Informal social communication. *Psychological Review, 57*, 271–282.

Fiedler, R. (1967). *A theory of leadership effectiveness.* New York: McGraw-Hill.

Filley, A. (1974). *Interpersonal conflict resolution.* Glenview, IL: Scott, Foresman.

Fischer, G. (1981). When oracles fail: A comparison of four procedures for aggregating subjective probability forecasts. *Organizational Behavior and Human Performance, 28*, 94–110.

Fish, J. (1973). *Placebo therapy.* San Francisco: Jossey-Bass.

Fisher, J. (1978). *Effective casework practice: An eclectic approach.* New York: McGraw-Hill.

Fisher, J., & Gochros, H. L. (1975). *Planned behavior change: Behavior modification for social work.* New York: The Free Press.

Fisher, R., & Ury, W. (1981). *Getting to yes.* New York: Houghton Mifflin.

Flowers, J. (1979). Behavior analysis of group therapy and a model for behavioral group therapy. In D. Upper & and S. Ross (Eds.), *Behavioral group therapy, 1979: An annual review* (pp. 5–37). Champaign, IL: Research Press.

Forester, J. (1981). Questioning and organizing attention: Toward a critical theory of planning and administrative practice. *Administration & Society, 13*(2), 181–205.

Fortune, A. (1979). Communication in task-centered treatment. *Social Work, 24*, 390–397.

Fortune, A. (1985, December). Planning duration and termination of treatment. In A. Fortune (Ed.), *Social Service Review* (pp. 648–661). Chicago: The University of Chicago Press.

Fortune, A. (1987). Grief only? Client and social worker reactions to termination. *Clinical Social Work Journal, 15*(2), 159–171.

Fortune, A., Pearlingi, B., & Rochelle, C. (1991, June). Criteria for terminating treatment. *Families in Society: The Journal of Contemporary Human Services, 366–370.

Fortune, A., Pearlingi, B., & Rochelle, C. (1992). Reactions to termination of individual treatment. *Social Work, 37*(2), 171–178.

Fox, E., Nelson, M., & Bolman, W. (1969). The termination process: A neglected dimension in social work. *Social Work, 14*(4), 53–63.

Frances, A., Clarkin, J., & Perry, S. (1984). *Differential therapeutics in psychiatry: The art and science of treatment selection.* New York: Brunner/Mazel.

Frank, J. (1961). *Persuasion and healing: A comparative study of psychotherapy.* New York: Schocken Books.

Freedman, B. (1974). *An analysis of social behavioral skill deficits in delinquent and undelinquent adolescent boys.* Unpublished doctoral dissertation, University of Wisconsin, Madison.

Freeman, A., Fleming, J., Simmons, K., & Pretzer, J. (1990). *Clinical applications of cognitive therapy.* New York: Plenum.

French, J., & Raven, B. (1959). The bases of social power. In D. Cartwright (Ed.), *Studies in social power.* Ann Arbor: Institute for Research, University of Michigan.

Freud, S. (1922). *Group psychology and the analysis of the ego.* London: The International Psychoanalytic Press.

Fuhriman, A., & Packard, T. (1986). Group process instruments: Therapeutic themes and issues. *International Journal of Group Psychotherapy, 36*(3), 399–525.

Galinsky, M., Rounds, K., Montaque, A., & Butowsky, A. (1993). *Leading a telephone support group for persons with HIV disease.* Chapel Hill: University of North Carolina.

Galinsky, M., & Schopler, J. (1977). Warning: Groups may be dangerous. *Social Work, 22*(2), 89–94.

Galinsky, M., & Schopler, J. (1980). Structuring co-leadership in social work training. *Social Work with Groups, 3*(4), 51–63.

Galinsky, M., & Schopler, J. (1989). Developmental patterns in open-ended groups. *Social Work with Groups, 12*(2), 99–114.

Garfield, S. (1986). Research on client variables in psychotherapy. In A. Garfield & A. Bergin (Eds.), *Handbook of psychotherapy and behavior change* (3rd ed., pp. 213–256). New York: John Wiley & Sons.

Garland, J., Jones, H., & Kolodny, R. (1976). A model of stages of group development in social work groups. In S. Bernstein (Ed.), *Explorations in Group Work* (pp. 17–71). Boston: Charles River Books.

Garland, J., & Kolodny, R. (1967). Characteristics and resolution of scapegoating. In National Conference of Social Welfare, *Social Work Practice* (pp. 198–219). New York: Columbia University Press.

Gartner, A., & Riessman, F. (Eds.). (1984). *The self-help revolution.* New York: Human Sciences Press.

Garvin, C. (1987). *Contemporary group work* (2nd ed.). Englewood Cliffs, NJ: Prentice-Hall.

Garvin, C. D., & Glasser, P. H. (1971). Social group work: The preventive and rehabilitative approach. In Robert Morris (Ed.), *The encyclopedia of social work* (pp. 1263–1272). New York: National Association of Social Workers.

Garvin, C., Reid, W., & Epstein, L. (1976). A task-centered approach. In R. Roberts & H. Northen (Eds.), *Theories of social work with groups* (pp. 238–267). New York: Columbia University Press.

Garwick, G. (1974). *Guideline for goal attainment scaling.* Minneapolis: Program Evaluation Project.

Gazda, G., & Mobley, J. (1981). INDS-CAL multidimensional scaling. *Journal of Group Psychotherapy, Psychodrama and Sociometry, 34*, 54–72.

Gentry, M. (1987). Coalition formation and processes. *Social Work with Groups, 10*(3), 39–54.

Germain, C., & Gitterman, A. (1980). *The life model of social work practice.* New York: Columbia University Press.

Gibb, C. (1969). Leadership. In G. Lindzey & E. Aronson (Eds.), *The handbook of social psychology* (2nd ed., pp. 205–273). Redding, MA: Addison-Wesley.

Gibb, J. (1961). Defensive communication. *The Journal of Communication, 11*, 141–148.

Gilbert, N., Miller, H., & Specht, H. (1980). *An introduction to social work practice.* Englewood Cliffs, NJ: Prentice-Hall.

Giordano, J. (1973). *Ethnicity and mental health.* New York: Institute of Human Relations.

Gitterman, A., & Schaeffer, A. (1972). The white professional and the black client. *Social Casework, 54*(5), 280–291.

Gitterman, A., & Shulman, L. (Eds.). (1986). *Mutual aid groups and the life cycle.* Itasca, IL: F. E. Peacock.

Glassman, U., & Kates, L. (1990). *Group work: A humanistic approach.* Newbury Park, CA.: Sage Publications.

Glisson, C. (1986). The group versus the individual as the unit of analysis in small group research. *Social Work with Groups, 9*(3), 15–30.

Goldfried, M., & D'Zurilla, T. (1969). A behavioral-analytic model for assessing competence. In C. D. Spielberger (Ed.), *Current topics in clinical and community psychology* (Vol. 1, pp. 151–196). New York: Academic Press.

Goldsmith, J., & McFall, R. (1975). Development and evaluation of an interpersonal skill training program for psychiatric inpatients. *Journal of Abnormal Psychology, 84*, 51–58.

Goldstein, A. (1973). *Structured learning therapy.* Elmsford, NY: Pergamon Press.

Goldstein, A., Keller, K., & Sechrest, L. (1966). *Psychotherapy and the psychology of behavior change.* New York: John Wiley & Sons.

Goldstein, H. (1983). Starting where the client is. *Social Casework, 64*, 267–275.

Goldstein, H. (1988). A cognitive-humanistic/ social learning perspective on social group work practice. *Social Work with Groups, 11*, 9–32.

Goldstein, S. (1985). Organizational quality and quality circles. *Academy of Management Review, 10*(3), 504–517.

Goodman, G. (1969). An experiment with companionship therapy: College students and troubled boys—assumptions, selections and design. In B. G. Guerney (Ed.), *Psychotherapeutic agents: New roles for non-professionals, parents and teachers* (pp. 121–128). New York: Holt, Rinehart and Winston.

Good Tracks, J. (1973). Native-American noninterference. *Social Work, 18*, 30–34.

Gordon, T. (1975). *P.E.T.* New York: Plume Books.

Gordon, W. (1961). *Synectics: The development of creative capacity.* New York: Harper & Row.

Gottman, J., & Leiblum, S. (1974). *How to do psychotherapy and how to evaluate it.* New York: Holt, Rinehart and Winston.

Gouran, D. (1982). *Making decisions in groups: Consequences & choices.* Glenview, IL: Scott, Foresman.

Graen, G., & Schiemann, W. (1978). Leader-member agreement: A vertical dyad linkage approach. *Journal of Applied Psychology, 63*, 206–212.

Gray, G. (1964). Points of emphasis in teaching parliamentary procedure. *The Speech Teacher, 13*, 10–15.

Green, J. W. (1982). *Cultural awareness in the human services.* Englewood Cliffs, NJ: Prentice-Hall.

Greenbaum, T. (1987). *The practical handbook and guide to focus groups research.* Lexington, MA: Lexington Books.

Grinnell, R. (1973). Environmental modification: Casework's concern or casework's neglect. *Social Service Review, 47*(2), 208–220.

Guetzkow, H., & Gyr, J. (1954). An analysis of conflict in decision-making groups. *Human Relations, 7*, 368–381.

Gulley, H. (1968). *Discussion, conference and group process* (2nd ed.). New York: Holt, Rinehart and Winston.

Gummer, B. (1987). *Groups as substance and symbol: Group processes and organizational politics, 10*(2), 25–39.

Gummer, B. (1988). Post-industrial management: Teams, self-management, and the new interdependence. *Administration in Social Work, 12*(3), 117–132.

Gutierrez, L., and Ortega, R. (1991). Developing methods to empower Latinos: The importance of groups. *Social Work with Groups, 14*(2), 23–43.

Hackman, J., & Morris, C. (1975). Group tasks, group interaction process and group performance effectiveness: A review and proposed integration. In L. Berkowitz (Ed.), *Advances in experimental social psychology* (Vol. 8, pp. 47–99). New York: Academic Press.

Haley, J. (1973). *Uncommon therapy: The psychiatric techniques of Milton H. Erickson, M.D.* New York: W. W. Norton.

Halpin, A. (1961). *Theory and research in administration.* New York: Macmillan.

Halstead, L. (1976). Team care in chronic illness: A critical review of the literature of the past 25 years. *Archives of Physical Medicine and Rehabilitation, 57*, 507–511.

Hammond, K., McClelland, G., & Mumpower, J. (1980). *Human judgment and decision making: Theories, methods and procedures.* New York: Praeger.

Hammond, L., & Goldman, M. (1961). Competition and non-competition and its relationship to individuals' non-productivity. *Sociometry, 24*, 46–60.

Hare, A. (1976). *Handbook of small group research* (2nd ed.). New York: The Free Press.

Harmon, J., & Rohrbaugh, J. (1990). Social judgement analysis and small group decision making: Cognitive feedback effects on individual and collective performance. *Organizational Behavior and Human Decision Processes, 46*, 35–54.

Harnack, R., & Fest, T. (1964). *Group discussion: Theory and technique.* New York: Appleton-Century-Crofts.

Hartford, M. (1962). *The social group worker and group formation.* Unpublished doctoral dissertation, University of Chicago, School of Social Service Administration, Chicago.

Hartford, M. (1964). Frame of reference for social group work. In *Papers toward a frame of reference for social group work*. New York: National Association of Social Workers.

Hartford, M. (1971). *Groups in social work*. New York: Columbia University Press.

Hartford, M. (1978). Groups in the human services: Some facts and fancies. *Social Work with Groups, 1*(1), 7–13.

Hasenfeld, Y. (1985). The organizational context of group work. In M. Sundel, P. Glasser, R. Sarri, & R. Vinter (Eds.), *Individual change through small groups* (2nd ed., pp. 294–309). New York: The Free Press.

Health Services Research Group. (1975). Development of an index of medical underservedness. *Health Service Research, 10*, 168–180.

Heap, K. (1979). *Process and action in work with groups*. Elmsford, NY: Pergamon Press.

Hemphill, J. (1956). *Group dimensions: A manual for their measurement*. Columbus, OH: Monographs of the Bureau of Business Research, Ohio State University.

Henry, S. (1992). *Group skills in social work: A four-dimensional approach*. (2nd ed.). Itasca, IL: F. E. Peacock.

Hersen, M., & Bellack. A. (1976). *Behavioral assessment: A practical handbook*. Elmsford, NY: Pergamon Press.

Hersey, R., & Blanchard, K. (1977). *Management of organizational behavior: Utilizing human resources* (3rd ed.). Englewood Cliffs, NJ: Prentice-Hall.

Hersey, R., Blanchard, K., & Natemeyer, W. (1979). Situational leadership, perception and the impact of power. *Group and Organization Studies, 4*(4), 418–428.

Herzog, J. (1980). Communication between co-leaders: Fact or myth. *Social Work with Groups, 3*(4), 19–29.

Higginbotham, J., & Cox, K. (1979). *Focus group interviews: A reader*. Chicago: American Marketing Association.

Hill, F. (1965). *Hill interaction matrix* (rev. ed.). Los Angeles: Youth Studies Center, University of Southern California.

Hill, W. (1977). Hill interaction matrix (HIM): The conceptual framework, derived rating scales, and an updated bibliography. *Small Group Behavior, 8*(3), 251–268.

Hirschowitz, R. (1974). Small-group methods in the promotion of change within interagency networks: Leadership models. In A. Jacobs & W. Spradlin (Eds.), *The group as agent of change* (pp. 228–251). New York: Behavioral Publications.

Hollis, F., & Woods, M. (1981). *Casework: A psychosocial therapy* (3rd ed.). New York: Random House.

Homans, G. (1950). *The human group*. New York: Harcourt Brace Jovanovich.

Homans, G. (1961). *Social behavior: Its elementary forms*. New York: Harcourt Brace Jovanovich.

Houle, C. (1960). *The effective board*. New York: Association Press.

Howard, J. (1970). *Please touch*. New York: McGraw-Hill.

Huber, G. (1980). *Managerial decision making*. Glenview, IL: Scott, Foresman.

Hudson, W. (1982). *The clinical measurement package*. Homewood, CA: Dorsey Press.

Huff, F., & Prantianida, T. (1968). The effect of group size on information transmitted. *Psychodynamic Science, 11*(10), 365–366.

Hunt, W., Barnett, L., & Branch, L. (1971). Relapse rates in addiction programs. *Journal of Clinical Psychology, 27*(4), 455–456.

Ivancevich, J., & Donnelly, G. (1970). Leader influence and performance. *Personnel Psychology, 23*(4), 539–549.

Jacobson, E. (1978). *You must relax*. New York: McGraw-Hill.

Jamieson, D., & Thomas, K. (1974). Power and conflict in the student-teacher relationship. *Journal of Applied Behavioral Science, 10*(3), 321–336.

Janis, I. (1972). *Victims of group think*. Boston: Houghton Mifflin.

Janis, I., & Mann, L. (1977). *Decision making: A psychological analysis of conflict, choice and commitment*. New York: The Free Press.

Jay, A. (1977). How to run a meeting. In F. Cox, J. Erlich, J. Rothman, & J. Tropman (Eds.), *Tactics and techniques of community practice* (pp. 255–269). Itasca, IL: F. E. Peacock.

Jayaratne S., & Levy, R. (1979). *Empirical clinical practice*. New York: Columbia University Press.

Jennings, H. (1947). Leadership and sociometric choice. *Sociometry*, (10), 32–49.

Jennings, H. (1950). *Leadership and isolation* (2nd ed.). New York: Longman.

Jessup, L., & Valacich, J. (1993). *Support group systems. Special Issue: Small Group Research*, 24, 427–592.

Johnson, D. W. (1993). *Reaching out: Interpersonal effectiveness and self-actualization* (5th ed.). Boston: Allyn and Bacon.

Johnson, J. (1975). *Doing field research*. New York: The Free Press.

Kadushin, A. (1972). *The social work interview*. New York: Columbia University Press.

Kahn, S. 1982. *Organizing: A guide for grassroots leaders*. New York: McGraw-Hill.

Kane, R. (1974). Look to the record. *Social Work*, 19, 412–419.

Kane, R. (1975a). The interprofessional team as a small group. *Social Work in Health Care*, 1(1), 19–32.

Kane, R. (1975b). *Interprofessional teamwork*. Syracuse, NY: Syracuse University School of Social Work.

Kane, R. (1976). Thoughts from the bleachers. *Health and Social Work*, 18, 52–59.

Kane, R., & Kane, R. (1981). *Assessing the elderly: A practical guide to measurement*. Lexington, MA: Lexington Books.

Kanfer, F., & Goldstein, A. (Eds.). (1975). *Helping people change*. Elmsford, NY: Pergamon Press.

Kart, G., Metress, E., & Metress, J. (1978). *Aging and health*. Redding, MA: Addison-Wesley.

Katz, A. H., & Bender, E. I. (1987). *The strength in us: Self-help groups in the modern world*. Oakland, CA: Third Party Associates.

Kaul, T., & Bednar, R. (1986). Research on group and related therapies. In S. Garfield and A. Bergin (Eds.), *Handbook of psychotherapy and behavior change* (3rd ed., pp. 671–714). New York: John Wiley & Sons.

Keith, R. (1991). The comprehensive treatment team in rehabilitation. *Archives of Physical Medicine and Rehabilitation*, 72, 269–274.

Kelleher, K., & Cross, T. (1985). *Teleconferencing: Linking people together electronically*. Englewood Cliffs, NJ: Prentice-Hall.

Kelley, H. (1951). Communication in experimentally created hierarchies. *Human Relations*, 4, 39–56.

Kelley, H., & Stakelski, A. (1970). Errors in perception of intentions in a mixed-motive game. *Journal of Experimental Social Psychology*, 6, 379–400.

Kelley, H., & Thibaut, J. (1969). Group problem solving. In G. Lindzey & E. Aronim (Eds.), *Handbook of social psychology* (2nd ed., pp. 1–101). Redding, MA: Addison Wesley.

Kelly, G. (1955). *The psychology of personal constructs*. New York: W. W. Norton & Company.

Kephart, M. (1951). A quantitative analysis of intragroup relationships. *American Journal of Sociology*, 60, 544–549.

Kiesler, S. (1978). *Interpersonal processes in groups and organizations*. Arlington Heights, VA: AHM Publishing.

Kinlaw, C. D. (1992). *Continuous improvement and measurement for total quality: A team-based approach*. San Diego, CA: Pfeiffer, and Homewood, IL: Business One Irwin.

Kinnear, T., & Taylor, J. (1991). *Marketing research: An applied approach* (4th ed.). New York: McGraw-Hill.

Kiresuk, T., & Sherman, R. (1968). Goal attainment scaling: A general method for evaluating comprehensive community mental health programs. *Community Mental Health Journal*, 4(6), 443–453.

Klein, A. (1953). *Society, democracy and the group*. New York: Whiteside.

Klein, A. (1956). *Role playing*. New York: Associated Press.

Klein, A. (1970). *Social work through group process*. Albany, NY: School of Social Welfare, State University of New York at Albany.

Klein, A. (1972). *Effective group work*. New York: Associated Press.

Kline, D., & Schieber, F. (1985). Vision and aging. In J. Birren & K. W. Schaie (Eds.), *Handbook of the Psychology of Aging* (pp. 296–331). New York: Van Nostrand Reinhold.

Kolodny, R. (1980). The dilemma of co-leadership. *Social Work with Groups, 3*(4), 31–34.

Konopka, G. (1949). *Therapeutic group work with children.* Minneapolis: University of Minnesota Press.

Konopka, G. (1954). *Group work in the institution.* New York: Association Press.

Konopka, G. (1983). *Social group work: A helping process* (3rd ed.). Englewood Cliffs, NJ: Prentice-Hall.

Koss, P., & Butcher, J. N. (1986). Research on brief psychotherapy. In S. L. Garfield & A. E. Bergin (Eds.), *Handbook of psychotherapy and behavior change* (3rd ed., pp. 627–670). New York: John Wiley & Sons.

Kramer, J., & Conoley, J. (1992). *Eleventh mental measurement yearbook.* Lincoln, NE: Buros Institute of Mental Measurements.

Kristein, M. (1980, January). *How much can business expect to earn from smoking cessation?* Paper presented at the Conference of the National Interagency Council on Smoking and Health, Chicago.

Krueger, R. (1988). *Focus groups: A practical guide for applied research.* Newbury Park, CA: Sage Publications.

Kurland, R. (1978). Planning: The neglected component of group development. *Social Work with Groups, 1*, 173–178.

Kurland, R. (1982). *Group formulation: A guide to the development of successful groups.* Monograph No. 3. Albany, NY: Social Welfare Continuing Education Program.

Labrecque, M., Peak, T., & Toseland, R. (1992). Long-term effectiveness of a group program for caregivers of frail elderly veterans. *American Journal of Orthopsychiatry, 62*(4), 575–588.

Lacoursiere, R. B. (1980). *The life cycle of groups: Group developmental stage theory.* New York: Human Sciences Press.

Lakin, M. (1991). Some ethical issues in feminist-oriented therapeutic groups for women. *International Journal of Group Psychotherapy, 4*, 199–215.

Lang, N. (1972). A broad range model of practice in the social work group. *Social Service Review, 46*(1), 76–84.

Lang, N. (1979a). A comparative examination of therapeutic uses of groups in social work and in adjacent human service professions: Part I—The literature from 1955–1968. *Social Work with Groups, 2*(2), 101–115.

Lang, N. (1979b). A comparative examination of the therapeutic uses of groups in social work and in adjacent human service professions: Part II—The literature from 1969–1978. *Social Work with Groups, 2*(3), 197–220.

Larsen, J., & Mitchell, C. (1980). Task-centered, strength-oriented group work with delinquents. *Social Casework, 61*(3), 154–163.

Lauffer, A. (1977). *Grantsmanship.* Newbury Park, CA: Sage Publications.

Lauffer, A. (1978). *Social planning at the community level.* Englewood Cliffs, NJ: Prentice-Hall.

Lawler, E., III, & Mohrman, S. (1985, Spring). Quality circles after the fad: There are benefits for managers and employees—and there are limitations. *Public Welfare,* 37–44.

Lazarus, A. (1971). *Behavior therapy and beyond.* New York: McGraw-Hill.

Lazarus, R. S., & Folkman, S. (1984). *Stress, appraisal, and coping.* New York: Springer.

League of Women Voters Educational Fund. (1977). How to plan an environmental conference. In F. Cox, J. Erlich, J. Rothman, & J. Tropman (Eds.), *Tactics and techniques of community practice* (pp. 111–152). Itasca, IL: F. E. Peacock.

Leavitt, H. (1951). Some effects of certain communication patterns on group performance. *Journal of Abnormal and Social Psychology, 46,* 39–56.

LeBon, G. (1910). *The crowd: A study of the popular mind.* London: George Allen & Unwin Ltd.

Lederman, L. C. (1989). *Assessing educational effectiveness: The focus group interview as a technique for data collection.* Paper presented at the meeting of the Speech Communication Association, San Francisco.

Lee, J. (Ed.). (1990). *Group work with the poor and oppressed.* New York: Haworth Press.

Lehmann, D. (1989). *Market research and analysis* (3rd ed.). Homewood, IL: Irwin.

Levine, B. (1979). *Group psychotherapy: Practice and development.* Englewood Cliffs, NJ: Prentice-Hall.

Levine, B. (1980). Co-leadership approach to learning group work. *Social Work with Groups, 3*(4), 35–38.

Levine, B., & Gallogly, V. (1985). *Group therapy with alcoholics: Outpatient and inpatient approaches.* Newbury Park, CA: Sage Publications.

Levinson, D., & Klerman, G. (1973). The clinician-executive: Some problematic issues for the psychiatrist in mental health organizations. *Administration in Mental Health, 1*(1), 52–67.

Levinson, H. (1977). Termination of psychotherapy: Some salient issues. *Social Casework, 58*(8), 480–489.

Levitt, J., & Reid, W. (1981). Rapid assessment instruments for social work practice. *Social Work Research and Abstracts, 17*(1), 13–20.

Lewin, K. (1946). Behavior as a function of the total situation. In L. Carmichael (Ed.), *Manual of child psychology* (pp. 791–844). New York: John Wiley & Sons.

Lewin, K. (1947). Frontiers in group dynamics. *Human Relations, 1,* 2–38.

Lewin, K. (1948). *Resolving social conflict.* New York: Harper & Row.

Lewin, K. (1951). *Field theory in social science.* New York: Harper & Row.

Lewin, K., & Lippitt, R. (1938). An experimental approach to the study of autocracy and democracy: A preliminary note. *Sociometry, 1,* 292–300.

Lewin, K., Lippitt, R., & White, R. (1939). Patterns of aggressive behavior in experimentally created "social climates." *Journal of Social Psychology, 10,* 271–299.

Lewis, B. (1978). An examination of the final phase of a group development theory. *Small Group Behavior, 9,* 507–517.

Lewis, E., & Ford, B. (1990). The network utilization project: Incorporating traditional strengths of African-American families into group work practice. *Social Work with Groups, 13*(4), 7–22.

Lewis, H. (1982, October). Ethics in work with groups: The clients' interests. In N. Lang &

C. Marshall (Chairs), *Patterns in the mosaic.* Symposium conducted at the Fourth Annual Meeting of Social Work with Groups, Toronto.

Lewis, R., & Ho., M. (1975). Social work with Native Americans. *Social Work, 20,* 379–382.

Lewis, R., & Ho, M. (1992). Social work with Native Americans. In A. Morales & B. Sheafor (Eds.), *Social work: A profession of many faces* (6th ed.). (pp. 193–204). Boston: Allyn & Bacon.

Lieberman, M. (1971). Reinforcement of cohesiveness in group therapy. *Archives of General Psychiatry, 25,* 168–177.

Lieberman, M. (1975). Groups for personal change: New and not-so-new forms. In D. Freedman & J. Dyrad (Eds.), *American handbook of psychiatry* (pp. 345–366). New York: Basic Books.

Lieberman, M. (1976). Change induction in small groups. *Annual Review of Psychology, 27,* 217–250.

Lieberman, M. (1990). Perspective on self-help groups. *International Journal of Psychotherapy, 40,* 251–278.

Lieberman, M., & Borman, L. (Eds.). (1979). *Self-help groups for coping with crisis.* San Francisco: Jossey-Bass.

Lieberman, M., Yalom, I., & Miles, M (1973). *Encounter groups: First facts.* New York: Basic Books.

Likert, R. (1961). *New patterns of management.* New York: McGraw-Hill.

Likert, R. (1967). *The human organization.* New York: McGraw-Hill.

Lippitt, R. (1957). Group dynamics and the individual. *International Journal of Group Psychotherapy, 7*(10), 86–102.

Lonergan, E. C. (1985). *Group intervention.* New York: Jason Aronson.

Long, K., Pendleton, L., & Winter, B. (1988). Effects of therapist termination on group processes, *International Journal of Group Psychotherapy, 38*(2), 211–223.

Longres, J. (1990). *Human behavior in the social environment.* Itasca, IL: F. E. Peacock.

Lopez, J. (1991). Group work as a protective factor for immigrant youth. *Social Work with Groups, 14*(1), 29–42.

Lowe, J., & Herranen, M. (1978). Conflict in teamwork: Understanding roles and relationships. *Social Work in Health Care, 3,* 323–330.

Luft, J. (1984). *Group processes* (3rd ed.). Palo Alto, CA: Mayfield.

Lum, D. (1992). *Social work practice and people of color: A process-stage approach* (2nd ed.). Pacific Grove, CA: Brooks/Cole.

MacLennon, B. (1965). Co-therapy. *International Journal of Group Psychotherapy, 15,* 154–166.

Mahler, C. (1969). *Group counseling in the schools.* Boston: Houghton Mifflin.

Mahoney, M. (1974). *Cognition and behavior modification.* Cambridge, MA: Ballinger.

Maier, N. (1963). *Problem-solving discussions and conferences: Leadership methods and skills.* New York: McGraw-Hill.

Maier, N., & Hoffman, L. (1960). Quality of first and second solutions in group problem solving. *Journal of Applied Psychology, 44,* 278–283.

Maier, N., Solem, A., & Maier, A. (1975). *The role-play technique.* LaJolla, CA: University Associates.

Maier, N., & Zerfoss, L. (1952). MRP: A technique for training large groups of supervisors and its potential use in social research. *Human Relations, 5,* 177–186.

Maloney, S. (1963). *Development of group work education in social work schools in U.S.* Unpublished doctoral dissertation, Case Western Reserve University, School of Applied Social Science, Cleveland.

Maltzman, I., Simon, S., Raskin, D., & Licht, L. (1960). Experimental studies in the training of originality. *Psychological Monographs, 7*(Whole No. 493).

Maluccio, A. (1979). *Learning from clients.* New York: The Free Press.

Manor, O. (1986). The preliminary interview in social groupwork: Finding the spiral steps. *Social Work with Groups, 9*(2), 21–39.

Maple, F. (1977). *Shared decision making.* Newbury Park, CA: Sage Publications.

Marks, M., Mirvis, P., Hackett, E., & Grady, J. (1986). Employee participation in a quality circle program: Impact on quality of worklife, productivity, and absenteeism. *Journal of Applied Psychology, 71,* 61–69.

Marsh, E., & Terdal, L. (Eds.). (1981). *Behavioral assessment of childhood disorders.* New York: Guilford Press.

Maultsby, M. (1975). *Help yourself to happiness.* New York: Rational Living.

Maultsby, M., & Carpenter, L. (1980). *The rational self-counseling coursebook: The ABC's of more personal happiness.* Lexington, KY: University of Kentucky Press.

Mayadas, N., & Glasser, P. (1981). Termination: A neglected aspect of social group work. *Social Work with Groups, 4*(2), 193–204.

Mayer, J., & Timms, N. (1970). *The client speaks: Working class impressions of casework.* New York: Atherton Press.

McCallion, P., Toseland, R., & Diehl, M. (1994). Social work practice with caregivers of frail older adults. *Research on Social Work Practice, 4,* 64–68.

McCaskill, J. (1930). *Theory and practice of group work.* New York: Association Press.

McClane, W. (1991). The interaction of leader and member characteristics in the leader-member exchange model of leadership. *Small Group Research, 22,* 283–300.

McCorkle, L., Elias, A., Bixby, F. (1958). *The highfields story: an experimental project for youthful offenders.* New York: Holt.

McDougall, W. (1920). *The group mind.* New York: G. P. Putnam's Sons.

McGee, T., & Schuman, B. (1970). The nature of the co-therapy relationship. *International Journal of Group Psychotherapy, 20,* 25–36.

McGrath, J. (1984). *Groups: Interaction and performance.* Englewood Cliffs, NJ: Prentice-Hall.

McGrath, J. (1992). Time, interaction, and performance (TIP): A theory of groups. *Small Group Research, 22,* 147–174.

McGrath, P., & Axelson, J. (1993). *Accessing awareness & developing knowledge: Foundation skills for a multicultural society.* Pacific Grove, CA: Brooks/Cole.

McKay, M., & Paleg, K. (Eds.). (1992). *Focal group psychotheraphy.* Oakland, CA: New Harbinger Pub.

McLaughlin, R., White, E., & Byfield, B. (1974). Modes of interpersonal feedback and leadership structure in six small groups. *Nursing Research, 23*(4), 207–318.

Meichenbaum, D. (1977). *Cognitive-behavior modification: An integrative approach.* New York: Plenum.

Meichenbaum, D. (1985). *Stress innoculation training.* New York: Plenum.

Meichenbaum, D., & Cameron, R. (1983). Stress innoculation training: Toward a general paradigm for training coping skills. In D. Meichenbaum & M. E. Jaremko (Eds.), *Stress reduction and prevention* (pp. 115–154).

Melnick, J. (1974). *Risk, responsibility, and structure: A conceptual framework for initiating group work.* Paper presented at the American Psychological Association Convention, New Orleans, LA.

Meltzoff, J., & Kornreich, M. (1970). *Research in psychotherapy.* New York: Atherton Press.

Merton, R., Fiske, M., & Kendall, P. (1956). *The focused interview.* Glencoe, IL: Free Press.

Merton, R., & Kendall, P. (1946). The focused interview. *American Journal of Sociology, 51*, 541–557.

Middleman, R. (1978). Returning group process to group work. *Social Work with Groups, 1*(1), 15–26.

Middleman, R. (1980). The use of program: Review and update. *Social Work with Groups, 3*(3), 5–23.

Middleman, R. (1982). *The non-verbal method in working with groups: The use of activity in teaching, counseling, and therapy.* An enlarged edition. Hebron, CT: Practitioners Press.

Middleman, R., & Wood, G. (1990). Reviewing the past and present of group work and the challenge of the future. *Social Work with Groups, 13*(3), 3–20.

Miller, H., & Tripodi, T. (1967). Information accrual and clinical judgment. *Social Work, 12*(3), 63–69.

Miller, S., Nunnally, E., & Wackman, D. (1972). *The Minnesota couples communication program couples handbook.* Minneapolis: Minnesota Couples Communication Program.

Mills, T. (1967). *The sociology of small groups.* Englewood Cliffs, NJ: Prentice-Hall.

Miner, F. (1979). A comparative analysis of three diverse group decision making approaches. *Academy of Management Journal, 22*, 81–93.

Morales, A., & Sheafor, B. (1992). *Social work: A profession of many faces* (6th ed.). Boston: Allyn & Bacon.

Moreno, J. (1934). *Who shall survive?* Washington, D.C.: Nervous and Mental Diseases Publishing Co.

Moreno, J. (1946). *Psychodrama* (Vol. 1). Boston: Beacon Press.

Morgan, D. (1988). Focus groups as qualitative research. *Qualitative research methods.* Newbury Park, CA: Sage Publications.

Mullen, E. (1969). The relationship between diagnosis and treatment in casework. *Social Casework, 50*, 218–226.

Mullen, E. (1981, November). *Evaluating social work effectiveness in a turbulent world.* Paper presented at the Seventh National Association of Social Workers Symposium, Philadelphia, PA.

Munzer, J., & Greenwald, H. (1957). Interaction process analysis of a therapy group. *International Journal of Group Psychotherapy, 7*, 175–190.

Murphy, M. (1959). *The social group work method in social work education* (a Project report of the Curriculum Study Vol. XI). New York: Council of Social Work Education.

Myers, D., & Arenson, S. (1972). Enhancement of the dominant risk in group discussion. *Psychological Reports, 30*, 615–623.

Nadler, D. (1977). *Feedback and organizational development: Using data base methods.* Redding, MA: Addison-Wesley.

Nadler, D. (1979). The effects of feedback on task group behavior: A review of the experimental research. *Organizational Behavior and Human Performance, 23*, 309–338.

Napier, H. (1967). Individual versus group learning: Note on task variable. *Psychological Reports, 23*, 757–758.

Napier, R., & Gershenfeld, M. (1981). *Groups: Theory and experience* (2nd ed.). Boston: Houghton Mifflin.

Newcomb, T. (1956). The prediction of interpersonal attraction. *American Psychologist, 2,* 575–586.

Newstetter, W. (1948). The social intergroup work process. In *Proceedings of the National Conference of Social Work* (pp. 205–217). New York: Columbia University Press.

Nixon, H. (1979). *The small group.* Englewood Cliffs, NJ: Prentice-Hall.

Northen, H. (1969). *Social work with groups.* New York: Columbia University Press.

Northen, H. (1982). *Clinical social work.* New York: Columbia University Press.

Novaco, R. (1975). *Anger control: The development and evaluation of an experimental treatment.* Cambridge, MA: Lexington Books.

Nunnally, J. (1978). *Psychometric theory.* New York: McGraw-Hill.

Ollendick, T., & Hersen, M. (Eds.). (1984). *Child behavioral assessment.* Elmsford, NY: Pergamon Press.

Olmsted, M. (1959). *The small group.* New York: Random House.

Olsen, M. (1968). *The process of social organization.* New York: Holt, Rinehart and Winston.

Orlinsky, D., & Howard, K. (1986). Process and outcome in psychotherapy. In S. Garfield & A. Bergin (Eds.), *Handbook of psychotherapy and behavior change* (3rd ed., pp. 311–381). New York: John Wiley & Sons.

Osborn, A. (1963). *Applied imagination: Principles and procedures of creative problem solving* (3rd ed.). New York: Charles Scribner's Sons.

Osgood, C., Suci, C., & Tannenbaum, P. (1957). *The measurement of meaning.* Urbana, IL: University of Illinois Press.

Oxley, G., Wilson, S., Anderson, J., & Wong, G. (1979). Peer-led groups in graduate education. *Social Work with Groups, 1,* 67–75.

Papell, C., & Rothman, B. (1962). Social group work models—Possession and heritage. *Journal of Education for Social Work, 2,* 66–77.

Papell, C., & Rothman, B. (1980a). Social group work models: Possession and heritage. In A. Alissi (Ed.), *Perspectives on social group work practice* (pp. 116–132). New York: The Free Press.

Papell, C., & Rothman, B. (1980b). Relating the mainstream model of social work with groups to group psychotherapy and the structured group approach. *Social Work with Groups, 3*(2), 5–23.

Parloff, M. (1961). Therapist-patient relationships and outcome of psychotherapy. *Journal of Consulting Psychology, 25,* 29–38.

Parnes, S. (1967). *Creative behavior guidebook.* New York: Charles Scribner's Sons.

Parnes, S., & Harding, H. (Eds.). (1962). *A sourcebook for creative thinking.* New York: Charles Scribner's Sons.

Parsons, R. (1991). Empowerment: Purpose and practice principle in social work. *Social Work with Groups, 14*(2), 7–21.

Parsons, T. (1951). *The social system.* New York: The Free Press.

Parsons, T., Bales, R., & Shils, E. (Eds.). (1953). *Working papers in the theory of action.* New York: The Free Press.

Patti, R. (1974). Organizational resistance and change: The view from below. *Social Service Review, 48*(3), 367–383.

Patton, M. (1989). *Qualitative evaluative methods.* Newbury Park, CA: Sage Publications.

Pearson, V. (1991). Western theory, eastern practice: Social group work in Hong Kong. *Social Work with Groups, 14*(2), 45–58.

Pepitone, A., & Reichling, G. (1955). Group cohesiveness and the expression of hostility. *Human Relations, 8,* 327–337.

Perlman, H. (1970). The problem-solving method in social casework. In R. Roberts & R. Nee (Eds.), *Theories of social casework* (pp. 129–180). Chicago: University of Chicago Press.

Pernell, R. (1986). Empowerment and social group work. In M. Parnes (Ed.), *Innovations in social group work* (pp. 107–118). New York: Haworth Press.

Peterson, J. (1974). The interface of institution and group process. In A. Jacobs & W. Spradlin (Eds.), *The group as agent of change* (pp. 5–17). New York: Behavioral Publications.

Pfeiffer, J., & Goodstein, L. (Eds.). (1984–1994). *The annual: Developing human resources.* San Diego: University Associates Inc.

Phillips, H. (1951). *The essentials of group work skills.* New York: Associated Press.

Phillips, J. (1948). Report on discussion 66. *Adult Education Journal, 7,* 181–182.

Pincus, A., & Minahan, A. (1973). *Social work practice: Model and method.* Itasca, IL: F. E. Peacock.

Pinderhughes, E. B. (1979). Teaching empathy in cross-cultural social work. *Social Work, 2*(4), 312–316.

Pinkus, H. (1968). *Casework techniques related to selected characteristics of clients and workers.* Unpublished doctoral dissertation, Columbia University, New York.

Piper, W., Debbane, E., Bienvenu, J., & Garant, J. (1982). A study of group pretraining for group psychotherapy. *International Journal of Group Psychotherapy, 32,* 309–325.

Piper, W., Debbane, E., Garant, J. & Bienvenu, J. (1979). Pretraining for group psychotherapy. *Archives of General Psychiatry, 36,* 1250–1256.

Polansky, N. (Ed.). (1960). *Social work research.* Chicago: University of Chicago Press.

Polansky, N. (1982). *Integrated ego psychology.* Chicago: Aldine.

Powell, T. (1987). *Self-help organizations and professional practice.* Silver Springs, MD: National Association of Social Workers Press.

Prince, G. (1970). *The practice of creativity.* New York: Harper & Row.

Prigmore, C. S. (1974). Use of the coalition in legislative action. *Social Work, 19*(1), 96–102.

Rahaim, S., Lefebvre, C., & Jenkins, T., (1980). The effects of social skills training on behavioral and cognitive components of anger management. *Journal of Behavior Therapy and Experimental Psychiatry, 5,* 3–8.

Reder, P. (1978). An assessment of the group therapy interaction chronogram. *International Journal of Group Psychotherapy, 28,* 185–194.

Redl, F. (1942). Group emotion and leadership. *Psychiatry, 5,* 573–596.

Redl, F. (1944). Diagnostic group work. *American Journal of Orthopsychiatry, 14*(1), 53–67.

Reid, K. (1981). *From character building to social treatment: The history of the use of groups in social work.* Westport, CT: Greenwood Press.

Reid, K. (1991). *Social work practice with groups: A clinical perspective.* Pacific Grove, CA: Brooks/Cole.

Reid, W. J. (1978). *The task-centered system.* New York: Columbia University Press.

Reid, W. J. (1992). *Task strategies: An empirical approach to clinical social work.* New York: Columbia University Press.

Reid, W. J., & Epstein, L. (1972). *Task-centered casework.* New York: Columbia University Press.

Reid, W. J., & Hanrahan, P. (1982). Recent evaluations of social work: Grounds for optimism. *Social Work, 27*(4), 328–340.

Reid, W. J., & Shapiro, B. (1969). Client reactions to advice. *Social Service Review, 43,* 165–173.

Reid, W. J., & Shyne, A. (1969). *Brief and extended casework.* New York: Columbia.

Resnick, H., & Patti, R. (Eds.). (1980). *Change from within: Humanizing social welfare organizations.* Philadelphia: Temple University Press.

Richards, T. (1974). *Problem solving through creative analysis.* New York: John Wiley & Sons.

Richmond, M. (1917). *Social diagnosis.* New York: Russell Sage Foundation.

Rimm, D., & Masters, J. (1974). *Behavior therapy.* New York: Academic Press.

Rivas, R., & Toseland, R. (1981). The student group leadership evaluation project: A study of group leadership skills. *Social Work with Groups, 4*(3/4), 159–175.

Roback, H., Ochoa, E., Bloch, F., & Purdon, S. (1992). Guarding confidentiality in clinical groups: The therapist's dilemma. *International Journal of Group Psychotherapy, 42*(1), 81–103.

Robert, H. (1970). *Robert's rules of order.* Glenview, IL: Scott, Foresman.

Roberts, R., & Northen, H. (Eds.). (1976). *Theories of social work with groups.* New York: Columbia University Press.

Robinson, J., & Shaver, P. (Eds.). (1973). *Measures of social psychological attitude* (2nd ed.). Ann Arbor, MI: University of Michigan Press.

Robson, M. (1982). *Quality circles: A practical guide*. Aldershat, Hants, England: Gower Publishing.

Roethlisberger, F. (1941). *Management and morale*. Cambridge, MA: Harvard University Press.

Roethlisberger, F., & Dickson, W. (1939). *Management and the worker*. Cambridge, MA: Harvard University Press.

Roethlisberger, F., & Dickson, W. (1975). A fair day's work. In P. V. Crosbie (Ed.), *Interaction in small groups* (pp. 85–94). New York: Macmillan.

Rohrbaugh, J. (1979). Improving the quality of group judgment: Social judgment analysis and the delphi technique. *Organizational Behavior and Human Performance, 24,* 73–92.

Rohrbaugh, J. (1981). Improving the quality of group judgment: Social judgment analysis and the nominal group technique. *Organizational Behavior and Human Performance, 26,* 272–288.

Rohrbaugh, J. (1984). Making decisions about staffing standards: An analytical approach to human resource planning in health administration. In L. Nigro (Ed.), *Decision making in the public sector* (pp. 93–116). New York: Marcel Dekker.

Rohrbaugh, J., & Harmon, J. (August, 1981). *Social judgment analysis: Methodology for improving interpersonal communication and understanding.* Paper presented at the 89th Annual Convention of the American Psychological Association, Los Angeles.

Rokeach, M. (1968). *Beliefs, attitudes and values: A theory of organization and change.* San Francisco: Jossey-Bass.

Rooney, R. (1992). *Strategies for work with involuntary clients.* New York: Columbia University Press.

Rose, S. (1981). Assessment in groups. *Social Work Research and Abstracts, 17*(1), 29–37.

Rose, S. (1989). *Working with adults in groups: A multi-method approach.* San Francisco: Jossey-Bass.

Rose, S. (1991). The development and practice of group treatment. In M. Hersen, A. Kazdin, & A. Bellack (Eds.), *Handbook of Clinical Psychology* (pp. 627–642). New York: Pergamon.

Rose, S., Cayner, J., & Edleson, J. (1977). Measuring interpersonal competence. *Social Work, 22*(2), 125–129.

Rose, S., & Edleson, J. (1987). *Working with children and adolescents in groups.* San Francisco: Jossey-Bass.

Rose, S., & Hanusa, D. (1980). *Parenting skill role play test.* Interpersonal skill training and research project, University of Wisconsin, Madison.

Rose, S., & LeCroy, C. (1991). Group treatment methods. In F. Kanfer & A. Goldstein (Eds.), *Helping people change* (4th ed., pp. 422–453). New York: Pergamon Press.

Rose, S., Tallant, S., Tolman, R., & Subramanian, K. (1987). A multimethod group approach: Program development research. *Social Work with Groups, 9*(3), 71–88.

Rosenblatt, A. (1962). The application of role concepts to the intake process. *Social Casework, 43*(1), 8–14.

Rosenthal, L. (1978). *Behavioral analysis of social skills in adolescent girls.* Unpublished doctoral dissertation, University of Wisconsin, Madison.

Rossi, P., Freeman, H., & Wright, S. (1979). *Evaluation: A systematic approach.* Newbury Park, CA: Sage Publications.

Rothman, J. (1974). *Planning and organizing for social change: Action principles for social science research.* New York: Columbia University Press.

Rotter, G., & Portugal, S. (1969). Group and individual effects in problem solving. *Journal of Applied Psychology, 53,* 338–341.

Rounds, K., Galinsky, M., & Stevens, L. S. (1991, January). Linking people with AIDS in rural communities: The telephone group. *Social Work, 36,* 13–18.

Rubin, A. (1985). Practice effectiveness: More grounds for optimism. *Social Work, 30*(6), 469–476.

Rubin, H., & Rubin, I. (1992). *Community organizing and development* (2nd ed.). New York: Macmillan.

Ryder, E. (1976). A functional approach. In R. Roberts & H. Northen (Eds.), *Theories of social work with groups* (pp. 153–170). New York: Columbia University Press.

Sage, P., Olmsted, D., & Atlesk, F. (1955). Predicting maintenance of membership in small groups. *Journal of Abnormal and Social Psychology, 51*, 308–331.

Sarri, R. (1974). Behavioral theory and group work. In P. Glasser, R. Sarri, & R. Vinter (Eds.), *Individual change through small groups* (pp. 50–70). New York: The Free Press.

Sarri, R., & Galinsky, M. (1985). A conceptual framework for group development. In M. Sundel, P. Glasser, R. Sarri, & R. Vinter (Eds.), *Individual change through small groups* (2nd ed., pp. 70–86). New York: The Free Press.

Sarri, R., Galinsky, M., Glasser, P., Siegel, S., & Vinter, R. (1967). Diagnosis in group work. In R. D. Vinter (Ed.), *Readings in group work practice* (pp. 39–71). Ann Arbor, MI: Campus Publishing.

Schachter, S. (1959). *The psychology of affiliation.* Stanford, CA: Stanford University Press.

Scheidel, T., & Crowell, L. (1979). *Discussing and deciding: A deskbook for group leaders and members.* New York: Macmillan.

Schinke, S. P., Gordon, A. N., & Weston, R. E. (1990). Self-instruction to prevent HIV infection among African-American and Hispanic-American adolescents. *Journal of Consulting and Clinical Psychology, 58*, 432–436.

Schinke, S. P., Orlandi, M. A., Forgey, M. A., Rugg, D. L., & Douglas, K. A. (1992). Multicomponent, school-based strategies to prevent HIV infection and sexually transmitted diseases among adolescents: Theory and research into practice. *Research on Social Work Practice, 2*, 364–379.

Schinke, S. P., & Rose, S. (1976). Interpersonal skill training in groups. *Journal of Counseling Psychology, 23*, 442–448.

Schlenoff, M., & Busa, S. (1981). Student and field instructor as group co-therapists. Equalizing an unequal relationship. *Journal of Education for Social Work, 17*, 29–35.

Schmitt, M., Farrell, M., & Heinemann, G. (1988). Conceptual and methodological problems in studying the effects of interdisciplinary geriatric teams. *The Gerontologist, 28*(6), 753–763.

Schopler, J., & Galinsky, M. (1981). When groups go wrong. *Social Work, 26*(5), 424–429.

Schopler, J., & Galinsky, M. (1984). Meeting practice needs: Conceptualizing the open-ended group. *Social Work with Groups, 7*(2), 3–21.

Schopler, J., & Galinsky, M. (1990). Can open-ended groups move beyond beginnings? *Small Group Research, 21*(4), 435–449.

Schopler, J., Galinsky, M., Alicke, M. (1985). Goals in social group work practice: Formulation, implementation and evaluation. In M. Sundel, P. Glasser, R. Sarri, & R. Vinter (Eds.), *Individual change through small groups* (2nd ed., pp. 140–158). New York: The Free Press.

Schutz, W. (1967). *Joy: Expanding human awareness.* New York: Grove Press.

Schwartz, W. (1966). Discussion of three papers on the group method with clients, foster families, and adoptive families. *Child Welfare, 45*(10), 571–575.

Schwartz, W. (1971). On the use of groups in social work practice. In W. Schwartz & S. Zalba (Eds.), *The practice of group work* (pp. 3–24). New York: Columbia University Press.

Schwartz, W. (1974). The social worker in the group. In R. W. Klenk & R. M. Ryan (Eds.), *The practice of social work* (pp. 208–228). New York: Wadsworth.

Schwartz, W. (1976). Between client and system: The mediating function. In R. Roberts & H. Northen (Eds.), *Theories of social work with groups* (pp. 171–197). New York: Columbia University Press.

Schwartz, W. (1981, April). *The group work tradition and social work practice.* Paper presented at Rutgers University, School of Social Work, New Brunswick, NJ.

Schwartz, W., & Zalba, S. (1971). *The practice of group work.* New York: Columbia University Press.

Seaberg, J., & Gillespie, D. (1977). Goal attainment scaling: A critique. *Social Work Research and Abstracts, 13*(2), 4–9.

Seashore, S. (1954). *Group cohesiveness in the industrial work group.* Ann Arbor, MI: University of Michigan Press.

Seely, H., & Sween, J. (1983, March). Critical components of successful U.S. quality circles. *Quality Circles Journal, 6,* 14–17.

Seligman, M. (1975). *Helplessness: On depression, development, and death.* San Francisco: W. H. Freeman.

Selltiz, C., Wrightsman, L., & Cook, S. (1976). *Research methods in social relations* (3rd ed.). New York: Holt, Rinehart and Winston.

Shaffer, J., & Galinsky, M. (1989). *Models of group therapy.* Englewood Cliffs, NJ: Prentice-Hall.

Shaw, C. (1930). *The jack roller.* Chicago: University of Chicago Press.

Shaw, M. (1964). Communication networks. In L. Berkowitz (Ed.), *Advances in experimental social psychology* (Vol. 1, pp. 111–149). New York: Academic Press.

Shaw, M. (1976). *Group dynamics: The psychology of small group behavior.* New York: McGraw-Hill.

Shaw, M. (1980). *Role-playing.* LaJolla, CA: University Associates.

Shelly, M., & Bryan, G. (Eds.). (1964). *Human judgment and optimality.* New York: John Wiley & Sons.

Shepard, C. (1964). *Small groups: Some sociological perspectives.* San Francisco: Chandler Publishing.

Sherif, M. (1936). *The psychology of social norms.* New York: Harper & Row.

Sherif, M. (1956). Experiments in group conflict. *Scientific American, 5*(195), 54–58.

Sherif, M., & Sherif, C. (1953). *Groups in harmony and tension: An introduction of studies in group relations.* New York: Harper & Row.

Sherif, M., & Sherif, C. (1969). *Social psychology.* New York: Harper & Row.

Sherif, M., White, J., & Harvey, O. (1955). Status in experimentally produced groups. *American Journal of Sociology, 60,* 370–379.

Shils, E. (1950). Primary groups in the American army. In R. Merton & P. Lazarsfeld (Eds.), *Continuities in social research* (pp. 16–39). New York: The Free Press.

Shipley, R., & Boudewyns, P. (1980). Flooding and implosive therapy: Are they harmful? *Behavior Therapy, 11*(4), 503–508.

Shulman, L. (1978). A study of practice skills. *Social Work, 23*(4), 274–280.

Shulman, L. (1981). *Identifying, measuring and teaching helping skills.* New York: Council on Social Work Education & Council on Accredited Schools of Social Work.

Shulman, L. (1992). *The skills of helping individuals and groups* (3rd ed.). Itasca, IL: F. E. Peacock.

Shuster, H. D. (1990). *Teaming for quality improvement: A process for innovation and consensus.* Englewood Cliffs, NJ: Prentice-Hall.

Silbergeld, S., Koenig, G., Manderscheid, R., Meeker, B., and Hornung, C. (1975). Assessment of environment-therapy systems: The group atmosphere scale. *Journal of Consulting and Clinical Psychology, 43*(4), 460–469.

Silverman, M. (1966). Knowledge in social group work: A review of the literature. *Social Work, 11*(3), 56–62.

Siporin, M. (1972). Situational assessment and intervention. *Social Casework, 53*(2), 91–109.

Siporin, M. (1975). *Introduction to social work practice.* New York: Macmillan.

Siporin, M. (1980a). Ecological system theory in social work. *Journal of Sociology and Social Work, 7,* 507–532.

Siporin, M. (1980b, November). *Group membership and experience: Older insights and current needs.* Paper presented at the Second Symposium of Social Work with Groups, Arlington, TX.

Slavson, S. R. (1945). *Creative group education.* New York: Association Press.

Slavson, S. R. (1946). *Recreation and the total personality.* New York: Association Press.

Smith, A. (1935). Group play in a hospital environment. In *Proceedings of the National Conference of Social Work* (pp. 372–373). Chicago: University of Chicago Press.

Smith, H., & Doeing, C. (1985, Spring). Japanese management: A model for social work administration? *Administration in Social Work, 9*(1), 1–11.

Smith, M. (1977). *Value clarification.* LaJolla, CA: University Associates.

Smith, M., Tobin, S., & Toseland, R. (1992). Therapeutic processes in professional and peer counseling of family caregivers of frail elderly. *Social Work, 37*(4), 345–351.

Smith, P. (1978). Group work as a process of social influence. In N. McCaughan (Ed.), *Group work: Learning and practice* (pp. 36–57). London: George Allen and Unwin.

Somers, M. (1976). Problem-solving in small groups. In R. Roberts & H. Northen (Eds.), *Theories of social work with groups.* New York: Columbia University Press.

Spergel, I. (1966). *Street gang work.* Redding, MA: Addison-Wesley.

Spergel, I. (1969). *Community problem solving.* Chicago: University of Chicago Press.

Spielberger, C., Gorsuch, R., Lushene, R., Vagg, P., & Jacobs, G. (1983). *Manual for the stait-trait anxiety inventory.* Palo Alto, CA: Consulting Psychologists Press.

Spilker, B. (Ed.). (1990). *Quality of life assessments in clinical trials.* New York: Raven.

Spivak, G., & Spotts, J. (1966). *Devereaux behavior rating scale.* Devon, PA: Devereaux Foundation.

Stanley, J., & Hopkins, K. (1972). *Educational and psychological measurement and evaluation.* Englewood Cliffs, NJ: Prentice-Hall.

Starak, Y. (1981). Co-leadership: A new look at sharing group work. *Social Work with Groups, 4*(3/4), 145–157.

Stattler, W., & Miller, N. (1968). *Discussion and conference* (2nd ed.). Englewood Cliffs, NJ: Prentice-Hall.

Steiner, I. (1972). *Group process and productivity.* New York: Academic Press.

Stern, R., & Drummond, L. (1991). *Practice of behavioural and cognitive psychotherapy.* New York: Cambridge University Press.

Stewart, D. W., & Shamdasani, P. N. (1990). *Focus groups: theory and practice.* Newbury Park, CA: Sage Publications.

Stogdill, R. (1974). *Handbook of leadership.* New York: The Free Press.

Stokes, T., & Baer, D. (1977). An implicit technology of generalization. *Journal of Applied Behavior Analysis, 10*(2), 349–367.

Stoner, J. (1961). *A comparison of individual and group decision including risk.* Unpublished master's thesis, Massachusettes Institute of Technology, Cambridge, MA.

Stoner, J. (1968). Risky and cautious shifts in group decisions: The influence of widely held values. *Journal of Experimental Social Psychology, 4*, 442–459.

Stotland, E. (1969). *The psychology of hope.* San Francisco: Jossey-Bass.

Stouffer, S. (1949). *The American soldier, combat and its aftermath.* Princeton, NJ: Princeton University Press.

Strauss, B., & Strauss, F. (1952). *New ways to better meetings.* New York: The Viking Press.

Stuart, R. (1970). *Trick or treatment: Who and when psychotherapy facts.* Champaign, IL: Research Press.

Stuart, R. (1977). *Behavioral self-management: Strategies, techniques, and outcomes.* New York: Brunner/Mazel.

Stuart, R., & Davis, B. (1972). *Slim chance in a fat world.* Champaign, IL: Research Press.

Sue, D. W., & Sue, D. (1990). *Counseling the culturally different: Theory and practice* (2nd ed.). New York: John Wiley & Sons.

Sundel, M., Glasser, P., Sarri, R., & Vinter, R. (1985). *Individual change through small groups* (2nd ed.). New York: Free Press.

Sundel, M., Radin, N., & Churchill, S. (1985). Diagnosis in group work. In M. Sundel, P. Glasser, R. Sarri, & R. Vinter (Eds.), *Individual change through small groups* (2nd ed., pp. 117–139). New York: The Free Press.

Swanson, A. (1978). *The determinative team: A handbook for board members of voluntary organizations.* New York: Exposition Press.

Swenson, J., Griswold, W., & Kleiber, P. (1992, November). Focus groups method of inquiry/intervention. *Small Group Research, 23*(4), 459–474.

Tannenbaum, R., & Schmidt, W. (1972). How to choose a leadership pattern. In J. Lorsch & P. Lawrence (Eds.), *Managing groups and intergroup relations.* Homewood, CA: Dorsey Press.

Taylor, D., Berry, P., & Block, C. (1958). Does group participation when using brainstorming facilitate or inhibit creative thinking? *Administrative Science Quarterly, 3,* 23–47.

Taylor, R. (1903). Group management. *Transactions of the American Society of Mechanical Engineers, 24,* 1337–1480.

Teger, A., & Pruitt, D. (1967). Components of group risk-taking. *Journal of Experimental Psychology, 3,* 189–205.

Thelen, H. (1954). *Dynamics of groups at work.* Chicago: University of Chicago Press.

Thibaut, J., & Kelley, H. (1954). Experimental studies of group problem-solving process. In G. Kindzey (Ed.), *Handbook of social psychology* (Vol. 2, pp. 735–785). Redding, MA: Addison-Wesley.

Thibaut, J., & Kelley, H. (1959). *The social psychology of groups.* New York: John Wiley & Sons.

Thomas, E. (1975). Uses of research methods in interpersonal practice. In N. Palansky (Ed.), *Social work research.* Chicago: University of Chicago Press.

Thomas, E. (1978). Generating innovation in social work: The paradigm of developmental research. *Journal of Social Services Research, 2*(1), 95–115.

Thomas, E. (1990). Modes of practice in developmental research. In L. Videka-Sherman & W. Reid (Eds.), *Advances in clinical social work research* (pp. 202–217). Silver Spring, MD: NASW Press.

Thoresen, C., & Mahoney, M. (1974). *Behavioral self-control.* New York: Holt, Rinehart & Winston.

Thorndike, R. (1938). On what type of task will a group do well? *Journal of Abnormal and Social Psychology, 33,* 409–413.

Thrasher, F. (1927). *The gang.* Chicago: University of Chicago Press.

Tolman, E. (1932). *Purposive behavior in animals and men.* New York: Appleton-Century-Crofts.

Tolman, E., & Brunswick, E. (1935). The organism and the causal texture of the environment. *Psychological Review, 42,* 43–77.

Tolman, R., & Edleson, J. L. (1989). Behavioral group treatment for men who batter. In B. A.

Thyer (Ed.), *Behavioral family therapy* (pp. 169–190). Springfield, IL: C. C. Thomas.

Tompkins, R., & Gallo, R. (1978). Social group work: A model for goal formulation. *Small Group Behavior, 9*(3), 307–317.

Torrance, E. (1957). Group decision making and disagreement. *Social Forces, 35,* 314–318.

Toseland, R. (1977). A problem-solving workshop for older persons. *Social Work, 22*(4), 325–327.

Toseland, R. (1980). Group problem solving with the elderly. In S. Rose (Ed.), *A casebook in group therapy: A behavioral-cognitive approach* (pp. 66–84). Englewood Cliffs, NJ: Prentice-Hall.

Toseland, R. (1981). Increasing access: Outreach methods in social work practice. *Social Casework, 62*(4), 227–234.

Toseland, R. (1987). Group versus individual decision-making: An experimental analysis. *Social Work with Groups, 10*(2), 95–105.

Toseland, R. (1990a). *Group work with older adults.* New York: New York University Press.

Toseland, R. (1990b). Long-term effectiveness of peer-led and professionally led support groups for family caregivers. *Social Service Review, 64*(2), 308–327.

Toseland, R. (1993). Choosing a data collection method. In R. Grinnell (Ed.), *Social work research and evaluation* (4th ed., pp. 317–328). Itasca, IL: F. E. Peacock.

Toseland, R., & Coppola, M. (1985). A task-centered approach to group work with the elderly. In A. Fortune (Ed.), *Task-centered practice with families and groups* (pp. 101–114). New York: Springer Publishing Co.

Toseland, R., Decker, J., & Bliesner, J. (1979). A community program for socially isolated older persons. *Journal of Gerontological Social Work, 1*(3), 211–224.

Toseland, R., & Ephross, P. (1987). *Working effectively with administrative groups.* New York: Haworth Press.

Toseland, R., & Hacker, L. (1982). Self-help groups and professional involvement. *Social Work, 27*(4), 341–347.

Toseland, R., & Hacker, L. (1985). Social workers' use of groups as a resource for clients. *Social Work, 30*(3), 232–239.

Toseland, R., Ivanoff, A., & Rose, S. (1987). Treatment conferences: Task groups in action. *Social Work with Groups, 10*(2), 79–94.

Toseland, R., Kabat, D., & Kemp, K. (1983). An evaluation of a smoking cessation group program. *Social Work Research and Abstracts, 19*(1), 12–20.

Toseland, R., Krebs, A., & Vahsen, J. (1978). Changing group interaction patterns. *Social Service Research, 2*(2), 219–232.

Toseland, R., Labrecque, M., Goebel, S., & Whitney, M. (1992). An evaluation of a group program for spouses of frail, elderly veterans. *The Gerontologist, 32*(3), 382–390.

Toseland, R., Palmer-Ganeles, J., & Chapman, D. (1986). Teamwork in psychiatric settings. *Social Work, 31*(1), 46–52.

Toseland, R., & Reid, W. (1985). Using rapid assessment instruments in a family service agency. *Social Casework, 66*, 547–555.

Toseland, R., & Rivas, R. (1984). Structured methods for working with task groups. *Administration in Social Work, 8*(2), 49–58.

Toseland, R., Rivas, R., & Chapman, D. (1984). An evaluation of decision making in task groups. *Social Work, 29*(4), 339–346.

Toseland, R., & Rose, S. (1978). Evaluating social skills training for older adults in groups. *Social Work Research and Abstracts, 14*(1), 25–33.

Toseland, R., & Rossiter, C. M. (1989). Group interventions to support family caregivers: A review and analysis. *The Gerontologist, 29*, 438–448.

Toseland, R., Rossiter, C., & Labrecque, M. (1989). The effectiveness of peer-led and professionally led groups to support family caregivers. *The Gerontologist, 29*(4), 465–471.

Toseland, R., Rossiter, C., Peak, T., & Hill, P. (1990). Therapeutic processes in support groups for caregivers. *International Journal of Group Psychotherapy, 40*(3), 279–303.

Toseland, R., Rossiter, C., Peak, T., & Smith, G. (1990). Comparative effectiveness of individual and group interventions to support family caregivers. *Social Work, 35*(3), 209–219.

Toseland, R., Sherman, E., & Bliven, S. (1981). The comparative effectiveness of two group work approaches for the evaluation of mutual support groups among the elderly. *Social Work with Groups, 4*(1/2), 137–153.

Toseland, R., & Siporin, M. (1986). When to recommend group treatment: A review of the clinical and research literature. *International Journal of Group Psychotherapy, 36*(2), 171–201.

Toseland, R., & Spielberg, G. (1982). The development of helping skills in undergraduate social work education: Model and evaluation. *Journal of Education for Social Work, 18*(1), 66–73.

Trecker, H. (1946). *Group process in administration.* New York: Women's Press.

Trecker, H. (1956). *Group work in the psychiatric setting.* New York: William Morrow.

Trecker, H. (1972). *Social group work: Principles and practices.* New York: Association Press.

Trecker, H. (1980). Administration as a group process: Philosophy and concepts. In A. Alissi (Ed.), *Perspectives on social group work practice* (pp. 332–337). New York: The Free Press.

Triplett, N. (1898). The dynamogenic factors in pacemaking and competition. *American Journal of Psychology, 65*(1), 93–102.

Tripodi, T., & Miller, H. (1966). The clinical judgment process: A review of the literature. *Social Work, 11*, 63–69.

Tropman, E. (1977). Staffing committees and studies. In F. Cox, J. Erlich, J. Rothmann, & J. Tropman (Eds.), *Tactics and techniques of community practice* (pp. 105–111). Itasca, IL: F. E. Peacock.

Tropman, J. (1980). *Effective meetings: Improving group decision-making.* Newbury Park, CA: Sage Publications.

Tropman, J., Johnson, H., & Tropman, E. (1979). *The essentials of committee management.* Chicago: Nelson-Hall.

Tropp, E. (1968). The group in life and in social work. *Social Casework, 49*, 267–274.

Tropp, E. (1976). A developmental theory. In R. Roberts & H. Northen (Eds.), *Theories of social work with groups* (pp. 198–237). New York: Columbia University Press.

Trotzer, J. (1977). *The counselor and the group: Integrating theory, training and practice.* Pacific Grove, CA: Brooks/Cole.

Tuckman, B. (1963). Developmental sequence in small groups. *Psychological Bulletin, 63,* 384–399.

Upper, D., & Cautela, J. (Eds.). (1982). *Covert conditioning.* Elmsford, NY: Pergamon Press.

Van de Ven, A. (1974). *Group decision making and effectiveness: An experimental study.* Kent, OH: Kent State University Press.

Van de Ven, A., & Delbecq, A. (1971). Nominal versus interacting group processes for committee decision-making effectiveness. *Academy of Management Journal, 9,* 203–212.

VanGundy, A. B., Jr. (1988). *Techniques of structured problem solving* (2nd ed.). New York: Reinhold.

Vannicelli, M. (1992). Removing the roadblocks: Group psychotherapy with substance abusers and family members. New York: Guilford Press.

Vinter, R. (Ed.). (1967). *Readings in group work practice.* Ann Arbor, MI: Campus Publishing.

Vinter, R. (1985a). The essential components of social group work practice. In M. Sundel, P. Glasser, R. Sarri, & R. Vinter (Eds.), *Individual change through small groups* (2nd ed., pp. 11–34). New York: The Free Press.

Vinter, R. (1985b). Program activities: An analysis of their effects on participant behavior. In M. Sundel, P. Glasser, R. Sarri, & R. Vinter (Eds.), *Individual change through small groups* (2nd ed., pp. 226–236). New York: The Free Press.

Vinter, R., & Galinsky, M. (1985). Extra group relations and approaches. In M. Sundel, P. Glasser, R. Sarri, & R. Vinter (Eds.), *Individual change through small groups.* (2nd ed., pp. 266–276). New York: The Free Press.

Vorrath, H. H., & Brendtro, L. K. (1985). *Positive peer culture* (2nd ed.). Chicago: Aldine.

Vroom, V. H. (1969). Industrial social psychology. In G. Lindsey & E. Aronson (Eds.), *Handbook of social psychology* (Vol. 5, pp. 196–268). Redding, MA: Addison-Wesley.

Vroom, V. H., Grant, L., & Cotton, T. (1969). The consequence of social interaction in group problem solving. *Journal of Organizational Behavior and Human Performance, 4,* 79–95.

Vroom, V. H., & Yetton, P. (1973). *Leadership and decision making.* Pittsburgh: University of Pittsburgh Press.

Waldo, C. (1986). *A working guide for directors of not-for-profit organizations.* New York: Quorum Books.

Walker, J. (1970). *Walker problem behavior identification checklist.* Los Angeles: Western Psychological Services.

Wallach, M., & Wing, C. (1968). Is risk a value? *Journal of Personality and Social Psychology, 9,* 101–106.

Walls, R., Werner, T., Bacon, A., & Zane, T. (1977). *Behavior checklists in behavioral assessment: New directions in clinical psychology.* New York: Brunner/Mazel.

Walton, M. (1990). *Deming management at work.* New York: G. P. Putnam's Sons.

Warren, R. (1977). *Social change and human purpose: Toward understanding and action.* Skokie, IL: Rand McNally.

Wasserman, H., & Danforth, J. (1988). *The human bond: Support group and mutual aid.* New York: Springer.

Watts, T. (1981). Ethnomethodology. In R. Grinnell (Ed.), *Social work research and evaluation* (pp. 361–372). Itasca, IL: F. E. Peacock.

Watzlawick, P., Weakland, J., & Fisch, R. (1974). *Change: Principles of problem formation and problem resolution.* New York: W. W. Norton.

Wayne, J., & Avery, N. (1979). Activities for group termination. *Social Work, 24*(1), 58–62.

Weed, L. (1969). *Medical records, medical education and patient care: The problem-oriented record as a basic tool.* Cleveland: Case Western Reserve University Press.

Weissman, A. (1976). Industrial social services: Linkage technology. *Social Casework, 57*(1), 50–54.

Weissman, H. (Ed.). (1969). *Individual and group services in the mobilization for youth experiment.* New York: Association Press.

Weisner, S. (1983). Fighting back: A critical analysis of coalition building in the human services. *Social Service Review, 57*(2), 291–306.

Wells, R. (1982). *Planned short-term treatment.* New York: The Free Press.

Whitaker, D. (1975). Some conditions for effective work with groups. *British Journal of Social Work, 5,* 423–439.

Whitaker, D., & Lieberman, M. (1964). *Psychotherapy through the group process.* New York: Atherton Press.

Whittaker, J. (1985). Program activities: Their selection and use in a therapeutic milieu. In M. Sundel, P. Glasser, R. Sarri, & R. Vinter (Eds.), *Individual change through small groups* (2nd ed., pp. 237–250). New York: The Free Press.

Whyte, W. (1943). *Street corner society.* Chicago: University of Chicago Press.

Wilson, G. (1956). *The practice of social group work.* New York: Report of the Committee on Practice, Group Work Section, National Association of Social Workers.

Wilson, G. (1976). From practice to theory: A personalized history. In R. W. Roberts & H. Northen (Eds.), *Theories of social work with groups* (pp. 1–44). New York: Columbia University Press.

Wilson, G., & Ryland, G. (1949). *Social group work practice.* Boston: Houghton Mifflin.

Wilson, G., & Ryland, G. (1980). The social group work method. In A. Alissi (Ed.), *Perspectives on social group work practice* (pp. 169–182). New York: The Free Press.

Wilson, S. (1978). *Informal groups: An introduction.* Englewood Cliffs, NJ: Prentice-Hall.

Wilson, S. (1980). *Recording: Working guidelines for social workers.* New York: The Free Press.

Wise, H. (1974). *Making health teams work.* Cambridge, MA: Ballinger.

Wodarski, J. (1981). *The role of research in clinical practice: A practical approach for the human services.* Baltimore: University Park Press.

Wolf, T. (1990). *Managing a nonprofit organization.* New York: Prentice-Hall.

Wolfe, M., & Proshansky, H. (1974). The physical setting as a factor in group function and process. In A. Jacobs & W. Spradlin (Eds.), *The group as agent of change* (pp. 206–227). New York: Behavioral Publications.

Wolins, M. (1959). The problem of choice in foster home finding. *Social Work, 4*(4), 40–48.

Wolpe, J. (1973). *The practice of behavior therapy* (2nd ed.). Elmsford, NY: Pergamon Press.

Wright, J., Thase, M., Beck, A., & Ludgate, J. (Eds.). (1993). *Cognitive therapy with inpatients: Developing a cognitive milieu.* New York: Guilford Press.

Wyss, D. (1973). *Psychoanalytic schools: From the beginning to the present.* New York: Jason Aronson.

Yalom, I. (1983). *Inpatient group psychotherapy.* New York: Basic Books.

Yalom, I. (1985). *The theory and practice of group psychotherapy* (3rd ed.). New York: Basic Books.

Yost, E., Beutler, L., Corbishley, M., & Allender, J. (1985). *Group cognitive therapy: A treatment approach for depressed older adults.* Elmsford, NY: Pergamon Press.

Zajonc, R., Wolosin, R., & Wolosin, W. (1972). Group risk-taking under various group decision schema. *Journal of Experimental and Social Psychology, 8*, 16–30.

Zander, A. (1977). *Groups at work.* San Francisco: Jossey-Bass.

Zastrow, C., & Kirst-Ashman, K. (1990). *Understanding human behavior and the social environment* (2nd ed.). Chicago: Nelson-Hall.

Ziller, R. (1957). Four techniques of group decision making under uncertainty. *Journal of Applied Psychology, 41*, 384–388.

Zimet, C., & Schneider, C. (1969). Effects of group size on interaction in small groups. *Journal of Social Psychology, 77*(2), 177–187.

Subject Index

Name Index